The Collected Works of J. Krishnamurti

Volume XII

1961

There Is No Thinker, Only Thought

COLLECTED WORKS VOLUME 12

Photo: J. Krishnamurti, ca 1962 by Cecil Beaton

P.O Box 1560, Ojai, CA 93024

Website: www.kfa.org

Printed in the United States of America

ISBN 13: 9781934989456
ISBN: 1934989452

Contents

Preface vii

Talks in New Delhi, India 1

First Talk, January 8, 1961 1
Second Talk, January 11, 1961 7
Third Talk, January 13, 1961 13
Fourth Talk, January 15, 1961 20
Fifth Talk, January 18, 1961 26
Sixth Talk, January 20, 1961 33
Seventh Talk, January 22, 1961 40

Talks in Bombay, India 49

First Talk, February 19, 1961 49
Second Talk, February 22, 1961 57
Third Talk, February 24, 1961 63
Fourth Talk, February 26, 1961 68
Fifth Talk, March 1, 1961 75
Sixth Talk, March 3, 1961 81
Seventh Talk, March 5, 1961 89
Eighth Talk, March 8, 1961 95
Ninth Talk, March 10, 1961 103
Tenth Talk, March 12, 1961 107

Talks in London, England 117

First Talk, May 2, 1961 117
Second Talk, May 4, 1961 122
Third Talk, May 7, 1961 128
Fourth Talk, May 9, 1961 133
Fifth Talk, May 11, 1961 139
Sixth Talk, May 14, 1961 142
Seventh Talk, May 16, 1961 147
Eighth Talk, May 18, 1961 153
Ninth Talk, May 21, 1961 157

Tenth Talk, May 23, 1961	163
Eleventh Talk, May 25, 1961	168
Twelfth Talk, May 28, 1961	174
Talks in Saanen, Switzerland	183
First Talk, July 25, 1961	183
Second Talk, July 27, 1961	188
Third Talk, July 30, 1961	193
Fourth Talk, August 1, 1961	198
Fifth Talk, August 3, 1961	203
Sixth Talk, August 6, 1961	207
Seventh Talk, August 8, 1961	213
Eighth Talk, August 10, 1961	217
Ninth Talk, August 13, 1961	223
Talks in Paris, France	229
First Talk, September 5, 1961	229
Second Talk, September 7, 1961	234
Third Talk, September 10, 1961	238
Fourth Talk, September 12, 1961	243
Fifth Talk, September 14, 1961	248
Sixth Talk, September 17, 1961	253
Seventh Talk, September 19, 1961	258
Eighth Talk, September 21, 1961	263
Ninth Talk, September 24, 1961	269
Talks in Madras, India	275
First Talk, November 22, 1961	275
Second Talk, November 26, 1961	281
Third Talk, November 29, 1961	288
Fourth Talk, December 3, 1961	293
Fifth Talk, December 6, 1961	299
Sixth Talk, December 10, 1961	305
Seventh Talk, December 13, 1961	313
Eighth Talk, December 17, 1961	319
Questions	327
Index	337

Preface

Jiddu Krishnamurti was born in 1895 of Brahmin parents in south India. At the age of fourteen he was proclaimed the coming World Teacher by Annie Besant, then president of the Theosophical Society, an international organization that emphasized the unity of world religions. Mrs. Besant adopted the boy and took him to England, where he was educated and prepared for his coming role. In 1911 a new worldwide organization was formed with Krishnamurti as its head, solely to prepare its members for his advent as World Teacher. In 1929, after many years of questioning himself and the destiny imposed upon him, Krishnamurti disbanded this organization, saying:

Truth is a pathless land, and you cannot approach it by any path whatsoever, by any religion, by any sect. Truth, being limitless, unconditioned, unapproachable by any path whatsoever, cannot be organized; nor should any organization be forced to lead or to coerce people along any particular path. My only concern is to set men absolutely, unconditionally free.

Until the end of his life at the age of ninety, Krishnamurti traveled the world speaking as a private person. The rejection of all spiritual and psychological authority, including his own, is a fundamental theme. A major concern is the social structure and how it conditions the individual. The emphasis in his talks and writings is on the psychological barriers that prevent clarity of perception. In the mirror of relationship, each of us can come to understand the content of his own consciousness, which is common to all humanity. We can do this, not analytically, but directly in a manner Krishnamurti describes at length. In observing this content we discover within ourselves the division of the observer and what is observed. He points out that this division, which prevents direct perception, is the root of human conflict.

His central vision did not waver after 1929, but Krishnamurti strove for the rest of his life to make his language even more simple and clear. There is a development in his exposition. From year to year he used new terms and new approaches to his subject, with different nuances.

Because his subject is all-embracing, the *Collected Works* are of compelling interest. Within his talks in any one year, Krishnamurti was not able to cover the whole range of his vision, but broad applications of particular themes are found throughout these volumes. In them he lays the foundations of many of the concepts he used in later years.

The *Collected Works* contain Krishnamurti's previously published talks, discussions, answers to specific questions, and writings for the years 1933 through 1967. They are an authentic record of his teachings, taken from transcripts of verbatim shorthand reports and tape recordings.

The Krishnamurti Foundation of America, a California charitable trust, has among its purposes the publication and distribution of Krishnamurti books, videocassettes, films and tape recordings. The production of the *Collected Works* is one of these activities.

New Delhi, India, 1961

First Talk in New Delhi

I think, before we begin, it should be made clear what we mean by discussion. To me it is a process of discovery through exposing oneself to the fact. That is, in discussing I discover myself, the habit of my thought, the way I proceed to think, my reactions, the way I reason, not only intellectually, but inwardly. It is really exposing oneself not merely verbally but actually so that the discussion becomes a thing worthwhile—to discover for ourselves how we think. Because, I feel if we could be serious enough for an hour or a little more and really fathom and delve into ourselves as much as we can, we shall be able to release, not through any action of will, a certain sense of energy which is all the time awake, which is beyond thought.

Surely, this discussion is related to our daily living—they are not two separate things. And as most of us have become so extraordinarily mechanical in our attitudes and conclusions, unless we break up the pattern of our thinking, we live so partially, we hardly live at all—live in the total sense of that word. And is it possible to live with all our senses completely awakened, with a mind that is not cluttered, with a perception that is total, a seeing that is not only visual but is beyond the conditioned thinking? If we could, it would be worthwhile to go into all that. So, if that interests you, we could discuss this sense of awareness, of total awareness of life, and thereby perhaps release an energy that will be awake all the time in spite of our shallow existence.

Do observe, watch your own mind when you are listening to what is being said. Then you learn.

Question: Sir, what do you mean by learn?

KRISHNAMURTI: I think if we could understand learning, then perhaps it would be a benefit. Is learning merely an additive process? Perhaps I add to something which I already have, or to the knowledge which I already possess. Is that learning? Is learning related to knowledge? If learning is merely an additive process through that which I already know, is that learning?

Then what is learning—like what is listening? Do I listen if I am interpreting, if I am translating, if I am merely corroborating to myself that which I am listening to, contradicting or accepting or denying? Does learning consist in transforming one's conclusions, altering one's conclusions, or adding more, or expanding one's conclusions? Surely, if one has to understand what is listening, what is learning, one has to explore somehow, doesn't one? Or is learning or listening or seeing unrelated to the past, and it is not a question of time at all? That is, can I listen so completely, so comprehensively that the very act of listening is perceiving what is true, and therefore the very perception has its own action without my interpreting what is seen into action?

Question: Aren't you using learning *in a very special sense? As we understand learning, it has a relation to knowledge—that is, getting more and more knowledge. There is no other meaning which can be put into that word learning. Are you not using it in a very special sense?*

KRISHNAMURTI: Probably we are using that word in a special sense. To me it is exploring and asking. I want to find out how to discuss this. Is a discussion merely an exchange of ideas, a debate, an exposition of one's own knowledge, cleverness, erudition, or is a discussion, in spite of knowledge, a further exploration into something which I do not know? Is it a scientific exploration where the scientist, if he is really worthy at all, inquires?—there is not a conclusion from which he inquires.

What are we trying to do? We are just laying the foundation for a right kind of discussion. If it is merely a schoolboy debate, then it is not worth it. If it is merely opposing one conclusion to another, then it does not lead very far. If you are a communist and I a capitalist, we battle with words, political activities, and so on; it does not get us anywhere. If you are entrenched as a Hindu or a Buddhist or whatever you are, and I am something else—a Catholic—we just battle with words, with conclusions, with dogmas, and that does not get us very far.

And if I want to go very far, I must know, I must be aware that I am discussing from a position, from a conclusion, from a knowledge, from a certainty, or that I am really not entrenched. If I am held to something and from there I proceed or try to find out, then I am so conditioned that I cannot think freely. All this is a self-revealing process, isn't it?

Discussions of that kind would be worthwhile, if we could do that. Now what shall we discuss?

Comment: Total living.

KRISHNAMURTI: A gentleman wants to know how to live completely.

Comment: Sir, I am interested in understanding the mechanism of thinking. At times thought seems to come from the bottom of conclusions, and at times from the top surface, like a drop from above. I am confused. I do not know thought apart from the background. I am unable to evaluate what the word thought *really means.*

KRISHNAMURTI: Yes, sir, shall we discuss that?

Thought is the mechanism of thinking. Is thinking merely a response to a question, to a challenge? If thinking is merely a reaction, is that thinking at all? I think perhaps I am going too fast. Somebody should tell me if I am going too fast.

Comment: I think we can understand you, sir.

KRISHNAMURTI: All right, sir. You asked me a question and I replied. The reply is provoked by your challenge, and I reply according to the content of my memory. And that is the only thinking I know. If you are an engineer and I ask you a question, you reply according to your knowledge. If I am a yogi, a Sanskrit scholar, or this or that, then I reply according to that, according to my conditioning. Isn't that so, sir?

So, is thinking—thinking as we know it—a reaction to a challenge, to a question, to a provocation, according to my background? My background may be very complex; my background may be religious, economic, social, or technical; my background may be limited to a certain pattern of thought—according to that background I reply. The depth of my thinking may be very superficial; if I am educated in the modern system, then I reply to your question according to my knowledge. But if you probe a little deeper, I reply according to the depth of my discovery into my unconscious. And if you still ask me further, probe, inquire more deeply, I reply either saying, "I don't know," or according to some racial, inherited, acquired, traditional answer. Isn't that so, sir? That we all know, more or less. Thoughts are all mechanical responses to a challenge, to a question. The mechanism may take time to reply. That is, there may be an interval between the question and the answer, to a greater or lesser extent, but it will be mechanical.

Now if I am aware of all that process—which few of us are; if I may, I am taking it for granted that we are aware—I realize that my whole response to a question, which is the process of thinking, is very mechanical and shallow; though I may reply from a very great depth, it is still mechanical. And we think in words, don't we, or in symbols. All thought is clothed in words or in symbols or in patterns. Is there a thinking without words, without symbols, without patterns?

And so the problem arises, doesn't it, sir, whether all our thinking is merely verbal. And can the mind dissociate the word from thought? And if the word is dissociated, is there a thought? Sirs, I do not know if you are experiencing or merely listening.

Question: What is thinking?

KRISHNAMURTI: I ask you a question, how do you reply to that?

Comment: From my background. Thinking is the most natural process.

KRISHNAMURTI: I ask you, "Where do you live?" And your response is immediate. Isn't it? Because where you live is very familiar to you, without a thought you reply quickly. Isn't that so, sir? And I ask you a further complex question. There is a time lag between the reply and the challenge. In that interval one is thinking. The thinking is looking into the recesses of memory. Isn't it?

I ask you, "What is the distance between here and Madras?" You say, "I know it, but let me look it up." Then you say the distance is so many miles. So you have taken an interval of a minute; during that minute, the process of thinking was going on—which is looking into the memory and the memory replying. Isn't that so, sir? Then if I ask you a still more complex question, the time interval is greater. And if I ask a question the answer to which you don't know, you say, "I don't know," because you have not been able to discover the reply in your memory. However, you are waiting to check, you ask a specialist, or go back home and look into a book and tell. This is the process of your thinking, isn't it?—waiting for an answer. And if we proceed a little further, if we ask a question of which you don't know the answer at all, for which memory has no response, there is no waiting, there is no expectation. Then the mind says, "I really do not know, I cannot answer it."

Now can the mind ever be in such a state when it says, "I really do not know"?—which is not a negation, which isn't still saying, "I am waiting for an answer." I ask you what truth is, what God is, what X is, and you will reply according to your tradition. But if you push it further and if you deny the tradition because mere repetition is not discovery of God, or reality, or what you will, a mind that says "I don't know" is entirely different from a mind which is merely searching for an answer. And isn't it necessary that a mind should be in such a state when it says, "I really do not know"? Must it not be in that state to discover something, for something new to enter into it?

Comment: Sir, we have come to this point: We think in terms of words, symbols, and we have to dissociate thought from the words and symbols.

KRISHNAMURTI: Sir, have we experienced directly that all thinking, as we know, is verbal? Or, it may not be verbal. I am just asking. And what has that to do with daily existence? Going to the office, meeting the wife, quarreling, jealousy—you know the whole business of daily existence, the appalling boredom and the fear and all that—what has that got to do with this question? Is thinking verbal? I feel we should not go too far away from the actual living—then it becomes speculative. But if we could relate it to our daily living, then perhaps we shall begin to break down some factors in our life which are distracting. That is all.

Sir, let us begin again. Words are very important to us, aren't they? Words like *India, God, communist, Gita, Krishna,* and also words like *jealousy, love* are very important to us. Aren't they?

Comment: Yes. The meaning of the word is very important.

KRISHNAMURTI: That is what I mean, the meaning of the word. And can the mind be free of the word which so conditions our thinking? Do you understand, sir?

Comment: That cannot be.

KRISHNAMURTI: Sir, it may be an impossible thing; it may not be possible at all, but we are slaves to words. You are a Theosophist, or you are a communist, or you are a Catholic with all the implications in the significance of those words. And if we do not understand those words and their meaning and their inwardness, we are just slaves to words. And should not the mind, before it begins to explore, to inquire, break down this slavery to words? Do you understand, sir? The communist uses the word *democracy* in one sense—people's government, etc.—and somebody else uses the same word in a totally different sense. And so a man begins to inquire what the truth is in this matter when he finds two so-called intelligent people using the same word with diametrically opposite meanings. So one becomes very, very cautious of words.

Can the mind break down the conditioning imposed by words? That is the first thing, obviously. If I want to find God, I have to break down everything—simple ideas, conclusions about it—before I can find it. And if I want to find out what love is, must I not break down all the traditional meaning, the separative, dividing meaning of love—such as the carnal, the spiritual, the universal, the particular, the personal? How does the mind free itself from words? Is it possible at all? Or do you say, "It is never possible"?

Question: Sir, can we temporarily suspend opinions from conclusions?

KRISHNAMURTI: Sir, in regard to discussing anything, what do you mean by "temporarily suspend"? If I temporarily suspend that I am a communist and discuss communism, then there is no meaning, no discovery.

Question: Sir, is it not like that one can go into the dark without even a torch?

KRISHNAMURTI: Yes, sir, probably; then its exploring may be like that. Real thinking is opposed to mechanical thinking. I do not know what mechanical thinking is and what real thinking is. Is your mind mechanical? To you, is thinking mechanical? Should not the mind be really interested in breaking down the words, the difficulties in problems, the danger of confusion created by words? Should not the mind be really interested, not intellectually, in the life and death problems of the world. Unless the interest is there, how will you start breaking down the accepted academical meaning? If you are inquiring into the question of freedom, into the question of living, must you not inquire into the meaning of those words? Merely to be aware that a mind is slave to words is not an end in itself. But if the mind is interested in the question of freedom, in the question of living, and all the rest of it, it must inquire.

Question: If the mind is not interested, how is the mind to get it?

KRISHNAMURTI: "How am I, who am not interested, to be interested?" I must sleep, and how am I to keep awake? One can take several drugs or counsel someone to keep oneself awake. But is that keeping awake?

Comment: When I see a thing, my seeing is automatic; then interpretation comes in and also condemnation.

KRISHNAMURTI: Sir, what do you mean by "seeing"? There is a visual seeing—I see you and you see me; I see the things that are very near, very close, and I also see visually things very far. And I also use that word *seeing* to mean understanding; I say, "Yes, I see that very clearly now." And the interpretative process is going on in the very seeing. And we are asking, if all seeing is interpretation, what is the principle which says that seeing is not interpretation? Can I look at something without interpreting? Is that possible?

Can I look at something without interpreting that which I see? I see a flower, a rose. Can I look at it without giving it a name? Can I look at it, observe it? Or in the very process of observing, is the naming taking place, the two being simultaneous and therefore not separable? If we say they are immediate, not separable, then there is nothing that can bring about the cessation of interpretation.

Let us find out if it is possible to look at that flower without naming it. Have you tried it, sir? Have you looked at yourself without naming, not only in a casual way, but inwardly? Have you looked at yourself without interpreting what you are? I see I am bad, I am good, I love, I hate, I ought to be this, I ought not to be that. Now have I looked at myself without condemning or justifying?

Comment: The difficulty is, sir, that we cannot just see ourselves without judging our action. Also, when we judge, immediately we stop action.

KRISHNAMURTI: Then it is not a difficult thing. You see the fact. The difficulty arises only when you don't see the fact. I see very clearly that when I see myself as I am, I condemn, and I realize that this condemnatory process stops further action. And if I do not want further action, it is all right. Isn't it? But if there is to be further action, this condemnatory process has to cease. Then where is the difficulty?

I see myself lying, not telling the truth. Now if I do not want to judge it, then there is no problem; I just lie. But if I want to challenge it, then there is contradiction. Isn't there? I want to lie and I do not want to lie; then the difficulty arises. Isn't that so?

If I see that I am lying and I like it, I go on with it. But if I don't like it, if it does not lead anywhere, then I don't say it is difficult. Because it doesn't lead anywhere, because to me this is a serious matter, I stop lying. Then there is no contradiction, there is no difficulty.

Words have condemnatory or appreciative meanings. As long as my mind is caught in words, either I condemn or accept. And is it possible for the mind not to accept or deny but observe without the word and the symbol interfering with it?

Question: But is action separate from that word?

KRISHNAMURTI: Is observing a thought process? Can I observe without the word, which we said is either condemnatory or appreciative?

Question: How is observing different from thinking, sir?

KRISHNAMURTI: I am using the word *observing*. Stick to that word observing. I observe you and you observe me. I look at you and you look at me. Can you look at me without the word *me*, the prejudice, your like and dislike? You are putting me on a pedestal, and I am putting you on a bigger pedestal. Can you look at me and can I look at you without this interpreting process?

Comment: It is not possible to observe without the thought process, which is memory coming into being.

KRISHNAMURTI: Then what? If that is so, then we are perpetual slaves to the past, and therefore there is no redemption. There is no redemption for a man who is always held a slave to the past. If that is the only process I know, then there is no such thing as freedom; then there is only the expansion of conditioning or the narrowing down of conditioning. Therefore, man can never be free. If you say that, then the problem ceases.

Question: My response to you now is one thing, and my response when I go outside is another. For maintaining my family and myself, certain basically essential things are necessary. In getting them, I also feel the need to ensure the continuity of these material things—food, clothing, and shelter—in the future also. My needs also tend to grow. Thus, greed steps in, and it develops. How is my mind to stop greed at any level?

KRISHNAMURTI: "How is greed to go when I am living in this world of constant growth in needs?" Is not that it, sirs? I think there are certain things I need, and those needs must continue. Why have I apprehension about them? I wonder if we cannot tackle this whole problem—fear, total living, what is thinking, and the things that we discussed—if we could discuss that awareness which awakens intelligence. I am putting it very briefly. If we could discuss how to be aware intelligently all through the day—not sporadically, not for ten minutes—then I think this problem would be answered for ourselves by ourselves. Is it possible for me to be aware—in the sense of being intelligently alert, wherever I may be, whether high or low, whether I have little or much—so that my mind ceases to be in a state of apprehension? Now is it possible to be aware intelligently?

What is it to be intelligent? Unless I understand that word and the meaning of that word, the significance, the inward sense of that word, we can ask thousands of questions, and there will be thousands of answers, but we shall remain as before. Now I am asking myself: Can I understand this feeling, the being intelligent, so that if I have that feeling of being intelligent, then there is no problem, as I will tackle everything as it comes along."

January 8, 1961

Second Talk in New Delhi

We said last time when we met that we would discuss the question of intelligence, and I think if we could go through it as deeply as possible and as fully, perhaps it might be very beneficial to see whether the mind has the capacity of fully comprehending problems and thereby discovering what it is to be really intelligent. To go into it very deeply, it seems to me, first we must understand what is a problem; then how the mind comprehends or is aware of the problem, how it understands the problem—which leads, does it not, to the understanding of self-knowledge. Knowledge is always in the past. Self-knowing is an active process of the present; it is an active present. And in understanding a problem, one discovers, doesn't one, the active process of knowing the instrument—that is, thinking, not theoretically, not academically, but actually—one experiences the process of knowing. We will go into that, and perhaps we will be able to discover what it is to be intelligent.

I don't see how we can discuss in a serious manner what is intelligence if we do not understand how we think. A mere definition of intelligence has no significance. The dictionary has a meaning, and you and I can give definitions, conclusions. But it seems to me that the very definition and giving a conclusion indicates a lack of intelligence rather than intelligence. So, if you think it is worthwhile also, we could go into this problem of intelligence rather widely and extensively, rather with fun, with a sense of gaiety—with a desirable seriousness which has also its own humor. So if you would let me talk a little bit, then you can pick up the threads, and afterwards we can discuss together.

I feel a mind that has a problem is incapable of really being free. A mind that is ridden with problems can never be really intelligent. I will go into all that. We will discuss all that presently. A mind that is increasing problems, that is the soil of problems, that starts to think from a problem, is no longer capable of intelligently approaching the problem. And a problem surely implies a thing that the mind does not understand, it finds hard to understand, cannot grapple with, cannot penetrate through to a solution. That is what we call a problem. It may be a problem with my wife, with children, with society, individually or collectively; the problem implies a sense of not being able to find a solution, an answer, and therefore that which we cannot find an answer or a solution for, we call that a problem. A mechanic who understands a piston engine knows all the things connected with a piston engine—to him it is not a problem because he knows; there is no problem to him. And also knowledge creates problems. I don't know if we could discuss that a little bit.

Knowledge invariably creates problems. If I didn't know anything about killing, then brutal violence and the rest of it would be no problem. It is only the knowledge that creates the problem, which is a contradiction in myself—I want to kill and I don't want to kill. It is the knowledge that is preventing me from killing, or it is the knowledge that creates a problem. And having created a problem, surely that very knowledge has forecast the solution also. I think this we must understand before we can go further into the question of comprehending what is intelligence.

Let us be clear that we are discussing—not academically nor theoretically as theoreticians, but actually—to experience what we are talking about. We are trying to find out, as we said, what it is to be intelligent. Can the mind be intelligent when it is burdened with problems? And in order not to be so burdened, we try to escape from problems. The very desire to find a solution is an escape from the problem. It is also an escape to turn to religions, to conclusions, to various forms of speculations. And as we have problems at every level of our existence—economic, social, personal, collective, national, international, all the rest of it—we are burdened with problems.

And is life a problem? And why is it that we have reduced all existence into a problem? Whatever we touch becomes a problem—love, beauty, violence—everything that we know of is in terms of problems. If the mind is capable of being free from problems, then to me that is the state of intelligence—which we shall discuss as we go along.

So, first we have problems. Problems exist because of our knowledge. Otherwise, we would have no problems. When the mind has a problem, the solution is already known. It is only the technique of finding the solution that we are seeking, not the answer, because we already know the answer. Shall we discuss that a little bit first?

Problems arise out of knowledge. And that very knowledge has already given the solution. The solution is already in the knowledge, consciously or unconsciously. What we are seeking is not the solution but the technique of achieving the solution which is already known. If I am an engineer or a scientist, I have a problem because I already know. The knowledge invites the problem. Because I know the problem which is the result of my knowledge, that knowledge also has supplied the solution. Now I say, "How am I to bridge the problem with the solution which is already known?" So, it is not that we are seeking solutions, answers, but how to bring about the solution, how to realize the solution. I think we have to realize that it is not the answer that we want because we know the answer; a problem indicates the answer, and the interval between the problem and the answer, the time interval is the technological interval of bringing that solution into effect. You see, it requires a great deal of self-knowledge to understand this, which means really the knowledge not only of the self that is active every day—going to the office, selling, buying, quarreling, being jealous, envious, ambitious, and all the rest of it, the outward symptoms of this egocentric activity—but also of the unconscious, the deep recesses of the mind, the untrodden regions of the mind. So, all this knowledge which is stored up creates the problem. The mere seeking of an answer to the problem is really, essentially, a technological search for the solution which is already known, and for this, one must go into the whole problem, into this whole thing called consciousness. I do not know if I am making myself clear, or I am making this a little more complex. After all, if I have intelligence, if there is intelligence, then there are no problems; I can tackle the problems as they arise. And can a mind be without a problem?

Let us go further. The state of the mind that is without a problem is what we call peace, what we call God, what we call the intelligent thing. That is essentially what we want, that is what the mind is constantly pursuing. But the mind has reduced all life into a series of problems. Death, old age, pain, sorrow, joy, how to maintain joy—everything is a nightmarish tale not only at the psychological level but at the individual level and at the collective level and also at the unconscious level of the whole human being. So it seems to me, to be actively participating in intelligence, one must go through all this; otherwise, it becomes merely a theoretical issue.

Now, after having said all this, can we discuss this question of problems arising from knowledge? Otherwise, there is no problem. And when we talk of a problem, we always imply that the answer is not known, the solution is not known. "If I only could find a solution to my problem"—that is our everlasting cry. But because of the very problem, we already know the solution. Could we just discuss that first and then proceed? And will that not lead to the uncovering of the solution, will that not be an active process of self-knowing?

Question: A mathematician has an unresolved problem. How is his mind to be free of it?

KRISHNAMURTI: Sir, are you a mathematician? Are you discussing this as a mathematician? Or are you discussing this question as a human being with a problem, not as a specialist with a problem?

Comment: I know a little of mathematics.

KRISHNAMURTI: We are discussing human problems. You say you have a problem of love.

Comment: Is that the result of prior knowledge? Sir, I love my children, I love my brother. I take their burden. I have a problem, and therefore I want to be free of that.

KRISHNAMURTI: What for? Why should you be free?

Comment: Because it is a disturbance to my mind.

KRISHNAMURTI: So, you see, mere escape is not the answer. You know the stupidity of escape, and yet you keep on escaping. So that is becoming your problem. My wife and I cannot get on. I drink. That is an escape. That drinking has become a problem. I have a problem with my wife, and now through escape I am taking a drink, and that has also become a problem. So life goes that way. We have innumerable problems, one problem bringing another. Isn't that so, sir?

So we are asking ourselves: Don't problems arise out of knowledge? Let us discuss. I said that problems arise out of knowledge and because of that knowledge and because of the problem, the answer is already known, the solution is already there.

Comment: Sir, the use of the word knowledge *is rather vague. You are covering so many things. Now take the instance of a car—that is technical knowledge. But that knowledge is quite different from a knowledge of the problem of life, or something where it is difficult to find a solution because of so many changing social conditions. And therefore knowledge does not always lead to a solution—it is not implied; sometimes in certain cases it may be implied, in certain cases it may not be.*

KRISHNAMURTI: I am not at all sure that it does not apply to everything. I am just suggesting, sir, I am not becoming dogmatic. Now wait a minute. You said the outward and inward, the outward knowledge and the inward knowledge. Why do we divide this as outward knowledge and inward knowledge? Are they to be kept in watertight compartments, or the outward movement is only the natural movement which becomes the inner? It is like the tide that goes out and then comes in. You don't say that it is the outward tide and the inward tide. The whole life is one movement going in and out, which we call the inner and the outer. It is one movement, isn't it, sir—not an outward movement apart from the inward movement. Essentially, is there a difference between outward knowledge and inward knowledge? It is not the outward knowledge that conditions the inward knowledge, and it is not the inward knowledge that modifies the outward knowledge. Can we so demarcate knowledge as the outward and the inward, and can we comprehend that knowledge is always in the past, it is something in which is implied the past?

Question: Sir, what about intuition?

KRISHNAMURTI: Intuition may be a personal projection, a personal desire rectified, spiritualized, and sublimated which becomes an intuition.

So, let us go back, if we may, to the point we were discussing. We have problems. As human beings we are cursed with various problems of life. The mind is always seeking an answer to these problems. But is there an answer which we do not already know, and therefore is it any good seeking it? You follow? I wish we could discuss this.

I have a problem, say, a problem of love, which is—I want to love universally, whatever that may mean; I want to love everybody without difference, without up and down, without color. I talk of universal love, and yet I love my wife. So, there is the universal and the particular, which becomes contradictory, not only verbally, but actually. We don't know what universal love means, first of all, but we glibly talk about it. Don't we? This country has been speaking everlastingly about nonviolence and preparing for war; there are class divisions and linguistic divisions. I am taking it as an example of our mind which talks about universal love and says God is love. You follow, sir? There is universal brotherhood, and I love my wife. How can I reconcile these two? That becomes a problem. How to transmute the personal, the particular, the "within-the-wall" to something which has no walls? You see, that becomes a problem. Doesn't it? Now let us discuss that.

First there is the knowledge, knowledge that there is universal love. Or we have an occasional feeling, an extraordinary sense of unity and the beauty of that quality which says, "There is nothing to bother about; why are you bothered about everything?" and then I go back home, and I have to battle with my wife. So there is this contradiction, and we are always trying to find an answer. Is that an intelligent approach to search for an answer? When I say there is universal love, that is knowledge. Isn't it, sir? Isn't that a knowledge, an idea, a conclusion, a thing which I have heard? No? The Gita says we are all one, and some other book says something like this, and so conclusions become our knowledge—either the conclusions imposed by tradition or by society, or our own conclusions which we have ourselves arrived at.

So, when we say we have a problem, what do we mean by that? Sir, you have problems, haven't you, of some kind or other. Now what do we mean by that? What is the state of mind that says I have a problem? What is the fact about the problem?

Comment: We want to come up to the standard we have set ourselves.

KRISHNAMURTI: You try to approximate to the standard, the ideal, the example, and as you cannot approximate yourself to it, it creates a problem. I want to be the manager, and I am a clerk, so that creates a problem. I do not know and you know, and I want to reach that state when I also can say, "I know," so that creates a problem. Isn't that so, sirs?

Comment: The feeling of insufficiency.

KRISHNAMURTI: Why do you make it a problem, sir? I feel an insufficiency, I feel envy, I have no capacity, I am not intelligent. I feel this emptiness in me. I see people happy and I am not. That is a very concrete example, sir. Now I feel insufficiency. And I am just asking myself why I make that into a problem. What is the quality that makes it into a problem? Do you understand, sir, what I am saying? I realize I am insufficient. Why should it become a problem, sir? I am insufficient, and I want to reach that state of mind which is sufficient. I realize through comparison, by seeing you, you have cleverness, position, money, prosperity, and I have none of these. I see that, and suddenly it has become a problem to me. You, the rich, and I, the poor—that has become a problem. I say to myself, "What has made the mind reduce this thing into a problem?" I see you beautiful and I am ugly, and the misery begins. I want to be like you—clever, beautiful, intellectual, you know all the rest of it. What has set the mechanism going? The mechanism is obviously comparison, isn't it? I am insufficient, you are sufficient; I am ugly, you are beautiful; you are this, and I am not—a contradiction. Now what creates this comparison? Why has the mind created the problem? Because, the mind has the capacity to compare, and this comparison has been cultivated from childhood. You are not so clever as your brother, you are not so good as your uncle, you are not so beautiful as your sister, and the rest of it—so from childhood this has been dinned into us. The mind says, "I am this and I must be that," and through comparison creates dissatisfaction. And this dissatisfaction, we say, leads to progress. This is the whole process.

I am dissatisfied with what I am because I have the capacity to compare with something greater, with something less, with something superior or inferior. Right? If by some miracle you could remove from the mind the comparative quality, then I will accept what I am. Then I won't have a problem. So, can the mind stop thinking comparatively, and why does it think comparatively? Because, the fact is my mind is small. That is a fact. Why do I compare it with something else and create a problem out of it? My mind is small, my mind is empty. It is a fact. Why don't I accept it? Is it possible to see the fact that I am this, not in terms of comparison? One of the major factors of the cause of problems is comparison. And we say that through comparison we understand, we say that through comparison we grow, and that is all we know. Is it possible for the mind to put away all comparison? If it is not possible, then we live in a state of perpetual problems. And a mind ridden with problems is a stupid mind, obviously.

Comment: Only an insane mind has no problem.

KRISHNAMURTI: A gentleman says that only the insane mind has no problem. The insane mind so identifies itself with something that all other things cease to exist. Psychologically when a mind identifies itself with something or says, "I am this," such a mind excludes every other issue and confines itself to that one thing. Now obviously it has no problem. Such a mind is an insane mind. But we are also insane because we have got innumerable conclusions with which we identify, and we exclude everything else. When I say, "I am a Muslim," or "I am a Hindu," and I refuse to recognize any other thing, I am insane.

Now, let us go back. Why does the mind create problems? One of the factors of this creation lies in comparison. Now, can the mind by investigation, by looking, observing, understand the futility of comparison, the waste of comparison?—because comparison leads to problems. Do you follow? A mind ridden with problems is not a mind at all; it is incapable of thinking clearly. So the truth is that comparison creates problems. I am ugly, I am violent; can I look at what I am without comparison?

Can you look at something without comparison? Can you look at the sunset without saying, "It is a lovely sunset, but not so beautiful as the sunset yesterday"? Have you ever tried it? The very observation of, looking at, something without comparison has an extraordinary sense of discipline—not imposed—to look at something with such attention that there is no question of comparing. Is it possible to look at something without comparison? Is it possible to look at myself without comparison? Is it possible for the mind to be aware of itself without saying it is not so good as that? If and when the mind can do that, there is no problem. Is there?

Comment: It is possible, but it is very difficult.

KRISHNAMURTI: Now what do you mean by "difficult"? You are using that word *difficult* because your mind is not free from comparison. When you say that it is difficult, you are thinking in terms of achievement—which means comparison. A problem is a waste of energy, and any engineer will tell you that waste is unused energy. Now, if a problem is a waste of energy, can this energy be brought to look at the problem without comparison? When I compare, it is a waste of energy. Obviously it is an escape from what I am. Now, to look at what I am, to be with the fact of what I am, requires all my energy. Doesn't it? Have you lived with something beautiful or ugly?

Question: Sir, what do you mean by "live"?

KRISHNAMURTI: Have you tried to live with something that is ugly or beautiful? If you live with something ugly, it either distorts you, or perverts you, or it makes you ugly. When you go down that street and you live in that street day after day, you are completely oblivious of the fact that you live in that dirt because you are used to it. So you have never lived with it—you are used to it; that has become your habit, and you are blind. And to live with a beautiful tree—there are beautiful trees and you have never even looked at them, which means you are totally oblivious of them. So you never live with anything, either ugly or beautiful. Now to live with something requires a great deal of energy. Doesn't it? To live with waste, doesn't it require a great deal of energy?

Comment: Then we will get caught up in the squalor.

KRISHNAMURTI: Either you are oblivious of it, or you are really caught up.

Comment: We are not caught if we are indifferent to it.

KRISHNAMURTI: As you are indifferent to the squalor, you are equally indifferent to the beauty. So, see the facts, sir. Something very interesting is coming out of this, which is the mind is dissipating its energy through problems. Obviously, the mind then through its dissipation becomes enfeebled and therefore cannot face facts. The fact is the mind is narrow, petty, stupid, and the mind cannot face that fact. And for the mind to live with *what is* is extraordinarily difficult, isn't it; that requires an enormous amount of energy so that it can observe without being distorted.

Question: When you use the word insufficiency, *does it not imply comparison?*

KRISHNAMURTI: Sir, I am only using that word in the sense the dictionary uses it, not comparatively. I am just saying I am insufficient. Insufficiency has a comparative meaning. But when I use the word *insufficient* in the dictionary sense, there is no comparison. I wish we could somehow, if we are really serious, disinfect all words so that we have just the meaning of the words. To live with sufficiency or insufficiency, it requires a great deal of energy so that the fact does not distort the mind.

Question: Sir, is insufficiency different from the mind? Can the mind look at it?

KRISHNAMURTI: When I say I am insufficient, the mind is aware that it is insufficient. It is not outside of itself as the observer watching something observed. Sir, would you try, just for the fun of it, to live the whole day today with yourself, without comparison, just to live, to see what you are and live with it? Try to live with that garden, with a tree, with a child so that the child does not distort your mind, so that the ugliness does not distort the mind, nor the beauty distort the mind. And you will find, if you do, how extraordinarily difficult it is and what an abundance of energy is necessary to live with something. And because we say one must have that energy to live with something totally, completely, we say there are various ways of gathering energy, but those are all dissipation of energy.

Please see the fact, the fact that the mind is insufficient, and live with it all day, see what happens, observe it, go into it. Let it have its way, see what happens. And when you can so live with it, there will be no insufficiency because the mind is freed from comparison.

January 11, 1961

Third Talk in New Delhi

We were discussing the day before yesterday the question of comparison and differentiation, whether a mind that is comparing and therefore thinking of its advancement is really advancing at all. And as long as a mind is in conflict, in comparison, is not the mind in fact deteriorating? Is not the conflict an indication of deterioration? And we were discussing what it is that makes the mind perceive, observe the fact as it is, and not interpret or offer an opinion about the fact, and whether a mind is capable of such perception if it is merely comparing. And also we went into the whole question of discontent. Most of us are dissatisfied, discontented with what we are, with what we are doing in our relationships, with the state of the world's affairs. And most of us who are at all thoughtful want to do something about all this. And is discontent a source of action? I do not know if we could explore that a little bit. I am dissatisfied politically with the situation in the world. The motive of my action is discontent. I want to change the situation in certain patterns—communist, socialist, or whatever it is, extreme left, or center, center from the left, or center from the right, and all the rest of it.

Now, is action born of discontent creative action? I do not know if I am going on to what we were discussing day before yesterday. But I think it is connected with what we were discussing the other day because we are always thinking, aren't we, in terms of the better. And is there creation in the field of the better? Is there intelligence where there is discontent? And discontent, surely, as we know it, is the incapacity to approximate totally or completely with the better, with the more.

Please, if I may point out here, this is rather a difficult thing which we are discussing. Unless we somehow give a little bit of our attention to it, it is going to be rather difficult. I feel that the mind in conflict is a most destructive mind. When a mind is in conflict and so destructive, any action springing from the mind—however erudite, however cunning, however capable of carrying out a plan, economic, social, whatever it is—is destructive. Because its very source is discontent—which is the comparative mind, which is the destructive mind—its action, whether partial, total, or whether it is capable of covering the world and all the rest of it, is destructive. And as most of us have this bug, this insect, this cancer of discontent and we are always seeking satisfaction because of this discontent—through drink, God, religion, yoga, political action, and so on—our action is surely the escape from this flame of discontent. And the more quickly we find a corner in the recesses of the mind, or in action, where we find we are more contented, there we settle down to stagnate. This happens for all of us in our everyday relationship, in our activities, and so on. If I can find a guru, a teacher, a theory, a speculation, I am out of my discontent; I am happy to find it, and I settle back. And surely such action is very superficial, isn't it? And is it possible for the mind to see, or perceive, the truth of discontent and yet not allow itself to stagnate but discover the source of discontent? Let me put it round the other way, sirs. Comparison—the better, the more—surely breeds discontent. And we think, don't we, that if there were no comparison, there could be no progress, there could be no understanding. Such comparison is essentially the expression of ambition. Whether the comparison is in the political, religious, or economic field, or in personal relationship, such comparison inevitably is based on ambition. The man wanting to become the manager, the minister wanting to become the prime minister, and the prime minister saying, "Everything is all right; I am in the right place; you don't be ambitious"—the whole of that process, surely, is the result of comparison to better the "I am" and "We are." When the mind is ambitious, surely, such a mind is incapable of love. Ambition is a self-centered action. Though it may talk in terms of peace and world welfare, God, truth, this or that, it is surely the self-centered movement expressing itself through comparison, ambition. Such a mind is incapable of love. That is one thing. And can the mind see the truth of all this? A mind which is concerned with itself, with its own advancement, with its own expression through fulfillment, economic, social, and all the rest of it—such a mind is incapable of affection, of love. And therefore it must inevitably create a world in which comparison, the hierarchical values of comparative existence is continued. So conflict is a continuous inevitability, and as far as one can see it, it is very destructive. Now we see all this as factual, as actual fact, in our daily life. And can the mind cease to think comparatively and therefore eliminate conflict—which does not mean stagnate in the thing which is?

What I am trying to say is: Can the mind cease to be in a state of conflict? And is conflict, which indicates self-contradiction, inevitable? You see that awakens an extraordinary question, which is: Is creation—I mean not printing, building, writing a poem, that is only an expression of the state of the mind; I am not talking of the expression but of that state of creativeness—is that state of being in creation the result of conflict? And truth, God, and whatever one likes to name that—that thing which human beings have been seeking century upon century—is that to be perceived, known, experienced, through conflict? Then why are we in conflict? And is it possible for the mind to be totally free of conflict, which means having no problems? But there are problems in the world, and a mind free of conflict will meet with those problems and cut through them like a knife through butter, like a sharp knife that cuts through without leaving any traces on the knife.

Now I do not know if you think along these lines or if you think differently. After all, sir, the individual as well as the collective, the unit as well as the community, the one as well as the society, is concerned, isn't it, really with a mind that is not in conflict, that is really a peaceful mind—not the politician's peace, not the communist's peace, not the Catholic's peace, but in the sense of a good, first-class mind, capable of reasoning, analysis, and also capable of perceiving directly and immediately. Can such a mind exist?

If the mind is in a state of comparison, it creates problems and is everlastingly caught in them, and therefore it is never free. Sir, from childhood we have been brought up to compare—the Greek architecture, the Egyptian, the modern—to compare with the leader, the better, the more cultured, the more cunning; to be the perfect example; to follow the Master; to compare, compare, compare, and therefore to compete. Where there is comparison, there must be contradiction obviously—which means ambition. Those three are linked together inevitably. Comparison comes with competition, and competition is essentially ambition. Is there a direct perception, is it possible to see something true immediately when the mind is caught up in this vortex of comparison, conflict, competition, and ambition? And yet you know the communist society as well as the capitalist society, and every society is based on this competition. The more, the more, the more, the better—the world is caught up in it, and every individual is in it. We say that if we have no ambition, if we have no goal, if we have no aim, we are just decaying. Sirs, this is so deeply rooted in our minds, in our hearts—this thing to achieve, to arrive, to be. And if you take that away, shall I stagnate? I will stagnate if it is forcibly taken away from me; if through any form of influence I cease to compete, I stagnate. But can I understand this process of comparative, competitive, ambitious existence, and through understanding and seeing the fact of it, be free of it? This is a very complex problem. It is not a matter of just agreement or disagreement. Can the mind be in a state in which all sense of influence has ceased?

I do not know if you have ever explored the problem of influence. In America, I believe, they tried subliminal advertising, which is to show a film on the screen at a very tremendous speed, advertising what you should buy; consciously, you have not taken it in, but unconsciously, you have taken it in; you know what that advertisement is, and when you leave the cinema or the place, as the propaganda has already taken root, you go and buy the advertised article, unconsciously. But fortunately the government stopped that.

But aren't we, all of us, unconsciously or perhaps even consciously, the slaves of such subliminal propaganda? After all, all tradition is that. A man who lives in tradition repeats whatever he has been told—which most of us do, either in platitudes or in certain forms of expansive modern words. We are slaves to that tradition, not only as custom, habit, but also as the word. I do not know if this interests you. Because, all this surely is implied when the mind begins to go into it to see if it can free itself from this comparative existence.

The world is in chaos. There is no question about it. From the communist point of view, it is in a mess. Some say you must have better leaders, bigger, wiser, more capable leaders. Others say you must go back to religion, obviously implying you must go back to your tradition, follow this and follow that, or create a plan which you must follow. You know what is happening in the world.

Looking at all this, is it a matter of leadership, is it a matter of better planning or creating a world according to a certain pattern, whether the left or the right—which means the pattern is much more important, the formula is much more important than the human being who will fit into the pattern? That is what most politicians, most leaders, most theoreticians, and the rest of them are concerned with. They create the plan and fit the human being into that plan. Is that the issue at all? At one level, obviously, that is the issue. But is that the fundamental issue, or is it that creativity in the immense sense of that word has completely stopped, and how is one to bring the human mind to that state of creativity?—not how to control the human mind and shape it according to a certain pattern as the Catholics and everybody else are doing in the world.

What are the things that hold the mind? The psychoanalysts have tried to unloosen the mind by analysis. But they have not succeeded. And I am not at all sure that any outward agency, as religion, as a guru, as a book, as a theorist, and so on and so on, can ever unloosen the blockages of the mind. Or is it really only possible through self-knowing from moment to moment? You understand? That means an awareness without the burden of previous knowledge which interprets what is being experienced. But, what is the state of the mind which is experiencing? I see a beautiful thing, a tree, a building, the sky, a human being lovely with a smile, with a job, and all the rest of it. I see it; the very perception of that is the state of experiencing.

Now, when the mind is conscious in the state of experiencing, is there an experiencing? I do not know. When there is silence in this immense world of noise, that experiencing of silence—is it a conscious process? And if it is conscious, if the mind says, "I am experiencing silence," is it experiencing silence? When you are happy—bursting with happiness, not for any reason, not because your liver is functioning well, or you have had a good drink, or any god's influence, but really feeling that sense of incredible source of bliss and joy without any foundation—if you say at that time, "I am experiencing a marvelous state," obviously it ceases to be. Can we, you and I, at a stroke, stop the mind thinking comparatively? It is like dying to something. Can we do that? That is really the issue, not how to bring about a state of mind which is not comparative.

Sir, we are aware consciously that we are in conflict, and that conflict arises out of self-contradiction. Now, there is a state of self-contradiction. How do we eradicate it? By analysis, going into it, analyzing step by step, and saying these are the causes of contradiction and these are the blocks? Ambition, obviously, is the result of self-contradiction. You don't live with the fact.

Sir, how do you live with a fact? The fact that I have ideals is one thing, and the fact that I realize that having ideals is the most stupid escape from the fact of *what is* is another thing. They are two stages. Now, I can reject ideals because I see the falseness of ideals. I see the falseness of an ideal; it has no value, so I brush it aside. But there is the fact that I am violent, that I am this and that. The fact is that, and can I live with the fact? And what is implied in living with something? Sir, I may live in a street full of noise, dirt, squalor. Is that living with it? I don't smell any more the filth, I don't see any more the dirt in the street because I get used to it by living in that street.

Getting used to something is one way of living—which is: The mind has become blunt, dull, which means the thing which is dirty, squalid, ugly, has perverted the mind, made the mind insensitive. There is something extraordinarily beautiful—the picture, the sunset, the face, the field, the trees, the river, a light on the river—I see these every day and these also I get used to. The marvelous mountains—I get used to them. And the mind has become insensitive to both, the ugly and the beautiful. That is one way of living.

Now, what does living with something mean? Obviously, to live with ugliness implies my mind must be much more sensitive, much more energetic, full of energy in order not to be perverted by the ugliness; and similarly, my mind must be astonishingly alive in order to live with something extraordinarily beautiful. Both should demand an intensity of energy, an intensity of perception, so that there is no question of getting used to it. Not getting used to it—that is what is implied in living with something.

Now, how is the mind to be sensitive?—not a method when I use the word *how*; method is what makes the mind most insensitive. But can the mind see the fact of this? The very perceiving of the fact—is that not the releasing of energy?

Take the mind which is being made dull every day by going to the office, seeing the stupid boss, or the bullying boss, or yourself not so clever as the boss and trying to imitate the boss, the nagging, the bus, the squalor, the poverty—all that is making the mind so dull. I see all this; I face this every day of my life. Then what am I to do? Will going to the temple, going to the god, going to the Sunday sermon sharpen my mind, make my mind exquisitely sensitive to everything? Will that do it? Obviously, it won't. Then why do I do it? Why don't you negatively cut away everything that is going to make the mind dull?

Comment: But being conscious of all this, I get a feeling of being unhappy.

KRISHNAMURTI: Be unhappy, what is wrong with being unhappy? Why should you not be unhappy? The world is unhappy. How do you get out of it? First you must know unhappiness. You must know what fear is before you can get out of it. If you are escaping from it, you are afraid of it; you have never faced the issue.

What do you mean by ambition? I am using the word *ambition* in the dictionary sense, which means an intense desire, the fulfillment of that desire. That is, I want to be the manager, I want to be the minister, I want to be on the top of the heap, I want to be something intensively. To see the absurdity of such a thing and at the same time talk about love and peace and goodness is utter nonsense. When I have seen that is ambition, I am out of it, I won't be ambitious; at least I won't talk about peace, love, and goodness.

Question: Can we run away from traditions, families, living on a desired pattern?

KRISHNAMURTI: Sir, who is suggesting that we should run away from family? Our minds are the result of tradition. You are a Hindu. I may not be a Hindu, a Muslim, or a communist, or whatever it is. You are the result of your environment, of your society, of your education, of the family, the name you know—you are the result of all this. At what level do I see this, the verbal, theoretical as an explanation, or do I see this as a fact? What do you say, sir? Surely, there is a vast difference between seeing, perceiving something as a fact and offering an opinion about the fact or indulging in explanations about the fact, verbal, intellectual, theoretical, spiritual, whatever it is. Do you see that your mind is the result of tradition, whether it is the modern tradition or is the tradition of one yesterday or a thousand yesterdays?

Some days ago, perhaps last year, some of my friends asked me to sit in front in a car, and several people were sitting behind in the car. And as we were driving along, they were talking about awareness, the complications of awareness, what was meant by awareness, and the chauffeur who was driving the car ran over a poor goat and broke its leg. And the gentleman sitting in the car was still discussing awareness; he never noticed that the poor goat had been run over; he was not concerned about anything but intellectually discussing awareness.

Sir, you are doing exactly the same thing. Can you be aware of the fact that your mind is dull?

Comment: There is the will to live. If my mind were to know that it is dull, it wouldn't be able to live.

KRISHNAMURTI: Oh The will to live prevents you from facing your dullness—is that what you call living? The gentleman says that seeing the fact that I am dull will horrify me, and I will cease to live. But I am asking, "Are we living now?" When we don't see the beautiful sky, when we don't see the beautiful tree, when we don't see the garden, sea, rain, when we don't know all that, feel love, feel sympathy, are we living?

Sir, take a very simple example which everybody talks about in India since I have been here—corruption. There is corruption everywhere, because everybody talks about it from top to bottom, and everybody says we cannot help it, and we don't bother over it. But suppose each one of us were really aware what corruption implies, what would happen? Would that prevent corruption, or would that make you more corrupt? Sirs, you have never thought about this.

Have you been aware of the fact of what you are? We are slaves to words—the word *soul*, the word *communist*, the word *congress*, the words *this* and *that*. Are you aware of this fact that you are slaves to words? For instance, you don't go into why you are used to the word *leadership*. Why? Because, you belong to a party, socialist, communist, congress, or something else. They have their leaders, and you accept them; it is the tradition, and you also see if you don't want to accept the same, you may lose your job. Therefore fear blocks you from looking. So you accept it as it is advantageous, it is profitable, it is less disturbing, so you live in the world of words and are slaves to words. So, the word *God* means very little to all of you. Does it really mean anything? We might spell it the other way and be slaves to that word *dog* as the altruists are. But, sir, can the mind break through all this slavery to words?

As long as the mind is seeking security through words, it is going to be dull. I don't mean that the mind must be very clever, read lots of books, and all the latest books and the enormous and the latest criticism—I am not talking about that sort of superficial cleverness. I am talking of perceiving the mind as it is.

Sir, let us take another problem, the same thing in a different way. We are all competitive, aren't we? In the office, at home, religiously, we are competitive. There is the guru and I am below him, and one day I will reach that state, and I will be the guru and so on—climbing the ladder. We are, aren't we, ambitious. Aren't we competitive?—which means we are ambitious, which means lack of love.

Comment: There is a distinction between rational ambition and irrational ambition. For example, I try to improve my work, that is a rational ambition; and if I want to become the prime minister, that is irrational ambition.

KRISHNAMURTI: Sirs, a gentleman says, "There is rational ambition and there is irrational ambition; when I try to become the prime minister—a post which is already occupied—it is irrational ambition, and it is rational ambition when I try to improve my job.''

Comment: He means personal efficiency. That is all.

KRISHNAMURTI: Personal efficiency? Can an ambitious mind ever be efficient? Have you noticed a child completely absorbed in a toy? Would you call that child efficient? You don't call it efficient because the toy to him is something amazing; he is completely in it. There is no incentive, there is no trying to become better, trying to become something else.

Question: This is play. If I have no ambition, if I don't want to work for my children, why should I improve?

KRISHNAMURTI: Are you improving, sir? Sir, if all incentive were taken away, would you stop working? Do you know what is happening in the world, in welfare states? Sweden is the most complete form of all welfare states, and there are many more suicides there than anywhere else. Why? Because, there is no incentive; everything from womb to tomb is settled. That is one form of not having an incentive. And here, in this country and elsewhere, you have incentive; you will become a better officer if you work hard—climb, climb, climb. Yet, efficiency is declining here also, isn't it? No? What do you say, sir? You have incentive and yet efficiency is declining. You have no incentive and thereby the mind is becoming dull. So, if you want to be really efficient, how do you set about it? Don't talk of efficiency; how do you become efficient? Only when you give your whole mind to it, when you love the thing which you are doing. Isn't that so, sir?

Comment: But we have no choice because of circumstances.

KRISHNAMURTI: Sir, each of us is a slave to circumstances, and we hold to them. Can't we realize to what extent one is a slave to circumstances and limit it, cut it and be free of it, instead of saying, ''I am a slave to circumstances''? Limit it to bodily needs and get on with it. We are not asking ourselves first why the mind is made dull.

Sir, we began this morning asking ourselves if we can understand this whole process of competition, conflict, and ambition and this attitude of the mind to accept leadership, to follow. This is what we are used to. You are sitting there, I am sitting here; you are listening to me with an attitude, with an idea, and you say, ''Let me listen.'' So there is this conflict which inevitably results in dulling the mind. Obviously, sir, all conflicts destroy the mind. Now, is it possible to see the process of this conflict? And the very perception of this conflict—perceiving, seeing the very source of this conflict, not what you should do about it—the very perception has its own action. Now, do we see that? That is all that I am asking. What is the good of saying, ''It is inevitable. What will happen if I don't compete in the society which is competitive, which is ambitious, which is authoritative? What will happen to me?''—that is not the problem. You will answer it later. But can we see the fact that a mind which is in conflict is the most destructive mind, and whatever it wants to do, any activity, however reformative, has in it the seed of destruction.

Do I see it as I see a cobra, that it is poisonous? That is the crux of the whole matter. And if I see it, I do not have to do a thing about it; it has its own action. Look, sir. You know, the saints, the leaders, and all the swamis and the yogis talk about building character, doing the right thing, living a right life, and they talk a great deal about what they do in the West, about sin. Now, is there sin when there is love? And when there is love, is there not character? Let love do what it will; it is always right. When there is love, what it does is right; and if it doesn't do anything, it is right. So why discuss everything else—how to build character, what should you do, and what should you not do, and how can we find it? Surely, sir, to uncover the source of love, the mind must be extraordinarily free from conflict. To look at the heavens, sir, your mind must be clear, mustn't it? It cannot be engrossed in your office, in your wife, in your children, in your security; it must look, mustn't it? So, can the mind be free from conflict, which means competition and all the rest of it?

Sir, how do you see things? Do you see things at all? Sir, do you see me and do I see you—see visually—or between you and me are there several layers of verbal explanations and curtains, opinions, and conclusions? You understand what I am saying? Do you see me, or do you see your verbal explanations about me? When you see a minister, do you see the man or the minister? What, sirs?

Comment: We usually see the minister and rarely the man.

KRISHNAMURTI: So, you never see the fact at all, you see the label and not the contents. You are slaves to words, slaves to labels. You don't say, "Let me look at that man and not that label, not the socialist, the congress, the communist, the capitalist, but look at the man"—which indicates that we are slaves to words. Sir, haven't you noticed with what respect we greet a big man, a big noise? What does that mean? Surely, all this is part of self-knowing. The very knowing is going to create its own action.

January 13, 1961

Fourth Talk in New Delhi

The last few times that we met here, we have been considering what it is to be intelligent, not merely at the functionary level, but right through one's whole being. And we were, I think, day before yesterday considering efficiency and competition, whether a competing mind, a mind that is ambitious, is really an intelligent mind. A mind that is comparing and in comparison is said to be progressing, achieving, arriving—is such a mind essentially an intelligent mind? You know, words are as a rider to understanding; words are meant to convey a certain significance, to open the door to further comprehension. But if we merely use words and are slaves to words, it seems to me, it is incredibly difficult with a group of people which is constantly changing, to pursue a particular line of thought completely and wholly because there are newcomers all the time, and it is rather difficult to maintain a certain verbal comprehension at a certain level at the same time. And we were discussing, considering, whether the mind could be free of this idea of comparison. And from that, the question arose as to efficiency in action: whether a mind which has comprehended the fullness, the deep significance of competition, achievement, arriving—whether such a mind can act at all efficiently. I think it might be worthwhile if we could this morning consider what is action.

I wonder what we consider is action. At what level does action cease and contemplation begin, or is there no such division as contemplation and action? I am not using the word *contemplation* in any ascetic or Christian sense of that word, but in the sense: to contemplate, to think, to fathom out things, to delve into the deep recesses of one's own mind, to meditate. Is there a difference between action and contemplation in that sense? But for most of us, action means doing, a physical action, doesn't it? For most of us, going to the office, writing, playing, doing something, cooking, bathing, talking, and so on, the doing is the action. And so we have a philosophy of action.

Let us think the problem out together, you and I together—not I think it out, and you listen, agree or disagree with what is being said. Because, when we are thinking out together a problem, there can be no agreement or disagreement. We are rowing the same boat down the same river, or up the same river. We must go together. And so, if I am talking, it is not that you are merely a hearer, but rather you are partaking, sharing in the thought; I may be talking now, but you cannot leave it all to me and just listen. So, please, while the speaker is saying certain things, you have not only to listen but also actually to experience the thing that is being said. Otherwise, we cannot possibly go any further.

Sirs, I have been saying we have a philosophy of action, a pattern of action. We have not only a pattern of action but a pattern of thought which has established the pattern of action according to which it is going to act, to do. For us there is a difference between idea, thought, and action; and we are everlastingly seeking to bridge over, to bridge thought and action. So we not only have a framework in which thought functions, within which thought lives, but also from that framework we create another framework of actions which we call philosophy of action. Whether it is the philosophy of action in daily life or philosophy of action in inward life, it is all according to a pattern.

And is there any other kind of action which is not merely the conformity to an idea, to an ideal, to a pattern? And if there is such an action, is not that action merely reaction and therefore not action at all? Obviously, a reaction is not an action. If you push me in a direction and I resist and do something in return, it is a reaction, and therefore it is not an action. If I am greedy and I do something out of that greed, it is a response to the original influence. If I am good because society tells me to be good, or I do something because I am afraid, or I do, act, in order to be something, in order to achieve, in order to become, in order to arrive, such activities are reactions.

And reaction is not obviously total action. I seek God, or truth, or something else, because I am afraid of life, and I pursue a pattern of views, denials, in order to achieve a result; such activities are obviously reactions which bring about, breed contradiction. And being in a state of contradiction, any action from that contradiction creates further contradictions, and therefore there is general reaction and not action. Sir, if you really go into it, it is very interesting to find out for oneself if the mind can be in a state of action without reaction. Because reaction involves the pattern of authority—whether it is the authority of the Catholic, the authority of the communist, the authority of the priest, or the authority which the reaction has brought about, an experience which becomes the knowledge from which there is action. I do not know if you are following all this. So, the mind has to understand what is action, not according to the Gita, not according to the various divisions which the human mind has broken action into—such as the political action, the religious action, the contemplative action, the individual action, the collective action—which, to me, are all reactions; communism is the reaction to capitalism, and

Marxism is the reaction to all the 18th century or the 19th century conditions.

So, can the mind perceive all this, not deny it? Because the moment you deny it, there is the reaction of denial, and resistance in any form brings a reaction, and from that reaction any action is still a reaction. So, the mind seeing this, comprehending this—can it discover an action which is not a reaction? Sir, this has, I think, immense significance because most of our lives are contradictory. We are in a state of contradiction, our lives are in a state of contradiction, our society is in a state of contradiction; and any activity born of that contradiction is bound to create more misery, more contradictions, more travail, more agony. And it is not that I am asking a theoretical question but an actual question to myself and therefore to society: Whether it is possible for the mind to understand this contradiction and therefore perhaps comprehend reaction and come upon, not intellectually, something which is action and which is not the result of reaction.

Sir, let us put it round the other way. Most of us know love through jealousy. Most of us know peace through violence or as the opposite of violence, the so-called nonviolence which we are everlastingly talking about in this country. The practicing of nonviolence is practicing reaction. But the mind has to go into the whole problem of violence, which is essentially a contradiction.

So, the understanding of the contradictions within oneself—not merely those at the conscious level, at the verbal, intellectual level, but also the deep contradictions within oneself—may perhaps reveal the reaction and its processes; and in understanding them, perhaps we shall be able to come upon that action which is not the outcome of influence. I do not know if this thing interests you at all.

A man says, "I am going to lead a religious life, I am going to lead a life of silence, a life of contemplation; I am not a businessman, I am not a shoddy-level politician, I am not interested in socialism, so I don't like any of these things as they don't appeal to me; I am going to withdraw and lead a contemplative life." Is such a mind an intelligent mind, which divides life as the contemplative, silent life and the business life and the political life and the religious life, and can it live? Whether I do go to the office or I don't go to the office, life is action, living is action. And is it possible to live so totally that there is no division? This means really there is only the active present of action, which is the acting—not the acting according to a pattern, not the doing according to something, but doing, living, acting—always in the present. Sirs, can we discuss this?

Sir, as one sees, tyranny is growing more and more in the world. Whether it is the tyranny of the fascist or the tyranny of the communist, or the tyranny of the church or of the politician, tyranny is extending, expanding. And one can only battle it not as a reaction, but by living a life which is not a reaction, which is a thing which is real, which is uninfluenced, which is complete, which is not conditioned. The fascists and the communists are the same because both are tyrannical, as the church is. One has to see this and not act in reaction to it, and the very seeing of it is action.

To put the question differently, sirs, the active present of doing—acting not with an end in view, not with a goal to achieve, not to conform to the pattern established either by society or by yourself for yourself through your own reactions—has got immense importance. You say that unless one belongs to a group, to a political party, to a particular organization, or to various sects, action effective in society is not possible; that if you want to do something to alter society, you must create an organization or join a group of people who want to do the same thing.

Such a group is a reactionary group, and so the reform is a continuous process of bringing about the seed of deterioration.

Now, one who sees this, who comprehends this—not one who is afraid of all this—obviously cannot belong to any group, and yet his action must be effective, but to judge the effectiveness of his action according to the effect on society seems to me to be naturally wrong.

Question: Is there not such a thing as purposeless action, action without a purpose?

KRISHNAMURTI: We are trying to find out what is meant by an action with a purpose, a purposive action. To be effective, apparently, you must have a purpose in action. If I want to create a school, the purpose is to create a school; I must act towards it. I go for a walk; the purpose is to enjoy the sunset, to get exercise, to look, to observe.

Comment: An action without a purpose is merely an event. But it cannot be called action which is movement, movement which may have a good end.

KRISHNAMURTI: So, to you, event is different from action. An action has a purpose towards something, and an event is an immediate incident. This is all hairsplitting. Don't do it.

I thought I made it clear at the beginning of the talk, or rather during the talk, that there is only action, and not action with a purpose. We are trying to investigate, to experience, to understand this extraordinarily complex thing called action. This gentleman says that an action is only an action where there is a purpose. And I am asking myself: Is that an action at all?

Comment: It seems to me that when I look at a flower, I have no purpose, and this is an action. When I hear a bird singing, that bird-song somehow affects me, and I have real joy in hearing that; this is an action, but without purpose.

KRISHNAMURTI: Yes sir. But there is poverty in this country, starvation, squalor, and all the rest of it. That has to be altered, it has to be wiped out; and you and I, being part of the society, we say, "What shall I do about it?" What you said about the flower is one thing, and the other thing is, "What am I to do about this?" And seeing that, I say, "I will join that group, or that party that will help to wipe this out." This is a purposive action also. Isn't it? Now I am just asking myself—I am sure you are doing the same—whether action needs a purpose. I am living rightly, and therefore the very act of living is right action. It seems to me that we are substituting purpose for living, and that from living there is an action which is not purposive in the ordinary sense of the word.

Sir, let us take another question, which is: Has love a purpose? And is not the very fact of loving, in itself, the righteous, the good, the complete action in the world, and in the world of thought and ideas and of flowers and everything else? Sir, this is not a matter of intellectual agreement with me. We are trying to understand whether an action with a purpose, or a purposive action, is the right way out of all this mess and difficulty. Or, is there a different way, a different approach, a different thing altogether? You follow, sir? I can live purposively, according to the Gita or the Koran or some other book, but that is not living at all; it is conforming, it is a reactionary process. Or, I can establish a righteous purpose, seeing the immediate purpose—which is Tibetans starving and poverty in India—and act on that immediacy. But always there is the act of doing. There is an entity as the thinker, the doer who is doing, and hence there is a gap; he is everlastingly trying to bridge over between the idea and the action. Now, can I wipe out all that, the whole thing, and look at action entirely differently? Then the very living is acting, which does not need any purpose, which does not have an end. Living has no end. It is only a dead being who says, "My end is there." So, if I can so live, why do I want a purpose? But the living is the thing, which is not a reaction.

Question: I see a boy drowning and I rescue him. Is that action a purposive action?

KRISHNAMURTI: Sir, don't please take a concrete example and draw conclusions from that example, whether an action such as rescuing a boy or somebody drowning is spontaneous or true. What we are trying to find out is: How to live? And the "how" is not a pattern. This is a question to comprehend a way of living which is not a reaction, which has no end in view—a living that is so complete, so total, that the very living is the action both outward and inner.

The fact is my life is in a state of contradiction. That obviously is a fact, and from that fact there are reactions which, in fulfilling those reactions, create further reactions and further misery. And I say that the pursuit of such fulfillment politically, religiously, economically in the present is most destructive. Now, if those are facts, my concern is with the understanding of self-contradiction within and without—which is society as well as within—which is a unitary process and not a separative process; and then in understanding this contradictory process, outward and within, the mind inevitably comes to this question of action without seeking a purpose, action which is not stimulated by a purpose.

A contradictory mind is an ineffectual mind. And look at our society; we do not have to go very far! Can there be a mind which is not in itself self-contradictory and therefore is not a slave to influence? I have put to you a question. Now, how do you listen to it? You have heard the words, you understand the verbal meaning, but how do you listen to it? To find an answer to it, or do you listen to find out what it means, not verbally but inwardly? I put to myself the question: Whether there is a mind which in the very act of living—living being thinking, living being alive—in its action includes all purposes, which is beyond all purpose? When I put this question to myself, the way this particular mind proceeds is: It does not want an answer, it does not want a solution, it tries to find out the actual experience of putting away the words; having understood the meaning of words, it actually experiences the state of the mind that says yes. It is no longer seeking a purpose, it is no longer seeking an answer; therefore, it is no longer seeking—which means the mind is in a state of complete perception. In the very act of having put that question, it is not waiting for an answer because the waiting for an answer implies that there is an answer. Such a mind is in a state of complete perception, seeing.

Look, sir, I want to live a life which is not contradictory. I see that everything around me—politically, religiously, traditionally, my education, my relationship, everything I do—is contaminated with this contradiction, tarred with this ugliness; and such contradiction is a sin, pain, is a thing that the mind says it must go beyond. First I have become aware of this contradiction within as well as in society, and seeing the brutality of contradiction, the question arises: Is it possible to go beyond it, not theoretically and verbally, but actually? When the mind puts that question to itself, it must inevitably come upon action; it cannot just theoretically say it is out of contradiction. Contradiction is an action in living. So then the mind asks itself: Is it possible to live—which is action itself—such that there is no purpose? Purpose is so silly in living. It is a small mind that is always asking for the goal of life, for the purpose of life.

So, sir, if you could understand this, if the mind could understand this sense of living which is action, then there would be no division between the political, religious, contemplative action and life. There is not a life according to the Gita, or according to the Bible, or the Christ or the Buddha, but there is living.

Question: I want to lead a life without contradiction. Does that become a purpose?

KRISHNAMURTI: If you want to lead a life without contradiction and that becomes a purpose, then you will never lead a life without contradiction. Sir, I am not being personal. Are you aware of a state of contradiction in your life? Are you not ambitious? A mind which is in a state of ambition is in a state of contradiction, obviously. I am just asking: Are you actually, apart from the verbal expression, aware that your life is in a state of contradiction? I am violent and nonviolent; that is contradiction, isn't it? Am I aware of this? Do I know that I live like that? Or living that way, do I say it is inevitable, rationalize it, and cover it up? What do I do, sir?

Sir, the society and the leaders of society who try to guide the society which they represent, politically or religiously, are in a state of contradiction, isn't it so? Yet, these people talk about peace. How can a mind which is in conflict ever have peace and talk about peace, or try to organize peace?

Question: Why should not a mind which is violent try not to be violent?

KRISHNAMURTI: The mind which is violent tries to be nonviolent. What does it mean? Is that possible? You have not tried it, you have been talking about nonviolence. Have you tried to become nonviolent? What is the thing which is more important—to understand *what is,* or to see *what is* and try to make *what is* into "what it is not"?

Comment: A person who is trying to be nonviolent may succeed ultimately.

Question: Sir, do you advocate spontaneous love?

KRISHNAMURTI: Sir, if you don't mind, I may put it differently. I don't know what love is, what it is to love, what it is to have humility. Can I know what love is by trying to love? Can I have humility, the quality of being humble, by trying to be humble?

Comment: Behind all this there is a certain pressure.

KRISHNAMURTI: This is your problem. A mind that is completely empty cannot be pushed around; it has no pressure behind it, to use that gentleman's word. And most of our minds have pressure which creates contradictions—pressure being desire. Can the pressures be removed, not as a reactionary process? Or can the mind perceive these pressures and be free of them? Put it anyway you like, the very perception of these pressures is the releasing of the mind from the pressures. That is the real issue, isn't it? What we are talking about is that action through pressure is a reaction, whether the pressure be good, noble or ignoble, it is still reaction, and such a reaction must create more confusion, misery. Seeing all this, the mind asks itself whether it is possible for it to exist without these pressures and what the action is that flows when there is no pressure.

Sir, you have heard all this for an hour and a half. What does it mean to you, not verbally as agreement or disagreement, but in fact? If you happen to hear something true, it does something to you. We know unfortunately that our life is miserable, contradictory, and very superficial. When we leave this room, are we going to continue in the same way? I am not trying to say you should or you should not. That is up to you.

January 15, 1961

Fifth Talk in New Delhi

We were discussing on Sunday morning what it is to act, what are the implications of action, what are reactions, and how far one can differentiate between reaction and action which is not merely the outcome of a response. I think we made it sufficiently clear that there is a vast difference, not only in quality, but in dimension, between action and reaction. For most of us, activity is reaction, and to be able to discern reaction at depth requires, does it not, a great deal of understanding of oneself. And I do not know how far each one of us has gone within himself to find out for oneself whether most of our activities—religious, political, family—and the relationship between us and society and between society and us are not based on reaction. And reaction, as we discussed, is the outcome of contradiction. And in the process of understanding the self-contradiction, there is, if one has gone into it sufficiently deeply, an action which is totally divorced from reaction. The greater the tension in self-contradiction, the greater the activity, the greater the response of that action, of that reaction.

You know there is a tension when a human being is contradicting, consciously or unconsciously, not only within himself, but between himself and society. When there is a contradiction, there is a tension; and the more violent the contradiction, the greater is the tension. And of course the ultimate tension is the asylum. But for most of us this contradiction does breed a certain tension. And from this tension, there is an action, there are activities. I think there is a well-known case about which an analyst has been talking to us. A good and well-known writer, who was in revolt, was analyzed. He wrote from a great deal of tension, a sense of contradiction within himself, with society, and with all the things that society stood for; and the feeling that he was in revolt was a reaction; and out of this reaction which created a great deal of tension, he wrote. And when he was analyzed, this tension was taken away, and he could not write at all afterwards. With most of us, this tension does exist in a mild form, but the greater the tension, the greater will be the emotional response to society as a reaction. And as most of us are casually, superficially aware of our contradictions, our tension is very mediocre, very small, superficial; and therefore our activities are superficial, and we lead a very mediocre life, though we are aware of our tensions. I do not know if you have not noticed all this within yourselves.

And is there an action which is devoid of this reaction? I think we should approach it negatively. I mean negative not in the sense of the opposite of the positive. Obviously action which is divorced from reaction cannot be cultivated because all that I know is reaction. Isn't it? You flatter me, I feel very alive; you insult me, I feel low. I am ambitious, I want to climb, and I am frustrated and I feel miserable. So there is the reaction. And if in myself there is contradiction without understanding the quality, the whole process of this contradiction within myself, merely to cultivate or to think about the action which is devoid of reaction is another form of reaction. Therefore we must approach the question of action which is extraordinarily positive, only negatively. I do not know if I am making myself clear on the point. To see something very clearly, one must have no blocks; there must be no hindrances. If I want to see very clearly this tree with all the beauty, with all the outlines—the trunk, the extraordinary grace, the strength and the movement of the tree—what do I do? I cannot see it very clearly if I am myopic, if I am thinking about something else, if I am worried, if I am distracted. I must give my whole attention, and I cannot give my whole attention to it if I am thinking of other things, if other things are worrying me. Therefore, to perceive, to see anything in life, the perception must be negative and not positive. The mind must cease to worry, the mind must put away its own problems—its myopic, shortsighted, limited view—and be negative; then only can it see *what is.* The quality of action is dynamic, not theoretical. I have a horror of theories because they have no meaning; a theory is merely conforming to an idea or creating an idea according to which you are going to live—which are all reactions.

So, in order to really comprehend action which is not the outcome of a contradiction, with its tensions and activities and responses, one must go to it negatively. Any positive action based on will is really conforming to a pattern, and it contradicts a true action which is not the response of reaction. So, if we understand very clearly that true perception can only come about through a negative approach, then we shall begin to see what are the limitations, rather than overcome the limitations.

So, we are going to examine and discuss the blockages, the hindrances, the limitations that create a tension, a contradiction from which there are activities which are what we call positive and negative. So, one of the fundamental hindrances to this action without response is the urge and the demand for power. Power is essentially the urge of a mind which is in a state of contradiction within itself and tries to cover it up by achieving success.

Sir, this is a very difficult subject, and one has to go very deeply into oneself to understand this. We all want power, power which comes through money, through position, through success, through some capacity which is recognized by society, and that recognition gives us a position of prestige. That is what we all want, the religious people as well as the nonreligious, the materialistic people as well as the scientist; every human being demands this recognition by society as an important person, as being a VIP, a big man. And this urge for power is really evil, if one may use that word *evil*—I am using that word in the dictionary sense without any condemnatory meaning behind it. But once one admits that to oneself or sees the truth of it, it becomes extremely difficult to fit into society. The power to do good, the power to alter human lives, the power of the husband over the wife, the power of the wife over the husband, the power of a leader, the power which the follower creates in the leader—all power breeds this sense of domination in the leader because there is no leader without a follower. If I don't follow, I have no leader. But we want to follow. We want to be told, we want to be urged, coerced, influenced, urged to do the right thing. And so there is power, whether it is the tyrannical power of a dictator or the democratic power of a prime minister. The prime minister has got immense power through our poverty, and the so-called saint—through austerity, through denial, through control—feels in himself tremendously self-centered power. I am sure you have felt all this—the moment you have a certain capacity, that capacity gives you an immense power; if you can do some thing very well, you are already on the top of the world. All such forms of power are essentially and basically evil. One has to see that for oneself and to observe that for oneself, not merely intellectually, verbally, but inwardly, and to eschew that because one understands it. Doesn't a man who has power direct, guide, change, move? Such a man we call a creative man, a good man; we say he is creating a new society, a new way of looking at life, a new public—you know the whole business of the political world. And then there is the vast field of power through religions. So, one has really to grasp that, understand it, not say, "Power is evil, and tell me how to get away from it," because there is no getting away from it. You have to understand it, you have to see it, and you have to have it in your blood; then you move away from it. And in the moving away from power, there comes the action which is divorced from reaction. I hope I am making myself clear.

As I said, a negative approach is necessary. The so-called positive action of power, doing good or doing evil, is based on the sense of power. But all power is evil; there is no good power—power being influence, power being the desire to achieve, the sense of personal power, or the power of a person identified with the community and the community advancing. All that sense of power is evil. If I see that, if the mind perceives that, then that very perception frees the mind from that sense of power. And then there is that quality of action which is not a reaction, which has no reaction; then, whether you are walking, working, or whether you are writing, talking, there is that sense of activity, action without a reaction.

Most of us are envious, and envy is a tremendous hindrance to that action. You may say, "How can I live in this world without envy?" You know envy. A man who is envious, who is perpetually seeking power, has no humility.

And another thing that blocks us is the sense of conformity—conformity being limitation, conformity to an example, conformity brought about through influence, a good influence, any influence, pressure. Can the mind understand this sense of conformity and free itself from that conformity? You know, sir, this is one of the most difficult things to do, if you have tried to understand conformity and whether the mind can ever be free from conformity. Because, after all, the leaders, political or religious, are all after shaping the mind of a human being according to their patterns. And can a mind which is the result of the conformity of centuries be free from conformity? I am talking of the mind, not just the superficial mind that is educated to learn a certain technique, but also the mind that has accepted tradition, that lives in tradition, that functions in tradition, that quotes, that repeats, that everlastingly cultivates good habits and calls it virtue following the pattern of tradition. All such limitations, acceptances, or denials are reactions of these things that we have accepted. Can the mind understand these things, and mustn't the mind be free from the sense of conformity which breeds authority? Mustn't the mind be free from this limitation?

Sir, I can go on talking, you can go on listening. But you see our lives are so twisted with fear, so warped, corrupt, corrupted by fear, conscious or unconscious. And it seems to me that a mind that understands the nature of this destructive thing called fear must go into this question of conformity with its authority, with its sanctions, with its limitations, acceptances. And can the mind understand conformity, unravel it? Not how not to conform because that has no meaning, because the moment you say "how," you have another pattern, and you become a slave to that pattern. But if we could unravel the way of conformity, then you would come to see that there is the verbal conformity—because I am speaking English and you also speak English, there is the possibility of communication between us, which is a conformity. There is also the conformity to put on a shirt, a coat, the conformity of certain accepted codes of conduct, such as keeping to the right side of the road or left side of the road and so on.

Now, when you go beyond those, is not all thinking, the patterns of thinking, a form of conformity, a form of imitation, projected by memory? Do you understand, sir? Our thinking is the response of memory, memory-association, and that memory-association is the pattern of conformity, like the electronic brains which function at astonishing speed, with such astonishing clarity, precision; memory, when it is very clear, sharp, alive, functions mechanically, which we call thinking. And is not that thinking a process of conformity? Please don't accept this because you have to see this for yourself; there is no acceptance or denial in all this. Whatever you call God, truth, that immense thing, immeasurable thing, cannot be measured by the mind which is shaped and held and put in the framework of conformity to ideas, to impressions, to memories, to influence, to tradition. Can the mind go beyond all this, or is the mind not capable of it but can only function within the framework of the pattern of conformity? It may be a bigger pattern or a smaller pattern, a more peaceful pattern, more good, more sociable, more amenable, more affectionate, but it is still within the pattern of conformity—conformity as idea, conformity as thought. If it cannot go beyond and if you say that is not possible, then we take root in the prison and make the prison more beautiful; then man can never be free. I think most of us accept that theory, though we all say we are this or we are that. And a mind that has gone into itself, delved into it—in the sense of meditation—will find out the limitations of conformity, without being told how to conform or not to conform.

So, when the mind understands, perceives, sees this imitative, conforming process, will not that very perception of conformity free the mind so as to be active without reaction? You see, sir, from that arises another question. I am not talking, I am observing the whole thing, experiencing the whole thing as we go along. There is another thing involved in this, which is maturity. Maturity, for most of us, is growing from boyhood to middle age and then to old age physically. Mentally we are not mature. A mature mind is not a mind which is in a state of contradiction. A mature mind is not a mind that is in a tension of that contradiction. A mature mind is not a mind that merely conforms through the urge or the demand for power, position, prestige. I feel a mature mind is that mind which comprehends all this—power, imitation, the evilness of power, the corruption of conformity through ambition, competition, the conformity to a pattern whether established by society or by the mind itself through its own experience. A mind which is held in all these patterns of activities is an immature mind and therefore a mediocre mind.

So, can a mind, seeing all this, go beyond it? That is the question. So, let us discuss this. What is the function of a talk like this? Is it not that you and I, though I am talking, should not only hear but experience these things in living? This, a talk should do. When you leave, you cannot be what you were when you came in. You have to discover what you are and break through; the very perception is the breaking through; you don't have to break through.

Question: Do you think a detached action will lead to this?

KRISHNAMURTI: Now, what do we mean by a detached action?

Comment: Not caring for the results.

KRISHNAMURTI: You say that detachment implies not seeking the results, the profits, the ends thereof. It is a theory, the Gita says so and we repeat it. It is not a fact in your life. You want to be a superintendent or a bigger boss or a still bigger boss; there is always the imitation, always the end in view. Now before we see whether detachment will lead or help one to understand action without reaction, we must find out what we mean, not only verbally, but semantically, by the word *detachment,* and from what we are to be detached. And before we ask what detachment is, should we not ask why we are attached? Detachment is not important, surely, but *why* we are attached. If I can understand the process of attachment, then there is no question of detachment.

Comment: Attachment is normal. It is instinct. And detachment is something you have to arrive at, a positive act.

KRISHNAMURTI: You say that attachment is natural, and detachment is something to arrive at through discipline. Now, is attachment natural? Have you seen the little puppies on the roadside, sir? The mother feeds them for about 4 to 6 weeks, and afterwards they are detached from the mother. This is true of birds and animals. They don't squeal about detachment. They don't practice attachment.

Comment: That is a biological process and this is an intellectual process.

KRISHNAMURTI: Oh, that is a biological process! Again, a mother is attached to a baby, why? It is a biological process. No? You are attached to your children; is it a biological process? Now, why are you attached? Please don't say that we must be attached or that we must not be attached. I am asking why we are attached; examine that first. Is it natural, biological, to be attached? Why are you attached? That is good enough, begin with that.

Comment: One should not be attached as soon as the children can stand on their own legs.

KRISHNAMURTI: What do you mean by "should not"? The fact is that we are attached. Why are you attached? We have to examine that first. But before we understand why we are attached, we want to detach. Sir, why are you attached? Why am I attached to this house? I feel secure in having a job, in being a big man, in being a big noise; and I say, "This is my house, my wife, my child—my, my, my." Now what is behind that? You know you are attached to your wife and children. Why are you attached? Sir, the psychological reason is insufficiency, fear, moodiness, loneliness; all these things compel me unconsciously or consciously to identify myself with this house, with a job, with a position of importance, never something below me, but always up, never with a cheap thing, but always with the prime minister, never with a man, but with God. So this process of identification creates attachment, obviously, doesn't it? Look how difficult it is to break down the idea to which you are so attached, the idea of Christ, the idea of somebody else, and the idea which one has created for oneself! You are attached to these ideas, and then you ask, "How am I to be detached?" If I know how, for what reasons, why I am attached, then my concern is not detachment but the understanding of attachment, and from there, there is no problem. I am attached—which means all the pain, all the misery, the confusion, the contradiction, the frustration, fears—I like that, and I say, "Yes, I like this and I live it." But without understanding this, if I talk about detachment, it has no meaning, it is just a pastime.

Do you know, do you feel, that you are seeking power, that your mind is conforming? Do you know that you are mediocre? Do you know it, feel it? Or are you afraid to face the fact that you are dull, mediocre? Sir, mustn't I recognize what I am before I do anything else? How can I undertake the job of a minister or a captain or a general or an admiral if I do not know the job? I must have the capacity, I must first see what I am, and not react. I must recognize the fact first, mustn't I?

Let us take a very simple thing. Sir, do I recognize that I am insensitive, dull, mediocre? If I don't recognize it, I am pretending, am I not? But in actuality, I cannot pretend; if I have got cancer, I cannot pretend that I have no cancer. And if I can recognize that I am dull, then a different action takes place. Either I become terribly depressed because I say, "I must be clever like that man," and I begin to discover that I am comparing and that the very dullness comes about through comparison. Or, when I recognize that I am dull, insensitive, then I am not insensitive, I am not dull. But the man who pretends that he is never dull—he is the most stupid man.

Have you, has the mind watched itself thinking, sir? We are not merely concerned with the movement of thought, with the nature of thinking, but what to think and what not to think. We do not watch the river flowing by, we do not see the boat or the little buoy on the river; but we say, "Now, can I use that water for hydroelectricity or take it to my garden or this or that?" We don't move with the thought. Now, we are thinking not in terms of how to change thinking, or to change the content of thinking, but about the very nature of thinking. You understand, sir? Now, to find out the nature of thinking, one has to follow it, not say, "I must change, I must not change"—which is to be aware of the movement of thinking. Sir, have you ever tried for a given period of time, say ten minutes, to put down precisely what you think? Please try this: just to put down on paper for ten minutes every thought. Try it, sir; then what happens? First you find your thought is moving very rapidly; then by writing down, your thought becomes slower. Doesn't it? But if you say that you cannot do it because the thought is too rapid or that it is difficult, it is finished. But if you say, "I am going to write down for ten minutes this morning every thought, whatever the thought may be—good, bad, vulgar, successful, nonsuccessful," and if you write it down, you will see that the mind, in the very process of putting it down, becomes slower. If you put it down as an exercise that you are doing, then there is a restriction, then there is an effort, then it is like putting on the brake of a car which you want to slow down. You may succeed, you may fail, but just do it for the fun of it, and then you begin to discover that the mind can be astonishingly slow, precise, and that the mind that is slow can be made tremendously fast.

We have seen that through contradiction a tension is created, and that tension in action produces certain results and, as most of us are in a state of self-contradiction, that self-contradiction produces a certain activity. All activities of a person whose mind is in a state of contradiction within itself are most destructive, whether that person is a marvelous writer or a great painter or a great politician. Sir, are you aware of your self-contradiction and the action born of that self-contradiction? Apparently, it is almost impossible to look at ourselves. We are always looking at ourselves through the mirror of somebody else. Sir, how do we discuss this thing? We can discuss only if you don't quote anybody, if you don't quote any book, but if you can experience something directly. Apparently that is not possible for most of us, and we do not even know that we are quoting.

Comment: Sir, if conformity leads to contradiction, absolute nonconformity may lead to absolute confusion.

KRISHNAMURTI: First of all, sir, is the present society in which we live in such good order, beautifully arranged, everything functioning beautifully? Is there not chaos in India, in the world? What do you mean by nonconformity and conformity? Sir, even the most ascetic man in power conforms when occasion, death or marriage, arises; though he says, "I don't conform," he conforms. Doesn't he? You see this everywhere. Ceremonies have no meaning, surely. Yet you people do ceremonies. Don't you, sir, in some form or other? You do ceremonies that have no meaning, and yet you are all professors and intellectuals, you call yourselves modern. This is an obvious contradiction, isn't it? We are totally unconscious, carrying on in what you call the modern way and living in an ancient world—which is a contradiction. You follow, sir? Don't bring them to clash, avoid the clash, that is all; one part of the mind says, "Let me carry on in the traditional way," and the other part of the mind says, "I will drive a car." You don't ever allow the two to meet. So, in order to avoid that conflict, we keep them apart—that is all what we are doing. And then in the middle of all this mess and confusion, we talk about God.

Comment: Sir, conformity is essential to some extent.

KRISHNAMURTI: Yes, sir. I conform by keeping to the right side of the road, I conform by buying the postage stamp, I conform by putting on cloth, I conform to certain activities which society demands—buying, taxes, and all the rest of it. Now, does conformity of such a kind interfere with the state of the mind which says, "I must find out what it is to live without conformity"?

Question: May I know the technique for comprehension?

KRISHNAMURTI: Sir, do you mean to say that you learn something through a technique? You know the jet? I do not know anything about the jet. I know a little about the piston engines because I have taken them out and put them together. I do not know anything about the jet. I want to learn and to know all about it. Do I have a method by which to learn? Do stick to this one point, sir. Do I have a method to learn, or do I go to somebody who teaches me, points out various parts of the jet machine, and I listen and learn? There is no technique to learning. Sir, to learn something, the mind mustn't know anything about it. Don't agree. If I know nothing about anything, then I can learn. If I know something about something, I am only adding to it. Sir, take your own example. You are all so-called religious people. I do not know what that means. But I accept it, that you are all religious people. You are all seeking God. But actually you know nothing about God, actually nothing. Now if you want to know, you cannot carry all your Upanishads, Gita, Koran, and all the rest of it; you must learn; your mind must be empty to learn; you cannot go to that God with all your prejudices, your compulsions and wants and hopes and fears; you must go to it empty to learn. To learn about something, there must be a sense of not knowing. If I know already about the jet, I learn along the same line. I add more to what I already know. That is not learning. That is only adding; addition is not learning.

Sir, look at a flower when you go out in your garden, or at a flower on the roadside;

just look at it; don't say, "It is a rose, it is this and that." Just look at it, and in looking at it that way, you learn—learn about the petal, what the stem is like, what the pollen is like, and so on. Can you keep on looking at it every time afresh, at every flower, not just say, "It is a rose," and finish with it? That means, can I look at my wife, my child, the neighbor, always with new eyes? Sir, this requires a great deal of self-penetration.

January 18, 1961

Sixth Talk in New Delhi

The last few times that we have met here, we have been discussing the question of action—what is action?—because it seems to us that it is a very vital question to be understood and thereby to be carried out in life. We have divided life, haven't we, into various categories of action: the political, the religious, the economic, the social, the individual, and the collective. And it seems to me, in so dividing life, we are never acting totally, we can never act totally. We act in fragments invariably leading to contradiction. And it is this contradiction, both in society and in the individual, that leads to all kinds of complex miseries and frustrations. These contradictions help us to avoid facing realities and escape to some illusory ideas, God, truth, behavior, and all the rest of it. And it seems to me that it is very important to understand what an action is which is total, which is comprehensive, which is not broken up into fragments. And to understand that total action, we have to investigate—not verbally or intellectually, but actually—and see how the mind that is broken up into fragments functions at one level vigorously, efficiently and lives at other levels in a state of chaos, misery, travail, and so on.

And as we were saying the day before yesterday, the action of which we are mostly aware is that of dependence—dependence on another, on society, on a job which gives satisfaction and thereby also invites misery. And if one goes into this question of dependence, one sees how extraordinarily we depend on belief psychologically, inwardly, for our happiness, for our sustenance, for our inward sense of well-being. I do not know if we have not noticed, in ourselves and in others, that our action is essentially very deeply based on this dependence. We depend on another for our happiness and, in our relationships, this dependence obviously does breed a certain kind of action which inevitably breeds fear. And it is this fear that is the motive for most of our action, the desire to be secure in our relationships; and thereby we bring about a necessity, don't we, of belonging to something. Most of us want to be committed to something. I do not know if we have investigated this extraordinary urge to belong to something, belong to some society, to some association, belong to a group, belong to a particular ideological structure, belong to a country, belong to a certain class. And I do not know if you have not noticed this: the so-called intellectual is so committed and, after having been committed to one form of activity, finds it futile, joins another and keeps on moving from one to another—which is called seeking—and thereby the very urge becomes the action which is the outcome of an urge to belong, to commit oneself to something.

Sir, this discussion this morning, it seems to me, would be utterly futile if we merely remain at the verbal level—that is, if we merely discuss intellectually or verbally, and not go into the problem deeply within ourselves to find out why we belong to something, why we are committed as a Hindu, as a Buddhist, as a communist, or committed to the urge to belong, which is very indicative of the fact that most of us cannot stand alone. We are either Catholics or one of the hundred things you know. We are committed not only to outward organizations but to ideas, to ideals, to examples, to a certain pattern of thought and action. We have to be aware of this commitment and to find out what lies behind it psychologically, inwardly. And it seems to me, unless we go into that whole question of what is the impulse that makes us commit ourselves to a certain course of action, a certain pattern of thinking, certain ways of activity, we will never come upon that feeling of living totally, in which the very living is action. And that is one of the problems.

The other problem is surely, is it not, that in understanding action, we must comprehend also function and status. Most of us use function to gain status. We use function to be something, to become something psychologically, inwardly. We use the very doing of something efficiently in order to achieve prestige, position, and power. So, to us action is not important, the function of doing something is not important, but what it is going to give us. Now we are going to get prestige, power, position—that is for us important. And as we were saying the other day, power, the feeling of dominance, the feeling of importance—which obviously is contrary to humility—this sense of power is evil. Whether it is exercised by the politician, by the guru, by the wife over the husband, by the husband over the wife, or by the master over the servant, the sense of power is obviously the most evil thing on earth. And we are so little aware of it. I do not know if you have not noticed all these things, what importance we give not to the function but to the status which is derived from function. You know the way you treat an important man, the tremendous respect and the garlands you put round his neck. So all this surely involves the understanding and the awareness of one's own thinking, of an inward perception of one's behavior and motive, the urges, the compulsions that lie behind action; this obviously involves, does it not, the awareness of every movement of thought and the motive behind our thought, the root from which thought, as a tree, grows. Until we are aware of this whole process of the structure of thought, action must inevitably be broken up, and therefore there can never be a total action, and so we live in a state of contradiction all our life.

So, perhaps, this morning we could profitably discuss not only function and status and the urge to commit oneself to something, to belong to something, but also go into this question of knowledge and the freedom from knowledge, which is essential to discover the unknowable. Could we go into all that this morning, could we discuss that, would that be of interest to you?

This is not a matter of agreement or disagreement. We are trying to investigate, we are trying to find out, we are trying to explore. And a mind that is merely assenting or disagreeing or agreeing is not exploring; it is just hearing certain words and is not self-examining.

You know, sir, the problem of knowledge is very interesting, and so is the question of knowing. Is there a knowing when we are pursuing knowledge? Most of us read a great deal. The more intellectual we are, the greater the capacity to read and to correlate, to argue, theorize. And knowledge seems to me to be a great hindrance to knowing. The machines, the calculators, the electronic brains have great knowledge all stored up in them; they are capable of doing astonishing calculations in a split second. They can tell you the history of any country, if the electronic brain has been informed about that country sufficiently. They can compose, they can write poems, they can paint. A monkey in America has painted pictures, and some of these pictures are hung in museums. We are all experts in technique, all the result of knowledge. The specialist obviously specializes in a particular technique, as a doctor, an engineer, a scientist. Is that specialist capable of creation? I do not mean inventing. Invention is entirely different from creation. And is the mind which is so burdened with knowledge capable of creation? Will the technique of the bureaucrat, of the man who is capable of functioning mechanically at a certain level, make him capable of this sense of creative being, creative reality, creative living? Sirs, this may not be your question. I think this is the question that is confronting the rest of the world. Because, in the world there is an increase of knowledge, of facts, how to do things better, greater insistency on capacity, and being a perfect functionary, based on knowledge, obviously; and so human beings are becoming more and more mechanical. Is that the way of realizing or unfolding human freedom? Is that the way to discover something which is not measured by the mind, the unnameable, the unknowable, to discover that thing which man has been seeking for centuries and centuries, millenniums? Can that be discovered through knowledge, through a system, a method, through yoga, through a path, or through the various philosophical ideas? For me, knowledge has nothing whatever to do with the other. And to discover the other, for the other to be, for the other to come, there must be an innocency of the mind, surely. And the mind is not innocent when it is crowded with knowledge. And yet, knowledge is worshiped as well as the man who has astonishing capacity, gift, talent. So, I think, it is essential to find out whether knowledge is essential, and to free the mind from knowledge so that it can move, it can fly, it can be in a state of innocency.

Knowledge is necessary for function, to do something efficiently, thoroughly, completely, well. Knowledge is essential to be a first-class carpenter. To work in a garden, you must know something about soil, about the plant, how to do this and that; to be a good administrator, you must know, you must have the experience, knowledge as an engineer or this or that. And surely the calamity comes when function is used to acquire a status. Perhaps, if we understood that, we could differentiate and keep clearly the limitations of knowledge and spill over from knowledge to freedom, if I can so put it; then there is the freedom from status. I am not sure whether I am making the issue clear. To go from here to your home, knowledge is essential. Knowledge is essential to communicate. I know English and you know English. If I spoke in French or Italian, you would not know it. Knowledge is essential to do your job. But that very knowledge we use to acquire position, power. And it seems to me the beauty of the abandonment of the world is the abandonment of status. The man who gives up the world—which is symbolized by putting on a robe, or joining a monastery, or eating one meal a day—has not given up the world at all; it is a farce; he is still pursuing power, power over himself, power over others, the urge to be, to become, to arrive. So, is it possible to see the importance and the necessity of functioning perfectly, capably, and not let that function take us willingly or unwillingly into the paths of destructive usages of that function?

Sir, it is no good your merely listening to me, hearing some words. I feel that you have to perceive the truth of the fact that function in itself is right, true, good, noble, but when it is used for status, it becomes evil because it leads to power, and the pursuit of power is an action that is destructive. Sir, if I see something, if I see a cobra, a poisonous snake, the very perception is action, isn't it? If I see a bottle marked "poison," that very seeing stops all action towards that poison. To see something false as false is complete action. You don't have to say, "What am I to do?" So, attention, not concentration, mere attention is the thing that is going to resolve.

Sir, I see very clearly for myself that humility is absolutely essential. A mind that is burdened with knowledge is never, can never be humble. And there is humility which is not cultivated. The humility that is cultivated is the most stupid form of vanity. And there is humility when I see the truth that function as knowledge is essential, and therefore it is not dependent on anybody. But when that function is utilized to become or to achieve, or to usurp a position, power, then status becomes evil. I see all that very clearly—not merely verbally, intellectually, but as I see a nail on the road, as I see very clearly my face in a mirror. I cannot alter it; it is a fact as it is. In the same way, to perceive this thing, to see it—that very seeing does something. And for us, the seeing is the difficulty—not the how or what to do after the seeing—because we are so committed to knowledge, using function in order to achieve power. After all, the clerk is bored with his job, and yet he does his best to get on to the next rung of the ladder, and he is climbing. He wants success, more money, more—you know all the rest of it. And the whole structure of society is based on achievement and acquisition.

Comment: Status comes automatically if one functions effectively. Status, in that case, is not evil because it is got without pursuing it.

KRISHNAMURTI: Look how clever we have become! If status comes to me without my asking, it is perfectly good. Is it? How cunning our minds are, isn't it so? One has to pursue function and, even if status comes, one has to avoid status like poison.

Question: Would not that be a reaction, sir?

KRISHNAMURTI: No, sir. For most of us action is reaction, and this reaction expresses itself in competition as the good and the bad, the big man and the little man, the example and the follower—all contradictions and competition and achievement. So, when I use the word *avoid*, it is not a reaction. I am using the word avoid in the ordinary dictionary sense of the word avoid. That is not a reaction. When you see something poisonous, you avoid it; it is not a reaction.

We want position, consciously or unconsciously, we want to be somebodies. Now, sir, take this town—appalling, flying with flags and power. We want to be in the center of the show and to be invited to the grand fair. Because you are a good functionary, you are a respectable citizen, you fit into the framework of this appalling structure of power and acquisition. But if you saw the real brutality of all this, not the loveliness of a blue sky, but the brutality, the harshness, the acquisitiveness, the demand for power and the worship of power, if you actually felt this, then status would be nothing to you, even to accept it or to reject it; you would be out of this.

Question: Sir, we have to function in some sphere or another in society, and that requires more and more knowledge relating to that sphere. Then, how can it be said that more and more knowledge takes us away from knowing?

KRISHNAMURTI: I need knowledge to function. I need more and more knowledge to function as a scientist or as an engineer, properly, fully. Now, where does that knowledge interfere with knowing? Knowing is in the active present, isn't it? Knowledge is in the past. And most of our knowing is an additive process—that is, we add to what we already know, and that we call increasing the knowledge. That is what we do. That is how we function, add, add, add to what we already know, and that gives us capacity, and that capacity gives us status. That gives us efficiency to which society adds status.

Question: Suppose I don't care for that status?

KRISHNAMURTI: No, sir. It is no use supposing. I know it is very nice to say, "suppose" and to proceed theoretically. But actually one has to see the deadliness of function which leads to status, and also to see what is knowledge and knowing. Knowing is always in the active present. Knowing, the verb itself—going, loving, doing, thinking—is always active in the present. Now, if you are merely using the knowing as an additive process to the past as knowledge, then surely there is no knowing; it is merely adding. To know something, for knowing, your mind must be fresh all the time, mustn't it? It must be a movement, mustn't it? But when the movement as knowing becomes knowledge, it ceases to be a movement. Sir, don't accept my word for this. This is a psychological, inward fact. Now, can I function always in the state of knowing, not with knowledge? Please think about it. Don't accept or reject it, but go into it.

Always I have to function, but that involves a much more complex problem, which is that of education. Society demands certain forms of functionaries—engineers, scientists, specialists in arms, and bureaucrats. Therefore society and government are concerned with the cultivation of those particular faculties which will be helpful to society, to organize society, and they say, "educate." But they are not concerned with the total education. Now, is not education the total development of man, not only of a particular function? The total development of man includes function. But mere pursuit of a function, and not the total development, leads obviously to contradiction in oneself, in society, as well as in the individual. So one has to begin again all anew to see if there cannot be a way of education, a school where education is given so that the mind is aware totally and not merely in one direction.

So, sir, to go back to this question which is, psychologically, very interesting—which is: Knowledge, and knowing whether the mind can function, be active in a function, knowing all the time, not active merely mechanically with knowledge.

Comment: Sir, in the process of doing, there is recognition, and recognition becomes knowledge.

KRISHNAMURTI: Knowledge implies recognition. Doesn't it? I know you, sir, because I have seen you half a dozen times. And the memory interferes with our meeting, with my seeing you. Now, I have already the memory, the prejudices, the imprints which block, which prevent my seeing you now. Can I not look at you now without the impediment of all that? Now can I not look at you in the active present without thought, though I have thought?

Sir, let us take a much closer example. Can I look at my wife anew, without all the thousand yesterdays, without the many yesterdays of rankle, bitterness, quarrels, jealousies, anxieties, images, and emotional, sexual urges? Or is it not possible? Don't agree, sir. It is not a matter of agreement or disagreement.

Can I look at somebody with whom I am living, with whom I live day after day, without all the recollections and reminiscences and remembrances? Though I have lived with that person for many days, can I look at him anew? Is that possible? Can I look at something without the past interfering with it? There is the past; I cannot help it. I lived yesterday. I cannot deny yesterday. But can I die to yesterday and look? Let us put it round the other way, sir. Is there sensitivity?

If there is no sensitivity, there is the blunting all the time, the becoming dull. To see anything, there must be sensitivity. To see the squalor, the beauty, the dirt, and all the poverty, the beauty of the skies, the flowers, there must be sensitivity. Now, to see beauty or ugliness and not make it mechanical, you must see it afresh each time. Sir, if I remember yesterday's sunset and the beauty of it, I cannot see the sunset of today. That is a psychological fact. Now can I look at the sunset today, though I have seen the sunset of yesterday? This means a constant movement—moving, moving—without establishment, without being fixed. Sir, the psychological pleasure, the glory of yesterday, the remembrance of yesterday prevents the glory of today.

Sir, let us put the problem differently. How is the mind to be very young, fresh? I don't know if you have ever thought about it. And it is only the young mind that is revolutionary, that sees, that is always in a state of determining, not in a state of determined action. So, how is a mind to be, to remain young in that sense?

Comment: Forget yesterday.

KRISHNAMURTI: Oh, no, you cannot forget that. You want your house; you cannot forget brutality, your ways, your habits, the brutality of society—it is there at your door nagging all the time. You cannot forget it. But you can see how the mind is made dull, stupid, by this incessant storing up. Sir, that is why I brought in the issue of commitment. If we are not committed to something in some form or other, we are lost human beings. If you don't call yourself a Hindu, a Christian or a Buddhist or a communist or a fascist, you will be completely lost; and therefore, to bring about a collective action, you join something, you belong to something with all the implications of power, position, prestige, and all the ugliness of all that. So, really what we want is not freedom but security, security in knowledge which is recognizable by you and by society. Why need I put on a sannyasi robe if I have abandoned the world in the sense: I do not want power in any form? What is the point of it? But I put on that robe essentially for recognition, though inwardly I may be boiling over.

So, sir, I think we must honestly, but not verbally and cheaply, tackle this problem of security, why the mind demands security in so many ways—in my relationships with my wife, with my child, in my relationship with society, ideas, ideations, and in function as power, position, status, in committing myself to something. Why is there this urge for security? I wish, sir, you would go into it and not merely listen to what I am saying because you have to live with yourself. Why this urge for security—for social welfare, for the welfare of society from the womb to the tomb? The feeling of security is the most destructive thing on God's earth, the feeling that I have achieved, the feeling that I know, the idea that there is a permanent soul, a permanent atma, Brahma. Why this constant demand? That is why we have methods, systems of yoga, systems of meditation, and all the other absurdities. If we could tackle this urge for security, the compulsion that makes the mind demand security, then we would understand this whole thing.

Comment: Sir, it is fear of the unknown.

KRISHNAMURTI: Yes, sir, fear of the unknown—fear of not having a job, fear of public opinion, fear of death, living, thinking, every form of fear—therefore, you want to be secure. Now, what do you mean by "fear"? Do examine it, sir. Don't give me or yourself a verbal explanation. What is the significance, what lies behind that word fear, what do you mean by fear? What is the nature of fear, not the content of fear, the thing itself, not a description of it? Sir, take a very simple thing. I am afraid of what my wife or husband or my neighbor says. Now I want to find out not the explanations for that fear but the nature, the quality of that fear, what it means to be afraid. Now, what does it mean? What is the nature of the mind that says, "I am afraid"? Sir, how do you find out the nature of something? I want to find out the nature of fear. What do I do? First of all, I must cease to give verbal explanations, mustn't I? I must look at fear. To know what fear is, I must look at it; I must not say, "It is red, blue, it is purple, it is not nice." I must look at it, which means I must cease to give an opinion or the description of the content of fear. Can I so look at fear?

Look, sir, I am afraid of death. I want to understand the nature of the fear which says, "I am afraid of death." Now, how do I look at it? I only know it because of something else, don't I? I only know fear because of the effect. I only know fear through words, through the effects, through the influence that it is going to bring, or may bring, or may not bring—which means I look at the thing with an opinion, with a conclusion. Can my mind look at fear without opinions and conclusions? Our mind is made up of conclusions, opinions, judgments, and evaluations, isn't it? When I say I am thinking, the thinking process is that. Now, can I look at something without that process? Don't say no, don't deny or accept it. Can you look, can I look at something without this mental intellectualism going on? Sir, look. I want to know all about death--to know, to experience, not just say, "I am afraid of death, what am I to do?" What do I do? I have never experienced death before. I have seen dead bodies being carried away. I have seen my relations die. I know there is death inevitably. But while living, functioning alive, feeling, I want to know what it means, not at the last moment when something is being carried away. I want to know now how to die. If you are going to lose your job, you will at once put your mind to that, you will have sleepless nights until you find a way out.

I want to find out what it means to die. I cannot take a drug and die; then I will be unconscious. So, how do I proceed? Sir, death is inevitable; at the end of fifty or sixty years, death is inevitable. I don't want to wait until that. I want to find out, to know what death means, so that in the very knowing, fear is gone. How do I set about it? You have been taught escapes, but not to find out how to die.

You know, sir, what it means to die. Don't you? Have you died to anything, to any pleasure, to any pain? Just to die to a pleasure—this means, what? I drink, and it gives me a certain relief, a certain pleasure, a certain dulling or a certain quickening effect. Can I die to that—die, in which no effort is involved? Because, the moment I exercise effort to die to something, it is merely a continuity of that something.

Sir, let us come a little nearer. You have insulted me, or you have flattered me. You have looked at me, you have not greeted me, you are jealous of me. Can I die to that memory without effort? What, sir? That is a dying, isn't it? You cannot bargain with death, you understand? You cannot say to death, "Please let me have a few days more." So, in the same way, can you die to memory? Perhaps you can die to some pain, but can you equally die to pleasure, can you? Sir, just try that a little bit; then you will know what it is to die to yesterday, yesterday being memory. You follow? I want to know what it is to die, to die to this demand for continuity, to die to this incessant urge for security, to die to the thing which I call fear, to die to something. If I die to these, then I will know what death is; then the mind will know what it is to be in a state where it has passed through death and is not contaminated by its pain.

So, the problem, sir, is this: A mind that is not innocent can never receive that which is innocent. God, truth, or whatever the thing that is not nameable—the immeasurable—that cannot be without an innocent mind, without a mind that is dead to all the things of society, dead to power, position, prestige, dead to knowledge. After all, power, position, prestige is what we call living. For us, that is life; for us, that is action. You have to die to that action, and you cannot do it because that is what you want. Sir, to die to the things which we call living is the very living. If you go down that street and see the power, those flags which are the measures of power, and if you die to all that, it means that you die to your own demand for power which has created all this horror.

Comment: It is some sort of total annihilation.

KRISHNAMURTI: Why not? What is living but total annihilation? Is the way you live now really living? Sir, we want to gain heaven without going through anything; we want to be mediocre human beings, completely comfortable and secure, and have our drinks and our sex and our power, and also have that thing which we call heaven.

So, sirs, to sum up: To be alone, which is not a philosophy of loneliness, is obviously to be in a state of revolution against the whole setup of society—not only this society, but the communist society, the fascist, every form of society as organized brutality, organized power. And that means an extraordinary perception of the effects of power. Sir, have you noticed those soldiers rehearsing? They are not human beings any more, they are machines, they are your sons and my sons, standing there in the sun. This is happening here, in America, in Russia, and everywhere—not only at the governmental level, but also at the monastic level, belonging to monasteries, to orders, to groups who employ this astonishing power. And it is only the mind which does not belong that can be alone. And aloneness is not something to be cultivated. You see this? When you see all this, you are out, and no governor or president is going to invite you to dinner. Out of that aloneness there is humility. It is this aloneness that knows love—not power. The ambitious man, religious or ordinary, will never know what love is. So, if one sees all this, then one has this quality of total living and therefore total action. This comes through self-knowledge.

Belief in God is detrimental to the experiencing of that reality. If I believe God is this or that, it is a detriment, and I cannot experience that at all. To experience, my mind must be clean, swept, purged of all these—which means my mind must be totally in a state in which no influence of any kind has touched it. And from that state, action is total, and therefore all action in that state is good and has an extraordinary capacity because it is not a contradictory, conflicting action. Sir, don't you know this: When you love to do something—not because somebody tells you, not because you have some reward—you do it most efficiently? You give your body, your mind, your whole being to it when you love something.

January 20, 1961

Seventh Talk in New Delhi

This is the last talk. The day before yesterday, when we met, we were considering the question of fear and the compulsive urge to seek power in different forms. And it seems to me that it is quite important to understand how to meet fear. For most of us fear is constant, unconsciously or consciously.

As most of us have this fear, it is quite important, I think, to meet that fear without engendering other problems. We were saying that we are afraid of death, we are afraid of insecurity, we are afraid of losing jobs, we are afraid of not advancing, we are afraid of not being loved, we are afraid of so many things. And how is it possible to meet fear openly, easily, and not let fear breed other problems, which consciously or unconsciously build up our lives? I think we could approach that issue by understanding what is sleep and what is meditation. You may think it is far-fetched, but I do not think it is, if we go along a little.

For most of us, effort seems to be the very nature of existence; every form of effort is our daily bread—effort to go to the office, effort to work, effort to get up, effort to achieve a certain result—we live by effort. And it has become part of us. And we fear that if there is no effort, we shall stagnate; and so we are constantly battling with ourselves to be alive by pressure, by discipline, and not only by pursuing ambition as a means of stirring us up, but also by making effort to think rightly, to feel rightly, to resist. That is our very existence. And I wonder if any of us has really seriously considered why we make effort at all and if effort is necessary. Or, does effort prevent understanding? Understanding, it seems to me, is the state of mind which is capable not only of listening to everything that is being said explicitly but also of directly perceiving things very simply. And a mind that is merely interpretative is not capable of understanding. A mind that merely compares is incapable of clear perception.

We will discuss this as we go along, but I am just laying the foundation, as it were, for our discussion. We do see things very clearly and sharply and precisely when we give our complete attention, not only verbally, intellectually, emotionally, but with our whole being. Then we are in a state of real perception, real comprehension. And that state, obviously, is not the result of effort. Because, if we are making an effort to comprehend, that effort implies struggle, resistance, a denial, and all our energy is taken away by that effort to resist, to try to understand, to try to resist.

So, I think, we have to understand that effort does prevent perception. You know when you try to hear something and you are making an effort to hear, you really don't hear; all your energy is gone in making the effort. And if we can merely see this issue, not how not to make effort, just see it, then we can go to something which is important in discussing effort and fear—namely, consciousness, which is broken up for most of us into the unconscious and the conscious. The conscious is the superficial layer which is often dull, which has been educated, which has acquired a certain technique and functions at the superficial level.

Please, sirs, you are not merely listening to a certain series of words or ideas, but actually in the very listening, you are experiencing what is being said; then only such a listening is worthwhile. But if you are merely listening to the words, to the ideas, then such a hearing has no value at all. If it is self-applicable, then your listening has real depth. So I hope you will so listen.

We function superficially, and our daily life is very superficial. But there is a great depth, hidden away in the vast recesses of the mind, which is the hidden, the unconscious. That is the racial, the traditional, the accumulated knowledge, experience of the race, of the human being, of the individual. So, there is a contradiction between the conscious mind which has acquired knowledge and technique and which is capable of adjusting itself to any environment, and that vast storehouse of hidden aspirations, compulsions, urges, motives, which is not so easily educated. And that contradiction shows itself in dreams during sleep, through symbols, through hints, intimations. And just before going to sleep, you have perhaps various forms of ideas, pictures, images, and as you dream, you have the interpretation of those dreams at the same time as you are asleep. So, the mind, the conscious as well as the unconscious, when it is asleep is in a constant turmoil, is constantly in a state of inquiring, searching, answering, responding, creating visions, symbols, which we call dreams. So, the mind is never at rest even though it is asleep. You must have noticed all this. There is nothing mysterious about it. These are obvious psychological facts which you can discover for yourself without reading any book. And I think one must investigate all that because that is part of self-knowledge, surely, of knowing the whole process of one's own mind.

So, without really understanding this process of contradiction within the mind, and the breeding of illusion which comes from this self-contradiction, meditation has very little meaning because meditation is an action, and we have been discussing action. I do not know what that word *meditation* means to you. Surely, meditation is, is it not, a process through exploration into the depths of the mind, and that exploration is the awakening of experience. This is not the experience according to a pattern, or a way, or a system, but the uncovering of the processes of conditioning so that the mind is actually experiencing those conditionings and going beyond. So, it seems to me, merely to have a desire to achieve a certain result in meditation does lead to various forms of illusion. You understand, sirs? Without knowing the process of thinking, without being aware of the contents, of the nature of thinking, meditation has very little value. But yet we must meditate because that is part of life. As you go to your office, as you read, as you think, as you talk, as you quarrel, as you do this and that, so also meditation is a part of this extraordinary thing called living. And if you do not know how to meditate, you are missing a vast field of life, perhaps the most important part of life.

I was told a lovely story of a disciple going to a Master, and the disciple taking a posture of meditation and closing his eyes; and the Master asks the disciple, "I say, what are you doing, sitting in that way?" And the disciple says, "I am trying to reach the highest consciousness," and the disciple shuts his eyes and continues. So, the Master picks up two pieces of rock and rubs and keeps on rubbing them together, and the noise awakens the disciple. And the disciple looks at it and says, "Master, what are you doing?" And the Master says, "By rubbing, I hope to produce in one of the pieces of stone a mirror." And the disciple smiles and says, "You can continue like that for ten thousand years, Master, but you will never produce a mirror." And the Master says, "You can sit like that for the next million years, and you will never find." You see, it reveals a great deal if you think about that story. We want to meditate according to a pattern, or we want a system of meditation; we want to know how to meditate. But meditation is a process of living; meditation is the awareness of what you are doing, of what you are thinking, of the motives, of the inner secrets of the mind, because we do have secrets. We never tell everything to another. There are hidden motives, hidden wants, hidden desires, jealousies, aspirations. Without knowing all these secrets, hidden urges, and compulsions, mere meditation leads to self-hypnosis. You can put yourself quietly to sleep through following a certain pattern, and that is what most of us are doing, not only in meditation, but in daily life. Great parts of us are asleep and blindly some parts of us are active—the part that is earning a livelihood, quarreling, successful; the part that is aspiring, hoping, achieving, breeding innumerable fears. So, we have to understand the totality of the mind. And the very understanding is meditation. Do you know how you talk to another, how you look at another, how you look at a tree, the evening sunset, the capacities that you have? Do you understand your vanity, the urge for power in which there is pride of achievement? Without understanding all this, there is no meditation. And the very understanding of this complex process of existence is meditation. And as one goes into this question very deeply, one begins to discover that the mind becomes extraordinarily quiet, not induced, not hypnotized by that word into a state of silence. Because most of us lead very contradictory lives, our lives are in a state of conflict all the time; whether we are awake or asleep, there is a burning conflict, misery, travail; and to try to escape from them through meditation only produces fear and illusion. So, it is very important to understand fear. And the very understanding of fear is the process of meditation.

If I may, let us go deeply into this question of fear because for most of us, fear is very near, very close to us. And without understanding that which is very close, we cannot go very far. So, let us spend a little time in understanding the extraordinary thing called fear. If we could understand that, then sleep has a totally different meaning. I will come to that presently. How to—I mustn't use the word *how,* because that only awakens in your mind the pattern of meeting fear. We are aware that we are afraid. I am sure you are aware of it. Now, before we inquire into fear, what do we mean by "being aware"? Let us examine that word and the feeling behind that word.

How do we see things actually, visually? And do we see anything, or do we merely interpret things? I hope you are following. Do I see you and you see me, or do you interpret what you see and I interpret what I see? Interpretation is not seeing. Is it? Please do spend a little time on this matter. Don't be too anxious to find out what meditation is. This is part of meditation. Can I see without interpretation? Can you see me without giving all kinds of tributes, without evaluation, without judgment—just see me, in which no name is employed? The moment you name, you have blocked yourself from seeing. I do not know if you have ever experimented with this thing. Sir, please give your attention to this because we are going to inquire into what it is to be aware of fear. We are examining what it means to be aware. What does it mean? It means, obviously, to be aware not only of the outward movement of thought and perception but also of the inward movement of thought and perception. Doesn't it? I see the trees and I respond; I see the people and I respond; I see beauty and there is a response to beauty; similarly, there is a response to ugliness, to all this squalor, the pomp, the sense of power. There is an observation externally, outwardly, which is interpreted, which is judged, criticized, and that very movement which goes outward also comes in—it is like a tide going in and out. By observing the outward movement, the mind also observes the inward movement of that same act with all its reactions. So awareness is this total process of the outward and inward movement of thought, of judgment, of evaluation, of acceptance, denial. Am I making it clear or not? Because unless we are clear on this point, we cannot go into the question of fear.

Sir, do we understand anything by naming it? You understand? Do I understand you when I say you are all Hindus, Buddhists, communists, this or that? Do I understand you by giving you a label? Or do I understand you when there is no naming, when there is no interference of the label? You follow, sirs? So, the process of labeling, giving a name, is really a hindrance to comprehension. And it is extremely subtle, extremely arduous, to observe something without giving a name, without giving a quality, because the very process of our thinking is verbalizing. Isn't it? What I am trying to convey is that awareness is a total process, not merely a state of mind which criticizes, evaluates, condemns, or compares. To understand why it compares, why it criticizes, why it evaluates, what is the process of this evaluation, what lies behind this judgment—the whole process of that is awareness, which is really the mind being aware of the whole process of its activities.

If one has grasped a little bit of that, we can then go into the question of fear, envy, and what jealousy means. Can you look at that feeling without giving it a name? Because, the naming process is the process of the thinker, who merely observes thought as though it were something apart from the thinker. We know the division between the thinker and the thought, the experiencer and the experienced. The thinker gives words to the thing that is being experienced, as pleasure and pain. When the thinker observes and does not give words to the things that it observes, then there is no difference between the thinker and the thing which is being observed; then it is one. Please do comprehend this thing because it is quite difficult. This is an extraordinary experience because the moment there is no division between the observed and the observer, there is no conflict. Do please understand this. This is really very essential because most of us live in a state of contradiction. And the problem is whether a mind can be so completely, totally whole that there is no observer and the thing observed, and thereby be free of contradiction. And so one must understand how this contradiction arises.

Sir, take a very simple example of envy, jealousy, anger. In all these things, in the moment of experiencing, there is no contradiction. But the second after that experiencing, there is contradiction as the thinker, the observer, looks at the thing and says, "It is good, or it is bad; it is anger, or it is envy." At the moment of experience, there is no contradiction—which is an extraordinary thing. Only when the experiencing is over, the second after, begins the contradiction. And this contradiction arises when the thinker is in the process of judging, evaluating what he has observed, either accepting or denying it—which is essentially a process of verbalizing or reaction according to his conditioning. So, to wipe away this contradiction, can the thinker observe without giving words to that thing which is being observed?

Have you ever gone into the question of words, how the mind is a slave to words—the Hindu, the Buddhist, the Muslim, the communist, the capitalist, the democrat, the congressman, the wife, husband, the word *God*, or no God? Our mind is a slave to words. And to free the thought from the word—is that possible? Don't accept anything that I am saying. Is it possible to free a thought from the word? And if it is possible, then can the thinker, the observer, look at the thing without the label, without the term, without the symbol? And when it can so directly look, without the interference of the label, the word, the symbol, then there is no thinker observing the thing. Now this is meditation. You understand, sirs? And that requires enormous attention, which is not concentration at all. Attention implies a totality, an extension of a totality, whereas concentration is a limitation. So, the mind inquiring into the problem of fear, which is essentially a problem of contradiction, must understand this process of looking at a thing without the verbalization, which is essentially the memory interfering with the observer.

Comment: That totalization of the mind is an abstraction, withdrawing from the world.

KRISHNAMURTI: It is not an abstraction, sirs. You see the difficulty? You give one meaning to a set of words and I give another meaning; and you come for the first time with your meaning, and though we have gone already into this, we have to begin all over again. So, I am sorry; I will not go into all that again. We are not talking in terms of abstraction. We are talking of the actual fact. We are not abstracting; we are looking into the process of the mind. The mind is looking at itself, which is not an abstraction. It is not deriving a conclusion from something. It observes, it is in a state of observation, and therefore there is no abstraction from which it judges, there is no deduction, there is no conclusion. The mind that is observing is never in a state of conclusion, and that is the beauty of a mind which is alive. A mind that functions from conclusion is no mind at all.

Look, sirs, let us begin again. Most of us have various forms of fear which distort our thinking, our way of life—we tell lies, we get angry, we are ambitious because we are afraid. A man who is not afraid, who has no fear, has no ambition. He does not want to say he lives; he is in a state of complete being. And from there you can begin to inquire into something that is not measurable. But a mind that is afraid, that tries to find that which is unnameable, not measurable—such a mind can never discover what is true. It can create illusions and it does, and lives in illusions. So, we really have to meet fear as it arises, and in the meeting of the fear, not bring about other series of reactions. How is one to meet it without reacting to it? Surely, the reaction arises only when you use the word *fear*, doesn't it?

Sir, look: you don't mind using the word *love;* when you use that word, you feel elated. But when you have a feeling, if you use the word *anger*, it has a condemnatory value already. So, to look at fear totally so that the observer is not separate from that feeling, there has to be no word or label which makes them separate. How do you look at, observe, fear? How do you know you are afraid?

Comment: If I find a cobra, I try to go back or do something, and that tells me afterwards that I was afraid of that cobra.

KRISHNAMURTI: Yes, sir. What do you mean by fear, what is the nature of fear—not what makes you afraid? A cobra makes you afraid, what public opinion says makes you afraid, death makes you afraid, your not achieving your marvelous height in the social ladder makes you afraid—they are the things that make you afraid. But do you know the nature of fear, not the things that make you afraid? Surely, there is a difference between the two, isn't there?

Have you ever really felt fear, lived with fear? Have you? Or, have you always avoided fear? Obviously, we have always avoided fear. When I am afraid, I turn on the radio, take a drink, go to the temple, go for a walk, or do a number of things, but I never live with fear. Do I live with fear as I have lived, or want to live, with pleasure? Both require a certain energy. Don't they? Sirs, to live with pleasure is something that gives you great pleasure, for that you must have great energy; otherwise, it destroys you. Now, to live with beauty and to live with ugliness demand energy. And this energy is destroyed when the word, the label, the symbol comes in and thereby creates a division in living with the thing. Do you understand?

Look, sir, I say you are dull. Can you look at yourself without reacting? You may not like to be told by somebody that you are dull, but when you look, when you observe, you realize that you are dull. Sir, aren't you dull when you don't see the beauty of the skies, the heavens, the earth, the trees, the squalor, the misery, the pomp, the power; when you don't observe all this, when you are blind, don't you realize that you are dull? Has somebody to tell you that you are dull? Is your dullness to be indicated by another, or do you realize yourself that you are dull? Sir, you see the difference between the two? When someone says you are dull, you accept it and merely react to it, or you say, "I am not dull. Who are you to tell me that I am dull?" The word *dull* has a condemnatory meaning, and you think you are so very clever, so very superior, though the fact is you are dull.

Take insensitivity. Insensitivity comes into being when the mind functions in habit, when it doesn't see, when it doesn't feel, when it is not alive to everything in life. I realize I am insensitive, I realize I am dull. What is my reaction? I immediately try to become clever, try to make an effort not to be dull. How can a dull mind make effort and be clever, be superior and free from dullness? It must realize that state fully. Now, to realize that state fully, completely, wholly, there must be no reaction. I must observe it. The mind must see it. And it may not observe, if it merely says, "Oh, I am dull, I must become clever, I must do this or I must do that." To observe, the mind must live with the fact. Every form of condemnation is an escape from the fact, and to live with the fact requires tremendous energy.

Sir, look: you see a tree there, don't you? You see over it the blue sky and the evening star, Venus, but you don't observe, you don't feel. Now to feel all this, the mind must be in a state of astonishing aliveness, with a sense of vibrant energy. And you cannot have energy if there is a contradiction between the observer and the observed. And the contradiction arises through reactions, through the employment of words or symbols, when the memory interferes between the observer and the observed. So, to look at fear, to live with fear, to meet fear without creating a contradiction between the fear and the observer is the problem. You understand, sirs? I may, through some trick, avoid one set of fears; but as I move in life, there is another fear and so on. Fear is like a shadow that suddenly comes, and it constantly comes. It is there. A mind that wants to understand fear and to be totally free of fear—not of just one form of fear—must have energy so that the mind is capable of being something else than being a slave to fear. For the mind to go into that, to live with it—it means being in this state of energy.

Now, the whole process of what we have been discussing is meditation. Meditation is not sitting in a room or a corner, cross-legged and all the rest of it, breathing and all that—which is self-hypnosis. But one has to go into this so that the mind during the day—as it walks, as it works, as it plays, as it observes—is aware without reacting, is aware, watching choicelessly, so that when it does go to sleep, there is some other process of action which is not the mere action of the conscious mind or the unconscious mind. When the mind has been very alert during the day watching, observing, unearthing every motive, every thought, every movement of thought, then, when it does sleep, it is in a state of quietness; then it can experience other things which are not merely experienced by the conscious mind. So meditation is a process not only during the waking period but also during the sleeping period. And then you will find that the mind has emptied itself of everything it has known, emptied itself of all its yesterdays—not that there are no yesterdays; there are the yesterdays, but the mind empties itself of all the responses of the yesterdays which condition the mind. You know, sirs, a thing that is completely empty is totally full. And it is only such a mind that can receive or comprehend that which is not measurable by a mind which is the outcome of time.

Question: Is not fear an instinct born with the child?

KRISHNAMURTI: So, you say fear is instinctive, is natural. Sir, as you are walking, you come across a cobra, a snake, and you instinctively jump back. Now, is that fear, and is it not natural? If you have no such instinctual reaction, you will be committing suicide. So, we have to draw a line between the sense of preservation, and the insensitivity which interferes with the psychological demand for security.

Let me put it round the other way. Sirs, we need food, clothes, and shelter. We need a certain cleanliness, a certain comfort, and that is essential. In probably fifty years or a hundred years the world will have an overflow of food because science is so advanced. Now, when do food, clothes, shelter interfere, or when does the mind use those things to be secure inwardly, psychologically? You are following what I am saying, sir? I need those things—you and I need food, clothes, and shelter. But we use this need for psychological purposes---a bigger house, bigger position; we use the need for power, position, prestige, and thereby create the whole picture of fear.

There is seeing a snake and the nervous reaction: that is one thing. The other thing is sitting in a room and imagining, thinking—thinking that this house might catch fire, that my wife might run away, that the snake might come in. This thinking process may engender or breed fear. There are two sets of neurological fears: one is with the meeting of a snake, and the other is the fear which thought awakens through the nerves, through imagination, through supposition.

Comment: This means that the instinctive response is not fear at all.

KRISHNAMURTI: Right. Fear is only there when thought is in operation. Don't say no, but examine it. There is the ordinary instinctual neurological response which, you say, is not fear. Perhaps it may be. The second is that thought awakens certain responses neurologically and thereby creates fear. Now these two are totally different. Is it possible to observe all neurological fears, including those awakened by thought, without the thought awakening fear?

Question: There are certain neurological responses which are awakened by thought which we call fear. How is it possible to observe the neurological responses of fear without the word fear, *without the name?*

KRISHNAMURTI: We have to understand the ways of thinking, the ways of thought, when we meet these neurological fears which are awakened through the word. I sit in a room, and my thought imagines and says, "I am going to lose my job, based on facts such as I am inefficient; or, my wife is going to run away, which may be or may not be factual; or there is death"; and this creates fear. Thought is creating fear through the future. In all fear, future is involved. That is tomorrow. I am living, I am functioning, but death may be there tomorrow. So, thought through time as the future creates fear. So, thought is time—thought based on the reactions and the responses of knowledge of many yesterdays through the present to the future.

We are talking of thought which is the content, which is the nature of time. I think I am going to become a big man, and I also think that I may not become a big man, and so there is fear. Thought creates fear. That is important. So, the question is: Can thought look at fear—that is, can thought look at neurological responses which are natural? Can thought which creates fear, look at fear? Do you look at anything with thought? Is thought in operation when you observe? You observe a rose, a flower; the very observation is verbalizing; it is the recognition that it is a rose—the word. Is there a looking at something without recognition? Can I look at fear without recognition?

When I use the word *fear,* there is inherent in it differentiation. The very employment of that word fear is a differentiation. The differentiation exists because there is the observer with his words, symbols, ideologies, and reactions—with these, he looks and thereby creates in the very observation a differentiation. Because he so observes through differentiation, he runs away from it or acts upon it. Is there observation of fear without differentiation? Fear can be met without differentiation only when there is no thinker with all the responsive reactions to the thing that he is observing. Can the observer look, without differentiation of the thing which he calls fear? He can only do that when he has understood the whole significance of living with that something entirely, totally. And he is not capable of living with that something totally when he is avoiding or accepting. And he avoids or accepts according to pain and pleasure—physical as well as psychological—which means that the word has assumed importance.

Sirs, you are all believers in God, aren't you, or in something else. You are believers in something, and that believing is conditioning your mind to certain responses. Now, we are asking whether the mind can look without the differentiation which the word makes. And to go into all that—which is the very essence, which is the process of self-knowledge—is meditation. And if you so meditate, then you will begin to discover for yourself that you can observe the feelings, the fears without this differentiation which the word creates, and you can therefore live with them so completely, totally, that the entire body of fear ceases. And such a mind is the creative mind; such a mind is the good mind; only such a mind can receive that which is immeasurable; only such a mind can receive the blessing of the eternal.

January 22, 1961

Bombay, India, 1961

First Talk in Bombay

We see throughout the world a dreadful and frightening chaos. Everywhere people are one against another, not only individually, but racially, communally, as a country, as a group, or as a race. Nationalism is rampant, increasing. The margin of freedom is very small, not only for the individual, but also for the community, for the mind. Religions are dividing people; they are not the unifying factor at all. And there is the increase of tyranny, either of the left or of the right. There are various forms of religions, sects—innumerable, in thousands—all over the world saying that they have the real stuff. Religious tyranny is equally abhorrent to a mind that is really seeking what is truth, as is political tyranny, and both are on the increase. Catholicism with its dogma, with its creeds, with its excommunications, and all the rest of it, is on the move, is spreading; so is communism also on the increase, with its excommunications, liquidations, and denials of human rights, thoughts, and freedom, spreading poverty, squalor, chaos. In fact, the house is burning, and literally burning; and there remains only the final explosion, which is the atomic bomb. All this we know in a minor or major degree.

Every individual not only has the feeling that something must be done to see the problem, not merely intellectually, but also feels the inward necessity of an urgent response to the whole total issue. When one does not feel the total issue, one goes about reforming socially, reviving the old religions, going back to the Upanishads, the Gita, or to some ancient thought, or following some leader who promises more. There is the feeling that as one cannot do it by oneself, one must leave it to somebody else—to the guru, to the political leader. And there is reform in patches—giving land, appeasing, pacifying, coexisting, twisting words to mean different things apart from the direct meaning in the dictionary, to suit one's own or one's party's ideological intentions. Sir, there is corruption, there is misery, there is increasing industrialization all over the world, and industrialization without revolution only leads to mediocrity and greater suffering.

A revolution of a different kind is necessary—that is what I want to discuss; that is what I want to go into. But I think one must see the utter futility of religious organizations completely, the absurdity of those organizations and of merely following a certain idea, a certain plan for the salvation of man. To a mind that is seeking truth, a religious leader has no meaning any more. I do not know how you feel about all this. But watching, going about, wandering about in the land, there is this sense of appalling death of human integrity because we have handed over ourselves politically to a party or parties, or religiously to books, or to the latest saint who wanders about in a loincloth with his particular social, political, or religious panacea, appeasing, pacifying. I do not think I am exaggerating what is actually taking place, not only in this unfortunate country, but also in the rest of the world.

Now, you know this. I have only described what is a fact. A mind that gives an opinion about a fact is a narrow, limited, destructive mind. You understand, sir? Let me explain a little bit further. This is a fact—what is actually taking place in the world. And you and I know it very well. You can translate the fact in one way, and I can translate it in another way. The translation of the fact is a curse which prevents us from seeing the actual fact and doing something about the fact. When you and I discuss our opinions about the fact, nothing is done about the fact; you can add perhaps more to the fact, see more nuances, implications, significance about the fact, and I may see less significance in the fact. But the fact cannot be interpreted; I cannot offer an opinion about the fact. It is so, and it is very difficult for a mind to accept the fact. We are always translating, we are always giving different meanings to it, according to our prejudices, conditionings, hopes, fears, and all the rest of it. If you and I could see the fact without offering an opinion, interpreting, giving a significance, then the fact becomes much more alive—not more alive—the fact is there alone; nothing else matters; then the fact has its own energy which drives you in the right direction. Opinions drive us, conclusions drive us, but they drive us away from the fact. But if we remain with the fact, then the fact has its own energy which drives each one of us in the right direction.

So, we know the fact of what is happening in the world, without interpretations. The interpretation should be left to the politicians who deal with the immediate, with possibilities, and who twist a possibility to suit their ideas, their feelings, their conclusions, their opinions, and all the rest of it. They are the most destructive people on earth, whether they are the highest politicians or the lowest vote-catchers. You can see this happening right through the world—separating the people, dividing the land, and enforcing certain ideas according to their prejudices, their petty, little opinions. So, seeing all this, we also see this perverse desire to be guided by a guru, by a priest, by a man who knows more—which is perverse because there is no such thing as a man who knows more; we, however, think that there are people who know more. It is our life that we have to live, it is our misery, it is our conflict, it is our contradiction, our sorrows that we have to deal with, not somebody else's; unfortunately, we are incapable of solving them ourselves, and so we turn to others to help us, and we are caught in those things that are of little importance.

So, seeing this whole picture and also the tremendous sorrow and the turmoil that is going on all over the earth, to respond rightly to this whole problem, we need a different mind—not the mind that is religious, not the mind that is political, not the mind that is capable in business, not the mind that is full of knowledge of the past, of books. We need a new mind because the problem is so colossal.

I think one has to see the importance and urgent necessity of having this new mind—not how to get it. We have to see the importance of having such a mind because the problem is really colossal, so intricate, so subtle, so diversified; and to approach, to understand, to go into it, to bring about right action, a totally different mind is needed. I mean by the *mind* not only the physical quality of the mind—the quality of the mind which is verbally, in thought, very clear; a good mind; a mind that can reason logically, sanely, without any prejudice—but also a mind which has sympathy, pity, affection, compassion, love; a mind that can look, see, perceive directly; a mind that can be still, quiet, peaceful within itself, not induced, not made still. I mean by the mind all that, not just an intellectual thing, a verbal thing. I mean by the *mind*, the mind in which all the senses are fully awake, sensitive, alive, functioning at their highest pitch; I mean the totality of the mind, and it must be new to meet this urgency.

Man has explored in the past, gone into it, watched it, knows all about the past; the scientist, as you know, has explored all that and is exploring in time, in space, with rockets, with satellites. The electronic machines are taking over the functions of the mind in regard to calculations, translations, composing this and that; they are taking over more and more of the functions of the mind because they can do the things more efficiently than the average brain or the most clever brain can. So again, seeing all this, you need a new mind, a mind that is free of time, a mind which no longer thinks in terms of distance or space, a mind that has no horizon, a mind that has no anchorage or haven. You need such a mind to deal not only with the everlasting but also with the immediate problems of existence.

Therefore the issue is: Is it possible for each one of us to have such a mind? Not gradually, not to cultivate it because cultivation, development, a process, implies time. It must take place immediately; there must be a transformation now, in the sense of a timeless quality. Life is death, and death is awaiting you; you cannot argue with death as you can argue with life. So is it possible to have such a mind?—not as an achievement, not as a goal, not as a thing to be aimed at, not as something to be arrived at, because all that implies time and space. We have a very convenient, luxurious theory that there is time to progress, to arrive, to achieve, to come near truth; that is a fallacious idea, it is an illusion completely—time is an illusion in that sense. Such a mind is the urgent thing, not only now, but always; that is quite necessary. Can such a mind come about, and what are the implications of it? Can we discuss this?

Sirs, the issue is: Can we wipe out the whole thing and start anew? And we must because the world is becoming something new totally. Space is being conquered, machines are taking over, tyranny is spreading. Something new is going on of which we are not aware. You may read the papers, you may read magazines, but you are not aware of the movement, the significance, the flow, the dynamic quality of this change. We think we have time. You know somebody goes and pacifies the people saying that time is there. Somebody else meditates according to a certain system; he says, "Still there is time." And we say, "Let us go back to the Upanishads, revive the religions; there is time; let us play with it leisurely." Please believe me, there is no time—not believe me—it is so. When the house is burning, there is no time to discuss whether you are a Hindu, a Muslim, or a Buddhist, whether you have read the Gita, the Upanishads; a man who discusses those things is totally unaware of the fact that the house is burning. And when the house is burning, you may not be aware of it, you may be dull or insensitive, you may have become weak.

So, can we discuss the possibility of such a mind? How do you discuss such a thing, sirs and ladies? How do you probe into this? I have put you a question, not merely verbally, but also with my whole being; you have to respond to it; you cannot say, "Well, I will carry on my way; I belong to that society, this society, and this is good enough; my saint is good enough for me; he has found his vocation, he is doing good, he is reforming, and I am doing a petty little thing in my corner, and all the rest of it"—all that is out.

How do you inquire into all this? How do you answer, what is your response to it? Is it possible? Obviously, you don't know. You cannot say it is, or it is not. If you say that it is not possible, then there is nothing that can be done; then you have closed the door yourself. When you say that it is not possible and that you must have your guru, your saint, you have blocked yourself psychologically, inwardly. If you say that it may be possible and if it is a hope, then that hope implies despair also. If you say that it may be possible and if it is not a hope, then it means it may be possible; you do not know. Do you understand the difference between the two?

The man who says, "No, such a mind is incredible, I won't have it, it is too beyond me, beyond my capacities, I cannot do it. It is not possible," has closed the door psychologically, inwardly. And there is the man who says, "Perhaps, it is possible, I do not know"; surely, he is devoid of all hope. We must be clear that the quality of hope is gone. The moment you have hope, inevitably there comes frustration. You understand, sir? A mind which hopes invites frustration, and a mind which is hoping, and therefore living in frustration, is incapable of inquiry. Please do see this. So, a mind that says it may be possible is not in a state of hope at all. It is not a mind that says, "It is possible to achieve," because again achievement implies hope; and therefore, where there is achievement, there is always failure, therefore invitation to frustration. So a mind that says, "It may be possible"—such a mind alone can begin to inquire. Please see the importance of this because it is not in doubt, it is not accepting, it is not denying.

There are three states of the mind—the mind that says, "It is not possible," the mind that hopes to achieve, and the mind which says, "It may be possible." The first two are different minds; they are only thinking in terms of time, in terms of hope, despair, achievement, frustration. But an inquiring mind is devoid of these two. Now, if that is clear—clear in the sense that you see the truth that a mind is capable only when it has freed itself from hope, despair, and all that, and from saying, "It is not possible, it is only for the few," then you wipe those two out—then the mind says, "It may be possible"; it is only such a mind that can inquire. Now, sir, what is the quality of your mind?

Comment: We are full of fear, we cannot get over this fear.

KRISHNAMURTI: A mind which is afraid is incapable of inquiry. It is not a question of how to be free of fear. If my feeling is to inquire, fear ceases; fear becomes of secondary importance. In trying to climb a mountain, if there is fear that you are too old, or you are too young, you may not have the capacity of climbing; therefore, you do not climb, but if you feel the necessity of climbing, the fear goes away. It may be in the background, but you climb.

Question: May I know what you mean by inquiry, or trying?

KRISHNAMURTI: I did not use that word *try.* I said *inquiry.* I am not using that word merely in the dictionary meaning but also to mean a mind that is inquiring, looking. To inquire, you must have freedom; the mind must not be tethered to any form of beliefs, conclusions. To inquire implies that all personal idiosyncrasies, vanities, hopes must be put aside for the time being; it means the result is not important. To inquire implies that in the very process, I am suffering, I may change, or there might be a tremendous revolution inwardly, outwardly. And to inquire into it, obviously fear, conclusions, all the things that weigh us down, must be put aside—not put aside, because the very urgency of inquiry puts all that aside. The very urgency, the very necessity for inquiry becomes essential; therefore, the other things become of secondary importance; they have no meaning at all for the moment. You understand, sir? It is like war—in war, as you know, all things, all factories, all resources of the human mind, everything comes to defend; they are not thinking of the possibility, fears, hopes—everything is gone. So is your mind. Now you are listening to all this; is your mind in a state of inquiry? Is your mind demanding of itself such an inquiry?

Comment: When you are talking, most of us are thinking of our own problems. That is the difficulty.

KRISHNAMURTI: That is wrong, if you will forgive me. Most of us are thinking of our problems because we are conditioned according to our problems, and so the problems are our chief concern, and we come here to see if we can solve the problems. I know that, and you know that. You want to know how to live with your husband, with your wife; you want to know what awareness is; you want to know whether this guru, that saint is right; whether there is life after death; what there is after death, if there is immortality; what happens if you are having a negative mind; you want to know how to meditate—problems, problems. When the house is burning, what happens? Don't you know? The fire is more important than your immediate problems—not that your problem does not exist; it is there, but the fire is more important. This does not mean what the communists say in a roundabout way—that it is important you act in a certain direction because your problems are there. I am not talking in that sense at all; that is double talk. I say that your problems matter, but you will deal with them much more completely, thoroughly, absolutely when you understand how to inquire.

Sir, don't you know there is corruption in this country? Don't you know there is poverty? Don't you know there is squalor, there is in everything that is going on in this country lack of beauty, lack of love, lack of sympathy, appalling squalor, degradation where the mind is dead? Don't you know all this?

Comment: That is in appearance, and it is something like a dream.

KRISHNAMURTI: If it is a dream, then live in it, sir. Then treat the world as a dream and maya, and don't bother, don't listen to what is being said. If you treat the world as an illusion, then there is no problem. But you don't treat the world as an illusion when you are hungry, when your job is gone, when you don't know whence your next meal comes, when your wife runs away from you, when you have no children and want children; when there is death awaiting any moment, you don't say the world is an illusion. The world is in chaos, whether you like it or not.

Question: Is feeling an aspect of mind, sir?

KRISHNAMURTI: Surely, I said that. The mind includes desires, love, hate, jealousy, emotions—the whole, total thing that is vibrating, alive. The man who says that the world is maya, illusion, or the man who says, "Settle the economic problem first, then everything will be all right; bread first"—all that is included in the mind. The thought, the contrary thought, the urgency, demands, cruelty, gentleness, the sense of love, tenderness—all that is the mind. So, sirs, how is it that you don't feel the urgency of the moment as you would feel if you were ill, if you needed an operation? And why don't you feel the urgency? How do you inquire into the urgency?

You want the good things of the world, and also you want a good mind. You cannot have both. By the "good things of the world," I mean not the clothes one wears but the things that power gives, that money gives, that position, prestige, gives. We want to live with those things and also to have a very good mind—a mind which has no ambition, which has a sense of delight in the very act of living. We want both; in other words, we are concerned with the immediate ambitions, fulfillment, frustration, quarrels, jealousies, envy, aspirations; and we also say, "Well, time is beyond measure," and we want these two to live together. To have both is not possible. It is possible to have a good mind, the real mind; then ambition has no place—you may have a few clothes, shelter, and money, and that is all. The good mind, the real mind, is important, not the other, but now the other is important for us.

Is your mind inquiring? Is your mind in a state of inquiry? Obviously not. Now, how do you proceed with your mind that does not feel the urgency? How is such a mind to feel the urgency? Are you aware of your own mind? We need a new mind, the totality of the new mind, to answer to this chaos in this world. Now if you say it is not possible, it is one thing; if it is something to be achieved, it is another thing, but such categories of mind are not capable of inquiry. I ask you: What is your state of mind; are you aware of it? Do you say it is not possible, or do you still think in terms of hope, and all the significance of it? Or, does your mind say, "Let me inquire."

Comment: It is somewhat difficult.

KRISHNAMURTI: Life is difficult. To get up in the morning in time to come here, wait here for one hour and a half, come by bus, sit around doing nothing is difficult. Everything is difficult. Pleasure is not difficult, but with it come difficulties, but we want pleasure without difficulties, regrets, remorse. It is only when the mind is capable of living in that totality that remorse, difficulty, pain have no meaning; it is only then there is living; then, there is movement.

So, are you aware? What do you mean by being aware? What do you mean by awareness?

Have you ever seen a tree? How do you look at a tree? How do you see a tree? Do you see the branch, do you see the leaf, do you see the fruit, the flower, the trunk and imagine the roots underneath? How do you see the tree? And besides, have you ever looked at a tree, or you have just passed it by? Probably you have just passed it by, and so you have never seen the tree. But when you look at a tree—look, see visually—do you see the whole tree or just the leaf, the whole tree or merely the name of the tree? How do you see a tree? Do you see the shape, the height, the beauty of a leaf, the wind playing with it, the tree moving with the wind, the nature of the leaf, the touch of the leaf, the perfume of the tree, the branches, the slender ones, the thick ones, the delicate ones, the leaf that flutters? Do you see the whole of the tree? If you don't see it as a whole, you don't see the tree at all. You may pass it by and say, "There is a tree, how nice it is!" or say, "It is a mango tree," or "I do not know what those trees are; they may be tamarind trees." But when you stand and look—I am talking actually, factually—you never see the totality of it; and if you don't see the totality of the tree, you do not see the tree.

In the same way is *awareness.* If you don't see the operations of your mind totally in that sense—as you see the tree—you are not aware. The tree is made up of the roots, the trunk, the branches, the big ones and the little ones and the very delicate one that goes up there, and the leaf, the dead leaf, the withered leaf, and the green leaf, the leaf that is eaten, the leaf that is ugly, the leaf that is dropping, the fruit, the flower—all that you see as a whole when you see the tree. In the same way, in that state of seeing the operations of your mind, in that state of awareness, there is your sense of condemnation, approval, denial, struggle, futility, the despair, the hope, the frustration; awareness covers all that, not just one part. So, are you aware of your mind in that very simple sense, as seeing a whole picture—not one corner of the picture and saying, "Who painted that picture?" Seeing the whole picture includes seeing the blue, the red, the contradictory colors, the shades, the movement of water, the sky. In the same way, are you aware of your mind in movement, the contradictory and the condemnatory attitudes, saying, "This is good, that is bad; I do not want to be jealous, I want to be good; I have not got that, I want that; I want to be loved"—all the everlasting chatter within the mind. Are you aware in that way? Don't say, "It is difficult; how am I to get it?" Don't begin to analyze, don't say, "Is this right, do I look at it rightly?" or "Oh, shouldn't I do it?" That is all part of awareness. Are you aware of your mind that way?

Comment: At a few moments one is aware.

KRISHNAMURTI: The gentleman says that only now and then he is so aware. That is good enough, is it not? You know the taste of what it feels like to be so aware. Only you say it must last, you must go on with it all day long. But are you aware of it now—not tomorrow, not the day after tomorrow? Are you aware of it as we are talking together now? Awareness implies the seeing of the whole—not just the quarrels, the anxieties, the hopes, but the whole thing. Some of you have been on an airplane, haven't you? From there, you see the whole earth, how the earth is divided into little plots; from there, there are no frontiers, no stages, the earth is not yours or mine; from there, you see the rivers, trees, rocks, mountains, desert; you get a whole perspective, the depth, the height, and the beauty of all that; from there, the arid land is as beautiful as the rich land—the totality of the earth is seen in that sense of awareness.

Now, let us go back. Is your mind inquiring—inquiring not into what is the good mind, not into what is the new mind? Because the new mind is something which comes out of the void, out of complete negation; the new mind comes only in that state of revolution when the mind is completely alone. And the mind cannot be alone and uninfluenced, solitary; it cannot be in a state of complete negation when you are caught in beliefs, in conclusions, in fears, in religious superstitions, in the ideological, ideational desires. And the mind has no sense of the void—in which state alone there is perception, there is the seeing of the total—when you are following somebody, when you have authority, when you are ambitious, when you are striving after being virtuous, nonviolent.

So, can you, with that totality of your feelings, inquire not into the new mind but into the whole structure of the urge for power, the ambitions which all of us have? The urge for power—you understand, sir? There is power spiritually—you know the saint, the man who has conquered himself, the man who says, "I know, I have read it, I have achieved it." There is the power physically through money, prestige, position, through function, through achieving a state of being near the powerful VIPs, the ICS, the chief engineer, the big bosses. You understand all this, sirs? Can you inquire into that? If you are going to inquire into it, completely cut it out—not in time, but immediately. So can you, with that sense of awareness, see the anatomy of power, inquire and break it up so completely that when you leave, you are out of time?—there is no time because, in this, time and space and distance are included. You understand? Can you, sirs? It is like absorbing, digesting power. Go into it with such complete awareness, see the whole structure of it and the part you want in that structure—following a guru who leads you to safety, going to the Masters, belief in the Master. Many among you have beliefs in something or other, and they come here year after year; I do not know why. Let them keep to their temples, Masters—play with them, have a good time with them—but not waste their time and mine here. You know what I think of all that. I am completely out of all that, as they all lead to power, prestige, position, security. But that is what you want, so have it then, chase, go after it.

Question: How to be free from all these things?

KRISHNAMURTI: How? You don't want to be free from all this; if you wanted, you would step out of it. So, please don't ask me "how"; I am asking you something entirely different. How little you pay attention! I am talking of the new mind, not the mind which says, "How am I to get somewhere?" The new mind does not come from a mind that is seeking achievement, wanting to be free. The new mind does not come through discipline. The new mind does not say, "How am I to be free?"; it bursts into that state, it explodes. I am showing you, I am pointing out to you how to explode with your whole being—not gradually, not when it suits you occasionally, not when you are thinking of something else, not when you have a little time for this, not when you have spent all your life in going to your work and earning your livelihood. I am suggesting that a mind that is aware requires that the mind must inquire into your ambition, your desire for power, prestige, position, the way you treat people; how you crawl on your knees when you meet a big man, your desire for security, a job, position. See the structure of all this, be aware of it. And when you are totally aware of it, you are out of it in a flash; it has dropped out.

Question: You deny stages in this sort of revolution, or discovering in parts?

KRISHNAMURTI: I certainly deny stages; I totally deny discovering in parts, gradually, in time, distance, space; I have explained why it is like that. "In parts" implies what? It implies conditioning, subtraction, time, gradualness, from here to there, from one state to another. It implies achievement, getting there, being somebody, arriving. And if you go into it, you will see that all this implies a sense of laziness, acceptance of things as they are—accepting the yesterdays, todays, and tomorrows, accepting the division of the land, of the people. Sirs, don't you see this simple thing? How do you see a tree—part by part, or do you see it as a whole thing? It requires such extraordinary, such dynamic energy to see a whole thing. And do you derive that energy by little parts? Are you kind little by little? Do you love little by little? If you do love little by little, it is a gradual process; it is habit, it is not love; it is repetition. Sirs, don't you know all this? Please, sirs, do consider whether you are inquiring into your ambitions, into the anatomy of power; you have to approach it not just little by little but see the whole thing, and when you see the whole thing, it goes away in a flash.

February 19, 1961

Second Talk in Bombay

We were considering, the other day when we met, what is necessary in the present chaotic, confused, and conflicting world. We were considering not only the immediate action necessary but also a continuous action, and we can only have such action when we comprehend the totality of the problem. And to comprehend the whole, we need a different mind, a new mind, a mind that is not merely concerned with the particular but with the total; and comprehending the total, the mind can play with the comprehension of the particular. And we were also talking about a state of exploration, rather than exploring. I think those two are different activities, are they not? A mind that is merely concerned with exploring, not only outwardly, but inwardly, is in a state of restlessness, a state of push, urge; but a state of exploration is a negative awareness in which there is perception without recording—it is a state of pure seeing.

I do not know how far we have understood the significance of seeing. I think it is necessary to consider it further. I wonder if we see anything. You know what I mean by seeing? Looking, observing, perceiving, the quality of listening—all these are implied in seeing, and the seeing is prevented when there is an opinion about the fact of that which you are seeing. I look at you and you look at me. I do not know most of you, but you know me. You have opinions about me, conclusions, ideas, certain judgments; you have pictures, images, symbols. You don't see me actually because you have ideas about me. So you never see, you never perceive, you never listen; these ideas, opinions, conclusions, a certain tradition, what you have read—those prevent you from seeing. Do experiment, as I am talking, with what I am talking about.

Surely, seeing implies putting aside all these and merely observing, listening, seeing, perceiving, absorbing, seeing actually what is the fact; it is much more vitalizing, and from that you derive enormous energy. Opinions don't give energy. Conclusions, ideas, give a certain form of energy which dissipates, which is destructive, which creates tension and contradiction because most of our actions are born out of the conflict of contradiction and the tension that contradiction brings about. So if you could see without bringing judgments, evaluation, acceptance, and denial, if you could merely perceive things, facts as they are, inwardly as well as outwardly, then that very perception brings an extraordinary quality of energy. Actually there is no outward state distinct from the inward state; they are not two different states, they are really one continuous movement like the tide going out and coming in. To be aware of the fact—that alone does bring about a certain sense of vitality, energy, a quality of beauty. So we are talking about the necessity of such perception. It is only a new mind that can comprehend the significance of seeing something totally.

The new mind is not something to be achieved, is not something to be worked for, is not an ideal—an end to be achieved, a goal, something to be striven after. It comes into being instantaneously, and it is only possible when there is such seeing. Time prevents this perception. A mind that thinks in terms of gradualness, in terms of distance, space, in terms of from here to there, as movement from here to there, as an achievement, as an end—such a mind cannot see a thing totally. So, perhaps it might be worthwhile if we could discuss a little bit of what time is because I think it is very important to go beyond time.

Time is thought, and thought is the process of memory that creates time as yesterday, today, and tomorrow, as a thing that we use as a means of achievement, as a way of life. Time to us is extraordinarily important, life after life, one life leading to another life that is modified, that continues. Surely, time is the very nature of thought, thought is time. And as long as time exists as a means to something, the mind cannot go beyond itself—the quality of going beyond itself belongs to the new mind which is free of time. Time is a factor in fear. By time, I don't mean the chronological time, by the watch—second, minute, hour, day, year—but time as a psychological, inward process. It is that fact that brings about fear. Time is fear; as time is thought, it does breed fear; it is time that creates frustration, conflicts, because the immediate perception of the fact, the seeing of the fact is timeless. The perceiving, the awareness, the state of exploration in which there is the immediate perception of the fact—for instance, the fact that one is angry—is timelessness. What you will do about anger, to get rid of it, what you cannot do and what you will do—all this is allowing time to enter into that.

So, to understand fear, one must be aware of time—time as distance, space; time which thought creates as yesterday, today, and tomorrow, using the memory of yesterday to adjust itself to the present and so to condition the future. So, for most of us fear is an extraordinary reality, and a mind that is entangled with fear, with the complexity of fear, can never be free; it can never understand the totality of fear without understanding the intricacies of time. They go together.

Sirs, to find out, to understand, one has to listen as you would just listen to the crow, to those boys shouting, to those bells, without commenting, without saying, "He is talking, and I must listen to find out what he means." If you listen to those birds, to those crows, to the noise in the street, to the boys shouting, to that gun going, and also to listen to what is being said here, then it is totality of listening. All these are facts—the noise of the gun, the crow, the children shouting, the bus rattling by, the noise in the street. And the moment you resist one fact against another, and decide to listen to one and not to the other, then you are not listening at all. Listening is a total process, and therefore there is no resistance, and therefore there is an immediate perception of the fact, if you are so listening with an extraordinary casualness. There must be a sense of casualness to catch the real. A mind which is merely serious and does not know what it is to be casual, to be playful, to be light, can never see the fact. And a serious mind which does not know what it is to be casual may have a certain amount of energy, but such energy is destructive.

Now let us consider the totality of fear. A mind that is afraid, that has deep within itself anxiety, a sense of fear, the hope that is born out of fear and despair—such a mind obviously is an unhealthy mind. Such a mind may go to temples, churches; it may spin every kind of theory, it may pray, it may be very scholastic, may outwardly have all the polish of sophistication, obey, have good manners and politeness, and behave righteously outwardly; but such a mind that, has all these things and its roots in fear—as most of our minds have—obviously cannot see things straight. Fear does breed various forms of mental illnesses. No one is afraid of God, but one is afraid of public opinion, afraid of not achieving, not fulfilling, afraid of not having the opportunity; and through it all there is this extraordinary sense of guilt—one has done a thing that one should not have done; the sense of guilt in the very act of doing; one is healthy and others are poor and unhealthy; one has food and others have no food. The more the mind is inquiring, penetrating, asking, the greater the sense of guilt, anxiety. And if this whole process is not understood, if this whole totality of fear is not understood, it does lead to peculiar activities, the activities of the saints, the activities of politicians—activities which are all explainable if you watch, if you are aware of this contradictory nature in fear, both the conscious and the unconscious. You know fear—fear of death, fear of not being loved or fear of loving, fear of losing, fear of gain. How do you tackle this, sirs?

Fear is the urge that seeks a Master, a guru; fear is this coating of respectability, which everyone loves so dearly—to be respectable. Sir, I am not talking of anything which is not a fact. So you can see it in your everyday life. This extraordinary, pervasive nature of fear—how do you deal with it? Do you merely develop the quality of courage in order to meet the demand of fear? You understand, sir? Do you determine to be courageous to face events in life, or merely rationalize fear away, or find explanations that will give satisfaction to the mind that is caught in fear? How do you deal with it? Turn on the radio, read a book, go to a temple, cling to some form of dogma, belief? Let us discuss how to deal with fear. If you are aware of it, what is the manner of your approach to this shadow? Obviously one can see very clearly that a mind that is afraid withers away; it cannot function properly; it cannot think reasonably. By fear I do not mean the fear at the conscious level only but also in the deep recesses of one's own mind and heart. How do you discover it, and when you do discover it, what do you do? I am not asking a rhetorical question; don't say, "He will answer it." I will answer it, but you will have to find out. The moment there is no fear, there is no ambition; but there is an action which is for the love of the thing, but not for the recognition of the thing which you are doing. So how do you deal with it? What is your response?

Obviously, the everyday response to fear is to push it aside and run away from it, to cover it up through will, determination, resistance, escape. That is what we do, sirs. I am not saying anything extraordinary. And so fear goes on pursuing you like a shadow; you are not free of it. I am talking of the totality of fear, not just a particular state of fear—death, or what your neighbor will say, fear of one's husband or son dying, one's wife running away. You know what fear is? Each one has his own particular form of fear—not one, but multiple fears. A mind that has any form of fear cannot obviously have the quality of love, sympathy, tenderness. Fear is the destructive energy in man. It withers the mind, it distorts thought, it leads to all kinds of extraordinarily clever and subtle theories, absurd superstitions, dogmas, and beliefs. If you see that fear is destructive, then how do you proceed to wipe the mind clean?

Comment: Try to probe into the cause of fear.

KRISHNAMURTI: You say that by probing into the cause of fear, you would be free of fear. Is that so? You know why you are afraid of what people might say, your neighbor might say, of public opinion; you might lose your job, you might lose several things, you might not be able to get your daughters married into respectability. Every person is afraid of some kind of thing or other and knows why he is afraid, and yet fear is not eradicated. Trying to uncover the cause and knowing the cause of fear does not eliminate fear. Can you deal with fear by running away from it? If it can be dealt with only by understanding fear, how do you understand fear?

How do you comprehend something? If you have a son, how do you understand him? Have you ever tried to understand your son, wife, your guru, neighbors, politicians, and the rest of it? Have you? What does it mean to understand your little girl? What do you do? First, you must observe the child—observe, watch, see the child when it is playing, when it is laughing, crying. It is necessary to observe, and you cannot observe if you project all your ideas—such as the child must be good, but she is naughty; she is to be compared with the other child, and so on. It is only when you are not projecting, into your observation, these ideas and opinions that you observe; and from that observation, you begin seeing the deeper meanings. That observation is the quality of affection. Sirs, haven't you tried all this? Probably not. In the same way how do you understand fear? It is essential that the mind be free of fear. Otherwise, your gods, your pujas, and your religiosity, respectability, mean nothing; they might just as well be dead. To you, fear is not something that you must understand, grapple with and put away, to be free from; you accept it as part of your existence; therefore, you treat it very casually; it does not matter.

Question: To observe fear alone—will it lead us to something?

KRISHNAMURTI: Look, sirs. We talked about a mind that is in a state of exploration, not exploring; we talked about seeing facts, and how thought is time, and thought produces fear. It is thought that says, "I am angry, I am ambitious, I must not be jealous and so on." We have not isolated fear, only I took that to go into, as you might just take sex or death or something else. But as fear is the most extraordinarily common thing for most of us, I thought of going into it, of seeing the nature of fear—not only a particular fear, but the whole nature of fear.

Comment: It is so terrifying that we have not got the capacity to understand or look at it; instead of that, we try to imagine some divine power which will protect us.

KRISHNAMURTI: Divine power protecting a petty little mind which is afraid to look at itself! Is that divine power so interested in you? Sir, you must get away from that kind of thinking.

How do you deal with fear? Fear is a result, fear is a process of thought—thought being the product of time as the consequence of memory—fear, not only the immediate fear, but the deep-down fear of several centuries of activities, impulse, compulsion, and all the rest of it, which is deep down in the unconscious. How do you deal with total fear, knowing all the causes?

In the totality of mind there is fear, there is anxiety, there is ambition, there is envy, there is frustration, there is fulfillment, there is aspiration, despair, a hoping, there are the Masters, the qualities, the discipline. When you are considering the totality of the mind, fear is not isolated, but for most of us fear is isolated. It is excellent to have that totality of perception; then you can deal with it, but most of us have not got that extraordinary, exquisite, subtle sense of totality. Most of us are caught in one particular fear which dogs all our lives for the rest of the time. Having isolated it, how do you deal with it? That is the problem for most of us, you understand, sir?

Comment: The moment you understand it, it falls away by itself.

KRISHNAMURTI: What is the significance of that word *understand?* Do you deal with fear one by one as it arises, or do you tackle the whole fear? And to tackle the totality of fear, you cannot approach it in isolation as the thing isolated. I do not know if I am conveying anything to you. Sir, look! I am afraid of what public opinion is; I see the cause of it, how childish, immature it is to be afraid of public opinion. I see the absurdity of it, but I am still afraid I may lose my job. I need not tell you what public opinion does to people. Now, do you deal with that in isolation, as a thing apart, or do you proceed with public opinion in such a way that it will lead you to the total comprehension of fear? If I had the capacity or a way of looking at the fear of public opinion, then that might open the door to the total, complete understanding of fear. That is my point, you understand? Every movement of thought strengthens fear; I am not concerned for the moment with that. I am afraid of public opinion; I know the cause thereof, I know the significance of all that. Now, will the exploration of that lead to the opening of the door to the totality of fear? That is all my concern, not how to get rid of fear. If one incident can lead to the totality, then the mind will be completely free of it. I do not know if I am making myself clear.

Sirs, let us move from fear for the moment. There is violence and nonviolence. I am violent, and there is the ideal of nonviolence; and I try to approach this through discipline, conflict, contradiction, this terrible adjustment to the ideational nonviolence which all your gurus, swamis, yogis, all the sacred crowd do—which is violence—and adjust myself to nonviolence. Now, please follow this. The fact is violence; the nonfact is nonviolence. Nonviolence is an illusion; it is a word, it has no reality. Violence is a reality; the other has no reality at all; it is just a speculative idea, thought, that you must be nonviolent because the leaders say it is profitable, because then you will achieve political independence, and you can play around with words—but the fact is you are violent. I have to understand something actually by looking at the fact, which is: The mind must never be caught in the illusion of words and ideas, away from the fact. Sirs, when a politician talks about nonviolence, peace, and all that, you have to set it aside because the fact is violence. Now, how do I understand violence?

How does the mind operate after discarding all the illusion of words, of ideals, and the conflict between the fact and the reality of the ideal, and the attempt to approach the fact with the ideal and therefore continuing the conflict? You have got to discard totally all that when you are dealing with the fact scientifically, to deal with the fact and not with illusion; the mind then has discarded the whole principle of imitation, conformity to a pattern, an idea. So the mind, by dealing with one fact, has discovered how the mind is taking to words, reaching conclusions which have no reality, and so there is only the fact. You understand? Then the mind is capable of looking at that fact. And what does it imply—"looking at a fact?"

Looking—what does it mean, sir? How do I look at anger? Obviously, I look at it as an observer being angry. I say, "I am angry." At the moment of anger there is no 'I'; the 'I' comes in immediately afterwards—which means time. So, can I look at the fact without the factor of time, which is the thought, which is the word? This happens when there is the looking without the observer. See where it has lead me. I now begin to perceive a way of looking—perceiving without the opinion, the conclusion, without condemning, judging. Therefore I perceive that there can be "seeing" without thought, which is the word. So the mind is beyond the clutches of ideas, of the conflict of duality, and all the rest of it. So, can I look at fear not as an isolated fact?

Sir, fear and violence are just examples. Through one example you can see the whole universe of thought; by taking one thing, "fear," your mind has opened the door. If you isolate a fact that has not opened the door to the whole universe of the mind, then let us go back to the fact and begin again by taking another fact so that you yourself will begin to see the extraordinary thing of the mind, so that you have the key, you can open the door, you can burst into that. You understand, sirs?

You always analyze fear very clearly, the cause of it, the results of it, the interrelated causes of it—you can see the whole pattern of fear. You are afraid of your neighbor, you are afraid of your wife, husband, death, losing the job, falling ill, not having enough money in old age, or that your wife might run away, your husband might look to somebody else, your sons, your daughters do not obey you, you know all this, sirs—fear, fear which each one of us has. And if it is not understood, it leads to every form of distortion, to mental illnesses. The man who says that he is as great as Napoleon is mentally unbalanced, like the man who is pursuing the Masters, gurus, the ideological patterns of existence. All that is unbalanced mental illness—I know you won't accept it, but it does not matter. To be sane is an extraordinarily difficult thing in a world of insanity, in a world in which people are mentally ill. Sirs, think of the absurdity of the churches with their dogmas, with their beliefs—not only the Catholic beliefs, but the Hindu, Islamic, Buddhist beliefs which millions of people cherish. It is all ill-health, mental illness born of fear. You would sneer at the dogma which the Catholics believe in, that Virgin Mary went physically to heaven; you say, "What absurdity!" But you have your own form of absurdity, so don't brush it aside. We know the causes of it. We know the extraordinary subtleties of it. By considering one fear—the fear of death, the fear of the neighbor, the fear of your wife dominating over you, you know the whole business of domination—will that open the door? That is all that matters—not how to be free of it—because the moment you open the door, fear is completely wiped away.

Sir, the mind is the result of time, and time is the word—how extraordinary to think of it! Time is thought; it is thought that breeds fear, it is thought that breeds the fear of death; and it is time which is thought, that has in its hand the whole intricacies and the subtleties of fear. So you cannot wipe away fear without understanding, without actually seeing into the nature of time, which means thought, which means the word. From that arises the question: Is there a thought without the word, is there a thinking without the word which is memory? Sir, without seeing the nature of the mind, the movement of the mind, the process of self-knowing, merely saying that I must be free of it has very little meaning. You have to take fear in the context of the whole of the mind.

To see, to go into all this, you need energy. Energy does not come through eating food—that is a part of physical necessity. But to see, in the sense I am using that word, requires an enormous energy; and that energy is dissipated when you are battling with words, when you are resisting, condemning, when you are full of opinions which are preventing you from looking, seeing—your energy is all gone in that. So in the consideration of this perception, this seeing, again you open the door.

February 22, 1961

Third Talk in Bombay

We were discussing, the day before yesterday when we met, the question of fear. Fear is a product of thought; thought is the word, and the word and thought are within the dimensions of time. We were also discussing how important it is for the mind, the totality of the mind, to be rid of fear because, obviously, fear does corrupt, does corrode the process of thinking. Fear creates all kinds of illusions, escapes, and various forms of conflict; it prevents the quality of that energy which is creative. And I would like this morning that we discuss this quality of energy. Please don't give deeper significance as yet to that word. Let us go slowly, because really to go very far and very deeply one must begin very, very close, and not merely just take things for granted.

Every form of motion is energy; every thought is energy; the energy in nature, the energy of water, the energy of a machine, and everything that we do is a form of energy; only with us energy takes various forms and expressions. Almost all our activities are forms of that mechanical energy because all our activities are born out of thought, whether conscious or unconscious. Do think it out with me slowly. Thought is mechanical; thought can never be free, and therefore energy is never free. Thought is mechanical—I mean by that that thought is the response of memory, and memory is obviously mechanical. All knowledge is mechanical. What is additive or taken away from is mechanical; all additive processes, surely, are automatic, mechanical responses. Thought creates for itself contradictions through conflict. For most of us, energy is the conflict arising from thought which is born of self-contradiction—the good and the bad, the 'what should be' and the *what is,* the division between poetry and mathematics, between enormity and immensity and the particular, the contradictions, the duality, the division. And the greater the division, the greater the consciousness of that division, the greater the tension; and the greater the tension, the greater the activity and the energy. I do not know if this is clear to you. These are obvious facts.

One has to be aware of this contradiction within oneself, of the fact that the greater the tension that contradiction produces, the greater the activity, the greater the energy. People who have this tremendous tension are extraordinarily active. The man who is completely addicted—I am using that word *addicted* in the dictionary sense—to a belief is extraordinarily active. We are not considering whether that activity is good or bad, whether it is socially beneficial or not—that is irrelevant for the moment. And the complete identification with a group, with a nation, with a party and its dogmas, gives astonishing energy. You know of such people, don't you? That energy is automatic, mechanical, because it is born out of thought. Thought is the response of memory or of knowledge or of past experience, and all additive processes are mechanical because they are the result of thought.

So we see that there is an extraordinary division in us and outside of us, and we always try to bring them together, to cement them—the duality in the metaphysical, the physical, the mental, the emotional. And this division, and the maintenance of this division, not only produces a certain energy but also brings imaginatively or theoretically the opposites together, creating an extraordinary energy. There is the physical energy which is expressed in every movement, every step that we take crudely or very beautifully; there is the energy of the superb athlete expressing physically this energy; there is the emotional energy when you feel very strongly about something, a righteous anger, a sense of what you must do; and there is that energy which comes into being when you find your vocation. The man who has found his vocation is extraordinarily active, full of energy, full of doings. Then there is the intellectual energy, when you are pursuing an idea, putting various ideas together, correlating, discussing, arguing, deducing, dissecting, inducing—it has tremendous energy.

Sir, I am not saying anything out of facts; I am just repeating what we all know. The man who hates has extraordinary energy, as in a war; look what astonishing things they do in a war. The energy, the fear which produces a defensive armament—that also produces extraordinary energy. Fear, hate, anger, jealousy, envy, ambition, seeking a result—all these do create an inward sense of vitality, a drive, a compulsive movement. Physically there is automatic energy. Everything else is surely energy produced by thought. So the energy that we expend and gather is within the field of time, which is within the field of thought, and so that energy is always destructive. The ambitious man is a most destructive human being, whether he is spiritually ambitious or wanting to be something in this world.

Now the question is: Is there an energy which is not within the field of thought, which is not the result of self-contradictory, compulsive energy, of self-fulfillment as frustration? You understand the question? I hope I am making myself clear. Because, unless we find the quality of that energy which is not merely the product of thought that bit by bit creates the energy but also is mechanical, action is destructive, whether we do social reform, write excellent books, be very clever in business, or create nationalistic divisions and take part in other political activities and so on. Now, the question is whether there is such an energy, not theoretically—because when we are confronted with facts, to introduce theories is infantile, immature. It is like the case of a man who has cancer and is to be operated upon; it is no good discussing what kinds of instruments are to be used and all the rest of it; you have to face the fact that he is to be operated upon. So, similarly, a mind has to penetrate or be in such a state when the mind is not a slave to thought. After all, all thought in time is invention; all the gadgets, jets, the refrigerators, the rockets, the exploration into the atom, space, they are all the result of knowledge, thought. All these are not creation; invention is not creation; capacity is not creation; thought can never be creative because thought is always conditioned and can never be free. It is only that energy which is not the product of thought that is creative. Can the mind of the individual, of each one of us, penetrate into that energy factually, not verbally?

Question: You say that all thought is mechanical, and yet you ask us to inquire and find out. Is not this reflection an aspect of thought?

KRISHNAMURTI: Sir, surely you must use reason to abolish reason. We must have the capacity to think precisely, clearly. It is only when you are clear that you can go beyond, not when you are confused, messy. We are going to use thought and see how far thought can go, what the implications of thought are, and not accept thought as being mechanical or not. Unless you have found it, there is no meaning. We live by thought—your jobs, all your relationships, everything is the result of thought. So one must understand this extraordinary organism. The process of all thinking is the inward nature of thought. Unless you understand this, unless you find it out yourself, there is no meaning in your saying that this extraordinary energy is there, or it is not there.

Sir, a nationalist—whether Russian or American or Indian or Chinese—when he feels very strongly for his nation, has a certain amount of energy; and obviously that energy is most destructive, cruel, stupid—I use the words *cruel, stupid,* in the dictionary sense without any condemnatory sense. For him that is extraordinarily important; driven by that energy, he does extraordinary things—he will kill, build; he will sacrifice; he will do all the various kinds of activities. Now, a mind that is caught in that nationalistic spirit or in the caste or the provincial spirit can, unless it profoundly cleanses itself, never understand the other energy, though it may talk about it. A mind that has fear in its deep recesses and functions in that fear cannot understand anything beyond its own energy. We have exorcised thought, but our fears remain. We have accepted ambition as a very noble thing; we have accepted competition and the conflict in competition as a part of our existence; and we do not know a life without conflict, inward, outward, deeply, and superficially; and this conflict does create a certain amount of energy. All scriptures, all saints, tell you that in order to have this extraordinary energy, you must be bachelors, you must discipline yourself, you must give up your homes, you must not look at women, you must discipline your mind so completely that nothing exists except a withered mind, you must destroy your desire, you must not look at a tree and enjoy a tree. Tradition says, "To have that energy, you must deny." So you follow it. Those who are very well-read, who discuss with me sometimes—they are full of this "sadhana" or whatever they call that, full of discipline, what they must do and what they must not do, because they want that energy—as though by sacrifice or suppression, by denial, they are going to have that extraordinary energy. Man, for centuries upon centuries, has been seeking that energy—which is timeless—he calls it God or some other name.

Question: Sir, is that energy God's?

KRISHNAMURTI: The gentleman asks if that energy is God's. That is one of our favorite hopes to call it soul, the permanent, spiritual entity which is asleep, which, when given a chance, will blossom. A mind that is so full of its own self-centered activities, with its own ambitions, drives, urges, has its everlasting hope to grasp the other; and as it cannot grasp the other, it invents the thing "soul," the permanent entity, and says that we are all of the essence of that energy.

Now, let us come back. We know contradiction. We know the divisions that exist—the mathematician, the poet, the writer, and the laborer. We know the conflict between the mathematician and the man who wants to be a poet. We know the contradiction in us—"I want to be a great man, the most well known man, the most famous man; and in the very process of becoming that, I am frustrated." In this there is conflict, and this very conflict produces another form of energy.

So from what source is our action? Let us begin from there. Why are you doing things, going to the office, making money, having a home, or writing an article, or criticizing government? From what source are you doing all this?

Question: To release tension, one writes—doesn't one?

KRISHNAMURTI: I wish the gentlemen and ladies who write articles would discuss this. Do I write an article; am I here talking to you out of self-contradiction which creates a tension which must have a release? Do I talk because I am in a state of self-contradiction? Do I go round talking to people, meeting them, and all the rest of it because inwardly I am in contradiction, and therefore that contradiction creates a tension? You know that the greater the contradiction, the greater is the tension, and that tension must have a release, and therefore the release is to talk or to write. Is that why I am talking? I know my talking is not out of contradiction; I do not care whether I talk or do not talk, write or do not write; therefore, it is not out of any self-centered, contradictory tension or trying to do good, to help people, and all the rest of it. So it is not that. Now, turn it on yourself. Why are you doing anything? Are you acting out of your contradiction, out of tension, or do you feel compelled to do this or pushed into it? We have also heard people say that the "inner voice" tells them to do this or that—which is their wish transformed into the "inner voice," a feeling of compulsion, a desire to do something. But please don't give me reasons; go into it yourself a little and find out why you are doing certain things.

There is the urge to commit oneself to something, to a party, to an idea, to a group, to a faith, to politics, to religion, to family, to a society, to a church, to the communist party, the socialist party, to a certain guru, to belong to something. You cannot be alone; there is no security in aloneness, there is no sense of well-being inwardly by yourself. Then there is the desire to commit yourself in order to do some action—a communal action, a collective action. Then there is the desire to help socially, economically, spiritually with the sense, "I know, you don't know; let me help." Therefore you are committing yourself to that. That commitment can be on specialized lines or on political lines or religious lines and so on. And we commit ourselves also to a party, to a group, to a country because that gives us an extraordinary sense of power, security. You may not have clothes, you may not have shelter, but to belong to the most powerful party—the socialist, the communist, the democratic, or the republican party—gives you a certain position, power, a certain status. So we commit ourselves, and this is translated as "I cannot live by myself; I am a social entity, and I must help society, I must repay to society what society has given me." You know the lovely words that we spin around—I am not saying this sarcastically. So, do you act through commitment? Are you functioning with the desire to be committed to something so that you are out of this world of insecurity? Is that the source of your action?—though you say it is social work, for the country, for the good of the people, for humanity, for God.

When a man says, "I want to help people," he must question why he wants to help people at all. Is there such a thing as helping somebody inwardly? Outwardly you can give another clothes, shelter, and a job, you can help him to specialize mechanically. Won't it be worthwhile to find out what is the urge? Is it charity, is it generosity, is it to appease one's conscience, is it love? Why do you write an article and convince people—give land, don't give land, do this and don't do that? What is the motive? All our action has a motive. Motive is thinking, thought, which says, "I am doing this for the good of the nation, of the world, for the good of my neighbor." And what you are doing then is very mischievous—whether the greatest saint does this or a petty little man does this.

The mind is of time; it is in itself the measurer, and the very measuring creates energy. When you feel that you have controlled your body completely, don't you know that extraordinary sense of power, the quality of energy which is the measurement of the mind? And therefore, such measurement is within the dimensions of time. Now the question is whether all functions of the mind—however subtle, however deep, however thoughtful, however unselfish—are still within the dimension, within the scope, within the field of thought, and therefore limited, and therefore its energy must be limited, and that energy must be contradictory. Can such a mind drop this whole process immediately and enter into the other—not gradually? The moment you say "gradually," you introduce time, and therefore gradualness becomes the enslavement of thought.

Question: In some moments we do feel that there are no contradictions and no confusion, and there is also no reference to time. Is that creativeness?

KRISHNAMURTI: The gentleman says that sometimes we do feel a state when there is no contradiction, when the mind is quiet, when there are no conflicts. He asks whether that would be a creative state. If there is such a state, the mind wants more of it or to continue it. Then you are a slave to your thought, to desire, to all things.

Somebody is telling you something, you listen. The very act of listening is the act of release. When you see the fact, the very perception of that fact is the release of that fact. The very listening, the very seeing of something as a fact, has an extraordinary effect without the effect of thought.

Have you really listened to what has been said? When you have translated what you have heard into your own terminology, into Sanskrit, into the Gita, interpreted it, your mind has not absorbed, has not listened; it has merely translated what is being said to terms of its own comprehension—which means you have not listened. Or you have listened to see how you can translate it into daily life—which again is not listening. Or you say, "How can the mind be without thought, without knowledge?" All these activities prevent one from listening.

Look, sir. Let us take one thing—say ambition. We have gone sufficiently into what it does, what its affects are. A mind that is ambitious can never know what it is to sympathize, to have pity, to love. An ambitious mind is a cruel mind—whether spiritually or outwardly or inwardly. You have heard it. You hear it; when you hear that, you translate it and say, "How can I live in this world which is built on ambition?" Therefore, you have not listened. You have responded, you have reacted to a statement, to a fact; therefore, you are not looking at the fact. You are merely translating the fact or giving an opinion about the fact or responding to the fact; therefore, you are not looking at the fact. Do you follow? If one listens—in the sense without any evaluation, reaction, judgment—surely then, the fact creates that energy which destroys, wipes away, sweeps away ambition which creates conflict.

Sirs, you will leave this room this morning going back to your work, and you will be caught up in ambition with your life, everyday life; you have listened this morning about ambition, and again you go and plunge into ambition. So you have created a contradiction, and the contradiction will become greater the moment you come here again. You follow? And the tension will grow, and out of that tension you give up ambition and become very religious and say, "I must not be ambitious"—which is equally absurd. But if you listen to what I am saying, you will have no contradiction any more, and ambition will drop away like a dead leaf from a tree.

The energy that ambition creates is destructive. Don't you see in this world destruction? So explanations, convictions, are not going to free the mind from this position of ambition. Any kind of your discipline, denial, sacrifice is not going to free the mind. But the act of listening to a fact will free the mind from conflict and from the tension from that conflict, and therefore it has discovered a source of energy which is not merely thought.

February 24, 1961

Fourth Talk in Bombay

We shall continue with what we were talking about the day before yesterday. We were talking about a different kind of energy than the energy generated by frustration and the tension of contradiction, and also about what is the actual, factual reason for most of our actions.

Are we aware of our actions, and to what extent and at what depth? Because, obviously everything that we do is a form of action—thinking, sitting, moving, feeling, going to the office, looking at a sunset, a flower, a child, a woman, a man. And we divide action as political, economic, social, religious, and scientific; and after categorizing action, we try to find our particular groove, our particular way, and thereby we hope through right vocation to find a release of the creative energy of which we were talking about day before yesterday.

I hope we are thinking together of the problem, and you are not merely listening to what is being said or being mesmerized by my words. Somebody wrote to me a couple of days ago that the audience is being mesmerized by me. Probably you are; I am not at all sure; I hope you are not because that is not my intention at all; it is too immature, and I do not think you can be mesmerized.

But it is important, is it not, that we should think out these problems together as deeply and as widely as possible—not that you are going to do anything about it. Obviously, most of us are old and we have settled in our grooves, and we do not want to be shaken out of them; we have committed ourselves to business, to the bureaucracy, to administration, to religious activity, or to political activity; or we feel we must "do something," and we do not want to be shaken out of our grooves. And if one is at all deeply interested in this question of energy, one must obviously inquire into the contradiction in which most of us live, the tension which that contradiction creates, and the action from that tension. The action from this tension which comes from self-contradiction is our life, it is our way of living—the everlasting conflict. And this conflict, we feel, is necessary, and so we have got used to the continuation of an energy which is destructive. We went into that sufficiently last time we gathered here.

But isn't it important to find out for ourselves what is the motive, what is the drive, the compulsion, that is making us do things? Take a very simple thing. Why are you here, sirs? What is the drive, what is the thing that makes you get up early and go through all this inconvenience, sitting in a very uncomfortable position for an hour or so, and being questioned by the speaker, being driven to discuss things which most of us have not even thought about? Why? I think if one can really go into this—not from what I say, but for yourself—I think one begins to discover a great many things, one begins to uncover the coil of confusion. Most of us are confused and don't know what to do. We are doing things—going to the office, going to a church, going to a temple, joining a political party, this or that, writing articles, preaching, walking with somebody, and so on and so on—we are doing something. But why we do it we are not clear. Obviously, when you go to the office, it is fairly clear why you go to the office—to earn a livelihood. And all the routine, the boredom, the insults, the immoral issues involved in it, being bossed over by a man who is just ambitious, being driven by his greed, and so on—is it not really important, if one is at all earnest, to uncover all these things? Life is a constant challenge and response; that is what we call living. You are challenged, questioned, asked, demanded, consciously or unconsciously, all the time, while sitting here, when you go outside, when you do anything; that is the process of existence. The constant challenge and the constant response, and their interplay, we call living and action.

Sirs, may I request you not to take notes? Do listen because you can't take notes and at the same time listen, because you are exploring into yourselves, you are not listening to what is being said; what is being said is only a means, a door through which you are going to go into yourself; and if you are taking notes, you are not paying attention to what is being said, or not going into yourself. You are just taking notes so that you can think it over at home; it is not the same thing as listening and exploring this yourself now.

So, life is this constant interplay of challenge and response. Let us look at it a little bit, explore into it, because it is going to reveal something extraordinary if we can go into it. We respond according to our limitations, and the challenge also is limited; a challenge is never pure. You respond to a political action, to a political idea, and politics is very limited; and if you are inclined politically, you respond to that limited challenge, and so your response is also limited, and the result is further limitation. You follow? There is the political challenge of a country which has recently acquired independence and which does not know what real democracy is, the real meaning and the significance of that word—the beauty, the feeling of equality, equal opportunity, the feeling of being together, the equality of relationship. We do not know all the implications. There is this challenge, and we respond to it because we do not understand. We are confused, we do not know. There is corruption, there is this and there are ten different things; so we respond to a partial challenge, we respond with confusion; the result is further confusion. I do not know if I am making myself clear on that point. So with religion, so with our relationships, so in the challenge of everyday little things—there is always a partial challenge and a partial response. The challenge is as confused as the response, so we try various avenues of action—the political, the religious—which are essentially confused; we see the utter futility of all that, and we wait and say, "Let me wait, let me do something in the meantime, it does not matter, write articles, go around, or walk around with somebody through the land, write, do this, do that"—wait, wait, wait, hope, hope, and hope, because every challenge that we have responded to has resulted in the burning away, the withering away of ourselves. This is the ordinary everyday course of our life. So having burned our fingers, now we say we should wait. We do feel in communism, politics, religious activities, we do feel in some other activity—feel, feel, feel, which makes us plunge into something. And then we see that our faith has been defeated, that our faith is being destroyed, and the feeling, the vitality, the intensity is being burned away through all these confused challenges and responses. Do follow this, sirs. Do pay a little attention to this—listen.

I am not saying anything extraordinary, I am not saying anything which you have perhaps not thought out; but I am thinking it aloud with you so that we go along together and at the end of it say, "I do not know what to do; I will wait, but in the meantime, I will do something, carry on." We do not wait, but we support something which is pernicious, which is evil, which confuses others. I do not know if I am making myself clear. If I wait, I will do nothing; I will remain quiet, I won't do a thing, I won't write an article because if I write, if I speak, if I join, if I do anything, I shall be responding partially to the challenge, and therefore the response will be confused and therefore misleading. The more so-called serious, intellectual, volatile and vibrant, capable of arguing we are, the more we are trying to do something to get on, not being able to sit quiet, to look, to delve into, so we are all the time responding to challenges which are confused, and our responses are also confused. Sirs, what is the harm in not doing anything?

Let us explore this. If you don't know, why should you do anything? What is the harm in saying, "I do not know, I will wait," and in waiting, not put your fingers and your mind to doing things? Why do you not wait like the blind man who does not take a step in any direction but says, "I do not know; I will wait, I will stand; let me get used to this feeling of my blindness and what it implies"? But most of us are afraid to wait because of public opinion. We have been leaders, we have done this and that, we have pushed around people, told them what to do, incited them; and now they look to you, the big man. And you feel you are somebody, you feel you must do something because society is giving you something, and you must respond to society, so you are back again in this confused response to confused challenges. Please see the importance of this. Don't push it aside. Please see the vanity of the people who want to do something when they themselves are confused, bedeviled by their own contradiction, tensions, and frustrations and lack of zest; they are the real mischief-makers. Now, that is what we are caught in.

Now, let us go a little step further. When you see this whole picture—I mean by *seeing* not verbally, not intellectually, but really comprehending—when you see, when you understand deeply, significantly, that any action born out of challenges and responses which are confused, which are partial, which are not total, are bound to lead to mischief, bound to bring about further misery, further confusion, not less, then will you ever listen to any challenge? The challenge is always from the outside. The man who has written so much, who has known so much, who has traveled wide, who has done this and that, who has got immense popularity—he says something and you respond. But when you look at that challenge without response, you see how small, petty, nationalistic, trivial it is! The communist challenge, the socialist challenge, the religious challenge, all the challenges of the various swamis, yogis, the Gita, the Upanishads—they are all from the outside. You follow? And when you respond to a challenge from the outside which is confused, limited, the response is also partial, incomplete, superficial. So you begin to ask, "Is there a challenge from the outside which can ever be complete?" You understand? Can a challenge from outside—the Western challenge; the challenge which the Romans and the Greeks made; which all the past civilizations made and got destroyed; the challenges which you meet everyday—your wife, your husband, your child, everything around you—which are all from outside—can that challenge from the outside be total, complete? Or is it not always partial because that never takes both the outside and the inside? It is partial. So having put that question and found the truth of that question, you put that question to yourself; you begin to inquire whether within yourself the response is also partial and therefore superficial, limited. Then you begin to ask: Is there not a state of mind which is its own challenge and which is its own response? And you go further and ask: Is there not a state of mind that has no challenge and no response? A thing that is, is its own challenge, its own response—it is beyond challenge and response.

We have divided life as outward movement and inward movement; there is the division between the outer and the inner. The outer is position, power, and other things which we renounce if we are inclined spiritually—whatever that word may mean. The outer is the BA, MA, PhD, the business man, the man who has a little more, and all the rest of it. The inner is the unconscious, the educated, the uneducated, the family, the racial inheritance. The outer is always asking, demanding, questioning, becoming, and the inner is always responding to the outer. And the outer being always partial, the interplay between the response and the challenge is also partial and not the total thing. But the movement of the outer and the inner is like the tide that goes out and the tide that comes in, and it would be stupid to say that is the outer and this is the inner; the tide is both the out and the in. And a mind that is aware of this unitary movement is not responding merely to the outer or merely to the inner. The very movement of the outer and the inner as a unitary process is the total challenge and response.

Sir, let me put the thing differently. We have divided all influences as the outward influence and the inner influence. The outward influence, society, pushes you; all traditions push you in one direction, and you react to it either along with it or in the opposite, in the same direction or in the opposite direction. So we are the playthings of influence, and being playthings, to respond to one set of influences and reject the other set of influences, or to react to one set in a certain way and not react in another way produces confusion. So you begin to inquire whether there is a state of mind which is beyond all influence.

Question: There is a response from the individual to the outer challenge. That response is from memory. How can the mind be devoid of memory so as to meet the challenge in the manner about which you are speaking?

KRISHNAMURTI: The question is: "All challenges are according to the response of memory, and how can memory, which must be conditioned, cease in order to respond totally?" That question is not a challenge to me. It is a challenge to you. Isn't it? How do you respond to it?

Do you understand the question, the challenge? He says all response to any challenge is according to memory, which is limited, so response is always limited. Therefore, there can be no total response. And yet the speaker has been saying: Is there a total response without the limited reaction of knowledge and memory? How do you respond to it? He has asked: "Can the mind, in order to respond totally, be free of memory, memory being always conditioned?" Is that the right question? It may be the right question; I do not know, but I want to find out if his question has validity in the context of what we are talking about.

Comment: The question is to find a solution.

KRISHNAMURTI: The gentleman says that question is asked in order to find a solution. Look at it, sirs. Is there a solution to a question? Do remain with that thing for two minutes please. Of course, you ask a question in order to find an answer. Now, is there an answer from another to a question of this kind? That is one thing. The other thing is: Why do you ask a question? For explanation, for inquiry? And when you do ask a question, it must be a problem; otherwise, you won't ask it. Are you asking to find an answer to the problem, or are you asking to find out why this problem exists at all? The moment you ask, the moment you put forth a problem, you already know the answer because the problem exists because of the answer. If you had not the answer—conscious or unconscious—the problem would not be there. You are not meeting my point, sir? Follow this please, step by step. That gentleman asked a question: Can there be a total response to a total challenge as long as the mind is a slave to memory? Now, that is his challenge to us. Now, before I respond, I want to know what it is all about.

I want to know why he asked that question. What made him ask that question, and if he asked the question, does he not know already the answer? Otherwise, he won't ask that question. If I did not know something about engineering or science or mathematics, the problems of mathematics, science, or engineering would not arise; because they arise, I know the answer; it may take time to find out, but I already know the answer; otherwise, the problem would not exist. You understand, sir? Therefore knowledge creates the problem, and knowledge supplies the answer. You understand?

Question: Is it that one knows the answer, or is it the assembly of information?

KRISHNAMURTI: Surely, it is the same thing. Don't let us use mere words. Let us go back to what we were considering. Before we respond to a question, we must find out first of all if it is a right question; and if it is a right question, why is it that he has asked it? Now, what is a problem? A problem is about something, and if I do not know about that something, there is no problem. Because I know something about it, I begin to assemble various particulars of knowledge in order to answer. So knowledge creates the problem, and the assemblage and putting together of knowledge finds the answer. So I know the problem and the answer. You see, sir, what it does, if you will go into it, it frees the mind from the problems and from the search for solutions for problems.

Now, the question is: Can the mind be free to respond totally if there is memory? Obviously not. Therefore the next step is: Why bother? That is our step. We always respond according to our conditioning—being a Hindu, being a Christian, and so on. We respond according to our conditioning. That is finished. Or, you put the question differently, which is: As the challenge can never be total, so my response also can never be total. As we have seen, a man who responds for a period politically, then for a period religiously, and for a period socially—he is responding partially all the time to partial demands. Don't go to sleep over this. Do think it out. So, I do not say to myself, "Can the mind be free of memory?"—I am but asking myself, "Can the mind be the challenge and the response at the same moment? Must a challenge always be from the outside and a response always from within, both being limited and confused? And can the mind step out of that and be the challenge and the response in itself?" You follow, sir? If it is capable of doing that, can it live in a state where there is no challenge and no response at all—which is not death?

Question: What is the use of a mind when there is no response and challenge? Such a mind does not lead us anywhere. What will come out of such a mind?

KRISHNAMURTI: "What will come out of that?" Why is that question being asked? A mind which has responded to challenges partially, and therefore created misery for others and for itself, sees that all responses and all challenges are limited; therefore, the mind asks itself, "Can I be the challenge as well as the response?" This means an astonishing state of questioning itself, and itself responding and knowing its limitations and the limitations of its own challenge. And the next step is: Can the mind be in a state in which there is no challenge and no response? Where will that lead to? Why should it lead anywhere? Please follow this; the thing of beauty is in itself; there is no need for it to be something else, to be more. You understand? A thing that in itself is pure—what need is there for it to be more?

Sirs, are you following the inwardness of all this? Don't you know people, don't you know yourself? You have responded to political independence in this country, then joined parties, then became frustrated, saw the futility, the corruption, the ambition, the cruelty, and then you left all that; and you took up something else, walked with a certain saint, and then you saw the futility; you then joined this movement, that movement, tore yourself; and at the end of it all you say, "I am finished, I am tired, I have burned myself out." You don't then say to yourself, "I am burned out; I shall remain with it," but you want to do something, and therefore you are back again entering the field of confusion, miseries, strife, creating for others the net in which you are caught.

So, see all this, sirs. I don't have to tell you verbally all this. Observe it and you will know. And from that observation see that all challenge is inevitably limited, and all response is also inevitably limited—which is a contradiction. And from that contradiction arises a tension, an action; and then you say to yourself, "Can the mind be so vital that it is itself the challenge and also the response?" And you see the limitations of that also. Then you go further, the mind goes still further, and says, "Is there a state where there is no challenge and no response, a state which is not death, stagnation, but something tremendously alive?" A live thing, sir, has no challenge or response. It is alive totally, completely. It is like fire—fire needs no response and no challenge; it is fire. It is like light, like goodness.

So, from that state where there is no challenge and no response, from that alone, is action—every other so-called action is destructive. So when one begins to say, "An activity that is partial is destructive," one must apply it to oneself. You have to put to yourself the question, "What is the motive of my action? Why am I doing a thing? Why do I write an article? Why do I sit on the platform and talk?" I went into all that the other day.

Comment: You have described the final stage and the initial stage; the middle is not clear.

KRISHNAMURTI: Responding is always to a conditioned challenge, and the response is also conditioned. Now, the next thing is a mind which challenges itself. The mind is free of the outer beliefs, and challenges itself why it believes in certain dogmas, why it does this and that—why you write, why you speak, what the reason of your thought is, what is behind your greed, envy. Don't you ask all this, sirs, and don't you respond? This response is again partial, obviously. I am anxious, I am greedy, I am afraid; and therefore I want this—this is an escape. This means that you are still responding to your partial demands. And that does not lead you very far because you have explanations, you know the causes, you know all the raisons d'être, your own intentions, unless you are deceiving yourself; then you don't have any problem. After going through all that, you are bound to come to the other: Is there a state when the mind is light, when the mind is fire which just burns—that is, when there is no challenge? Sir, the mind then is something which is just alive totally; every atom, every sense, everything in it is completely vibrating. There is then no challenge and no response. And from that there is action which will never be destructive. You don't have to accept my word for it, sirs. You can experiment with it yourself. If you follow this, you can see this in a flash.

Question: Does it mean one does not select between a response and a challenge?

KRISHNAMURTI: Sir, how can a mind which is confused, which is partial, choose a challenge which is partial? Can a confused mind choose? But what it chooses will be confused. Sir, don't you know what is happening in regard to political gangs, political threats, and votes? You go and vote for Mr. or Mrs. so-and-so. Their promise is there, but what have they done? They have made confusion worse, confounded, and you have chosen. And you have also tyranny where you have no choice. So when does the choice come in, how does the choice come in? When you see a mind confused, what it chooses is also confused. How can it choose anything?

Comment: You said that we should stop and wait. But I do not see the point of this when most of us are having certain responsibilities like families, going to the office, and so on.

KRISHNAMURTI: Sir, I did not say that. I will repeat it again. Some of us who had gone into the gamut of all this, as students, joined some movement, gave up college in order to serve the country, fought for freedom, went to prison; then when they came out of prison, they got big jobs in the political world; they are now big men, so they are out of our clutches. But we are being prisoners, we have burned ourselves, and we see that the people who are big are corrupt with power, position, and we say, "How empty all that is!" So we push that aside. Then we join some other movement, and we go around, and then at the end, we say, "Oh, what a mess it has made of me!" Have you not gone through all this? I am not talking about jobs, routine. That is a different thing, sir. We have got to go to our offices. But inwardly, we want to commit ourselves to something, don't we? We have committed ourselves to this and that, one thing after another, burned ourselves; we have withered away in these commitments, and at the end of it we say, "We are burned out." But we do not wait; we are scribbling, talking, yelling, following, doing something all the time.

Question: It seems most of the people who come to listen to you come because they are desperate, because they are skeptics, cynics. Is it not difficult to wait, as far as the job is concerned?

KRISHNAMURTI: I said you cannot wait for your job; if you do, you will miss the bus, you will miss your job. That has got to go on. I have to support my family, I have my children, wife, I have got to go on with that. But I am talking with regard to the inward response to the challenge, this constant battle which is going on—the fulfillment, the capacity for a job, the inefficiency which is preventing the fruition of my job. Even if I ask you not to go to your jobs, you would go; that is absolutely clear. You are not to be told; if I ask you to wait, you smile and get up and go away. But I am talking of the people like you, who have been through all these things one after the other and have burned their fingers, their hearts, their minds; and they are waiting, hoping, for some new challenge to come along to shake them, to wake them up. You are not actually waiting—waiting in the sense: "I will wait until the right moment comes, and I will find out whether I respond to a right challenge." If you have gone as far as that, you are bound to ask if your mind is capable of living in itself as the challenge and the response.

So, the mind—I mean by the mind, the senses, the feelings, the desires also—that is being ambitious, that is caught in ambition and has divided itself into the outer and the inner is not free. But when the totality of the mind is completely awake, then what need does it have for a challenge and a response?

If you are half asleep, you are to be shaken, and out of the sleep you respond. If you have some gifts, you make a mess of everything, and that is why you have to be terribly careful about all talents and gifts because you can persuade people so easily—that is what the politicians as well as saints do, through threats, through promises, through rewards, through prayers. So, when you have seen all this, not only in India, but throughout the world, the same pattern repeated over and over and over again, then you are bound to sweep away all this and find out whether there is not action which is born out of fullness. But you cannot find that fullness if you have not gone through all this, or seen all this in a flash. You don't have to go through all this if the mind sees this clearly—not mesmerized, not hypnotized. When you see all this, you put away with a full sweep all your vanities, your ambitions, your urges, your competitive anxieties. It is really a very simple thing. Anything that is beautiful and true is always very simple.

February 26, 1961

Fifth Talk in Bombay

It seems to me that it is rather an important thing to go into the question of challenge and response, and see how far we can go into it because perhaps that will open the door to many things. Now, in discussing, it seems to me, it is essential not merely to think of function at the verbal level—that is, I say something and you either listen, agree or disagree, and brush it aside, which is of very little value—but to be self-critically aware at what level, from what depth, we respond to all the challenges of life. Though we may be specialized human beings, mechanics, professors, engineers, politicians, or the so-called religious people, however much we may be specialized, the challenge at whatever level will be equally sterile, limited, or special. If I am a politician, then I respond to the challenge as a politician; or if I am a religious person, I respond according to that. I am in contact; I open my heart or mind to a limited extent according to my conditioning, environmental, circumstantial influences. And as life is a series of continuous, conscious or unconscious challenges and responses all the time, there is no time limit to it. It is there all the time—when you sit down, look, when you hear, taste, when you go out—everything is a constant challenge and a constant response.

Is it not important for each one of us to find out actually at what depth and from what level we respond? Do I respond according to my belief, to my experience, to my limited knowledge, to my prejudices—as a doctor, as a professor, as a believer or nonbeliever, as a communist, socialist, nationalist, Parsi, Hindu, Buddhist, Muslim, Christian, and so on? From what depth are we actually reacting? Are we aware of it? Because, it seems to me that it is important to be conscious of this fact. If we are merely responding to a series of challenges according to the categories in which our minds are being caught, then our life is obviously very limited, very superficial; and at the end of our work, of our travail, of our suffering, of our inquiry, we are burned up entities; there is nothing left but ashes. I do not know if you have not noticed—not only within oneself, but outwardly with people who have been through all these things—that at the end they are left with nothing because they have responded according to the demands of the immediate circumstances, according to the immediate possibilities—to the immediate urgency only. If we observe, all outward challenges are very limited, whether they are historical or actual or theoretical; challenges of such kinds are superficial, they are on the surface; you may react to them from a greater depth, but all challenges are from the outside, like all influences. So if you are merely responding all the time to immediate necessities, to immediate demands, to an immediate urgency, then we are slaves to time. Our response is small, according to the limited sphere of our capacities.

Look, sirs, what is happening in the world? The world is broken up into nations with nationalistic ideas, into political parties, into groups—Islam, Hindu, Parsi, India—and we are all reacting to that; there is little poverty or great poverty, and we are reacting to that as immediate, and some superficial reformations are going on—we say it is marvelous, and we are working for it. Or, we are afraid of death, so we go to somebody who explains it away, and we believe in some theory. So we are always reacting on a very superficial level, though the superficiality may have a little depth. That is a fact.

Now, when you see the fact, when you see the truth of the fact, you invariably go beyond—that is, the mind itself becomes the challenger and also the entity that responds. Because, when the mind itself has critically challenged itself, it is much more potent than the superficial challenge. If I ask myself: What am I doing; why do I think and in what manner do I think; what are the limitations of my action; am I a nationalist; do I believe, do I not believe, why do I believe; what is the process of my thinking; do I know what it is to love, do I know what it is to be generous out of a pure heart without a motive; am I a citizen of a small dotted space on the earth called India on the colored map, and I, fighting for that India, feeling extremely, tremendously important for that little spot or that little color or for a party, why do I belong; am I afraid?—if I ask myself, then such a challenge is much more vital, much more intense, much more potent than the superficial challenges; that makes my mind intensely aware, makes my mind sharp, inquiring, ceaselessly acting in the right sense—not in the superficial sense like a monkey that grabs one thing after the other. The mind cannot be a challenge and a response to itself unless we have understood the outward challenge as much as possible; when the outer challenge has lost its impetus, its strength, its vitality—which means actually when we are not reacting to the immediate challenge—the mind becomes its own challenger, makes its own response; then you will begin to understand the extraordinary vitality of thought and the limitations of thought.

If we respond at the same level as the challenge, the problems will not be solved. The political problems which create certain challenges are being answered on that level, all through the world. No challenge, no problem can be answered on its own level, and yet that is what we are doing. The politicians who fill the pages of the newspapers are doing that, and we are responding to all those printed speeches, all the machinery of politics. When we have really understood these influences—every kind of influence—then we can go still further, which is not a mere continuation of the outer challenge and a superficial response. A mind that is challenging itself all the time is not a continuation of that process at all; it is something entirely different. Then the mind is so aflame that it is like a pillar of fire; it has no challenge and no response. Then only is there right action, and that is the only action that will not create misery, confusion, and mess in the world. But one cannot come to that without understanding all this. You cannot jump to it or say, "How can I get that?"—it is a childish question.

Sirs and ladies, don't you know at what depth you are reacting, at what level you are reacting? You are reacting only to the security of the present job, livelihood, wife, child—just at that level. I don't say it is an ugly level or marvelous level or the only level. Are you aware that you are reacting as a Hindu, as a nationalist, as a member of a party—communist, socialist, congress, or some other party? Do you know, sir, at what level you are acting, responding?

Comment: As long as there is duality, challenge and response will remain.

KRISHNAMURTI: Is that what we are discussing? You see, sirs, this is one of those wild statements unrelated to what is being said. I asked you: At what level are you acting, reacting, functioning, thinking, feeling? And you answer something else; you are not aware of it. Sirs, do you understand the purpose of our discussion? I feel if we can really discuss very seriously and consistently, go into it deeply, we will be transformed human beings—not in a century or in a couple of years, but now. Something happens to you if you can think clearly, purposefully, directly and face things as they are.

Do you know at what level you and I are reacting, responding? If you don't, shouldn't you find out? Because, that is the waking up of the mind, isn't it? And then you can go into the next thing; why should the mind at all feel challenged by the outside? Because, the mind itself then becomes the force that questions, challenges, and such a challenge is much more vital. Then you cannot deceive yourself, you cannot dodge the issue; the mind cannot create illusions and answer something because it is faced with itself.

In the world at present there is the scientific spirit that is rampant. The scientific spirit thinks precisely, observes clearly under the microscope; it cannot deceive itself. Through the microscope, through every form of research, it looks, observes precisely, without any equivocation, without any prejudice. The scientist may be prejudiced outside his laboratory—he may be a communist, he may be a nationalist, he may be merely seeking security for his family, he may want to be famous, he may want to be this and that. But the "scientific spirit" which we are talking about is not the human being who is the scientist. The scientific spirit is the spirit of precision, efficiency; and essentially, it is the spirit and the continuation of the spirit as knowledge. This is obvious—they could not plan to go to the moon if they had no knowledge behind it. Knowledge can invent, but knowledge is never creative. The scientist is never creative; he is the inventor because his very profession is of invention, and his invention is based on knowledge, on what he has learned. I am not saying anything extravagant, outrageous; it is not a fancy; it is a fact. For me, knowledge is essentially the accumulated knowledge of many, many centuries.

Comment: I think, sir, you are doing an injustice to the scientist. For instance, there is the adventure of performing an experiment to challenge the statements of ages ago, which is something new.

KRISHNAMURTI: It is perfectly true, sir; I did not deny that. But I am trying to put very succinctly the feeling of the scientific spirit. Knowledge, whether it is of centuries or of thousands and thousands of years, is the additive process; and occasionally there is a burst through this knowledge to something new—it is the scientific spirit of adventure, of entering a field which has not yet been investigated. The scientific spirit of adventure requires a precision of thought in which there are no personal idiosyncrasies allowed, in which nationalism, provincialism, linguistic feeling such as Gujarati and Maharashtrian do not exist. I am talking of that sense of research which demands knowledge and occasionally bursts through the cloud of knowledge. You follow what I mean, sir? After all, every experiment is the result of that. That is why I say there is an occasional breakthrough. That scientific spirit is rampant in the world. Every boy wants to be a scientist, a physician, an engineer, a mathematician, not only because it is profitable, but also for the fun of it. That is what is happening.

Then there is the religious spirit. I mean by the religious spirit not the sectarian spirit, not the secular spirit, not the spirit of the Hindu as a religious person. The man who belongs to an organized religion—I do not call him a religious man at all. Hindu, Christian, Muslim, Parsi—they are all conditioned by their society, by their circumstances, by their education; either they believe or they don't believe because they are being taught. That is not the religious spirit at all, that is merely the acceptance of a tradition which enslaves the mind. That entity which performs rituals, believes in dogmas, repeats certain words, quotes endlessly the Gita or the Upanishads or the latest this and that is not a religious mind. The man who goes to the temple is not a religious man; he is doing it according to his tradition, or he is afraid, or he feels he will lose his job; he does not know what to do; he will not be able to marry off his daughter if he does not go to the church—that is not religion. So one has to find out what is the right religious spirit as well as the right scientific spirit because the marriage of the two is the challenge.

You have to inquire into what is the religious spirit, what is the religious mind. Sir, you understand through negation; you find out what is true through negative thinking—which is not the reaction to the opposite, to the positive. A mind that goes to the church or to the temple, that is merely functioning automatically like a machine according to tradition, with fear that has superstition because it is conditioned—such a mind is not a religious mind. Why do I say so? Is that my reaction? Is that merely reaction? Is that a response because I want to be free? I say, "How ugly all this is," and therefore I react. I say, "How stupid, crippled people are who are going to the church, though they get a little kick out of it, out of repeating the Gita or quoting something! How silly all that is! They are not religious," and I revolt, but my revolt is still within the field of challenge and response. So, is there a way of thinking which is not merely a response, a reaction? And that can only be found out if I understand what it is to think out negatively.

What do we mean by negative thinking? If negative thinking is merely a reaction to positive thinking—which merely leads to conformity—then such negative thinking also leads to actions which form another series of imitations and conformities. I mean by negative thinking not reaction to the positive. Let us be clear on that point before we go further. We are inquiring into what is the religious spirit. How do you begin to inquire? If you are inquiring, if inquiry is the process of reaction to a positive system of thought, to a positive tradition as going to church and all the rest of it, then such a response only creates further limitations, further cages for the mind. Is that clear? Sir, I leave Christianity and become a Hindu. I join Hinduism, as Hinduism may be a little more expansive, a little more decorative, philosophical, and all the rest of it, but it is a reaction. Or, if I have been brought up in a family which believes in God—I wonder if there is such a thing—I react to it, and from that reaction any action is further limitation. That is fairly simple, sir, isn't it?

Sir, you are not agreeing with me; this is not a matter of agreement, but it is a matter of perception, seeing, because I want to go into the next question: What is negative thinking? If I leave Hinduism to become a communist, it is a reaction; and that reaction does produce a certain activity which superficially is more beneficial but essentially limited, essentially conditioned, essentially destructive; if I leave communism and become a socialist or a fascist, it is likewise a reaction; and if I leave all this and go off to the Himalayas or to Manasarovar, it is still a reaction. Now, such a reaction, though it looks negative, is a response to the positive. And what I am talking about as "negative thinking'' has nothing to do with either of these two. The mind has to see the falseness of the so-called positive action and of the reaction to the positive—which it calls negative. The entirely negative action comes into being only when you see the falseness in the positive and the falseness in the negative, which is a reaction to the positive.

If I see something false in what has been said, in what has been maintained, then the action is not a reaction. The action of a man who sees that all spiritual organizations are false, that they cannot lead man anywhere except to slavery—such perception and the consequent dissolution of the spiritual organization is not a reaction. It is a fact.

Question: Thinking is associated with word formation. When you use the words negative thinking, *does it mean that word formation continues?*

KRISHNAMURTI: The questioner says: ''All thinking is the continuation of the word, all thinking is in the field of the symbol and the word. The word, the symbol is memory; and the reaction to the word, to the memory, may be negative, but it is still in the field of word and memory; has negative thinking no verbal limitation, no symbolic conditioning?''

All thinking is the verbal continuity of a word. Have you ever thought without a word? All thinking is based on memory; memory is the symbol, the visual response of stored-up experience which is expressed by words like: ''I have been hurt; I have been flattered; I hate; I am envious.'' That is the process of thinking with words and the continuation of the words. The questioner asks: ''Is negative thinking free of the words?''

All religious organizations, whether the little ones or the colossal ones or the most efficient ones or the feeble ones—organizations such as the Catholic church, the Hindu, the Theosophical, all religious organizations, the pseudoreligious organizations, or the pseudoscientific organizations—such organizations will not free the mind to discover what is truth; they are false, they are destructive. Now, when I say that, that is merely to communicate what I feel, what I think. Now, how do I see, how do I understand, how do I comprehend the fact that spiritual organizations are destructive? It is very important; please listen to the question. Do I see it as a reaction—because I cannot be the head of the whole organization of all the religions, I react? Because I won't be the head of the biggest organization in the world, I say that that organization is very bad—which will be a reaction. All this is still within the field of memory—wanting to be ''something''—the feeling of power, position, prestige, having followers and worshipers and all the rest of it. Therefore all this is still within the field of the word, as thought expressing itself through the desire to be something.

Sir, you insult and I react—that is, I feel insulted. I react because I did not like your insult, and that reaction is still the opposite of your action; therefore, it is still within the field of thought. Now, when I say, ''What is the religious spirit?'' and inquire into it, I am inquiring into it not as a reaction, therefore not as the continuation of the word. It would be a continuation of thought which says, ''This is wrong and that is right.'' But only a mind that has no reaction perceives. This question of negative thinking is very interesting—perhaps, one should not use these two words together—*negative* and *thinking*.

Question: Could not that be real perception instead of negative thinking?

KRISHNAMURTI: Sir, look! You know what positive thinking is, don't you? If you tell me something, I deny or agree with you. The agreement with what you said is part of a positive process, or you say something and I disagree with you; that is negative, but it is still within the field of agreement and disagreement, which is a reaction. You follow, sir? Now, when I say let us inquire into religion negatively, I mean by that: Let us see the fact of the so-called religious spirit—see the fact, not verbally, not in thought—see the fact, which demands a mind that is free from the word.

I see the fact that all spiritual organizations—from the most holy to the most degrading, from the most powerful to the most weak—are destructive to the human spirit. I see that. It is a fact. Now, either that fact is a reaction because I want to be the head of all religious organizations, and I cannot—it is a frustrated perception, and therefore I say, "I am out of it"—or, I see the fact, not what the results are, whether they are profitable, beneficial, superficially helpful, but I see the fact. Now you might ask, "How do you see the fact?" I see the fact because my mind is in a state of negation—there is no verbal continuity, no desire to be something, and no frustration. "This institution is wrong, and so I am out of it; this institution is right, and so I am joining it"—both these statements are within the positive-negative field; they are both reactions. But when the mind sees the fact, then its perception is from a negative state which is not the positive-negative reaction. I see that when a man is seeking the truth or a guru or whatever you call it, when a man is belonging to something, it has no meaning. I do not want to convince; I see, and it has no meaning for me. The statement that it has no meaning is not a reaction.

What is the true religious spirit? I want to find out the real thing, the real fact. Obviously the man who goes to the temple, who believes, who goes to churches, believes in dogmas, who belongs—that is not the religious spirit at all, nor is the reaction to that the religious spirit. So out that goes. Then I ask what is the religious spirit? When you deny, when you see the fact, the falseness of belonging and the reaction of not-belonging, then the mind is in a state of negation—which means the mind is alone; it has no authority, it has no goal, it is not the product of influence of any society, communists, socialist, democratic, or this and that. It is alone, it is not dependent for its security, for its happiness, for its well-being, for its experiences. It is completely alone—not isolated, not lonely. Therefore it is not in a state of fear which is a reaction. So it means what? A religious mind is free of the past, a religious mind is free of time because time belongs to the positive and negative reactions. So a religious mind is a mind that is capable of thinking precisely, not in terms of negative and positive. Therefore, such a religious mind has within it the scientific mind, but the scientific mind has not the religious mind in it. The religious mind contains the scientific mind, but the scientific mind cannot contain the religious mind because that is based on time, on knowledge, on achievement, success, utilization.

The religious mind is a mind that is capable of thinking precisely, clearly, sharply, which is the scientific mind; and it is the religious mind that is creative, not the scientific mind. The scientific mind can invent; invention, capacity, gift has nothing to do with creative being; writing a poem, painting a few pictures, composing music is not the creative thing of the religious mind. So the religious mind is the only mind that can respond totally to the present challenge and to all challenges at all times.

Now when you go home, fight with this and find out if you have got the religious spirit—not the phony religious spirit and the reaction to it, but the real religious spirit—the mind that is alone, not as the opposite of the community or the society, because it has finished with the opposites, the positive and the negative. It is alone—in the sense a flame is alone—and it is only that mind that can answer these challenges, these compelling problems of the present day. And if you have the intention, as you go out of this room, fight it out with yourselves, sirs, whether you have got that religious mind. You must have a religious mind as you are human beings with all these crushing, destructive, sorrowful problems. To answer these problems totally, completely, with all your being, you must have such a mind.

Why have you not got such a mind? Not "how to get such a mind"—because the "how" is a reaction of the positive. You may say, "I do not know, but if you tell me, I will do it"; that is still a reaction of the positive-negative reaction. But if you challenge yourself ceaselessly—why you do puja, why you go to a guru, follow rituals, do these terrible things that are destructive, why you are a nationalist, why you belong to anything at all, Parsi, Hindu, Muslim, and all the rest of it—it will tell you the whole story of why you belong; but if you react, you won't find it. To find out, you cannot react to it, but look at it.

Then, is such a mind possible at all? Can the mind be so uninfluenced that it is not the product of time, the product of space, the product of distance as the past and the future? Can the mind be so solitary, solid in its aloneness, like fire? Until your mind is that, whatever your answer may be, it is going to be a destructive answer.

March 1, 1961

Sixth Talk in Bombay

The day before yesterday, we went into the question of the religious spirit and the scientific spirit. What is the religious spirit, the religious mind? And what is the scientific mind? I feel those are the only two real minds that can resolve the problems of the world. The really scientific mind is contained in the religious mind. We know more or less what the scientific mind is. There is the logical mind, the mind that can think clearly, freely, without prejudice, without fear, can investigate into the whole problem of matter, life, and speed, and so on. Can that mind enter into the religious mind, or are they two different things? The religious mind is the mind that in no way follows tradition, that is utterly free from all authority; it is not investigating from a center as knowledge, as the scientific spirit does. When the scientific mind breaks through the limitations of knowledge, then perhaps it approaches the religious mind.

Can we discover for ourselves what is the religious mind? The scientist in his laboratory is really a scientist; he is not persuaded by his nationalism, by his fears, by his vanities, ambitions, and local demands; there, he is merely investigating. But outside the laboratory, he is like anybody else with his prejudices, with his ambitions, with his nationality, with his vanities, with his jealousies, and all the rest of it. Such a mind cannot approach the religious mind. The religious mind does not function from a center of authority, whether it is accumulated knowledge as tradition, or it is experience—which is really the continuation of tradition, the continuation of conditioning. The religious spirit does not think in terms of time, the immediate results, the immediate reformation within the pattern of society. I do not know if you have thought about this matter since we last met here, and what your responses are. We said the religious mind is not a ritualistic mind; it does not belong to any church, to any group, to any pattern of thinking. The religious mind is the mind that has entered into the unknown, and you cannot come to the unknown except by jumping; you cannot carefully calculate and enter the unknown. The religious mind is the real revolutionary mind, and the revolutionary mind is not a reaction to what has been. The religious mind is really explosive, creative—not in the accepted sense of the word *creative,* as in a poem, decoration, or building, as in architecture, music, poetry, and all the rest of it—it is in a state of creation.

How does one discover the religious mind—not discover it—how can the radical transformation from the very roots of one's being come about? Now, the question arises: How to recognize a religious mind, how to recognize a saint? Are there any religious people in the world now? I think we shall be able to answer this perhaps irrelevant question if we could understand what we mean by the word *recognize.* What does that word mean? I recognize you and you recognize me because we have knowledge—you know me from the past and I know you from the past. To recognize is to see again, not only physically, visually, but also psychologically, inwardly. To recognize a saint, he must comply with the rules, he must conform to the conditions which society has laid down. Society says, "You are a saint because you have a loincloth, you don't get angry, you have one meal, you are not married, you are this and that." He is a saint according to the pattern which we have, but if you explode the pattern—which you must, in order to find the religious mind—then there is no saint at all. I think it is very important to understand this. The Catholic church recognizes saints, canonizes them; it is very strict in this canonization—the saints must conform to certain regular rules, they must be under certain conditions and carefully watched over, they must do certain things, they must lead a certain kind of life, they must serve the church, they must conform to the pattern established by the church. Here, in this country, the saint must conform to your ideas about what a saint should be: He must have a saffron robe, lead the monastic life, do good work, be a religio-socio-political entity; he must please the government, he must please the public, and he must conform to the authority of a book, the Gita, the Upanishads, or something else. And when you shatter the whole pattern of existence, of recognition, then who is the saint? He may be around the corner unrecognized.

Why do we want to recognize? We want to recognize a saint because we want to follow, we want to be led, we want to be told. The pernicious desire to follow, to be told what to do, is essentially the urge which everyone feels, the urge of insecurity. Obviously, if one comprehends the word recognize, it is an extraordinary word. We not only recognize somebody as being something, but also recognize in ourselves experience. When I recognize an experience as being this or that, I have categorized that experience—that is, put it back in my memory, captured it by memory—and therefore it is not a living thing. It is very important to understand this, sirs. But one can find out for oneself—not who is a saint, that is snobbishness—how to approach the religious mind, and we said it is possible only when the mind is no longer reacting to the positive as a negative. The perception, the seeing of something as the true or false is not a reaction, and that perception is only possible when the mind is in a state of negation which is not the opposite of the positive.

We act: our action, as it is now, is a reaction, isn't it? A insults B; B reacts, and that reaction is his action. If A flatters B, then also B reacts, and his action is a reaction. B is pleased with it; he remembers that he is a good man, he is a friend, and all the rest of it, and from that there is a subsequent action—which is, A influences B, and B reacts to that influence, and from that reaction is further action. So, that is the process we know, a positive influence, a response which may be the positive continued or the opposite negative action—reaction and action. In that way we function. And when we say, "I must be free from something," it is still within the field of it; when I say, "I must be free from anger, from vanity," the desire to be free is a reaction; because anger, vanity might have brought you misery, discomfort, you say, "I must not be that." So the "must not" is a reaction to "what was" or "what is," and from that negative there is a series of actions as discipline, control—"I must not, I must." From an influence, from a conditioning, there is a reaction, and that reaction creates further action. Therefore there is a positive and a negative response, a positive push and a negative push; and from the negative push there is a response, an answer, an action.

Now, in that state of mind which is reacting, can you observe anything? If I react to the rituals which all religions insist upon, and say, "Oh, what nonsense it is!" and push it away from me, do I understand the whole significance of rituals? I understand the whole significance of rituals when I do not react but examine the rituals—which is the scientific spirit.

So the examination of something is not possible if it is a reaction. A says that all spiritual organizations—whether they are small or colossal, perfectly organized and controlled from Rome or from Banaras or from somewhere else—are detrimental to man's freedom and discovery of what is truth, and all the rest of it. Now is that statement a reaction on the part of the individual A? It is not a reaction when A has looked at it, and out of comprehension, out of seeing the truth of it, says, "Don't belong to any organization of such a kind." Organizations are necessary as educational institutions, as post offices, as government, as this and that; but even those, when the mind is not extraordinarily alert, capture the mind and make the mind a slave—though not so much as the religious organizations based on belief, on authority, and all the rest of it. Am I making the thing clear? So a negative approach, perception, reveals the truth or the falseness of action.

Can the mind look, observe, without reaction? Can I look at those flowers without reaction? There is bound to be a reaction if the mind is observing from a center, the center which is the positive and the negative state. Sir, don't accept what I am saying. Observe yourself. Observe your own mind. I say, "How immature it is to call yourself a Hindu or an Indian or a Catholic or a communist or what you will!" You react to me; don't you? You are bound to react though you may pretend not to react. You say, "That man says so and so; let me be quiet and hold myself in." But you are bound to react because I have used very strong words—"how silly, how stupid, how unhealthy, how immature, infantile." Now when you react, you don't find the truth or the falseness of that statement; you are merely reacting. Now to find the falseness or the truth of that statement, the mind cannot react; it must observe, it must comprehend that statement.

You can comprehend the truth or the falseness of a statement only if you have no center from which you are observing—which means if you are not being committed. If I am committed to communism, to a party, I push away anything that you say about communism; I do not want to listen to it because I have seen what Marx has said, and that is all I accept; and from that center of commitment, acceptance, security, I react; and in that process, I do not observe, I am incapable of observing, examining. So can the mind look at something without the center? Observation without the center is the negative process.

Comment: The sense of recognition has always been there ever since our childhood; we have been brought up in that manner by means of our education, our background, and all that; therefore, whatever we see, whatever we observe, there is bound to be reaction.

KRISHNAMURTI: I understand, sir. But is it possible for the mind to break through the conditioning and observe?

Sirs, you presume you are believers in God; you have been brought up in that idea, you are conditioned with that idea. Whether there is God or there is no God, you don't know, but you believe in God; you have been brought up from childhood in that way, and so your mind is conditioned to that word; your tradition, your literature, your songs, puja, myths—all say that you must believe. You have been brought up in that way to believe just as a communist in Russia has been brought up not to believe, so there is not much difference between that and this. One is brought up to believe in something, the other is brought up not to believe in it. Now, to find out if there is God or if there is no God, or if there is something more than mere thought, you must shatter the whole background, mustn't you? You must break through the conditioning in which you have been brought up. When the mind sees the truth that any form of conditioning is destructive to perception, then the mind is capable of breaking through; then the breaking through is not a reaction.

And that opens the whole field of self-knowing—to observe the whole process of thought, the motives. The awareness without judgment of the whole structure of one's own mind, the knowing of one's own mind, is self-knowing. But leave that for the moment—we may probably discuss it another time.

The mind that observes from a center is bound to react, and such a mind is incapable of discovering what is true. If A's mind functions from a center, and A meets a saint—a man who puts on a sannyasi's robe, has one meal a day or half a meal, meditates, and goes to sleep—A reacts only from that center, from the pattern of his conditioning. But if there is no center from which to recognize, observe, then A sees the truth or falseness of that entity—which has much more vitality than merely accepting the conditioned human being, which is the process of recognition.

So, in finding out what is a religious mind, obviously one can see certain things. The ritualistic mind is obviously not the religious mind; it is too immature. You get a little kick out of doing puja, going to the temple, to the church; it is like going to a cinema because you get a certain pleasure, a certain kick out of it. Obviously the authority of the scriptures, the authority of the saint, the authority of what is being said, the authority of a guru—all authority is obviously destructive. And can the mind break through authority, not as a reaction, but seeing the falseness of authority? The perception is not a reaction. Therefore a mind which can look without the center is in a state of negation—not the negation of the opposite.

You can understand verbally what is being said, but that is not relevant; are you applying it; is it a thing that you are actually going through? When you really put aside authority, God, the books, the Gita, the Upanishads, the authority of the saint—not as a reaction, but because there is perception through negation which is not the reaction to the positive—then through this negation the mind is not working from a center, from a conclusion, from an idea; and therefore the mind is timeless—because a mind that is using a word, symbol, is caught in time.

Sir, I do not know if you have ever thought out or gone into this whole process of verbalizing, giving a name. If you have done so, it is really a most astonishing thing and a very stimulating and interesting thing.

When we give a name to anything we experience, see or feel, the word becomes extraordinarily significant; and the word is time. Time is space, and the word is the center of it. All thinking is verbalization; you think in words. And can the mind be free of the word? Don't say, "How am I to be free?" That has no meaning. But put that question to yourself and see how slavish you are to words like India, Gita, communism, Christian, Russian, American, English, the caste below you, and the caste above you. The word *love,* the word *God,* the word *meditation*—what extraordinary significance we have given to these words, and how slavish we are to them. Think of it, sirs—a sannyasi going about interpreting the Gita and thousands following him—the word *Gita* is enough. So the mind is a slave to words. Can the mind be free of words? Play with it a little, sirs.

Comment: The word disappears but comes again.

KRISHNAMURTI: The word disappears but comes back. So you are so greedy, aren't you? You want to capture the mind which is without the word, always, permanently, everlastingly. We are talking of no time, and you are talking of time, which disappears but which you want to maintain. You follow? Do see the difficulty, sir. I am not saying it is not difficult, but see how slavish we are to words. The word is the process of recognition, and with the recognizing process we want to enter into something unknown, and you can't. God is not something to be recognized—to be recognized would be very cheap; your pictures, your statues, or this or that are not God. So the word creates the mind, and the mind creates time as thought. Is there a thinking without the word? When the mind is not cluttered up with words, then thinking is not thinking as we know; but it is an activity without the word, without the symbol; therefore, it has no frontier—the word is the frontier.

The word creates the limitation, the boundary. And a mind that is not functioning in words has no limitation; it has no frontiers; it is not bound. Look, sirs! Take the word *love* and see what it awakens in you, watch yourself; the moment I mention that word, you are beginning to smile, and you sit up, you feel. So the word love awakens all kinds of ideas, all kinds of divisions such as carnal, spiritual, profane, infinite, and all the rest of it. But find out what love is. Surely, sir, to find out what love is the mind must be free of that word and the significance of that word.

The scientific mind is functioning from knowledge to knowledge. It is the additive mind. But a scientific mind may explode, break through, go beyond knowledge; then it may enter into the religious mind which can contain it. And the religious mind is obviously a mind that has finished with the past—not the factual past, but the psychological past. The religious mind is never in the process of accumulating memory as a psychological impetus, as a means to psychological action. A religious mind is not giving root to the word, and so it is free from the authority of the word.

Question: Is there not the undefined barrier of inchoate propensity beyond the word?

KRISHNAMURTI: I do not quite understand that, sir. Now, what does that mean? The questioner asks: "Is there not a clear, precise state beyond the word which is inchoate, not formed?" From where are you looking? Are you looking from beyond the center or looking from the center? Are you speculating, or are you actually experiencing as we are going along? You do not know what a religious mind is, do you? From what you have said, you don't know what it means; you may have just a flutter or a glimpse of it, just as you see the clear, lovely, blue sky when the cloud is broken through; but the moment you have perceived the blue sky, you have a memory of it, you want more of it, and therefore you are lost in it; the more you want the word for storing it as an experience, the more you are lost in it.

Question: From a nonverbal state in childhood we have come to the verbal state. Now you tell us to eliminate all the past that we have gathered. Is it possible to go now, instantaneously, to that state of being nonverbal?

KRISHNAMURTI: The questioner asks: "Is it possible instantaneously to wipe away the verbal state?" The verbal state has been carefully built up through centuries, in relation between the individual and society; so the word, the verbal state is a social state as well as an individual state. To communicate as we are doing, I need memory, I need words, I must know English, and you must know English; it has been acquired through centuries upon centuries. The word is not only being developed in social relationships but also as a reaction in that social relationship to the individual; the word is necessary. The question is: It has taken so long, centuries upon centuries, to build up the symbolical, the verbal state, and can that be wiped away immediately?—which implies, "Don't we need time?" Can you use time to abolish time, or is some other factor necessary to break time? If I say, "It must be done gradually," the gradual may be a day or a thousand days or a million days, the gradual means employment of time. Through time are we going to get rid of the verbal imprisonment of the mind, which has been built up for centuries? Or must it break immediately? Now, you may say, "It must take time, I can't do it immediately." This means that you must have many days, this means a continuity of what has been, though it is modified in the process, until you reach a stage where there is no further to go. Can you do that? Because we are afraid, we are lazy, we are indolent, we say, "Why bother about all this? It is too difficult," or "I do not know what to do"—so you postpone, postpone, postpone. But you have to see the truth of the continuation and the modification of the word. The perception of the truth of anything is immediate—not in time. Time implies distance, space; in that space lots of varieties of experiences and changes from your center take place, and you are reacting to them; therefore, each prolongation of a second means a modification of "what has been." Don't say that you can't understand what we are talking about. This is very simple if you apply your mind. The question involved is: Can the mind break through instantly on the very questioning? Can the mind see the barrier of the word, understand the significance of the word in a flash and be in that state when the mind is no longer caught in time? You must have experienced this; only it is a very, very rare thing for most of us.

Question: From the scientific, evolutionary point of view, we have developed from a nonword state to a word state. Can we reject the word now?

KRISHNAMURTI: I did not reject the word. I see its effect, its influence, its imprisoning quality; I see the truth of it; it does not mean that I react; it does not mean I defend it or accuse it; it does not mean that I am free from it; but it means that there is a state when I recognize something as truth, and that state is a different state.

Question: How would you then distinguish the preword state—that is, the primitive or the nondeveloped state—from the wordless state of which you are speaking?

KRISHNAMURTI: I do not understand, sir. The questioner asks what is the difference between the very primitive mind which has no words but only makes sound, and the other mind which has gone through centuries of cultivation of the word, the symbol, the idea? What is the difference between the two?

Why should we go through all this verbal cultivation for centuries if we have to come to that state when the mind is no longer a slave to the word, as is the primitive mind? Must I know sobriety only through drunkenness? Must I go through sorrow to know what happiness is? We say yes; that is our tradition, that is our everyday life. And everyone tells us, "You go through this in order to get that." This we accept as inevitable. But I do not accept this as inevitable.

Let us consider suffering. Will suffering lead man to sorrow if he understands suffering—not in time, not in space? We all know suffering. Seeing somebody suffering, dying, seeing the wife blind, seeing the son dying, seeing the poverty, seeing the stupidity of one's mind and comparing—such as one has everything and the other nothing—we suffer. Suffering is a reaction from the center; therefore, it is destructive and does not lead to the purity of the mind. Is it necessary to suffer?

The mind is being developed through centuries in the employment of the word, and the word is the result of social communication and individual response. The questioner asks: When we talk about freeing the mind from the word, is not that state the same as that of the primitive? I do not think so, sir. But perhaps the man who is really primitive may be closer to the other than the man who is waddling through all this. But unfortunately, we are neither the primitive kind nor the other; we are in-between, and the state of in-betweenness is mediocrity.

Question: When something happens unanticipated, it has a terrific impact on us, and at that moment there is a state which can be called timeless; in that state there is no word at all, and one is stunned. Would you call that experience a timeless experience?

KRISHNAMURTI: No, sir. When you see something beautiful, you are stunned; you have a shock, an experience, and you are stunned; when you have a brutal attack, you are stunned; there is the state of being paralyzed—are all such states the same as the state without the word? No, sir, there is a difference. You see a beautiful sunset, a lovely thing, and for the moment you are speechless. What has happened? That is merely a paralyzed state for a few seconds, as when a clot of blood going to the brain paralyzes half the body. In that state, of course, the mind does not react. But the mind which is in that state is not the same thing as the religious mind.

When we have seen all this, there arises the problem of aloneness and loneliness. Aloneness is the state when the mind is alone, has no companion, has no shadow, but is really alone—which is not the product of influence, which is not put together. But one cannot possibly envisage or capture or understand that state of mind which is really alone unless one understands what it is to be lonely—the process of isolation which leads to that state which we call loneliness. Now, sir, aren't you isolating yourself? Is not India isolating itself, calling itself India and thus cutting itself from relationships, from contact with other countries? Aren't you isolating yourself when you consider yourself as belonging to a particular nation? You may not accept that word *isolating*, but that is a fact. When a politician uses that word *nation* in order to build up his country, isn't that an isolating process? Is not calling yourself a Hindu, a Christian, a Buddhist, a Muslim an isolating process? When you have a gift, a talent, and you use that talent to build up yourself, is there not an isolating process? Aren't you isolating yourself when you are identifying yourself with your family—not that there is not the family, but when you say, "It is my family," and go quivering about it? When you go into this deeper, whether you are walking or sitting quietly in the woods or in a bus, suddenly you realize how extremely lonely you are, suddenly you feel cut off from everything. Haven't you ever known that feeling with its darkness, with its isolation, with its fear, with its peculiar sense of helplessness, the sense of complete despair without a shadow of hope? Haven't you felt all this? Sir, any man who is at all awake must have felt this, and the ultimate expression of this is frustration. The man who has felt it runs away from it—turns on the radio, goes to the temple, chatters, rushes to the husband or wife—seeking escape from this feeling called loneliness. We isolate ourselves socially, nationally, religiously, economically, and in every way, though we may talk of brotherhood, peace, nation. This isolated mind says, "I am going to find out"—it is just nonsense; it cannot find out. If one observes, one will find that in the process of isolation there is a sense of loneliness. I wonder if you have felt this. When you have felt loneliness, what have you done, sir?

Comment: Read a book.

KRISHNAMURTI: Read a detective book, turn on the radio, pick up the newspaper and read—which is what? All this is to fly away from loneliness.

When you fly away from something, it is the flight that creates the fear; it is not facing the fact that creates the fear, but it is the flight away from the fact. If I say, "Yes, I am lonely," and see that fact, then I am incapable of having fear. But the moment I wander away, take a flight, escape, the very process of wandering away from the fact is the process of creating fear; and then escaping from the fact to something else becomes all-important, absorbing; then I will protect, defend, fight, and wrangle about that something; I escape from myself, and I go to the guru; then I protect the guru. The guru, the object of escape becomes all-important because that is your refuge from the fact. The fact is not the illusion, but the object to which you fly away from the fact is an illusion, and it creates fear—whether it is the nation, the guru, the idea, the conclusion—you are battling with this all through life. Sir, that is a fact; see the fact, don't say, "What can I do?" Don't do anything; just see the fact.

When you say, "I am lonely," and are facing that feeling, what does that mean? It means that you are through with the process of isolation; you have come to the ultimate thing. Now, how do you observe this feeling? Observation is not something colossal, intellectual, marvelous; it is just the logical observation of the fact, and that in itself is sufficient. Now, how do you observe the feeling? Is the mind observing the feeling without the word? Or is the mind observing the feeling with the word—that is, using the word to observe the feeling? If you look at it through the word, do you look at it at all? When you look at that feeling with the word, then you are a slave to the word, and the word prevents you from looking; therefore, you are not capable of looking at it.

How to be free of the word? The "how" has no meaning; there is no method. You have to see the fact that you cannot look at something if you are caught by the word; you have just to see the fact. If you are interested in seeing, in observing, the feeling, then the word becomes irrelevant. Look, sir, I want to understand a child—it may be my son or somebody else. To understand the child, I watch it playing, crying, doing everything, all day long. But if I watch him as "my" son, with the word from a center, I am incapable of watching; I watch, but it has no significance. Similarly, to watch, to observe something clearly, the word must be irrelevant. Now, can you observe what you have called "loneliness" without any escape; can you face it without the word? The word *God* may create the feeling, but we know no God at all; but to find out God, the word must go out.

So, can the mind look at itself without the word? That requires an extraordinary precision of thought, precision of observation into oneself without any deviation. When the word is gone with its feeling, what remains? Find out, sirs. I am not telling you what you should do—telling you has no meaning; to a hungry man, describing what food is has no value. But you have to come to the door of perception, which you must yourself open and look. If you are not capable of all that, that is your affair; but since you are here, that is what we are doing.

So, the mind has to understand the whole significance of isolation. Everyone has tasted at some moments this extraordinary sense of loneliness which is there like a dark shadow. The mind will have to go through it to understand the meaning and significance of the word, whether the word is creating the feeling; and having seen the fact of the word, the mind will go beyond that—which means it will really be free of all influence. And if you have gone through this, there is a jump—which means being completely alone, like a column of fire. When the mind is in that state, it is religious mind; from that, there is action which is completely different from the action of a self-frustrated, isolated mind with its loneliness. Don't cover up the action of the self-frustrated mind with the sannyasi's robe, with the words of the Gita, and all the nonsense of sainthood.

March 3, 1961

Seventh Talk in Bombay

I think it would be a great mistake if we treat these talks as a theoretical affair, approximating our lives to ideas or ideals. That surely is not what we are doing. We are moving very carefully and advisedly from fact to fact which is after all the approach of a scientist. The scientist may have various theories, but he pushes those aside when he is confronted with facts; he is concerned with the observation of outward things, the things that are about matter, whether it is near or far; to him there is only matter and the observation of that matter—the outward movement. The religious mind is concerned with the fact and moving from the fact, and its outward movement is a unitary process with its inward movement—the two movements are not separate. The religious man moves from the outward to the inward like a tide, and there is this constant movement from the outer to the inner and from the inner to the outer, so that there is a perfect balance and a sense of integration, not with the outer and the inner as two separate movements, but as a unitary movement.

If one observes very carefully, one sees what an extraordinary thing anonymity is. The anonymous approach, after all, is required to understand a fact. To see the reality of what is false or to find out what is truth, there must be the approach of the anonymous, not the approach of tradition, of hope, of despair, of an idea—which are all identified with something or other, and therefore can never be anonymous. A monk who withdraws into a monastery and takes a name is not anonymous, nor the sannyasi, because they are still identified with their conditioning. One has really to be aware of this extraordinary movement of the outer and the inner as a unitary process, and the understanding of this whole thing must be anonymous. Therefore it is very important to understand all conditioning and to be aware of that conditioning, and to shatter through that.

I hope you are aware of the significance of "listening." You are not merely listening to me, to the speaker, but you are also at the same time listening to your own mind—the mind is listening to itself—because what is being said is merely an indication. But what is more important is that through this indication one begins to listen—the mind begins to listen to itself and is aware of itself, aware of every movement of thought. Then I think these talks would be of significance and worthwhile. But if you merely treat them as a theory, something to be thought over, and after thinking over, to come to a conclusion and then approximating your daily life with that conclusion, these talks would seem to be utterly futile. When there is a condemnatory process or justification, there is an identification with thought. One has to see the significance of all this as we go along. We have been talking about the religious mind and the scientific mind. Every other mind is a mischievous mind, whether it is of a learned person or of a very erudite person or of the sannyasi who has given up this and that; the political mind is, of course, the most destructive mind. The real scientific mind observes, analyses, dissects, goes into the outward movement of life without any compromise; the scientist may compromise outside the laboratory where he is still a conditioned human being, but inside the laboratory there is that spirit of inquiry and research as a ruthless pursuit of fact; that is the only spirit in the scientific field, and our minds must be that to understand. The mind must also have this comprehension of the outer as well as the inner, and as these are the only two actual facts, one begins to understand these two as a unitary process, and it is only the religious mind that can comprehend the unitary process. Then whatever action springs from the religious mind—that is the action that will not bring about misery, confusion.

Also we have been discussing to some extent the question of fear, and perhaps it might be worthwhile this morning to consider suffering and compassion. I have been told by physicists that when they focus strong light on an atom, that light awakens the movement in the atom; and in that movement—with the mind that is looking at the movement—there is an indeterminism: that is what the scientists say. Now, there is, I feel, the light of silence with which to approach all the problems—the light of silence which can be turned on, if one may use that phrase. And that light of silence brings into being precision, clarity, preciseness to the actual movement of every thought. It is only in that light of silence there is comprehension. I think we have discussed enough of that to see the implications involved in it. Then with that understanding let us consider what is suffering. We have thought of fear, we have gone into it somewhat. Now let us go into the question of suffering because I feel that fear and suffering are very close to the comprehension of what is compassion. The scientific mind is not a compassionate mind; it can't, it does not, know what compassion means. But it is the religious mind that knows, lives, has its being in compassion. And to comprehend that thing, one must understand what is suffering.

Please, I hope you are not merely listening to my words because you can really get into a hypnotic state, mesmerized by words, by learning phrases. I can quite imagine how you will repeat "the light of silence," and the mind will keep on repeating it. You have not understood what it means, but that is a new phrase, it sounds nice—that would be mesmerizing yourself. But perhaps if we could really approach this question of suffering actually, not theoretically, then out of this struggle with words, with thought, with the mind, the flame of compassion might come into being.

What is suffering? We are all suffering, every human being is in some kind of suffering. The death of someone whom one likes breeds sorrow; poverty, the outward and inward sense of poverty, also breeds an extraordinary sense of fruitlessness. And the inwardly poor human being, when he is aware of it, is caught in the world of sorrow; it is a terrible thing to realize that you have absolutely nothing inside. You may have degrees, titles, ministerships, good clothes, places, and all the rest of that; strip them off and you will find inside an empty shadow and ashes. Strip the man of his knowledge, of words, of the things he has accumulated, and there, too, there is immense sorrow for him. We suffer in so many things—the sorrow of frustration, the anxiety of ambition, the solitary existence, the woman who has no child everlastingly crying, the man who has no capacity and sees capacity and cleverness, the man who has a gift and the one who is stupid wants to have that gift and many other gifts. Incapacity and capacity both lead to suffering. There is the suffering of a man who knows that he is not loved, that there is another whom he loves but who does not return the love. So there are so many varieties and complications and degrees of suffering. We all know that. You know it very well, and we carry this burden right through life, practically from the moment we are born until the moment we collapse into the grave. Watch yourself, sir, not my words. Is suffering essential? Is it a part of existence to suffer? Is it inevitable? Is it the human law?

Man has suffered for thousands upon thousands of years and still goes on—from the poorest beggar to the richest man, from the most powerful to the least. If we say that it is inevitable, then there is no answer; if you accept it, then you have stopped inquiring into it. You have closed the door to further inquiry; if you escape from it, you have also closed the door. You may escape into man or woman, into drink, amusement, into various forms of power, position, prestige, and the eternal chatter of nothingness. Then your escapes become all-important; the objects to which you fly assume colossal importance. So you have shut the door on sorrow also, and that is what most of us do. Can we talk a little bit to each other openly? I suffer as my son dies; there is an empty void, utter misery, confusion, the sense of loss, degradation. You know all this; I run away from it into the belief in reincarnation; then resurrection and all the rest of it follow—which means I have escaped from the fact. And when I have escaped, obviously I can't understand what is suffering. Now, can we stop escape of every kind and come back to suffering? You understand, sirs? That means not seeking a solution for suffering. There is physical suffering—a toothache, stomachache, an operation, accidents, various forms of physical sufferings which have their own answer. There is also the fear of future pain, which would cause suffering. Suffering is closely related to fear and, without comprehension of these two major factors in life, we shall never comprehend what it is to be compassionate, to love. So a mind that is concerned with the comprehension of what is compassion, love, and all the rest of it must surely understand what is fear and what is sorrow.

Take the physical fact first. I may have a disease or a certain form of disease which is apparently inevitable. Or the doctors may find a new antibiotic or a new drug which will perhaps prolong life—instead of living a hundred years, you may live a hundred and twenty years. Once a person has been ill, he is always afraid of the future, afraid of the recurring disease, recurring pain, recurring anxiety—the fact of "what has been" projects itself into the future: I may become ill and thus it begins; sorrow, the wheel of sorrow goes on, which is the projection of the thought of "what has been" into the future "which may be." We are aware of it, and it requires a very sharp mind not to project thought, not to project itself into the future—because once it has pain, it may have pain again, and through that, death; so fear sets in; the wheel of sorrow goes on. So the comprehension of sorrow as physical fear projected by the mind has to be understood. You cannot brush that aside and say that we are only concerned with sorrow which is inward, psychological. Not that there is no inward and psychological suffering, but one has to understand this physical fact first. Most of us have dental trouble or various forms of pain; we have got to know them. The mind has remembered the past pains and says, "look," gets frightened, anxious, and so it is afraid of a future pain. And thought has been the seed that has caused this future pain and anxiety. Just listen to it to see this process. I wonder if you have understood it when I say: Just listen to it—the psychological fact that a person who has had pain is afraid of pain recurring in the future. Thought has created that fear; in the future, you may not have the pain, but the mind is already preparing for it; that is the actual psychological fact. Merely observe the fact—you can't do anything about the fact—see that is how the mind operates. The nervous system, the whole defensive organism gets going; it is very anxious to do the right thing, always with the background of fear, of pain, or sorrow.

Then what is sorrow? We have understood the physical process that engenders fear and suffering. Then what are the other kinds of sorrow—not other kinds—what is sorrow otherwise? Take the fact that most of us have experienced the death of someone whom we loved. There is a terrific sense of loss, there is a sense of anguish, a sense of complete loneliness, of being left alone, stranded. We know that; most of us have had that experience in various degrees of intensity. Why is there suffering? What do you say, sir?

Comment: The thought of fear is there.

KRISHNAMURTI: Yes, sir, there is the thought of fear. Go into it.

Comment: A feeling of utter helplessness.

KRISHNAMURTI: The feeling of utter helplessness—but why should that cause sorrow? Why should death cause sorrow, why should living cause sorrow? Why should this thing called death be such an extraordinary factor which produces untold fear and sorrow, as living also apparently causes untold suffering and sorrow? So life and death are synonyms when there is sorrow. Do understand this, sirs. It is not that you are afraid only of death which causes sorrow, but you will also see you are afraid of living which causes sorrow—living, being good, being respectable, having a job or no job, being loved or not loved, ambition with its frustrations, the incapable or the capable mind which has its own tortures, the feeling of being frustrated. You know the life you lead—going every day to the office, the routine, the boredom, the insults, the anxiety. Not approximating, not reaching, not arriving—that is also our living, is that not so? The eternal competition with somebody and with some idea—that is what we call living. Such living also produces an astonishing kind of this thing called sorrow, as death does.

Why are we so frightened of death—not what happens after? We are not talking abut the aftereffects, whether there is continuity or not, whether there is a soul or not, and all that. We are discussing the fact that we are all acquainted with this terrible thing called death which causes pain, suffering, anxiety, a sense of utter helplessness, the loneliness, the isolation, the feeling that you are stranded. Don't you know this feeling, sirs?

Comment: We are in sorrow because when he was living, the person we loved was filling some space in us and helping us to live.

KRISHNAMURTI: That is so, and that is why we loved the person. I love my son because he is going to immortalize me, I am going to carry my name through him, I am going to perpetuate myself, because he is going to support me when I am old, he will be better than me, he will go to college, be clever and get better degrees, have a better job, become an important man, and so he will be recognized as an important man, and in that importance I also glory, and so on and on. And therefore I say, "I love my son," and the mother says, "I love my son." This extraordinary process goes on everlastingly from the known existence of man thousands and thousands of years ago until now. The religions, the great teachers have talked about it, and we are caught in it.

Comment: We instinctively avoid pain and sorrow.

KRISHNAMURTI: The gentleman says that we instinctively avoid pain and sorrow. When you say you avoid pain and sorrow, then why do you suffer? Such a question has no meaning. If you say, "I instinctively avoid a snake," then that has an answer; that is a fact. But when you say you instinctively want to avoid pain and suffering, you are living in suffering; you can't avoid it. You are following all this, sirs? Why do you suffer? Go into it, sirs. That is your challenge. What is your response to that challenge, sirs? Why do you suffer?

Comment: Because we are not full, because our mind is not full. There is the utter emptiness of life.

KRISHNAMURTI: You have given explanations, and at the end of it you suffer—which means that you accept suffering as inevitable. A healthy mind does not accept suffering, sir. Now after explaining, do you want to go into it? How do you go into it so that when you leave this room, you are finished with suffering once and for all, you do not go back to the eternal wheel of sorrow?

Comment: Accept the fact that there is suffering. Attachment is the cause of sorrow.

KRISHNAMURTI: You say that attachment is the cause of sorrow. Therefore, you cultivate detachment, and in the meantime you are agonizing. You are in a state of agony, and you accept the fact that you are suffering. Why do you accept it? You don't accept sunshine, do you? Suffering is there; you don't have to accept it. Pain with its burning intensity is agonizing you, and you don't say, "I must accept it." It is there. You can explain, you can gradually push it away—that is what you are doing. You might say, "I accept it, I will bear with it," but you can't bear with an intense pain more than a few hours or so.

And the mind says sorrow is created by attachment—which means you will be free from sorrow if you are detached. So you begin to cultivate detachment which all the books talk about. Why are you attached first of all? You say that you are inwardly empty, and therefore you are attached to the wife, to the child, to an idea, to power, position, to fill that emptiness. You don't tackle the emptiness, but you run away from the emptiness. So how do you face this fact of suffering?

Question: What are the implications of suffering?

KRISHNAMURTI: How do you inquire into suffering? That is my point—not "what are the causes?" You know the causes. But you are not facing the fact. You are suffering; how do you tackle it, sirs?

Comment: Stop thinking of it.

KRISHNAMURTI: Take a drug, go to a cinema, take a tranquilizer? Will that help me? You are advising me how to kill suffering, you are advising me with a lot of words, aren't you? You give me explanations, and at the end of it all I am still empty-handed.

I want to know, when I suffer, how to be free of it. Not with words, not with explanations. When I have a toothache actually, I go to the nearest dentist; I don't sit down, explain, explain. If that is the mind that asks and that responds to the challenge, that wants to be out, then what will you do? It can only then look at the fact and stop escaping altogether. I want to know why I suffer; therefore, I cannot escape away from this thing through explanations, through drink, through women, through the radio, through something else. I want to understand the thing, I want to break through it, crash through it, put it away everlastingly so that it will never touch my mind again. That means, I want to be with it, I want to know all about it—not give words to it, not give explanations to it. As I would go to the nearest doctor and see that there is no pain, in the same way I end suffering.

I am not going to escape from it because I see that through escape—however subtle, however cunning, however reasonable—there is no solution. Then what happens to the mind that has stopped escaping, that has no longer the Gita, the Upanishads, the guru, reincarnation, tradition? It has stopped everything. What is the state of mind that is no longer escaping, that wants to grapple with this thing and come out of it clean-washed, bright, spotless? The mind has realized that to look at something, there must be no escape of any kind, and it has to be scientifically ruthless with itself, and so it has no self-pity.

Then for the first time you have no words; you have stopped the use of all words. Before, you had indulged in words, explanations, quotations; now, you have no words, words have stopped. So the mind that knows suffering, that has suffered, that has gone through the travail of existence, is faced with the stark fact, and it observes.

Now, let us look into the word *observation*—not into the thing that you are looking at, but the state of observation. How do you observe? How do you look at your wife, husband, child, or a tree or a flower? What happens generally is: all kinds of pictures, ideas, desires surge forward. If you could understand how you observe, then you will come to something which will help you to understand sorrow.

When you see a most lovely thing, a beautiful mountain, a beautiful sunset, a ravishing smile, a ravishing face, that fact stuns you, and you are silent; hasn't it ever happened to you? Then you hug the world in your arms. But that is something from outside which comes to your mind, but I am talking of the mind which is not stunned but which wants to look, to observe. Now, can you observe without all this upsurging of conditioning? To a person in sorrow, I explain in words; sorrow is inevitable, sorrow is the result of fulfillment. When all explanations have completely stopped, then only can you look—which means you are not looking from the center. When you look from a center, your faculties of observation are limited. If I hold to a post and want to be there, there is a strain, there is pain. When I look from the center into suffering, there is suffering. It is the incapacity to observe that creates pain. I cannot observe if I think, function, see from a center—as when I say, "I must have no pain, I must find out why I suffer, I must escape." When I observe from a center, whether that center is a conclusion, an idea, hope, despair, or anything else, that observation is very restricted, very narrow, very small, and that engenders sorrow.

So, when I want to understand suffering, because of the intensity of wanting to understand, I do not look at it from a center. I want to be free from sorrow—free, so that it will never touch the mind again. The mind says, "It is an ugly thing, it is a brutal thing, it distorts perception, it distorts living, death, and everything." There must be a total comprehension and therefore a total wiping away of it from the whole of the mind. That is the challenge. When the mind responds according to its conditioning, according to its background, from its center, the observation of the fact is prevented. When I look at the world as a nationalist, I can't look at another human being who comes from abroad; I have no relationship with him, though I may talk of brotherhood, peace, and all such things. When I am looking, observing, from a center which I call "nationalist," I am functioning within the boundaries of a petty, small island. So I can only look at the full, whole world and be with the world totally, wholly, when I have no center as a nationalist, as a Hindu, and all the rest of it.

So what is important is to look at, observe without the center, and then there is no suffering ever more. There will be physical suffering—the kidneys may go wrong, you may have cancer, blindness, death may occur—but you are then able to look at physical suffering, every torturous, psychological suffering, without the center. Therefore you will never have psychological suffering.

And it is only the mind that does not suffer that has no fear. It is only such a mind that is in a state of compassion. Sirs, do go out of this room with that intensity; when the challenge is so great, you have to respond greatly, not from a little corner of the universe as the 'me'.

March 5, 1961

Eighth Talk in Bombay

The last time we met here, we were talking about fear, sorrow, and compassion. One could see very clearly that when the mind is crippled with fear, there cannot be compassion, nor sympathy, nor pity; a mind that is tortured by suffering, to whatever degree, to whatever depth, cannot feel the extraordinary power of compassion. The scientific mind, being precise, clear in its investigation, cannot feel this compassion which can only be when the mind has understood itself. The outward investigation of things does not necessarily lead to the inward comprehension of things, but the inward comprehension of things does bring about an understanding of the outer. The inner comprehension is of the religious mind. The totality of the mind includes all its feelings, ambitions, fears, anxieties, capabilities, the power of observation, the power of position, the power of prestige, cruelty, the venomous hatred, and all the rest of it.

Today, let us go into and understand time and timelessness. To understand this whole process of time with all the complexities involved in it, one has to understand what is influence. Let us investigate this a little; through the understanding of influence, we shall understand what is time and timelessness. If we could, instead of merely discussing it at the verbal level or intellectually splitting it all up, understand the mind that is conditioned by time—which is essentially the word and the influence—perhaps we shall come to understand what it is to be timeless. So let us investigate what is influence.

We are, each one of us, influenced by environment; we are the result of all kinds of influences—good and bad, beautiful and ugly, the influence of the past, the racial inheritance, the family tradition; we are influenced by the food we eat, the dress we wear; every thought, every movement is the result of influence. We are influenced by newspapers, by the magazines, by the cinema, the books we read; we are influenced by each other, consciously or unconsciously. There is this process of response to a challenge, which is from past influence. Please, sirs, when I am saying this, do not accept it or deny it but just observe it—how you live, how you are influenced by the Gita, the Upanishads, the guru, the politician, the newspapers. We are the result of propaganda, the subliminal propaganda or the obvious propaganda—the subliminal propaganda being very, very subtle, suggestive. The immediate yesterday is not so important, but the memories of ten years ago have hypnotic vitality. If we observe, religiously, economically, socially, we are the result of the traditions that this country has inherited, you and I have inherited, from the past. When you say you believe in God, you are influenced, you have been told; and also there is your own desire to find some safety, some security, some permanency; so you are brought up to believe. There are others, those in the communist world, who are brought up not to believe—again influenced. So you are no more religious than those who are brought up not to believe because you are the result of propaganda, you are the result of your circumstances, you are the product of your environment; obviously, whether you accept it or not, that is a psychological fact. Calling yourself a Hindu, a Parsi, is obviously the result of your conditioning. So also is calling yourself a Russian and all the rest of it.

So the mind is the result of conditioning, of innumerable influences, conscious and unconscious. The unconscious is much more powerful, much more potent than the conscious mind; the unconscious mind is the residue, the storehouse of innumerable memories, traditions, motives, impulses, compulsions. Please, watch your own mind, watch yourself when I am talking; you are not just listening to a vague description to which you are approximating.

Question: Sir, how did the first mind come into being?

KRISHNAMURTI: We can observe theoretically how the first mind came into being. Obviously it came into being through sensation, through hunger, through taste, smell, touch. We have developed the arm to stretch, to catch. That is not the problem, sir. How we began we can inquire into, we can suppose, we can investigate; but the fact is, here we are. To investigate the origin of all things is to approach it scientifically, as the scientists, the biologists are investigating the origin of life. You have to investigate what you are actually now. When you investigate, the problem arises whether there is a beginning or an ending—not what was the beginning.

We started with the question of time and timelessness. If we investigate the problem of time, we must investigate the problem of existence which is living, which is influence, which is the result, what we are. And to discover what we are, we have to take ourselves as we are, and be ruthless in our investigation of what we are—not suppose that we were something in the beginning of all things. If we can understand what is in the present, then we will see the beginning and the ending of the thing. There is no beginning and no ending, and you cannot comprehend that extraordinary sense of timelessness unless you understand the mind that is in the present. I am not avoiding the question about what was in the beginning. How will you find it out? You are not biologists, investigators; you are not specialists who can investigate the whole problem of what was, how all life came into being. The specialists have experimented, they have created life in a test-tube. What does it matter if we are not going to find out the origin of all things?

Let us see the mind, our minds, yours and mine. The human mind, as it is now, is the result of the environment. You can see that very clearly if you observe yourselves in your relationship with society, with your neighbors, with the country. We object to being told we are the result of our environment because we think we are something extraordinarily spiritual, as though the environment is also part of the whole existence of man. So it is very important to understand if it is possible to extricate the mind—for the mind to extricate itself—from all influences. Is that possible? Because it is only when the mind has extricated itself from all influences that it can find what is the timeless. To understand what is time—not put it aside, not create a theory, not involve your mind in suppositions and wishes and all that—you actually have to investigate your own mind, and you cannot investigate if you are not aware of the extraordinary impacts of influences.

Obviously, when you listen to me, you are being influenced, aren't you? When you listen to that bell in the street which that garbage-collecting lorry makes, that very sound is influencing; everything is influencing. Can the mind be aware of these influences, watch every influence that is shaping the mind and extricate itself, or be aware of it and walk through it? So that is a problem, which means really the understanding of the whole, of the many yesterdays. There is now, as I am talking to you, the impact of influence in the present, and your response to what is being said is, surely, the memory of a thousand yesterdays. The thousand yesterdays are the result of a thousand previous yesterdays with their influences and with their challenges and responses, with their conditioning—which is memory, which is time. Isn't it? Sir, have you noticed in yourself that yesterday is not so very important; the memories of yesterday fall away very quickly, but the memories of the past ten years have an extraordinary hypnotic vitality? I do not know if you have noticed it. What you did ten years ago, how you felt ten years ago—or what you felt when you were a young boy running about, suddenly capturing the light on the trees, the memory of swimming, that freedom, no responsibility, the fullness of living where there was no conflict, where there was a complete sense of joy—you remember all that, all that has extraordinary vitality, much more than the memories of yesterday. That is influencing us, that is shaping our thinking.

So we understand time as the influence of a thousand yesterdays. So we begin to investigate time as memory, as yesterday, time as today, and time as tomorrow—time as yesterday going through the passage of today, coming out shaped, conditioned, molded into tomorrow. So there is not only the time by the watch, the chronological time, but also there is the time as memory, stretching backwards and forwards, this memory as the unconscious, hidden deep down in the vast recesses of one's mind.

So, there is time by the watch, by the chronometer as yesterday, today, tomorrow; there is time from place to place, from here to there, before and after; and there is the time of 'becoming': I am this, and I shall be that; I am today brutal, violent, ugly, stupid; and tomorrow or perhaps after ten tomorrows, I will be that. So there is time from here to there. All aspiration is that—one day I shall achieve, one day I shall become the manager, one day I shall become the chief boss of the whole show. So there is in this time the urge to fulfill, and with the urge of fulfillment there is the inevitable frustration and sorrow, which is still a part of time. We know this, we accept this as inevitable, as a part of our natural existence, and hope that one day through time, gradually, life after life, or after a series of many tomorrows, we shall arrive there. We say a seed becomes the tree, and there must be time for the seed to become the tree. I planted it yesterday; I watch it today, and in ten years time, it will be a lovely thing, full of leaves, shadows innumerable. So I pretend that I shall also be one day reaching that place where there is permanency. So we begin to introduce permanency and the transient, and say that eventually we shall arrive at the permanent.

Is there anything permanent? Permanency in relationship, permanency of house, of government, permanency of something or other, permanency of truth, God—this means a continuity which means time. We accept all this like children who are told what to do, and for the rest of our life we are slaves to what is being said. So unless we understand this whole process of time, we shall not enter into that state which may exist or may not exist.

Should I accept the state of timelessness? All that we know is time. Because we are slaves to it, it tortures us; there is a continuous battle from *what is* to 'what shall be'. So we have to understand that; let us be clear.

There is a time according to the watch, there is a time when the train leaves, there is a time when the airplane leaves the earth, there is a time when you just go to your office, there is a time when you must sow, there is a time when you must reap—that is one kind of time. Then there is the time—inward time—which is memory; that is extraordinarily complex, extraordinarily subtle; and without grappling with it, without understanding it, without going into it ruthlessly like a scientist who investigates something, you cannot find out if there is or if there is not a state when time is not. As long as there is cause and effect, there must be time; as long as there is action based on an idea, there must be time—the time being: bridging the act or approximating the act according to an idea. You see the difficulty? When I am dull and I am trying to become clever—that is also part of time. When I realize I am violent, and I am trying to practice, to discipline, to control, to become nonviolent, the gradation, the gradual process to 'become' demands time. We are all brought up that way. When in the school, you are told that you must be the best boy—at once, there is time. All competition is time—competition of the clerk to become the manager, and the manager competing to become the supermanager, the director, and eventually something bigger. There is not only chronological time but also psychological time, the time of 'becoming'.

Comment: Mind, time, and experience seem to be one thing, but memory cannot be time because memory is of the past. It is part of the conception of time.

KRISHNAMURTI: Are we discussing this theoretically or factually? Look at your own minds, sirs. Your mind is the result of experience, which is the result of time, isn't it?

And the mind varies with the experiences, but it is still within the field of time. You may have different experiences, and I may have different experiences, but that experience, which has created memory from which springs thought, is still within the field of time. Now, we are discussing time, unfolding it; we are not even discussing, we are just exposing it. It is not a question of my agreeing or your denying. We are just looking at the map.

Question: When I listen to you, I am being influenced by your thought; then I say: I will investigate what you are talking about. Don't you think the question, "I will investigate," also involves time?

KRISHNAMURTI: Of course, sir. The whole process of thinking involves time.

Question: How do you ask us to be aware of facts without being influenced?

KRISHNAMURTI: I never said that, sir, you are assuming it. I said: First let us be aware of the facts—neither accepting nor denying them. Where is the difficulty, sir? Before I enter into timelessness, if there is such a state, I must know first what time is—not according to Einstein, according to the Gita, or according to the latest professor, or the interpreter of the Gita. I want to know what my mind is like, which is the result of time, and I want to understand time.

If you want to understand something, you must approach it simply, mustn't you? If you want to understand a very complicated machinery, you must begin to unscrew little by little, taking one thing after another, bit by bit; you can't jump into it—you can, if you have the mind. But most of us have not got that sharp, clear, scientific mind which is not prejudiced, which is not conceiving, formulating. So you have to look at time. There is the time of going to the office, the train time, time by the watch, and that is one time. Then there is this vast field of time which is experience, memory, thought, mind, aspirations, the becoming, the denying, the fulfilling, the mind which says, "I must be something"—all that is time, which we are discussing. We are looking at it, observing it; we are not denying it, we are not accepting it, but we are seeing something as it is.

So your mind is that—not what it was at the beginning and not what it will be at the end. I do not know what it was at the beginning, and what it will be at the end. But I take a slice off in this vast time, a gap, and look at it, which is 'myself'. If you don't want to look at yourself, that is quite a different matter. I do not see how you can investigate—investigate in the sense that you directly experience, directly observe, directly feel your way, taking the thing as you are, not assuming what you were—which may be merely tradition and acting according to that tradition, not having any hope of what you will be, which too is within the field of time.

Question: Has time any relationship with God?

KRISHNAMURTI: Do you believe in God, sir? Belief in God, what does that mean, believing in something which you don't know? You hope and you believe there is God and that you will eventually reach God. We have to understand this process of time, and that is real meditation. Meditation is not sitting in a corner and doing all kinds of self-hypnotic processes. But to investigate the mind whether it is caught in time or whether the mind can be free of time—that is real meditation.

I want to find out if there is a timeless state because as long as the mind is a slave to time, there is no freedom. It is a slave to cause-and-effect. I love you because you give me something; I go from here to there because I want to get something; I see that to be nonviolent is very profitable; economically and inwardly it gives me a sense of success—so there is cause-and-effect. The mind which investigates wants to find out if there is a state where there is no cause-and-effect, which is pure energy—energy which has a cause-and-effect is limited energy. If I say, "Be good," you may be good; this involves a pressure, an influence—is that goodness? If you are good with a motive, is that goodness? Or is goodness something which has no motive at all? Has love a motive? If I love my wife because she gives me her body, because she bears me children, she cooks for me, she looks after my laundry and the house when I earn a livelihood, is that love? Has love, compassion, a cause? You follow all this, sirs? I want to find out, my mind is curious to find out; I cannot be curious if I accept various stupid, vague theories, however pleasant they may be; I must investigate, find out, be ruthless with myself.

So, let us begin. The mind is of time, is of experience, and that experience is based on memory; that memory is the record held within the mind—memory not only of my own personal experience but also the memory of man held within the unconscious, which is conditioning my thinking all the time, which is shaping my thoughts all the time, consciously and unconsciously. Can the mind which is the result of all that be free? You follow the problem? You understand the problem, sirs? Then only can I find out if there is a timeless state; otherwise, I cannot possibly understand it. Theoretically it may be that a few saints—not saints that recognize themselves as saints; the public, the church may call them saints; they never experience the timeless—a few people out somewhere have experienced this. But let us not go into that now. Here I am, here you are; we are the products of influence which shapes our experiences, and those experiences being conditioned, our future experiences are also conditioned. I am asking myself, are we conscious of this fact? You understand? This is a very simple thing. Am I conscious when I say I am a Hindu or Buddhist or a Parsi? Do I know, am I conscious that I am believing, that my mind is operating in a conditioned state which is within the field of time? Do I know that mind—not that it is right or wrong? Do I know that much? Then, if I know that, then I say to myself, "Is it possible, being in that state, to see, to observe?"

I cannot see anything, I cannot observe clearly, precisely, when I call myself a Hindu, a Christian, a Buddhist—which is the whole tradition, the weight of tradition, the weight of knowledge, the weight of conditioning. With that mind I can only look at life, at something, as a Christian, as a Buddhist, as a Hindu, as a nationalist, as a communist, as something or other, and that state prevents me from observing. That is simple.

When the mind watches itself as a conditioned entity, that is one state. But when the mind says, "I am conditioned," that is another state. When the mind says, "I am conditioned," in that state of the mind, there is the 'I' as the observer, watching the conditioned state. When I say, "I see the flower," there is the observer and the observed; the observer is different from the thing observed; therefore, there is distance, there is a time-lag, there is duality, there are the opposites; and then there is the overcoming of the opposites, the cementing of the dual—that is one state. Then there is the other state when the mind observes itself as being conditioned in which there is no observer and the thing observed. You see the difference?

You observe that your mind is conditioned: there is the observer who says, "I am conditioned"; therefore, the observer is different from the conditioned state. When you say, "My mind is conditioned, I am the result of time, I am the experiencer, and I have the experience," you are talking of the state when there is duality. When you say, "I am angry, and I must not be angry," when you say, "I know I am conditioned," and "How am I to be free from conditioning?" there is the 'you' as the observer, as the thinker, saying, "I must be free." So there is the dual process going on; that is a fact. It is not that I am trying to establish it; that is a fact, that is how you think. You say, "I am violent, and I must become nonviolent"—this country is ridden with that idea; in other countries it is something else. Here nonviolence is a most extraordinary, lovely state, and you hug this and you say, "I must become that." I say that is the fact, that is what you think. There is the observer, the thinker, and the observed and the thought. So there is the duality which is time, the observer saying, "I must become nonviolent"; this involves time. It is a gradual process, and how to cement the two becomes the problem. You want to bring the two together, to bridge over. Then you say, "I must discipline, practice," and you go through various forms of discipline, control, subjugation, this and that, in order to bring these two together—which implies all the time an outside factor, the entity who is disciplining, the mind which is controlling, the mind which chooses, the mind which denies, the mind which accepts, as though it is separate from this thing itself. This is what you are doing. I am not describing, I am not telling you; you don't have to approximate to what is being said; this is what you are doing, and I say that all that involves time. Do you see that you are doing this? Do you observe that you are doing this?

I am ambitious; I want to be something for various reasons: power, prestige, this gives me power, there is patronage involved in this, I like that, I am ambitious, ambitious to be something. That involves time: I must work, I must be cunning, I must be ruthless, I must see the right people, pull strings, go and bow down, lick somebody's boots, pay false respect, bend down, almost touch their feet, crawl on my knees. This is what is happening in the world. I want to be something—that involves time; there is the observer, the thinker who says, "I am going to be that." Now, with that mind, you are asking, "Is there timelessness?" You are caught in time; the mind is held within that framework, held in that mold, and in that mold you are asking, "Is there timelessness?" I say it is a vain question. When you shatter the mold, you will find out. Then you will say, "Please tell me how to shatter this in order to enjoy that lovely state"—which means achieving an end; that becomes your ambition; then there is practice, discipline, change, again all in time.

When you observe, you are aware without the division as observer and the observed. The mind is aware of itself being conditioned—not the mind and the thought being separate. You see the difference, sirs? This is very difficult, very complicated. The mind observes itself as the observer; this is not a hypnotic thing. Watch yourself. When the mind is a slave to this "I want to be this or that," it is in the state in which there is the observer and the observed, the division, the duality, and all the rest of it. For that mind to realize that the observer is the observed, that there is no separation—it is an extraordinary experience. It is not a rare thing which you do experience. When you are angry, when you are in a tremendous experience, when you are passionate, when you are joyous, when you are carried away by something, in that state of experience, there is not the observer nor the observed. Haven't you noticed it, sirs? When you are tremendously angry, in that moment, in that split second, there is neither the observer nor the observed; you are in that state of experience. Later on you say, "How am I not to be angry? I must not be angry," and all that. Then time begins. These are facts, sir; I am not saying something outside facts. This is not a theory. So, when the mind separates itself as the observer, thinker, as thought and the observer, you are perpetuating time; and then the problem arises: How to bridge the two, the idea and the action, approximating the action to the idea. This is what you are doing.

The idealist, the utopian; the idea and the action; the idea as a cause and the act also as a cause—all this involves time. So the mind is caught in a cause-and-effect chain. Now, when the mind observes itself as being conditioned, there is only action, there is no idea; at the moment of anger there is action, at the moment of passion there is action, there is no idea; the idea comes later. When you feel tremendously about something, strongly about something, there is no idea; you are in that state which is action without the idea; there is no approximating action to an idea—which is a curse of modern civilization, the curse of the idealist. Now we have gone through all that. Do you follow this? This is meditation, this is real work.

Can your mind be aware that it is conditioned, not as an observer watching itself being conditioned, experiencing now—not tomorrow, not the next minute—the state in which there is no observer, the same as the state you experience when you are angry? This demands tremendous attention, not concentration; when you concentrate, there is duality. When you concentrate upon something, the mind is concentrated, watching the thing concentrated upon; therefore, there is duality. In attention, there is no duality because in that state, there is only the state of experiencing.

When you say, "I must be free from all conditioning, I must experience," there is still the 'I', who is the center from which you are observing; therefore, in that there is no escape at all because there is always the center, the conclusion, the memory, a thing that is watching, saying, "I must, I must not." When you are looking, when you are experiencing, there is the state of the nonobserver, a state in which there is no center from which you look. At the moment of actual pain, there is no 'I'. At the moment of tremendous joy, there is no observer; the heavens are filled, you are part of it, the whole thing is bliss. This state of mind takes place when the mind sees the falseness of the state of mind which attempts to become, to achieve, and which talks about timelessness. There is a state of timelessness only when there is no observer.

Question: The mind that has observed its own conditioning—can it transcend thought and duality?

KRISHNAMURTI: You see how you refuse to observe something very simple? Sir, when you get angry, is there an idea in that stage, is there a thought, is there an observer? When you are passionate, is there any other fact except that? When you are consumed with hatred, is there the observer, the idea, and all the rest of it? It comes later on, a split second later, but in that state there is nothing of this.

Question: There is the object towards which love is directed. Is there duality in love?

KRISHNAMURTI: Sir, love is not directed to something. The sunshine is not directed to you and me; it is there.

The observer and the observed, the idea and the action, the *what is* and 'what should be'—in this, there is duality, the opposites of duality, the urge to correlate the two; the conflict of the two is in that field. That is the whole field of time. With that mind, you cannot approach or discover if there is time or if there is not. How is it possible to wipe that away? Not how, not the system, not the method, because the moment you apply a method, you are again in the field of time. Then the problem is: Is it possible to jump away from that? You cannot do it by gradation because that again involves time. Is it possible for the mind to wipe away the conditioning, not through time, but by direct perception? This means the mind has to see the false and to see what is truth. When the mind says, "I must find out what is timeless," such a question for a mind involved in time has no answer. But can the mind which is the product of time wipe itself away—not through effort, not through discipline? Can the mind wipe the thing away without any cause? If it has a cause, then you are back again in time.

So you begin to inquire into what is love, negatively, as I explained before. Obviously, love which has a motive is not love. When I give a garland to a big man because I want a job, because I want something from him, is that respect, or is it really disrespect? The man who has no disrespect is naturally respectful. It is a mind which is in a state of negation—which is not the opposite of the positive, but the negation of seeing what is false and putting away the false as a false thing—that can inquire.

When the mind has completely seen the fact that through time, do what you will, it can never find the other, then there is the other. It is something much vaster, limitless, immeasurable; it is energy without a beginning and without an end. You cannot come to that, no mind can come to that—it has only to 'be'. We must be only concerned with the wiping away, if it is possible to wipe it clean, not gradually; that is innocency. It is only an innocent mind that can see this thing, this extraordinary thing which is like a river. You know what a river is? Have you watched up and down in a boat, swam across the river? What a lovely thing it is! It may have a beginning and it may have an end. The beginning is not the river and the end is not the river. The river is the thing in between; it passes through villages; everything is drawn into it; it passes through towns, all polluted with bad chemicals; filth and sewage are thrown into it; and a few miles further, it has purified itself; it is the river in which everything lives—the fish below, and on top, the man that drinks its water. That is the river, but behind that, there is that tremendous pressure of water, and it is this self-purificatory process that is the river.

The innocent mind is like that energy. It has no beginning and no end. It is God—not the temple-god. There is no beginning and no end; therefore, there is no time and timeless. And the mind cannot come to it. The mind which measures in time must wipe itself away and enter into that without knowing that because you cannot know it, you cannot taste it; it has no color, no space, no shape. That is for the speaker, not for you, because you have not left the other. Don't say there is that state—it is a false state when that statement is made by a person who is being influenced. All that you can do is to jump out of it, and then you will know—then you won't even know—you are part of this extraordinary state.

March 8, 1961

Ninth Talk in Bombay

During these talks, we should not merely listen to what is being said but also listen to our minds because mere description or explanation is not sufficient in itself—it is like describing food to a hungry man, and such description has no value at all; what he needs is food. Mere theorizing or speculating 'what should be' and 'what should not be' seems to me so utterly futile and immature. So, the listening has to be such that there is observation of the immediate facts, and that apparent observation is only possible when we are aware of our own minds and the operations of our own minds. The scientist in his laboratory puts aside theories and observes facts; he does not approximate the fact to the theory. When the fact denies an old theory, he may have a new theory, a new hypothesis, but he is always going from fact to fact. But we unfortunately have a theory which becomes extraordinarily vital, strong, potent, and we try to approximate or adjust the fact to that theory—that is our existence. We have a permanent idea, a lasting idea that society should be this way, and relationship should be that way, and so on and on; these are our permanent conditions, demands, and traditions, and according to them we live, ignoring facts.

Now, why does the mind demand permanency? Is there anything permanent? Theoretically we say there is no permanency because we see life is in a flux—constantly changing, an endless movement; there is never a moment when you can say, "This is permanent." You may lose your job; your wife, your husband may leave; you may die; everything is in a movement that is without end, in a state of flux, constantly changing—these are obvious facts. But yet we want something very permanent. And to us that permanency is safety, comfort; from that we try to establish all action, don't we? We want permanency in our relationships, in occupation, in character, and in a continued experience; we want the permanency of pleasure and the avoidance of pain permanently. We want to be in a state of peace which will be constant, enduring, long lasting. We want to make permanent every good form, every good feeling, the feeling which explodes as affection, as sympathy, as love. We seek ways and means to make all this permanent. Then realizing that all this is not permanent, we try to establish within ourselves a spiritual state which is constant, enduring, timeless, eternal, and all the rest of it. That is our constant demand and state.

How upset we are if the wife, the husband, leaves; how tremendously shaken when death comes! We want everything solidified, made permanent; we want to capture and put into the frame a lovely experience that goes by in a fleeting second. The incessant demand for permanency is one of our constant urges. Is there such a thing as permanency? Is any thing permanent? And why does the mind refuse to see the fact that there is nothing permanent in the world, inside or outside?

The man who has a good job wants it to last forever, he is afraid to retire; and when he retires, he begins to inquire for some other permanency. And this demand, the difference between the fact and the urge for something contrary to the fact, creates conflict. I want a permanent, lasting, enduring relationship with my wife, my children. My wife is like me, a human being, living, moving, thinking, changing; she may look at another or run away; then the trouble begins, the conflict begins—jealousy, envy, fear, hope, despair, frustration. And to overcome that conflict, we try to discover various ways and means not to face the conflict but to find something that will introduce a new factor which will give us another state, another experience of permanency. I do not know if you have not noticed all this within yourself? I am not talking about something extraneous, absurd, or theoretical.

So, there is conflict. To me conflict is death. A mind in conflict is a most destructive mind; it does not face facts. It is very difficult to face facts, to look at facts, to be capable of observing facts, to see things actually as they are outwardly and inwardly, without bringing in our prejudices, our conditionings, responses and desires, hopes, fears, and all the rest of it. And this demand for permanency does blind the mind, does make the mind dull, and therefore there is no sensitivity. Sensitivity implies a mind that is constantly not only adjusting but also going beyond the mere actual adjustment, flowing, moving with the fact. The fact is never still; it is like the river always moving, always flowing; the moment there are little pools, little diversions where the water remains, there is stagnation. A moving, living mind is never still; there is never a sense of permanency, and it is such a mind that is sensitive not only to the ugly but also to the beautiful, to everything; it is sensitive. So it is the sensitive mind that is capable of appreciating or being in that state which is called beauty or ugliness. I do not know if you have thought at all of what is beauty and what is ugliness.

Unfortunately, in this country desire has been suppressed as a religious act. The sannyasis, the saints, and the so-called holy people have urged and constantly maintained that desire should be rooted out. When you destroy anything within or without, obviously there is the state of insensitivity; and when the mind is insensitive, it is incapable of seeing what is beautiful.

I do not know if you have noticed as you ride in the bus to go to the office, as you talk to the people, as you sit at a table how crude, how thoughtless the people are in their speech and manners, and their complete disregard of another. I am not moralizing, I am merely describing, stating the fact. Beauty is not really the opposite of ugliness; beauty contains the ugly, but the ugly does not contain beauty. Without this sense of what is beautiful—not merely physical adornment, but the beauty of gesture, courtesy, consideration, the sense of yielding in which there is a great gentleness, tenderness—without that sense of beauty, surely man is incapable of living in that movement, that moving quality which has no permanency. It is only the mind that demands permanency that is aware of death.

How is it possible—how, not in the sense of a method—for the mind to be aware of this conflict between the fact and what the mind wants, and so live in a constant movement which has no resting place, no anchorage, which deeply, inwardly does not demand anything permanent? I do not know if you have noticed or asked yourself whether there is anything permanent in life. That is one of our greatest difficulties, isn't it? We love somebody, the wife, the husband, the child, perhaps the community, perhaps the world, and perhaps the universe; but through it all runs the sense of endurance, constancy, a thing that will know no change. I wonder if you ever asked yourself why the mind is on the quest for permanency, why it demands permanency. We do not find permanency here because all relationships change, all things move; there is death, there is a mutation. And so we say there is God, there is something which is changeless, which is what we are not, and we are seeking God.

Is the mind capable of putting away all this—not only this urge for permanency, but also the memory which has become permanent, the knowledge which prevents the movement of life, its living quality? Is it possible to enter into that movement, and yet at the same time have the capacity of recollection which will not interfere with the quality of living, with the quality of something that is dynamic, moving?

Most of us think that knowledge, information, is necessary, and that gives a certain sense of security, permanency, which colors all our lives. From that question there arises another question: What is learning?

Is learning merely addition, an accumulative process, and therefore, it is additive, adding, adding, adding—which is mechanical? Is learning mechanical or something entirely different? The schoolboy is only gathering information, accumulating, adding, putting it by in his storehouse of memory; and when a question is asked, he responds. This is the process of acquisition, this is the process of adding. Is that learning? Unless you answer this for yourself, you are pursuing the path of permanency which is mechanical.

The electronic brains, the computers are machines which do astonishing calculations, astonishing things; they are more accurate, more swift, more subtle, more capable of solving difficult problems than the human being because they are all based on a mechanical process. At present, they are incapable of learning. Is learning mechanical, or is there only learning when the mind is nonmechanical?—which means when the mind is not in habit. When I have got a dogma or a belief, when I am a devotee of somebody—some saint or some book—I am incapable of learning anything new; I am only translating the new in my devotion, in my identification with the picture, my social work, this and that; and when I do change, it is the change in reaction as reaction, and therefore it is not learning.

You cannot learn if you are merely using the mind as a mechanical process of adding, continuing the habit or altering the habit to another series of habits. Have you not noticed that as you grow older, you settle down in habits? How difficult it is to eat some strange food when you are used to eating a particular kind of food! Do watch yourself next time how you sit at the table, your mannerisms. Your mind has solidified itself in habits, in mannerisms. You have already established a certain pattern of existence, of living, and it is extraordinarily difficult to break it, and the breaking is merely a reaction, and learning is not reaction. A mechanical process is a reactive process, but learning never is.

The quality of sensitivity is not mechanical. It is the sensitive mind that is capable of learning and not the mind that functions in habits, and the mind functions in habit when it is held by tradition.

What is the state of your mind when you are learning about something which you do not know? When it says, "I do not know, I am going to find out," it is waiting to know, it is not blank, it is not humble; it is in a state of expectancy, waiting to gather. But when it says, "I don't know," and is not in a state of expectancy, it is capable of learning because it is intensely active, not in the activity of gathering information, but active in itself; it has brushed aside everything it has known—all beliefs, all ideas, all dogmas, all anchorages.

So conflict exists when the mind refuses to face the fact, to see the truth or the falseness which is in the fact, because it has certain ideas about the fact; and the conflict is between the idea, hope, tradition, conclusion, and the facts.

There is such a thing as death—the physical mechanism wearing itself out, like everything that is used up. I want to learn what is death—not the conclusion or opinion about death, not whether there is reincarnation or if there is continuity after death. I have seen dead bodies being carried, I have seen people in tears, in anxiety, agony, being alone, being frustrated, empty, and I must know about death. The accumulation of information about death—such as resurrection, reincarnation, continuity—is a mechanical, additive process which will give comfort to a mind which is already mechanical. But that is not learning about death. There is death, the ending of the physical body, but there may be an ending of a different kind also; I want to learn. I do not say I must be eternal, continuous, or there is something in me which is everlastingly continuous. I am not interested in what others have said or what is said in books. I have to discard the whole world of information, the mechanical process of knowledge. If there is any power that is mechanical left in my mind, which is accumulating, I shall not learn; therefore, I must die to that without argument. Because my interest is to learn about death, can I die to everything which has become mechanical?—to my sex, to my ambition, to position, power, prestige, which are all mechanical. Can I die to all this without an argument? When the mind dies to the mechanical process of accumulation with its identifications, to the things it has known, then it is in a state of learning. The interest in learning puts away, destroys the mechanical process of living. If the mind wants to destroy the mechanical process, it cannot because the thing that wants to destroy is still mechanical, because it wants to get somewhere. But when the interest in learning about death has destroyed the mechanical process, the mind is in a state of not-knowing, a state of emptiness, because it is dead to all the mechanical processes of memory, insults, hopes, fears, despairs, joy; therefore, the mind itself is in a state of the unknown. The unknown is death. When the mind is itself in a state of the unknown, is aware of itself as the unknown, there is no search any more—it is only the mind that is functioning mechanically that is seeking, and seeking is essentially from knowledge to knowledge. As the mind is no longer seeking—that is an extraordinary state, never seeking any more—it is never in conflict, it is astonishingly alive, sensitive.

The unknown cannot be described. All description is the process of giving you more accumulative knowledge and therefore making you more mechanical. You have to come to the state when you say to yourself, "I do not know"—not out of bitterness, not out of despair, but with that sense of love. Love says, "I do not know," always. Love never says, "I know." It is the very essence of humility that says, "I do not know," and humility is absolute innocence.

March 10, 1961

Tenth Talk in Bombay

This is the last talk of this series. We have been discussing for the last few weeks that the present world situation demands a new mind that is dimensionally quite different, that is not directive, that does not function merely in particular directions, but wholly. Such a new mind is the real "religious mind." The religious mind is entirely different from the scientific mind. The scientific mind is directive; it breaks through from the piston engine to the jet engine through various physical barriers, in direction. But the religious mind explodes without direction, it has no direction. And that explosive nature of the new mind is not a matter of discipline, is not a thing to be got, to be reached, to be obtained; if you are reaching, obtaining, gaining, having that as a goal, then it becomes directive and therefore scientific. The religious mind comes into being when we understand the whole structure of our whole thinking, when we are very familiar with knowing oneself, self-knowing. One has to understand oneself, all the thoughts, the movements, the envy, ambitions, compulsions and urges, fear, sorrow, the aspirations, the clogging nature of belief and dogma and the innumerable conclusions to which the mind comes, either through experience or through information. Such self-knowing is absolutely essential because it is only such a mind that can, because it has understood itself, wither itself away for the new to be.

Logic, reason, clear verbal thinking is not sufficient; it is necessary, but it does not get anywhere. An ambitious man can talk, same as a politician who is generally very ambitious about nonambition, about the dangers of ambition—that is verbal logic but has no significance. But if we would understand, if we would inquire into ourselves, we should not only go through the verbal explanation but also drop away all explanations completely because the explanations are not the real things. I know several people who have listened for years to what is being said; they are experts in explanations; they can give explanations far better than the speaker, verbally, logically, clearly. But look into their hearts and their minds—they are ridden, confused, ambitious, pursuing one thing after the other, always the monkeyish activity. Such a mind can never comprehend the new mind.

I think it is very important that this new mind should come into being. It does not come by wishing, by any form of desire, sacrifice. What it demands is a mind that is very fertile, not with ideas, not with knowledge—fertile like the soil that is very rich, the soil in which a seed can grow without being nurtured, carefully watched over, because if you plant a seed in sand, it cannot grow, it withers away, it dies. But a mind which is very sensitive is fertile, is empty—empty, not in the sense of nothingness, but it does not contain anything else except the nourishment for the seed. And you cannot have a sensitive mind if you have not gone into yourself far, deeply inquiring, searching, looking, watching. If the mind has not cleansed itself of all the words, of conclusions, how can such a mind be sensitive? A mind which is burdened with experience, with knowledge, words—how can such a mind be sensitive? It is not a matter of how to get rid of knowledge—that is merely direction—but one has to see the necessity for the mind to be sensitive. To be sensitive implies sensitive to everything, not in one particular direction only—sensitive to beauty, to ugliness, to the speech of another, to the way another talks and you talk, sensitive to all the responses, conscious and unconscious. And a mind is not sensitive when it has a bloated body, eating too much, when it is a slave to the habit of smoking, the habits of sex, the habit of drinking, or the habits which the mind has cultivated as thought—obviously such a mind is not a sensitive mind. Do you see the importance of having a sensitive mind, not how to acquire a sensitive mind. If one sees the necessity, the importance, the urgency of having a sensitive mind, then everything else comes, adjusts itself to that. A disciplined mind, a mind that is conformed, is never a sensitive mind. Obviously, a mind that follows another is not a sensitive mind. Only that mind is sensitive which is exquisitely pliant, that is not tethered to anything.

And a mind that is fertile, not in the invention of new ideas, does not relish or indulge in explanations as though in themselves words are a reality. The word is never the thing. The word *door* is not the door; these two are entirely different things. But most of us are satisfied with words, and we think we have understood the whole structure of the universe and ourselves by words. Semantically we can reason logically, verbally, very clearly, but that is not a fertile mind. A fertile mind is empty like the womb before it conceives; as it is empty, it is fertile, rich—which really means it has purged itself of all the things that are not necessary for the new mind to be. And that comes into being only when you see the urgency of having such a mind, a fertile mind without any belief, without any dogma, without any frustration, and therefore without hope and despair, without the breath of sorrow which is really self-pity. Such a mind is necessary for the new mind, and that is why it is essential to enter into the field of self-knowing.

We know several people who have listened to these talks for thirty, forty years and have not gone beyond their own skins inwardly; outwardly, they are incessantly active. Such people are racketeers, exploiting, and therefore very destructive people, whether they are politicians or social workers or spiritual leaders who have not really deeply, inwardly, penetrated into their own beings, which is after all the totality of life. You and I are the totality of life, the whole of life—the life: the physical life, the organic life, the automatic nervous responses, the sensation, the life that pursues ambitiously its end, the life that knows envy and so everlastingly battles with itself, the life that compares, competes, the life that knows sorrow, happiness, the life that is full of motives, urges, demands, fulfillment, frustrations, the life that wants to reach ultimately the permanent, the lasting, the enduring, and the life that knows that every moment is a fleeting moment, and that there is nothing permanent or substantial in anything—all that is the totality of you and me: that is life. And without really understanding all that, mere explanation of all that has no value at all; and yet we are so easily satisfied with explanations, with words—which indicates how shallow we are, how superficial our life is, to be satisfied by cunning words, by words which are very cleverly put together. After all, the Upanishads, the Gita, the Bible, the Koran are just words, and to keep on repeating, quoting, explaining the same is still the continuation of the word; and apparently we are extraordinarily satisfied by these—which indicates how empty, how shallow, how easily satisfied we are by words which are ashes.

So it is absolutely essential to understand oneself. The word *understanding* has nothing to do with the word *explanation*. The description is not the understanding; the verbal thing is not the understanding. To understand something requires a mind that is capable of observing itself without distortion. I cannot understand, look at these flowers if my attention is not given to them. In attention there is no condemnation, there is no justification, no explanation, or conclusion. You understand? You observe, and such a state of observation comes into being when there is the urgency to understand, to look, to observe, to see, to perceive; then the mind strips itself of everything to observe. For most of us observation is very difficult because we have never watched anything, neither the wife nor the child, nor the filth on the street, nor the children smiling; we have never watched ourselves—how we sit, how we walk, talk, how we jabber away incessantly, how we quarrel. We are never aware of ourselves in action. We function automatically, and that is how we want to function. And having established that habit, we say, "How can I observe myself without the habit?" So, we have a conflict, and to overcome the conflict, we develop other forms of discipline, which are a further continuation of habits.

So, habit, discipline, the continuation of a particular idea—these prevent understanding. If I want to understand a child, I have to look, I have to observe, not at any given moment only, but all the time, while the child is playing, crying, doing everything. I have to watch it, but the moment there is a bias, I have ceased to watch. The discovery for oneself of the biases, the prejudices, the experiences, and the knowledge that prevents this observation is the beginning of self-knowledge. Without that inquiry of self-knowledge you cannot observe. Without stripping the 'I' of the glasses of prejudices and the innumerable conditionings, can you look? How can the politicians look at the universe, the world, because they are so ambitious, they are so petty, concerned with their advancement, with their country? And we too are concerned with our service, wife, position, achievements, ambitions, envies, conclusions; and with all that we say, "We must look, we must observe, we must understand." We can't understand. Understanding comes only when the mind is stripped of all these—there must be a ruthless stripping. Because, these engender sorrow, they are the seeds, the roots of sorrow, and a mind that has roots in sorrow can never have compassion.

I do not know if you have ever taken up one thing and gone into it, probed into it—such as *envy*. Our society is based on envy, our religion is based on envy. Envy is expressed in society as 'becoming', socially climbing the ladder of success. Envy includes competition, and that word *competition* is used to cover up envy; our society is built on that. And the structure of our thinking is built on envy with its comparisons and competition to be something. Take that one thing, envy, understand it and go right through it. Put your teeth into it and strip the mind of envy. And it requires energy, doesn't it, to go through envy, to watch it in operation outside of us and inside the skin, to watch the expression of envy, the fulfillment of envy, and the frustration of envy which include ambition, jealousy, hatred, and to take that and go right through it, not only semantically, verbally, logically, precisely in thinking, but also actually strip the mind of all envy so that it does not think in terms of competition, of reaching, gaining; I am sure you have not done it—not only the people who have come here for the first time, but also the people who have heard me for thirty years. They have not done this; they skirt round it, explain, play. But to take stock of themselves, day after day, every minute, ruthlessly, to penetrate into this appalling thing called envy—that requires energy. That energy is not commitment to nonenvy, you understand? When one is concerned with the understanding of envy, there is no duality as nonenvy to which one is committed, as violence and nonviolence. The desire to become nonviolent is a directional commitment, and that directional commitment gives you energy. Don't you know that when you are committed to some form of activity—saving the Tibetan children, saving the Indian nationality, or something else—it gives you an extraordinary vitality. The people who have fought for this unfortunate country, who have been in prisons—they have had extraordinary energy to do all that because they were committed to something. This commitment is self-forgetfulness in something; it is a substitution, and the self is in identification with that something, and that gives energy. But to inquire into envy which is nondirective requires a totally different form of energy because you are not committed to nonenvy, you are not committed to a state when you have no envy. In the search to go into envy, you need an astonishing, potent, vital, energy which has no relation to any form of commitment. Do please understand this: Because you are inquiring ruthlessly into yourself—never letting a single thought go by which has the quality of envy—that energy comes which is nondirectional, which does not come through commitment. That energy comes only when you begin to understand yourself, when the mind is stripping itself of all the contradictory processes which mean conflict.

The mind in conflict has no energy. Rather than have conflict, it is much better for it to live in a state of nonconflict, whatever it be—ambitious, sluggish, lazy, indolent, idolatrous. There, you are wherever you are; you are stupid, that is all. But a mind which is stupid, saying, "I must become clever, spiritual, and all the rest of it"—such a mind is in conflict. And a mind in conflict can never have understanding; it has not the energy to understand. Please do see this: A tortured mind, a mind caught in this duality has not the energy to understand; it is wasting itself in conflict. But the mind that is inquiring into itself, seeking out the corners, the recesses, the deep hidden regions of the mind in which the mind lurks, looking, looking, looking—in that, there is no conflict because it moves from fact to fact; it does not deny the fact or accept the fact; it is so, and that engenders an extraordinary energy without motive. Do experiment with this, sirs, see it. Take as I said one thing like envy or ambition or what you will and work it right through. Not to strip the mind of envy—which you can't do—then it becomes conflict, a duality, and your conflict takes away the energy; it is like a man who is violent trying to become nonviolent. All the saints, the mahatmas, and the great ones of the land have been battling in themselves all day long, and that battle creates an energy which is not the energy of purification. But to have the energy of purification, you have to go into one thing, to observe, to understand, to see whether you can find out.

The mind is a vast thing; it is not just a little spot in the universe—it is the whole universe, and to investigate the whole universe, the mind requires an astonishing energy. That energy is greater than all the rockets because it is self-perpetuating, because it has no center from which to move. And you cannot come by this energy unless there is real inquiry into the movement of the mind as the outer and the inner, the inner with its division as the unconscious which is the storehouse of all the racial inheritance of the family, the name, the motives, the urges, the compulsions; and that inquiry is not a process of analysis. You cannot inquire into something that is nebulous, that is unknown, that is not predictable; you can theorize about it, you can speculate about it, you can read about it, but that is not the comprehension of the unconscious. Or you can look at it through Jungianism, Freudianism, or with the help of the latest analyst or psychologist; or you can go back to the eternal books like the Gita or the Upanishads—that does not give you the understanding of the unconscious of which you are a part.

What brings about the understanding of the unconscious? We are not trying to understand the unconscious. We are understanding more or less the conscious mind, its everyday activity. But the unconscious thing that is hidden, dark, from which all urges, compulsions, cleavages, the intuitive, compulsive fears come in—how do you understand that? We dream either at night or during the day; the dreams are the hints of that unconscious, the intimations of the things which are hidden, taking new forms, symbols, images, visions, and all the rest of it; and merely interpreting these visions, symbols, pictures is not the solution.

I do not know if you are following all this. Until the mind understands the unconscious as well as the superficial mind, there is no understanding of oneself. You understand the issue, sir, of what I am saying? The mind is the conscious as well as the unconscious, the hidden. The conscious mind has recently acquired education as an engineer or as a physicist or a biologist or a professor or a lawyer; it is being imposed upon by the necessity of circumstances; it acquires a certain level of capacity. But behind the depth of the unconscious, there is the storehouse of experiences, of the culture, of the story of man; the story of man is there. So you are the story of man, and how do you go into that? Can the conscious mind go into it? Obviously not. The conscious mind cannot enter into something of which it is not aware. The conscious mind functions on the top; it may receive the intimations, the hints through dreams from below, from the unconscious, from the hidden, but that conscious, open, surface mind cannot enter into the deep recesses of the unconscious. And yet, the mind has to understand the totality of itself. You follow the issue?

Understand the question first—not what the answer is. If you put the question to yourself, the question is put because you already know the answer. Otherwise you won't put the question. Do please see the importance of this. An engineer or a scientist puts a question because he has a problem, and that problem is the outcome of his knowledge, and the problem exists only in the exploration of that knowledge, and because of that knowledge, he has the answer. For example, because of the scientific knowledge about the jet engine and all its implications, the problem arises: How to cover the distance from the earth and go to the moon. If we had not the knowledge, we would not have the problem. The problem arises because of the knowledge, and the answer is already there because of the knowledge. Inquiry into the knowledge, how to find it out—that is the problem.

So I am putting to you the same question differently. The mind is both the conscious and the unconscious. We all know the conscious. The unconscious has deep, hidden recesses containing hidden desires, hidden wants, hidden longings. How can the superficial mind enter into that, uncover it, and wipe it all away and be refreshingly innocent, fresh, youthful, new? That is the quality of the new mind. Having put the question, you already know the answer; otherwise, you would not have put the question.

I can analyze the unconscious by taking one experience at a time and analyzing it very carefully, but this analysis does not solve the problem because the unconscious is a vast treasure-house, and it will take a lifetime to go into one experience after another, and also it requires an extraordinary mind to analyze, as the problem gets more complicated if I miss the true analysis. Yet it is imperative to cleanse the unconscious—whether it is possible or not, it is irrelevant now. The unconscious is the story of man, the historical story, the cultural story, the accumulative story, the inherited story, the story that has been adjusting, that has adjusted itself to contradictory urges, demands, purposes; it is the story of 'you'. You perhaps know yourself on the top very superficially; you may say, "I am a lawyer," or "I am a judge," on the surface. But there is the whole mind and the whole story, and the whole entity has to be cleansed. How will you do it? If it is a problem to you, and you say, "I have got to find this out," then you will find tremendous energy to find it out.

How do you look at anything? How do you observe anything? How do you observe me? You are sitting there and seeing me, and how do you see me? Do you see me as I am? Or do you see me verbally, theoretically, traditionally as an entity who has a certain reputation as the Messiah and all the rest of it? Be clear yourselves how you observe the speaker who is sitting here. Obviously, you are looking with various eyes and various opinions, with various hopes, fears, experiences—all that is between you and the speaker, and therefore you are not observing the speaker. That is, the speaker says one thing, and what is heard is interpreted in terms of your knowledge of the Gita or the Upanishads or your infinite hopes and fears; therefore, you are not listening. You follow this? So, can the mind strip itself of its conclusions, of what it has heard, of what it has known, of what it has experienced, and see the speaker and listen to him directly without any interpretation?

What is actually happening to you directly, now, as you are listening? Now if you are listening, if you are observing, stripping the mind of all the stupid conclusions and all the rest of it, then you are listening directly, seeing the speaker directly. So your mind is capable of observing negatively—negatively in the sense that the mind has no conclusions, has no opposites, has no directive; it looks; in that observation it will see not only what is near but also what is far away. You understand? Some of you have driven a car, haven't you? If you are a very good driver, you see three hundred to four hundred yards ahead, and in that seeing you take in not only the near—the lorry, the passenger, the pedestrian, the car that is going by—but you also see what is far ahead, what is coming. But if you keep your eyes very close to the front mudguard, you are lost—that is what the beginners do. The mind can look far as well as very near; it sees much more than the eye when you are driving.

The mind cannot observe, see what is near as well as what is far away if there is a conclusion, if there is a prejudice, if there is a motive, if there is fear, if there is ambition. Now, that state of mind which observes is the negative mind because it has no positive and the reaction to the positive. It just watches, it is just in a state of observation without recollection, without association, without saying, "This is what I have seen, and this is what I have not seen"; it is in a state of complete negation, and therefore there is complete attention of observation. So your mind, when you observe, is in a state of negation. It is simply aware, not only of the thing very far, but also of the very near—not the ideal, there is no ideal in observation; when you have an ideal, you cease to observe, you are then merely approximating the present to the idea, and therefore there is duality, conflict, and all the rest of it. In that state of negation in which there is no reaction as the opposite of the positive, in that state of awareness, in that state of observation there is no association, you merely observe. And in that state of observation there is no observer and the observed. This is important to understand—understand in the sense of experiencing it, not verbally seeing the reason and the logic of it—because the experience of the observation in which there is no observer and the observed is really an astonishing state. In that there is no duality.

Sir, can you observe that way? You can't because you have never gone into yourself, never played with your mind, and the mind is never being aware of itself as thinking, watching, hoping, looking, searching; if you have not done that, obviously you can't come to this. Don't ask how to do this, don't ask for an answer. It requires hard, logical, steady work, which very few of us are willing to do, to bring about a mind which is in a state of negation, which has stripped the totality of itself, both the conscious and the unconscious, of the story.

All that is important is: The mind has to be in the state when it can see, observe. It cannot see because of all its foolish conclusions, theories. But as it is interested in observing, it wipes out all these with one stroke. The wiping away of the totality of the mind, the conscious and the unconscious, is not an act of discipline, sacrifice. In that state of mind there is neither the conscious nor the unconscious. It is the unconscious that prevents you from seeing, observing, looking, because the moment you look, fear comes in—you may lose your job, or ten other different things which the unconscious is aware of, but the conscious is not aware of; because of fear, the mind says, "I won't look, I won't see." But when there is an intense urge, an intense interest to see, to observe, there is no longer the interference of all the stories of man; all the stories have been wiped away; then the mind is in the negative state when it can see, observe directly. Such a mind is the new mind. Such a mind has no direction, and therefore it is not the political mind, it is not the Indian mind, it is not the economic, the scientific, the engineering mind, because it has exploded without direction, it has broken through everywhere, not merely in a particular direction. So, that is the religious mind.

The religious mind does not touch politics, the religious mind does not touch the economic problems, the religious mind does not talk of, is not concerned with divorce, nondivorce, the temporary reforms, pacifying this part or that part, because it is concerned with the totality and not with the part. So when the mind is functioning in particular directions saying, "I must be peaceful, I must not be angry, I must observe, I must be more kind," those partial directive activities do not result in a new mind.

The new mind comes into being without a direction and explodes. And that is hard, arduous work; it requires constant watching. You can't watch yourself from morning till night, vigilant, never blinking; you can't. So you have to play with it. When you play with something, you can carry on for a long time. If you do not know how to play with this sense of awareness lightly, you get lost; there again begins the conflict: How am I to be aware, what is the method, what is the system? As you are playing, you learn. So learning is not a matter of accumulation; the moment you accumulate, you have ceased to learn. The mind which is full of knowledge can only add to itself further knowledge, further information. But we are talking of something in a totally different dimension, and you have to learn about it, and therefore it is not a problem; if it is a problem, it has come from your knowledge, and therefore it has the answer in the knowledge. But the state of the new mind is not within the field of knowledge; it is something entirely different. It is that state of creation which is exploding all the time. You do not know a thing about it; you cannot say that it is a problem to you because it is a problem to you only when you know about it, and you do not know anything about it. Therefore to understand a thing, knowledge has to come to an end. They are coming to that in the West, they are beginning to understand that knowledge is not at all enough; they know most things of life, but that is not leading them anywhere; they know about the universe, how it came into being, they know about the stars, they know the depth of the earth, the depth of human relations, the physical organism they know, they have added to the knowledge. They say we must not hate, we must be kind, we must be brotherly, but it has not led them very far.

So the new mind cannot come into being with authority, with the Masters, with gurus. You have to wipe off all that and start with a clean slate. And knowledge is not the way to clean the slate, knowledge is an impediment; knowledge is useful at a certain level, but not in the new mind. So the mind has to divest itself of its own fears, its depths of sorrow and despair, to understand, to observe and to be aware of itself, to know itself and then see the futility of knowing itself. If you have once seen the absurdity of spiritual organizations—even of one organization, just one, whether you are a little group or a world organization as the church or as something else—when once you have seen it, it is over; when you have understood once, you have wiped the whole thing off completely. So you never belong to anything; therefore, there is no need to follow anybody.

So, you may be one of the happy few who say, "I have seen it," and who, in the breath of understanding, enter into the mind that is the unknown. One can do it and from there reason logically, discuss. But most of you are unfortunate; you cannot do that because you have not the energy. Look at your lives, sirs! You spend forty to fifty years working in an office with its routine, boredom, anxieties, fear, the mechanical nature of it, and at the end you say you must look into this. You are burned out, and you want to turn to something which is alive; you cannot, though you may walk to the Himalayas or up and down the land—because you have not a fresh, eager, live mind. This does not mean that the bureaucrat, the office worker has not got it, but he is destroying himself. He can get it there or anywhere, but it requires extraordinary energy. The yogis and the saints tell you, "You must be bachelors; you must not smoke; you must not get married; you must not do this or that," and you follow them, but such following does not give that energy; that creates only conflict and misery. What releases that energy is direct perception, and that brings about the new mind.

It is only the mind that explodes without any direction that is compassionate—and what the world needs is compassion, not schemes. And compassion is the very nature of the new mind. Because the new mind is the unknown mind, it is not to be measured by the known; and one who has entered into it knows what it is to be in a state of bliss, to be in that state of benediction.

March 12, 1961

London, England, 1961

First Talk in London

I think we should be fairly clear from the beginning as to what is the intention of this gathering. It should not, I feel, degenerate in any way into a mere intellectual exchange of words and ideas or an exposition of one's own point of view. We are not dealing with ideas because ideas are merely the expression of one's own conditioning, one's own limitations. To argue over ideas, who is right and who is wrong, is surely utterly futile. Rather let us explore our problems together. Instead of being lookers-on, as at a game being played, let us take part, each one of us, in these discussions and see if we can penetrate very deeply into our problems—not only the problems of the individual, but of the collective. I feel it should be possible for us to go beyond the mutterings, the chattering of the mind, beyond all worldly demands and influences, and to discover for ourselves what is true. And in discovering what is true, we shall be able to confront, to be with, the many problems which each one of us has.

So perhaps we can discuss intelligently, leisurely, hesitantly, so as to capture the whole significance of life, of our existence—what it is all about. And I feel that is possible only if we can be very honest with ourselves, which is rather difficult. In the process of discussing, we should be exposing ourselves, not somebody else, so that by our own intelligence, our own precise thinking, we can penetrate into something really worthwhile.

I think most of us know, not only from the newspapers but from our own direct experience, that there is a tremendous change going on in the world. I am not thinking of the change of going from one thing to another but of the rapidity of change itself, not only in one's own life but in the collective, the national, among all the various peoples of the world.

For one thing, machines are doing astonishing things. In many spheres the electronic brains, the computers, are doing things much more accurately and quickly than we human beings can. And they are investigating how to make machines which will operate further machines without the interference of man at all. So man is gradually being eliminated. These machines function on the same principle as the human mind, the human brain. Perhaps in time they will compose, write poems, paint—as the monkey has been taught to paint pictures, and so on. There is an extraordinary wave of change, and the world will never again be as it has been for us. I think we are all aware of that. But I am not at all sure that we are aware of our own individual relationship to this whole process because we consider knowledge an immensely important thing; we worship knowledge—but the machines are capable of much vaster knowledge. That is one side of the problem.

Then there is the existence of every type of communism, fascism, and all the rest of it. One observes the enormous, the crushing, the degrading poverty of Asia, and human beings seeking a system to solve that problem. But the problem remains unsolved because of our limited, nationalistic points of view, because each country, each system, wants to dominate.

So it seems to me that to meet all these problems from a totally different point of view, a fundamental revolution is necessary—not the communist, socialist, American, or Chinese revolution, but an inward revolution, a completely new mind. I think that is the issue—not the atom bomb, or going to the moon, or who has traveled round the earth half a dozen times in a rocket; the monkey has done it, and more and more people will do it. Surely, to meet life as a whole, with all its incidents and accidents, one must have a totally different mind—not the so-called religious mind which is the product of organized belief, whether of the East or of the West; such a mind only perpetuates division and creates more and more superstition and fear. All the absurd divisions and limitations—belonging to one group or another, joining one society or another, following a particular form of belief or pattern of action—these things are not going to solve our immense problems.

I feel it is only possible to meet these issues if we can enter into something which is not merely the outcome of experience, because experience is always limited, always colored, always within the bondage of time. We have to find out for ourselves, have we not, if it is possible to go beyond the frontiers of the mind, beyond the barrier of time and uncover the immense significance of death—which means, really, to unravel what it is to live. For that, surely, a new mind is absolutely essential—not an English, Indian, Russian, or American mind, but a mind that can capture the significance of the whole, that can break down nationalism, the conditionings, the values, and go beyond the words to which it is a slave.

That, for me, is the real issue, the real challenge. I would like to discuss with you intelligently, precisely, without sentiment, without parables, to find out if there is a way or no way to come by a new mind. Is there a path, a method, a system of discipline which will lead us to it; or have all methods, disciplines, systems, and ideas to go completely overboard, be wiped away, if the mind is to be made fresh, young, innocent?

You know, in India—that ancient land with so many traditions, where there are, unfortunately, so many people—they have had several so-called teachers who laid down what is right and what is wrong, what method one should follow, how to meditate, what to think and what not to think; and so they are bound by, they are held in, their various patterns of thinking. And here, too, in the West, the same process is going on. We do not want to change. We are more or less constantly seeking security in everything we do—security in the family, in relationships, in ideas. We want to be sure, and this desire to be sure inevitably breeds fear, and fear brings about guilt and anxiety. If we look into ourselves, we will see how intensely afraid we are of almost everything and how there is always the shadow of guilt. You know, in India to put on a clean loincloth makes one feel guilty; to have one square meal makes one feel guilty because there is so much poverty, dirt, squalor, and misery everywhere. Here it is not so bad because you have the welfare state, jobs, and a large measure of security, but you have other forms of guilt and anxiety. We know all this, but unfortunately we do not know how to shake ourselves free from all the ugly, limiting factors; we do not know how to throw them off completely so that our mind is again fresh, innocent, and young. Surely, it is only the mind that is made new which can perceive, observe, discover if there is a reality, if there is God, if there is something beyond all these words, phrases, and conditionings.

So, considering all this, what is one to do? And if there is something to be done, what is it, and in what direction does it lie? I do not know if what I am saying means anything to you at all. For me it is very serious—not in the way of a long face, a mood—but in the sense of being intense, urgent, immediate. And if you also feel the necessity of a new mind, let us discuss where one is to begin, what one is to do.

Comment: The mind seems to go round and round, but never seems to go beyond its own limitations.

KRISHNAMURTI: Shall we discuss this a little?—because we do not just want a question and answer meeting. First of all, before we say that the mind goes round and round, we must discover, must we not, what is the whole content of the mind, what we actually mean by the mind. Now, how do we answer a question of that kind? What is the process that is set going when that question is asked? Please observe your own minds and do not wait for me to answer. I have put a question: What is the mind? How do you respond, and what is responding? How do you observe anything? How do you observe a tree? Do you glance at the surface of it, or do you observe the trunk, the branches, the leaves, the flowers, the fruit—the whole of the tree? How do you observe a thing, totally? I hope I am not making it too abstract, but I think one has to go into all this. When we ask the question, "What is the mind?" how do you respond to that challenge? From what center, from what background do you observe? And to observe something entirely, newly, totally, what do you do?

Comment: One has to look with comprehension, not with the mind.

KRISHNAMURTI: And what does one mean by comprehension? Please, sir, I am not just quibbling, but I suggest that we do not introduce other words as a substitution. Let us go along together for a bit. What do we mean by observing, seeing, perceiving? When I say that I see something very clearly, what does that mean? It means that we have not merely seen the thing physically, with the eyes, but also that we have gone beyond the words, does it not? I see that nationalism is a stupid form of emotionalism, without any rationality, without any sense. I see it, please, not you. First, there is immediate perception of the falseness of it; then I give the explanations: how it separates people, the poisonous nature of it, how destructive it is to call oneself an Indian, Englishman, German, or whatever it is. I do not have to be told about it, I do not have to reason about it, to come to a conclusion through deduction or induction. I just see it all at one glance: there is immediate perception—just as I see that belonging to any organized religion is the most corruptive, destructive existence.

Now what is this capacity to see? And do I see the totality of the mind? Not the segments of the mind, the intellectual part, the emotional part, the part which retains and uses knowledge, the part which is ambitious and which is contradicting itself by wanting not to be ambitious, and so on and so on. Do I see the totality of the whole thing, or am I waiting for someone to tell me about it?

I think it would be very interesting and profitable—if I may use that commercial word—if we could, each one of us, find out what we mean by "seeing." You know, I do not have to be told when I am hungry. I know that I am hungry. No amount of description would give me the experience of hunger. Now, can you and I have direct experience of the mind as a total thing? And when you do have an experience of something as a whole, as a total thing, is there then a center from which it is being experienced?

You want to experience the totality of the mind, do you not? You want to experience the sense of the total feeling of life, the total feeling of not holding on to something. But how will you know what the totality of the mind is? Experience is always in terms of the known, is it not, and if you have never experienced the totality of the mind, how will you know it? Do you see the problem? Please do not just agree, because this involves a great deal.

You know, when you fly from place to place in an airplane, there is the earth 30,000 to 40,000 feet below you; and as you go across Pakistan, Iran, the Middle East, Crete, Italy, France, England, America, and so on, you know they are all divided with the artificial divisions created by man, but there is the feeling of the totality of the earth, of this whole earth, which is so extraordinarily beautiful.

Now to feel the quality of that totality—can you experience it in terms of what you have already known? Or is it something that is not experiencable in terms of recognition?

Perhaps I am going too fast into the question, so let us ask ourselves again: What is the mind? Let us go into it, unravel it.

The mind is the capacity to recognize, to hoard knowledge as memory; it is the result of centuries of human endeavor, experience, and conflict, and of the present individual experiences in relation to the past and the future; it is the capacity to design, to communicate, to feel, to think rationally or irrationally. There is the mind that feels gentle, quiet, serene, and also brutal, ruthless, superior, arrogant, vain, that is in a state of self-contradiction, pulled in different directions. It is the mind that says, "I am English," or "American," or "Indian." There is the unconscious mind, the deep-down collective, the inherited; and there is the superficial mind that has been educated according to a certain technique, a code of behavior, action, and knowledge. It is the mind that is seeking, searching, wanting permanency, security; the mind that lives on hope, but knows only frustration, failure, and despair; the mind that can remember, recollect; the mind that is very sharp, precise; the mind that knows what it is to love, and to want to be loved.

Surely, all that is the totality, is it not? That is the mind which you and I have—and the animals, too, only much less of it. And then there is the mind which says it must go beyond all this, must reach out somewhere, must experience a totality, a timeless, immeasurable thing.

So, all that is the mind. We know of it in segments when we are jealous, angry, hateful, or we are aware of it in self-contradiction, or there are dreams, hints, intimations from the past. All that is the mind. It is the mind that says, "I am the soul, I am the atma, the higher self, the lower self, this, that, and the other." It is the mind that is caught within the limits of time because all that is of time. And it is the mind that is a slave to words, like the English are slaves to the words *the Queen, the Christ;* and the Indian is a slave to his set of words; and the Chinese, the communists, to theirs, and so on.

Now realizing all this, then how do you proceed? What, actually, is the mind?

Let us approach it differently. You see, sirs, there must be a change, and a calculated change is no change at all. The change to achieve a certain result through practice, discipline, control, ruthless domination—all that is merely the continuity of the same thing in a different guise. And the progressive, evolutionary change—that has gone, too; we have finished with it. The only change is the radical, immediate change. How is the mind to come to that change so that it has wiped away its conditioning, its brutalities, its stupidities, its fears, its guilt, its anxieties and is new? I say it is possible, not through the analytical process, not through investigation, examination, and all that. I say it is possible to wipe the slate clean at one stroke, on the instant. Do not translate this as the grace of God; do not say, "It is not possible for me, but it may be for someone else"—then we are not facing the issue, we are avoiding it. That is why I said at the beginning that we need very clear, precise thinking, a ruthless inquiry.

Comment: This instantaneous wiping away—surely, there can be no thought of any kind in it.

KRISHNAMURTI: But how is it to be done, what is the action? You understand, sir, what I mean? You know very well what is happening in the world—probably better than I do because I do not read newspapers, I do not study them, but I travel and I see people, the big ones and the insignificant ones, and I listen. You know that there must be a tremendous revolution within one to meet the challenge of this chaotic, messy world. I say it is possible, and I would like, if I may, without stopping you from discussing, to continue to inquire along those lines. To bring about a radical change—is not that your problem, whether you are young or whether you are old? So, how do we tackle this thing?

Comment: That seems to be something we are trying to grasp but cannot.

KRISHNAMURTI: When we try to grasp, when we try to capture something, surely we are already translating this into terms of the old. Sir, must you not be very clear whether this is your problem? If I am imposing the problem upon you, then there will be a state of contradiction between you and me. I am not imposing, I am only stating the problem. If you do not see it, let us discuss it. But if you do see it, then it is your problem, not mine. Then you and I have a relationship; then we are in contact with each other to find out an answer to it. And if it is not your problem, then I say: Why isn't it? Please look at what is happening in the world: there is more and more externalization; the outward things are becoming more and more important—going to the moon, who gets there first; you know all the infantile things that are becoming tremendously important. So, if this is a problem for all of us, then how do we answer it, how do we set about it?

Comment: We can only say we do not know.

KRISHNAMURTI: When we say, "I do not know," what do we mean?

Comment: I mean just that.

KRISHNAMURTI: No, excuse me, you do not mean that. Let me unravel it a little bit because there are different states of "knowing" and "not-knowing." If you were asked a familiar question, you would answer immediately, would you not? Because you are familiar with it, your response is instantaneous. If you were asked a more complicated question, you would take time to reply, and the lag between the question and the response is the process of thinking, is it not? That thinking is a looking into memory to find the answer. This is obvious; it is not a complicated thing I am talking about, it is very simple. Then if another question were asked, still more complicated, and to which for the moment you do not know the answer, you say, "I do not know"; but you are waiting—waiting to find out the answer either from the reservoir of your own memory or for somebody else to tell you. So when you say, "I do not know," it means that you are waiting, expecting to find out. Now, just a minute. Can you honestly say, "I do not know"—which means there is no expectation, and no looking into memory? So there are the two states when there is the question of how is there to be a new mind: you can either say, "I do not know," meaning you are waiting for me to tell you, or you actually do not know, and therefore there is no expectation, no wanting to experience something—and that may be the essential.

Let us go back a little because I feel it is important to understand what is meant by perceiving, seeing, observing. How do we really see something?

Comment: It seems to me that we can only see through words.

KRISHNAMURTI: Do you understand through words? Of course, we use words to communicate so that you can talk to me, and I can talk to you, but that is not slavishness to the words. Are we aware how slavish we are to words? The words *English, Russian, God, love*—are we not slaves to these words? And being slaves to words, how can you comprehend something that is total, not held within a word? Being a slave to the word *love*—that word which is so misused, corrupted, divided as sexual and divine—can I understand the total nature of what it is?—which must be an astonishing thing. The whole universe is contained in the meaning, the significance of that word.

Most unfortunately, you see, we are slaves to words, and we are trying to reach something which is beyond words. To uproot, to shatter the words and be free of words gives an extraordinary perception, vitality, vigor. And does it take time to free yourself from words? Do you say, "I must think about it first," or "I must practice awareness," or "I will read Bertrand Russell"? Or do you actually see that a mind which is a slave to words is incapable of looking, observing, feeling, seeing?—therefore that very clarity, that very truth destroys slavishness.

Comment: One might see for an instant, and then the mind comes in again.

KRISHNAMURTI: Do you see for an instant that nationalism is poisonous, and then go back to it? Do we realize that we are slaves to the word? The communist is a slave to the words *Marx, Stalin,* and so on. And the so-called Christian is a slave to the symbol, the cross, and the whole wordplay on it. Go to Rome, go anywhere, and all there is, is the word.

And perhaps we are also slaves to the word *mind.* We worship the mind, and all our education is the cultivation of the mind. And surely, what we are trying to find out is the totality of something—which is not the word—the feeling that one embraces the whole thing without the barrier of the word.

May 2, 1961

Second Talk in London

We were saying the last time we met that a great revolution must take place not only because of the appalling world situation but because it is imperative for the human mind to be free to discover what is true. It seems to me that it is essential to bring about a new mind, a mind that is not limited by nationality, by organized religions, by belief, by any particular dogma or by the limitations of experience. It is urgent, surely, to bring about a creative state—a state which is not merely the capacity to invent, to paint, to write, and so on, but creative in a much deeper and wider sense. We were wondering how it is possible to bring about such a revolution, and what action is necessary. And I hope we can continue along this line of investigation.

One has tried, has one not, by joining various groups, attending various schools of thought and meditation, to find out what to do. We feel the need to find out what to do, not only in daily life, but we also want to know if there is a way of action—in a much larger sense of that word—of a total nature, not only at a given moment. I think it is fairly obvious that most of us are eager to find out what to do, and perhaps that is why you are here and why you belong to so many groups, religious bodies, and societies—to find out what to think and what to do.

For me, that is not the problem at all. The "what to do" demand, the demand for a mode of conduct, a particular way of life, is really very detrimental to action. It implies, does it not, a system which you can follow from day to day in order to reach a particular goal, a particular state of being. Living as we do in this mad, chaotic, ruthless world, we try to find, through all the mess, a way of living, a way of action which will not create more problems. And I feel that to understand this whole matter really deeply, one has to understand effort, conflict, and contradiction.

Most of us live in a state of self-contradiction, not only collectively, but individually. I hope I am not making absolute statements, but I think it is more or less accurate that we very rarely know moments when there is no conflict, no contradiction within ourselves; we do not know of a state when the mind is completely quiet and when that very quietness is an action in itself. Most of us live in contradiction, and from this contradiction there is conflict. And we are concerned with how to be free of this conflict, not only outwardly, but inwardly. If we can discuss and go on from there, perhaps we shall be able to find an action which is not merely a reaction.

For most of us action is a reaction. And is it possible to act without reaction and therefore create no contradiction within ourselves? I hope I am making myself clear. I should like us to discuss this together and go into it very thoroughly. Because for me, conflict in any form is, to put it mildly, detrimental to comprehension, to penetration, to understanding. We are bred, educated on conflict and competition; our whole acquisitive society is based on it. So is it possible for the mind to free itself from conflict and thereby uncover this whole process of self-contradiction? Perhaps we could intelligently discuss this and thereby come by that mind which is in a state of revolution, and so understand what it is to act without the conditioning effects of experience and knowledge.

Question: Would that not be acting without thought?

KRISHNAMURTI: Surely, that would be rather chaotic, would it not? Perhaps we should first discuss the process of thinking, the mechanism of thinking. So let me ask you the question: What is thinking?

Comment: I should say that thinking is a nervous reaction to that which has been experienced. We cannot react to something we do not know.

KRISHNAMURTI: You know, there are machines that think—the electronic brains, the computers. Is our thinking much along the same lines? Is it the response of memory,

memory being stored-up experiences, individual and collective, in which is included the nervous response? I ask you: What is thinking? Do please experiment a little bit. Before you answer, should you not be aware of the process, aware of the mechanism of replying? In the interval between the question and your response, the process of thinking is going on, is it not? The challenge of the question sets the mechanism of thought in motion, and then there is the response. Is that not so? If I ask you what your religion is or what your nationality is, you reply, do you not, according to your education, your upbringing, according to your belief or nonbelief. Now what is this background from which you respond?

Comment: Memory.

KRISHNAMURTI: That is so, is it not? If I am born in a certain place, educated there, molded by the society, the tradition in which I live, then I have a certain storehouse of experiences, memories, and I respond to any challenge from that background. That is the mechanism, and that is what we call thinking. And according to that inherited and acquired experience, I live, I act. So my thinking is always very limited, and so there is no freedom in thinking.

Question: Is it not possible to have creative thinking—for example, to make new discoveries in science or mathematics? Is thinking entirely the result of conditioning?

KRISHNAMURTI: When do we really discover anything? When do we perceive something new, either inwardly or objectively?

Comment: I would say when the known ways have been exhausted.

KRISHNAMURTI: Let us go into it a little bit. I have a problem in mathematics, and I work at it, tackle it in many different ways until I am exhausted, and then I let it alone, and the next morning or sometime later the answer pops up. So when my mind has gone into the problem thoroughly without finding an answer, and gives it up, then there is a certain quietness with regard to that problem, and later on the answer comes.

Question: Do you say that this process is not thinking?

KRISHNAMURTI: We are trying to find out, are we not? There is a lot involved in this. Thinking is not just at one level of the mind; the whole unconscious has to be considered also. We are trying to find out what thinking is. And we see that most of our thinking is from the background of memory, experience, knowledge, and all the rest of it. And there are moments when we see something in a flash, apparently unrelated to the past, and what we see may be false or may be true, depending on how we translate it, on what our background is. When the superficial mind is quiet, there may be discovery in the sense of a new invention or a new idea, but is all new discovery of the same nature? Because we have to consider the total mind, have we not?—not only the superficial mind, but the unconscious mind also.

We function at a very superficial level most of the time, do we not? The activities we engage in are very superficial; they do not demand the total response of our whole being. It is fairly obvious that all our education and background is geared to the superficial response; we are living on the surface of the mind. But there is also the deep, unexplored unconscious mind which is always giving hints, intimations, dreams, and so on, and again these are translated by the conscious mind according to its conditioning.

And is not the entire consciousness conditioned? The unconscious is, surely, the reservoir of the racial memories—the recollections, reflections, traditions, and memories, the accumulated knowledge of man. Whereas the conscious, superficial mind is educated to the techniques of this modern world. So obviously there is a contradiction between the unconscious and the conscious. The conscious mind may be educated to have no belief in God, to be an atheist, a communist, or what you will, but the unconscious has been trained for centuries in belief, and when the crisis comes, the unconscious responds much more than the conscious mind. You know all this, do you not? So the totality of consciousness, not only the superficial, but also the unconscious, is conditioned, and any response from the unconscious is not a liberating factor. Do please think about this and discuss with me—not just agree or disagree. If a mathematician has a problem and after exploring it, going into it, solves it without thought, then is that solution something totally new, not generated, not springing from the unconscious?

Question: If it comes from the unconscious, it is actually old stuff. It is not really new, is it?

KRISHNAMURTI: If I may say so, one must be very careful here not to be merely speculative. Either one speaks from direct comprehension after exploring the whole business, or else one may be merely repeating what somebody has said or what one has read. If we could for the moment, or even forever, discard what other people have said—the yogis, the swamis, the analysts, the psychologists, the whole lot of them—then we shall be able to find out for ourselves, directly, whether it is possible for the total consciousness to be free of conditioning. If it is not possible, then all one can do is to continue the old process of making the total consciousness better—more worthwhile, more good, noble, and all the rest of it. That is like living in a prison and decorating the prison. Whether the brain has been washed by the communists, the Catholics, the Protestants, the Anglicans, or by any other sect, it is the same. And it is really a very important and vital matter to consider whether it is at all possible to go beyond the limited, conditioned consciousness, whether the mind can ever be free in the deepest sense of that word. There are those who say that the mind, being the result of time and environment, must always remain a slave to those influences, but we are asking if it is possible to go beyond the mind, beyond time.

Question: How could such a thing be possible?

KRISHNAMURTI: We are going into the whole issue, are we not? Either the mind is capable of freeing itself from all influences and therefore from all environments—whether of the past, the present, or the future—or it is not possible. The communists do not believe it is possible, nor do the Catholics or any of the religious people. They talk about freedom, but they don't believe in it because the moment you leave them, you have become a heretic—they excommunicate you, burn you, liquidate you, and all the rest of it. So, is it possible for an action to take place which does not spring from the field of consciousness, of limitation, of conditioning? Do you see the question, sirs?

Comment: The experience of most of us is that it is not possible, and yet we have intimations that it may be possible, but we do not know how to achieve it.

Comment: I feel it is not possible.

KRISHNAMURTI: Are you just waiting for me to say something? You see, I do not know how far you have gone into all this for yourselves.

Comment: I am sure that the conscious mind can be free, but it seems to me that a tremendous difficulty is the unconscious mind.

KRISHNAMURTI: Is it possible, by analyzing, to go into the unconscious step by step and unravel it, and thereby go beyond it? Is that possible?

You see, the unconscious is a positive process, is it not? And can you approach a positive process with a positive demand? Both the conscious and the unconscious are under the same limitation, are they not? The conscious mind has its own motives for wishing to investigate the unconscious. The motive is there; it wants to be free. The motive is positive, and the unconscious is not something vague; it is also positive. But although the unconscious is positive—with all its hints, intimations, dreams, and so on, you do not know for yourself its content; you do not know what it actually is. So can the conscious mind investigate something which it does not know? Please do not brush this aside; it is very important. Will analysis, whether by another or by yourself, uncover the whole content of this thing called the unconscious, of which you are totally unaware?

Comment: I think the unconscious is too vast.

KRISHNAMURTI: No, no, do not just say it is too vast; then you are not meeting the actual question, you are going off at a tangent. You see, I do not think you have ever gone into the whole process of thinking. Is there a thinking which is without the word, the image, the idea, the symbol—because the symbol is in the unconscious as well as in the conscious, is it not? And I think the process of investigating the unconscious by means of analysis is a faulty process. I want to suggest that there is a way which is immediate perception.

Let us be clear, first, that all thinking is mechanical. Thinking is the response of memory, the response of knowledge, of experience, and all thinking from this background is conditioned. Therefore thinking can never be free; it is always mechanical.

Comment: Yes, I see that.

KRISHNAMURTI: What do you mean when you say, "I see"? Please, this is very important.

Comment: Something inside me makes me realize it.

KRISHNAMURTI: Then something inside you makes you realize that you must be a nationalist, does it not? It makes you believe that there is God, that you must have a religion. If you depend on something which tells you from inside, then you are also apt to have illusions, are you not? So what do we mean by "I see"? If I say nationalism is a poison, do you see the truth of that?

Comment: It is obvious.

KRISHNAMURTI: And when I say that to have any belief, to belong to any society, to any organized religion is detrimental to discovery, do you see that too?

Comment: Not so clearly because I belong to a group that is working for the United Nations, and I think that is a good thing.

Comment: The disunited nations, he means.

KRISHNAMURTI: Obviously they are disunited, but we are wandering off. You said very clearly that you saw nationalism as a poison. You all agreed. But unconsciously you are all nationalistic, are you not? You feel you are English, French, or whatever it is. It is there, deep-rooted, is it not? And you say that you do not see with the same clarity that belief is destructive to discovery. But look at it this way: I want to find out if there is God. I really want to find out for myself if there is or there is not. So I must first brush aside every concept of God, must I not, not only in the conscious, but in the unconscious. To really find out, I must first tear out all the roots of the culture in which I have been brought up, educated; there must be no shelter, no refuge in which I feel I am doing good work. Since my intention is to find out, I must ruthlessly get rid of everything that I have accepted so that I have no shelter, physical, verbal, intellectual, or emotional; then I do not belong to anything.

We started off this discussion with the question of what to do in this mad world. A new way of looking at life, a new mind altogether, is necessary; and such a new way must be born out of a complete revolution, a total cutting away from the past. And the past is the unconscious as well as the conscious. So to belong to any particular organized group of thought is poisonous.

And any effort we make to be new also belongs to the past, does it not? Because the whole present structure of society is based on acquisitiveness, which is effort. The whole process of "I must be this" or "I must not be that" involves effort, conflict; I see that. And when I say, "I see it," I mean I see it factually, not emotionally, sentimentally, intellectually, or verbally. I see it as I see that microphone. And the very perception of that fact has wiped away that conditioning completely. I wonder if I am conveying anything to you? Please do not just agree with me. This is not a social game. Because if you see it the same way, then you also are out of it all, completely, instantly.

Comment: We feel we are bound to our conditioning by our duties to society, to the family.

KRISHNAMURTI: The gentleman says, quite rightly, that we are bound by our duties to our family, to society, to our work, to the country, to the religion we have been brought up in, and all the rest of it. So, when faced with the necessity of a completely new mind, we put the family, society, in opposition to the fact. And therefore there is a conflict between the fact and what you conceive to be your duty. Is that not so? So to escape from this conflict, one enters a monastery, becomes a monk, or inwardly isolates oneself; one builds a habit round oneself and lives in it. You see, sirs, when you use the words *duty* or *responsibility,* you have put yourself in opposition to freedom. But if you have perceived the fact of what we have been talking about, then you would have a totally different action towards your family and society.

You see I am trying to get back to action, and perhaps I am forcing the issue. After all, we all want to "do something" about life. I know people all the world over who have disciplined themselves ruthlessly because they want to find out what is right to do. They have isolated themselves, renounced, obeyed religious edicts, and made tremendous efforts, and at the end of it they are dead, withered human beings. It is the constant effort to be something, to become something that has destroyed them. And when you put society and the family in opposition to freedom, all you have done is to introduce the factor of conflict. And I say, do not introduce the element of conflict into it at all. See the truth of it, and that seeing will itself take care of the relationships. You see, as I was saying, for most of us action is merely reaction. I flatter you, and you respond; I insult you, and you respond. Our action is always reaction. I am talking of something else, of action which is not a reaction but which is total action. This is not some queer, odd, fantastic idea of my own. But if you have gone into the whole thing for yourself, if you have observed the world, watched people, studied them, really looked at them—the great ones, the insignificant ones, the so-called saints, and the so-called sinners—you would see that they have all built their lives on conflict, strife, suppression, and fear, and you would see the horror of it. To be free of all that, you must first see it.

Comment: There is so much conditioning that is unconscious.

KRISHNAMURTI: Please look at this. We all live in the superficial conscious mind, and how am I to unravel every layer, every detail of the unconscious, without missing a point? Is it possible for the conscious mind to enter into something which is unconscious, hidden? Surely, all I can do is to watch, to be wide awake, alert all day—as I work, as I rest, as I walk, as I talk—so that I have a dreamless night.

We began by talking about a revolution which is not the result of calculation and thought because thought is mechanical, and thought is a reaction. Communism is a reaction to capitalism; if I give up Catholicism and become something else, it is still a reaction. But if I see the truth that to belong to anything, to believe in anything is holding on to a form of security and therefore preventing the actual perception of what is true, then there is no conflict, no effort.

So, I see that action which is a reaction is no action at all. I want to find out what freedom is. I see the imperative urgency, the necessity of a new mind, and I do not know what to do. So I am concerned with the "what to do," and therefore I have laid the emphasis on "what to do" and not on a new mind. And the "what shall I do?" becomes all-important, and I say, "Please tell me"—which creates the authority, and authority is the most pernicious thing in the world.

So can we realize inwardly, see the actual fact that all our action is reaction, all our action is born from the motive to achieve, to arrive, to become something, to get somewhere? Can I just realize that fact, without introducing the "what shall I do," "what about the family, my job," and all that? Because if the mind does see the fact without translating it in terms of the old, then there is immediate perception; then one will understand that action which is not a reaction, and that understanding is an essential quality of the new mind.

May 4, 1961

Third Talk in London

We have been talking previously about the necessity of having a new, fresh mind. Everywhere one goes there is an awful mess and a great deal of suffering, not only physically, but also inwardly, and there is endless confusion. And it seems to me that instead of tackling the suffering and confusion, we are trying to escape from it all, either to the moon or in entertainments or in various forms of delusion. But whatever we do, there is the continuity of suffering and confusion, and to break through it all, I feel one needs a fresh, new mind.

So I would like to continue where we left off, and to consider if it is at all possible to live in this world without conflict. Because it seems to me that a mind occupied with conflict is a dull mind, a mediocre mind. We are all in conflict of one kind or another, at various levels, in different forms. And we either put up with it or too readily escape from it in entertainments, social reforms, and in all that the churches and religions offer with their rituals, strange words, their beliefs, and dogmas which are romantic forms of consolation. And as we grow older and the escapes become more and more habitual, constant, the mind gets ever more dull, heavy, stupid. I think that is a fact with most of us. There may be a few moments when, in spite of all this misery of conflict, there is a break in the clouds and one sees something very clearly, and a sense of quietness, of depth comes into being, but that is very rarely.

I think we should inquire deeply into this matter, and that is an arduous task. It is not a matter of just discussing a few ideas, but rather it means to penetrate very far into ourselves, to see whether it is possible to eradicate conflict in every form. It requires a keen, sharp mind, a mind that does not allow itself to be caught in a net of words. We are apt, I am afraid, to listen merely to hear certain words, phrases, and ideas, which is just to skate on the surface. And probably that is why we come to all these talks, year after year, and why it all becomes rather stupid in the end because we merely bandy with ideas and never go deeply into the matter for ourselves and actually eradicate conflict.

So I think we should confine ourselves this morning to seeing if it is actually possible—not theoretically or verbally—to really understand the nature of conflict and perhaps come out of it renewed, fresh, young, and innocent. An innocent mind is never in conflict; it is in a state of action. A mind in action, moving, renewing all the time, can never be in conflict. It is only the mind which has contradictions within itself that is perpetually struggling. Please, as I am talking, do not merely listen to the words because words by themselves have only a very ordinary meaning. And I am sure if you will look into yourselves, you will find many contradictions. So please actually follow it through, actually experience as we go along, and then perhaps at the end of this discussion you will have a sense of clarity, a sense of freedom from this appalling weight of conflict.

We have accepted conflict from childhood. In our education, all the schools throughout the world are breeding grounds of conflict, and there is the constant struggle to compete with others who are much cleverer than we are. And as we grow older, we follow the example, the leader, the authority, the ideal; and then there arises this cleavage between 'what should be' and *what actually is,* and hence there is contradiction. There is not only the outward, worldly conflict, the competition, the ideals, the ambition to achieve, the perpetual drive of modern society to become clever, more beautiful; not only the copying of the neighbors, but also the copying of Jesus, of God; not only the copying of fashion, but the copying of virtue. All this results in outward war between peoples, races, nations, and statesmen. And if one rejects all that as too stupid, then one turns inward and here again is the problem of achieving peace, quietude, happiness, God, love, heaven. The inward search is a reaction to the outer search, and therefore it is still the same movement. It is like the tide which goes out and comes in. These are obvious psychological facts, and if one is aware of it all, then there is no arguing about it; it is so. You may dispute whether it is possible to go beyond it all, but the actual fact is that there is conflict both inwardly and outwardly, and it does breed an astonishing sense of brutality, an efficiency that leads to ruthlessness. The outward movement may bring about a certain progress, prosperity, but one can see what is happening in the world: Where there is great prosperity, there is less and less freedom. One can observe it in America very clearly, how there is this great prosperity and how the sense of pioneering, of freedom, is gradually disappearing. Inwardly, too, the greater the intensity of conflict, the greater the urge to activity; and so you get the do-gooders, the people who go around reforming, the so-called saintly people, and the intellectuals who are forever writing books, and so on. The greater the tension in conflict, the more it expresses itself through capacity.

We all know about this, we all feel the pull in different directions. We know the drive of ambition. And where there is ambition, there is no love in any form, there is no quietness, no sympathy, pity, or affection. And the escape from conflict, whether it is the conflict between two people or between the nations, and whether the avenue of the escape is God, drink, nationalism, or one's bank account, it leads more and more deeply into an illusory sense of security. Our minds live in myths, in speculative ideas.

So conflict increases, and from that state there is action, and that action breeds further contradiction. And so we are caught in this wheel of struggle. I am only putting into words what is actually happening. This is the lot of everyone. We can see for ourselves that the mind is always trying to escape through suppression, through discipline—which the saints throughout the world advocate and which is really just putting the lid on everything. And if it is not discipline we escape to, it is some form of activity: social reform, political reform, the taking of courses, the furthering of brotherhood—you know about all this activity, agitation, the urge to do something about something.

So all we know is that our action breeds further misery, further distortion, further illusion and suffering, inwardly and outwardly. Every relationship, which begins so freshly, so newly, deteriorates into something ugly, dull, or venomous. We must all be aware of this dual process of love and hate. And our everlasting prayer is that we may cover it up—and the gods reply, unfortunately, because the escapes are there for the taking.

That is the picture: the picture of an idea, an ideal, and the resulting action towards that idea. The mind creates the idea and then tries to act in approximation to that idea. So there is a cleavage, and we are always trying to build a bridge over that gap. And we never succeed because the idea is stable; we have created it firmly, fixed it, but action must be varied, changing, in constant movement because of the demands of life. And so there is ever conflict.

And while being aware of all these tremendous tensions, these wrenching demands, we have never asked ourselves whether it is possible to live in this world without conflict. Is it possible? I feel that it is only the mind that does not have a single movement of conflict that is creative. I do not mean the creativity of the poets, the painters, the architects, and so on. They may have certain gifts, a certain capacity; they may occasionally see a flash of something and put it in marble, write a poem, or design a building, but they are not truly creative because they are still at war within themselves and with the world; they are driven by their ambitions, jealousies, their angers, and hatreds like the rest of us. Whereas to find God—or whatever name you like to give it—to find, to really discover if there is such a thing, the mind must be totally free from conflict. All this requires tremendous work, and perhaps some of us older ones are already finished, done for. We may be, or we may not be.

I do not know if you have seen the pictures in the caves in Dordogne, seventeen thousand years old. The colors are very bright because the wind and the rain have never come there. They depict man struggling with animals, horses, bulls with lovely horns, and they are full of extraordinary movement. But the struggle is the same.

So the question is: What shall we do about it all? And you have to answer this question because it is you who suffer, who are in conflict. You cannot just sit back and wait for somebody else to answer. And this has nothing really to do with age, you know; it is not a matter of whether you are old or young.

To put the problem differently, to live is to act. You cannot live without action. Every gesture, every idea, every wave of thought is action, and every action gives rise to a reaction, and from that reaction there is further action. So all our action is reaction, and we are caught in it. Now is it possible to live with an extraordinary abundance of action which has no roots whatever in conflict? That is the question, and I hope I am making myself clear.

Comment: I think it happens to us occasionally; it comes and goes in spite of ourselves, like the wind in the trees or the blowing along of dead leaves.

KRISHNAMURTI: That is, it happens occasionally, and the memory of it remains, and the desire for the repetition of it arises, and so there is conflict again. Do you see this? I have an experience of delight: looking at a lovely cloud, a beautiful face, a sweet smile, and it has left an imprint of pleasure, joy, and ecstasy. And I want it repeated again, and the conflict begins. Please follow this right through, and you will see something for yourself.

Comment: The conflict starts from wanting.

KRISHNAMURTI: Does it? What is wrong with wanting something beautiful?

Comment: Wanting it back again, I mean.

KRISHNAMURTI: Wait a minute, sir. All wanting is wanting again. There would be no wanting at all if there had been no previous tasting of it, no previous recollection. All wanting is a further recognition of what has been.

Question: What about our want of God?

KRISHNAMURTI: It is the same thing, is it not? To want a woman, a baby, to see a beautiful sunset, or to want God, and to want the repetition of the experience—it is all the same, surely. I think you are missing the point.

Comment: It is the resistance to the wanting that creates the contradiction.

KRISHNAMURTI: Wanting breeds conflict, and any form of resistance breeds conflict, but is that the issue? After all, the everlasting cry of the artist is that he has known this occasional flutter of beauty, and he wants to capture it, so he struggles with it, takes to women, to drink, and so on. And we do the same; we live in the past, the "happy days that have gone," the remembered faces and memories, all the things we want to recapture. There is the desire, and there is the resistance to that desire, but is that the issue? All the saints have said, "Wipe away desire"; they tell you to turn your back on it, smother it, control it, not be passionate. But is that the issue we are following?

Comment: I do not think I understand desire.

KRISHNAMURTI: Is that the problem? Look, sirs, when you have had an experience and you want to have more of it, to continue it, have you not created a problem? Whether you resist or whether you yield, have you not created a problem? We have created the problem of how to maintain a certain state, have we not? Right? Now what is a problem? A problem, surely, is something I have not understood. When I have understood something, the problem ceases. To a mechanic, something wrong with a motorcar is no real problem; he knows what to do. Here we do not know what to do, and the not-knowing is a problem. We cannot destroy desire, that would be too appalling, too stupid; it would be the vulgarity of the saint—sorry if I shock you. And resistance is a form of suppression. Right?

And what is there to understand about desire? Not very much. You know what desires are and how they come into being, and you know also the resistance and how it comes—through our education, our traditions, our background, the "this is right and that is wrong" attitude, the feeling that I must be respectable at any price, and my respectability must be recognized by society. You know it all.

Now can we go a little bit further? What is a problem, what creates a problem?

Comment: The memory of the experience.

KRISHNAMURTI: You cannot cut out experience, can you? That would be to die, to shut your eyes to life, to become insensitive. Living is experience. Listening to all this, looking out of the window—it is all experience. But with us, each experience leaves its residue as memory, the scar of memory. Are you following all this? So memory is the problem, not desire or resistance. So can the mind live in a state of experiencing without leaving a residue as memory?

You may understand this verbally, but it is really an extraordinary thing to go into; it requires a tremendous vitality and energy. The mind cannot escape from experience, but we all try to escape from a vital experience. We accept things as they are; we thicken the walls of belief; we refuse to see that the world is one, that the earth is yours and mine; we have divided it up as the British, the European, the Indian, the Russian, and we stay, paralyzed, within those walls. So we really refuse experience because we do not want any change; we cultivate memory, adding to it instead of taking away.

So the issue is: Can the mind receive everything without its leaving an imprint? You cannot say it is possible or it is not possible. Do please think about it. Because it is only a mind that is experiencing, seeing, looking, vibrating, that is alive. A mind is not alive when it is burdened with centuries of memory, which is what we call knowledge, tradition. But yet we cannot wipe out knowledge; it must be there; otherwise, you would not know how to get home. But can we live without the interference of the past?

Comment: The problem is that to prevent memory from leaving its imprint on the mind, we must be possessed of a tremendous interest in every one of our experiences.

KRISHNAMURTI: Please, sir, look at what you have said—"we must." The "must" has already sown the seed of conflict, has it not?

Question: I suppose I should have said: How can this interest be brought about?

KRISHNAMURTI: To find a right answer, you must ask a right question. Is your question a right question?

Question: Is it rather: Why am I not interested?

KRISHNAMURTI: You know, it is like playing the right tone on a violin. You can only get the right tone when the string is at the right tension. Are you putting your question with the right tension? I don't mean a state of conflict, but right tension. If you will look at it, you will answer it for yourself. Perhaps the very question you are putting is preventing you from discovering for yourself? Do you see this? I will put it differently.

I see actually, visually, the conflict in the world and in myself. There is contradiction inside and outside. And the effort to do something about it—to be peaceful, to avoid all suffering—involves conflict. My whole being is torn in different directions, and so there is self-contradiction. This is, inescapably, the fact. You are following? And the wanting to do something about the fact is the reaction of trying to escape from it, to repudiate it, to resist it, to go beyond it. Right? So the desire, the urge, the impulse to do something about it is the problem. But if the fact is there, and you see you cannot do a thing about it, then the fact gives the answer. Then, is there a problem?

May 7, 1961

Fourth Talk in London

We have been talking about the new mind, and I am sure it cannot be brought about by any form of will, by any desire, or through any intention or purposeful thought. But it seems to me that if we can understand the various factors that prevent that state from coming into being, then perhaps we can discover for ourselves what the nature of the new mind is. So I would like to discuss with you an issue which may be rather complicated, but I hope we can go into it fully, and if necessary, continue with it next time.

I do not know whether you have ever asked yourselves why there is this compulsive urge to commit oneself to a certain way of thought, to belong to something, to identify oneself with an idea, to commit oneself to a particular course of action. One commits oneself, let us say, to communism, and one completely identifies oneself with those ideas, those activities. One can see why one does this; it is because one hopes ultimately for utopia, and all the rest of it. But I think that is only a superficial explanation. I think there is a much deeper psychological reason why each one of us wants to belong to something—to a certain person, to a group, to certain ideas and ideals. And perhaps we can examine the inward nature of this urge. What exactly is it?

I think, first of all, there is the desire to act. We want to bring about some kind of reform, to change the world according to a certain pattern. There is the feeling that we must do something together, that there must be cooperative action. And at some levels—to improve the roads, to bring about better sanitation, and so on—it is perhaps necessary that we commit ourselves to a particular idea. But if one inquires more deeply, I think one begins to find out, does one not, that there is this urge to identify ourselves with something in order to have a sense of assurance, a sense of security.

I am sure we all know many people who have committed themselves to a particular political party or a particular course of action or a certain group of religious thought. And after a time they begin to find that it does not suit them, and so they drop it and take up something else.

I think it is important to find out why there is this urge. Why is it that we commit ourselves to something or someone? I think if we inquire into this, we can open the door into the whole problem of fear.

The mind, surely, is always seeking security, permanency. It seeks permanency in relationship with the wife, the husband, the children, in an idea, in knowledge, and in experience. And the more experience we have, the more knowledge we accumulate, the greater is the sense of security. And may I say here that it is one thing to listen to the words that are being said, but it is quite another thing to experience what those words convey. I am merely describing the nature of our own minds, and if one is not aware of one's own thoughts and activities, the description becomes a very superficial thing. But if, by going through the words, one begins to understand oneself, see how one is actually seeking security and what it implies, then it will have extraordinary significance. To be merely satisfied with words and explanations, which most of us are, seems to me utterly futile. No hungry man is satisfied with the word *food*.

So can we go into this whole question of fear, but not what we should do about it? We can come to that later, or perhaps it may not be necessary at all. Why does fear arise? And why is the mind always seeking security, not only physically, outwardly, but inwardly?

We are talking about the "outward" and the "inward," but for me, it is all one movement which expresses itself outwardly as well as inwardly. It is a movement going out and coming in, like a tide. There is no such thing as an outward world and an inward world, and to separate the two is to bring about a division, a conflict. But to understand the inward tide, the inward movement, one must understand the outward-going movement also. And if one is aware of things outwardly, and if there is no reaction to the outer in the form of a resistance, a defense, or an escape, then it can be seen that the same movement goes inward, very deeply and profoundly, but the mind can follow it only if there is no division.

If we think about it a little, we can see that most so-called religious people divide the outer and the inner; the outward activity is regarded as largely superficial, unnecessary, and even evil, and the inner is regarded as very significant. And so there is conflict—which we went into rather thoroughly the other day. We are now inquiring into the question of fear, not only the fear caused by outward events, but also by the inner demands and compulsion, the everlasting search for certainty. All experience, obviously, is a search for certainty. An experience of pleasure makes us demand more of it, and the 'more' is this urge to be secure in our pleasures. If we love someone, we want to be quite sure that that love is returned, and we seek to establish a relationship which we at least hope will be permanent. All our society is based on that relationship. But is there anything which is permanent? Is there? Is love permanent? Our constant desire is to make sensation permanent, is it not? And the thing which cannot be made permanent, which is love, passes us by. I wonder if I am making myself clear? Take the question of virtue. The cultivation of virtue, the desire to be permanently virtuous is essentially the desire to be secure. And is virtue ever permanent? Please, sirs, do not just nod your heads in agreement, but do follow this in yourselves.

Let us say one is angry, or feels one lacks goodness, sympathy, affection. By cultivating nonanger, tolerance, one hopes to bring about a state of virtue, the virtue then being merely a commodity for convenience, a means to something else. And surely virtue, goodness, is not cultivable at all. Goodness, like humility, only comes into being when there is full attention, without trying to gain anything from it. Take the question of being loved, or to love. Is it possible for the mind which is ambitious to love or be loved? The clerk who wants to become the manager, the so-called saint who wants to realize God—they are ambitious, occupied with their own achievements, and such a mind obviously cannot know love. The mind that would understand the nature of the word we call *love* must obviously be utterly free of that whole sense of security—which makes us essentially vulnerable. So is it ever possible to be really free of fear?

We want to be secure in this world, materialistically, and we want to be secure in our respectability, in our ideas; we want to be told what will happen to us after death, and our mind is everlastingly pursuing—if you will observe it—this desire to be certain. And I do not see how the mind can be free of fear, with all its frustrations, so long as the mind is seeking security. Obviously there must be some measure of physical security; we must know where our next meal is coming from, that we have somewhere to sleep, some clothes, and all the rest of it; and a fairly decent society tries to provide all that. Probably in about fifty years time the whole world will have some form of physical security. Let us hope so, but that is irrelevant for the moment. But we want to be secure both in our actions and inwardly; and is that not the cause of fear?

Fear is ever with us, is it not? Fear of darkness, fear of one's neighbor, of public opinion, fear of losing health, fear of not having capacity, fear of being a nobody in this monstrous, acquisitive, aggressive world, fear of not arriving, of not realizing some state of supreme happiness, bliss, God, or whatever it is. And of course there is the ultimate fear of death. We are not discussing death for the moment, but we are just trying to see, to uncover fear. Obviously fear is always in relation to something else. There is no fear by itself, per se. There are dozens of fears, all in relation to something. And is it possible to stand completely alone? Is it possible for the mind to be completely alone without isolating itself, without building walls, ivory towers, around itself? A mind is alone when it is no longer seeking security. And can it free itself so totally from all fear?

You see, time is involved in fear. Shall we go into it a little bit? Time as yesterday, today, and tomorrow is a factor of fear. I am getting old, and there is death waiting for me, from now to all the tomorrows. And the thought of death is the thought of fear. Would there be fear of death, of an ending, if there were no thought of tomorrow, of the future? Please do not agree with me. Agreeing with an explanation is valueless. If you have actually gone into this question of fear for yourself, you must have uncovered this question of time, which includes not only the tomorrow but the past—which means, does it not, experience. Can the mind be so alone, so totally away from the past and the future that it is not enclosed at all in the field of time?

The mind is seeking security, is it not, through identifying itself with an idea, a belief, a particular course of action, belonging to a group, to Christianity, to Hinduism, to Buddhism, this or that—and all of this is contrary to being alone. Most of us are terribly frightened of being alone. Then there is the conflict which arises from contradiction, and the root of this contradiction is the urge for fulfillment. So there is this constant urge to fulfill, to be, to become something permanent, and there is the question of time. These are all the factors of fear, and I do not think there is any need to go into further detail.

Now, having seen the totality of the picture, the total feeling of it, the question arises: Can the mind put away all fear? This means, really, if one can so put it without being misunderstood, can one be alone, without relationship? Can there be an aloneness which is not merely an opposite to the conflict of contradiction which relationship creates? I feel that in that aloneness, there is real relationship, not the other. In aloneness there is no fear.

After all, man has tackled this problem of fear for centuries, and we are not free from it. And the extreme forms of fear lead to various kinds of neurosis, and so on. Now the question is: Can you and I, seeing all this, be totally free from fear, on the instant? Not hypnotizing ourselves and saying, "I am now free from fear," because that is just silly. Seeing the whole of fear means, essentially, does it not, a state of non-being.

Comment: It appears to me that I am frightened of being forced into circumstances, like living in some great city or working in a factory, where there is nothing I can love or feel is worthwhile.

KRISHNAMURTI: So what will you do about it, sir? I have to work from morning to night, let us say, in a little London office, with an unpleasant boss. Going every day, by bus or tube, to work—the routine, the excruciatingly boring people, the horror of it all. What shall I do? Circumstances are forcing me to do it. I have a responsibility: the wife, the children, the mother, and all the rest of it. I cannot go away, escape into a monastery—which would be another horror: the routine of getting up every morning at 2 o'clock, saying the same old prayers to the same old deities, and all the rest of it. In this world of routine, boredom, dirt, and squalor we all do everything to escape; we all ask, "What can I do to get out of it?"

First of all, we are educated wrongly—we are never educated to love the thing we do. So we are caught and cannot escape, and so we ask, "What shall I do?" Right, sirs? To escape into romanticism, into beliefs, churches, organizations, ideas of utopia, is obviously absurd. I see the futility of it, and therefore I discard it. There is no longer the temptation to escape, and I am left with the fact—the brutal, hard fact. What shall I do? Tell me, sirs!

Comment: Surely, you cannot do anything about it.

KRISHNAMURTI: Sirs, have we ever lived with something without any resistance? Have I ever lived with my anger without resistance?—which is not the same as accepting it, which is merely continuing it. Living with anger, knowing the whole inward nature of it; living with envy, not trying to overcome it, to suppress it, or transform it—have you ever tried it? Have you ever tried to live with something really beautiful, a picture, lovely scenery, a magnificent mountain with a view that is superb? And what happens if you do live with it? You soon get used to it, do you not? You see it for the first time, and it gives you a certain sense of release, perception, and you get used to it; after a few days it fades away. Look at the peasants in all parts of the world, living with marvelous scenery around them; they have got used to it. And the squalor of the cities all over the world, the dirt, the filth, the ugliness, the cruelty, the appalling brutality involved—we get used to that also. To live either with beauty or with ugliness, and never to get used to it—that requires an astonishing energy, does it not? Not to be overpowered by ugliness, nor to be dulled by beauty, but to be able to live with both of them requires extraordinary sensitivity and energy. And can one do it? Do, please, sirs, think it out a little bit.

The problem of energy is quite complicated. Food does not give the energy of which I am talking. It gives energy of a certain type, but to live with something, to live with love demands a totally different kind of energy. And how does one come by this energy, which is, essentially, the energy, the nature of the new mind? Surely one comes by it when there is no fear, when there is no conflict, when you do not want to be something, when you live totally, anonymously.

But what is the good of my talking about all this? It implies an extraordinary perception of the outer and the inner search for security. And most of us are too tired, too old, committed to living in the past, or in our work, or in some other dark dungeon of our being. So what shall we do?

Let us come back to our first question. Can the mind free itself, on the instant, from all the urge, the demand to be secure? Can one live in a state of complete uncertainty—without in the least going mad?

Question: If one has work which one enjoys very much, is there fear in that also?

KRISHNAMURTI: Yes, sir, because you may lose your capacity. You know, capacity is a dreadful thing; it gives you such a good escape. If you are a good painter, a good talker, if you have the capacity to put words together, to write, if you are a clever engineer or have any gift at all, it gives you such an extraordinary sense of security, confidence in yourself in this competitive, acquisitive world. And if you have no confidence in your own abilities, you feel utterly lost. But surely, to find God or whatever name you like to give, the mind must be completely empty, must it not? It must be free from knowledge, from experience, from capacity, and therefore free from fear, completely innocent, fresh, and young.

Comment: That seems to be the end of myself as I know myself, completely.

KRISHNAMURTI: Surely, sir, that is so. I do not know if you have tried to live a whole day so completely that there is no yesterday or tomorrow. That requires a great deal of understanding of the past. The past is not only the word, the language, the thought, but the looking back into yesterday with all its roots in the present. To completely let go of the past—the wrong that one has done, the things said which were not true, the hurtful things, the damage one has done—to let go of all the pleasures, pains, and memories. I do not know if you have ever tried it—just to walk out of it. And one cannot walk out of it if there is either regret or pleasure in the things remembered. Try it sometimes, not because I say so, or because you hope to get a reward out of it, or to have some wonderful experience—that would be just an exchange, a barter. But it is really quite extraordinary for the mind, which is the result of time, to be completely timeless.

Question: Habit forms quite a large part of what you are talking about, surely?

KRISHNAMURTI: You see, we have to find out. I am not just answering questions; we are discussing. And we see that the mind is always occupied. With most of us that is so. It is occupied with teaching, with babies, with the house, the job; it is occupied with its own vanities and virtues—you know the innumerable things with which it is occupied. And the occupation denotes habit. Now why has the mind to be occupied? Whether it is occupied with sex or with God or with virtue, it is just the same. There is no noble or ignoble occupation. Is that not so? I do not know if you really see this. Mere substitution of occupation is no release from occupation. Now, why has the mind to be occupied?

Comment: It may be a way of escape.

KRISHNAMURTI: Yes, sir, it is escape all right, but you see, explanations do not get us very far. Go a little bit further, sir. Go into it.

Question: It is fear, is it not? It is greed also, I think.

KRISHNAMURTI: One can go on and on and on, adding more and more explanations: escape, fear, greed. And then what? I am not being cynical, rude, or rough. We have given explanations—but the mind is not free from occupation.

Comment: Because the mind is occupation.

KRISHNAMURTI: You say the mind is occupation, which means, does it not, that the mind that is not occupied, not active, thinking, functioning, inquiring, responding, challenging—those are all symptoms of the mind—is not a mind. Is that so? The word *door* is not the door, and the word *mind* is not the mind. Does the mind realize itself as occupation? Or is there a mind which says, "I am occupied"?

I want to find out why the mind insists on being occupied. Why do we say that if the mind is not occupied, active, searching, defending, having anxiety, fear, guilt, it is not a mind? If all those things are not there, is there no mind?

Comment: Those things are the mind on one level, but not all the mind.

KRISHNAMURTI: The anxiety, the guilt, the fear, the responses—that is all we know, is it not? And what is the totality of the mind, as we know it? The totality of the mind, as we know it, is the unconscious and the conscious. Let us go back a bit. Why is the mind occupied? And what would happen if the mind were not occupied?

Comment: If the mind is not occupied, there is deep attention.

KRISHNAMURTI: Not "if"—that is speculation. You see, we are not going through.

Comment: The mind is all the time reacting to various stimuli. That is the process of being occupied.

KRISHNAMURTI: All right, sir, all right. Have you ever tried having no thought at all? Because every thought is occupation with something or other.

Comment: It is impossible to try it because if the mind is empty, one cannot.

KRISHNAMURTI: No, no, sir! Again, it is not a question of "if," and I do not mean "try" in that sense. We are caught in words. Has it ever happened to you that thought has come to an end? Not just ending one thought because you have gone out and beaten it to death—I do not mean that. But when there is thought, there is occupation. Thought sets habit going, which brings us back to the fact that thought is fear. Have you ever looked at anything without thought? I do not mean a state of blankness. You are all there, fully attentive, your whole being is there. Have you ever looked at something in that state in which there is no thought? Have you ever looked at a flower without naming it, saying how beautiful it is, what a lovely color it has, and so on? You know how the mind chatters. Have you looked at anything without any judgment, any evaluation?

You see, if we could look at fear without any resistance, without accepting or condemning or judging, merely observing it taking place within oneself and living with it, then, would it be fear? But the living with it requires enormous energy so that the mind is giving its attention completely.

Let us say that somebody says to me, "You are a very arrogant man." Many people tell me things—that I am this or I am that. Every statement that they make, I live with. If you will forgive me for talking a minute about myself, I live with it, I do not resist it; I neither say it is right nor it is wrong. And to live with it requires attention to see if it is true. Attention is energy. Attention, energy, is the whole universe—but that is irrelevant for the moment. Can one live with it, not distort it; not say, "I have been told that before; I am not like that," or "I am like that, and I must change." Do you follow? Is it not possible to live with the pleasant and the unpleasant; to live with suffering—whether it is a toothache or some other form of suffering—to live with fear, without getting unbalanced? You see, we want to live with the pleasant things, the lovely experiences we have had. They are dead and gone, but we want to live with them; therefore, we are only living with a dead memory. Suffering we do not want to live with; we want to find a way out. But is it not possible to live with both, not asking for a solution, not asking for an answer, and not just going to sleep over it? You see, this is meditation.

May 9, 1961

Fifth Talk in London

We were talking the last time about fear and whether it is at all possible for the mind to be totally free of it—not partially, not gradually, but to throw it out entirely. I would like to go into it further this evening.

Our minds are influenced in every direction—by the books we read, by the food we eat, by climate, by tradition, and by innumerable challenges and responses. All these impressions make up the conditioning of the mind. We are the result of influences: the so-called good and the so-called bad, the superficial and the deep, unthought-out, unrecognized, unknown influences. And most of us are unaware of this fact. When I use the expression *unknown influences,* I do not mean anything mysterious. Actually, we are not aware, when riding in a bus or in the underground, of the noises, of the advertisements, of the propaganda in the newspapers and in the speeches of the politicians, of all that is going on. And yet we are shaped by these things, and when one begins to be aware of it all, it is rather terrifying, rather disturbing.

So the question is whether the mind is capable of ever being really free of influence, the unconscious as well as the conscious influences. We all know that they have been trying, in America I think, a method of advertising in the cinemas, on the radio, and elsewhere, by saying things so fast that the conscious mind cannot take it in, but the unconscious does; the imprint is left. It was called subliminal advertising, and fortunately the government stopped it. But unfortunately, even though one form of it has been stopped, we are all slaves to this unconscious, subliminal propaganda. We pass it on to our children from generation to generation, and we are held in the framework of influence.

We are not doing propaganda here; let us be very clear about this. For me, every form of influence is destructive of what is true. If the mind is ever to be free to discover the unknowable, the thing that cannot be measured, that is not put together by the mind of man, then one must penetrate through all these influences. Fear has its roots in the imprint of time, and goodness cannot flower in the field of time. So can one inquire into influence—the influence of the word, the word *communist,* the word *belief,* and the word *nonbelief*—and find out for oneself whether the mind can free itself from the word, the symbol?

I think it is important to inquire into this, and I wonder what we mean by "inquire." How do we inquire? How does one penetrate into things? What does inquiry imply? Do you consciously look into fear, into the various forms of influence, into the hypnotic effect of the word—do you consciously, deliberately look? And when you do so look, does it reveal anything? Or, is there another form of seeing, looking, inquiring? Through the exercise of the will, through the urge, the desire, the compulsion to inquire, to search out, will you find out about fear? Will you uncover all the implications of it? Will you gather information about it little by little, page by page, chapter by chapter? Or will you understand the whole thing at once, totally? Surely, there are the two ways of inquiry, are there not? I do not know if you have thought about it at all. There is the so-called positive process of deliberately setting about to investigate every form of fear by watching every step, every word, being aware of every movement of thought. And it is an extraordinarily destructive process, is it not, this constant tearing of oneself to pieces in order to find out. It is the analytical, the introspective process.

Is there another way of inquiry? Please, I am not trying to make you think in a certain direction—which is what the propagandist does. But can we see for ourselves what is true and what is false without any influence, without any verbal directive? Can we see the truth in the false, and what is true, as true? The question is: Will the analytical process of inquiry free the mind from every form of fear? And is it possible at all to be free of fear? There is the self-protective fear, physically, when you come across a snake or a mad dog or an onrushing bus. That form of self-protective fear is sanity, surely. But every other form of protective reaction is based on fear. And can the mind, through this positive process of inquiry, unravel all the knots, the ways, the means of fear?

I think we ought to be very clear before we go further that this is not a question of your accepting or not accepting what is being said. We are not inquiring in terms of argumentation but trying to see what is the actual fact. If one sees a fact, one does not need to argue about it or be convinced.

So the question is: Through introspective examination, through the will, through effort, can the mind free itself, unravel the causes of fear, and step out of it?

You have tried, I am sure, to discipline yourself against fear or to rationalize it—fear of darkness, fear of what people may say, fear of dozens of things. We have all tried discipline, and yet fear is still there. Resistance will not wipe it away. So, if the positive process—if I may use that word because "analytical" is not a sufficient description—if the positive process is not effective for the freeing of the mind, then is there another way?

I am not using the word "way" in the sense of a gradual movement leading somewhere, implying a distance from here to there. It is in the so-called positive way that there is gradualness, the space of postponement, the "in the meantime," the "eventually I will arrive," and "it has to be conquered sooner or later," and so on. In that process there is always an interval between the fact of *what is* and the idea of 'what should be'. For me, that will not free the mind at all because it implies time, and time becomes all-important. For me, time implies fear. If there were no such thing as tomorrow or yesterday, and all the influences of yesterday leading through today to tomorrow—which implies not only chronological time but also psychological time, which is the will to achieve, to arrive, to conquer—then there would be no fear because then there would be only the living moment, the gap in which time is not.

So the so-called positive approach, positive inquiry, activity, is essentially a prolongation of fear. I do not know if we really comprehend that—not just the words I am saying, which are not important, but the actual fact.

Now, if the positive process is not the releasing factor, then what is? But first we must understand that the inquiry into what is the releasing factor is not merely a reaction to the positive process. This must be very clearly seen. Please wait, wait just a minute and look at it. I am thinking aloud. I have not thought all this out beforehand. We must give each other time to really look at it.

We can see that the inquiry which we have called the positive process does not free the mind from fear, for it maintains time—time as tomorrow, which is shaped by the influences of the past acting through the present. Please do not just accept this—see it. If you see the truth or the falseness of it, then your further inquiry is not just a reaction to the positive process.

You know what I mean by "reaction." I do not like Christianity for a dozen reasons, so I become a Buddhist. I do not like the capitalistic system because I cannot acquire immense riches or whatever the reason is, so as a reaction, I become a fascist, a communist, or something else. Being afraid, I try to develop courage, but it is still a reaction and therefore still within the same field of time.

So, a fact emerges from this: which is that when you see something as false, which is not a reaction, then a new process comes into being—not a process; a new seed is born.

I do not know if I am making myself clear. First of all, to see something as false or to see something as true, a very alert mind is needed: a mind that is completely free of any motive.

Now we understand what we mean by the analytical process, and if one sees the falseness of it or the truth of it, or sees the truth in the false, then how will you tackle fear? If that is not the way, then you have to turn your back on it wholly, have you not? The turning of your back on it is not a reaction; it has no motive; it is just that you have seen it as false and therefore turned away from it. Please, I do not know if you understand all this. I think it is very important to comprehend it because then you cut at the very roots of effort and will.

Now, what is the state of the mind which has turned away from the analytical process, with all its implications? Please do not just listen to my words but look at your own mind.

Comment: The mind is completely uncertain.

KRISHNAMURTI: Sirs, please do not answer! Please do not give verbal expression to it yet. Wait, please. Do not express it, even to yourselves, because it is something entirely new; you follow? And therefore you have no words for it yet. If you already have the words, you are still not actually looking.

You see, that state is the revolution, is it not, the revolt which is not a reaction, the revolt from the whole tradition of how to be free, how to achieve, how to arrive. I do not know if you capture this. Let us change a little bit; let that simmer for a little while.

You know, most of us know what it is to feel anxious, to feel guilty—to put on clean clothes when millions in the East have no clothes at all, to have a good meal when millions are hungry. Perhaps, living in a prosperous country where you are safe from the womb to the tomb, you do not know what that feeling is. There is not only the collective guilt of the race, there is the guilt of the family, the name, the big name and the little name, the guilt of the VIP's and of the nobodies, and the guilt of the individual, the things we have done wrong, the things we have said and thought, the despair of it all. I am sure you all know it. And out of this despair we do the most extraordinary things. We rush around, joining this and that, becoming this and denying that, all the time hoping to wipe away the inward despair. And despair, again, has its roots in fear. And despair breeds many philosophies, and through it one goes through many deaths. I am not being dramatic or romantic. This is the ordinary state that everybody goes through, either intensely or very superficially. When it is superficial, one turns on the radio, picks up a book, goes to a cinema, goes to a church, or watches a parade. When it is very deep, one goes off the deep end and becomes a neurotic or joins one of the new, fashionable movements of the intellect.

This is what is happening throughout the world. We have denied God, the churches have lost their meaning, the authority of the priest is washed out. The more one thinks, the more one cleanses the mind of all these absurdities.

So, you have got to tackle fear, you have got to understand fear. You follow? You have got to find out. Because there is not only the fear of death, the fear of the things that you have done and the things that you have not done, but there is the despair, anxiety, and guilt born of fear. These are all the expressions of fear. So if the mind is not to go to pieces or deteriorate, if it is to be alive, active, rich, it has got to wipe away fear. Until we do that, I do not think we can know what it means to love and what it means to have peace—not political peace and all the rest of that, but a real sense of inward quietness, untouched by time, incorruptible; it has no relation to that thing called peace which is put together by the mind of man.

So it is imperative for the mind to be free of fear because it is only the free mind that can discover if there is something beyond. You can call it truth, God, or what you will—it is that which man has been seeking for centuries, for millennia.

May 11, 1961

Sixth Talk in London

We have been talking about complete freedom from fear, and obviously it is really necessary to be free of it because fear creates so many illusions, so many forms of self-deception. A mind which is in any way bound to fear, consciously or unconsciously, can never find out what is true or what is false. Without being free from fear, virtue has very little meaning. And I would like to discuss with you what virtue is—if there is such a thing at all or whether it is merely a social convention which has nothing whatever to do with reality. I think one must approach the subject with an understanding of the necessity for the mind to be free of fear. When there is no fear at all, is there virtue? Is morality, virtue, merely a social convention, changing from time to time? For most of us, virtue is a quality, a morality which is the outcome of resistance, conflict, but I feel that virtue may have quite a different meaning if we can uncover its significance.

We can brush aside all the social morality, which is more or less necessary—like keeping the room in order, having clean clothes—but apart from those things, virtue or morality is, for most of us, a cloak of respectability. The mind that conforms, the mind that obeys, that is pursuing authority, convention, is obviously not a free mind; it is a puny, narrow, limited mind. So we have to ask whether the mind can ever be free from all forms of imitation. And to understand this problem, one has really to wipe away from one's mind every form of fear. Social morality is essentially based on authority and imitation. So, if we may, let us for the moment consider whether the mind can understand the limitations of imitation, of conformity to a pattern. And is it ever possible for the mind to uncondition itself?

It seems to me that goodness, the flowering of goodness, can never take place when the mind is merely respectable, conforming to the social pattern, to an ideological or a religious pattern, whether imposed from outside or cultivated from within. So the question is: Why does one follow? Why does one follow not only the social pattern but the pattern one has set up for oneself through experience, through the constant repetition of certain ideas, certain forms of behavior? There is the authority of the book, the authority of someone who says he knows, the authority of the church, and the authority of the law, and where is one to draw the line as to where there can be no following and where there must be following?

The following of the law is obviously necessary in the sense of keeping to the right or left side of the road, depending on the country you are in, and so on, but when does authority become detrimental, in fact evil?

In going into all this, one can see, can one not, that most of us are seeking power. Socially, politically, economically, religiously, we are seeking power: the power that knowledge gives, the power that a technique gives, the extraordinary power one feels when one has complete control over one's body, the power which asceticism gives. Surely all that is an imitative process; it is conforming to a pattern in order to derive a certain power, position, vitality. So it seems to me that without understanding the whole anatomy of power, the urge, the desire for it, the mind can never be in that state of humility which is not the humility man has invented.

So, why does one follow at all? Why are you following me, the speaker, if you are following? And are you following, or are you listening? Those are two different states altogether, are they not? You are following if you want to achieve, to arrive, or to gain something which you think the speaker is offering. But if the speaker is offering something, then he is really a propagandist; he is not a truth-seeker. And if you are following someone, it obviously means that you are afraid, uncertain; you want to be encouraged, to be told how to arrive, succeed.

Whereas if you actually listen—which is entirely different from following authority or seeking power—then you are listening to discover what is true and what is false, and that discovery does not depend on opinion, on knowledge. Now how do you discover what is false and what is true if you are listening? Obviously, a mind that is merely arguing within itself or with a person who is stating certain things is not discovering what is true or false. One is not listening at all when that listening merely provokes a reaction—a reaction according to one's knowledge, experience, opinion, education, which is one's conditioning. Also you are not listening when you are making an effort to find out what the other person is saying because your whole concern then is taken up with the effort. But if all those states could be set aside, then there is the state of listening which is attention.

Attention is not at all the same as concentration. Concentration is bringing the mind to focus on a particular point through the process of excluding. Whereas attention is full comprehension. There is attention when you are not only listening to the speaker but when you are listening also to the church music going on next door and to the traffic outside, when the mind is totally attentive, without a frontier and therefore without a center. Such a mind is listening, and such a mind sees what is true and what is false immediately, without reaction, without any form of deduction, induction, or other tricks of the mind. It is actually listening, and therefore in that very act of listening, there is a revolution, there is a fundamental transformation.

That attention, for me, is virtue; it is only in that attention that simple goodness flowers, the goodness that is not the product of education, society, and all the intellectual trimmings of influence. And perhaps, also, such attention is love. Love is not a virtue, as we know virtue. And where there is such love, there is no sin; then one can do what one will; then one is beyond the clutches of society and all the horrors of respectability.

So, one must find out for oneself why one follows, why one accepts this tyranny of authority—the authority of the priest, the authority of the printed word, the Bible, the Indian scriptures, and all the rest of it. Can one reject completely the authority of society? I do not mean the rejection brought about by the beatniks of the world; that is merely a reaction. But can one really see that this outward conformity to a pattern is futile, destructive to the mind that wants to find out what is true, what is real? And if one rejects the outer authority, is it possible also to reject the inner, the authority of experience? Can one put away experience? For most of us, experience is the guidance of knowledge. We say, "I know from experience," or "Experience tells me I must do this," and experience becomes one's inward authority. And perhaps that is far more destructive, far more evil than outward authority. It is the authority of one's conditioning and leads to every form of illusion. The Christian sees visions of Christ, and the Hindu sees visions of his own gods, each because of his own conditioning. And the very seeing of those visions, the very experiencing of those illusions, makes him highly respected, and he becomes a saint.

Now, can the mind entirely wipe away the conditioning of centuries? After all, conditioning is of the past. The reactions, the knowledge, the beliefs, the traditions of many thousands of yesterdays have gone to shape the mind. And can it all be wiped away? Do please seriously consider this and not just brush it aside by saying, "It is not possible," or "If it is possible, how am I to do it?" The "how" does not exist. The "how" implies "in the meantime," and a mind that is concerned with "in the meantime" is really postponing. You may think that though the mind can be brainwashed to become a communist or a capitalist or whatever it is—which merely implies a different form of conditioning—it is impossible to be free from all conditioning. You see, I do not know if you are following all this. I do not know whether you are conscious of your own conditioning, what it implies, and whether it is possible to be free or not. You see, conditioning is the very root of fear, and where there is fear, there is no virtue.

To go into this really profoundly requires a great deal of intelligence, and I mean by intelligence the understanding of all influence and being free of it. Influence is the cause of conditioning. You have been brought up to believe in God, in Christ, repeating things day after day, whereas in India they brush all that aside because they have been brought up with their own saints and gods. So the question is: Can the mind, which has been influenced by the heavy weight of tradition for centuries upon centuries, put it all aside without any effort? Can you walk out of it all, out of all this background, as freely as you can walk out of this hall? And is not this background the mind itself? The story of the mind is the mind. I do not know if I am making myself clear.

The mind is the background. The mind is tradition. The mind is the result of time. And seeing the hopelessness of its own activities, it finally says there is the grace of God which it must wait for, accept, receive—that is another form of influence—and such a mind is not an intelligent mind.

So what is one to do? I am sure you must have gone through all this. You must have experimented with it: not to accept, not to rely on authority, not to allow yourself to be influenced. You must have realized that the mind itself cannot do anything. It is its own slave; it has created its own conditioning, and any reaction to that conditioning merely furthers the conditioning. Every movement, every thought, every action that is going on within the mind is still within the limited field of its own values. If one has—not theoretically, not intellectually, not verbally, but actually—gone into it as far as that, then what happens? I hope you understand the issue. The issue is that for the mind that would discover what is true and if there is such a thing as the immeasurable, the unnameable, all authority must cease—the authority of the law as well as the authority of experience. This does not mean I will drive on the wrong side of the road. It means that the mind rejects the authority of all experience, which is knowledge, which is the word, and that it rejects the extraordinarily subtle forms of influence, the "waiting to receive," the expectations. Then the mind is a really intelligent mind.

To go into oneself so deeply, thoroughly, is quite an arduous work. To apply oneself to anything requires energy, not effort. And if one has gone as far as that, then is there anything left of the mind as we know it? And is it not necessary to arrive at that state? Because that, surely, is the only creative state. Writing a poem, painting pictures, putting up a building, and all the rest of it—surely, that cannot be called creative in the true sense of the word.

You see, one feels that creation, the thing that we name as God, or truth, or whatever you like to call it, is not for the select few. It is not for those who merely have capacity, a gift, like Michelangelo, Beethoven, or the modern architects, poets, and artists. I feel it is possible for everyone—that extraordinary feeling of immensity, of something that has no barrier, no frontier, which cannot be measured by the mind or put into words. I feel it is possible for everybody. But it is not a result. It comes into being, I think, when the mind starts with the nearest thing, which is itself—not when it goes after the farthest thing, the unimaginable, the unknown. Self-knowing, the understanding of oneself, is to open it up; go into it, see what it is, do not seek something outside. The mind is a really extraordinary thing. As we know it, it is the result of time; and time is authority—the authority of the good and the bad, of what must be done and what must not be done, the tradition, the influences, the conditioning.

So can the mind, your mind—I am not being personal—can your mind uncover its conditioning totally, both the conscious and the unconscious, and walk out of it? The "walk out" is only a verbal expression. But when the mind sees itself as conditioned and understands the whole works of it, the whole machinery of it, then, at one stroke, the mind is on the other side.

Question: Does one perceive one's conditioning through the provocations, the challenges of life?

KRISHNAMURTI: Do you really see anything through a provocation? If you react to a provocation, would you call that seeing?

Comment: I suggest that the type of awareness or heightened perception which you are talking about is sometimes experienced when one is witnessing an accident.

KRISHNAMURTI: Does the sudden freezing, narrowing down of attention, make you see—"see" in the sense that we are discussing? We are talking about conditioning and the perceiving of that conditioning. What does this perception mean? Are you trying to see your conditioning just because I say that if your mind is conditioned you cannot see what is true? Do you hope that out of seeing your conditioning there will be eternal bliss, and all the rest of it? You know, experience is an extraordinary thing. Either you try to experience because somebody is telling you about something, or else you are actually experiencing the thing itself, for yourself. Nobody has to tell you about hunger or envy or anger. The discovery of your conditioning because somebody tells you about it is not your discovery. I do not know if you are following this. Take a very simple thing. Nationalism is a form of conditioning. The nationalistic mind is a provincial mind, a mediocre mind. Do you see the truth, the fact of that for yourself? Or do you say, "It may be so. I must find out. Quite possibly he is right."

I will put it differently. I see very clearly that to belong to any organized religion is very destructive to the discovery of God, or whatever name you like to give it. The mind cannot commit itself to any form of organized thought, belief, or dogma. I see that very clearly, nobody has to tell me. For me it is so, and I say it. Then, because I have a certain reputation, etc., you say to yourself, "I must give it up." Then you are caught—wanting to belong, and yet something telling you not to belong. So it is not your experience. In direct perception there is no conflict. A mind that sees the actuality of something, whether it is false or whether it is true, is perceiving immediately, without any conflict, without any cause, without seeking any result. So the quality of perception is quite different from the imitative experience of copying, which has an ulterior motive.

So, we have been talking of fear, authority, virtue, and conditioning. Does one see the fact of one's own conditioning, the fact? And when you do see it, do you see totally, or only the part of the whole? Do you see the whole volume, or only one page of the volume? If you are not seeing the totality but only one page, then there will be a battle, a war within yourself.

Question: How does one know if one is seeing the whole volume or only a page?

KRISHNAMURTI: Do you want to be made certain that you see the whole and not the part? If you want to be assured, are you not seeking authority? It is a wrong question, if you will pardon my saying so. The question is: Is it possible to see the whole?

Comment: May I suggest that to find the correct answer, you must ask no questions and expect no answers.

KRISHNAMURTI: Is not that quoting Zen Buddhism? You see, sir, trying to find out for oneself is much more vital, real, than reading a book.

Comment: We all have moments when there is an awareness of everything, and then one wants to trap it and keep it continuously.

KRISHNAMURTI: Can you capture understanding? And can you keep it continuously? What has continuity is not the real, it is merely a habit. We all say, "I must have this thing continuously; I must have your love, your affection for all time." We say that to the husband, the wife, and we say it to God. What has continuity is not new; it is not the state of creation. It is only when there is the dying to each minute that there is the new.

Let us get back to the point. What is the state of the mind that sees the whole, the total? Please do not try to answer. You are trying to find out for yourself. Do you ever see anything totally? Take a tree—I know it is a very simple, common thing—but do you see the totality of the tree, the tree-ness, if I may use such a word? When you see a river, is it only "the Thames," or do you see the totality of all rivers, the river-ness?

You see, sirs, I want to find out now, before I leave this hall, what it means to see totally, and whether I have seen anything totally. And we are talking of something, and perhaps we do not even know what it means. Have you ever watched a flower—not just given it a name and passed it by, but watched it—which means seeing, listening, feeling with all your being? Surely, to watch, to see a flower, the river, the person, the trees, the conditioning, implies, does it not, being aware without a center, without the word.

Look—when one is angry, lustful, in that there is no center, is there? At the very moment of anger there is no center, is there? You are completely the anger. Is that not so? And the next minute comes the center which says, "I should not have been angry. Silly of me."

Question: Is not that anger a state of self-centeredness?

KRISHNAMURTI: Please, I do not think that you see this. In the actual state of anger there is no condemnatory reaction of calling it self-centered; that comes after. We are asking whether the mind can see the totality of its own conditioning—the conscious, the unconscious influences of tradition, values, beliefs, dogmas, nationalism, the word *British*—this whole thing?

Comment: I should say that we never see anything.

KRISHNAMURTI: You are probably quite right, sir. But we are asking the question now.

Comment: We can only feel totally.

KRISHNAMURTI: And when you do feel totally, is there a center which says, "I feel totally"? Please do not answer. Please follow this right through. It is very important to be free of this conditioning, obviously, because every way you look at it, it is so utterly stupid. To be conditioned as a Catholic, as a Protestant, as a Hindu, as a communist, or this or that; to be conditioned by a label, a word, and all the content behind the label and the word—it is so silly. Now, can the mind wipe it all away with one stroke? You see, virtue lies in that perception. The only virtuous man is the man who sees the totality of his conditioning and wipes it away. The rest are not virtuous at all; they are merely playing about with the toys of so-called civilization.

This means, really, can the mind be totally attentive? Can you be completely aware with all your senses, with all your body, with all your mind? Even if you are so aware for a fleeting second, then you will never ask, "How am I to be totally aware? Is it possible?" You see, I feel we miss so much beauty and love and such a profound sense of immensity when we surround ourselves with all our words, quarrels, beliefs, dogmas, and all such things. We do not kick them out, and so we are slaves to time.

May 14, 1961

Seventh Talk in London

During the last few times we have met, we have been talking about fear, and perhaps we could approach it from a different angle. Fear breeds every form of illusion and self-deception, and it seems to me that unless one's mind is totally free from every form of fear, then every thought, every action is colored by it. Though we have talked about it in some detail, I think it might be worthwhile to approach it differently. I think it would be a good thing if one could find out for oneself how to go into a thing like fear, how to unravel it, not only at the conscious level, but at the deeper layers, the hidden recesses of one's own consciousness. How does one penetrate, for instance, into desire? Because desire, with its urgency, its incessant demand for self-fulfillment, breeds fear and brings about self-contradiction.

Now, what significance has desire? And in the process of uncovering it, can one come to understand the urge to fulfill, with its frustrations and miseries? And can one understand the process of comparison? Because, it seems to me that where there is comparison, there is also the urge for power. All these things are linked together, and perhaps this evening we can go into it fairly deeply.

You see, I feel there is a state of mind which is above and beyond feeling and thought, but to come to that, it requires an enormous understanding of the process of feeling and also the process of thinking. The only thing we have is our feeling and thinking. The feeling is prompted by desire; it is strengthened and maintained by the urge of desire, and desire is always in terms of the furthering of pleasure and the avoidance of pain and suffering. Therefore, behind desire there is always the shadow of fear. So it seems to me that a mind that would think precisely, without any perversion, any twist, must inquire into the whole issue of desire.

Now, how does one inquire? How does one set about unraveling this extraordinarily subtle thing called desire, which is the basis of all psychological promptings? The urge to fulfill invariably brings frustration, fear, and sorrow; and so the so-called religious people have said that we must put away desire, so we try to dominate it, suppress it, sublimate it, or escape from it through various forms of identification with something. Desire means conflict. I want to be something, and in the very process of trying to become that something, there is conflict, and then comes the demand, the effort to escape from the conflict. Outwardly desire is expressed in society as acquisitiveness, the pursuit of the 'more', and inwardly it is expressed as progress towards certainty.

And can desire be controlled? Should it be controlled? Or must one give full vent, full expression to it? That is the problem. If one gives full expression to it, there is always the uncertainty of what may be the result, and therefore a sense of frustration and fear. If one disciplines it, controls it, shapes it, that also involves conflict between that *which is* and that 'which should be'. And of course if one suppresses it, sublimates it through various forms of identification—with a particular group, a particular set of ideas, a belief, and so on—there is still conflict. Desire seems to breed conflict, and I think most of us are aware of this. If we are at all intellectual, we find a safety valve in order not to give it full rein, and our desires take the form of intellectual conceits, vanities, and purposes, the acquisition of knowledge, cleverness.

And desire, hoping to achieve, to fulfill, is always comparing. I do not know if you have noticed how one is forever comparing—comparing oneself with another, comparing one's dress, one's looks, one's experiences, comparing ideas, pictures, and so on. Do we really comprehend anything through comparison? And can the mind cease to compare altogether? Can one, perhaps, begin to understand what desire is and not seek to suppress it? I think it is fairly obvious that suppression is futile, though it is extraordinarily prevalent throughout the world, especially among those people who are trying to record their own saintliness. Whether one suppresses a little or completely, it is still there, only it takes a different form of expression.

Now, passion and lust are two different things, though they are both forms of desire. You must have passion. To live with something beautiful or with something ugly, there must be passion; otherwise, the beauty dulls the mind, and the ugly thing distorts the mind. Passion is energy, and merely suppressing desire does not bring about this extraordinary sense of intensity, of passion. Of course, if desire identifies itself with an idea, with a symbol, with a philosophy, it does bring about a certain kind of intensity. You know the people who trot around the world doing all kinds of good work, trying to tell people what they should be and what they should not be. I do not mean that kind of intensity because if they were to stop talking, stop doing good works, and all the rest of it, they would find themselves caught in their own miseries, their own travail. But there is an intensity which comes into being when you understand desire and when you see the complete significance of all suppression, sublimation, substitution, escape.

I hope you are not merely listening to the words but are aware of your own forms of desire, and that you quickly, swiftly perceive the road along which it is going and where it leads, and how you have suppressed desire, identified it with something. After all, the purpose of these discussions is not for you to listen to me but to listen so as to discover, to see the whole map of oneself, the extraordinary complexity of oneself, the twists, the narrow paths, the ambitions, the urges, the compulsions, the beliefs, the dogmas. After all, if one does not see all that, is not aware of all that, then these meetings are absolutely useless; they become just another form of entertainment, perhaps a little more intellectual, but at the end of it one is left with ashes. Words are ashes, and to live on explanations, on words, gives rise to an empty life, an arid existence.

So I think it would be worthwhile if we could, during the process of these discussions, really battle with ourselves, unravel things, and then perhaps go beyond and above this process of feeling and thought. I would like us this evening to come to that, but one cannot come to it unless one really understands—not merely verbally or intellectually—the extensiveness of desire and all its significance.

I think one can see that every form of disciplining, controlling, suppressing, substituting, or sublimating perverts the beauty of desire and therefore makes the mind and heart incapable of being young, swift. I think that must be very clearly perceived. And is it possible to really see this, trained, as one has been, in a society whose values are acquisitive, whose religious dogmas and beliefs entail every form of twisting, suppressing desire? Desire obviously means comparison, and comparison, if one goes into it more deeply, leads to the urge for power.

You see, we talk a great deal about peace and love and all that kind of thing. Every politician throughout the world is everlastingly talking about his god, his peace, his love. And can a mind that has not understood the whole significance of desire know what love is? And the religious people consider desire evil—except the one desire for God, or Jesus, or somebody; and the monasteries are filled with such people. Can such minds see the immensity of that thing which we cover by the word *love?*

So, if one sees the significance of suppression, and therefore there is no longer the urge to suppress, transmute, and all the rest of it, then what is one to do with desire? It is there, burning, urging us to fulfill, to get ahead, to get a car, a bigger house, and so on. It is there, so what is one to do? I wonder if we have ever asked ourselves that question? We are so used to controlling it, shaping it, curbing it, adding ballast to it, or approximating it to something else—which is comparison. And can we ever stop that process? You see, it is only when that process has stopped completely that one can ask what one is to do with desire. I do not know if you have got to that point.

It means, really, can one live in this world without ambition? Can you go to the office and work without ambition? And if you did, would not your competitor wipe you out? And is there not the fear that if there were no ambition, one would just fade away? If I may suggest it, do put this question to yourself. When do you ask: What to do with desire? Must you first go through all the forms of fulfillment with their frustrations, miseries, fears, guilt, and anxiety? Or perhaps you never put that question at all, but only suppress all the time. Perhaps if you have not found happiness, position, prestige in one direction, you turn in another direction; these are the outward and the inward expressions of it. When one is a nobody in this disintegrating world, one turns inward for fulfillment. You never put that question when you are right in the wake of it, do you?

For a mind that is really inquiring, that really wants to find out if there is God, truth, something beyond all words, it is surely very important to understand this thing called desire. Is it right to be desireless? And if you kill desire, do you not also kill all feeling, with all its qualities of sensitivity? Feeling is a part of desire, is it not?

So, if one has gone into all the implications of suppression, then is one no longer suppressing, no longer substituting? It is not merely a matter of verbally mesmerizing yourself; it is quite an arduous thing—if you have gone that far. Because, a part of this desire is discontent—discontent with what we are—and at the back of this discontent is the urge for power, to be something, to fulfill in some way. Most of us are caught in this wheel of fulfillment and frustration, and with the everlasting battle of self-pity, one ultimately goes through the door of despair.

Now, can one actually see all this, and not take days, months, years over it? Can one see this everlasting search for fulfillment—how we know it is going to bring misery, and yet we keep on with it? Can we see it all as the whole content of our life and cut at the very root of it? And then, if one has gone that far—or rather, that near—what is one to do with desire? Is there any need, then, to do anything about desire? Do you follow?

So far, we have always done something about desire, given it the right channel, the right slant, the right aim, the right end. And if the mind—which is conditioned, which is always thinking in terms of achievement through training, through education, and so on—is no longer trying to shape desire as something apart from itself, if the mind is no longer interfering with desire, if I may use that word, then what is wrong with desire? Then, is it the thing we have always known as desire? Please, sirs, go along with it, come with me.

You see, we have always thought of desire in terms of fulfillment, achieving, gaining, getting rich, inwardly or outwardly, in terms of avoidance, in terms of the 'more'. And when you see all that, and put it away, then the feeling, which we have so far called desire, has a totally different meaning, has it not? Then you can see a beautiful car, a lovely house, a lovely dress without any reaction of wanting, identifying.

You know the whole social approach to existence in which you have been brought up, educated since childhood—all the ideation, the search for fulfillment, that you must be better than the next man, and so on. When you see the whole content of this conflict, and when it has fallen away from you from within, dropped from your hand, then is desire that which it previously was?

After all, to feel is to think, is it not? The two are inseparable. When I see a child in misery, starving, then I want to cut out society, the politician, and all the rest of them, and do something about it. The feeling always goes with the thought. And feeling is perception, sensation, touch, and all the rest of it. To feel is to be sensitive, and the more sensitive you are, the more you get hurt, so you begin to build a defense, a shield. All this is a form of desire. To cease to be sensitive is obviously to become inwardly paralyzed, to die. Perhaps most of us are paralyzed; that is what happens to us through education, through social relationships, contacts, knowledge—everything makes us dull, stupid, insensitive. And living in a tomb, we try to feel.

Realizing all this, then is there a limit to desire? I do not know what other word to use for that thing which we have called desire. Do you see what has happened—if you have gone into it? It is no longer feeling or thought—it is something entirely different, in which feeling and thought are included. Do go into it. Most of our lives are so terribly dull, full of routine, boredom—you know very well the horrors of your existence, the mediocrity of it—and we have not understood even a day or even a minute of our lives if we have not understood some of all this. And that is probably why we are all so terribly "spiritual," mediocre!

So we come to this issue—which is really very interesting, if you have gone into it. The thing that we have called desire, with all its corruptions, its travail, its miseries, its suffering, impotence, enthusiasm, interests, and so on—one has seen the full depth of it all; at one glance one can see it. You know how you do not have to get drunk to know what sobriety is. In the same way if one sees the process of fulfillment completely, it is finished; every form of fulfillment, every form of being or becoming something, has ended.

Comment: I think one needs to get drunk to know what drunkenness is.

KRISHNAMURTI: Surely that is rather far-fetched, is it not?—that one needs to know what it is to be drunk, and therefore one must drink? Must one go through murder to know what murder is? Sirs, do not let us be clever. Let us really apply our minds to all this.

Comment: It is the contradictions in desire that make it so impossible to deal with it.

KRISHNAMURTI: Why are there contradictions, sir? Do please follow it through. I want to be rich, powerful, important, and yet I see the futility of it because I see that the big people, with all their titles and so forth, are just nobodies. So there is a contradiction. Now, why? Why is there this pull in different directions; why is it not all in one direction? Do you follow what I mean? If I want to be a politician, why not be a politician and get on with it? Why is there this withdrawal from it? Do please let us discuss it for a few minutes.

Comment: We are afraid of what might happen if we give ourselves over entirely to one desire.

KRISHNAMURTI: Have you given yourself to anything once, totally, completely?

Comment: Once or twice, for a few minutes.

KRISHNAMURTI: Been completely in it? Perhaps sexually, but apart from that do you know when you have given yourself to something, totally? I question it.

Comment: Perhaps in listening to music.

KRISHNAMURTI: Look, sir. A toy absorbs a child. You give a child a toy, and he is completely happy; he is not restless, he is taken up with it, completely there. Is that giving yourself to something? The politicians, the religious people—they give themselves over to something. Why? Because it means power, position, prestige. The idea of being a somebody absorbs them like a toy. When you identify yourself with something, is that giving yourself over to something? There are people who identify themselves with their country, their queen, their king, and so on, which is another form of absorption. Is that giving oneself over to something?

Question: Is it possible ever actually to give oneself over to something insofar as there is always a schism between?

KRISHNAMURTI: That's it, sir. That is exactly right. You see, we cannot give ourselves over to something.

Question: Is it possible to give oneself over to someone?

KRISHNAMURTI: We try to. We try to identify ourselves with the husband, the wife, the child, the name—but you know better than I do what happens, so why talk about it? You see, we are deviating from the thing we are talking about.

Comment: A desire is right and good when it does not damage anything else.

KRISHNAMURTI: Is there wrong desire and right desire? You see, you are going back to the beginning; we covered the whole field, surely. Do you see how we have translated it already—the desire that is good and bad, worthwhile and not worthwhile, noble and ignoble, harmful and beneficial? Look deep into it. You have divided it, have you not? That very division is the cause of conflict. Having introduced the conflict by the division, you have then introduced a further problem: How to get rid of the conflict?

You see, sirs, we have been talking for fifty minutes, this evening, to see if one can really see the significance of desire. And when one really sees the significance of desire, which includes both the good and the bad, when one sees the total meaning of this conflict, this division—not just verbally, but comprehends it fully, puts one's teeth into it—then there is only desire. But, you see, we insist on evaluating it as good and bad, beneficial and nonbeneficial. I thought at the beginning we could wipe away this division, but it is not so easy; it requires application, perception, insight.

Question: Is it possible to get rid of the object and stay with the essence of desire?

KRISHNAMURTI: Why should I get rid of the object? What is wrong with a beautiful car? You see, you are creating conflict for yourself when you make this division of the essence and the object. The direction of the essence changes the object all the time, and that is the misery of it. When one is young, one wants the world; and as one grows older, one is fed up with the world.

You see, we were trying to understand desire and thereby let conflict die away, wither away. We have touched on so many things this evening. The urge for power which is so strong in all of us, so embedded, and which includes the dominance over the servant, the husband, the wife—you know it all. Perhaps some of you, in the course of the discussion this evening, have gone into this thing, have seen that where the mind is seeking fulfillment, there is frustration and therefore misery and conflict. The very seeing of it is the dropping of it. Perhaps some of you have not merely followed the words but understood the implications of the feeling of wanting to fulfill, to be something—the ignobleness of it. The politician seeks fulfillment, the priest does it, everybody does it, and one sees the vulgarity of it all, if I may use that word. Can one really drop it? If you see it as you see a poisonous thing, then it is like a tremendous burden taken off your shoulders. You are out of it; with a flick, it is gone. Then you will come to that point which is really extraordinarily significant. Not all this—all this has its own significance—but something else, which is a mind that has understood desire, the feeling and the thought, and therefore goes beyond and above it. Do you understand the nature of such a mind—not the verbal description of it? The mind, then, is highly sensitive, capable of intense reactions without conflict, sensitive to every form of demand; such a mind is above all feeling and thought, and its activity is no longer within the field of so-called desire.

For most of us, I am afraid, this is a lot of froth, a state to be desired or created. But you cannot come to it that way nor by any means. It comes into being when one really understands all this, and you do not have to do a thing.

You see—if you will not misunderstand what is being said—if you could leave desire alone, either to let fly or wither away—just leave it alone—that is the very essence of a mind which is not in conflict.

May 16, 1961

Eighth Talk in London

It seems to me that when we are thinking about fear, we have to consider its relation to conflict. For me, any form of conflict, outward or inward, is very destructive; it perverts one's thinking. When there is conflict, every problem leaves its mark on the mind; the mind becomes the soil in which the root of the problem grows. For most of us conflict seems so natural and inevitable that we accept it without question. We strive against it; we say we must not be in conflict, but invariably we are. So perhaps this evening we could go into it and see if it is at all possible, living in this rather mad world, for the mind to be free of it totally.

Now, before we go into that, I would like to talk about whether there is a way of thinking which is not positive. Because it seems to me that all our positive thinking is really only a reaction. I mean by "positive" when we say, "I must, I must not; I should be, I should not be," and this positive thinking brings about its own reaction of resistance, negation. I do not know if I can communicate this easily; it requires a great deal of understanding to comprehend what is involved in what we call a positive approach to our problems.

The positive approach seeks an explanation of the problem, the rationalizing of it, trying to escape from it, trying to do something definite in order not to be caught in it. That is what we do in everyday life. That process I call positive thinking: it is a reaction to the problem.

The problem is conflict. We seem to be perpetually in conflict about so many things—in our relationships with the husband, the wife, the children, society; and in our relationship with ideas, beliefs, dogmas. We are in conflict in the search for fulfillment and in the frustration it brings, in the search for truth, God, what to do, what to think, how to behave, how to correct something which has gone wrong—there is this constant war going on within. And our approach to it all, it seems to me, is always positive—which is, to do something about it, to escape from it, to join societies, seek some kind of drug, whether a religious drug, a tranquilizer, or what you will. And this positive approach is really a reaction to the problem, is it not?

Now, I feel there is a negative approach which is not a reaction, and not the opposite to the positive approach. At present, when I have a problem like conflict, I do not know how to resolve it; and so I resort to various forms of escape—through memory, thinking it out, battling with myself, hoping to get some kind of result, hoping that something will happen. For me, such an approach does not help us to be free from conflict. And I think there is an approach which is not the positive as we know the positive, but which is a negative process of understanding—not a reaction. I would like to go into it a little bit.

You see, the mind must be totally empty to see something new. And newness is not brought about by the investigation of the problem, the analyzing of it. If you are a mathematician, a scientist, or engineer, and so on, and you have a problem, you try to analyze it, look at it from every angle until the mind is exhausted and goes to sleep over it or forgets it for a time; and in that interval, after an hour or so or a few days, the solution may appear. We all know this. But that answer is not the outcome of a mind which is new, fresh, empty. A new mind is entirely devoid of conflict. It has no problem. And whatever problem arises, whatever challenge comes to it, does not leave a mark, even for a second, because the mark which endures even for a second leaves an imprint, and so conditions the mind. You see, only the empty mind, not the blank mind, but a mind that is fully alive, responding to every challenge—not as a reaction, not as a problem, but completely absorbing it—can instantly fathom it and finish with it immediately. And it is only an empty mind with that quality, of that nature, which can be free of conflict. It is only such a mind that is passionate. For me that word *passionate* has quite a different meaning from the ordinarily accepted meaning. I think one has to be passionate, one has to be intense—but not about something. This intensity is different from enthusiasm, which is only temporary. A mind that is in conflict can never be passionate, and it is only a passionate mind that sees the beauty of life, the beauty of everything, and that beauty is an extraordinary thing.

So the question is: Is it possible to be free of conflict—not theoretically, intellectually, verbally, not in a hypnotic state of mesmerizing oneself into saying it is or it is not possible, but actually? Is it really possible, living in this world, having relationships, going to the office, thinking, feeling, being brutalized by society, to be free of conflict? I do not know if you have asked yourself that question. Or am I imposing the question on you? Perhaps we have accepted conflict as inevitable and made God into the ultimate refuge of peace, calmness, and all the rest of it.

But if one has asked oneself whether the mind can really be free of conflict, then, I think, one has to go very much deeper into the problem—which I hope we can this evening. Why does conflict arise? Why does conflict arise between me and my wife, my husband my neighbor, between me and an idea? I will answer in my way, but if you can discover for yourself why you are in conflict, then I think my explanation and your own feeling will meet. Otherwise communication is impossible. I hope you understand what I mean.

So, I want to know why I am in conflict—not merely the superficial explanation, but I really want to go to the root of it. There is conflict consciously and also unconsciously, deep down in the innermost recesses of my mind, the secret conflicts of which nobody knows; and I want to go into the very depth of it. Now, does one analyze it, go into the reasons, or does one see it in a flash?

You know, even the Freudians and the Jungians and the analysts are beginning to change their ideas. They feel that they do not have to take months and years to unravel the poor individual. It is too expensive; only the rich can afford it, so they are trying to find a quicker means. Instead of having the patient rattle on day after day, month after month, they are trying, some of them, drugs, chemicals, and a direct personal approach. Not that I have read books about it, but I have friends, analysts and nonanalysts, who come and talk with me about all this. In the process of analysis, unless you are very, very careful, minutely observing and never twisting what you observe, you will miss something, misinterpret something, and the next examination will strengthen the fault. Do please follow this and realize that analysis, dissecting, tearing to pieces, is not the way. Nor is controlling, escaping.

I want to know why there is conflict, this mass of contradictions. Now, how are you going to find out the very root of the matter? Because, if one can find the root of it, then that very discovery will bring a negative approach, and it will not create a reaction which will have a positive action on what is discovered. Do you understand? I will go into it.

I want to know what is the cause of conflict, the total conflict—the contradictions, desire pulling in different directions, and the fear which arises. Now knowing is one thing, and actually experiencing is another. Is that not so? Knowing implies an observer who is looking on, and experiencing is a state in which there is no experiencer. That is, I can tell you verbally what is the radical cause of conflict, and you can agree or disagree or accept it and add it to your further explanations, or there is an entirely different thing, which is that, in listening to the very description, you are at the same time experiencing the central issue that is creating conflict. Am I making it clear?

Look—knowing is one thing, and experiencing is another. Knowing about God or truth is one thing, but actually experiencing something of that immensity is quite different. Most of us are aware that we are functioning from a center, the center which has become knowledge, the center which is experience, the center from which all compulsive urges and resistances take place, the center that is always seeking security. Please do not accept my words but actually experience the center from which you think, the self. And where there is a center, there must be a circumference and the battle is to reach the circumference, the 'what should be'. The circumference is always something different from *what is.* Is that not so?

We know all this. We know that having experienced that, all our activities, thoughts, and feelings are shaped, projected, conditioned by the center; the center at once says, "I must get rid of it." So there is a division between the center and the thing that should be or the thing that has been. There is always this division, and conflict is essentially the war between the 'what should be' and *what is.* The *what is,* which is the center, is always trying to shape itself into the 'what should be', and from that duality arises conflict.

Now, the center is the accumulated memories of experience, the result of the conflict with the opposite, with 'what should be'—I am a lustful man, and I feel I should not be—and the conflict between the two creates memory which forms the center. Is that not right? The center is memory. Now, memory has no reality; it is not a fact; it is something dead, gone, finished, though at a certain level it can be used when necessary. But it is dead, and yet our life is guided by this dead thing, by something which is not real. From this we function, and so fear grows, and so there is the contradiction of desire.

Let us leave it there for the moment and look at it differently.

I think most of us know what it is to be lonely. We know that state when all relationship has been cut off, when there is no sense of the future or of the past, a complete sense of isolation. You may be with a great many people, in a crowded bus, or just sitting next to your friend, your husband or wife, and suddenly this wave comes upon you, this sense of an appalling void, an emptiness, an abyss. And the instinctive reaction is to turn away from it. So you turn on the radio, chatter, or join some society, or preach about God, truth, love, and all the rest of it. You may escape through God or through the cinema; all escapes are the same. And the reaction is fear of this sense of complete isolation, and escape. You know all the escapes—through nationalism, your country, your children, your name, your property, for all of which you are willing to fight, to struggle, to die.

Now, if one realizes that all escapes are the same, and if one really sees the significance of one escape, then can you still escape? Or, is there no escape? And if you are not escaping, is there still conflict? Do you follow? It is the escape from *what is,* the endeavor to reach something other than *what is,* that creates conflict. So a mind which would go beyond this sense of loneliness—this sudden cessation of all memory of all relationship, in which is involved jealousy, envy, acquisitiveness, trying to be virtuous and all that—must first face it, go through it, so that fear in every form withers away. So, can the mind see the futility of all escapes through one escape? Then there is no conflict, is there? Because, there is no observer of the loneliness—there is the experiencing of it. You follow? This loneliness is the cessation of all relationship; ideas no longer matter; thought has lost its significance. I am describing it, but please do not just listen because then, when you leave this hall, you will be left with ashes. After all, the purpose of these discussions is to free oneself actually from all these terrible entanglements, to have something else in life than conflict, the fear and the weariness and boredom of existence.

Where there is no fear, there is beauty—not the beauty the poets talk about and the artist paints, and so on, but something quite different. And to discover beauty one has to go through this complete isolation—or rather, you do not have to go through it, it is there. You have escaped from it, but it is there, always following you. It is there, in your heart and your mind, in the very depths and recesses of your being. You have covered it up, escaped, run away, but it is there. And the mind must go through it, like going through a purgation by fire. Now, can the mind go through it without reaction, without saying it is a horrible state? The moment you have a reaction, there is a conflict. If you accept it, you still have the burden of it; and if you deny it, you will still come across it round the corner. So the mind has to go through it. Are you following all this? Then the mind is that loneliness; it has not got to go through it; it is that. The moment you think in terms of going through and reaching something else, you are again in conflict. The moment you say, "How am I to go through, how am I to really look at it?" you are caught in conflict again.

So there is emptiness, there is this extraordinary loneliness which no Master, no guru, no idea, no activity can take away. You have fiddled with all of them, played with all of them, but they cannot fill this emptiness—it is a bottomless pit. But it is not a bottomless pit the moment you are experiencing it. Do you understand?

You see, if the mind is to be entirely free of conflict—totally, completely without apprehension, fear and anxiety—there must be the experiencing of this extraordinary sense of having no relationship with anything, and from that comes a sense of aloneness. Don't please imagine that you have it; it is quite an arduous thing. It is only then, in that sense of aloneness in which there is no fear, that there is a movement towards the immeasurable, because then there is no illusion, no maker of illusion, no power to create illusion. So long as there is conflict, there is the power to create illusion; and with the total cessation of conflict, all fear has ceased, and therefore there is no further seeking.

I wonder if you understand. After all, you are all here because you are seeking. And, if you examine it, what are you seeking? You are seeking something beyond all this conflict, misery, suffering, agony, anxiety. You are seeking a way out. But if one understands what we have been talking about, then all seeking ceases—which is an extraordinary state of mind.

You know, life is a process of challenge and response, is it not? There is the outward challenge—the challenge of war, of death, of dozens of different things—and we respond. And the challenge is never new because all our responses are always old, conditioned. I do not know if this is clear. In order to respond to the challenge, I must recognize it, must I not? And if I recognize it, it is in terms of the past, so it is the old, obviously. Do please see this because I want to move a little further.

To a man who is very inward, the outward challenges no longer matter, but he still has his own inward challenges and responses. Whereas I am talking of a mind that is no longer seeking, and therefore is no longer having a challenge and a response. And this is not a satisfied, contented state, a cow-like state. When you have understood the significance of the outward challenge and the response, and the significance of the inward challenge which one gives to oneself and its response, and have gone through all this swiftly—not taking months and years over it—then the mind is no longer shaped by environment; it is no longer influenceable. The mind that has gone through this extraordinary revolution can meet every problem without the problem leaving any mark, any roots. Then, all sense of fear has gone.

I do not know how far you have followed all this. You see, listening is not merely hearing; listening is an art. All this is a part of self-knowing, and if one has really listened and gone into oneself profoundly, it is a purification. And what is purified receives a benediction which is not the benediction of the churches.

May 18, 1961

Ninth Talk in London

This morning, I would like, if I may, to talk about time and death. And as it is rather a complex subject, I think it would be worthwhile to understand what is the meaning of learning. Life is a vast complex, with all its turmoil, suffering, anxieties, love, jealousies, and accumulations; and we learn through travail. This learning is a process of accumulation. For us, all learning is an additive process; and when there is addition, a gathering-in, is there any learning at all? Is accumulation learning? Or is there learning only when the mind is totally innocent? I think we should inquire into this a little because to understand time and death, one has to learn, one has to experience, and experiencing is never an accumulative process.

In the same way, love is never accumulation. It is something always new. It is not a thing that is born out of remembrance. It is totally unrelated to the picture on the mantelpiece. So perhaps if we could, hesitantly but rather intelligently, understand what it means to learn, then we can probe into the question of time and death, and perhaps also discover what it means to love.

For me, learning implies a state of mind which is never gathering, never accumulating. If one learns with a mind that has already gathered, then such learning is merely the acquisition of more knowledge, is it not? The accumulation of knowledge is not learning. The electronic machines are doing that; they are acquiring more and more knowledge, and they are incapable of learning. The acquisition of knowledge is a mechanical process, and learning can never be a mechanical thing. A mind must always be fresh, young, innocent, to learn. And a mind which is learning is always, surely, in a state of humility—not the humility cultivated by the monk, the saint, or the erudite person. A mind that is learning has its own dignity because it is in a state of humility.

I am using the word *learn* in quite a different sense, not as a process of acquiring knowledge. Living with a thing and acquiring knowledge about it are two different states. To learn about something, you must live with it, and if you already have knowledge about it, you cannot live with it because then you are only living with your own knowledge. To find out for ourselves about the extraordinarily complex problem of time and death, one must learn, and therefore live with it; and this is completely impeded if we approach it with the accumulation of what we already know, with knowledge. I will go into it a little, and perhaps we shall be able to communicate with each other.

We were talking the other day about desire. We went into it fairly sufficiently, but I think we missed something—that desire is intimately connected with will. Will implies, surely, not only desire but also choice. Where there is choice, there is will, and therefore the problem of time arises.

Please, if I may suggest it, listen to the whole thing right to the end. Do not stick at parts of it with which you agree or disagree, but look at the totality of it, the whole content of it. It is a matter of perception, of seeing something directly, and when you see something very directly then you neither agree or disagree—it is so.

So, as I was saying, through conflict, outward and inward, we develop will. And will is a form of resistance, obviously, whether it is the will to achieve or the will to be, the urge to deny or the determination to sustain something. Will is the many threads of desire, and with that we live. And when we inquire into time, we require an insight which is quite different from the will to understand. I do not know if this is clear, but I will go along with it, and perhaps you will see it. This is an informal talk, not a prepared talk; it is more or less an inquiring into oneself, and to go into it publicly is one thing, and to go into it all by oneself is quite another. What we are trying to do is to communicate it to each other—this journey into time. The inquiry implies time also, and the putting of words together implies time, and all communication is based on time. And perhaps there is a comprehension of what is time and what is timelessness, not through words, not through verbal or intellectual communication, but perhaps by sidestepping the whole process. But unfortunately we must first inquire verbally, intellectually, into time. And this inquiry is the sense of learning about it—which is not remembering what you have read, or merely hearing the words I am saying, but the perception of it, seeing it directly for yourself. And I think that may have immense value.

Time is both chronological and psychological, outward and inward. And conflict arises when time is introduced into our lives as "I will be, I will not be; I must arrive; I must fulfill." And if the mind could eliminate all that process, then we might find that the mind is no longer measurable, has no frontier, and yet can live in this world totally, completely, with all its senses.

For most of us, chronological time as today, tomorrow, and yesterday is essential. Time is involved in learning a technique, to earn a livelihood. It is there, and you cannot avoid it; it is a reality. It took time for you to come here; it takes time to learn a language; there is time as growing from youth to old age. It takes time, involving distance and space, to go from here to the moon. These are all facts, and it would be absurd and insane to deny it.

Now, is there any other time at all, as a fact? Or has the mind invented psychological time as a means of achievement, as a means of becoming something? I am envious, acquisitive, brutal; but, given time, I will gradually be free from envy, be nonviolent. Is that a reality, is it a fact, as the distance from London to Paris is a fact? Is there any other fact as definite and real as space and distance? In other words, is there psychological time at all? Though we have invented it, though we live with it, though it is a fact to us, is there such a thing? We accept chronological time, and we also accept psychological time, and these two, we say, are facts. The one, the chronological time, is a fact, but I am questioning whether the other is a fact. Is time necessary in order to see something clearly, immediately? To see acquisitiveness, envy, all the things, the suffering involved in envy, to see the truth of it, is time necessary? Or does the mind invent psychological time in order to enjoy the fruits of envy and avoid the pain of it? So, time may be the refuge of an indolent mind. It is the lazy mind that says, "I cannot see the thing immediately, give me time, let me look at it for a longer period; later I will do something about it"; or "I know I am violent, and gradually, when it no longer pleases me, when it is no longer profitable to me, when I am no longer enjoying it, I will give it up." Therefore the ideal is born: the idea of 'what should be' is placed at a distance, away from the fact of *what is*. So there is a gap between 'the fact' and 'what should be'. And I am asking: Is the ideal, the 'what should be', a fact? Or is it a convenient invention of the mind to enable it to carry on with the pleasures and pains, the indolence of postponement?

Now to see something immediately—the absurdity of envy, of competition, of social morality—to see the falseness of it immediately, does that require time? To transform the mind, for the mind to free itself of its own conditioning, does it require time? You see, as it is generally understood, a revolution implies carrying out an economic, social, political, or other pattern as a reaction to what has been before. For me, a reaction is not a revolution. A revolution is instantaneous and is unrelated to a reaction.

The mind is, after all, the result of many thousands of yesterdays, and being itself the result of time, it always thinks in terms of yesterday, today, and tomorrow. And to find out if there is a timelessness, to really find out, to learn about it, there must be a complete revolution in the mind itself. Am I conveying anything, or not at all?

Look, you are an Englishman, an Italian, a Frenchman, a Hindu, or whatever it is, and with it goes all the nationalism—the conditioning, the separative, divisive attitudes towards life. And this conditioning has been put together through time, through education, through propaganda; for two thousand years the church has brainwashed you to be a Christian. And this conditioning of religion, of nationalism, of separativeness must obviously be broken down completely because those things are all frontiers, limitations of the mind. And the breaking down of it all, is that a matter of time?

Let us look at it differently. Where does time exist? Not only time by the watch but the inward time, where does it exist? Please, this is not a rhetorical question, an argumentative question, or a question put just to stimulate your mind—that is all too silly. I am asking this because space, time, and distance must exist in a state where there is no time at all. That state must exist first, and everything else comes into that. Without timelessness, there is no space and distance. Please do not accept or deny it; we must feel our way into it. I have not yet communicated to you the feeling of it, so you cannot say it is so, or it is not so, or that what I say has no meaning to you.

You see, you exist in space. Without space, you would not be. Without the space between two words, the words have no meaning. Without the space between two notes, there would be no music. The space is the thing unknown, in which the known exists. Without the unknown, the known is not. I do not know if I am conveying it to you. Please, this is not just sentimental stuff to be grinned over or agreed with. I am going to go on into something else. If whatever one says becomes dead, there is no life.

Most of us want a life which has continuity, which is time and space. So, for us death is a horror, to be avoided, and life is something to be prolonged through medicine, through doctors, and so on. Or, faced with the inevitability of death we say, "I will believe in something: that I will continue and that you will continue—always in space."

So, if one can put it this way, in the womb of the unknown, time and space exist. But without feeling one's way into the unknown, the mind becomes a slave to time and space. It took us time to get here, but does it take time to perceive anything, to see something which is not a matter of time? To see something as false, does it take time? To see the falseness of nationalism, the poisonousness of it, does it take time? Please wait a minute, do not agree. I do not mean the intellectual, verbal seeing but the actual seeing, the actual feeling of it so that you never again touch it—surely, that does not take time? Time is relied upon only when the mind is ineffective, indolent.

And death—why is there such fear of death? Not only for the aged but for everyone there is this fear. Why? And being afraid, we have invented all the lovely comforting theories: reincarnation, karma, resurrection, and all the rest of it. It is fear that has to be understood, but do not let us go back into fear. We are trying to understand what it means to die.

Most of us want physical continuity—the remembrance of the things we have been, the hopes, the satisfactions, the fulfillments—most of us live with the memories, the associations, the pictures on the mantelpiece, the photographs. And all that may be cut off when the physical body ceases, and that is a very disturbing thing. I have lived so long, for fifty or sixty years; I have struggled to cultivate certain virtues, to acquire knowledge, and what is the value of life if I am to be cut off from it all, to cease on the moment? So, time-space comes in. You follow? Time, as space and distance. So for us, death is a matter of time. But that which has continuity, which knows no ending, can never renew itself, can never be young, fresh, innocent. It is only something that dies that has the possibility of a creation, a newness, a freshness. So, is it possible to die while living, to know the vitality, the energy of death, with all the senses fully awake? What does death mean? Not the death of old age, disease, and accident, but the death of a mind that is fully active, that has tasted, experienced, and has acquired knowledge, which means, really, the death of yesterday. Do you understand?

I do not know if you have ever tried it, for the fun of it—to die to everything that you have known. Then you will say, "If I die to all my remembrances, to my experience, my knowledge, my photographs, my symbols, my attachments, and my ambitions, what is left?" Nothing. But to learn about death, the mind must be in a state of nothingness, surely. Let us take one thing. Have you ever tried to die, not only to suffering, but to pleasure? We want to die to suffering, to unpleasant memories, but to die also to pleasure, to joys, to things that give you an enormous sense of vitality—have you tried it? If you have, you will see that you can die to yesterday. To die to everything so that when you go to the office, to your work, your mind is new—surely, that is love, is it not, not the remembered things.

So, the mind has been put together through time; the mind is time. Every thought shapes the mind in time. And not to be shaped by time, thought must completely come to an end. Not an enforced ending, not a mechanical ending, not a cutting off, but the ending which is the seeing of the truth that it must end.

So, if one is to learn about death, one must live with death. If you would learn about a child, you must live with the child and not be frightened by the child. But most of us die a thousand deaths before real death. To live with death is to die to yesterday so that the yesterday leaves no imprint on the today. You try it. When the perception of what is true about this is there, then living has quite a different meaning; then there is no division between living and death. But we are frightened of living and frightened of dying, and we understand neither living nor death. To live with something we must love it, and to love is the dying to yesterday—then you can live. Living is not the continuity of memory, or going back into the past and saying, "What a marvelous time I had when I was a boy."

We do not know death, and we do not know life. We know the turmoils, the anxieties, the guilt, the fears, the appalling contradictions and conflicts, but we do not know what living is. And we only know death as something to be dreaded, feared; we put it away and do not talk about it, and we escape into some form of belief, like flying saucers or reincarnation or something else.

So, there is a dying and therefore a living when time, space, and distance are understood in terms of the unknown. You see, our minds work always in terms of the known, and we move from the known to the known, and we do not know anything else, and when death cuts off this continuity of the known with the known, we are frightened, and there is no comfort. What we want is comfort, not the understanding of, the living with something we do not know.

So, the known is yesterday. That is all we know. We do not know what tomorrow is. We project the past, through the present, into the future, and thereby hope and despair are born. But really to comprehend the thing called death, which must be something extraordinary, something unknowable, unthinkable, unimaginable, one must learn about it, one must live with it, one must come to it without knowledge and without fear. And I say it is possible that one can die to the many yesterdays. After all, the many yesterdays are pleasure and pain. And when you die to yesterday, the mind is empty, and it is frightened of that emptiness, and so it begins again, going from one known to another. But if one can die to pleasure and pain—not a particular pleasure or a particular pain—then the mind is without time and space. And such a mind then has time and space without the conflict of time and space. I do not know if you follow. I am afraid language is very limited. Perhaps we can discuss it.

Question: I have always thought that where there is space, there must be time, and you seem to make it rather different. Is not the space between two words, time?

KRISHNAMURTI: Sir, we know both psychological time and time by the watch. And how is the mind which is bound to these two times—in which are involved space and distance—to find out if there is a time without space and distance? You follow? I want to find out if there is a timelessness, in which no measurement exists as time and space. Is it possible, first of all, to find out such a thing? It may not be. If it is not possible, then the mind is a slave to time and space always; then it is finished. Then it is merely a matter of adjustment, trying to have a little less suffering and so on. Understanding all that, can the mind, without authority, find out for itself if there is a timelessness? And how is it to find out? It can find out only by abandoning psychological time—as when it sees something immediately. Which means, does it not, that the mind frees itself from the center round which it moves, that there is a dying to the center which has accumulated pleasure and pushed away pain. And I think that has direct relationship to our daily living.

Question: Is not chronological time the same as psychological time?

KRISHNAMURTI: In a certain sense they are both the same.

Is there not the urge for the mind to be in a state of something permanently? For us, permanency is very important, is it not? But there is no such thing as permanency because there is war, there is death, my wife runs away with somebody, and so on. The urge to have permanency is the desire to be secure. But the mind objects to insecurity, so it invents hopes and the idea of God who is permanent. A god who is made permanent in time and space cannot be God. So, if the mind could see, immediately, the truth, the fact that there is nothing permanent, then I think time, death, and love will have a totally different significance.

Question: After the stopping of the heart, is there thought as the person?

KRISHNAMURTI: Oh, how eager we are to find out about this! How we sit up and take notice!

Let us go into it. Is there personal thinking and collective thinking? Or, is all thinking collective, only we personalize it? You are all British: it is collective thinking. You are all Christians: it is collective thinking. There is individual thinking only when you break away from the collective, when you are no longer confined, limited, conditioned. So, surely we are only individuals in the sense that one organism is separate from another organism, in the sense that there is a space and a distance between us. Is not all our thinking collective?—which is rather a horrible idea, but is it not so?

Question: If you were told you were going to die tomorrow, would that have any effect on you personally?

KRISHNAMURTI: None whatever; I would carry on. But the question is: Is there individual thinking apart from the collective? What I am trying to say is this. I am brought up as a Hindu, a Christian, a Buddhist, or whatever it is, believing in all the things that society believes in and being a part of it all.

Is there thought separate from that? Any thought separate from that can only be a reaction, is that not so? I can break away from the framework of the collective and say I am separate, but actually that is only a reaction within the framework, is it not? I am talking of the total rejection of the framework. Is it possible? If it is possible, then there is an individual thinking which is not merely a reaction to the collective.

After all, death is the breaking away from the collective. Death is a breaking away from the framework in which there is collective thinking and the reaction to the collective which you call individual thinking, but which is still part of the collective. Dying to all that may be, and must be, something entirely different, something which cannot be measured in terms of the collective or in terms of the individual, something unknowable, unknown. And I say that if the unknown does not exist, and if the known does not exist within the unknown, then we are merely slaves to the known, and there is no way out. The unknowable is only possible when one dies to the known.

May 21, 1961

Tenth Talk in London

I would like to talk this evening about the quality of the meditative mind. It may be rather complex and abstract, but if one goes into it thoroughly—not so much in detail, but to discover the nature of it, the feeling of it, the essence of it—then perhaps it will be worthwhile; then perhaps without conscious effort and deliberate purpose, we shall be able to break through the shallow mind which makes our lives so empty, so superficial, and so habit-ridden.

And I think it would be worthwhile, first of all, if we could realize for ourselves how shallow we are. It seems to me that the shallower we are, the more active we become, the more collective we become, the more social reforms we indulge in. We collect works of art, we chatter endlessly, take up social activities, concerts, books, go to picture galleries, and the everlasting office and business. These things make us dull, and when we realize this dullness, we try to sharpen ourselves with words, with the intellect, with the things of the mind. And being shallow, we also try to escape from that emptiness into religious activity, prayers, contemplation, the pursuit of knowledge; we become idealists, hang pictures on the wall, and so on. I think we know fairly well, if we are at all aware, how shallow we are, and how a mind which is following a habit or practicing a discipline in order to become something is made more and more dull, stupid, so that it loses its sharpness, its sensitivity. It is very difficult for a shallow mind to shatter its own narrowness, its own limitations, its own pettiness. I do not know if you have thought about it at all.

What I am going to talk about this evening demands not only a certain activity of the mind, of the intellect, but also an awareness of the word and its limitations. And if we can communicate with each other, not only verbally, but beyond the symbol which the words evoke in our minds, and also feel our way along together, then we shall begin to discover for ourselves what it is to meditate, what is the quality of the mind that is capable of meditation.

It seems to me that without the comprehension of the extraordinary beauty of meditation, however seemingly intelligent, gifted, capable, penetrating one may be, such a life is very superficial and has little meaning. And realizing that our lives have very little meaning, we then seek a purpose in life; and the greater the purpose that is offered to us, the nobler we think our endeavors to be. I feel that the search for a purpose is a wrong approach altogether. There is no purpose; there is only a living beyond measure. And to discover that state which is beyond measure requires a very astute, sharp, clear, precise mind, not a mind that has been made dull by habit.

I think it is fairly clear that our lives are empty, shallow. And a shallow mind is easily satisfied. As soon as it becomes discontented, it follows a narrow groove, establishes an ideal, pursues the 'what should be'. And such a mind, do what it will—sit cross-legged, meditate upon its navel, or think about the supreme—will remain shallow because its very essence is shallow. A stupid mind can never become a great mind. What it can do is to realize its own stupidity, and the moment it realizes for itself what it is, without imagining what it should be, then there is a breaking down of stupidity. When one realizes that, all seeking comes to an end—which does not mean that the mind becomes stagnant, goes to sleep. On the contrary, it faces *what is* actually—which is not a process of seeking, but of understanding.

After all, most people are seeking happiness, God, truth, love everlasting, a permanent abode in heaven, a permanent virtue, a permanent love. And it seems to me that a mind that is seeking is a very superficial mind. I think we ought to be a little clear on this point, we ought to investigate it, we ought to look at the absurdity of a shallow mind and its activities because we shall not be able to penetrate into what we are exploring this evening if we are still thinking in terms of seeking, making an effort, trying to discover. On the contrary, we need an extraordinarily sharp, quiet, still mind. A shallow mind, when it makes an effort to become silent, will still be only a shallow pool. A petty mind that is so learned, so cunning, so full of the acquisitive pursuit of God, of truth, or of some saint because it wants to get somewhere is still superficial because all effort is superficial, is the outcome of a mind that is limited, narrow. Such a mind can never be sensitive, and I think one has to face the truth of that. The effort to be, to become, to deny, to resist, to cultivate virtue, to suppress, to sublimate—all that is in essence the nature of a shallow mind. Probably most people will not agree with this, but it does not matter. It seems to me an obvious psychological fact.

Now, when one realizes this, when one is aware of it, sees the truth of it actually, not verbally, not intellectually, and does not allow the mind to ask innumerable questions as to how to change it, how to get out of this shallowness—all of which implies effort—then the mind realizes that it cannot do anything about itself. All that it can do is to perceive, to see things ruthlessly, as they are, without distortion, without bringing in opinions about the fact—merely to observe. And it is extremely difficult, merely to observe, because our minds are trained to condemn, to compare, to compete, to justify, or to identify with what is seen. So it never sees things exactly as they are. To live with a feeling as it is—whether it is jealousy, envy, greed, ambition, or what you will—to live with it without distorting it, without having any opinion or judgment about it, requires a mind that has energy to follow all the movements of that fact. A fact is never still; it is moving, it is living. But we want to make it still by capturing it with an opinion, a judgment.

So, a mind that is aware, sensitive, sees the futility of all effort. Even in our education, the child, the student who makes an effort to learn, never really learns. He may acquire knowledge, he may get a degree, but learning is something beyond effort. Perhaps this evening we shall be able to learn together without effort, and not be caught within the realms of knowledge.

To be aware of the fact, without distortion, without coloration, without giving it any bias, to look at ourselves as we are—with all our theories, hopes, despairs, sufferings, failures, and frustrations—makes the mind astonishingly sharp. What makes the mind dull is belief, ideals, habits, the pursuit of its own enlargement, growth, 'becoming' or 'being'. And as I have said, to follow the fact requires a precise, subtle, active mind because the fact is never still.

I do not know if you have ever looked at envy as a fact and followed it. All our religious sanctions are based on envy, from the archbishop down to the lowest clergyman; and all our social morality, our relationships, are based on acquisitiveness and comparison, which is again envy. And to follow that right through in all its movements in all our daily activities requires a very alert mind. It is very easy, is it not, to suppress it, to say, "I see I must not be envious," or "As I am caught up in this rotten society, I must accept it." But to follow its movement, to follow every curve, line, its nuances, its subtlety—that very process of following the fact makes the mind sensitive, subtle.

Now, if one does that, if one follows the fact without trying to alter it, then there is no contradiction between 'the fact' and 'what should be', and therefore no effort. I do not know if you really see this—that if the mind is following the fact, then it is not caught up in trying to alter the fact, trying to make it different. This, again, is a psychological truth. And this following of the fact needs to be done all the time, night and day, even in sleep. Because the activity of the mind when the body is asleep is much more deliberate, purposive, and those activities are discovered by the conscious mind through symbols, hints, dreams.

But if the mind is alert throughout the day, all the time watching every word, every gesture, every movement of thought, then there is no dreaming; then the mind can go beyond its own consciousness. We will not go further into that at the moment because what we want to bring out is the necessity of a sensitive mind. If one would find out about truth, God, or whatever name you like to give it, it is absolutely necessary to have a good mind—not in the sense of being clever, intellectual, argumentative, but a mind that is capable of reasoning, of discussing, of doubting, of questioning and inquiring in order to find out. A mind that has frontiers, that is conditioned, is not sensitive; a nationalist, a believer, obviously has not a sensitive mind because his belief, his nationalism, limits his mind. So in following the fact, the mind is made sensitive. The fact makes the mind sensitive; you do not have to make the mind sensitive.

If that is somewhat clear, then what is the nature of the beauty which such a mind discovers? Beauty, for most of us, is in the things that we see objectively—a building, a picture, a tree, a poem, a flowing river, a mountain, the smile on a lovely face, the child in the street. And for us also there is the denial of beauty, the reaction to it, which is to say, "That is ugly." But a mind that is sensitive is sensitive both to the ugly and to the beautiful, and therefore there is no pursuit of that which it calls beautiful and no avoidance of the ugly. And with such a mind we discover that there is a beauty which is quite different from the valuations of the limited mind. You know, beauty demands simplicity, and the very simple mind which sees facts as they are is a very beautiful mind. But one cannot be simple if there is no abandonment, and there is no abandonment if there is no austerity. I do not mean the austerity of the loincloth, the beard, the monk, the one-meal-a-day, but the austerity of a mind that sees itself as it is and pursues what it sees endlessly. And the pursuit of that is abandonment because there is no anchorage to which the mind can cling. It must completely abandon itself to see *what is*.

So the perception of beauty demands the passion of austerity. I am using the words *passion* and *austerity* deliberately. I have explained austerity, and passion you must have to see beauty, obviously. There must be an intensity and there must be a sharpness. A mind that is dull cannot be austere, it cannot be simple, and therefore it has no passion. It is in the flame of passion that you perceive beauty and can live with beauty.

Perhaps to you these are all words to be remembered, conjured up, to be felt later. There is no "later"; there is no "in the meantime." It must take place now, as we are discussing, communing with each other. And this perception of beauty is not only in things—in vases, statues, and the heavens—but also one begins to discover the beauty of meditation and the intensity, the passion, of the mind which is meditative.

Now I would like to go into meditation because meditation is necessary, and we are laying the foundations of it. For meditation, one needs a mind that is capable of being silent—not a mind that has been made silent by tricks, by discipline, by coaxing, by suppression, but a mind that is completely quiet. That is absolutely essential for a mind that is in a state of meditation. Therefore the mind must be free of all symbols and words. The mind is a slave to words, is it not? The British are slaves to the word *queen*, and the religious person is a slave to the word *God*, and so on. A mind that is cluttered up with symbols, with words, with ideas, is incapable of being silent, quiet. And a mind that is caught up in thought is incapable of being quiet. Such quietness is not stagnation, not a blank state, not a state of hypnosis, but one comes to it darkly, unexpectedly, without volition, and without desire when you understand the process of thought.

Thought, after all, is the reaction of memory, and memory is the residue of experience, and the residue of experience is the center, the self. So there is the formation of the center, the self, the 'me', which is essentially the accumulation of experience, past and present, in relation to the collective as well as to the individual. From that center, which is the residue of memory, thought springs; and that process must be understood completely, which is self-knowing. So without self-knowing, consciously as well as unconsciously, the mind can never be quiet. It can only hypnotize itself into quietness—which is too childish, too immature.

So self-knowing is immediate, it is necessary, and it is urgent because the mind, knowing itself and all its tricks, imaginings, and activities, then comes without effort, without demand, without premeditation, to that state of complete quietness. The knowing of oneself is the knowing of the whole of thought and how it divides itself as the higher self and the lower self. It is the seeing of this whole movement of experience, memory, thought, and the center—the center becoming the thought, memory, and experience; and the experience again becoming memory with the further conditioning of experience.

I hope you are following all this because if you observe yourself closely, you will see it. The center is never static. What was the center becomes the experience, and the experience becomes the center, and the center is transformed into memory. It is like cause and effect. What was the cause becomes the effect, and the effect becomes the cause. And this process is not only conscious but unconscious. The unconscious is the residue of the race, of man, whether of the East or the West; those inherited traditions, meeting the present, are transformed into another tradition. To be aware of the many layers of the unconscious and of its movement requires a mind that is extraordinarily sharp and alive, never for a moment seeking security, comfort. Because the moment you seek security, comfort, you are finished, bogged down, held. A mind that is anchored to security, to comfort, to a belief, to a pattern, to a habit cannot be swift.

So, all this is the knowing of oneself, and the knowing of oneself is the discovering of the fact and the pursuing of the fact without the urge to change the fact. And that requires attention. Attention is one thing, and concentration is quite another thing. Most people who want to meditate hope to gain concentration. Every schoolboy knows what concentration is. He wants to look out of the window, and the teacher says, "Look at your book," and there is an inward battle between the desire to look outside and the urge of fear, of competition which makes him look at the book. So concentration is a form of exclusion, is it not, and in that process, though you may become sharp, you are limiting the mind. Please follow all this without accepting or denying, but just observe it.

A mind that is merely concentrating knows distraction, but a mind that is attentive, not held in concentration, knows no distraction. Then everything is a living movement. Do please take this to your hearts, and you will see that you will throw off all the burdens of the religious edicts that have been put on you and look at life differently. Life then becomes something amazing, enormously significant—the very living, and not escaping.

You know, when you give a child a toy, all his restlessness subsides, and he becomes quiet, absorbed by the toy. And it is the same with us; we have our toys, our Masters, saviors, pictures; and the mind absorbs them and becomes quiet. But that absorption is death for the mind.

Now attention is not the opposite of concentration; it is unrelated to concentration, and therefore it is not a reaction to concentration. Attention is when your mind is aware of every movement that is taking place within itself and outside. It implies not only hearing all the noises of the buses, the cars, but also what is being said, and being aware of your reaction to what is being said, without choice, so that the mind has no frontier. When the mind is so attentive, then concentration has quite a different meaning; then the mind can concentrate, but that concentration is not an effort, not an exclusion, but part of this awareness. I do not know if you are following this.

Such attention is goodness; such attention is virtue, and in that attention there is love, and therefore, do what you will, there is no evil. Evil comes into being only when there is conflict. An attentive mind, a mind that is completely aware of itself and all the things within itself—such a mind is then capable of going beyond itself.

So meditation is not a process of knowing how to meditate, being taught to meditate—that is all totally immature; then it becomes a habit, and habit makes the mind dull. A mind caught in its own conditioning may have visions of Christ or of the Indian gods or whatever it may be, but it is still conditioned. A Christian will only see visions of Christ, and the Indian will only see his own pet gods. A meditative mind is not an imaginative mind; therefore, it has no visions.

So, when the mind, which has been floundering around within its own movements, pursues the activity of its own thoughts, is in love with its center, its movement, its experiences, then only can it follow, then only is it quiet.

Now wait for a minute. The speaker can tell you verbally what then takes place, but that is of very little importance because you have to discover it. You have to come to the state when you open the door; if another opens the door for you, or seeks to, then the other becomes your authority and you become his follower. Therefore there is death for truth. There is death for the person who says he knows, and there is death for the person who says, "Tell me." The craving to know breeds authority, so the leader and the follower are caught in the same net.

Now, the speaker is going into this not to convince you, not to entice you, not to show you, or anything of that kind, but because when you understand this, you will see what relationship time and space have.

You know, when the mind is completely without barriers, without limitation, it is full; and being full, it is empty; and being empty, it can contain time—time as space and distance; time as yesterday, today, and tomorrow. But without that emptiness, there is no time, no space, no distance. Because of that emptiness, time exists, and therefore distance and space. And when the mind discovers this, experiences this—not verbally but actually, not as a remembered thing—then that mind knows what is creation—creation, not the thing created. And then you will see that when you go round the corner, when you walk in a wood or along some filthy street, wherever it may be, you will meet the everlasting.

So the mind has journeyed into itself, into the very depths of itself, without holding back. It is not like the journey in a rocket to the moon, which is fairly easy, mechanical; but it is the journey within, the inward look which is not just a reaction to the outer. It is the same movement, the outer and the inner. And when there is this deep, inward look, inward pursuit, inward flow, inward going, then the mind is not anything apart from that which is sublime. Therefore all search, all seeking, all longing, comes to an end.

Please do not be hypnotized, influenced by what is being said. If you are influenced, you will not know for yourself what love is. Meditation is the discovery of this extraordinary thing called love.

May 23, 1961

Eleventh Talk in London

We were talking last time about meditation and beauty, and I think if we could go back into it a little, we could then go on with what I want to discuss this time.

We were saying that there is beauty, a feeling of beauty beyond the senses, a feeling not provoked by the things put together by man or by nature. It is beyond these, and if one were to pursue the inquiry into what is beauty—which is not merely subjective or objective—one would come to that same intense awareness of the feeling of beauty that one comes to through meditation. I think that meditation, the meditative mind, is absolutely essential. We went into it fairly thoroughly and saw that a meditative mind is an inquiring mind which goes through the whole process of thought and is capable of going beyond the limitations of thought.

Perhaps for some of us it is extremely difficult to meditate, and it may be that we have not thought about the matter at all. But if one has gone carefully into this question of meditation—which is not self-hypnosis or imagination or the awakening of visions and all that immature business—one comes invariably, I think, to that same feeling, to that same intensity as when the mind is capable of perceiving what is beautiful, unprovoked. And a mind that is silent, still, and in that intensity discovers a state which is not bound by time and space.

I would like to talk this time about what is the religious mind. As we have been saying from the beginning of these informal talks, we are trying to communicate with each other, we are taking a journey together. Therefore you are not listening to the speaker with prejudice, with favor, with likes or dislikes; you are listening to find out for yourself what is true. And to find out what is true, caught as one is in so much false, immature thought, hope, and despair, one must not accept anything at all of what the speaker is saying. One has to investigate, explore; and that requires a free mind—not merely the reaction of a prejudiced, opinionated mind, but a really free mind which is not anchored to any particular belief, dogma, or experience, but which is capable of following a fact very clearly and precisely. And to follow facts requires a very subtle mind. As we were saying the other day, a fact is never static, never still; it is always moving—whether it is the fact that one observes within oneself, or it is an objective fact. The observation of a fact demands a mind that is capable, precise, logical, and above all, free to pursue.

It seems to me that in this present world, with all its confusions, misery, and turmoil, the scientific mind and the religious mind are necessary. Those, surely, are the only two real states of mind—not the believing mind, not the conditioned mind, whether it is conditioned by the dogma of Christianity, Hinduism, or by any other belief or religion. After all, our problems are immense, and living has become much more complex. Outwardly, perhaps, there is more sense of security, the feeling that perhaps there will be no atomic wars because of the great fear of them. One feels that while perhaps there may be a distant war, it will not be in Europe; and so one may feel more secure, physically and inwardly. But it seems to me that a mind seeking security becomes a dull mind, a mediocre mind, and such a mind is incapable of solving its own problems.

So, living in this world—with its routine, its boredom, with its superficial middle class, upper class, or lower class existence—to solve our problems, to go beyond them, to go deeply inwardly, there are only two ways: a scientific approach or a religious approach. The religious approach includes the scientific approach, but the scientific approach does not contain within it the religious approach. But we need the scientific spirit because the scientific spirit is capable of examining ruthlessly all the causes that bring about man's misery; the scientific spirit can bring about peace in the world, objectively, can feed mankind, give it houses, clothes, and so on—not just for the English or for the Americans, but for all the world. One cannot live in prosperity at one end of the earth, and at the other end have degradation, disease, hunger, and squalor. Probably most of you do not know anything about all that, but you should. To solve all these immense problems, to break through all the stupidities of nationalism, all the political bargainings, the ambitions, the avariciousness of power, one needs the scientific spirit. But unfortunately, as one sees, the scientific spirit is mostly concerned with going up to the moon and beyond, improving our comforts, better refrigerators, better cars, and all the rest of it. That is all right so far as it goes, but it seems to me a very limited point of view.

We know what the scientific spirit is—the spirit of inquiry, of never being satisfied with what it has found, always changing, never remaining static. It is the scientific spirit which has built the industrial world, but an industrial world without an inward revolution brings about a mediocre form of living. Without an inward revolution, all the so-called glories and beauties of intellectual life only make the mind more dull, more contented, satisfied, secure. Progress in certain ways is essential, but progress also destroys freedom. I do not know if you have noticed that the more you have of things, the less free you are. And so the religious people in the East have said, "Let us put away material things; they do not matter. Let us pursue the other thing," but they have not found that either. So we know, more or less, what the scientific spirit is—the spirit that exists in the laboratory. I am not talking about the individual scientist; he is probably like you and me, bored with his daily existence, avaricious, seeking power, position, and prestige, and all the rest of it.

Now it is much more difficult to find out what is the religious spirit. How does one go about it when one wants to discover something true? We want to find out what is the true religious spirit—not the strange spirit that prevails in organized religions, but the true spirit. So, how does one set about it?

I think one begins to discover what is the true religious spirit only through negative thinking, because for me negative thinking is the highest form of thinking. I mean by negative thinking the discarding, the tearing through of false things, breaking down the things that man has put together for his own security, for his own inward safety, all the various defenses and the mechanism of thought which builds these defenses. I feel one must shatter them, go through them rapidly, swiftly, and see if there is anything beyond. And to tear through all these false things is not a reaction to what exists. Surely, to find out what is the religious spirit and to approach it negatively, one must see what one believes, why one believes, why one accepts all the innumerable conditionings which organized religions throughout the world impose on the human mind. Why do you believe in God? Why do you not believe in God? Why do you have so many dogmas, beliefs?

Now, you may say that if one goes through all these so-called positive structures behind which the mind takes shelter, goes through them without trying to find something more, then there will be nothing left, only despair. But I think one has to go through despair also. Despair only exists when there is hope—the hope of being secure, being permanently comfortable, perpetually mediocre, perpetually happy. For most of us despair is the reaction to hope. But to discover what is the religious spirit, it seems to me that inquiry must come into being without any provocation, without any reaction. If your search is only a reaction—because you want to find more inward security—then your search is merely for greater comfort, whether in a belief, an idea, or in knowledge, experience. And it seems to me that such thought, born of reaction, can only produce further reactions, and therefore there is no liberation from the process of reaction which prevents discovery. I do not know if I am making myself clear.

I feel there must be a negative approach, which means that the mind must become aware of the conditioning imposed by society with regard to morality, aware of the innumerable sanctions which religion imposes, and aware also of how, in rejecting these outward impositions, one has cultivated certain inward resistances, the conscious and unconscious beliefs which are based on experience, knowledge, and which become the guiding factors.

So, the mind which would discover what the true religious spirit is must be in a state of revolution—which means the destruction of all the false things which have been imposed on it, either by the outward pressures or by itself, for the mind is always seeking security.

So it seems to me that the religious spirit has within it this constant state of a mind which never builds, never constructs for its own safety. Because if the mind builds with the urge to be secure, then it lives behind its own walls and so is not capable of discovering if there is something new.

So death, the destruction of the old, is necessary—the destruction of tradition, the total freedom from what has been, the removal of the things that it has accumulated as memory through the centuries of many yesterdays. Then, you might say, "What remains? All that I am is this story, this history, the experiences; if all that is gone, wiped away, what remains?" First of all, is it possible to wipe all that away? We may talk about it, but is it actually possible? I say it is possible—not by influence, not by coercion; that is too silly, too immature. But I say that it can be done if one goes into it very deeply, brushing aside all authority. And that state of wiping the slate clean—which means dying every day, and from moment to moment, to the things one has accumulated—requires a great deal of energy and deep insight; and that is a part of the religious spirit.

Another part of the religious spirit is the spirit of power in which is included tenderness and love. I am trying to express it in words; please do not stay with the words. I have said that another part of the religious spirit is the power which comes through love. And by the word *power* I mean something entirely different from the urge to be powerful, the feeling of dominance, of control—the power that comes through abstinence, or the power of a sharp mind which is ambitious, greedy, envious, wanting to achieve—such power is evil. The domination of one person over another, the power of the politician, the power to influence people to think in a certain way, whether it is done by the communists, the churches, the priests, or by the press—such power, to me, is utterly evil. I mean something entirely different, not only in degree, but in quality, something totally unrelated to the power of domination. There is such a power, a something outside, not provoked by our will or by our desire. And in that power there is that extraordinary thing which is love, and that is a part of the religious spirit.

Love is not sensual; it has nothing to do with emotion; it is not the reaction to fear; it is not the love that the mother has for her child, or the husband for the wife, and all the rest of it.

Please follow this, go into it, do not accept or reject because we are taking a journey together. You may say, "Such love, such a state of mind which is not based on a recollection, a remembrance, an association, is not possible." But I think one will find it. One comes upon it darkly when one begins to investigate this whole process of thought, the ways of the mind. It is a power which has its own being in itself; it is energy without a cause. It is entirely different from the energy that is generated by the self, the 'me', in the pursuit of the things it desires. And there is such an energy, but it can only be found when the mind is free, not tethered to time and to space. That energy comes into being when thought—as experience, as knowledge, as the ego, the center, the self, the 'me' which is creating its own energy, volition, with its sorrows, miseries, and all the rest of it—is dissolved. When that center is dissipated, then there is that energy, that power which is love.

Then there is another layer of the religious mind which is a movement—a movement which is not divided as the outer and the inner. Please follow this a little. We know the outward movement, the objective movements; and from that there is a reaction to it, which we call the inward movement, a going away from the outer, a renouncing of it, or else accepting the outer as inevitable and resisting it, and cultivating as a reaction an inward movement, with its beliefs, its experiences, and so on. There is the outward movement, the going outwards, being ambitious, aggressive, and so on; and when that fails, there is a turning inward. We never seek truth when the mind is happy. When the mind is pleased, delighted, it is in itself so lively that it does not want to even whisper the name of God. It is only when we are miserable, when outward things have failed, when you are no longer successful, when you have trouble in the family, when there is death, conflict, and so on, that you turn to the inward, as old people do. We never turn to religion when we are young because all our glands are working at top speed. We are satisfied with sex, position, prestige, money, fame, and all the rest of it. When those things begin to fail us, then we turn inward; or if we are still young, we become beatniks. All that is a reaction, and revolution is not a reaction.

Now, if one sees the truth of all that very clearly, then there is a movement which is both the outer and the inner; there is no division. It is a movement: a movement of seeing the outward things precisely, clearly, objectively as they are, and that same movement going within—not as a reaction, but like the tide that goes out and the tide that comes in being the same water. The going out is keeping the eyes, the senses—everything—open, alive. And the going within is the closing of the eyes—I am using that as a way of telling you; you do not have to keep your eyes closed. The going within is the inward look. Having understood the outer, the eyes turn inward, but not as a reaction. And the inward look, the inward understanding is complete quietness, stillness, because there is nothing more to seek, nothing more to understand.

I do not like to have to use the word *inward*, but I hope we have understood. It is this inward state that is creation. It has nothing to do with the power that man has to invent, to produce things, and so on. It is the state of creation. This state of creation comes into being only when the mind has understood destruction, death. And when the mind has lived in that state of energy, which is love, only then is there that state of creation.

Now, the part is never the whole. We have described the parts, but the spoke of a wheel is not the wheel, though the wheel contains the spokes. You cannot approach the whole through the part. The whole is understood only when you have the feeling of the totality of what has been said about the various parts of the religious mind. When you get the total feeling of it, then in that total feeling is included death, destruction, the sense of power through love, and creation. And this is the religious mind. But to come to that religious mind, the mind has to be precise, to think clearly, logically, never accepting the outward things or the inward things it has created for itself as knowledge, experience, opinion, and all the rest of it.

So the religious mind contains within itself the scientific mind, but the scientific mind does not contain the religious mind. The world is trying to marry the two, but it is impossible, so they will try to condition man to accept the separation. But we are talking about something entirely different. We are trying to take a journey of discovery, which means that you have to find out. To accept what is being said has no value at all; then you are back in the old routine; you are slaves to propaganda, influence, and all the rest of it.

But if you have taken the journey also, and if you are capable of discovering, then you will find that you can live in this world; then the turmoils of this world have a meaning. Because, in this total content, in this total feeling, there is order and disorder. Is that not so? Do you understand? You must destroy to create. But it is not the destruction of the communists. The disorder, if I can use that word, which exists in the religious mind is not the opposite of order. You know how we like order. The more bourgeois, limited, mediocre we are, the more we like order. Society wants order; the more rotten it is, the more orderly it wants to be. That is what the communists want—a perfectly orderly world. And the rest of us want it too; we are afraid of disorder. Please understand, I am not advocating a disorderly world; I am not using the word *disorder* in a reactionary sense at all. Creation is disorder, but that disorder, being creative, has order in it. This is difficult to convey. Do you get it?

So the religious mind is not a slave to time. Where time exists—that is, yesterday with all its memories, moving through today and so creating the future and conditioning the mind—this creative disorder is not. So the religious mind is a mind which has no future, which has no past, nor is it living in the present as an opposite to the yesterday and tomorrow because in that religious mind time is not included. I do not know if you understand.

So the mind can come to that religious state. And I am using the word *religious* to convey something totally new—not related to the religions of the world, which are all dead, dying, decaying. So the religious mind is a mind that can only live with death, with that extraordinary energy of power, of love. Do not translate it. Do not ask about loving the one or the many; that is childish. It is only the religious mind that can go within, and the going within is not in terms of time and space. The going within is limitless, endless, not to be measured by a mind that is caught in time. And the religious mind is the only mind that is going to solve our problems because it has no problems. Any problem that exists is absorbed and dissolved on the instant; therefore, it has no problems. And it is only the mind that has no problems, a really religious mind, that can solve all problems. And therefore such a mind has an intimate relationship with society, but society has no relationship with it.

So, in that sense of the word *religious,* a revolution is necessary in each one of us—a total revolution, not partial. All reaction is partial, and the revolution we are talking about is not partial; it is a total thing. And it is only such a mind that can be intimate with truth. Only such a mind can be friendly with God—or whatever name you like to give it. Only such a mind can play with reality.

Question: Does the same mind create disorder and order?

KRISHNAMURTI: I am afraid, sir, you have not taken the journey. There must be death for something new to be. Words, phrases, the intellectual formulation of questions—these have no relation to what we have been talking about. You know, when you see something very lovely, immense—the mountains, the rivers—the mind becomes silent, does it not? The beauty of what is seen sweeps from your mind all inquiry, all sentimentality, every whisper of thought; for the second, they are wiped out, because the thing seen is too great. But if the wiping away is done by something outside you, then it is a reaction; then you go back to your remembrances afterwards. But if you have actually taken the journey, then your mind is in that state when it does not ask questions, when it has no problems. Sir, a mind that is dying, dead, has problems—not a mind that is vital, living, moving like a river, intense.

Question: I think you will agree that the state of human society leaves a lot to be desired. Is it possible for a religious person to act upon that society in an effective way against all the other people who are acting differently?

KRISHNAMURTI: I was going to talk about that next time. What value has all this upon society? What is the point of the few, of one or two getting this? What is society, and what does society want? It wants position, prestige, money, sexuality; its very structure is based on acquisitiveness, competition, success. If you say something against all that, they do not want you. You cannot help it. If some of these so-called spiritual people, the priests and all the rest of them, began talking about not being ambitious, not having any wars, any violence at all, do you think they would have a following? Nobody would listen. And I am sure you will not listen to what is being said because you are going to carry on your own lives; you are going to pursue the path of ambition, frustration, and security, which is really the path of death. You will take little bits of this away to add to what you already know. What we are talking about is something entirely different, something really quite extraordinary in its beauty, its depths. But to come to it, to understand it, to live with it, requires enormous work, the work of going within, unraveling the conscious and the unconscious mind, and the world about you. Or you can see it all with one flash and wipe it away. Both require an astonishing energy.

May 25, 1961

Twelfth Talk in London

This is the last talk of this series, and we have been considering, during all the meetings we have had together, what kind of attitude or action is necessary to meet the challenge of a world which is so completely confused and destructive. There is a process of destruction, of degeneration going on everywhere, not only within society, but also within the individual. There is a wave of deterioration which always seems to be catching up on us. There are so many divisions between people, not only economically, but also racially and religiously. There is terrible suffering and squalor throughout the East, not only physically, but also emotionally, psychologically; there is tension, conflict, confusion everywhere.

Considering all this, it seems to me that a totally new mind is necessary—not a reconditioned mind, not a mind that has been brainwashed by the communists, the capitalists, the Christians, or the Hindus, but a totally new mind. And we have been considering how to bring about this new mind.

We have approached it from practically every point of view, outwardly and inwardly, and we have seen, I think, that the more we try to change the mind outwardly—through propaganda, which most religions are, or through economic or social pressure—the more the mind is conditioned, the shallower, emptier, more dull, more insensitive it becomes. It is fairly obvious, I think, to anyone who has at all observed these things, that a mind that is conditioned, consciously or unconsciously, a mind that is influenced, however subtly, is utterly incapable of dealing with the many problems that arise in modern civilization.

Most of us, I feel, are inwardly, psychologically, so petty and narrow, ridden with information and knowledge. And we have so many problems—the problems of relationship, the problems that arise in our daily lives, what to do and what not to do, what to believe and what not to believe, the everlasting search for comfort, for security, and for an escape from suffering—that when one has taken a grandstand view of them all, there seems to be very little hope. So, obviously, what is necessary, what is eminently desirable and essential is the quality of a completely new mind because now, whatever we touch brings about a new problem.

So, as we were saying at our last meeting, a religious mind is necessary. And we can see, can we not, that a religious mind is a mind that has purged itself of all beliefs, of all dogmas; it is capable of an inward awareness, a comprehension which brings about a certain stillness, quietude. And, being inwardly quiet, there is an intense awareness of everything outside itself. That is, because it has understood all the conflicts, frustrations, troubles, turmoils, suffering within itself, and is therefore still, outwardly it becomes intensely active in the sense that all the senses are vitally awake, capable of observing without any distortion, of following every fact without giving it a bias.

So the religious mind is not only capable of observing outward things clearly, logically, precisely, but through self-knowing it has become inwardly still, with a stillness that has a movement of its own. And we said that such a religious mind is therefore in a state of constant revolution. We are not talking about any form of partial revolution, not a communist, socialist, or capitalist revolution. The capitalists do not generally want a revolution anyhow, but the others do; and their kind of revolution is always partial—economic and so on. Whereas a religious mind brings about a total revolution, not only within but without; and I feel that it is the religious revolution, and no other, that can solve the many problems of human existence.

And what can such a mind do? What can you and I, as two individuals, do in this monstrous, mad world? I do not know if you have ever thought about it. What can a religious mind do?

We have explained very clearly that a religious mind is not a Christian, Hindu, or Buddhist mind, not a mind that belongs to some tawdry sect, or some society with fantastic beliefs and ideas; but a truly religious mind has inwardly perceived its own validity, the truth of its own perceptions, without distortion, and is therefore capable of logically, rationally, and sanely thinking out the problems that arise and never allowing any problem to take root. The moment a problem is allowed to take root in the mind, there is conflict; and where there is conflict, the process of deterioration is taking place, not only outwardly in the world of things, but also inwardly in the world of ideas, of feelings, of affections.

So what can the religious mind do? Probably very little. Because, the world, society, is made up of people who are ambitious, greedy, acquisitive, who are easily influenced, who want to belong to something, to believe, and who have committed themselves to certain forms of thought and patterns of action. You cannot change them except through influence, through propaganda, through offering them new forms of conditioning. Whereas the religious mind is telling them to completely denude themselves, inwardly, of everything. Because, it is only in freedom that one can find out what is true and if there is truth, God. The believing mind can never find what is true or if there is God; it is only the free mind that can discover. And to be free one must go through all the bondages which the mind has imposed upon itself and which society has created around it. That is an arduous task; it requires great penetration, outwardly and inwardly.

After all, most of us are caught in suffering. We all suffer in one way or another, physically, intellectually, or inwardly. We are tortured, and we torture ourselves. We know despair and hope and every form of fear, and in this vortex of conflict and contradictions, fulfillments and frustrations, longings, jealousies, and hatred, the mind is caught. Being caught, it suffers, and we all know what that suffering is—the suffering that death brings, the suffering of a mind that is insensitive, the suffering of a mind that is very rational, intellectual, that knows despair because it has torn everything to pieces and there is nothing left. A mind that is suffering gives birth to various types of philosophies of despair; it escapes into various avenues of hope, reassurance, comfort, into patriotism, politics, verbal argumentations, and opinions. And to a suffering mind there is always a church, an organized religion, ready, waiting to receive it and to make it even more dull by its offers of comfort.

We know all this, and the more we think about it all, the more intense the mind becomes, and there is no way out. Physically you may be able to do something about suffering—take a pill, go to a doctor, eat better food—but apparently there is no way out of it all except through escape. But escape makes the mind very dull. It may be sharp in its arguments, in its defensiveness, but the mind that is escaping is always afraid because it has to protect the thing to which it has escaped, and anything that you protect, possess, obviously breeds fear.

So suffering goes on; consciously we may be able to brush it aside, but unconsciously it is there, festering, rotting. And can one be free of it, totally, completely? I think that is the right question to ask because if we ask, "How to be free from suffering?" then the "how" creates a pattern of what to do and what not to do, which means following the avenue of escape instead of facing the whole issue, the cause and effect of suffering itself. So I would like, before we begin to discuss, to go into this question.

Suffering perverts and distorts the mind. Suffering is not the way to truth, to reality, to God, or whatever name you like to give it. We have tried to ennoble suffering, saying it is inevitable, it is necessary, it brings understanding, and all the rest of it. But the truth is that the more intensely you suffer, the more eager you are to escape, to create an illusion, to find a way out. So it seems to me that a sane, healthy mind must understand suffering, and be utterly free from it. And is it possible?

Now, how is one to understand the totality of suffering? We are not dealing merely with one type of suffering which you may be going through or I may be going through; there are, as we know, many forms of suffering. But we are talking of suffering as a whole, we are talking of the totality of something, and how does one comprehend or feel the whole? I hope I am making myself clear. Through the part, one can never feel the whole, but if one comprehends the whole, then the part can be fitted in, then the part has significance.

Now, how does one feel the whole? Do you understand what I mean? To feel, not just as an Englishman, but to feel the whole of mankind; to feel not merely the beauty of the English countryside, which is lovely, but the beauty of the whole earth; to feel love as a whole, not only for my wife and children, but the total feeling of it; to know the total feeling of beauty, not the beauty of a picture framed on the wall, or the smile on a lovely face, or a flower, a poem, but that sense of beauty which is beyond all the senses, beyond all words, beyond all expression—how does one feel it?

I do not know if you have ever asked yourself that question. Because, you see, we are so easily satisfied with a picture on the wall, with our own particular garden, with a tree we have singled out in a field. And how does one come to feel this entirety of the earth and the heavens, and the beauty of mankind? You know what I mean, the deep feeling of it?

I am going to go into it, if you will kindly follow, but let us leave it aside for the moment. We will let the question boil, simmer, go on unraveling, and we will approach it differently.

A mind that is in conflict, in battle, at war within itself, becomes dull; it is not a sensitive mind. Now, what makes the mind sensitive, not just to one or two things, but sensitive as a whole? When is it sensitive not only to beauty but to ugliness, to everything? It is only, surely, when there is no conflict—that is, when the mind is quiet within and therefore able to observe everything outwardly, with all its senses. Now what creates conflict? And there is conflict not only in the conscious, outward mind—the mind which is terribly conscious of its own reasonings, its own knowledge, its technical achievements, and so on—but also in the inward, unconscious mind which probably, if one is at all aware, is at boiling point all the time. So what creates conflict? Please do not answer because mere mental analysis or psychological investigation does not solve the problem. Verbal examination may show intellectually the causes of suffering, but we are talking of being totally free of suffering. So we must experience while we are talking, and not remain at the verbal level.

What creates conflict is obviously the pull in different directions. A man who is completely committed to something is generally insane, unbalanced; he has no conflict; he *is* that. A man who completely believes in something, without a doubt, without a question, who is completely identified with what he believes—he has no conflict, no problem. That is more or less the state of an ill mind. And most of us would like to be able to so identify ourselves, so commit ourselves to something that there is no further issue. Most of us, because we have not understood the whole process of conflict, only want to avoid conflict. But as we have pointed out, avoidance only brings further misery.

So, realizing all that, I am asking myself the question, and therefore putting it to you also: What creates conflict? And conflict implies not only the contradictory desires, the contradictory wills, fears, and hopes, but all contradiction.

Now why is there contradiction? Please, I hope you are listening, through my words, to your own minds and hearts. I hope you are using my words as a doorway through which you are looking, listening to yourselves.

One of the main causes of conflict is that there is a center, an ego, the self, which is the residue of all memory, of all experience, of all knowledge. And that center is always trying either to conform to the present or to absorb the present into itself—the present being the today, every moment of living, in which is involved challenge and response. It is forever translating whatever it meets into terms of what it has already known. What it has known are all the contents of the many thousand yesterdays, and with that residue it tries to meet the present. Therefore it modifies the present, and in the very process of modification it has changed the present, and so it creates the future. And in this process of the past, translating the present and so creating the future, the self, the 'me', the center, is caught. That is what we are.

So, the source of conflict is the experiencer and the thing which he is experiencing. Is it not so? When you say, "I love you," or "I hate you," there is always this division between you and that which you love or hate. So long as there is a division between the thinker and the thought, the experiencer and the thing experienced, the observer and the observed, there must be conflict. Division is contradiction. Now, can this division be bridged over so that what you see, you are; what you feel, you are?

Let us first be quite clear that so long as there is a division between the thinker and the thought, there must be conflict because the thinker is forever trying to do something about the thought, trying to alter it, to modify it, to control it, to dominate it, trying to become good, not to be bad, and all the rest of it. So long as there is this division, which breeds conflict, there must be this turmoil of human existence not only within but without.

Now, is there a thinker apart from thought? Am I making the question clear? Is the thinker a separate entity, something distinct, something permanent, apart from the thought? Or, is there only thought, which creates the thinker, because then it can give to that a permanency? You follow? Thought is impermanent; it is in a constant state of flux, and the mind does not like to be in a state of flux. It wants to create something permanent in which it can be secure. But, if there is no thought, there is no thinker, is there? I do not know if you have ever experimented with this, thought at all along these lines, or investigated the whole process of thinking and who is the thinker. Thought has said that the thinker is supreme, that there is the soul, the higher self, and so has given the thinker a permanent abode, but all that is still the result of thought. So, if one observes that fact, if one actually perceives that fact, then there is no center.

Please, this may be fairly simple to state verbally, but to go into it, to see it, to experience it, is very difficult. I feel that the source of conflict is this division between the thinker and thought. This division creates conflict, and a mind in conflict cannot live, in the highest sense of that word; it cannot live totally.

I do not know if you have ever noticed that when you have a very strong feeling, either of beauty or of ugliness, provoked from outside or awakened inwardly, in that immediate state of intense feeling there is, for the moment, no observer, no division. The observer comes in only when that feeling has diminished. Then the whole process of memory comes in; then we say, "I must repeat it," or "I must avoid it," and the process of conflict begins. Can we see the truth of this? And what do we mean by seeing? How do you see the person who is sitting on the platform? You not only see visually, but you also see intellectually; you are seeing that person through your memory, through your likes and dislikes, through your various forms of conditioning, and therefore you are not seeing, are you? When you really see something, you see without any of that. Is it not possible to look at a flower without naming it, without giving it a label—just to look at it? And is it not possible when you hear something lovely—not just organized music, but the note of a bird in a forest—to listen to it with all your being? And in the same way, can one not really perceive something? Because, if the mind is capable of actually perceiving, feeling, then there is only experiencing and not the experiencer; then you will find that conflict, with all its miseries, hopes, defenses, and so on, comes to an end.

When you see the whole truth of something, when you see the truth that conflict ceases only when there is no division between the observer and the observed, when you actually experience that state, without bringing all the forces of memory, all the yesterdays into it, then conflict ceases. Then you are following facts and are not caught in the division which the mind makes between the observer and the fact.

The fact is: I am stupid, weary, bound to a dull routine of daily existence. That is a fact, but I do not like it, so there is a division. I loathe what I am doing, so the mechanism of conflict is set going, with all the defenses, the escapes, and the miseries it entails. But the fact is that my life is an ugly thing, it is shallow, empty, brutish, habit-ridden.

Now, without creating this sense of division, and therefore conflict, can the mind simply follow the fact, follow all the routine, the habits, follow it without trying to alter it? That is perception in the sense that we are using that word. And you will find that the fact is never static; it is never still. It is a moving, living thing, but the mind would like to make it static, and therefore conflict arises. I love you, I want to hold on to you, to possess you, but you are a living thing; you move, you change, you have your own being; and so there is conflict, and out of that comes suffering. And can the mind see the fact and follow it? Which means, really, that the mind is very active, alive, intense outwardly, and yet quiet within. A mind that is not absolutely quiet within cannot follow a fact—it is so rapid. And it is only such a mind that is capable of this process, capable of following every fact as it presents itself all the time, without saying that the fact should be this or should be that, without creating the division, the conflict and the misery—only such a mind cuts at the root of all suffering.

Then you will see, if you have gone that far—not in space and time, but in understanding—that the mind comes to a state when it is completely alone.

You know, for most of us, to be alone is a dreadful thing. I am not now speaking of loneliness, which is a different thing. To walk alone, to be alone with somebody or with the world, to be alone with a fact. Alone in the sense of a mind that is uninfluenced, a mind that is no longer caught in yesterday, a mind that has no future, a mind that is no longer seeking, no longer afraid—alone. A thing that is pure is alone; a mind that is alone knows love because it is no longer caught in the problems of conflict, misery, and fulfillment. It is only such a mind that is a new mind, a religious mind. And perhaps it is only such a mind that can heal the wounds of this chaotic world.

Question: Would you tell us a little more of what love is?

KRISHNAMURTI: There are two things involved in this, are there not? There is the verbal definition according to the dictionary, which is not love, obviously. The word *love* is not love any more than the word *tree* is the tree. That is one thing, and in that is included all the symbols, the words, the ideas about love. The other is that you can find love only through negation, you can discover it only through negation. And to discover, the mind must first be free from the slavery to words, ideas, and symbols. That is, to discover, it must first wipe away everything it has known about love. Must you not wipe away everything of the known if you would discover the unknown? Must you not wipe away all your ideas, however lovely, all your traditions, however noble, to find out what God is, to find out if there is God? God, that immensity, must be unknowable, not measurable by the mind. So the process of measurement, comparison, and the process of recognition must be completely cut away if one would find out.

In the same way, to know, to experience, to feel what love is, the mind must be free to find out. The mind must be free to feel it, to be with it, without the division of the observer and the observed. The mind must break through the limitations of the word; it must see all the implications of the word—the sinful love and the Godly love, the love that is respectable and the love that is unholy—all the social edicts, the sanctions, and the taboos which we have put around that word. And to do that is a tremendously arduous work, is it not?—to love a communist, to love death. And love is not the opposite of hate because what is opposite is part of the opposite. To love, to understand the brutality that is going on in the world, the brutality of the rich and the powerful, to see a smile on a poor man's face as you go by on the road and to be happy with that person—you try it sometime, and you will see. To love requires a mind that is always cleansing itself of the things it has known, experienced, collected, gathered, attached itself to. So there is no description of that word; there is only the feeling of it, the wholeness of it.

Comment: In other words, in that moment one is love.

KRISHNAMURTI: I am afraid not, sir, because there is no known moment as that moment. There is no process of recognizing that you are love. Have you not ever been angry; have you not ever hated someone? At that moment, do you say, "I am that"? There is no recognizable moment, is there? You are that completely.

Comment: Christ taught us how to love in his words, "Love thy neighbor as thyself."

KRISHNAMURTI: Please, sir, I hope I can put it so that you will not misunderstand. To find out what is true, there can be no authority, no teacher, no follower. The authority of the book, the prophet, the savior, the guru, must completely, totally come to an end if one would find out how to love the neighbor. There is no teaching, and if there is a teaching and you are following it, the teaching has ceased to be. What difference is there between the dictator and the priest who is full of power and authority.

Comment: None.

KRISHNAMURTI: It is no good just answering me, sir. That was not a rhetorical question. After all, we all have authorities: the authority of the professor who knows, the authority of the doctor, the authority of the policeman, the authority of the priest, or the authority of our own experience. To see where authority is evil requires an intelligent mind, and to eschew authority is quite arduous. It means to perceive the totality of authority, the whole of it, the evilness of power, whether in the politician, in the priest, in the book, or your own authority over the wife, the husband. And when you do see it, really feel it completely, then you are no longer a follower. It is only such a mind that is capable of discovering what is true because a mind that is free can pursue the fact. To pursue the fact that you hate, you do not need authority; you need a mind that is free from fear, free from opinion, and that does not condemn. All this requires hard work. To live with something beautiful or something ugly requires intense energy. Have you noticed that the villager, the mountaineer, who lives with a magnificent mountain does not even see it; he has got used to it. But to live with something and never get used to it, one has to be so intense, to have such energy. And this energy comes when the mind is free, when there is no fear, no authority.

Question: Is the process of cleansing the mind a process of thought?

KRISHNAMURTI: Can thought ever be clean? Is not all thought unclean? Because thought is born of memory, it is already contaminated. However logical, however rational it may be, it is contaminated, it is mechanical. Therefore there is no such thing as pure thought, or "free" thought. Now to see the truth of that demands going into the whole process of memory, which is to see that memory is mechanical, based on the many yesterdays. Thought can never make the mind pure, and seeing that fact is the purification of the mind. Please do not agree or disagree. Go into it, go after it as you go after money, position, authority, and power. Put your teeth into it, and out of that comes a marvelous mind, a mind that is purged, innocent, fresh, a thing that is new, and so in a state of creation and therefore in revolution.

Question: At the moment of perception of what is, *will you tell us what happens?*

KRISHNAMURTI: I can give you a description of it, but will that help? Let us look at it. The fact is that we hate, we are jealous, envious. And you condemn it, saying, "I must not," so there is a division. Now what creates the division? First of all, the word. The word *jealousy* is in itself separative, condemnatory. The word is the invention of the mind, caught in the knowledge of centuries, and therefore made incapable of looking at the fact without the word. But when the mind does look at the fact without condemnation, which means without the word, then the feeling is not the same as the verbal description; it is not the word. Take the word *beauty.* You all seem to purr when that word is mentioned! To most of us beauty is a thing of the senses. It is again descriptive—"He is a nice looking man. What an ugly building!" There is comparison—"This is more beautiful than that." Always the word is used to describe something we feel through the senses, the manifested, as the picture, the tree, the sky, a star, a person.

Now is there beauty without the word, beyond the word, beyond the senses? If you ask the artist, he will say that without the expression, beauty is not, but is that so? To find out what beauty is, the immensity of it, the totalness of it, there must be the quickening of the senses, a going beyond the things we have labeled as beauty and ugliness. I do not know if you are following all this. Similarly to follow a fact like jealousy requires a mind that gives full attention to it. When one see the fact, in the very perception of it, in the instant you see it, the jealousy is gone, gone totally. But we do not want the total disappearance of jealousy. We have been trained to like it, to live with it, and we think that if there is no jealousy, there is no love.

So to follow a fact requires attention, watching. And what happens after? What happens as you are actually watching is much more important than the end result. You understand? The watching itself is much more significant than being free of the fact.

Question: Can there be thinking without memory?

KRISHNAMURTI: In other words, is there thought without the word? You know, it is very interesting, if you go into it. Is the speaker using thought? Thought, as the word, is necessary for communication, is it not? The speaker has to use words—English words—to communicate with you who understand English. And the words come out of memory, obviously. But what is the source, what is behind the word? Let me put it differently.

There is a drum; it gives out a tone. When the skin is tightly stretched and at the right tension, you strike it, and it gives out the right tone which you may recognize. The drum, which is empty, in right tension, is as your own mind can be. When there is right attention and you ask the right question, then it gives the right answer. The answer may be in terms of the word, the recognizable, but that which comes out of that emptiness is, surely, creation. The thing that is created out of knowledge is mechanical, but the thing which comes out of emptiness, out of the unknown, that is the state of creation.

May 28, 1961

Saanen, Switzerland, 1961

First Talk in Saanen

I think we should be very clear from the beginning why we have come here. For me these meetings are very serious, and I am using that word with a special significance. Seriousness, for most of us, implies adopting a certain line of thought, a particular way of life, following a chosen pattern of conduct; and gradually that pattern, that mode of life becomes the rule by which we live. For me, that does not constitute seriousness, and I think it would be very profitable and worthwhile if we could, each one of us, try to find out what it is that we take seriously.

Perhaps most of us, consciously or unconsciously, are seeking security in some form or another—security in property, in relationships, and in ideas. And these pursuits we take as being very serious. For me, again, that is not seriousness.

For me, the word *seriousness* implies a certain purification of the mind. I am using the word *mind* generally, not specifically, and we shall later go into the meaning of that word. A serious mind is constantly aware, and thereby purifying itself, and in it there is no search for security of any kind. It is not pursuing a particular fancy, does not belong to any particular group of thought, or to any religion, dogma, nationality, or country; and it is not concerned with the immediate problems of existence, though one has to take care of everyday events. A mind that is really serious has to be extraordinarily alive, sharp, so that it has no illusions and does not get caught in experiences that seem profitable, worthwhile, or pleasurable.

So it would be wise if we could, from the very beginning of these gatherings, be very clear for ourselves to what extent and to what depth we are serious. If our minds are sharp, intelligent, and serious, then I think we can look at the whole pattern of human existence throughout the world, and from that total comprehension come to the particular, to the individual. So let us see the totality of what is taking place in the world, not merely as information, not investigating any particular problem—one of a country or of a particular sect or society, whether democratic, communist, or liberal—but rather let us see what is actually taking place in the world. And from there, after seeing the whole, after grasping the significance of the outer events—not as information, opinion, but seeing the actual facts of what is taking place—then we can come to the individual. That is what I would like to do.

You know, opinion, judgment, and evaluation are all utterly futile in front of a fact. What you think, what opinions you have, to what religion or sect you belong, what experiences you have had—these have no meaning at all in front of a fact. The fact is far more important than your thought about the fact; it has a much greater significance than your opinion, which is based on your education, religion, particular culture, conditioning. So we are not going to deal with opinions, ideas, judgments; we are going, if we can, to see facts as they are. That requires a free mind, a mind that is capable of looking.

I wonder if you have ever thought over the question of what it means to look, to see? Is it merely a matter of visual perception, or is seeing, looking, something much more profound than mere visual seeing? For most of us, seeing implies the immediate—what is happening today and what is going to happen tomorrow—and what is going to happen tomorrow is colored by yesterday. So our looking is very narrow, very close, confined, and our capacity to look is very limited. I feel that if one wants to look, to see—beyond the hills, beyond the mountains, beyond the rivers and green fields, beyond the horizon—there must be a certain quality of freedom. It requires a very steady mind, and a mind is not steady when it is not free. And it seems to me very important that we should have this capacity of seeing, not merely what we want to see, not what is pleasurable according to our narrow, limited experiences, but seeing things as they are. To see things as they are frees the mind. It is really an extraordinary thing—to perceive directly, simply, totally.

Now, with that generality we will go on and look at all the things that are happening in the world, and you probably know much more about it because you read the newspapers, the magazines, the articles which are all produced in accordance with the prejudices of the author, the editor, the party. The printed word is very important for most of us. I do not happen to read newspapers, but I have traveled a great deal and have seen a great many people. I have been in the narrow lanes where the very poor live, and I have talked to the politicians, the very important people—at least they think they are important—and you know for yourselves what is happening. There is starvation, misery, degradation, poverty in the East. They will do anything to have a square, full meal, and therefore they want to break down the frontiers of thought, of custom, of tradition. And then there is the other extreme, places where there is immense prosperity, a prosperity that the world has never known, and places where food is abundant, clothes plentiful, houses clean, comfortable, as in this country. And one notices that these comforts breed a certain satisfaction, a mediocrity, a certain attitude of accepting things and not wanting to be disturbed.

The world is broken up into fragments, politically, religiously, economically, in thought and in philosophy. And the events in the world are fragmentary. The religions and the governments are after the minds of men; they want to control them, to shape them into technicians, soldiers, engineers, physicists, mathematicians, because then they will be useful to society. And organized religion or belief—as Catholicism or communism—is spreading. You must know all this very well. Organized belief is shaping the mind of man, whether it is the organized belief of democracy, communism, Christianity, or Islam. Do consider all this and do not say, "You are wasting your time repeating all this." I am not because I want to see first what is actually taking place, and then, if it is possible, to destroy all that within ourselves—totally destroy it. Because the outward movement, which we call the world, is the same tide that turns inward. The outward world is not different from the inward world, and without understanding the outward world, to turn inward has no meaning at all. I feel it is essential to understand the outward world, the brutality, the ruthlessness, the tremendous urge for success—how strongly one wants to belong to something, to commit oneself to certain groups of ideas, thoughts, and feelings. If we can understand all the outward events, not in detail, but grasp the totality of it by seeing it all with an eye which is not prejudiced, not afraid, not seeking security, not sheltering behind its own favorite theories, hopes, and fancies, then the inward movement has quite a different meaning. It is the inward movement which has understood the outer that I call seriousness.

So, you see, throughout the world the mind of man is being shaped and controlled—by religions, in the name of God, in the name of peace, eternal life, and so on; and also by governments, through everlasting propaganda, through economic enforcements, through the job, the bank account, education, and so on. So at the end of it you are merely a machine, though not as good a machine in some directions as the electronic computers. You are full of information—that is what our education does for us. So we are gradually becoming more and more mechanical. You are either a Swiss, an American, a Russian, an Englishman, or a German, and so on. You are all stamped for life in a pattern, and only very few escape from this horror, except into some fanciful religion or fantastic belief.

So that is life, that is the environment in which we live; there may be an occasional hope, a brief delight, but behind it all there is fear, despair, and death. And how do we meet that life? What is the mind that meets that life? Do you understand the question? Our minds accept these things as inevitable; our minds adjust themselves to that pattern, and slowly but definitely our minds deteriorate. So the real problem is how to shatter all this—not in the outward world; you cannot; the historical process is going on. You cannot stop politicians from having wars. There are probably going to be wars—I hope not, but there probably will be. Not here, perhaps, or there, but in some poor far off unfortunate country. We cannot stop it. But we can, I think, shatter within ourselves all the stupidities that society has built into us, and this destruction is creativeness. That which is creative is always destructive. I am not talking of the creation of a new pattern, a new society, a new order, a new God, or a new church. I am saying that the state of creation is destruction. It does not create a mode of conduct, a way of life. A mind that is creative has no pattern. Every moment it destroys what it has created. And it is only such a mind that can deal with the problems of the world, not the cunning mind, not the informative mind, not the mind that thinks of its own country, not the mind that functions in fragmentation.

So, what we are concerned with is the shattering of the mind so that a new thing can take place. And that is what we are going to discuss at all these meetings—how to bring about a revolution in the mind. There must be a revolution; there must be a total destruction of all the yesterdays; otherwise, we shall not be able to meet the new. And life is always new, like love. Love has no yesterday or tomorrow; it is ever new. But the mind that has tasted satiety, satisfaction, stores up that love as memory and worships it, or it puts the photograph on the piano or on the mantelpiece as the symbol of love.

So, if you are willing, if it is your intention also, we will go into the question of how to transform the dull, weary, frightened mind, the mind that is ridden with sorrow, that has known so many struggles, so many despairs, so many pleasures, the mind that has become so old and has never known what it is to be young. If you will, we will go into that. At least, I am going to go into it, whether you will or will not. The door is open and you are free to come and go. This is not a captive audience, so if you do not like it, it is better not to hear it because what you hear, if you do not want to hear, becomes your despair, your poison. So you know from the very beginning what is the intention of the speaker: that we are not going to leave one stone unturned, that all the secret recesses of the mind are to be explored, opened up, and the contents destroyed, and that out of that destruction there is to be the creation of something new, something totally different from any creation of the mind.

For this you require seriousness, earnestness. We must pursue slowly, hesitantly, but relentlessly. And perhaps at the end of it all—or at the very beginning of it because there is no beginning and no end in the destructive process—one may find that which is immeasurable, one may suddenly open the door of the eye, the window of the mind, and receive that which is unnameable. There is such a thing beyond time, beyond space, beyond measure; it cannot be described or put into words. Without discovering that, life is utterly empty, shallow, stupid, a waste of time.

So perhaps we can now discuss it a little bit, ask questions. But first we must find out what it means to discuss, what we mean by a question. A wrong question receives a wrong answer. Only a right question receives a right answer, and to ask a right question is extraordinarily difficult. To ask a right question—not of me alone, but of yourself and all of us—requires a penetrating mind, a mind that is astute, alert, aware, willing to find out. So please do not ask questions which are not relevant to what we are discussing. And in discussing, let us not discuss like schoolboys, you taking one side and I taking the other—which is all right in colleges or debating societies—but let us discuss to find out, which is the approach of the scientific mind and of the mind which is unafraid. Then such discussion becomes worthwhile; then we will proceed and discover for ourselves what is true and what is false. Therefore the authority of the speaker ceases because there is no authority in discovery. It is only the dull, lazy mind that demands authority. But a mind that wants to find out, to experience something totally, completely, has to discover, has to push through. And I hope these meetings will help each one of us to see for ourselves—not through somebody else's eyes—what is worthwhile, what is true, and what is false.

Question: Why do we find it difficult to put a right question?

KRISHNAMURTI: Do you find it difficult to put a right question? Or, do you want to put a question? Do you see the difference? We ourselves are not concerned with putting a right question, are we? It was I who stated that only a right question receives a right answer. You are concerned, surely, with putting forward a problem you have, so you are not concerned at all about a "right question." But if you want to understand your own problem, then you have to inquire into what the problem really is, and the very inquiry into what your problem actually is will bring about the right question. Do you understand? It is not that you must ask a right question. You cannot; you do not know. But if the problem is intense, if it has been studied, then you cannot help asking a right question. We generally do not study the problem, we do not look at it closely. We skim on the surface of it, and from the surface we ask a question, and the superficial question will only bring a superficial answer. And the superficial answer is all we want to know. If we are afraid, we ask, "How am I to get rid of fear?" If we have no money we ask, "How am I to get a better job, be successful?" But if you begin to investigate the whole problem of success which every human being is after, and if you go into it, find out what it means, why there is this urge, why there is this fear of not being a success—and I hope we will go into it—then in the very process of going into it, you are bound to ask the right question.

Question: What is it that is preventing us from going into a problem deeply?

KRISHNAMURTI: What is holding us back? A lot of things, are there not? Do you really want to go very deeply into the problem of fear? Do you know what it means? It means probing into every corner of the mind, tearing away every shelter, shattering every form of escape in which the mind has taken refuge. And do you want to do that, do you want to expose yourselves? Please do not so easily say yes. It means giving up so many things you are holding on to. It may mean giving up your family, your jobs, your churches, your gods, and all the rest of it. Very few people want to do that. So they ask superficial questions like how to get rid of fear, and think they have solved the problem. Or they ask if there is such a thing as God—just think of the stupidity of asking such a question! To find out if there is God, you must give up all gods, surely. You must be completely naked to find out; all the silly things that man has built up concerning God must be burned out. That means to be fearless, to wander alone, and very few people want to do that.

Comment: It is very painful to go into a problem.

KRISHNAMURTI: No, no, madame. It is difficult, but it is not painful. You see, we use a word like *painful*, and the very word prevents you from going into the problem. So first, if we would go into a problem, we must understand how the mind is a slave to words. Do please listen to this: We are slaves to words. You know, at the word *Swiss* the Swiss person is thrilled, as is the Christian at the word *Christ* and the Englishman at the word *England*. We are slaves to words, to symbols, and to ideas. And how can such a mind go into a problem? Before it can do so, it must first find out what the word means. It is not just an easy thing; it requires a mind that understands totally, that does not think in fragments.

Look, sir, the problem is simple. There is starvation in the world—probably not much of it in Switzerland or Europe, but in the East; you have no idea of the poverty, the starvation, the degradation, and the horrors of it all. The problem is not being solved because they all want to solve it according to their own pattern, the communist pattern or the democratic pattern, or according to their own national conceptions. They are approaching it in fragments, and therefore it will never be solved. It can only be solved when we approach it totally, irrespective of nationalities, party politics, and all the rest of it.

Comment: So to deal with this trouble in the world, we need order.

KRISHNAMURTI: Just a minute, sir. Do we want order in the world? Do please think it out. After all, order is what the communists offer. First create a mess, confusion, misery; and then produce order according to a certain pattern of ideas. Do you want order in your life, sir? Do think it out.

Question: What is the price we have to pay for it?

KRISHNAMURTI: That is not the problem. You can have order and pay the price through military dictatorship, through subjugating your mind, through adjusting yourself to authority, and so on. And you are paying the price when you belong to a certain group, to a certain religious society, are you not? There is Jesus, there is Mohammed, there is somebody else in India, and you follow; and there is order—you have paid the price for centuries. Now, do you want order? Do think about it and see the implications of it. Or, is it that in the very action of living, which is destructive, there is order?

Question: Fear is no doubt one of our biggest stumbling blocks and prevents progress. But we cannot tear down everything right from the start. Should we not be satisfied for the moment with halfway measures?

KRISHNAMURTI: You say that to tear down everything in order to be free of fear is too difficult for ordinary people like us, and is there not a gentler, a slower way of doing things? I am afraid not. You see, you have used the word *progress* and the word *fear.* Outward progress creates fear, does it not? The more you have—the more cars, luxuries, bathrooms, and so on—the more you are afraid of losing them. But if you are concerned with the understanding of fear, then progress does not make the mind dull and satisfied. And is there progress inwardly? For me there is not. There is only seeing immediately, and to see immediately, the mind must not be lazy. No, please do not agree with me, because it is very difficult. Just follow it. To see clearly, which is always in the immediate, the mind must no longer have the capacity to choose. To see things as they are, immediately, the mind must cease to condemn, to evaluate, to judge. That does not demand progress, it does not demand time. Sir, you do see things immediately when there is something dangerous—your response is immediate. There is no progress in it. When you love something with your whole being, the perception is immediate.

Comment: But to reach that possibility of seeing immediately. . . .

KRISHNAMURTI: Sir, you see, the word *reach* again implies time and distance. So the mind is a slave to the word reach. If the mind can free itself from the words *attain, reach, arrive,* then the seeing may be immediate.

July 25, 1961

Second Talk in Saanen

I think it is very important, especially during these discussions, to find out how to listen. Very few of us listen; we mostly hear. We hear superficially, as we hear that noise outside in the street, and that hearing enters the brain very little. What we only superficially hear, we throw off on the least provocation. But there is a different kind of listening in which the brain is alert without effort, interested, serious, wanting to find out what is true and what is false, not putting forward any opinion, any judgment and not translating or comparing what is said with what it already knows. For example, it is the latest fashion now to be interested in Zen; that is the craze. And if during these talks you try to compare what is being said with what you have read, in that process you are not listening at all, are you? You are merely comparing, and this comparison is a form of laziness. Whereas, if you listen without the intermediary of what you have learned or heard or read, then you are listening directly and responding directly without any prejudice. You are seeing the truth or the falseness of what is being said, and that is much more important than merely comparing, evaluating, judging.

So I hope you will not mind if I keep repeating that it is very difficult to learn the art of listening—it is as difficult as seeing. And both seeing and listening are necessary.

We were saying the last time that there is a great deal of chaos in the world. Outwardly there is poverty, starvation, and corruption; and inwardly also there is confusion, sorrow, and poverty of being. There is contradiction in the world. The politicians are declaring for peace and preparing for war; there is talk of the unity of man and at the same time a breaking up of it. And out of this chaos, disorder, we all want order. We have a passion for order. As we have a passion for keeping our rooms clean, orderly, so we have a passion to bring about orderliness in the world. I wonder if we have thought at all deeply about that word, what it implies. We want order inwardly, we want to be without contradiction, without a struggle, without confusion, so that there is no sense of disharmony and struggle; and so we turn to spiritual leaders to give us order, or join groups, or follow a certain set of ideas, disciplines. So we set up authorities; we want to be told what to do. We try to bring about order through conformity, imitation.

In the same way also, we want to have outward order, in politics, in the world of business. Therefore there are dictators, tyrants, totalitarian governments which promise total order, where you are not allowed to think at all. You are told what to think in the same way as you are told what to think when you belong to a church or to a group which believes in a certain set of ideas. The tyranny of the church is as brutal as the tyranny of governments. But we like it because we want order at any price. And we have order. War does bring about an extraordinary order in the state. Everybody cooperates to destroy each other.

So this obsession for order must be understood. Does the subjection of one's own confusion to authority, inward or outward, bring about order? Do you understand the question?

I am confused, I do not know what to do. My life is narrow, petty, confused, miserable; I am in a state of contradiction, and I do not know what to do. So I go to someone—a teacher, a guru, a saint, a savior—and probably some of you also come here with that attitude. So, out of your confusion you choose your leader, and when you act out of confusion, your choice only breeds further confusion. You give yourself over to authority—which means that you do not want to think at all, you do not want to find out for yourself what is true and what is false. To discover what is true and what is false is arduous work; you have to be on your toes, you have to be alert. But most of us are lazy, dull, not deeply serious; we would rather be told what to do, and so we have the saints, the saviors, the teachers for our conduct inwardly; and outwardly there are the governments, the tyrants, the generals, the politicians, the specialists. And we hope that by following them, gradually all our troubles will be over and thereby we shall have order.

Surely, the word *order* implies all that, does it not? Now, does the demand for order bring about order? Do please consider this because I want to go into it. I think authority and power of any kind are destructive. Power in any form is evil. And yet we are so eager to accept that evil because we are confused, because we do not know, we want to be told.

So I think from the very beginning of these talks we should understand that the speaker has no authority of any kind, nor are you, who are listening, followers of what is being said. We are trying to investigate, to find out, together. If you have come with the idea that you will be told what to do, you will go away empty-handed.

For me, what is important is to see that there is disorder, outwardly and inwardly, and that the demand for order is merely the demand for security, safety, certainty. And unfortunately there is no security, either outwardly or inwardly. The banks may fail, there may be war, there is death, the stock markets may collapse—anything might happen, and frightful things are happening. So the demand for order is the demand for security, safety; and that is what we all want, whether we are old or young. We do not care so much about inward security because we do not know how to set about getting it, but at least we hope we can have outward security through good banks, good governments, through a tradition which will continue indefinitely. So the mind gradually becomes satisfied, dull, safe, tradition-bound, and such a mind obviously can never find out what is true or what is false; it is incapable of meeting the tremendous challenge of existence.

I hope you are not being mesmerized by my words, but that you are listening so that you actually discover for yourselves whether there is such a thing as security or not. That is an enormous problem. To live in an outward world in which there is no security, and to live in an inward world in which there is no tradition, no yesterday or tomorrow, means that either one becomes unbalanced, totally insane, or one becomes extraordinarily alive and sane.

It is not a matter of choice. You cannot choose between security and insecurity, but one can see the fact that there is no security inwardly, psychologically. No relationship is secure, and however much you may cling to a certain doctrine, a belief, with it always goes doubt, suspicion, and therefore fear. Such an inquiry is necessary when there is a passion for order.

The opposite is not true either: that one must live in disorder, in chaos. That is only a reaction. You know that we live and act through reaction. All our actions are reactions. I do not know if you have noticed it. And if we see that order is not possible, then invariably we think that there must be the opposite—disorder, the reaction to order. But if one sees the truth that the demand for order implies all that we have just indicated, then out of that discovery of what is true, real order comes. Am I making myself clear? I will put it differently.

Peace, surely, is not the state where there is no war. Peace is something different. It is not the interval between two wars. To find out what peace is, one must be totally free of violence. To be free of violence demands a tremendous inquiry into violence. It means to actually see that in violence is implied competition, ambition, the desire for success, being tremendously efficient, disciplining yourself, and following certain ideas and ideals. Obviously, forcing the mind to conform—whether the pattern is noble or ignoble is irrelevant—implies violence.

We say that if we do not conform, there will be chaos, but such a statement is a reaction, is it not? Violence is not a superficial thing; to fathom it requires a great deal of inquiry. Anger, jealousy, hate, envy are all expressions of violence. To be free of violence is to be in peace, not to be in a state of disorder. That is why the knowing of oneself is not just a matter of casually looking into things for one morning and forgetting about it for the rest of the week. It is a very serious matter.

So, to understand order is much more important than the reaction of saying, "If there is no order, there will be chaos," as though the world we are living in were marvelous, beautiful, lovely, without chaos or misery! One has only to look at oneself to see how poor one is inwardly. We are without affection, without sympathy, without love, ugly, and so easily persuaded; and there is all this seeking of company, never being able to be alone.

So it is important to see the totality of order, not just take little bits of it which suit you. And it is very difficult to see something totally—as you see the total tree. I have talked a little bit about order, authority, and conformity; and if you can see the totality of that, then you will see that the brain, the mind, is free from this demand for order, and therefore free from following—whether it is the following of a national hero, the legend, and all that absurdity, or whether it is your particular teacher, guru, saint, and all the rest of it.

Now, what is "seeing totally"? First of all what is "seeing"? Is it only the word? Please follow this a little carefully, if you do not mind. When you say, "I see," what do you mean? Do not answer me, please, but just go with me. I am not setting myself up as your authority, and you are not my followers. I have not got any, thank God! We are together inquiring into this question of seeing because it is very important, as you will discover for yourselves.

When you say, "I see that tree," do you actually see it, or are you merely satisfied with the words "I see"? Do think about it. Let us take it slowly. Do you say, "That's an oak, a pine, an elm," whatever it may be, and pass it by? If so, it indicates that you are not seeing the tree because you are caught in the word. It is only when you understand that the word is not important and can set aside the symbol, the term, the name, that you can look. It is a very arduous thing, to look, because it means that the name, the word, with all the remembrances, the reminiscences associated with the word must be put aside. You do not look at me. You have certain ideas about me; I have a certain reputation and all that, and that is preventing you from seeing. If you can strip the mind of all that absurdity, then you can see, and that seeing is entirely different from the seeing through the word.

Now, can you look at your gods, your favorite pleasures, your feelings of nobility, of spirituality, and all that business—stripped of the word? That is very arduous, and very few people are willing really to look. Such seeing is total because it is no longer associated with the word and the memories, the feelings the word evokes. So, seeing something totally implies that there is no division, that there is no reaction to what is being seen—there is merely the seeing. And the seeing of the fact in itself brings about a series of actions which are dissociated from the word, the memory, the opinions, and ideas. This is not an intellectual feat, though it may sound to be one. Being intellectual or being emotional is rather stupid. But to see fear totally frees the mind from fear.

Now, we do not see anything totally because we are always looking at things through the brain. This does not mean that the brain should not be used; on the contrary, we must use our brain to its highest capacity. But it is the function of the brain to break up things; it has been educated to observe in parts, to learn in parts, not totally. To be aware of the world, of the earth totally, implies no sense of nationality, no traditions, no gods, no churches, no dividing up of the land and breaking up of the earth into colored maps. And seeing mankind as human beings implies no segregation as Europeans, Americans, Russians, Chinese, or Indians. But the brain refuses to see totally the earth and the man upon it because the brain has been conditioned through centuries of education, tradition, and propaganda. So the brain, with all its mechanical habits, its animal instincts, its urge to remain in safety, in security, can never see anything totally. And yet it is the brain which dominates us; it is the brain that is functioning all the time.

Please do not jump to the idea that there must be something besides the brain, that there must be a spirit in us which we must get into touch with, and all that nonsense. I am going step by step, so please follow it, if you will.

So the brain is conditioned—through habit, through propaganda, through education, through all the daily influences, the pettiness of life, and through its own everlasting chatter. And with that brain we look. That brain, when it listens to what is being said, when it looks at a tree, at a picture, when it reads a poem or listens to a concert, is always partial; it always reacts in terms of "I like" and "I dislike"—what is profitable and what is not profitable. It is the function of the brain to react; otherwise, you would be destroyed overnight. So it is the brain, with all its reactions, memories, urges, and compulsions—conscious as well as unconscious—which looks, sees, listens, and feels. But the brain, being in itself partial, in itself the product of time and space, of all education—which we have described—cannot see totally. It is always comparing, judging, evaluating. But it is the function of the brain to react and to evaluate, so to see things totally, the brain must be in abeyance, quiet. I hope I am explaining myself clearly.

So, the total seeing of something can only take place when the brain is highly sensitive, highly responsive to reason, to doubt, to questioning, and yet recognizes the limitations of reasoning, doubting, questioning, and therefore does not allow itself to interfere with what is being seen. If you really want to discover something other than the product of the brain, the brain must first go to its limit, questioning, arguing, discussing, wanting to find out and knowing its own limited, partial existence; and that very experience of knowing the limitation quietens the mind, the brain. Then there is total seeing.

When one can see the totality of order—with all the implications which we have more or less gone into—then one will see that out of that total comprehension comes a wholly different kind of order. Surely, the right order can only come when there is the destruction of the mind that demands order for its own satisfaction, security. When the brain has shattered its own creation, destroyed the soil in which it breeds all kinds of fancies, illusions, desires, wishes, then out of that destruction there is a love which creates its own order.

Comment: I think more creative activity in the classroom would help to uncondition the mind.

KRISHNAMURTI: We must understand what we mean by creativity. You see, we use the word *creative* so sloppily, so easily. A painter, a poet, an inventor, a teacher in a classroom—they all say they are creative. Do you know when you are creative, and can you use creativity in a classroom? It is like this—a painter has a moment of lucidity in which he sees, experiences, and then he puts it on the canvas. Please follow this a little. And in expressing it on the canvas, he begins to find that he has lost that moment of lucidity; and when he cannot recapture it, he goes after it through drink, through women, entertainment, amusement, hoping it will come back. And when he has abandoned all that and is walking quietly by some stream or in a lane, suddenly he has the same feeling again, which he once more expresses on the canvas. And the expression becomes a marketable thing; it is sold. And he becomes ambitious, he wants to produce, he wants to create more.

Now an ambitious man, a man who wants popularity, fame—whether in the schoolroom or in the business world or through invention or art—is he creative? Directly he wants to do something with "creativeness," directly he becomes ambitious to utilize it, help others with it, and so on; in that moment has he not destroyed all creativeness? You see, we want to put creativity, or God, or whatever it is, to use; we want to make profit out of it, and I am afraid it cannot be done. You may have a capacity, a gift in a certain direction, but do not call it creative action, creative thinking. No thinking is creative because thinking is merely a reaction. And can creation be a reaction?

Question: How can one see the totality of fear?

KRISHNAMURTI: I am afraid we cannot go into that now because we have to stop, but we shall take it up during the course of our talks. You see, what is important is to understand what is meant by "seeing totally," not just seeing one thing totally, like fear, love, hate, this or that. In wanting to see fear totally, you are wanting to get rid of fear, are you not? And the very desire to "get rid of" or "to gain" prevents the total seeing. You know, all this implies a great deal of self-knowing—knowing everything about yourself, every corner of yourself. When you look at your face in the mirror, you know it very well—every curve, every line, every angle—and in the same way one must know very deeply about oneself, not only the conscious self, but the hidden layers of the unconscious.

There is only one thing which I want to convey this morning, if I may—not ideas, not feeling, not some extraordinary "spiritual" thing, but how important it is to see totally. And to see totally implies seeing without judgment, without condemnation, without evaluation. It also implies that the brain is not reacting to what it sees, but merely observes in that state in which there is no thinker as separate from the thing observed. That is enormously difficult, so do not think you will get it by just playing with words. It means understanding the whole question of contradiction, because we are in a state of contradiction.

July 27, 1961

Third Talk in Saanen

As I said at the beginning of these discussions, I think it is very important to be serious. We are not talking here about ideas, and unfortunately most of us seem to be in communion with ideas and not with *what is.* It seems to me very important to pursue *what is,* the fact, the actual state of one's own being. To pursue the factual to the very end and discover the essence of things is, after all, seriousness. We like to discuss, to argue, and to be in contact with ideas, but it seems to me that ideas do not lead anywhere; they are very superficial, they are only symbols, and to be attached to symbols leads to a very shallow existence. It is quite an arduous task to put aside or go through the ideas and be in contact with *what is,* with the actual state of our own mind, our own heart; and for me, to penetrate into that very deeply, completely and thoroughly, constitutes seriousness. Through the process of going to the very end, there is the discovery of the essence so that one experiences the totality, and then our problems have quite a different meaning altogether.

I would like this morning to go into the question of conflict, and to go to the very end of it if we can, not merely as an idea, but to actually experience for ourselves whether the mind is capable of being completely and totally free of all conflicts. To really discover that for oneself, one cannot possibly remain at the level of ideas.

Obviously one cannot do anything about the conflict in the outside world; it is generated by a few uncontrolled people throughout the world, and we may be destroyed by them, or we may live on. Russia, America, or someone else may plunge us all into a war, and we can't do very much about it. But I think one can do something very radical about our own inward conflicts, and that is what I would like to discuss. Why within us, inside our skins, psychologically, are we in such conflicts? Is it necessary? And is it possible to live a life in which there is no conflict at all, without vegetating, going to sleep? I do not know if you have thought about it and whether it is a problem to you. For me, conflict destroys every form of sensitivity; it distorts all thought, and where there is conflict, there is no love. Conflict is essentially ambition, the worship of success. And we are in a state of conflict inwardly, not only at the superficial level, but also very deep down in our consciousness. I wonder if we are aware of it, and if we are, what do we do about it? Do we escape from it through churches, books, the radio, through amusements, entertainments, sex, and all the rest of it, including the gods we worship? Or do we know how to tackle it, how to grapple with this conflict, how to go to the very end of it and find out if the mind can be totally free from all conflict?

Conflict implies, surely, contradiction: contradiction in feeling, in thought, in behavior. Contradiction exists when one wants to do something but is forced to do the opposite. With most of us, where there is love, there is also jealousy, hate; and that also is a contradiction. In attachment there is sorrow and pain, with its contradiction, conflict. It seems to me that whatever we touch brings conflict, and that is our life from morning to night; and even when we go to sleep, our dreams are the disturbing symbols of our daily lives.

So when we consider the total state of our consciousness, we find we are in the conflict of self-contradiction, the everlasting attempt to be good, to be noble, to be this and not to be that. I wonder why it is? Is it at all necessary, and is it possible to live without this conflict?

As I said, we are going into this not ideologically but actually, which is to be aware of our state of conflict, to understand its implications, and to be in actual contact with it—not through ideas, words, but actually in touch. Is that possible? You know, one can be in contact with conflict through the idea, and actually we are more in contact with the idea of conflict than with the fact itself. And the question is whether the mind can put away the word and be in contact with the feeling. And can one discover why this conflict exists if we are not aware of the whole process of thinking—not somebody else's process of thinking, but our own?

Surely, there is a division between the thinker and the thought, with the thinker everlastingly trying to control, to shape thought. We know this is happening, and as long as this division exists, there must be conflict. So long as there is an experiencer and the experience, as two different states, there must be conflict. And conflict destroys sensitivity, it destroys passion, intensity; and without passion, intensity, you cannot go to the very end of any feeling, any thought, any action.

To go to the very end and discover the essence of things, you need passion, intensity, a highly sensitive mind—not an informed mind, a mind crammed with knowledge. You cannot be sensitive without passion, and passion, this drive to find out, is made dull by the constant battle within ourselves. Unfortunately we accept struggle and conflict as inevitable and grow daily more insensitive and dull. The extreme form of it leads to mental illness, but usually we find an escape in churches, ideas, and all kinds of superficial things. So, is it possible to live without conflict? Or, are we so deeply conditioned by society, by our own ambitions, greed, envy, and the search for success that we accept conflict as being good, as a noble thing with a purpose? It would be profitable, I think, if each one of us could find out what we actually think about conflict. Do we accept it, or are we caught in it and do not know how to get away from it, or we are satisfied with our many escapes?

It means, really, going into the whole question of self-fulfillment and the conflict of the opposites, and to see if there is any reality for the thinker, the experiencer who is everlastingly craving for more experience, more sensation, wider horizons.

Is there only thinking and no thinker, only a state of experiencing and no experiencer? The moment the experiencer comes into being through memory, there must be conflict. I think that is fairly simple if you have thought about it. It is the very root of self-contradiction. With most of us the thinker has become all-important but not the thought, the experiencer but not the state of experiencing.

This really involves the question we were discussing the other day of what we mean by seeing. Do we see life, another person, a tree through ideas, opinions, memories? Or are we directly in communion with life, the person, or the tree? I think we see through ideas, memories, and judgments, and that therefore we never see. In the same way, do I see myself as I 'actually am', or do I see myself as what I 'should be', or what I 'have been'? In other words, is consciousness divisible? We talk very easily about the unconscious and the conscious mind and the many different layers in them both. There are such layers, such divisions, and they are in opposition with each other. Have we to go through all these layers one by one and discard them or try to understand them—which is a very tiresome and ineffectual way of dealing with the problem—or is it possible to brush all the divisions, the whole thing aside and be aware of the total consciousness?

As I was saying the other day, to be aware of something totally, there must be a perception, a seeing, which is not tinged by an idea. To see something entirely, wholly, is not possible if there is a motive, a purpose. If we are concerned with alteration, we are not seeing what actually is. If we are concerned with the idea that we must be different, that we must change what we see into something better, more beautiful, and all the rest of it, then we are not capable of seeing the totality of *what is*. Then the mind is merely concerned with change, alteration, betterment, improvement.

So can I see myself as I am, as a total consciousness, without being caught in the divisions, the layers, the opposing ideas within consciousness? I do not know if you have ever done any meditation—and I am not going to discuss it just now. But if you have, you must have observed the conflict within meditation, the will trying to control thought and the thought wandering off. That is a part of our consciousness—that urge to control, to shape, to be satisfied, to be successful, to find security; and at the same time the seeing of the absurdity, the uselessness, the futility of it all. Most of us try to develop an action, an idea, a will of resistance to act as a wall around ourselves, within which we hope to remain in a state of nonconflict.

Now, is it possible to see the totality of all this conflict and to be in contact with that totality? This does not mean being in contact with the idea of the totality of conflict or identifying yourselves with the words I am using, but it means being in contact with the fact of the totality of human existence, with all its conflicts of sorrow, misery, aspiration, and struggle. It means to face the fact, to live with it.

You know, to live with something is extraordinarily difficult. To live with these surrounding mountains, with the beauty of the trees, with the shadows, the morning light and the snow, to really live with it is quite arduous. We all accept it, do we not? Seeing it day after day, we all get dull to it, as the peasants do, and never really look at it again. But to live with it, to see it every day with freshness, clarity, with sensitivity, with appreciation, with love—that requires a great deal of energy. And to live with an ugly thing without the ugly thing perverting, corroding the mind—that equally requires a great deal of energy. To live with both the beautiful and the ugly—as one has to in life—needs enormous energy; and this energy is denied, destroyed when we are in a perpetual state of conflict.

So, can the mind look at the totality of conflict, live with it without accepting or denying it, without allowing the conflict to twist our minds, but actually observing all the inward movements of our own desires which create the conflict? I think it is possible—not only possible, but when we have gone very deeply into it, when the mind is merely observing and not resisting, not denying, not choosing, it is so. Then, if one has gone as far as that, not in terms of time and space, but in actual experience of the totality of conflict, then you will discover for yourself that the mind can live much more intensely, passionately, vitally; and such a mind is essential for that immeasurable something to come into being. A mind in conflict can never find out what is true. It may everlastingly jabber about God, goodness, spirituality, and all the rest of it, but it is only the mind that has completely understood the nature of conflict and is therefore out of it which can receive the unnameable, that which cannot be measured.

Perhaps we can discuss or ask questions about all this. To ask a right question is very difficult, and in the very asking of a right question, I think we shall find the answer for ourselves. To ask the right question implies that one must be in contact with the fact, with *what is,* and not with ideas and opinions.

Question: What is the nature of creation?

KRISHNAMURTI: Sir, what is the nature of beauty? What is the nature of love? What is the nature of a mind which is not in conflict? Do you want a description of it? And if the description satisfies you, and you accept it, then you are only accepting the words, you are not actually experiencing for yourself. You see, we are so easily satisfied by explanations, by intellectual ideas, but all that process is just playing with words, and out of that arises the wrong question. Sir, don't you want to find out for yourself if it is possible to live in this world without conflict?

Comment: One feels one must take a stand against the outer world, and in the very act of opposing the world, there is conflict.

KRISHNAMURTI: I wonder if we really do anything just because we like to do it. Do you know what I mean? I love to do what I am doing—not that I get any kick out of sitting on a platform and talking to a lot of people; that is not the reason I am doing it. I am doing it because I like it, even if there were only one person or no one at all. And if it does create conflict, what of it? After all, none of us wants to be disturbed. We like to create a backwater of our own and live in it comfortably, with our ideas, our husbands, our wives, our children, and our gods. And somebody or something—life, a storm, an earthquake, a war—comes along and shakes us up. And we react, we try to build stronger walls, we create a further resistance in order not to be disturbed; and God is our last refuge, in which we hope there will be no more disturbance. If we are disturbed, and out of that disturbance there is turmoil, what is wrong with that? I am not forcing you to listen; the door is there, open. What we are trying to do in here is to understand conflict. And what is wrong with standing up against the world? After all, the world we are standing up against is the world of respectability, of innumerable false gods, churches, and ideas; we are standing up against hate, envy, greed, and all such things we have invented in order to protect ourselves. If you do that, and it creates disturbance, what is wrong about it?

Comment: I think there is no conflict if we live from moment to moment.

KRISHNAMURTI: Now, just a minute. You see how we go off into ideas? The "if we live from moment to moment" is conditional, it is an idea—which means we have never died to anything, died to pleasure, to pain, to our demands and ambitions. Can you actually die to it all?

Question: How do we know if we are facing the real fact or the idea about the fact?

KRISHNAMURTI: Now, this is a problem of yours, is it not? So how will you set about to find out? Have you ever looked at something or had a feeling without an idea? Suppose I have a feeling of anger; do I know that feeling only through the word? Do we feel through ideas? By saying I am an Indian, which is an idea, I get a certain emotion of nationality, so it is the idea that creates the emotion, is it not? Because I have been educated to think of myself as an Indian and have identified myself with a particular piece of earth, a particular color, that gives me certain sensations; and with those sensations I am satisfied. But if I were educated differently, to be just a human being, not identified with a particular race or group, my feeling would be entirely different, would it not? So for us words have certain connotations—a communist, a believer, a nonbeliever, a Christian—and through those words we have certain feelings, certain sensations. For most of us words are very important. I am trying to find out whether the mind can ever be free of the word, and when it is free, what is the state of the mind which feels? Am I making myself clear?

Look, sir, we have been talking about conflict this morning, and I want to find out, without playing with words, if the mind is capable of being free from conflict. I want to find out, to go to the very end of it, which means I must actually be in contact not with ideas but with conflict itself. Right? So I must not be sidetracked by ideas; I must feel my way into the whole of it, be in contact with the pain, the suffering, the frustration, the whole conflict, not finding excuses or justifications, but go deeply, profoundly into it. Do I do that verbally, with words? Are you meeting my point? That is why I asked this morning how we see something—through the screen of words or by actual contact? Is it possible to feel without the word? After all, a hungry man wants food; he is not satisfied with the description of food. And do you, in the same way, want to find out about conflict and go right to the end of it? Or are you satisfied with a verbal description of the state of the mind which is not in conflict? If you want to go to the very end of it, you must experience conflict, know all about it. One conflict, if you can live with it, study it, sleep with it, dream with it, eat it up, will reveal the totality of all conflicts. But that requires passion, intensity. To live on the surface and discuss leads nowhere and dissipates what little energy one has.

Question: If you go to the end of conflict for yourself, must you then just accept the conflict which is in the world?

KRISHNAMURTI: Can you divide the world so very neatly and definitely from yourself? Is the world so very different from yourself? You see, sirs, I think, if I may say so, that there is something which has not been understood by us. For me, conflict is a very destructive thing, inwardly as well as outwardly, and I want to find out if there is a way of living without being in conflict. So I do not say to myself that it is inevitable, and I do not explain to myself that as long as I am acquisitive, there must be conflict. I want to understand it, to go through it, to see if I can shatter it, to see if it is possible to live without it. I am hungry to do that, and no amount of description, explanation is going to satisfy me—which means that I have to understand this whole process of consciousness, which is the 'me', and in understanding that, I am understanding the world. The two things are not separate. My hate is the hate of the world; my jealousy, acquisitiveness, my urge for success—all this belongs also to the world. So can my mind shatter all this? If I say, "Tell me the way to shatter it," then I am merely using a method to conquer conflict, and that is not the understanding of conflict.

So I see that I must keep awake to conflict, be aware of it, watch every movement of it in my ambitions, my greed, my compulsive urges, and so on. And if I just watch them, perhaps I shall find out, but there is no guarantee. I feel I know very well what is essential if I would find out—namely, a passion, an intensity, a disregard for words and explanations so that the mind becomes very sharp, alert, observant of every form of conflict. That is the only way, surely, to go to the very end of conflict.

July 30, 1961

Fourth Talk in Saanen

We were saying the last time we met that seriousness is that urge, that intention to go to the very end of things and discover the essence; and if there is not that compulsive energy which drives one to discover what is true, then I am afraid these talks will have very little significance. It seems a pity to talk on a lovely morning like this, but I would like to go into the question of humility and learning.

By humility I do not mean, of course, that pretentious vanity which cloaks itself under the name of humility. Humility is not a virtue because anything that is cultivated, dragged out of one, disciplined, controlled, is a false thing. It is not a thing to be sown and reaped; it must come into being. And humility is not the subjugation of that desire which seeks fulfillment in success. Nor is it the religious humility of the monks, the saints, the priests, or which cultivated austerity brings about. It is something entirely different. To actually experience it, I think one has to go to the very end so that every corner of one's mind, all the dark, secret, hidden places of one's own heart and mind, are exposed to this humility, soaked in it. And if we would uncover the very essence of humility, I think we have to consider what is learning.

Do we ever learn? Is not all our learning mechanical? Learning, to us, is an additive process, is it not? The additive process forms a center, the 'me', and that center experiences, and the experience becomes memory, is memory, and that memory colors all further experience. Now, is learning an accumulative process, as knowledge is? And if there is the accumulative process of experience, knowledge, being, and becoming, is there then humility? If the mind is crammed full with knowledge, experience, memory, it cannot possibly receive the new. So is not the total emptying of the mind necessary for that which is timeless to come into being? And does that not mean the total, complete sense of humility, a state when the mind is not becoming, not accumulating, no longer seeking or learning?

I wonder if one has learned anything? One has gathered, one has had many experiences; there have been many incidents which have left their mark and been stored up as remembrances. I can learn a new language, learn a new way of exploring the heavens, but those are all accumulative, mechanical processes which we call learning. Now, this mechanical process of learning leaves a center, does it not? And this center—which accumulates knowledge, experiences—resists, desires to be free, asserts, accepts, and discards, is always in battle, in conflict. And it is this center that is always accumulating and emptying itself; there is the positive movement of acquiring and the negative movement of denying. This process we call learning.

If you will forgive me for saying so, I am sure some of you are trying to learn something from the speaker. But you are not going to learn anything from me because you can only learn something which is mechanical, like ideas. We are not dealing with ideas; we are not dealing with the description of something else; we are concerned with the fact, with *what is*. And to understand *what is* is not a mechanical process; it is not a process of looking at something in order to gather, not a process by means of which you can add to the center or diminish it. It is from this center, accumulated through the centuries, conditioned by society, by religion, by experiences, by education, that we are always trying to change. Functioning from this center, we try to change our qualities, change our way of thinking, implant a new set of ideas and discard the old. So this center is always trying to reform itself or to destroy itself in order to get something more, and that is what we are doing all the time.

Do please listen to this. This center is what we call the ego, the self, or whatever name you like to give it. The name is irrelevant, but the fact is important, which is *what is*. And in this process of change, there is violence. All change implies violence, and through violence there can be nothing new. When one says, "I must control myself, I must subjugate myself"—which means conforming to a pattern—it implies violence. The saints, the leaders, the teachers, the prophets—all talk about changing and controlling. And obviously the process of the center disciplining itself to conform to a pattern implies violence. And when we talk about nonviolence, it means the same thing.

So change implies, does it not, violence within the field of time—"I am this and I am going to force myself to be that." The "that" is in the distance—the ideal, the example, the norm. In this process of trying to turn violence into peace is the whole conflict of the opposites. So when we say, "I must learn all about myself," we are still caught in the accumulative process which only strengthens the center. So, can one see, not merely verbally, intellectually, but actually experience the fact that where there is a center which demands change—in which is involved violence—there can never be peace?

So, for me, there is no learning; there is only seeing. Seeing is not accumulative; it is not a process of gathering-in or of denying. Seeing *what is* is destructive, and in destruction there is peace, not violence. Violence, revolution, or change exists in the process of accumulating, maintaining the center. But when one sees the whole of that process totally, completely, with all one's being, then the fact, that *which is*, is completely destructive, and what is destruction is creation.

So humility is the state of that mind which has discarded completely all the accumulative process and its opposite, and is from moment to moment aware of *what is*. Therefore it has no opinion, no judgment; and such a mind knows what freedom is. A mind caught in violence has no freedom, and a mind that is seeking freedom can never be free because to it, freedom is a further accumulation.

Humility implies total destruction—not of outward, social things, but complete destruction of the center, of oneself, of one's own ideas, experiences, knowledge, traditions—completely emptying the mind of everything that it has known. Therefore such a mind is no longer thinking in terms of change. It is really a marvelous thing, if one can feel that. You see, that is a part of meditation.

So, first we must thoroughly understand the process of change because that is what most of us want—to change. The world is changing very rapidly in outward things. They are going to the moon, inventing rockets and all that; values are changing; Coca-Cola has spread throughout the world; the ancient civilizations are toppling over. The rapidity of change is greater than the fact of change. All the ancient gods, the traditions, the saviors, the Masters—they are all going, or gone. A few people hold on to them, building a wall of defense around themselves, but everything is going. And the mind is not concerned with destruction, it is not concerned with creation, it is only concerned with defending itself, always seeking a further shelter, a new refuge.

So if you go very deeply and seriously into the question of humility, you are bound to question this whole process of learning—the learning at the word-level which prevents one from seeing things as they actually are. A mind that is no longer concerned with change has no fear and is therefore free. And it seems to me that a mind which has understood the thing we have been talking about—such a mind is absolutely essential. Then it is no longer trying to change itself into another pattern, no longer exposing itself to further experiences, no longer asking and demanding, because such a mind is free; therefore, it can be quiet, still; and then, perhaps that which is nameless can come into being. So humility is essential, but not of the artificial, cultivated kind. You see, one must be without capacity, without gift; one must be as nothing, inwardly. And I think that if one sees this without trying to learn how to be as nothing—which is too stupid and silly—then the seeing is the experiencing of it, and then perchance the other thing can come into being.

Can we talk about this—about this thing only—not how we are going to change the world, or what some great politician is going to do next?

Question: Is understanding a capacity?

KRISHNAMURTI: Is understanding a capacity, something to be cultivated, to be slowly nurtured? Capacity implies a process of time, and do I understand something through time, through many days? Or do I understand something, see it immediately? Do I understand that being a nationalist, identifying oneself with a particular group, sect, or belief, is actually stupid? Do I see completely the whole significance of belonging, committing oneself to something? You know, we all want to belong to a particular group, society, race or family, name; we want to commit ourselves to a form of action—communist, socialist, religious, or moral. And why is this? There are several things involved in it, are there not? We like to act "cooperatively" together. That may be all right at a certain level, but to be inwardly committed to something surely prevents one from understanding and pursuing enlightenment. Does the seeing of that take time? It takes time because I am lazy, because I have committed myself, and I am afraid that if I withdraw from commitments, it will create trouble. So I say, "I'll take time to think it over." A lazy mind prevents itself from seeing directly, clearly, actually. Surely, to see oneself being stupid does not require time. I can see it; nobody has to tell me about it. But when I want to change it, when I want to become clever, when I want to be more this and less that, then it implies time and it implies violence. But to see that I am stupid, to really see it and be completely in it not only demands understanding, but the very seeing, of itself, destroys everything that I have built in and around myself. And that is what I am afraid of.

So to see that I am stupid, narrow, petty-minded, bourgeois, mediocre, and to live with that without trying to change it, without trying to polish it and give it a new name, a new title, and all the rest of it; to watch all its movements, its pretenses, to see the stupidity of trying to become clever—all that does not require time, it does not require capacity. It requires seriousness to go to the very end of it.

You know, sirs, we do act immediately, feel immediately, see immediately when there is danger. All our instincts, our senses are fully awake, and we don't talk about time.

Comment: One seems to see the stupidity of desire and be free of it, but then it comes in again.

KRISHNAMURTI: I have never said that a free mind has no desire. After all, what is wrong with desire? The problem comes in when it creates conflict, when I want that lovely car which I cannot have. But to see the car, the beauty of its line, the color, the speed it can do, what is wrong with it? Is that desire to watch it, look at it, wrong? Desire only becomes urgent, compulsive, when I want to possess that thing. We see that to be a slave to anything, to tobacco, to drink, to a particular way of thinking implies desire, and that the effort to break away from the pattern also implies desire, and so we say we must come to a state where there is no desire. See how we shape life by our pettiness! And therefore our life becomes a mediocre affair, full of unknown fears and dark corners. But if we understand all that we have been talking about by seeing it actually, then I think desire has quite a different meaning.

Question: Is it possible to distinguish between being identified with what we see and to live with what we see?

KRISHNAMURTI: Why do we want to be identified with anything? In order to become something bigger, nobler, more worthwhile, is it not? We want to give significance to life because life has no significance for us. Why should one identify oneself with the family, the friend, an idea, a country? Why not brush all identification away and live with *what is* all the time, which is always changing, never still?

Question: If one does not identify oneself with things, then I suppose one can live outside it all?

KRISHNAMURTI: The fact is, is it not, that we live within our own narrow circle, with our petty jealousies, our vanities, our stupidities. That is our life, and we have to face that and not identify ourselves with the gods, the mountains, and so on. It is much more arduous, it demands greater intensity and intelligence to live with the thing that is, without trying to change it, than it does to live with Jesus—which is merely an escape.

Question: In discovering, there is joy and pleasure; and is not discovering learning?

KRISHNAMURTI: Do we discover our sorrow and live with it in joy and delight? One can discover the beauties of the earth and revel in them, or discover the stupidities of the politician and reject them, but to discover the whole significance of sorrow is quite a different thing, is it not? It means I have to discover the sorrow of myself and the sorrow of the world. Studying the book of sorrow, learning about it, means that you are trying to learn what to do and what not to do so that you can safeguard yourself. Do please let us talk about this; I am not an authority. I do not think you can learn about sorrow. Then learning becomes mechanical. But a mind that sees the danger of mechanical gathering ceases to learn; it observes, it sees, it perceives, which is entirely different from learning. To be with sorrow, to live with it, without accepting or justifying, to know its movement as a living thing, requires a great deal of energy and insight.

Comment: It seems to me that one of the first things is to know what the mind is made up of.

KRISHNAMURTI: What is the mind made up of? The brain, the senses, capacity, judgment, doubt, superstition, fear; there is the mind which divides itself up, which denies, which longs, which has aspirations, which seeks security, permanency; this whole consciousness which is inherited, and which has implanted upon it the present, with its education, experiences, and so on—surely all that is the mind. It is the center that is seeing, evolving, changing, struggling, suffering; it is the thinker and the thought, with the thinker always trying to control thought.

And is it possible for the mind to empty itself of all this? You cannot say yes or no. All that one can do is to find out whether it is possible or not to see the frontiers of consciousness and their limitations, whether it is necessary to have a frontier, and whether it is possible to go beyond all that.

A serious mind knows its own limitations, is aware of its own mediocrity, stupidity, anger, jealousies, ambitions; and having understood them, it remains quiet, not seeking, not wanting, not groping after anything more. Only such a mind has brought about order within itself and is therefore still, and only such a mind can perhaps receive something which is not a product of the mind.

Comment: To know oneself requires a certain effort.

KRISHNAMURTI: I wonder! Sirs, aren't you making efforts already? We are always making an effort to be something, to acquire, to do something. Does seeing require effort? I am interested in looking at that mountain and the green slope, just in looking at it, and does that require effort? It requires effort when I am not interested, when I am told I must look. And if I am not interested and not forced to look, why bother about it?

Question: How does one get the energy for all this?

KRISHNAMURTI: I said that to live with *what is* requires energy, and the question is: "How does one get energy?" Please inquire into it. You get energy when you have no conflict, when there is no contradiction in your mind, no struggle, no violence, when you are not being torn in opposite directions by innumerable desires. You dissipate that energy by worshiping success, by wanting to be something, wanting to be famous, wanting to fulfill—you know the innumerable things we do which produce contradiction. We dissipate our energy in going to the psychiatrist, to the churches, in the innumerable escapes we pursue. If there is no contradiction, if there is no fear of the gods, of the ultimate, or of your neighbor, of what another says, then you have energy, not in meager quantity, but abundantly. And you must have that energy, that passion to pursue to the very end every thought, every feeling, every hint, every intimation.

August 1, 1961

Fifth Talk in Saanen

I would like to talk over with you this morning a rather complex subject, but before I begin to do that, I think, as I have said previously, that a certain amount of seriousness is necessary. Not the seriousness of a long face or of eccentricity, but that compulsive insistence to go to the very end, yielding where it is necessary, but nevertheless continuing. I want to deal this morning with a subject which needs all your seriousness and attention; the Orient calls it meditation, and I am not at all sure that the Occident fully understands what is meant by that word. We are not representing the Occident or the Orient, but we are trying to find out what it is to meditate, because for me, that is very important. It encompasses the whole of life, not just a fragment of it. It deals with the totality of the mind, and not only a part of it. Most of us, unfortunately, cultivate the fragment and become very efficient in that fragment. To go into the whole process of unraveling and revealing the dark recesses of one's own mind, exploring without an object, not seeking an end, coming to the total comprehension of the whole mind and, perhaps, going beyond, is for me meditation.

I would like to go into it rather hesitantly because each step reveals something. And I hope that we, all of us, will not merely remain at the verbal level or the level of intellectual analysis, not merely emotionally, sentimentally gather up some tidbits, but, being somewhat serious, go to the very end of it. And it may be necessary to continue with it the next time.

We are all seeking something, not only at the physical level, but at the intellectual level and in the deeper levels of one's own consciousness. We are always seeking happiness, comfort, security, prosperity, and certain dogmas, beliefs, in which the mind can settle down and be comfortable. If you observe your own mind, your own brain, you will see that it is always seeking and never being satisfied, but always hoping somehow to be satisfied permanently, everlastingly. We are seeking physical well-being, and most of us, unfortunately, are satisfied to remain with physical comforts, a little prosperity, a little knowledge, with mediocre relationships, and so on. If we are dissatisfied, as perhaps some of us are, with physical things, then we seek psychological, inward comforts and securities, or we want greater intellectual outlets, more knowledge. And this seeking, searching, is exploited by all the religions throughout the world. The Christians, the Hindus, and the Buddhists offer their gods, their beliefs, their securities which the mind accepts, and being conditioned, thereby it seeks no further. So our seeking is canalized, exploited. If we are thoroughly miserable, dissatisfied with the world and with ourselves, with our lack of capacities, then we try to identify ourselves with something greater, something vaster. And when we find something which satisfies us for the time being, we soon find ourselves shaken out of it, only to search further.

This process of discontent, of holding on to something until we are shaken loose from it, does breed, does it not, the habit of following, the habit of creating an authority for ourselves—the authority of the churches and of the various priests, saints, sanctions, and so on, which exists throughout the world.

Now, a mind that is crippled by authority—whether it be the authority of a religion, of capacity, of experience, or of knowledge—can never be free to find out. The mind must surely be free to discover. And one of the immense problems is to free the mind from all authority. I do not mean the authority of the policeman and the law. Going on the wrong side of the road will obviously lead to accidents, and if you break the law, you will find yourself in jail. Shunning authority at that level, not paying taxes and so on, is too silly and absurd. I am talking of the authority which is self-created or imposed by society, by religion, by books, and so on because of our desire to find, to seek.

So it seems to me that one of the essential things, an absolute necessity, is for the mind to free itself from all sense of authority. It is very, very difficult because each word, each experience, each image, each symbol leaves its mark as knowledge which becomes our authority. You may shun outer authority, but each one of us has his own secret authority, the authority which says, "I know." Authority, the following of a pattern, breeds fragmentary action. One may be very good at music or at some other thing, but whatever it may be, it is still fragmentary action. And we are talking of a total action in which the fragment is included. This total action covers the whole of life—the physical, the emotional, the intellectual. It is the action which comes into being when one has gone deeply into the unconscious and uncovered all the dark secrets of one's own mind, and when the mind comes out of that cleansed. It is that total action which is meditation.

So, it requires a great deal of arduous work, an inward looking, to uncover all the bypaths and lanes of authority which we have established for ourselves throughout the centuries, and in which we are constantly wandering. It is one of the most difficult things, to be free—to forget everything that one has known, inwardly, of yesterday; to die to every experience one has had, pleasurable or painful. But only then is the mind free to live, to act totally.

To do this requires an awareness without choice, a passive awareness in which all the secret longings, urges, compulsions, wishes, and desires are revealed; where the mind does not choose but merely observes. The moment you choose, you have subtly established authority, and therefore the mind is no longer free. To be aware inwardly of every movement of thought, the implications of every word, the significance of every desire, wish, and not to deny or accept, but pursue, watch choicelessly—this does free the mind from authority. It is only when the mind is free that it can discover what is true and what is false, and not before; and this freedom is not at the end but at the beginning. Therefore, meditation is not a process of controlling, disciplining, shaping the mind by desire, by knowledge.

I hope you are following all this. Probably some of it is new to you, and you may reject it. You know, to accept or reject indicates the incapacity to follow what another is saying to the very end, and since you have taken the trouble to come all the way here, I feel it would be absurd for you just to say, "He is right" or "He is wrong." So please listen to find out not what your own mind thinks but if the speaker is saying something false or true, to see the false in the truth or the truth as the truth, factually. This is impossible if you have read some book on meditation or on psychology and are comparing what is said with what you know. Then you are off on a sideline, you are not listening. But if you listen, not with effort, but because you want to find out, then you will find there is a certain joy in listening. I feel the very act of listening to what is true is the key. You have to do nothing except actually to participate in listening—which is not to identify. In meditation there is no identification, no imagination.

So, when the mind begins to understand the whole process of its own thinking, then you will see how thought becomes authority; you will find that thought, based on memory, knowledge, experience, and the thinker who guides thought, becomes the authority. So the mind has to be aware of its own thoughts, the motives from whence they have arisen, the cause of them. And you will find, as you inquire very deeply, that the authority of thought ceases altogether.

So one must lay the right foundation upon which to build the house of meditation. Obviously, every form of envy, which is essentially comparison—you have something beautiful and I have not; you are clever and I am not; you have a gift and I have not—all this must go. The mind that is envious—envious of possessions, envious of capacity—cannot go very far, nor can a mind that is ambitious. Most of us are ambitious, and a mind that is ambitious is always wanting to be successful, wanting to fulfill, not only in this world, but inwardly. A mature mind knows no success and no failure.

So the mind must be totally free, not just casually free, in fragments, but wholly free. And that too is very arduous. It means cleansing the mind that has been educated for centuries to compete, to want to succeed.

You know, to be free of envy is not a matter of time. It is not a matter of gradually getting rid of envy, or creating the opposite and identifying yourself with that opposite, or trying to bring about an integration with the opposite, all of which implies a gradual process. If you are ambitious and establish the ideal of no ambition, then to cover the distance, to achieve the ideal, you must have time. For me, that process is utterly immature. If you see something clearly, it drops away. To see envy totally with all the implications of it—which surely is not very difficult—does not take time. If you look, if you are aware, it opens itself up rapidly, and the seeing of it is the dropping of it.

Obviously a mind that is envious, ambitious, self-centered, cannot see the fullness of beauty; it cannot know what love is. One may be married, one may have children, one may have houses and perpetuate one's name; but a mind that is envious and ambitious cannot know love. It knows sentiment, emotionalism, attachment, but attachment is not love.

And if you have gone that far, not merely intellectually or verbally, you will find there is the flame of passion. Passion is necessary. And with that flame of passion one can see the mountains and the long slopes with green trees; one can see the misery everywhere, the appalling divisions man has created in his urge for security; one can feel intensely, but not self-centeredly. So this is the foundation, and having laid the foundation, the mind is free; it can proceed, and perhaps there is no further proceeding. So unless this totality is completely established in the mind, all seeking, all meditation, all following of the word, whoever has said it, leads only to illusion, to false visions. A mind that is conditioned in Christianity may obviously have visions of Jesus, but such a mind lives in illusions based on authority, and such a mind is very limited and narrow.

So if one has gone that far, inwardly, it must be of the immediate—it is not for the day after tomorrow, or next month, but actually at this present moment. The words I am using do not express the actuality; the words are not the thing. And if you are merely following the speaker, you are not inwardly following yourself. So meditation is essential. Meditation is not sitting cross-legged, breathing in a certain way, repeating phrases or following a formula; those are all tricks, though you may get what the system offers.

But what you will get will be a fragment and so, useless. Surely, one can see at a glance the whole process of discipline, following and conformity, and drop it on the instant because one understands it completely. But the immediacy of understanding is prevented when the mind is lazy. And most of us are lazy; that is why we prefer methods, systems which tell us what to do.

There is a certain form of laziness which is very good—it is a certain passivity. To be passive is good because then you see things very clearly, sharply. But to be physically or mentally lazy makes the mind and body dull, so that it is incapable of looking, seeing.

So, having laid the foundation—which is actually denying society and the morality of society—one can see that virtue is a marvelous thing, it is a lovely thing, it is a pure thing. You cannot cultivate it, any more than you can cultivate humility. Only the vain man cultivates humility, and to make an effort to be humble is most stupid. But one comes upon humility easily, hesitantly, when the mind begins to understand itself, all the dark, unexplored corners of one's consciousness. In self-knowing you come upon humility, and such humility is the very ground, the very eyes, the very breath through which you see, tell, communicate. You cannot know yourself if you condemn, judge, evaluate; but to watch, to see *what is* without distortion, to observe as you would observe a flower without tearing it to pieces, is self-knowing. Without self-knowing, all thought leads to perversion and to delusion. So in self-knowing one begins to lay the foundation of true virtue, which is not recognizable by society or by another. The moment society or another recognizes it, you are in their pattern, and therefore your virtue is the virtue of respectability and so no longer virtue.

So self-knowing is the beginning of meditation. There is a great deal more to be said about meditation; this is only an introduction, as it were, it is only the first chapter. And the book never ends; there is no finishing, no attaining. And the marvel of all this, the beauty of it all is that when the mind—in which is included the brain, everything—has seen and emptied itself of all the discoveries it has made, when it is entirely free of the known, without any motive whatsoever, then the unknowable, that which cannot be measured, may perhaps come into being.

Comment: I don't quite understand that freedom must be at the beginning and not at the end because at the beginning there is all the past, and not freedom.

KRISHNAMURTI: You see, sir, this involves a question of time. Will you be free at the end? Will you be free after many days, many centuries? Please, this is not a question of arguing with you, or your accepting what I am saying; we have to see it. I am conditioned as a Hindu, as a Christian, as a communist, or what you will; I am shaped by society, by events, by innumerable influences. Is the unconditioning a matter of time? Do please think it over. If you say it is a matter of time, then in the meantime you are adding more and more conditioning, are you not?

Sir, look at this. Every cause is also an effect, is it not? Cause and effect are not two separate, static things, are they? What was the effect becomes the cause again; it is a chain, continually undergoing modification, being influenced, maturing, diminishing or increasing through time, and so on. You are conditioned as an Englishman, a Jew, or a Swiss, or whatever it is, and do you mean to say that it takes time to see the absurdity of it? And seeing the absurdity of it, does it take time to drop it? You see, we do not want to see the pernicious nature of it because we like it, we have been brought up on it. The flag means something to us because we derive benefit from it. If you say, "I am no longer a Swiss," or this or that, you might lose your job, society might throw you out, you might not be able to marry off your son or daughter respectably. So we cling to it all, and that is what prevents us from seeing it immediately and dropping the thing.

Look, sir. If I have been working all my life to achieve, to become famous, to be successful, do you think I am going to drop it? Do you think I am going to drop the profit of it, the prestige, the name, the position? One can drop it immediately if one really sees the absurdity of it all, the brutality, the ruthlessness of it in which there is no affection, no love, but only self-calculated action. But one does not want to see it, and therefore one invents excuses, saying, "I will do it eventually, in time, but please do not disturb me just now." That is what most of us are saying, I am afraid. Not only the gifted, but we who are ordinary, mediocre people—we are all doing this. To cut the string does not take time. What it needs is immediate perception, immediate action, as when you see a precipice, a snake.

Question: How can we see so clearly and forget every experience?

KRISHNAMURTI: Must you not have an innocent mind to see anything clearly? Obviously every experience shapes the mind, adds to the conditioning of the mind; and through all that conditioning, we try to see something new. I am not saying there is something new; that is not the point. But if the mind wishes to see if there is something totally new, something that is creation, surely it must have an innocent mind, a young, fresh mind. I am not saying that we must forget every experience; obviously, you cannot forget every experience. But one can see that the additive process of experience makes the mind mechanical, and a mechanical mind is not a creative mind.

August 3, 1961

Sixth Talk in Saanen

We have been talking a great deal about facing the fact, observing the fact without condemnation or justification, approaching it without any opinion. Especially where psychological facts are concerned, we are apt to bring in our prejudices, our desires, our urges which distort *what is* and give rise to a certain sense of guilt, of contradiction, a denial of *what is*. We have been talking also of the importance of the complete destruction of all the things which we have built up as a refuge, as a defense. Life seems much too vast, too fast for us, and our sluggish minds, our slow way of thinking, our accustomed habits, invariably create a contradiction within us, and we try to dictate terms to life. And gradually, as this contradiction and conflict continue and increase, our minds become more and more dull. So I would like this morning, if I may, to talk about the simple austerity of the mind, and suffering.

It is very difficult to think directly, to see things clearly and to pursue what we see to the very end, logically, reasonably, sanely. It is very difficult to be clear and therefore simple. I do not mean the simplicity of the outward garments, of having few possessions, but I mean an inward simplicity. I think simplicity of approach to a very complex problem, as to suffering, is essential. So before we approach sorrow, we have to be very clear as to what we mean by the word *simple*.

The mind, as we know it now, is so complex, so infinitely cunning, so subtle; it has had so many experiences, and it has within it all the influences of the past, the race, the residue of all time. To reduce all this vast complexity to simplicity is very difficult, but I think it has to be done; otherwise, we shall not be able to go beyond conflict and sorrow.

So the question is: Given all this complexity of knowledge, of experiences, of memory, is it at all possible to look at sorrow and to be free of sorrow?

First of all, I think that in finding out for oneself how to think simply and directly, definitions and explanations are really detrimental. Definition in words does not make the mind simple, and explanations do not bring about clarity of perception. So it seems to me that one must be greatly aware of the slavery to words, though one has also to be aware that it is necessary to use words for communication. But what is communicated is not merely the word; the communication is beyond the word; it is a feeling, a seeing, which cannot be put into words. A really simple mind does not mean an ignorant mind. A simple mind is a mind which is free to follow all the subtleties, the nuances, the movements of a given fact. And to do that the mind must, surely, be free from the slavery of words. Such freedom brings about an austerity of simplicity. When there is that simplicity of approach, then I think we can look directly and try to understand what sorrow is.

I think simplicity of mind and sorrow are related. To live in sorrow throughout our days is surely, to put it mildly, a most foolish thing to do. To live in conflict, to live in frustration, always entangled in fear, in ambition, caught in the urge to fulfill, to be a success—to live through a whole life in that state seems to me so utterly futile and unnecessary. And to be free of sorrow, I think one must approach this complex problem very simply.

There are various kinds of sorrow, physical and psychological. There is the physical pain of disease, toothache, losing a limb, having poor eyesight and so on; and the inward sorrow that comes when you lose somebody whom you love, when you have no capacity and see people who have it, when you have no talent and see people with talent, with money, position, prestige, power. There is always the urge to fulfill, and in the shadow of fulfillment there is always frustration, and with it comes sorrow.

So there are these two types of sorrow, the physical and the psychological. One may lose one's arm, and then the whole problem of sorrow comes in. The mind goes back into the past, remembers what it has done, that it is no longer able to play tennis, no longer able to do many things; it compares, and in that process sorrow is engendered. We are familiar with that type of thing. The fact is that I have lost my arm, and no amount of theorizing, of explanations, of comparison, no amount of self-pity will bring that arm back. But the mind indulges in self-pity, in going back to the past. So the fact of the present is in contradiction with what has been. This comparison invariably brings conflict, and out of that conflict there is sorrow. That is one kind of sorrow.

Then there is the psychological suffering. My brother, my son, is dead, he has gone. No amount of theorizing, explaining, believing, hoping will ever bring him back. The ruthless, uncompromising reality is the fact that he has gone. And the other fact is that I am lonely because he has gone. We were friends, we talked together, laughed together, enjoyed together, and the companionship is over, and I am left alone. The loneliness is a fact, and the death is a fact. I am forced to accept the fact of his death, but I do not accept the fact of being lonely in this world. So I begin to invent theories, hopes, explanations as an escape from the fact, and it is the escapes that bring about sorrow, not the fact that I am lonely, not the fact that my brother is dead. The fact can never bring sorrow, and I think that is very important to understand if the mind is to be really, totally, completely free from sorrow. I think it is possible to be free from sorrow only when the mind no longer seeks explanations and escapes, but faces the fact. I do not know whether you have ever tried this.

We know what death is and the extraordinary fear which it evokes. It is a fact that we will die, each one of us, whether we like it or not. So either we rationalize death or escape into beliefs—karma, reincarnation, resurrection, and so on—and therefore we sustain fear and escape from the fact. And the question is whether the mind is really concerned to go to the very end and discover if it is possible to be totally and completely free of sorrow, not in time, but in the present, now.

Now, can each one of us intelligently, sanely, face the fact? Can I face the fact that my son, my brother, my sister, my husband or wife, whoever it is, is dead, and I am lonely, without escaping from that loneliness into explanations, cunning beliefs, theories, and so on? Can I look at the fact, whatever it is: the fact that I have no talent, that I am a dull, stupid sort of person, that I am lonely, that my beliefs, my religious structures, my spiritual values are just so many defenses? Can I look at these facts and not seek ways and means of escape? Is it possible?

I think it is possible only when one is not concerned with time, with tomorrow. Our minds are lazy, and so we are always asking for time—time to get over it, time to improve. Time does not wipe away sorrow. We may forget a particular suffering, but sorrow is always there, deep down. And I think it is possible to wipe away sorrow in its entirety, not tomorrow, not in the course of time, but to see the reality in the present, and go beyond.

After all, why should we suffer? Suffering is a disease. We go to a doctor and get rid of disease. Why should we bear sorrow of any kind? Please, I am not talking rhetorically—which would be too stupid. Why should we, each one of us, have any sorrow, and is it possible to get rid of it completely?

You see, that question implies: Why should we be in conflict? Sorrow is conflict. We say that conflict is necessary, it is part of existence; in nature and in everything around us there is conflict, and to be without conflict is impossible. So we accept conflict as inevitable, within ourselves and outside in the world.

For me, conflict of any kind is not necessary. You may say, "That is a peculiar idea of your own, and it has no validity. You are alone, unmarried, and it is easy for you, but we must be in conflict with our neighbors, over our jobs; everything we touch breeds conflict."

You know, I think right education comes into this, and our education has not been right; we have been taught to think in terms of competition, in terms of comparison. I wonder if one understands, if one really sees directly, by comparing? Or does one see clearly, simply, only when comparison has ceased? Surely, one can only see clearly when the mind is no longer ambitious, trying to be or to become something—which does not mean that one must be satisfied with what one is. I think one can live without comparison, without comparing oneself with another, comparing what one is with what one should be. Facing *what is* all the time totally wipes away all comparative evaluations, and thereby, I think, one can eliminate sorrow. I think it is very important for the mind to be free from sorrow because then life has a totally different meaning.

You see, another unfortunate thing that we do is to seek comfort—not merely physical comfort, but psychological comfort. We want to take shelter in an idea, and when that idea fails, we are in despair, which again breeds sorrow. So the question is: Can the mind live, function, be without any shelter, without any refuge? Can one live from day to day, facing every fact as it arises and never seeking an escape, facing *what is* all the time, every minute of the day? Because then I think we will find that not only is there the ending of sorrow but also the mind becomes astonishingly simple and clear; it is able to perceive directly, without words, without the symbol.

I do not know if you have ever thought without words. Is there any thinking without verbalizing? Or is all thinking merely words, symbols, pictures, imagination? You see, all these things—words, symbols, ideas—are detrimental to clear seeing. I think that if one would go to the very end of sorrow to find out if it is possible to be free—not eventually, but living every day free from sorrow—one has to go very deeply into oneself and be rid of all these explanations, words, ideas, and beliefs so that the mind is really cleansed and made capable of seeing *what is.*

Question: When there is sorrow, surely it is inevitable to want to do something about it?

KRISHNAMURTI: Sir, as we were saying the other day, we want to live with pleasure, don't we? We do not seek to change pleasure; we want it to continue all day and all night, everlastingly. We don't want to alter it, we don't want even to touch it, to breathe upon it, lest it should go; we want to hold on to it, don't we? We cling to the thing that delights us, that gives us joy, pleasure, a sensation—things like going to church, going to Mass, and so on. These things give us a great deal of excitement, sensation, and we do not want to alter that feeling; it makes one feel near to the source of things, and we want that sensation, don't we? Why can we not live equally, with the same intensity, with sorrow, not wanting to do a thing about it? Have you ever tried it? Have you ever tried to live with a physical pain? Have you ever tried to live with noise?

Let us make it simple. When a dog is barking of a night and you want to go to sleep, and it keeps on barking, barking, what do you do? You resist it, do you not? You throw things at it, curse it, do whatever you can against it. But if instead you went with the noise, listened to the barking without any resistance, would there be annoyance? I don't know if you have ever tried this. You should try it sometime: not to resist. As you do not push away pleasure, can you not in the same way live with sorrow without resistance, without choice, never seeking to escape, never indulging in hope and thereby inviting despair—just live with it?

You know, to live with something means to love it. When you love someone, you want to live with that person, to be with him, don't you? In the same way one can live with sorrow, not sadistically, but seeing the whole picture of it, never trying to avoid it, but feeling the force, the intensity of it, and the utter superficiality of it also—which means that you cannot do anything about it. After all, you do not want to do anything about that which gives you intense pleasure; you do not want to alter it, you want to let it flow. In the same way, to live with sorrow means, really, to love sorrow, and that requires a great deal of energy, a great deal of understanding; it means watching all the time to see if the mind is escaping from the fact. It is terribly easy to escape; one can take a drug, take a drink, turn on the radio, pick up a book, chatter, and so on. But to live with something entirely, totally, whether it is pleasure or pain, requires a mind that is intensely alert. And when the mind is so alert, it creates its own action—or rather, the action comes from the fact, and the mind does not have to do anything about the fact.

Question: In the case of physical pain should we not go to a doctor?

KRISHNAMURTI: Surely, if I have a toothache, I go to the dentist. If you have some kind of physical ailment, should you not go to the doctor? Are we not being rather superficial when we ask such a question? We are talking not only of physical pain but also of psychological suffering, of all the mental tortures one goes through because of some idea, some belief, some person; and we are asking ourselves whether it is possible to be totally free from inward sorrow. Sir, the physical organism is a machine, and it does go out of order, and you have to do the best you can about it and get on with it, but one can see to it that the mechanical organism does not interfere with the mind, does not pervert, twist it, and that it remains healthy in spite of physical disease. And our question is whether the mind, which is the source of all enlightenment as well as of all conflict, misery, and sorrow, can be free from sorrow, uncontaminated by our physical diseases and all the rest of it.

After all, we are all growing older every day, but surely it is possible to keep the mind young, fresh, innocent, not weighed down by the tremendous burden of experience, knowledge, and misery. I feel that a young mind, an innocent mind, is absolutely necessary if one would discover what is true, if there is God, or whatever name you like to give it. An old mind, a mind that is tortured, full of suffering, can never find it. And to make sorrow into something necessary, something that will eventually lead you to heaven, is absurd. In Christianity suffering is extolled as the way to enlightenment. One must be free from suffering, from the darkness; then only the light can be.

Question: Is it possible for me to be free from sorrow when I see so much sorrow around me?

KRISHNAMURTI: What do you think about it? Go to the East, to India, to Asia, and you will see a great deal of sorrow, physical sorrow, starvation, degradation, poverty. That is one type of sorrow. Come to the modern world, and everybody is busy decorating the outward prison, enormously rich, prosperous, but they also are very poor inwardly, very empty; there also is sorrow. What can you do about it? What can you do about my sorrow? Can you help me? Do think it out, sirs.

I have talked this morning, for about half an hour, about sorrow and how to be free of it. Do I help you, actually help you in the sense that you are rid of it, do not carry it with you for another day, being totally free from sorrow? Do I help you? I do not think so. Surely you have to do all the work yourself. I am only pointing out. The signpost is of no value, in the sense that it is no use sitting there reading the signpost everlastingly. You have to face loneliness and go to the very end of it, of all that is implied in it. Can I help the sorrow of the world? We not only know our own anguish and despair, but we also see it in the faces of others. You can point out the door through which to go to be free, but most people want to be carried through the door. They worship the one who, they think, will carry them, make him a savior, a Master—which is all sheer nonsense.

Question: Of what use is a free person to another if he cannot help him?

KRISHNAMURTI: How terribly utilitarian we are, are we not? We want to use everything for our own benefit or to benefit somebody else. Of what use is a flower on the roadside? Of what use is a cloud beyond the mountains? What is the use of love? Can you use love? Has charity any use? Has humility any use? To be without ambition in a world which is full of ambition—has that any use?

To be kind, to be gentle, to be generous—these things are of no use to a man who is not generous. A free person is utterly useless to a man who is ridden with ambition. And as most of us are caught in ambition, in the desire for success, he is of very little significance. He may talk about freedom, but what we are concerned about is success. All that he can tell you is to come over to the other bank of the river and see the beauty of the sky, the loveliness of being simple—to love, to be kind, to be generous, to be without ambition. Very few people want to come to the other shore; therefore, the man who is there is of very little use. Probably you will put him in a church and worship him. That is about all.

Comment: To live with sorrow implies the prolongation of sorrow, and we shrink from the prolongation of sorrow.

KRISHNAMURTI: I did not mean that, surely. To live with something, whether ugliness or beauty, one has to be very intense. To live with these mountains day after day—if you are not alive to them, if you don't love them, if you do not see the beauty of them all the time, their changing colors and shadows—would be to become like the peasants who have become dull to it all. Beauty corrupts in the same way as ugliness does, if you are not alive to it. To live with sorrow is to live with the mountains because sorrow makes the mind dull, stupid. To live with sorrow implies watching endlessly, and that does not prolong sorrow. The moment you see the whole thing, it is gone. When something is seen totally, it is finished. When we see the whole construction of sorrow, the anatomy, the inwardness of it, not theorize about it, but actually see the fact, the totality of it, then it drops away. The rapidity, the swiftness of perception depends on the mind. But if the mind is not simple, direct, if it is cluttered up with beliefs, hopes, fears, despairs, wanting to change the fact, the *what is,* then you are prolonging sorrow.

Comment: Our preconceptions are in the way and we have to tackle them, and that may take time.

KRISHNAMURTI: Sir, to see that one is lonely and also to be aware that one wants to escape from it are both instantaneous, are they not? The fact that I am lonely and the fact that I want to escape, I can perceive immediately, can't I? I can also see instantly that any form of escape is an avoidance of the fact of loneliness, which I must understand. I cannot push it aside.

You see our difficulty is, I think, that we are so attached to the things to which we escape; they are so important to us, they have become so extraordinarily respectable. We feel that if we ceased to be respectable, God knows what would happen. Therefore our attachment to respectability becomes all-important, and not the fact that we want to understand loneliness, or any other thing, totally.

Question: If we don't have the intensity, what can we do about it?

KRISHNAMURTI: I wonder if we want that intensity? To be intense implies destruction, does it not? It means shattering everything that we have considered so important in life. So perhaps fear prevents us from being intense.

You know, we all want to be terribly respectable, do we not?—the young as well as the old. Respectability means recognition by society, and society only recognizes that which is successful, important, the famous, and ignores the rest. So we worship success and respectability. And when you do not care whether society thinks you respectable or not, when you do not seek success, do not want to become somebody, then there is intensity—which means there is no fear, which means there is no conflict, no contradiction within, and therefore you have abundant energy to pursue the fact to the very end.

August 6, 1961

Seventh Talk in Saanen

If we may, we shall continue what we were talking about the day before yesterday, which was the whole content of what is meditation. In the East meditation is a very important daily event to those people who have gone into the matter very deeply, and perhaps it is not so urgent or serious in the Occident. But as it involves the total process of life, I think we should consider what is involved in it.

As I was saying, it would be utterly futile and empty if you merely followed the words or phrases and remained merely at the verbal level. When you only intellectually follow this question, it is like following a coffin to the grave. But if you go into it very deeply, it reveals the most extraordinary things in life. As I said, we are not dealing with the first chapter of a complete book because there is no end to the whole process of living. But we have to consider the issues as they arise.

We are going into it rather more deeply and comprehensively, as you will see, but first I think it is necessary to understand what is negative and what is positive thinking. I am not using those two words *negative* and *positive* in the opposing sense. Most of us think positively, we accumulate, add; or when it is convenient, profitable, we subtract. Positive thinking is imitative, conformative, adjusting itself to the pattern of society or to what it desires; and with that positive thinking, most of us are satisfied. For me, such positive thinking leads nowhere.

Now, negative thinking is not the opposite of positive thinking; it is quite a different state, a different process, and I think one has to understand that clearly before we can go any further. Negative thinking is to denude the mind totally; negative thinking is to make the brain, which is the repository of reactions, quiet.

You must have noticed that the brain is very active, constantly reacting; the brain must react; otherwise, it dies. And in its reaction, it creates positive processes which it calls positive thinking, and these are all defensive, mechanical. If you have observed your own thinking, you will see that what I am talking about is very simple, it is not complicated.

It seems to me that the primary thing is for the brain to be fully aware, to be sensitive without reacting, and therefore I feel it is necessary to think negatively. We may be able to discuss this further later on, but if you grasp this, you will see that negative thinking implies no effort, whereas positive thinking does imply effort—effort being conflict, in which is involved achievement, suppression, denial.

Please watch your own minds in operation, your own brains at work; do not merely listen to my words. Words have no deep significance; they are used merely to convey, to communicate. If you remain at the verbal level, you cannot go very far.

So all of us—through education, through culture, through the influence of society, religion, and so on—have very active brains, but the totality of the mind is very dull. And to make the brain quiet and yet fully sensitive, active but not cultivating defenses, is quite an arduous task, as you will know if you have gone into it at all. And for the brain to be tremendously active but totally quiet involves no effort.

For most of us, effort seems to be part of our existence; apparently we cannot live without it—the effort to get up in the morning, the effort to go to school, the effort to go to the office, the effort to sustain a continued activity, the effort to love somebody. Our whole life, from the moment we are born to the moment we enter the grave is a series of efforts. Effort means conflict, and there is no effort at all if you observe things as they are, the fact as it is. But we have never observed ourselves as we are, consciously or unconsciously. We always change, substitute, transform, suppress what we see in ourselves. All that implies conflict, and a mind, a brain that is in conflict is never quiet. And to think profoundly, to go very deeply, we need not a dull brain, not a brain that goes to sleep, not a brain drugged by belief, by defenses, but a brain that is intensely active, yet quiet.

It is conflict that makes the totality of the mind dull, so if we are to go into this question of meditation, if we are to enter profoundly into life, we have from the beginning to understand conflict and effort. If you have noticed, you will know that our effort is always to achieve, to become something, to be successful; and therefore there is conflict and frustration, with its misery, hope, and despair. And that which is in conflict all the time becomes dull. Don't we know people who are continually in conflict, and how dull they are? So, to travel very far and very deeply, one has to completely understand the question of conflict and effort. Effort, conflict, comes in when there is positive thinking; when there is negative thinking, which is the highest form of thinking, then there is no effort, no conflict.

Now, all thinking is mechanical because all thinking comes as a reaction from the background of experience, of memory. And thinking, being mechanical, can never be free. It can be reasonable, sane, logical, depending on its background, its education, its conditioning, but thinking can never be free.

I do not know if you have experimented at all to find out what is thinking? I do not mean the dictionary definition of it, or the philosopher's idea about it, but whether you have observed that thinking is a reaction.

Please follow this because one has to go into it. If I ask you a familiar question, you respond immediately because you are familiar with the answer. If a slightly more complicated question is asked, there is a time lag during which the brain is in operation, looking into memory to find the answer. If a still more complicated question is asked, the time interval is longer while the brain is thinking, searching, trying to find out. And if you are asked a question with which you are not at all familiar, then you say, "I do not know." But that state of "I do not know" is one in which the brain is waiting to find the answer, either by looking through books or asking someone, but it is waiting for the answer. This whole process of thinking is, I think, quite simple to see; it is what we are all doing all the time; it is the reaction of the brain from the store of experience, of knowledge which we have gathered.

Now the state of the mind that says, "I do not know," and is waiting for an answer, is entirely different from the state of the mind, which says, "I do not know," and is not waiting for an answer. I hope you follow this because if it is not clear, I am afraid you will not be able to follow the next thing. We are still talking about meditation, and we are probing into the whole problem of the brain and the mind. If one does not understand the root of all thought, to go beyond thought is impossible.

So there are two states: There is the brain which says, "I do not know," and is looking for an answer, and there is the other state of not-knowing because there is no answer. If one keeps that clear, then we can proceed and inquire into the question of attention and concentration.

Everybody knows what concentration is. The schoolboy knows it when he wants to look out of the window and the teacher says, "Look at your book." The boy forces his mind to look at the book when he really wants to look out of the window, and so there is a conflict. Most of us are familiar with the process of forcing the brain to concentrate. And this process of concentration is an exclusive process, is it not? You cut out, you shut away anything that disturbs the concentration. Therefore, where there is concentration, there is distraction. Do you follow? Because we have been trained to concentrate, which is a process of exclusion, cutting out, therefore there is distraction, and therefore conflict.

Now, attention is not the process of concentration, and in it there is no distraction. Attention is something entirely different, and I am going into it.

Please, this is a very serious thing we are talking about, and coming here is not like going to a concert, wanting to be entertained. It requires tremendous work on your part; it means a going within without any sense of wanting or not wanting. If you cannot follow seriously, then just listen quietly, hear the words, and forget it. But if you go into it deeply, a great deal is involved. Because you will see, as I go into it a little more, that freedom is necessary. Where a mind is in conflict, making an effort, there is no freedom; and where there is concentration and a resistance to distraction, there is no freedom either. But if we understand what attention is, then we are beginning to understand also that all conflict has ceased, and therefore there is the possibility of the mind being totally free—not only the superficial mind, but also the unconscious in which the secret thoughts and desires are hidden.

Now, we know what concentration is, so what is attention? I ask that question, and the instinctive response of each one of us is to find an answer, to give an explanation, to define it; and the more clever the definition, the more satisfied one is. I am not giving a definition; we are inquiring, and we are inquiring without words, which is quite an arduous thing; we are inquiring negatively. If you are inquiring with positive thinking, then you will never find the beauty of attention. But if you have comprehended what negative thinking is—which is not thinking in terms of reaction, the brain not asking for an answer—then you will find out what attention is. I am going to go into it a little.

Attention is not concentration; in it there is no distraction; in attention there is no conflict, there is no seeking for an end; therefore, the brain is attentive, which means that it has no frontiers; it is quiet. Attention is a state of mind when all knowledge has ceased, but only inquiry exists.

Try, sometime, a simple thing. When you go out for a walk, be attentive. Then you will find that you hear, you see much more than when the brain is concentrated because attention is a state of not-knowing, and therefore inquiring. The brain is inquiring without a cause, without a motive—which is pure research, the quality of the really scientific mind. It may have knowledge, but that knowledge does not interfere with inquiry. Therefore an attentive mind can concentrate, but the concentration is not a resistance, an exclusion. Are some of you following this?

So, to go on from that, this state of attention is of a mind which is not crammed with information, knowledge, experience; it is a state of mind which lives in not-knowing. This means that the brain, the mind has completely discarded every influence, every edict, every sanction; it has understood authority, has dissolved ambition, envy, greed, and is totally opposed to society and all its morality. It no longer follows anything. Such a mind can then proceed to inquire.

Now, to inquire profoundly requires silence. If I want to look at those mountains and listen to the stream as it rushes by, not only must the brain be quiet, but the entire mind, the conscious and the unconscious, must also be entirely quiet, to look. If the brain is chattering, if the mind wants to grasp, to hold, then it is not seeing, it is not listening to the beauty of the sound of the stream. So inquiry implies freedom and silence.

You know, people have written books about how to get a quiet mind through meditation and concentration. Volumes have been written about it—not that I have read any of them. People have come to me and talked about it. To train the mind to be silent is sheer nonsense. If you train the mind to be silent, then you are in a state of decay, as every mind that conforms through fear, through greed, envy, or ambition is a dead, dull, stupid mind. A dull, stupid mind can be quiet, but it will remain small and petty, and nothing new can ever come to it.

So, a mind that is attentive is without conflict, therefore free, and such a mind is quiet, silent. I do not know if you have gone so far; if you have, you will know that what we are talking about is meditation.

In this process of self-knowing you will find that the silent mind is not a dead mind, that it is extraordinarily active. It is not the activity of achievement, not the activity which is adding and subtracting, going, coming, and becoming, because that intensely active state has come into being without any seeking, without any effort; all along it has understood everything, every phase of its being. There has been no suppression of any kind, and therefore no fear, no imitation, no conformity. And if the mind has not done all these things, there can be no silence.

Now, what happens after? So far one has used words to communicate, but the word is not the thing. The word *silence* is not silence. So please understand this: that for silence to be, the mind must be free of the word.

Now, when the mind is actually still and therefore active and free and is not concerned with communication, expression, achievement—then there is creation. That creation is not a vision. Christians have visions of Christ, and Hindus have visions of their own little gods or big gods. They are reacting according to their conditioning; they are projecting their visions, and what they see is born from their background; what they see is not the fact but is projected from their wishes, their desires, their longings, their hopes. But a mind that is attentive and silent has no visions because it has freed itself from all conditioning. Therefore such a mind knows what creation is—which is entirely different from the so-called creativity of the musician, the painter, the poet.

Then, if you have gone that far, you will see that there is a state of mind which is without time and without space, and therefore seeing or receiving that which is not measurable; and what is seen and felt and the state of experiencing are of the moment and not to be stored away.

So, that reality which is not measurable, which is unnameable, which has no word, comes into being only when the mind is completely free and silent, in a state of creation. The state of creation is not just alcoholic, stimulated; but when one has understood and gone through this self-knowing and is free from all the reactions of envy, ambition, and greed, then you will see that creation is always new and therefore always destructive. And creation can never be within the framework of society, within the framework of a limited individuality. Therefore the limited individuality seeking reality has no meaning. And when there is that creation, there is the total destruction of everything that one has gathered, and therefore there is always the new. And the new is always true, measureless.

Question: The state of total attention and desire without a motive—are they the same?

KRISHNAMURTI: Sirs, desire is a most extraordinary thing, is it not? For us, desire is racked with such torture; we know desire as conflict, and therefore we have placed such limitations on it. And our desires are so limited, so narrow, so petty, so mediocre: wanting a car, wanting to be more beautiful, wanting to achieve. Look, how petty it all is! And I wonder if there is a desire without any torture, without any hope and despair! There is. But it cannot be understood while desire breeds conflict. But when there is the total comprehension of desire, of the motives, the tortures, the self-denials, the discipline, the travail that one goes through, when all that is understood, dissolved so that it completely disappears—then perhaps desire is something else. It may be love. And love may have its expression. Love has no tomorrow, and it does not think of the past—which means that the brain does not operate on love. I do not know if you have ever watched it—how the brain interferes with love, says that it must be respectable, divides it as divine and sinful, is always shaping it, controlling it, guiding it, making it fit in with the pattern of society or of its own experience.

But there is a state of affection, of love, in which the brain does not interfere, and perhaps that love may be found. But why compare? Why say, "Is it like this or like that?"

You see, sirs, I do not know if you have ever watched a raindrop as it falls from the heavens. That one drop is of the nature of all the rivers, all the oceans, all the streams, and the water that you drink. But that one raindrop is not thinking that it will be the river. It just drops, complete, total. In the same way, when the mind has gone through all this self-knowing, it is complete. In that state there is no comparison. What is creation is not comparative, and because it is destructive, there is nothing within it of the old.

So, not verbally or intellectually, but actually, one has to go through this process of self-knowing, from now everlastingly because there is no ending to self-knowing. And having no ending, it has no beginning, and therefore it is now.

There is one other thing I would like to talk about—which is, why one wants to worship. You know we all want to worship a symbol, a Christ, a Buddha. Why? I can give you a lot of explanations: You want to identify yourselves with something greater; you want to offer yourselves to something which you think is true; you want to be in the presence of something holy, and so on. But a mind that worships is a mind that is dying, decaying. Whether you worship the hero who is going to the moon, the hero of the past or of the present, or the one sitting on the platform, it is all the same; if you worship, then that creation can never come into being, will never come near you. And a mind that does not know that extraordinary state is everlastingly suffering. So, when one has understood this problem of worship, then it dies away as the falling of a leaf in the autumn. Then the mind can proceed without any barrier.

August 8, 1961

Eighth Talk in Saanen

We were talking yesterday about the way of meditation and how, if there is freedom, the mind can go very deeply within itself. And I would like this morning, if I may, to consider several things. First fear, and then time and death. I think they are interrelated, and that without understanding the one, we cannot possibly understand the others. Without understanding the whole process of fear, we shall not be able to comprehend what time is; and in the process of understanding time, we shall be able to go into this extraordinary question of death. Death must be a very strange fact. As life is—with its abundance, with its richness, with its varieties, fullness—so must death be. Death, surely, must bring with it a newness, a freshness, an innocence. But to comprehend that vast issue, the mind must obviously be free from fear.

Each one of us has many problems, not only outward problems, but inward, and the inward problems outweigh the outer ones. If we understand the inner, go into them profoundly, then the outward problems become fairly simple and clear. But the outward problem is not different from the inward problem. It is the same movement, as the ocean tide that goes out and comes in again. And if we merely follow the outward movement and remain there, we shall not be able to comprehend the inward movement of that tide. Nor shall we understand the inward movement if we merely escape from, abandon, the comprehension of the outer. It is the same movement, which we call outer and inner.

Most of us are trained to look at the outward tide, the movement that goes outward, and in that direction the problems increase more and more. And without understanding those problems, the inward movement, the inward look, is not possible.

Unfortunately, we have both outer problems—social, economic, political, religious, and so on—and also the inward problems of what to do, how to behave, how to respond to the various challenges of life. It seems that whatever we touch, outwardly or inwardly, creates more problems, more miseries, more confusion. I think that is fairly clear for most of us who are watching, observing, living: that whatever we touch with our hands, with our minds, with our hearts, increases our problems; there is greater misery, greater confusion. And I think all our problems can be understood when we understand fear.

I am not using that word *understand* intellectually, or verbally, but I am speaking of that state of understanding which comes into being when we perceive, see the fact, not only visually, but inwardly. Seeing the fact implies a state wherein there is no justification or condemnation but merely an observing, a seeing of a thing without interpretation. For all interpretation distorts. Understanding is instantaneous when there is no justification, condemnation, or interpretation.

For most of us this is difficult because we think understanding is a matter of time, a matter of comparison, a matter of gathering more information, more knowledge. But understanding does not demand any of these. It demands only one thing, which is direct perception, direct seeing without any interpretation or comparison. So without understanding fear, our problems invariably increase.

Now, what is fear? Each one has his own series of fears. One may be afraid of the dark, afraid of public opinion, afraid of death, afraid of not making a success in life, of frustration, not being able to fulfill, having no capacity, feeling oneself inferior. At every turn of the mind there is fear; every whisper of thought, consciously or unconsciously, breeds the dreaded thing called fear.

So what is fear? And please put that question to yourself. Is it something isolated, by itself, unrelated, or is it always related to something? I hope you understand what I mean, because we are not indulging in psychoanalysis. We are trying to find out if it is possible to rid the mind totally of fear—not bit by bit, but wholly, completely. And to find that out, we must inquire into what is fear, how it comes into being; and to find that out, we must inquire into thought, not only conscious thinking, but also the unconscious, the deep layers of one's own being.

To inquire into the unconscious is not, surely, a process of analysis because when you analyze, or another analyzes, there is always the observer, the analyst who is analyzing, and therefore there is a division, a dissimilarity, and so conflict.

I want to find out how fear comes into being. I do not know if we are aware of our own fears, and how we are aware of them. Are we aware merely of a word, or are we directly in contact with the thing that causes fear? Is the thing that causes fear fragmentary? Or is it a total thing which has varying expressions of fear? I may be afraid of death; you may be afraid of your neighbor, of public opinion; another may be afraid of being dominated by the wife, the husband; but the cause must be one. There are not, surely, several different causes which produce several types of fear. And will the discovery of the cause of fear free the mind from fear? Knowing, let us say, that I am afraid of public opinion, does that rid the mind of fear? The discovery of the cause of fear is not the liberation from fear.

Do please understand this a little; we have not the time to go into it in great detail because we have a vast field to cover this morning.

Knowing the cause, or the innumerable causes that breed fear, will that empty the mind of fear? Or is some other element needed?

When inquiring into what is fear, one has not only to be aware of outward reactions, but also to be aware of the unconscious. I am using that word *unconscious* in a very simple way, not philosophically, psychologically, or analytically. The unconscious is the hidden motives, the subtle thoughts, the secret desires, compulsions, urges, demands. Now, how does one examine or observe the unconscious? It is fairly simple to observe the conscious through its reactions of likes and dislikes, pain and pleasure, but how does one inquire into the unconscious without the help of another? Because if you have the help of another, that other may be prejudiced, limited so that what he interprets he perverts. So, how is one to look into this enormous thing called the hidden mind without interpretation—to look, to absorb, to comprehend it totally, not bit by bit? Because if you examine it fragmentarily, each examination leaves its own mark, and with that mark you examine the next fragment, thereby furthering the distortion. Therefore there is no clarity through analysis. I wonder if you are getting what I am talking about?

We can see, surely, that the discovering of the cause of fear does not free the mind from fear, and that analysis does not bring freedom from it either. There must be a total understanding, a complete uncovering of the totality of the unconscious, and how does one set about it? Do you see the problem?

The unconscious cannot, surely, be looked at through the conscious mind. The conscious mind is a recent thing, recent in the sense that it has been conditioned to adjust itself to the environment; it has been newly molded through education to acquire certain techniques in order to live, to achieve a livelihood; it has cultivated memories and is therefore capable of leading a superficial life in a society which is intrinsically rotten and stupid. The conscious mind can adjust itself, and its function is to do so. And when it is not capable of adjusting itself to the environment, then there is a neurosis, a state of contradiction, and so on. But the educated, the recent mind cannot possibly inquire into the unconscious which is old, which is of the residue of time, of all the racial experiences. The unconscious is the repository of infinite knowledge of the things that have been. So, how is the conscious mind to look at it? It cannot because it is so conditioned, so limited by recent knowledge, recent incidents, experiences, lessons, ambitions, and adjustments. Such a conscious mind cannot possibly look at the unconscious, and I think that is fairly simple to understand. Please, this is not a matter of agreement or disagreement; if we start that business of "You are quite right" or "You are quite wrong," then it has no meaning; we are lost. If one sees the significance of this immediately, then there is no agreement or disagreement because one is inquiring.

Now, what is necessary if one is to look into the unconscious, to bring out all the residue, to cleanse the unconscious totally so that it does not create all the contradictions which breed conflict? How is one to proceed to inquire into the unconscious, knowing that an educated mind is not capable of looking at it, nor the analyst, whose examination is fragmentary? How is one to look at this extraordinary mind which has such vast treasures, the storehouse of experiences, racial and climatic influences, tradition, the constant impressions; how is one to bring it all out? Do you bring it out fragmentarily, or is it to be brought out totally? If you do not understand the problem, then the further inquiry has no meaning. What I am saying is that if the unconscious is to be examined fragmentarily, then there is no end to it because the very fact that you examine and interpret fragmentarily strengthens the layers of the hidden mind. It must be examined as a whole picture. Surely, love is not fragmentary; it is not to be broken up into divine and profane, or put into various categories of respectability. Love is something total, and a mind that dissects love can never know what love is. To feel, to understand love there must be no fragmentary approach to it.

So, if that is really clear—that the totality cannot be understood through fragmentation—then a change has taken place, has it not? I do not know if you are meeting my point.

Now, the unconscious mind must be approached negatively because you do not know what it is. We know what other people have said about it, and we occasionally know of it through intimations, hints. But we do not know all the twists and turns of it, the extraordinary quality of the unconscious, all the roots. Therefore, to understand something which we do not know, one must approach it negatively, with a mind that is not seeking an answer.

We talked the other day about positive thinking and negative thinking. I said that negative thinking is the highest form of thinking; and that all thinking, whether positive or negative, is limited. Positive thinking is never free, but negative thinking can be free. Therefore, the negative mind, looking at the unconscious which it does not know, is in direct relationship with it.

Please, this is not something strange, a new cult, a new way of thinking; that is all immature and infantile. But when one wants to find out for oneself about fear and to be totally rid of it, not in fragments but completely, then one must inquire into the depths of one's mind. And that inquiry is not a positive process. There is no instrument which the superficial mind can create or manufacture in order to dig. All that the superficial mind can do is to be quiet, to put aside voluntarily, easily, all its knowledge, capacities, gifts, be independent of all its techniques. When it does that, it is in a negative state. To do that, one must understand thought.

Does not thought, the totality of thought—not just one or two thoughts—breed fear? If there were no tomorrow, or the next minute, would there be fear? The dying to thought is the ending of fear. And all consciousness is thought.

We come, then, to the thing called time. What is time? Is there time? There is time by the watch, and we think there is also inward, psychological time. But is there time apart from the chronological time? It is thought which creates time because thought itself is the product of time, of many yesterdays—"I have been that; I am this, and I shall be that." To go to the moon requires time; it takes many days, many months to put the rocket together, and to acquire the knowledge of how to put the rocket together also requires time. But all that is mechanical time, time by the watch. Distance is involved in going to the moon, and distance is also within the field of time, within the field of hours, days, months. But apart from that time, is there time at all? Surely, thought has created time. There is thought—I must become more intelligent, I must find out how to compete, I must try and become successful; how am I to become respectable, to subjugate my ambitions, my anger, my brutalities? And this constant process of thinking, which is part of the mechanistic brain, does breed time. But if thought ceases, is there time? Do you follow this? If thought ceases, is there fear? I am afraid, let us say, of public opinion—what people say about me, what they think of me. That thinking about it breeds fear. If there were no thought, I wouldn't care two pins for public opinion, and therefore there would be no fear. So, I begin to discover that thought breeds fear, that thought is the result of time. And thought, which is the result of many yesterdays, modified by all the experiences of the present, creates the future—which is still thought.

So the whole content of consciousness is a process of thought; therefore, it is bound within time. I hope you are following all this.

Now, can the mind be free of time? I am not talking of being free of chronological time—that would be insane, to be mentally unbalanced. I am talking of time as achievement, as success, as being something tomorrow, as becoming or not becoming, as fulfilling and frustration, as getting over something and acquiring something else. Which means that the question is: Can thought—which is the totality of consciousness, the revealed and the unrevealed—completely die, cease to be? When it does, you have understood the totality of consciousness.

So, dying to thought—to thought that knows pleasures, to thought that suffers, to thought that knew virtue, that knew relationship, that had become and had expressed itself in various ways, always within the field of time—surely, is total death. I am not talking of the mechanical, organic death, bodily dying. The doctors may invent some drug which will make it possible for the organic existence of the body to continue for a hundred and fifty or two hundred years—God knows what for! But that is all irrelevant. What is relevant is the dying in which there is no fear.

So, can the mind die to everything it has known, which is the past—which is death? That is what we are all afraid of: death, suddenly ceasing, in which there is no argumentation. You cannot argue with death; it is the ending. And to cease means to die to thought, and therefore to time.

I do not know if you have experimented with this at all. It is fairly easy to die to suffering; everybody wants to do that. But is it not possible to die to the pleasures, the things you have cherished, the memories that give you stimulation, that give you a feeling of well-being, to die to all that which is within time? If you have gone into it, if you have done it, then you will see that death has quite a different meaning from the death of decay.

You know, we do not die to it all; instead, from moment to moment we are decaying, corrupting, deteriorating, withering away. To die implies to have no continuity of thought. You may say, "That is very difficult to do, and if one has done it, what is the value of it?" It is not difficult, but it requires enormous energy to go into it. It requires a mind that is young, fresh, unafraid and therefore rid of time. And what value has it? Perhaps not any utilitarian value; to die to thought and therefore to time means to discover creation—creation which is destroyed and creating everything anew, every second. In that there is no deterioration, no withering away. It is only thought that withers—thought that creates the center as the 'me' and the 'not me'—it is only that which knows decay.

So, to die to everything that the mind has accumulated, gathered, experienced, to cease on the instant is creation, in which there is no continuity. That which has continuity is always decaying. I do not know if you have noticed this perpetual longing for continuity, which most of us have, the desire for the continuity of a particular relationship between the husband and wife, father and son, and all the rest of it. Relationship, when it is continual, is decaying, dead, worthless. But when one dies to continuity, there is a newness, a freshness.

So, the mind can directly experience what death is, which is quite extraordinary. Most of us do not know what living is, and therefore we do not know dying. Do we know what living is? We know what struggling is, we know what envy is, we know the brutalities of existence, the vulgarity of it all, the hatreds, the ambitions, the corruptions, the conflicts. We know all that; that is our life. But we do not know death, and so we are afraid of it. Perhaps if we knew what living is we should also know what dying is. Living, surely, is a timeless movement in which the mind is no longer accumulating. The moment you have accumulated, you are in a state of decay. Because whether it is a vast experience or a little experience, around that you build the wall of security.

So, to know what living is means to die every minute to the things one has acquired—the inward pleasures, the inward pains—not in the process of time, but to die as it arises. Then you will find, if you have gone that far, that death is as life. Then living is not separate from dying, and that gives an extraordinary sense of beauty. That beauty is beyond thought and feeling, and it cannot be put together and used in painting a picture, writing a poem, or playing an instrument. Those are irrelevant. There is a beauty that comes into being when life and death are the same, when living and dying are synonymous, because then life and death leave the mind completely rich, total, whole.

Question: Can we ask questions about this?

KRISHNAMURTI: It seems that a few are so ready with questions that I am wondering if you have listened to the speaker. Were you listening, or were you busy formulating your questions? Do you understand? You were already forming your questions and therefore not listening. Please, I am not being rude, believe me. I am just pointing it out. If one had listened to this talk, one's questions would be answered.

Question: Through the exploration of fear, will there not be danger of mental disorder?

KRISHNAMURTI: Could there be a greater danger of mental disorder than in the mentality with which we live now? Are we not all, if you will forgive me for pointing it out, a little bit disorderly, mentally? I am not being rude; it is not my intention or my thought to judge you. But there is this extraordinary concern about the danger of increased mental illness. Do you know what is making us ill? Not the inquiry into fear. Wars, communism, religious bigotry, ambition, competition, snobbery—these things are the indications of a mentally ill person. Surely, the inquiry into fear and ridding the mind totally of fear is the highest sanity. The question indicates, does it not, sirs, that we think the present society is a marvelous thing. Probably those of us who have a good bank account and are well-to-do feel that things are all right, and they do not want to be disturbed. But life is a very disturbing thing, a very destructive thing, and that is what we are afraid of. We are not interested in living, in being free from fear; but we want to find a corner where we are secure and comfortable, and to be left alone to rot. Sirs, this is not rhetoric; it is our inward, secret desire. We seek this safety in every relationship. What jealousy and envy there is in relationship! What hatred when the wife turns away from the husband, or the husband goes off with another! How we seek the approval of society and the benediction of the church! Surely, it is all these many things that bring about deterioration, the destruction of sanity.

Comment: These things are quite new to us, and I think we must continue with them.

KRISHNAMURTI: Sir, you cannot continue with them. If you continue with them, they are mere ideas, and ideas are not going to create anything new. I have been talking about the total destruction of the things that the mind has built inwardly. You cannot continue with destruction; if you do, it is merely construction, building up again that which must be destroyed.

We need a new mind, a fresh mind, a new heart, an innocent, young, decisive mind; and to have such a mind, there must be destruction; there must be a creation which is ever new.

August 10, 1961

Ninth Talk in Saanen

This is the last talk of this gathering. During these talks we have covered a great many subjects, and I think we should consider this morning what is a religious mind. I would like to go into it fairly deeply because I feel only such a mind can resolve all our problems, not only the political and economic problems, but the much more fundamental problems of human existence. Before we go into it, I think we should repeat what we have already said—that a serious mind is a mind that is willing to go to the very root of things and discover what is true and what is false in it, that does not stop halfway and does not allow itself to be distracted by any other consideration. I hope this gathering has shown sufficiently that there are at least a few who are capable and earnest enough to do this.

I think we are all very familiar with the present world situation, and we do not need to be told of the deceptions, the corruption, the social and economic inequalities, the menace of wars, the constant threat of the East against the West, and so on. To understand all this confusion and bring about clarity, it seems to me that there must be a radical change in the mind itself, and not just patchwork reform or a mere adjustment. To wade through all this confusion, which is not only outside us but within us, to grapple with all the mounting tensions and the increasing demands, one needs a radical revolution in the psyche itself, one needs to have an entirely different mind.

For me, revolution is synonymous with religion. I do not mean by the word *revolution* the immediate economic or social changes, but I mean a revolution in consciousness itself. All other forms of revolution, whether communist, capitalist, or what you will, are merely reactionary. A revolution in the mind, which means the complete destruction of what has been so that the mind is capable of seeing what is true without distortion, without illusion—that is the way of religion. I think the real, the true religious mind does exist, can exist. I think if one has gone into it very deeply, one can discover such a mind for oneself. A mind that has broken down, destroyed all the barriers, all the lies which society, religion, dogma, belief have imposed upon it, and gone beyond to discover what is true, is the true religious mind.

So first let us go into the question of experience. Our brains are the result of the experience of centuries; the brain is the storehouse of memory. Without that memory, without the accumulated experience and knowledge, we should not be able to function at all as human beings. Experience, memory, is obviously necessary at a certain level. But I think it is also fairly obvious that all experience based on the conditioning of knowledge, of memory, is bound to be limited. And therefore experience is not a factor in liberation. I do not know if you have thought about this at all.

Every experience is conditioned by the past experience. So there is no new experience; it is always colored by the past. In the very process of experiencing, there is the distortion which comes into being from the past—the past being knowledge, memory, the various accumulated experiences, not only of the individual, but also of the race, the community. Now, is it possible to deny all that experience?

I do not know if you have gone into the question of denial, what it means to deny something. It means the capacity to deny the authority of knowledge, to deny the authority of experience, to deny the authority of memory, to deny the priests, the church, everything that has been imposed on the psyche. There are only two means of denial for most of us—either through knowledge or through reaction. You deny the authority of the priest, the church, the written word, the book, either because you have studied, inquired, accumulated other knowledge, or because you do not like it, you react against it. Whereas true denial implies, does it not, that you deny without knowing what is going to happen, without any future hope. To say, "I do not know what is true, but this is false," is surely the only true denial because that denial is not out of calculated knowledge, not out of reaction. After all, if you know what your denial is leading to, then it is merely an exchange, a thing of the marketplace, and therefore it is not true denial at all.

I think one has to understand this a little, to go into it rather deeply because I want to find out, through denial, what is the religious mind. I feel that through negation one can find out what is true. You cannot find out what is true by assertion. You must sweep the slate completely clean of the known before you can find out.

So we are going to inquire what the religious mind is through denial, that is, through negation, through negative thinking. And obviously there is no negative inquiry if denial is based on knowledge, on reaction. I hope this is fairly clear. If I deny the authority of the priest, of the book, or of tradition because I do not like it, that is just a reaction because I then substitute something else for what I have denied; and if I deny because I have sufficient knowledge, facts, information, and so on, then my knowledge becomes my refuge. But there is a denial which is not the outcome of reaction or knowledge but which comes from observation, from seeing a thing as it is, the fact of it; and that is true denial because it leaves the mind cleansed of all assumptions, all illusions, authorities, desires.

So is it possible to deny authority? I don't mean the authority of the policeman, the law of the country, and all that; that is silly and immature and will end us up in jail. But I mean the denying of the authority imposed by society on the psyche, on the consciousness, deep down; to deny the authority of all experience, all knowledge, so that the mind is in a state of not knowing what will be, but only knowing what is not true.

You know, if you have gone into it so far, it gives you an astonishing sense of integration, of not being torn between conflicting, contradictory desires; seeing what is true, what is false, or seeing the true in the false, gives you a sense of real perception, of clarity. The mind is then in a position—having destroyed all the securities, the fears, the ambitions, vanities, visions, purposes, everything—in a state that is completely alone, uninfluenced.

Surely, to find reality, to find God, or whatever name you like to give it, the mind must be alone, uninfluenced, because then such a mind is a pure mind, and a pure mind can proceed. When there is the complete destruction of all the things which it has created within itself as security, as hope, and as the resistance against hope, which is despair, and so on, then there comes, surely, a fearless state in which there is no death. A mind that is alone is completely living, and in that living there is a dying every minute, and therefore for that mind there is no death. It is really extraordinary, if you have gone into that thing; you discover for yourself that there is no such thing as death. There is only that state of pure austerity of the mind which is alone.

This aloneness is not isolation; it is not escape into some ivory tower; it is not loneliness. All that has been left behind, forgotten, dissipated, and destroyed. So such a mind knows what destruction is, and we must know destruction; otherwise, we cannot find anything new. And how frightened we are to destroy everything we have accumulated!

There is a Sanskrit saying: "Ideas are the children of barren women." And I think most of us indulge in ideas. You may be treating the talks we have been having as an exchange of ideas, as a process of accepting new ideas and discarding old ones, or as a process of denying new ideas and holding on to the old. We are not dealing with ideas at all. We are dealing with facts. And when one is concerned with facts, there is no adjustment; you either accept it or you deny it. You can either say, "I do not like those ideas, I prefer the old ones, I am going to live in my own stew," or you can go along with the fact. You cannot compromise, you cannot adjust. Destruction is not adjustment. To adjust, to say, "I must be less ambitious, not so envious," is not destruction. And one must, surely, see the truth that ambition, envy, is ugly, stupid, and one must destroy all these absurdities. Love never adjusts. It is only desire, fear, hope, that adjusts. That is why love is a destructive thing, because it refuses to adapt itself or conform to a pattern.

So, we begin to discover that when there is the destruction of all the authority which man has created for himself in his desire to be secure inwardly, then there is creation. Destruction is creation.

Then, if you have abandoned ideas, and are not adjusting yourself to your own pattern of existence or a new pattern which you think the speaker is creating—if you have gone that far—you will find that the brain can and must function only with regard to outward things, respond only to outward demands; therefore, the brain becomes completely quiet. This means that the authority of its experiences has come to an end, and therefore it is incapable of creating illusion. And to find out what is true, it is essential for the power to create illusion in any form to come to an end. And the power to create illusion is the power of desire, the power of ambition, of wanting to be this and not wanting to be that.

So, the brain must function in this world with reason, with sanity, with clarity, but inwardly it must be completely quiet.

We are told by the biologists that it has taken millions of years for the brain to develop to its present stage, and that it will take millions of years to develop further. Now, the religious mind does not depend on time for its development. I wish you could follow this. What I want to convey is that when the brain—which must function in its responses to the outward existence—becomes quiet inwardly, then there is no longer the machinery of accumulating experience and knowledge, and therefore inwardly it is completely quiet but fully alive, and then it can jump the million years.

So, for the religious mind there is no time. Time only exists in that state of a continuity moving to a further continuity and achievement. When the religious mind has destroyed the authority of the past, the traditions, the values imposed upon it, then it is capable of being without time. Then it is completely developed. Because, after all, when you have denied time, you have denied all development through time and space. Please, this is not an idea; it is not a thing to be played with. If we have gone through it, you know what it is, you are in that state; but if you have not gone through it, then you cannot just pick up these ideas and play with them.

So, you find destruction is creation, and in creation there is no time. Creation is that state when the brain, having destroyed all the past, is completely quiet and therefore in that state in which there is no time or space in which to grow, to express, to become. And that state of creation is not the creation of the few gifted people—the painters, musicians, writers, architects. It is only the religious mind that can be in a state of creation. And the religious mind is not the mind that belongs to some church, some belief, some dogma—these only condition the mind. Going to church every morning and worshiping this or that does not make you a religious person, though respectable society may accept you as such. What makes a person religious is the total destruction of the known.

In this creation there is a sense of beauty, a beauty which is not put together by man, a beauty which is beyond thought and feeling. After all, thought and feeling are merely reactions, and beauty is not a reaction. A religious mind has that beauty—which is not the mere appreciation of nature, the lovely mountains and the roaring stream, but quite a different sense of beauty—and with it goes love. I do not think you can separate beauty and love. You know, for most of us love is a painful thing because with it always come jealousy, hate, and possessive instincts. But this love of which we are talking is a state of the flame without the smoke.

So, the religious mind knows this complete, total destruction, and what it means to be in a state of creation—which is not communicable. And with it there is the sense of beauty and love, which are indivisible. Love is not divisible as divine love and physical love. It is love. And with it goes, naturally, without saying, a sense of passion. One cannot go very far without passion—passion being intensity. It is not the intensity of wanting to alter something, wanting to do something, the intensity which has a cause so that when you remove the cause the intensity disappears. It is not a state of enthusiasm. Beauty can only be when there is a passion which is austere, and the religious mind, being in this state, has a peculiar quality of strength.

You know, for us, strength is the result of will, of many desires woven into the rope of will. And that will is a resistance with most of us. The process of resisting something or pursuing a result develops will, and that will is generally called strength. But the strength of which we are talking has nothing to do with will. It is a strength without a cause. It cannot be utilized, but without it nothing can exist.

So, if one has gone so deeply in discovering for oneself, then the religious mind does exist, and it does not belong to any individual. It is the mind, it is the religious mind, apart from all human endeavors, demands, individual urges, compulsions, and all the rest of it. We have only been describing the totality of the mind, which may appear divided by the use of the different words; but it is a total thing, in which all this is contained. Therefore such a religious mind can receive that which is not measurable by the brain. That thing is unnameable; no temple, no priest, no church, no dogma can hold it. To deny all that and live in this state is the true religious mind.

Question: Can the religious mind be acquired through meditation?

KRISHNAMURTI: The first thing to understand is that you cannot acquire it, you cannot get it; it is not to be brought about through meditation. No virtue, no sacrifice, no meditation—nothing on earth can buy this. This sense of attaining, achieving, gaining, buying must totally cease for that to be. You cannot use meditation. What I have been talking about is meditation. Meditation is not a way to something. To discover in every moment of daily life what is true and what is false is meditation. Meditation is not something to which you escape, something in which you get visions and all kinds of thrills—that is self-hypnosis, which is immature, childish. But to watch every moment of the day, to see how your thought is operating, to see the machinery of defense at work, to see the fears, ambitions, greeds, and envies—to watch it all, inquire into it all the time, that is meditation, or a part of meditation. Without laying the right foundation, there is no meditation, and the laying of the right foundation is to be free of ambition, greed, envy, and all the things that we have created for our self-defense. You do not have to go to anybody to be told what meditation is or to be given a method. I can find out very simply by watching myself, how ambitious I am or not. I do not have to be told by another; I know. To eradicate the root, the trunk, the fruit of ambition, to see it and totally destroy it is absolutely necessary. You see, we want to go very far without taking the first step. And you will find if you take the first step that it is the last step; there is no other step.

Question: Is it true that we cannot use reason to discover what is true?

KRISHNAMURTI: Sir, what do we mean by reason? Reason is organized thought, as logic is organized ideas, is it not? And thought, however clever, however wide, however well-informed, is limited. All thought is limited. You can observe it yourself; this is not something new. Thought can never be free. Thought is a reaction, a response of memory; it is a mechanical process. It can be reasonable, it can be sane, it can be logical, but it is limited. It is like the electronic computers. But thought can never discover what is new. The brain, through the centuries, has acquired, has accumulated experiences, responses, memory; and when that thing thinks, it is conditioned, and so cannot discover the new. But when that brain has understood the whole process of reason, logic, inquiring, thinking—not denied it, but understood it—then it becomes quiet. Then that state of quietness can discover what is true.

Sir, reason tells you that you must have leaders. You have had leaders, political or religious. They have not led you anywhere except to more misery, more wars, greater destruction and corruption.

Question: One sees the absurdity of condemning things, outwardly and inwardly, but one keeps on condemning. So what is one to do?

KRISHNAMURTI: When we say, "I see that I must not condemn," what do we mean by that word *see?* Please follow this a little slowly. I am examining that word see. What do we mean by that? How do we see a thing? Do we see the fact through the words? When I say, "I see that condemnation is absurd," do I see it? Or am I looking at the words *I must not condemn?* I do not see the true fact that condemnation does not lead anywhere, do I? I do not know if I am making myself clear. The word *door* is not the door, is it? The word is not the thing, and if we confuse the thing with the word, then we do not see it. But if we can put the word away, then we can look at the thing itself. If I see the whole implication of Catholicism, Hinduism, communism—see the thing, not the word—then I have understood it, I have finished with it. But if I cling to the word, then the word is an impediment to seeing.

So, to see, the mind must be free of the word but see the fact. I must see the fact that condemnation of any kind prevents the mind from really looking at something. If I merely condemn ambition, I do not see the whole anatomy, the structure of ambition. If the mind wants to understand ambition, there must be the cessation of condemnation; there must be the perception of the fact, without resisting it, without denying it. Then the seeing of the fact has its own action. If I see the fact of the whole structure of ambition, then the fact itself reveals to the mind the absurdity, the callousness, the infinitely destructive nature of ambition, and ambition drops away; I do not have to do a thing about it.

And if I see, inwardly, the full significance of authority, study it, watch it, go into it, never denying, never accepting, but seeing, then authority drops away.

August 13, 1961

Paris, France, 1961

First Talk in Paris

It is always difficult, I think, to communicate with another about serious things, and more especially is it so at these meetings where you speak French and I, unfortunately, must speak in English. But I think we shall be able to communicate with each other sufficiently clearly if we do not remain merely at the verbal level. Words are meant to communicate, to convey something, and the words in themselves are not significant. But most of us, I am afraid, remain at the verbal level, and therefore communication becomes much more difficult because what we want to talk about is also at the intellectual and emotional level. We want to communicate with each other comprehensively, as a whole, and for that we need a total approach—verbally, emotionally, and intellectually. So let us take the journey together, go along together, and look at our problems comprehensively, though that is extremely difficult.

First of all, the speaker is not talking as a Hindu, and he does not represent the Orient—though he may have been born in a certain place and have a certain passport. Our problems are human problems, and as such they have no frontiers; they are neither Hindu, French, Russian, nor American. We are trying to understand the whole human problem, and I am using the word *understand* in a very definite way. The mere use of words does not give understanding, nor is understanding a matter of agreement or disagreement. If we want to understand what is being said, we must consider it without prejudice, neither doubting nor accepting, but actually listening.

Now, in listening, which is quite an art, there must be a certain sense of quietness of the brain. With most of us our brains are incessantly active, ever responding to the challenge of a word, an idea, or an image, and this constant process of responding to a challenge does not bring about understanding. What brings about understanding is to have a brain that is very quiet. The brain, after all, is the instrument which thinks, which reacts; it is the storehouse of memory, the result of time and experience, and there can be no understanding if that instrument is all the time agitated, reacting, comparing what is being said with what it has already stored up. Listening, if I may say so, is not a process of agreeing, condemning, or interpreting, but of looking at a fact totally, comprehensively. For that the brain must be quiet but also very much alive, capable of following rightly and reasonably, not sentimentally or emotionally. Only then can we approach the problems of human existence as a total process and not fragmentarily.

As most of us know, the politicians of the world, unfortunately, are ruling our affairs. Probably, our very lives depend upon a few politicians—French, English, Russian, American, or Indian—and that is a very sad thing. But it is a fact. And the politician is only concerned with the immediacy of things—with his country, his position, his policy, his nationalistic ideals. And as a result there are the immediate problems of war—of the conflict between East and West, communism fighting capitalism, and socialism against any other form of autocracy—so that the immediate pressing problem is of war and peace, and how to manipulate our lives so as not to be crushed by these enormous historical processes.

But I think it would be a very great pity if we merely concern ourselves with the immediate—with the French position in Algiers, with what is going to happen in Berlin, whether there is going to be a war, and how we are to get through to survive. Those are the problems which are being pressed on us by the newspapers, by propaganda, but I think it is far more important to consider what is going to happen to the human brain, the human mind. If we are only concerned with present events and not with the totality of the development of the human mind and brain, then our problems will only increase and multiply.

We can see, can we not, that our minds, our brains have become mechanical. We are influenced in every direction. Whatever we read leaves its imprint, and all propaganda leaves its mark; thought is ever repetitive, and so the brain and the mind have become mechanical, like a machine. We function in our jobs mechanically, our relationships with each other are mechanical, and our values are merely traditional. The electronic computers are much the same as the mind of man, only we are a little more inventive, as we have made them; but they function as we function, through reaction, repetition, and memory. And all we seem to ask is how to make the mechanism, which is rooted in habit and tradition, run more smoothly, without any disturbance, and perhaps that will be the end of human life. All this implies, does it not, no freedom, but only a search for security. The prosperous demand security, and the poor of Asia with barely a meal a day—they also want security. And the response of the human mind to all this misery is merely mechanical, habitual, indifferent.

So the urgent question, surely, is: How to free the brain and the mind? Because if there is no freedom, there is no creativeness. There is mechanical invention, going to the moon, finding out new means of locomotion, and so on; but that is not creation, that is invention. There is creation only when there is freedom. Freedom is not just a word; the word is entirely different from the actual state. Nor can freedom be made into an ideal, for the ideal is merely a postponement. So what I want to discuss during these talks is whether it is possible to free the mind and the brain. Just to say that it is possible, or that it is not, is idle; but what we can do is to find out for ourselves, through experiment, through self-knowing, through inquiry, through intense search. And that demands the capacity to reason, to feel, to break with tradition, and to shatter all the walls which one has built up as security. If you are not prepared to do that from the very first talk to the last, then I think you are wasting your time coming here. The problems that confront us are very serious; they are the problems of fear, death, ambition, authority, meditation, and so on. Every problem must be tackled factually—not emotionally, intellectually, or sentimentally. And it requires precise thinking, great energy, so as to be able to pursue each inquiry to the very end and discover the essence of things. That seems to be essential.

If we observe, not only the outside events in the world, but also what is happening inwardly in ourselves, we find, do we not, that we are slaves to certain ideas, slaves to authority. For centuries we have been shaped through propaganda to be Christians, Buddhists, communists, or whatever it is. But to find out the truth, surely, we must not belong to any religion at all. It is a very difficult thing not to commit oneself to any pattern of action or thought at all. I do not know if you have ever tried not belonging to anything, if you have denied completely the traditional acceptance of God—which does not mean becoming an atheist, which is as silly as believing, but to deny the influence of the Church with all its propaganda of two thousand years.

Nor is it easy to deny that you are a Frenchman, a Hindu, a Russian, or an American; perhaps that is even more difficult. It is fairly easy to deny something if you know where the denial is leading you; that is merely going from one prison to another. But if you deny all prisons, not knowing where it is going to lead you, then you stand alone. And it seems to me that it is absolutely essential to stand completely alone, uninfluenced, for then only can we find out for ourselves what is true—not only in this world of daily existence, but also beyond the values of this world, beyond thought and feeling, beyond measure. Then only shall we know if there is a reality which is beyond space and time, and that discovery is creation. But to find out what is true, there must be this sense of aloneness, of freedom. You cannot travel far if you are bound to something—to your country, your traditions, your habitual ways of thought. It is like being tied to a peg.

So, if you want to find out what is true, you must break all links and inquire not only into the outside, your relationship with things and people, but also inwardly, which is the knowing of oneself—not only superficially in the waking consciousness, but also in the unconscious, in the hidden recesses of the brain and mind. That requires constant observation, and if you will so observe, you will see that there is no real division—as between the outside and the inside—for thought, like a tide, flows both outward and inward. It is all the one process of self-knowing. You cannot just reject the outer, for you are not something apart from the world. The world problem is your problem, and the outer and inner are the two sides of the same coin. The hermits, the monks, and the so-called religious people who reject the world are merely escaping, with all their disciplines and superstitions, into their own illusions.

We can see that outwardly we are not free. In our jobs, our religions, our countries, in our relationship with our wives, our husbands, our children, in our ideas, beliefs, and political activities, we are not free. Inwardly, too, we are not free because we do not know what our motives are, our urges, our compulsions, the unconscious demands. So there is freedom neither outwardly nor inwardly, and that is a fact. But we have to see that fact first, and most of us refuse to see it; we gloss over it, cover it up with words, with ideas, and so on. The fact is that psychologically as well as outwardly we want security. Outwardly we want to be sure of our job, our position, our prestige, our relationships; and inwardly we want the same security; and if one stronghold is broken up, we go to another.

So realizing this extraordinarily complex situation in which the brain and mind function, how is it possible to break through it all? I hope I am conveying the impasse to which we have come. The question is: Do we ever really face the fact? The fact is that the brain and the mind seek security in any form, and where there is this urge for security, there is fear. We never really face that fact; we either say it is inevitable or else ask how to get rid of fear. Whereas if we can come face to face with the fact, without trying to escape, interpret, or transform it, then the fact acts of itself.

I do not know if psychologically you have gone that far, experimented that far, for it seems to me that most of us do not realize to what depths our minds, our brains have become mechanical, and we have not asked ourselves whether it is possible to face that fact completely, with intensity.

Please let us be very clear that I am not trying to convince you of anything; that would be too immature. We are not doing propaganda here—we can leave that to the politicians, the churches, and the other people who sell things. We are not selling new ideas because ideas have no meaning; we can play with them intellectually, but they do not lead anywhere. What is significant, what has vitality is to face a fact; and the fact is that the mind, our whole being, has for centuries been made mechanical. All thought is mechanical, and to realize that fact and go beyond, one must first see that it is so.

Now, how does one come into contact, emotionally, with a fact? Intellectually I may say that I know I drink and that it is very bad to drink—physically, emotionally, and psychologically—and yet I still keep on drinking. But to come into contact emotionally with the fact is quite a different thing. Then the emotional contact with the fact has an action of its own. You know how, if you are driving a car for a long time, you get sleepy and you say, "I must wake up," but go on driving. Then later, as you pass dangerously close to another car, there is suddenly an immediate emotional contact, and you at once wake up and draw to one side and have a rest. Have you ever suddenly seen a fact in the same way, come into contact with it totally, completely? Have you ever actually seen a flower? I doubt it because we do not really look at a flower; what we do is immediately to categorize it, give it a name, call it a "rose," smell it, say how beautiful it is, and put it aside as the already known. The naming, the classification, the opinion, the judgement, the choice—all those things prevent you from really looking at it.

In the same way, emotionally to come into contact with a fact, there must be no naming, no putting it into a category, no judgment; there must be the cessation of all thinking, all reaction. Then only can you look. Do try, sometimes, to look at a flower, a child, a star, a tree, or what you will without all the process of thinking, and then you will see much more. Then there is no screen of words between you and the fact, and therefore there is an immediate contact with it. To evaluate, to condemn, to approve, to put into a category, has been our training for centuries, and to be aware of all this process is the beginning of seeing a fact.

At present the whole of our life is bound by time and space, and the immediate problems swamp us. Our jobs, our relationships, the problems of jealousy, fear, death, old age, and so on—these things fill our lives. Is the mind, the brain, capable of breaking through it all? I say it is because I have experimented with it, gone into the very depths of it, broken through it. But you cannot possibly accept what the speaker says because acceptance has no value. The only thing that has value is for you also to take the journey, but for that there must be freedom at the very beginning, there must be the demand to find out—not to accept, not to doubt, but to find out. Then you will see, as you go deeply into the question, that the mind can be free, and it is only such a free mind that can discover what is true.

Perhaps some of you would like to ask questions on what we have been saying. You know, to discuss, to ask questions is quite difficult. To ask the right question, you must know your problem. Most of us do not know our problems; we skim on the surface, but we do not tackle the actual problem, and so we ask wrong questions. If we can discuss rightly, then I think it will be quite fun; one learns much more by playing with the right problem than in being deadly serious about superficial things, as most people are.

Question: How is one to come into contact with a fact emotionally?

KRISHNAMURTI: To be in direct contact with something demands a total approach which is not merely intellectual, emotional, or sentimental. It requires a total comprehension.

Question: Must one not be attentive to the dual process that is going on within us all the time, and is that not self-knowledge?

KRISHNAMURTI: We have used the words *attentive, duality,* and *self knowledge.* Let us look at those three words, one by one, because if we do not understand these three words, we shall not be able to communicate with each other.

Now, what does it mean to be *attentive?* Do please listen to this because I am not just being finical; I want to be clear that we both understand the words we use. You may have one meaning and I another. For me, when one gives full attention, in that there is no concentration, no exclusion. You know how a schoolboy who wants to look out of the window is forced to look at his book, but that is not attention. Attention is seeing what is taking place outside the window and also what is in front of you. To observe, without exclusion, is quite a difficult thing to do.

Then what do you mean by *dual process?* We know there is a dual process, the good and the bad, hate and love, and so on; and to be attentive to these is very difficult, is it not? And why do we establish this dual process? Does it exist in actuality, or is it an invention of the brain in order to escape from the fact? I am violent, let us say, or jealous, and it bothers me; I do not like it, so I say I must not be jealous, violent—which is an escape from the fact, is it not? The ideal is an invention of the brain in order to escape from *what is,* and so there is duality. But if I completely face the fact that I am jealous, then there is no duality. Facing the fact implies that I go into the whole issue of violence and jealousy, and either I find that I like it, in which case the conflict must continue, or else I see the full implications of it and am free of the conflict.

Then what do we mean by *self-knowledge?* What does *knowing oneself* mean? Do I know myself? Is the self a static thing, or is it a thing that is always changing? Can I know myself? Do I know my wife, my husband, my child, or do I know only the picture which my mind has created? After all, I cannot know a living thing, I cannot reduce a living thing to a formula; all that I can do is to follow it, wherever it may lead; and if I follow it, I can never say I know it. So the knowing of the self is the following of the self, following all the thoughts, the feelings, the motives, and never for a moment saying, "I know it." You can only know something which is static, dead.

So, you see the difficulty of the three words involved in this question—attention, duality, and knowing oneself. If you can understand all these words and can go further, beyond them, then you will know the full significance of facing a fact.

Question: Is there a means to quieten the mind?

KRISHNAMURTI: First of all, when you ask that question, do you realize that your mind is agitated? Are you aware that your mind is never quiet, constantly chattering? That is a fact. The mind is ceaselessly talking, either about something or talking to itself; it is active all the time. Why does one ask that question? Please think it out with me. If it is because you are partially aware of the chattering and want to escape from it, then you might as well take a drug, a pill, to send the mind to sleep. But if you are inquiring and really want to find out why the mind chatters, then the problem is entirely different. The one is an escape, the other is to follow chattering right to the end.

Now why does the mind chatter? By "chattering" we mean, do we not, that it is always occupied with something—with the radio, with its problems, its job, its visions, its emotions, its myths. Now why is it occupied, and what would happen if it were not occupied? Have you ever tried not being occupied? If you have, you will find that the moment the brain is not occupied, there is fear. Because it means that you are alone. If you find yourself with no occupation, the experience is very painful, is it not? Have you ever been alone? I doubt it. You may be walking alone, sitting in the bus alone, or alone in your room, but your mind is always occupied, your thoughts are ever with you. The cessation of occupation is to discover that you are completely alone, isolated, and it is a fearsome thing; and so the mind goes on chattering, chattering, chattering.

September 5, 1961

Second Talk in Paris

I would like to talk over with you the question of authority and freedom. And I would like to go very deeply into it because I feel it is very important to understand the whole anatomy of authority.

So, first of all I would like to point out that I am not discussing academically, superficially, verbally; but if we are really serious then, I think, by the very act of listening rightly, there comes about not only understanding but also immediately the freedom from authority. After all, time does not free the mind from anything. Freedom is possible only when there is direct perception, complete comprehension without effort, without contradiction, without conflict. Such an understanding frees the mind immediately from whatever problem it is burdened with. If we follow the problem and see how far the mind can go into it, thoroughly, totally, then we will be free of this burden.

I do not know if you have thought very deeply about the matter of authority. If you have, you will know that authority destroys freedom, it curtails creation, it breeds fear, and it actually cripples all thought. Authority implies conformity, imitation, does it not? There is not only the outward authority of the policeman, the law—which to a certain extent is understandable—but there is the inward authority of knowledge, of experience, of tradition, the following of a pattern laid down by society, by a teacher, of how to behave, how to conduct oneself, and so on.

We are going to deal entirely with the understanding of the inward, psychological authority, with the psyche which establishes a pattern of authority for its own security.

Have you ever wondered why, throughout the ages, human beings have been relying for their pattern of conduct upon others? We want, do we not, to be told what to do, how to behave, what to think, how to act under certain circumstances. The search for authority is constant because most of us are afraid of going wrong, afraid to be a failure. You worship success, and authority offers success. If you follow a certain mode of conduct, if you discipline yourself according to certain ideas, they say eventually you will find salvation, attainment, freedom. For me, the idea that discipline, control, suppression, imitation, and conformity can ever lead to freedom is totally absurd. Obviously you cannot cripple the mind, shape it, twist it, and in that process find freedom. The two are incompatible; they deny each other.

Now, why do the human mind and brain always seek a pattern to which to conform? And may I say here that my explanation is worthless, has no meaning at all if you are not, each one of you, aware of your own inclination to follow—to follow an idea or a teacher. But if the explanation is actually awakening your own perception of the state of your own mind, then the words have significance. So why is there this urge to follow? Is it not the outcome of the desire to be certain, to be safe? Surely, the desire for security is the motive, the background of this urge to follow. Which means, does it not, the feeling that through success, through conformity, one will avoid all fear. But is there such a thing as inward security? Surely, the very search for security is fear. Outwardly, perhaps, it may be necessary to have a certain degree of security—a house, three meals a day, clothes, and so on—but inwardly, is there any such thing as security? Are you secure in your family, in your relationships? You dare not question it, dare you? You accept that it is so, it has become a tradition, a habit; but the moment you really question your relationship with your husband, your wife, your child, your neighbor, that very questioning becomes dangerous.

All of us, in some form or other, are seeking security, and for that there must be authority. And so we say there is God who, failing all else, will be our ultimate security. We cling to certain ideals, hopes, beliefs which will ensure for us a permanency, now and in the hereafter. But is there such a thing as security? And I think each one of us must discover, battle with, and clearly understand whether or not there is such a thing as security.

Outwardly, there is hardly any security nowadays. Things are changing so rapidly; mechanically there are new inventions, atomic bombs, and socially there are outward revolutions, especially in Asia, the threat of war, communism, and so on. But the threats to our inward security create in us a far greater resistance. When you believe in God or in some form of inward permanency, it is almost impossible to break that belief. No atom bomb will break your belief because in that hope you have taken root. We have committed ourselves, each one, to a certain way of thinking, and whether it is true or false, whether it has any reality or reason does not seem to matter; we have accepted it, and we hold on to it.

Now, to break through all that, to find out the truth of the whole matter, means a far greater revolution than any communist, socialist, or capitalist revolution. It means the beginning of freedom from authority, and the actual discovery that there is no such thing as inward permanency, security. Therefore it means the discovery that at all times the mind must be in a state of uncertainty. And we are afraid of uncertainty, are we not? We think that a brain that is in a state of uncertainty must go to pieces, become mentally ill. Unfortunately, there are a great many mental cases because people cannot find security. They have been shaken loose from their moorings, from their beliefs, ideals, fancies, myths, and so they become mentally ill. A mind that is truly uncertain has no fear. It is only the mind that is afraid—that follows—that demands authority. And is it possible to see all this and to put authority and fear away totally, completely?

And what do you mean by "seeing"? Is seeing merely a matter of an intellectual explanation? Will explanations, reasoning, sane logic, help you to see the fact that all authority, obedience, acceptance, conformity cripples the mind? For me, this is a very important question. Seeing has nothing whatsoever to do with words, with explanations. I feel that you can see something directly without any verbal persuasion, argument, or intellectual reasoning. If you put away persuasion, influence—which is all immature, childish—then, what is it that is preventing you from seeing and therefore being free immediately? For me, seeing is an action of immediacy; it is not of time. And therefore freedom from authority is not of time; it is not a question of "I will be free." But so long as you take pleasure from authority, find the process of following attractive, you are not allowing the immediacy of the problem to become urgent, vital.

The fact is that most of us like power—the power of the wife over the husband or the husband over the wife, the power of capacity, the feeling that one is clever, the power which austerity and control of the body gives. Any form of power is authority—whether it is the power of the dictator, political power, religious power, or the domination of one over another. It is utterly evil, and why can we not see that, simply and directly? I mean by "seeing" a total comprehension in which there is no hesitancy but only a complete response. What prevents that complete response?

This brings up the question of the authority of experience, of knowledge, does it not? After all, to go to the moon, to build a rocket, there must be scientific knowledge, and the accumulation of knowledge we call experience. Outwardly you must have knowledge. You must know where you live, you must be able to build, to put things together and take things apart. Such outward knowledge is superficial, mechanical, merely additive, finding out more and more. But what happens is that knowledge and experience become our inward authority. We may reject the outward authority as being childish—such as belonging to a particular nation, group, family, attaching ourselves to a particular society with its special manners, codes, and all that nonsense—but to put away the experiences that one has gathered, the authority of the knowledge one has accumulated, is extremely difficult.

I do not know if you have gone into this problem at all, but if you have, you will see that a mind which is burdened, heavy with knowledge and experience, is not an innocent mind, a young mind; it is an old mind, a decaying mind, and it can never meet freely, fully, totally, a living thing. And in the present world today, both inwardly and outwardly, a new mind, a fresh mind, a young mind is urgently needed to tackle all our problems—not one specific problem of science, medicine, politics, and so on, but the whole human problem. The old mind is weary, crippled, but the young mind sees quickly, without distortion, without illusion. It is a keen, decisive mind, not held within the frontiers of accumulated knowledge or bound by past experience.

After all, what is that experience which gives us such a feeling of nobility, of wisdom, of superiority? Experience is, surely, the response of our background to a challenge. The response is conditioned by the background, and so every experience strengthens the background. If you are churchgoing, a devotee of a certain sect, of a certain religion, then you have experiences, visions, according to that background—which only strengthens the background, does it not? And this conditioning, this religious propaganda—whether it is two thousand years old or quite recent—is shaping our minds, influencing the response of our brains. You cannot deny these influences; they are there. The communist, the socialist, the Catholic, the Protestant, the Hindu, dozens and hundreds of influences are all the time pouring in, consciously or unconsciously, and shaping the mind, controlling the mind. So experience does not free the mind, make it young, fresh, innocent. It is the destruction of the entire background that is necessary.

Understanding of this is not a matter of time. If you set out to understand each influence separately, you will be dead before you understand all of them. But if you can understand one influence fully, completely, then you smash through all forms of influence. But to understand one influence, you have to go into it thoroughly, completely. Merely to say that it is good or bad, noble or ignoble, is quite irrelevant. And to go into it completely, there must be no fear. To go into this whole question of authority is very dangerous, is it not? To be free of authority is to invite danger because no one wants to live in uncertainty. But the certain mind is a dead mind; it is only the uncertain mind that is young, fresh.

So, to understand authority, both outward and inward, is not a matter of time. It is one of the greatest blunders, greatest impediments, to rely on time. Time is really a postponement. It means we are enjoying security, imitation, following, and that all we are saying is, "Please do not disturb me. I am not ready yet to be disturbed." I do not see why one should not be disturbed; what is wrong with being disturbed? Actually, when you do not want to be disturbed, you are in fact inviting disturbance. But the man who wants to find out—whether it is disturbing or not—is free of the fear of disturbance. I know some of you smile at this, but it is far too grave a matter for that. It is a fact that none of us wants to be disturbed. We have fallen into a rut, a narrow groove, intellectual, emotional, or ideological, and we do not want to be disturbed. All we want, in our relationships and everything else, is to live a comfortable, undisturbed, respectable, bourgeois life. And to want to be nonbourgeois, nonrespectable, amounts to the same thing.

Now, if you are listening with self-application, then you will find that the freedom from authority is not a fearsome thing. It is like throwing off a great burden. The mind undergoes a tremendous revolution immediately. For a man who is not seeking security in any form, there is no disturbance; there is a continual movement of understanding. If that is not taking place, you are not listening, you are not seeing; you are merely indulging in the acceptance or rejection of a certain set of explanations. So, it would be very interesting for you to discover for yourself what is your actual response.

Question: Does the mind carry within itself the elements of its own understanding?

KRISHNAMURTI: I think it does, does it not? What prevents understanding? Are not the barriers created by the mind itself? Therefore the understanding as well as the barriers are elements of the mind.

Look, sir, to live with a sense of uncertainty without becoming mentally ill requires a great deal of understanding. One of the chief barriers is, is it not, that I insist that I must be secure inwardly. Outwardly I see that there is no security, so inwardly the mind creates its own security in a belief, a god, an idea. This prevents the actual discovery of whether there is inward security or not. So the mind creates its own slavery, and also has the elements of its own liberation.

Question: Why is a free man not disturbed?

KRISHNAMURTI: Is that a right question? As you do not know anything about the free man, the question is only a matter of speculation. If you will forgive me for saying so, that question has no meaning, for me or for you. But if you put the question the other way round, "Why am I disturbed?" then the question has validity and can be answered rightly. So why is one disturbed—if my husband turns away from me, at the death of someone, at failure, feeling I am not making a success of my life? If you really went into that, to the very end, you would see the whole essence of it.

Question: Is belief in God always based on fear?

KRISHNAMURTI: Why do you believe in God? What is the necessity? Do you bother about belief in God when you are very happy, or only when there is trouble ahead? Do you believe because you have been conditioned to do so? After all, for two thousand years we have been told that there is God, and in the communist world they are conditioning the mind not to believe in God. It is the same thing; in both cases the mind has been influenced. The word *God* is not God, and to really discover for yourself if there is such a thing as God is far more significant than to attach yourself to a belief or a nonbelief. And to find out for oneself requires enormous energy—the energy to break through all beliefs—which does not mean a state of atheism or doubt. But belief is a very comfortable thing, and very few people are willing to shatter themselves inwardly. Belief does not bring you to God. No temple, no church, no dogma, no ritual will bring you to reality. There is that reality, but to find that out, you must have an immeasurable mind. A petty, small mind can only find its own petty little gods. Therefore we must be willing to lose all our respectability, all our beliefs, to find out what is real.

I do not think you can listen to more. If you have listened lazily, merely hearing the words, then no doubt you could go on for another couple of hours. But if you have listened rightly, attentively, with a sense of going deeply, then ten minutes would be enough because in that period, you could have shattered the barriers which the mind has created for itself and discovered what is true.

September 7, 1961

Third Talk in Paris

It seems to me that most of us want some kind of peace. The politicians talk a great deal about it; all over the world that is their pet jargon, their pet word. Also each one of us wants peace. But it seems to me that the kind of peace which human beings want is more an escape; we want to find some state into which the mind can retreat, and we have never considered whether it is possible actually to break through our conflicts and thereby come to real peace. So I would like to talk about conflict because it seems to me that if conflict could be done away with—fundamentally, deeply, inwardly, beyond the level of the conscious mind—then perhaps we would have peace.

The peace I am talking about is not the peace which the mind and the brain seek; it is something entirely different. I think it will be a very disturbing factor, that peace, because it is very creative and therefore very destructive. To come to that comprehension of peace, it seems to me essential that we understand conflict because without going fundamentally, basically, radically into the problem of conflict, we cannot have peace either outwardly or inwardly, however much we may seek it, long for it.

To talk over something with each other—not as a speaker and an audience, which is an absurd relationship—demands that you and I think and feel on the same level and investigate from the same point of view. If you and I could together go into this question of conflict with tremendous eagerness and vitality, then perhaps we shall come upon a peace which is entirely different from the kind of peace which most of us try to find.

Conflict exists when there is a problem, does it not? A problem implies a conflict; a conflict of adjustment, of trying to understand, of trying to get rid of something, to find an answer. And most of us have problems of many kinds—social, economic, problems of relationship, of the conflict of ideas, and so on. And those problems remain unresolved, do they not? We never really think them through to the very end and free ourselves of them, but we go on day after day, month after month throughout life, carrying every kind of problem as a burden in our mind and heart. We seem unable to enjoy life, to be simple, because everything we touch—love, God, relationships, or what you will—becomes reduced in the end to an ugly, disturbing problem. If I am attached to a person, it becomes a problem, and then I want to know how to detach myself. And if I love, I see that in that love there is jealousy, anxiety, and fear. And not being able to resolve our problems, we carry them along with us, feeling incapable of coming upon a solution.

Then there is competition, which gives rise also to problems. Competition is imitation, trying to be like somebody else. There is the pattern of Jesus, the pattern of the hero, the saint, the neighbor who is better off, and there is the inward pattern which you have established for yourself and which you try to follow, to live by. So competition awakens many problems.

There is also the urge for fulfillment. Each one wants to fulfill in one way or another—through the family, the wife, the husband, or the child. And if one goes a little beyond that, there is the desire to fulfill socially, by writing a book, by somehow becoming famous. And when there is this urge to fulfill, to become something, there is also frustration, and with frustration comes sorrow. Then arises the problem of how to avoid sorrow and yet be able to fulfill. And so we are caught in this vicious circle so that everything becomes a problem, a conflict.

And we have accepted conflict as inevitable; it is even considered respectable and necessary for evolution, for growth, for becoming something. We feel that if there is no competition, no conflict, we shall stagnate, deteriorate; so mentally and emotionally we are always sharpening ourselves, fighting, being everlastingly in conflict with ourselves, our neighbors, and the world. This is no exaggeration; it is a fact. And I think we all know what a terrific burden this conflict is.

So it seems to me that the urgent question is whether you see the real importance of being free from conflict—but not in order to achieve something else. Is it at all possible to be free, *per se*, for itself, so that the mind is no longer in conflict under any circumstances whatsoever? At present we do not know whether it is possible or not. All we know is that we are in conflict, and we know the pain of it, the feeling of guilt, despair, the hopelessness and bitterness of modern existence; that is all we know.

So how is one to find out—not verbally, intellectually, or merely emotionally, but actually discover—if it is possible to be free? How does one set about it? Surely, without completely understanding this conflict at all the different levels of consciousness, we cannot possibly be free from it and understand what truth is. A mind in conflict is a confused mind. And the greater the tension of conflict, the greater is the productivity of action. You must have noticed how the writers, the speakers, the so-called intellectuals, are forever producing theories, philosophies, explanations. If they have got any talent at all, then the greater the tension and frustration, the more they produce; and the world calls them great authors, great speakers, great religious leaders, and so on.

Now if one observes closely, one can surely see that conflict distorts, perverts; it is, in its essence, confusion and is destructive to the mind. If one can really see this—without saying that the conflict of competition is inevitable, that the social structure is built on it and you must have it, and so on—then I think our attitude to the problem would be entirely different. I think that is the first thing: to see not intellectually, verbally, but actually to be in contact with that fact. From the moment we are born to the moment we die, there is this incessant battle within and without, and can we actually see the fact that this conflict is unintelligent? What is it that gives one the energy, the vitality to come into emotional contact with a fact?

You see, for centuries we have been educated to live in conflict, to accept it or to find some way to escape from it. And as you know, there are endless escapes—taking to drink, to women, to churches, to God, becoming terribly intellectual, full of knowledge, turning on the radio, overeating. And we also know that none of these escapes solves the problem of conflict; they only increase it. But do we deliberately confront the fact that there is no escape of any kind? I think our primary difficulty is that we have established so many escapes that we have made ourselves incapable of seeing the fact directly.

So one has to go deeply into the question of these conscious and unconscious escapes. I think it is fairly simple to find out the conscious escapes. You are conscious, are you not, when you turn on the radio, or when you go to church on Sunday, having led a brutal, ambitious, envious, ugly life all the week. But it is much more difficult to find out what the hidden unconscious escapes are.

I would like to go a little into this whole problem of consciousness. Consciousness, in its totality, is put together through time, is it not? It is the result of thousands of years of experience; it is made up of the racial, the cultural, the social influences of the past and carried through to the family, the individual, through education, and so on. The totality of all that is consciousness, and if you will examine your own mind, you will find that in consciousness there is always a duality, the observer and the observed. I hope this is not too difficult. This is not a psychological class nor an analytical, intellectual amusement. We are talking about an actual, living experience which you and I must deliberately go into if we are not to remain merely at the verbal level.

There must be conflict in the totality of consciousness so long as there is a division in consciousness as the thinker and the thought. This division entails contradiction, and where there is contradiction, there must be conflict. We know, do we not, that we are in contradiction, both outwardly and inwardly. Outwardly there is contradiction in our actions, wanting to live in a certain way and being caught up in activities of a different kind; and inwardly there is contradiction in our thoughts, feelings, and desires. Feeling, thought, desire, will, and the word make up the totality of our consciousness, and in that totality there is contradiction because there is always a division in it—the censor, the observer, who is always watching, waiting, changing, suppressing, and the feeling or thought which is operated upon.

If one has gone into this problem oneself—not through books, philosophies, and reading all the things other people have said, which are all empty words, but gone into it very deeply, insistently, without choice, without denial or acceptance—then one is bound to discover the fact that the totality of consciousness is in itself a state of contradiction because there is always the thinker operating on the thought, and this gives rise to endless problems.

So the question arises as to whether this division in consciousness is inevitable. Is there a separate thinker at all, or has thought created "the thinker" in order to have a center of permanency from which to think and feel?

You see, if one wants to understand conflict, one has to go into all this. It is not enough just to say, "I want to escape from conflict." If that is all we want, we may as well take a drug, a tranquilizer, which is fairly simple and cheap. But if one wants to go into it really profoundly and totally eradicate all sources of conflict, one must investigate the totality of consciousness—all the dark corners of one's mind and heart, the secret recesses where contradiction lurks. And one can understand profoundly only when one begins to inquire as to why there is this division between the thinker and the thought. You must ask if there is a thinker at all, or only thought. And if there is only thought, why is there this center from which all thought comes?

One can see, can one not, why thought has created a center as the 'me', the self, the ego; the name one gives to it is irrelevant so long as one recognizes that there is a center from which all thought arises. Thought craves permanency, and seeing that its expressions are impermanent, it creates a center as the 'self'. Then the contradiction arises.

To actually see all this, not merely take it in verbally, one must first of all totally deny all the escapes—cut off, like a surgeon, every form of escape. That requires intense awareness in which there is no choice, no clinging on to the pleasurable escapes and avoiding the painful ones. It requires energy, constant watchfulness, because the brain has so accustomed itself to escaping that the escape has become more important than the actual fact from which it is running away. But only when there is a total denial of all escapes is one able to confront, to face the conflict.

Then, when one has gone so far, when one has physically, emotionally, and intellectually denied every form of escape, then what happens? Then is there a problem? Surely, it is the escape which creates the problem. When you are no longer competing with your neighbor, no longer trying to fulfill, no longer trying to change what you are into something else, then is there conflict? Then you are able to face the fact actually of what you are, whatever it is. Then there is no judgment as good or bad. Then you are what you are. And the fact itself acts; there is no 'you' acting upon the fact.

All this is really quite interesting if you actually go into it. Take jealousy. Most of us are jealous, envious, either acutely or lazily. When you actually see that you are jealous, without denying it, condemning it, then what happens? Then is jealousy merely a word, or a fact? I hope you are following this because, you see, the word has an extraordinary importance for most of us. The word *God*, the word *communist*, the word *Negro* have an immense emotional, neurological content. In the same way, the word *jealousy* is already weighted. Now, when the word is put aside, then there is a feeling that remains. That is the fact, not the word. And to look at the feeling without the word requires freedom from all condemnation and justification.

Sometime, when you are jealous, angry, or more especially when you are enjoying yourself about something, see if you can distinguish the word from the feeling, whether the word is all-important or the feeling. Then you will discover that in looking at the fact without the word, there is an action which is not an intellectual process; the fact itself is operating, and therefore there is no contradiction, no conflict.

It is really quite extraordinary to discover for oneself that there is only thinking and not the thinker. Then you will find that one can live in this world without contradiction because then one needs very little. If one needs a great deal—sexually, emotionally, psychologically, or intellectually—there is dependence on another; and the moment there is dependence, there is contradiction and conflict. When the mind frees itself from conflict, out of this freedom there comes a totally different kind of movement. The word *peace* as we know it does not apply to it because for us, the word has many different kinds of meaning, depending on the kind of person who uses it—whether a politician or a priest or someone else. It is not the peace that is promised in heaven after you are dead; it is not found in any church, in any idea, or in the worship of any god. It comes into being when there is the total cessation of all inward conflict, and that is possible only when there is no need. There is no need, then, even for God. There is only an immeasurable movement which cannot be corrupted by any action.

Question: How is it possible, without destroying or suppressing desire, to give it freedom; and does looking at desire without condemnation make it disappear?

KRISHNAMURTI: First of all, we have an idea that desire is wrong because it produces various forms of conflict and contradiction. There are many desires within one, tearing at each other in different directions. That is a fact; we have desires, and they do create conflict. The question is: How to live with desire intensely without destroying it? If one yields to desire, when one fulfills a desire, in that very yielding there is also the pain of frustration. I do not want to take an example because explaining through a particular example perverts the understanding of the totality of desire.

One has first to see very clearly that every form of condemnation of desire is merely an avoidance of the understanding of it. If that fact is seen clearly, then the question arises as to what one is to do with desire. There it is, burning. Up to now we have condemned it or accepted it or enjoyed it, and in the very enjoyment of it, there is pain. In the suppression, in the control of it there is also pain. But if one does not condemn or evaluate, then it is there, burning, and what is one to do? Now, does one ever come to that state? Because in that state you are the desire; there is no longer 'you' and 'desire' as two separate things.

What always happens is, is it not, that we want to make the painful desires disappear and to hold on to the pleasurable ones. I say that is an altogether wrong approach. I say: Can you look at desire without condemning, without judging, without choosing between the various desires? Have you ever done it? I doubt it.

To understand the significance of desire, to live with it, to understand it, actually to look at it without judgment of any kind—that needs immense patience, inwardly. I do not think you have ever done it. But if you will try it, you will find that then there is no contradiction, no conflict. Then desire has quite a different meaning. Then desire may be life.

But so long as we are saying, "Desire is wrong" or "Desire is right," "Should I yield?" or "Should I not yield?"—in that whole process you are creating a division between yourself and desire, and therefore there is bound to be conflict. What gives understanding is to go into yourself quietly, to go deeply into yourself, inquiring, searching out why you are condemning, what you are seeking. Then out of that inward inquiry, in which there is no choice at all, you will discover that you can live with desire, and it has quite a different meaning. To live with anything, you need energy, vitality; and there is no energy left when you are all the time condemning and judging. To live with desire is to discover a state in which there is no contradiction at all. That means that then there is love, without jealousy, without hatred, without any form of corruption; and that is a really marvelous thing to find out for oneself.

Question: What did you mean when you said the other day that we must be disturbed?

KRISHNAMURTI: Please do not regard me as an authority; that would be dreadful. But you can see for yourself that the desire not to be disturbed is one of our main demands. And it may be that the mind, the brain, when it stops its incessant chattering, will discover that there is a great disturbance within. You can see for yourself that your mind is occupied all the time—with the wife, the husband, with sex, with nationality, with God, with where you are to get the next meal, and so on. And have you ever tried to find out why it is occupied, and what would happen if it were not occupied? Then you are confronted with something which you have never thought about, and that may be an extraordinarily disturbing fact. And it is. This constant occupation of the mind may merely be an escape from the fact of tremendous loneliness, emptiness. And you have to face that disturbance and go into it.

September 10, 1961

Fourth Talk in Paris

We were talking the other day about desire and the conflict which arises from desire and I would like to continue with that, and to talk also about need, passion, and love because I think they are all related. If we can go into it all deeply and fundamentally, then perhaps we shall be able to understand the whole significance of desire. But before we can understand desire, with all its conflicts and tortures, I think we ought to understand the question of need.

We do, of course, need certain superficial outward things, like clothes, shelter, and food. Those are absolutely essential for all. But I wonder if we need anything else, at all? Psychologically, is there actually any need for sex, for fame, for the compulsive urge of ambition, the everlasting inward demand for more and more? What do we need, psychologically? We think we need a great many things, and from that arises all the sorrow of dependence. But if we really go into it deeply and inquire, is there any essential need at all, psychologically, inwardly? I think it would be worthwhile if we would seriously ask ourselves this question. The psychological dependence on another in relationship, the need to be in communion with another, the need to commit oneself to some form of thought and activity, the need to fulfill, to become famous—we all know such needs, and we are everlastingly yielding to them. And I think it would be significant if we could, each one of us, try to find out what our needs actually are, and to what extent we depend on them. Because without understanding need, we shall not be able to understand desire, nor shall we be able to understand passion and therefore love. Whether one is rich or poor, one obviously needs food, clothes, and shelter, though even there the need can be limited, small, or expansive. But beyond that, is there any need at all? Why have our psychological needs become so important, such a compelling, driving force? And are they merely an escape from something much deeper?

In inquiring into all this, we are not talking in terms of analysis. We are trying to face the fact, to see exactly *what is,* and that does not need any form of analysis, psychology, or roundabout, cunning explanations. What we are trying to do is to see for ourselves what our psychological needs are, not to explain them away, not to rationalize them, not to say, "What shall I do without them? I must have them." All those things shut the door to further inquiry. And obviously the door is also closed tightly when the inquiry is merely verbal, intellectual, or emotional. The door is open when we really want to face the fact, and that does not need a great intellect. To understand a very complex problem, you need a clear, simple mind, but simplicity and clarity are denied when you have a lot of theories and are trying to avoid facing the issue.

So, the question is: Why have we such a driving need to fulfill, why are we so ruthlessly ambitious, why has sex such an extraordinary importance in our life? It is not a matter of the quality or number of one's needs, whether one has the maximum or the minimum, but why there is this tremendous urge to fulfill in family, in a name, in a position, and so on, with all the anxiety of it, the frustration, the misery—which society encourages and the church blesses.

Now, when you examine it, pushing aside the superficial response of saying, "What would happen to me if I did not succeed in life?" I think you will find that there is a much deeper issue in it, which is the fear of not-being, of complete isolation, of emptiness and loneliness. It is there, deeply hidden—this tremendous sense of anxiety, this fear of being cut off from everything. That is why we cling to all forms of relationship. That is why there is this need to belong to something—to a cult, to a society, to engage in certain activities, to hold on to some belief—because thereby we escape from that reality which is actually there, deep within. It is that fear, surely, which forces the mind, the brain, the whole being, to commit itself to some form of belief or relationship which then becomes the necessity, the need.

I do not know if you have gone that far in this inquiry, not verbally but actually. It means to find out for yourself and to face the fact that one is completely nothing, that inwardly one is as empty as a shell, covered with a lot of jewels of knowledge and experience which are actually nothing but words, explanations. Now, to face that fact without despair, without feeling how terrible it is, but just to be with it, it is first necessary to understand need. If we understand the significance of need, then it will not have such sway over our minds and hearts.

We will come back to it later, but let us go on to consider desire. We know, do we not, the desire which contradicts itself, which is tortured, pulling in different directions—the pain, the turmoil, the anxiety of desire, and the disciplining, the controlling. And in the everlasting battle with it, we twist it out of all shape and recognition; but it is there, constantly watching, waiting, pushing. Do what you will, sublimate it, escape from it, deny it or accept, give it full rein—it is always there. And we know how the religious teachers and others have said that we should be desireless, cultivate detachment, be free from desire—which is really absurd because desire has to be understood, not destroyed. If you destroy desire, you may destroy life itself. If you pervert desire, shape it, control it, dominate it, suppress it, you may be destroying something extraordinarily beautiful.

We have to understand desire, and it is very difficult to understand something which is so vital, so demanding, so urgent, because in the very fulfillment of desire, passion is engendered, with the pleasure and the pain of it. And if one is to understand desire, obviously, there must be no choice. You cannot judge desire as being good or bad, noble or ignoble, or say, "I will keep this desire and deny that one." All that must be set aside if we are to find out the truth of desire—the beauty of it, the ugliness, or whatever it may be. It is a very curious thing to consider, but here in the West, the Occident, many desires can be fulfilled. You have cars, prosperity, better health, the ability to read books, acquire knowledge, and accumulate various types of experience, whereas when you go to the Orient, they are still wanting food, clothing, and shelter, still caught in the misery and degradation of poverty. But in the West as well as in the East, desire is burning all the time, in every direction; outward and deep within, it is there. The man who renounces the world is as crippled by his desire to pursue God as the man who pursues prosperity. So it is there all the time, burning, contradicting itself, creating turmoil, anxiety, guilt, and despair.

I do not know if you have ever experimented with it at all. But what happens if you do not condemn desire, do not judge it as being good or bad, but simply be aware of it? I wonder if you know what it means to be aware of something? Most of us are not aware because we have become so accustomed to condemning, judging, evaluating, identifying, choosing. Choice obviously prevents awareness because choice is always made as a result of conflict. To be aware when you enter a room, to see all the furniture, the carpet or its absence, and so on—just to see it, to be aware of it all without any sense of judgment—is very difficult. Have you ever tried to look at a person, a flower, at an idea, an emotion, without any choice, any judgment?

And if one does the same thing with desire, if one lives with it—not denying it or saying, "What shall I do with this desire? It is so ugly, so rampant, so violent," not giving it a name, a symbol, not covering it with a word—then, is it any longer the cause of turmoil? Is desire then something to be put away, destroyed? We want to destroy it because one desire tears against another, creating conflict, misery, and contradiction; and one can see how one tries to escape from this everlasting conflict. So can one be aware of the totality of desire? What I mean by totality is not just one desire or many desires but the total quality of desire itself. And one can be aware of the totality of desire only when there is no opinion about it, no word, no judgment, no choice. To be aware of every desire as it arises, not to identify oneself with it or condemn it, in that state of alertness, is it then desire, or is it a flame, a passion that is necessary? The word *passion* is generally kept for one thing—sex. But for me, passion is not sex. You must have passion, intensity, to really live with anything; to live fully, to look at a mountain, a tree, to really look at a human being, you must have passionate intensity. But that passion, that flame is denied when you are hedged around by various urges, demands, contradictions, fears. How can a flame survive when it is smothered by a lot of smoke? Our life is but smoke; we are looking for the flame, but we are denying it by suppressing, controlling, shaping the thing we call desire.

Without passion how can there be beauty? I do not mean the beauty of pictures, buildings, painted women, and all the rest of it. They have their own forms of beauty, but we are not talking of superficial beauty. A thing put together by man, like a cathedral, a temple, a picture, a poem, or a statue may or may not be beautiful. But there is a beauty which is beyond feeling and thought and which cannot be realized, understood, or known if there is not passion. So do not misunderstand the word *passion*. It is not an ugly word; it is not a thing you can buy in the market or talk about romantically. It has nothing whatever to do with emotion, feeling. It is not a respectable thing; it is a flame that destroys anything that is false. And we are always so afraid to allow that flame to devour the things that we hold dear, the things that we call important.

After all, the lives we lead at present, based on needs, desires, and the ways of controlling desire, make us more shallow and empty than ever. We may be very clever, very learned, able to repeat what we have gathered, but the electronic machines are doing that, and already in some fields the machines are more capable than man, more accurate and swifter in their calculations. So we always come back to the same thing—which is that life as we live it now is so very superficial, narrow, limited, all because deep down we are empty, lonely, and always trying to cover it up, to fill up that emptiness; therefore, the need, the desire becomes a terrible thing. Nothing can fill that deep void within—no gods, no saviors, no knowledge, no relationship, no children, no husband, no wife—nothing. But if the mind, the brain, the whole of your being can look at it, live with it, then you will see that psychologically, inwardly, there is no need for anything. That is true freedom.

But that requires very deep insight, profound inquiry, ceaseless watching; and out of that perhaps we shall know what love is. How can there be love when there is attachment, jealousy, envy, ambition, and all the pretense which goes with that word? Then, if we have gone through that emptiness—which is an actuality, not a myth, not an idea—we shall find that love and desire and passion are the same thing. If you destroy one, you destroy the other; if you corrupt one, you corrupt beauty. To go into all this requires not a detached mind, not a dedicated mind or a religious mind, but a mind that is inquiring, that is never satisfied, that is always looking, watching, observing itself, knowing itself. Without love you will never find out what truth is.

Question: How can one find out what is one's main problem?

KRISHNAMURTI: Why divide problems as major and minor? Is not everything a problem? Why make them little or big problems, essential or unessential problems? If we could understand one problem, go into it very deeply however small or big it is, then we would uncover all problems. This is not a rhetorical answer. Take any problem: anger, jealousy, envy, hatred—we know them all very well. If you go into anger very deeply, not just brush it aside, then what is involved? Why is one angry? Because one is hurt, someone has said an unkind thing; and when someone says a flattering thing, you are pleased. Why are you hurt? Self-importance, is it not? And why is there self-importance? Because one has an idea, a symbol of oneself, an image of oneself, what one should be, what one is or what one should not be. Why does one create an image about oneself? Because one has never studied what one is, actually. We think we should be this or that, the ideal, the hero, the example. What awakens anger is that our ideal, the idea we have of ourselves, is attacked. And our idea about ourselves is our escape from the fact of what we are. But when you are observing the actual fact of what you are, no one can hurt you. Then, if one is a liar and is told that one is a liar, it does not mean that one is hurt; it is a fact. But when you are pretending you are not a liar and are told that you are, then you get angry, violent. So we are always living in an ideational world, a world of myth, and never in the world of actuality. To observe *what is,* to see it, actually be familiar with it, there must be no judgment, no evaluation, no opinion, no fear.

Question: Can one liberate oneself by following any particular religion?

KRISHNAMURTI: Certainly not. You know, two thousand years or five thousand years of teaching which persuades you to believe in a certain thing is not religion. It is propaganda. You have been told for centuries that you are a Frenchman, an Englishman, a Catholic, Hindu, Buddhist, or a Muslim, and you repeat those words endlessly. And do you mean to say that a mind which has been so conditioned, so influenced, and become such a slave to propaganda, ceremony, and the show of religion can, within that conditioning, be liberated?

Question: You have said that by believing in God one does not find God, but can one find God through revelation?

KRISHNAMURTI: Why do you want things to be revealed to you when you do not know your own self? Your own self has been revealed to you this evening; the way you think, the way you act, your motives, ambitions, urges, your incessant battles with yourself. It has been revealed to you, but you do not know anything about it. You only know your theories, visions. And if you do not know what is immediate, near at hand, how can you know something which is immense? So it is much better to begin with that which is very close, which is yourself. And when all deceptions, illusions have been wiped away, you will find out for yourself what is the real. Then you do not have to believe in God, you do not have to have a doctrine; it is there, that which is sublime, unnameable.

Question: Why does fear come upon us when we become conscious of our own emptiness?

KRISHNAMURTI: Fear only comes into being when you are escaping from the thing which is—when you are avoiding it, pushing it away. When you are actually confronted with the thing, facing it, then is there fear? Escaping, moving away from the fact causes fear. Fear is the process of thought, and thought is of time, and without understanding the whole process of thought and time, you will not understand fear. To look at the fact without avoidance is the ending of fear.

Question: You have said that our essential needs are food, clothing, and shelter, whereas sex belongs to the world of psychological desires. Can you explain that further?

KRISHNAMURTI: I am sure this is a question everyone is waiting to find out about! What is sex? Is it the act, or the pleasurable images, the thought, the memories around it all? Or is it just a biological fact? And is there the memory, the picture, the excitement, the need when there is love—if I may use that word without spoiling it? I think one has to understand the physical, biological fact. That is one thing. All the romanticism, the excitement, the feeling that one has given oneself over to another, the identification of oneself with another in that relationship, the sense of continuity, the satisfaction—all that is another thing. When we are really concerned with desire, with need, how deeply does sex play a part? Is it a psychological need, as it is a biological need? It requires a very clear, sharp mind, brain, to differentiate between the physical need and the psychological need. Many things are involved in sex, not just the act. The desire to forget oneself in another, the continuity of a relationship, children, and trying to find immortality through the children, the wife, the husband, the sense of giving oneself over to another, with all the problems of jealousy, attachment, fear—the agony of it all—is all that love? If there is no understanding of need, basically, deep down, completely, in the dark recesses of one's own consciousness, then sex, love, and desire play havoc in our lives.

Question: Can liberation be realized by everyone?

KRISHNAMURTI: Surely. It is not given to the few. Liberation is not a form of snobbishness; it is there for anyone who will inquire into it. It is there with an ever-widening, deepening beauty and strength when there is self-knowing. And anyone can begin to find out about himself by watching himself, as you watch yourself in a mirror. The mirror does not lie; it shows you exactly what your face looks like. In the same way you can watch yourself without distortion. Then you begin to find out about yourself. Self-knowing, learning about yourself is an extraordinary thing. The way to reality, to that unknown immensity, is not through a church door, not through any book, but through the door of self-knowing.

September 12, 1961

Fifth Talk in Paris

I think it would be good if we could actually experience that which I am going to talk about. For most of us, experience is a very casual affair. We respond to any challenge halfheartedly, languidly; there is hesitation, fear of what the consequences will be. We never respond to a challenge completely, with all our being. So there is always a lack of total attention when there is a challenge, and therefore our responses are very limited, restricted; they are never free, complete. One must have noticed that. And I feel it is very important to consider this carefully because we have so many experiences all day long, so many influences pass through us, each leaving its mark. The casual word, a gesture, an idea, a passing phrase or glance—these all leave their imprint, and we never give our total attention to any of them. To experience anything completely, there must be total attention, and we can see that attention is very different from concentration. Concentration is a process of exclusion, a narrowing down, a cutting out, whereas attention takes everything in.

As I am going to talk about something rather complex, I think one should be aware that experiencing demands total attention, not merely to listen to the words, but also to actually experience the thing. Listening is quite difficult. We hardly ever really listen to anything—to a bird, to a voice, to the husband, wife, or child; we just casually take a few words in and discard the rest, always interpreting, changing, condemning, and choosing. Listening demands a certain quality of full attention where none of these happens, where you give your whole being to finding out.

So to find out about fear—which I am going to talk over with you now—to go into it rather deeply demands sustained attention, not listening to a few phrases only and then going off thinking about your own ideas and problems, but actually going through the whole problem of fear to the very end. To be really serious is to have the capacity to go to the very end of any issue, whatever the consequences, whatever the final result may be.

I want to talk about fear because fear distorts all our feelings, our thoughts, and our relationships. It is fear that makes most of us turn what is called spiritual; it is fear that drives us to the intellectual solutions offered by so many people; it is fear which makes us do all kinds of odd and peculiar things. And I wonder if we have ever experienced actual fear, not the feeling that arises before or after an event. Is there such a thing as fear, by itself? Or is there only fear when there is the thought of tomorrow or yesterday, of what has happened or what will happen? Is there ever fear in the living, active present? When you are confronted with the thing of which you say you are afraid, in that actual moment is there fear?

For me, it is very important, this question of fear. Because unless the mind is totally, completely, absolutely free of fear of every kind: fear of death, of public opinion, of separation, of not being loved—you know the many types and varieties of fear—unless the total consciousness is free of fear, it is impossible to go very far. One may potter anxiously around in the enclosures of one's own brain, but to go very, very deeply into oneself and to see what there is and beyond, there must be no fear of any kind, neither the fear of death nor of poverty, nor of not attaining something.

Fear, because of its very nature, inevitably prevents inquiry. And unless the mind, the whole being is free from fear, not only the conscious fears, but the deep, secret, hidden fears of which one is hardly aware, there is no possibility of finding out what is actually there, what is true, what is factual, and if there actually is that sense of sublimity, of immensity which man has been talking about for centuries upon centuries.

I feel that it is possible to be totally free of fear, not during a period, not eventually, but literally to be free of it completely. The experience of that total state of nonfear is what I want to go into with you.

I want to make it clear that I am not talking from memory. I have not already thought out beforehand the question of fear and come here to repeat what I have rehearsed—that would be terribly boring, for me and for you. I also am inquiring. It must be new every time. And I hope you are taking the journey of inquiry with me and not merely being concerned with your own particular form of fear, whether it is of darkness, the doctor, hell, disease, God, what your parents will say, what the wife, the husband will say, or any of the dozens of forms of fear. We are inquiring into the nature of fear and not into any particular expression of fear.

Now, if you examine, you will see that there is fear only when thought dwells on the yesterday or tomorrow, the past or the future. The active verb is never fearful, but in the past or the future of the verb there is always fear. There is no fear in the actual present, and that is an extraordinary thing to discover for oneself. There is no fear of any kind when there is the actual, living moment, the active present. So thought is the origin of fear, the thought of tomorrow or yesterday. Attention is in the active present. The thought of what happened yesterday or what will happen tomorrow is inattention, and inattention breeds fear. Is that not so? When I can give my whole attention to any issue, without withholding, without denying, without judging, evaluating, in that state of attention there is no fear. But if there is inattention, that is, if I say, "What will happen tomorrow," or if I am caught up in what happened yesterday, then that engenders fear. Attention is the active present. Fear is thought caught in time. When you are confronted with something real, actual, when there is danger, in that moment there is no thought; you act. And that action may be positive or negative.

So thought is time—not time by the watch, but the psychological time of thought. So time breeds fear—time as the distance from here to there, which is the process of becoming something; time as the things I have said and done yesterday, the hidden things which I do not want anyone to know; time as what will happen tomorrow, what becomes of me when I die.

So thought is time. And in the active present is there time and is there thought? One can see, can one not, that fear only exists when thought projects itself forwards or backward, and that thought is the result of time—time as becoming something or not becoming, time as fulfillment or frustration. We are not talking of chronological time; obviously, to try to dispense with that would be lopsided and silly. We are talking of time as thought. If that is clear, then we must go into the question of what is thought, what is thinking. And I hope you are not merely listening to the words but actually listening to the challenge of what is being said, and responding for yourself. I am asking, "What is thinking?" Unless you know the mechanism of thinking and have gone into it very deeply, you cannot answer; your response will be inadequate. And if your response is inadequate, there will be conflict, and in trying to get away from the conflict, there is the avoidance of the fact—the fact that you do not know. The moment you realize that you have no answer, that you do not know, there is fear. I wonder if you are following all this.

So, what is thinking? Obviously, thinking is the reaction between challenge and response, is it not? I ask you something, and there is a time interval before you reply; in that interval thought is acting, searching for an answer. It is fairly simple to listen to this explanation, but to actually experience the process of thinking for yourself, to go into the question of how the brain responds to a challenge and what is the process of manufacturing the response, requires active attention, does it not? Please watch your response to the question: What is thinking? What is taking place? You cannot answer; you have never looked to find out; you are waiting for some response from your memory. And in that time lag, in the interval between the question and the response, there is the process of thinking; is that not so? If I ask you a question with which you are familiar, such as "What is your name?" you answer instantaneously because after constant repetition, you know the answer so well. If one asks something a little more serious, there is a time interval of several seconds, is there not, during which the brain is set in motion and is looking into memory for the answer. If one asks a much more complex question, the time interval is greater, but the process is the same—looking into memory, searching for the right words, finding them, and then responding. Please follow this slowly because it is really very amusing and interesting to watch this process taking place. It is all a part of self-knowing.

One can also ask a question, such as "What is the mileage between here and New York?" to which, after searching in memory you have to say, "I do not know, but I can find out." This takes more time. And one can ask a question to which you have to say, "I do not know the answer," but at the same time you are waiting for an answer, waiting to be told the answer. So, there is the familiar question and the immediate response; the not-so-familiar question, taking a little time; there is something which you are not sure of but can find out, again taking time; and something you do not know but think that if you wait, you will get an answer.

Now, if one asks the question, "Is there God, or not?" what happens? There is no answer to be found from memory, is there? Though you may like to believe, though you have been told, you have to brush all that nonsense aside. Investigation in memory does not help; waiting to be told is no good, for nobody can tell you, and the time interval is of no avail. There is only the fact in the active present, the absolute certainty that you do not know. This state of not-knowing is complete attention, is it not? And every other form of knowing or not-knowing comes from time and thought, and is inattention.

In following all this, are you learning? Surely, learning implies not-knowing. Learning is not additive; you cannot gather it. In the process of gathering, accumulating, you are merely adding to knowledge, which is static. Whereas learning is constantly changing, moving, living.

Therefore, what happens if you are learning about fear? You are pursuing fear, are you not? You are after fear, fear is not after you. And then you find that there is no such thing as 'you' and 'fear'. There is no such division. So attention is the active present in which the mind, the brain says, "I absolutely do not know." And in that state there is no fear. But there is fear when you say, "I do not know, but I hope." I think this is a very crucial point to understand. Let us look at it differently.

After all, fear arises when you are seeking security, outward or inward—when you want a state which is permanent, enduring, lasting, in relationship, in the things of this world, in the assurance that knowledge gives, in emotional experience. And ultimately we say there is God who is absolutely, everlastingly permanent—where we can find a peace, a security, which can never be disturbed. Each one is seeking security in one form or another, and you know how one plays at it all—seeking security in love, in property, in virtue, vowing to oneself to be good, to be without sex. We all know the horrors involved in openly or secretly seeking security. And that is fear because you have never found out if there is security. You do not know. I am using those words in the sense that it is a fact that absolutely and completely you do not know. You do not know if there is God or not. You do not know whether there will be another war or not. You do not know what is going to take place tomorrow. You do not know if there is anything permanent inwardly. You do not know what is going to happen in your relationships, with your wife, your husband, your children. You do not know, but you have to find out, have you not? You have to find out for yourself that you do not know. And that state of not-knowing, that state of complete uncertainty is not fear; it is full attention in which you can find out.

So one sees that the totality of consciousness, the whole of it—which includes the superficial, the conscious, the hidden, and the utmost depths of the racial residue, the motives, all that which is thought—is essentially fear. Though it may have certain forms of pleasure, pain, amusement, joy, and all the rest of it, you will see that it is the result of time. Consciousness is time; it is the result of many days, months, years, and centuries. Your consciousness as a Frenchman, historically, has taken many generations of propaganda. The fact that you are a Christian, a Catholic, or whatever it may be, has taken two thousand years of propaganda, during which you have been made to believe, to think, to function and act in a certain pattern which you call Christian. And not to have any belief, to be as nothing seems very fearful. So the total consciousness is fear. That is a fact, and you cannot merely agree or disagree with a fact.

Now, what happens when you are confronted with a fact? Either you have opinions about the fact, or you merely observe the fact. If you have opinions, judgments, evaluations of the fact, then you are not seeing. Then time comes in because your opinion is of time, of yesterday, what you have known previously. The actual seeing is the active present, and in that seeing, there is no fear. I am not mesmerizing you by saying there is no fear. This is an actual fact. It is the experiencing of an actual fact which frees the total consciousness from fear. I hope you are not too tired and are experiencing this because you cannot take it home and think it over. Then it has no value. What has value is directly to face it and go into it. Then you will see that the whole of our thinking mechanism with its knowledge, its subtleties, its defenses and denials—the whole of that is thought and the actual cause of fear. And we see also that when there is total attention, there is no thought, there is merely perception, seeing.

When there is attention, there is complete stillness, for in that attention there is no exclusion. When the brain can be completely still, not asleep, but active, sensitive, alive—in that state of attentive stillness there is no fear. Then there is a quality of movement which is not thought at all, nor is it feeling, emotion, or sentiment. It is not a vision, not a delusion; it is a totally different kind of movement which leads to the unnameable, the immeasurable, the truth.

But unfortunately you are not really listening, experiencing, because you have not actually gone into it, you have not inquired that far. Therefore before long, fear will surge over you again and overwhelm you. So you have to go into it, and as you go into it, it is being resolved. That is the foundation, and when you have laid the foundation, you will never seek because all search after reality is based on fear. When the mind, the brain, is free of fear, then you will find out.

Question: I have read a book by you on education. Could we not found a school of that kind while you are here in Paris?

KRISHNAMURTI: First of all, sir, we have been talking of fear, not of founding schools. If you want to found a school of that sort, it is up to you, not to me, because I am going at the end of next week. And schools are not so easily founded. There must be fire behind it. This question is right in its own place, but perhaps we can ask more relevant questions.

Question: Why do children have fear?

KRISHNAMURTI: Is not the question: Why do you have fear? It is fairly obvious why children have fear. They are surrounded by a society which is based on fear. The parents are afraid, and the child needs security essentially, and when he is deprived of security, he is afraid. You see, you are not facing the fact that you are afraid.

Question: Is it possible to be always in the state of full attention which excludes fear?

KRISHNAMURTI: In attention there is no exclusion; it is not a process of resistance. We went into the question of fear, and we saw that there is no fear when you are attending. In attention there is not an exclusive process of thought. You can use thought, but there is no exclusiveness. I do not know if you see the point. I am attending; at the moment I am completely there. But I am using words to communicate. The use of words is limited to that only, to the communication, not to the experiencing of the actual fact.

And then there is the question as to whether one can maintain full attention. To "maintain" implies time, and therefore you have already destroyed attention. If there is the cessation of attention, leave it, and let it arise. Do not say, "I must maintain it," for that means effort, time, thought, and all the rest of it.

Question: Is all memory connected with knowledge, or is that silence a memory of a different kind?

KRISHNAMURTI: The whole process of knowing, gathering experience, results in memory, which is time. We know the mechanical process of accumulating memory. Every experience not understood, incomplete, leaves its mark, which we call memory.

And is that stillness a memory of a different quality? It has nothing whatsoever to do with memory. Memory implies, does it not, continuity: the past, the present, and the future. Stillness has no continuity, and this is important to understand. One can induce, discipline the brain to be still, and that disciplining has a continuity; but the stillness which is a result of discipline, of memory, is not stillness at all.

We are talking of a stillness which comes without invitation when there is no fear of any kind, open or secret. And when there is that stillness, which is an absolute necessity and which is not of memory, then there is a totally different type of movement.

September 14, 1961

Sixth Talk in Paris

I want to talk over something which seems to me important: It is the question of mutation and change. What do we mean by change? And at what level, to what depth do we change? Obviously change is necessary; not only must the individual change, but the collective must change. I do not believe there is any collective mind, except the inherited racial instincts and knowledge stored up in the unconscious, but obviously collective action is necessary. But to make that collective action complete, not discordant, the individual must change in his relationship to the collective. In the very action of the individual changing, surely, the collective will also change. They are not two separate things opposed to each other, the individual and the collective, though certain political groups try to separate the two and to force the individual to conform to the so-called collective.

If we could unravel together the whole problem of change, how to bring about a change in the individual and what that change implies, then perhaps, in the very act of listening, participating in the inquiry, there might come about a change which is without your volition. For me, a deliberate change, a change which is compulsory, disciplinary, conformative, is no change at all. Force, influence, some new invention, propaganda, a fear, a motive, compels you to change—that is no change at all. And though intellectually you may agree very easily with this, I assure you that to fathom the actual nature of change without a motive is quite extraordinary.

Most of us have such ingrained, deep-rooted habits of thought, of ideas, of physical addictions that it seems almost impossible to give them up. We have established certain ways of eating, a certain kind of food we insist on, various habits of dress, physical habits, emotional habits, and habits of thought and so on; and to bring about a deep, radical change without some compulsive threat is really quite difficult. The change we know of is always very superficial. A word, a gesture, an idea, an invention can cause one to break a habit and adjust oneself to a new pattern, and one thinks one has changed. To leave one church and join another, to stop calling oneself a Frenchman and to call oneself a European or an internationalist, that sort of change is very superficial; it is merely a matter of commerce, of exchange. A change in the way of living, going on a trip round the world, changing one's ideas, one's attitudes, one's values—all this process seems to me very superficial because it is the result of some compulsive force, outwardly or inwardly.

So, we can see very clearly that to change because of any outside influence—through fear, or because of the desire to achieve a result—is not a radical change. And we do need a complete change, a tremendous revolution. What we need is not a change of ideas, of patterns, but the breaking up, the total destruction of all patterns. We can see, historically, that every revolution, however promising, however violent at the beginning, invariably ends in the old pattern repeated; and that every change brought about by the compulsion of fear or reward, profit, is only another adaptation. And there must be a change because you cannot continue to live with these petty, narrow, limited attitudes, beliefs, and dogmas. They must be shattered, they must be broken down. And how are they to be broken down? What are the processes which will totally break the formation of habits? Is it possible not to have patterns at all—not to be leaving one habit and establishing another?

If the whole question is understood up to now, then we can proceed to find out if it is possible to bring about a quality of the mind or brain which is always fresh, always young, new, never creating a habit of thought, nor clinging to a dogma or belief. So it seems to me that one has to inquire into the whole framework of consciousness in which we function. The whole of our consciousness, the hidden and the superficial, functions within a framework, a border; and to break down the border is the issue with which we are confronted. It is not merely a matter of a change in the way of thinking because you can think in a new way, as the latest communist, or adopt a new belief, but it is still within the framework of consciousness, of thought—and thought is always limited. So a change in the pattern of thought is not the breaking down of the limitations of consciousness.

Most of us are quite satisfied with a superficial adjustment, and we think it is an improvement to learn a new technique, acquire a new language, get a new job, find another way to make money, or form a new relationship when the old one becomes irksome. For most of us life is at that level: adjustment, compulsion, the breaking of old patterns and being caught in new ones. But that is not change at all, and the present human issues demand a complete revolution, a total mutation. So one has to go much deeper into consciousness to find out whether it is possible to bring about a radical change so that the limitations of thought are broken down and consciousness set free.

Perhaps superficially, consciously, you can do some wiping away of what is on the top of the slate; but to cleanse the deep recesses of one's own heart and mind, the hidden, the unconscious, seems almost impossible, does it not, because you do not know what is there; the superficial mind cannot penetrate into the dark storehouse of memory. But it has to be done.

I hope you are not merely following all this verbally, intellectually, because that is a stupid game to play; it is like playing with ashes. But if you are following experimentally, factually—not following the speaker, but following the experiment which you yourself are making—then I think it will have great value. So how can one go into the unconscious, into the hidden recesses of one's own heart, mind, and brain? The psychologists and the analysts try to take you back into infancy, and all the rest of it, but that does not solve the fundamental problem at all because there is the interpreter, the evaluator, and you are merely adjusting yourself to a pattern again. We are talking of completely destroying the pattern, because the pattern is merely the experiences of thousands of years forced onto the brain, which is fantastically sensitive and adaptable, by repetition.

So, how is one to set about breaking down the pattern? First, we must be sure that the analytical process done by the psychologist, the analyst, or yourself has no value when we are concerned with complete transformation, complete mutation. It may have some value in making a person who is mentally ill able to fit in more with the present unhealthy society, but we are not talking about that. Before one can proceed further, one must be completely sure that analysis cannot bring about a total revolution in consciousness. What is implied in analysis? Whether it is done by an outsider or yourself, there is always the observer and the observed, is there not? There is the observer, watching, criticizing, censoring, and he is interpreting what he observes according to a set of values which he already has. So there is a division between the observer and the observed, a conflict; and if the observer is not observing accurately, there is misrepresentation; and that misrepresentation is carried forward indefinitely, causing deeper misunderstanding. So there is no end to miscalculation in analysis. Of that you must be absolutely sure—sure in the sense that you can see that that is not the right way to free consciousness.

So if, not knowing what the right approach is, one can nevertheless deny the wrong approach, then the mind is in a state of negation, is it not? I wonder if you have ever tried negative thinking? Most of our thinking is positive thinking which also includes a certain form of negation. Our thinking at present is based on fear, on profit, on reward, on authority; we think according to a formula, and that is positive thinking with its own negations. But we are talking about the negation of the false without knowing what is the true. Can one say to oneself, "I know analysis is false; it will not break down the limitations of consciousness or bring about a mutation, so I will not indulge in it." Or, "I know nationalism is poison, whether it is the nationalism of France, Russia, or India, so I deny it. Not knowing what else there may be, I can see that nationalism is wrong." And to see that the gods, the saviors, the ceremonies man has invented, whether they are of ten thousand years, two thousand years, or the latest of forty years, to see that they have no validity and deny them completely—that demands a mind and a brain that is very clear, that has no fear in its denial. Then, by denying what is false, you are already beginning to see what is true, are you not? To see what is true, there must first be the denial, the negation of what is false. I wonder if you are following all this!

To find out what is beauty, you must deny all the beauty which man has created. To experience the essence of beauty, there must first be the destruction of everything that has been created so far because the expression, however marvelous it is, is not beauty. To find out what virtue is, which is an extraordinary thing, there must be a complete tearing down of the social morality of respectability, with all its silly taboos of what you must do and what you must not do. When you see and deny what is false, without knowing in advance what is true, then there is the real state of negation. It is only the mind and brain which is empty of what is false that can discover what is true.

So if the analytical process does not break up the framework within which consciousness functions, if you have denied that process, then one must ask oneself what are the other false things which must be denied. I hope you are following all this.

Surely the next thing to deny is the demand for a change. Why does one demand a change? You never demand a change if the present conditions suit you, satisfy you. You do not want a revolution if you have a million dollars. You do not want a revolution if you are comfortable, bourgeois, settled in society with your wife, your husband, your children. Then you say, "For God's sake, leave everything alone." You want a change only when you are disturbed, discontented, when you want more money, a better house. So if you go into it very deeply, our demand for change is the demand for a more comfortable, more profitable life. It is based on a motive, to acquire a new pattern of comfort, security. Now, if you see that process as false, as you must if you would find out what is true, then is there a seeking for a change? Is there a search at all?

After all, you are all here, are you not, wanting to find out. What are you seeking, and why are you seeking? If you go into it deeply, you will find that you are dissatisfied with things as they are and are wanting something new. And the new must always be gratifying, comfortable, assuring, secure. The so-called religious people are seeking God. At least they say so. But search surely implies something which you have lost, or something which you have known, and want to get back. How can you seek God? You do not know anything about God except what you have been told—which is propaganda. The church goes in for propaganda, and the communists also. But you do not know anything about God, and to find out, you must first totally deny, put aside all forms of propaganda, all the tricks that the churches and others have played.

So for the complete mutation in consciousness to take place, you must deny analysis and search, and no longer be under any influence—which is immensely difficult. The mind, seeing what is false, has put the false aside completely, not knowing what is true. If you already know what is true, then you are merely exchanging what you consider is false for what you imagine is true. There is no renunciation if you know what you are going to get in return. There is only renunciation when you drop something not knowing what is going to happen. That state of negation is completely necessary. Please follow this carefully because if you have gone so far, you will see that in that state of negation you discover what is true; because, negation is the emptying of consciousness of the known.

After all, consciousness is based on knowledge, on experience, on racial inheritance, on memory, on the things one has experienced. Experiences are always of the past, operating on the present, being modified by the present, and continuing into the future. All that is consciousness, the vast storehouse of centuries. It has its usefulness in mechanical living only. It would be absurd to deny all the scientific knowledge acquired through the long past. But to bring about a mutation in consciousness, a revolution in this whole structure, there must be complete emptiness. And that emptiness is possible only when there is the discovery, the actual seeing of what is false. Then you will see, if you have gone so far, that emptiness itself brings about a complete revolution in consciousness—it has taken place.

You know, so many of us are afraid, scared to be alone. We always want a hand to hold, an idea to cling to, a god to worship. We are never alone. In our room, in a bus, we have the companionship of our thoughts, our occupations; and when with other people, we adjust ourselves to the group, to the company. We are actually never alone, and for most people the very thought of it is frightening. But it is only the mind, the brain that is completely alone, empty of every demand, every form of adjustment, every influence, completely emptied—only such a mind discovers that that very emptiness is mutation.

I assure you that everything is born out of emptiness; everything new comes out of this vast, immeasurable, unfathomable sense of emptiness. This is not romanticism, it is not an idea, it is not an image, it is not an illusion. When you deny the false completely, not knowing what is true, then there is a mutation in consciousness, a revolution, a total transformation. Perhaps then there is no longer consciousness as we know it, but something entirely different; that consciousness, that state can live in this world because we are not denying mechanical knowledge. So, if you have gone into it, there it is.

But most of us want a change which is only a modified continuity. In that there is nothing new. In that there is no fresh, young mind. And it is only the fresh, innocent, young mind that can discover what is true, and it is only to such a mind which is free of the known that the unnameable, the unknowable can come.

Question: If one visually sees the false as the false and drops it, is that denial, or is there something more to it?

KRISHNAMURTI: I think there is something more to denial than that. What makes you deny, what is the reason, the motive? What urges you to deny something is either fear or profit. If you no longer find comfort in your church, you join another or some other stupid sect. But if you deny every form of church, every form of clinging to something that will give you comfort, not knowing where it is going to lead you in that state of uncertainty, in that state of danger, then that is denial. It requires a very clear perception that any religious organization is detrimental, is something ugly, that holds man in bondage; and when you deny that, you deny all spiritual organizations. And that means you will have to stand alone, does it not? Whereas you all want to belong to something or other, to call yourselves Frenchmen, Englishmen, Germans, Catholics, Protestants, and all the other things. To be a complete outsider to all this is denial.

Question: When one comes to this sense of emptiness, how can one live in this world practically?

KRISHNAMURTI: First of all, do you come to it? And then, we have not denied mechanical knowledge, have we? You must have mechanical knowledge to live in this world, to go to your office, to function as an engineer, an electrician, a violinist, or what you will. We are talking of a revolution in consciousness, in the psyche, in the entire being. The superficial technical knowledge, the mechanical machinery of the daily operational job, that you must have. But if the mind that uses this technical knowledge is not completely free, is not in a state of mutation, then the superficial mechanism becomes destructive, harmful, ugly, brutal—and that is what is happening in the world.

Question: Can you tell us again why analysis is wrong? I didn't quite get it.

KRISHNAMURTI: Let us look at it differently. What are dreams? Why do we dream? I am not diverging from the question. You dream because during the day your brain is so occupied that it has no quietness in which, and with which, it can go deeply. And you know how it is occupied—with the job, with competing, a thousand things. So while you are asleep, there are hints, intimations from the unconscious, which become symbols, dreams; and upon waking, you remember them and try to interpret them or to get them interpreted. You know this whole process. Now why do you dream at all? Why should you dream? Is not dreaming, if I may use the word, wrong? Because if you are observant, if you are aware of everything that is happening around you and inside you all the waking hours, then in that watching, you uncover everything as you go along; all the unconscious motives, desires, impulses come out into the conscious mind and are understood. Then when you sleep, dreaming is not possible. Then sleeping has quite a different significance. It is the same with analysis. If you can perceive the total process of analysis with one look—and you can—then you see very well that so long as there is an observer, a censor interpreting, the analysis must always be wrong. Because the condemnation or approval of the censor is based on his conditioning.

Question: You spoke of freedom from all influence, but are not these meetings influencing us?

KRISHNAMURTI: If you are being influenced by the speaker, then you might just as well go to the cinema, to the church, or to Mass. If you are being influenced by the speaker, then you are creating authority, and any form of authority prevents you from understanding what is real, what is true. And if you are influenced by the speaker, you have not understood what he has been saying for the last hour, the last thirty years. To be free of all influence—the books you read, the newspapers, the cinema, the education you have had, the society to which you belong, the influence of the church—to be aware of all influences and not to be caught in any of them is intelligence. That requires alertness, watchfulness, awareness of everything that is going on within, every response—which means not to let a single thought go by without knowing the content, the background, the motive of that thought.

September 17, 1961

Seventh Talk in Paris

If I may, I would like to talk over rather a complex issue with you, which is death. But before we go into that, I would like to suggest that those who are taking notes should not do so. The speaker is not giving a lecture where you take notes and later you or someone else interprets what is being said. Interpreters are exploiters, whether they are well-intentioned or merely want to make a name for themselves. So, I would earnestly suggest that you listen to, experience, and not think over what is said later, or listen to other people's comments on it—which is all so utterly futile.

I would also like to point out that words have very little meaning in themselves. They are symbols, used for the purpose of communication. I must use certain words, but they are used in order to commune, and one must feel one's way through them into things that are not explicable by words, and there is a danger in that because we are liable to interpret words according to our own likes and dislikes, and thereby miss the significance of what is actually being said. We are trying to find out what is false and what is true, and to do that, one must go beyond words. And in going beyond words, there is this danger of our own personal, individual interpretation of those words. So if we wish to go into this question of death really profoundly, as I intend to do, one must be aware of words and their significance and beware of interpreting them according to our likes and dislikes. If our minds are free of the word, the symbol, then we can commune with each other beyond the word.

Death is quite a complex problem, really, to experience and go into profoundly. We either rationalize it, intellectually explain it away, and comfortably settle back; or else we have beliefs, dogmas, ideas to which we run. But dogmas, beliefs, and rationalizations do not solve the problem. Death is there; it is always there. Even if the doctors and scientists can prolong the physical machinery for another fifty years or more, death is waiting. And to understand it, we must go into it, not verbally, intellectually, or sentimentally, but really face the fact and go into it. That requires a great deal of energy, a great clarity of perception; and energy and clarity are denied when there is fear.

Most of us, whether we are young or old, are scared of death. Though we see the hearse going by every day, we are frightened of death; and where there is fear, there is no comprehension. So to go into the question of death, the first, the essential requirement is to be free of fear. And by "going into it" I mean to live with death—not verbally, not intellectually, but actually to see what it feels like to live with something so drastic, so final, with which you cannot argue, with which you cannot bargain. But to do that, one must first be free of fear, and that is extraordinarily difficult.

I do not know if you have ever tried to be free of the fear of anything: the fear of public opinion, of losing your job, of being without a belief. If so, you will know that it is extremely difficult to put fear aside completely. Do we actually know fear? Or is there always an interval between the thought process and the actuality? If I am afraid of public opinion, what people say, that fear is merely a thought process, is it not? But when the actual moment arises of facing the fact of what people are saying, in that very moment there is no fear. In total awareness there is no experiencer. I do not know if you have ever tried to be completely aware without any choice, to be wholly perceptive without any borderline to attention. If one is so aware, one can see that one is always running away from the things of which one is afraid, always escaping. And it is this running away from the thing which thought calls fearful that creates fear, that is fear—which means, really, that fear is caused by time and thought.

And what is time? Apart from chronological time by the watch, as the tomorrow, the yesterday, is there time, inwardly, psychologically? Or has thought invented time as a means of attaining, a means of gaining, in order to cover the interval between *what is* and 'what should be'? The 'what should be' is merely an ideological statement; it has no validity, it is only a theory. The actual, the factual is *what is*. Face to face with *what is* there is no fear. One is afraid to know actually what one is, but in really facing *what is*, there is no fear. It is thought, thinking about *what is*, that creates fear. And thought is a mechanical process, a mechanical response of memory, so the question is: Can thought die to itself? Can one die to all the memories, experiences, values, judgments one has gathered?

Have you ever tried to die to something? To die without argument, without choice, to a pain, or more especially to a pleasure? In dying there is no argument; you cannot argue with death; it is final, absolute. In the same way one must die to a memory, die to a thought, to all the things, the ideas that one has accumulated, gathered. If you have tried it, you will know how extraordinarily difficult it is—how the mind, the brain holds on to a memory, clings to it. To give up something totally, completely, without asking anything in return, needs clear perception, does it not?

So long as there is continuity of thought as time, as pleasure and pain, there must be fear, and where there is fear there is no understanding. I think that is fairly simple and clear. One is afraid of so many things, but if you will take one of those things and die to it, completely, then you will find that death is not what you have imagined it to be; it is something entirely different. But we want continuity. We have had experiences, gathered knowledge, accumulated various forms of virtue, built character, and so on, and we are afraid that that will come to an end, and so we ask, "What will happen to me when death comes?" And that is really the issue. Knowing the inevitability of death, we turn to belief in reincarnation, resurrection, and all the fantasies involved in belief—which is really a continuity of what you are. And actually, what are you? Pain, hope, despair, various forms of pleasure bound by time and sorrow. We have a few moments of joy, but the rest of our life is empty, shallow, a constant battle, full of travail and misery. That is all we know of life, and that is what we want to continue. Our life is a continuity of the known; we move and act from the known to the known, and when the known is destroyed, the whole sense of fear arises, fear of facing the unknown. Death is the unknown. So can one die to the known and face it? That is the issue.

I am not talking of theories. I am not peddling in ideas. We are trying to find out what it means to live. Living without fear may be immortality, being deathless. To die to memories, to the yesterday and the tomorrow, is surely to live with death, and in that state there is no fear of death and all the absurd inventions which fear creates. And what does it mean, to die inwardly? Thought is a continuity of yesterday into the future, is it not? Thought is the response of memory. Memory is the result of experience. And experience is the process of challenge and response. You can see that thought is always functioning in the field of the known, and so long as the machinery of thought is functioning, there must be fear. Because, it is thought that prevents the inquiry into the unknown.

Please, we are trying to think this thing out together. I am not talking to you as a person who has discovered something new and is just telling you about it for you merely to follow verbally. You must go along with it and search out your own mind and heart. There must be self-knowing, for the knowing of oneself is the beginning of freedom from fear.

We are asking if it is possible to live with death, not at the last moment when the mind is diseased or there is old age or an accident, but actually to find out now. To live with death must be an extraordinary experience, something totally new, unthought of and which thought cannot possibly discover. And to find out what it means to live with death, you must have immense energy, must you not? To live with your wife, your husband, your children, your neighbor and not be perverted, twisted, to live with a tree, with nature, you need to have energy to meet it. To live with an ugly thing, you must have energy; otherwise, the ugly thing will distort you, or you will get accustomed to it, mechanically, and the same applies to beauty. Unless you live intensely, completely, fully in a world of this kind where there is every form of propaganda, influence, pressure, control, false values, you get accustomed to it all, and it dulls the mind, the spirit. And to have energy, there must be no fear, which means there must be no demand on life at all. I do not know if you can go as far as that: not to ask a thing of life.

We discussed "need" the other day. We do need certain physical comforts—food and shelter—but to make psychological demands on life means that you are begging, that you are afraid. It requires an intense energy to stand alone. To understand this is not a matter of thinking about it. There is understanding only when there is no choice, no judgment, but merely observation. To die each day means not to carry over from yesterday all your ambitions, your grievances, your memories of fulfillment, your grudges, your hatred. Most of us wither away, but that is not dying. To die is to know what love is. Love has no continuity, no tomorrow. The picture of a person on the wall, the image in your mind—that is not love, it is merely memory. As love is the unknown, so death is the unknown. And to enter the unknown, which is death and love, one must first die to the known. Then only is the mind fresh, young, and innocent; and in that there is no death.

You know, if you observe yourself as in a mirror, you are nothing but a bundle of memories, are you not? And all those memories are of the past; they are all over, are they not? So can't one die to it all in one clean sweep? It can be done, only it demands a great deal of self-inquiry and awareness of of every thought, every gesture, every word, so that there is no accumulation. Surely, that one can do. Then you will know what it is to die every day, and then perhaps we shall also know what it is to love every day, and not merely know love as memory. All that we know now is the smoke of attachment, the smoke of jealousy, envy, ambition, greed, and all that. We do not know the flame behind the smoke. But if one can put away the smoke completely, then we shall find that living and dying are the same thing, not theoretically, but actually. After all, that which continues, which does not come to an end, is not creative. That which has continuity can never be new. It is only in the destruction of continuity that there is the new. I do not mean social or economic destruction; that is very superficial. And if you have gone into it very deeply, not only at the conscious level, but deep down, beyond the measure of thought, beyond all consciousness—which is still in the framework of thought—then you will find that dying is an extraordinary thing. Dying then is creation. Not the writing of poems, painting pictures, or inventing new gadgets—that is not creation. Creation comes only when you have died to all techniques, to all knowledge, to all words.

So death, as we conceive of it, is fear. And when there is no fear because you are inviting death each minute, then every minute is a new thing; it is new because inwardly the old has been destroyed. And to destroy, there must be no fear but only the sense of complete aloneness—to be able to stand completely alone, without God, without family, without name, without time. And that is not despair. Death is not despair. On the contrary, it is living each minute completely, totally, without the limitations of thought. And then you will find that life is death, and death is creation and love. Death which is destruction is creation and love; they always go together; the three are inseparable. The artist is only concerned with his expression, which is very superficial, and he is not creative. Creation is not expression—it is beyond thought and feeling, it is free of technique, free of word and color. And that creation is love.

Question: How are future generations to exist if one dies each minute?

KRISHNAMURTI: I think, if I may say so, that you have misunderstood it entirely. Are you really concerned with what is going to happen to the coming generations? Is love incompatible with bearing children? Do you know what it means really to love somebody? I am not talking of lust. I am not talking of that complete identification, one with another, so that you feel carried away. That is comparatively easy when you are driven by emotion. I am not talking of that. I am talking of that quality of flame when you or the other completely ceases. But I am afraid very few have known that; very few have ceased, even for a moment. If you really know what it means, then there is no question of future generations. After all, if you were really concerned about the future generations, you would have different schools, a totally different kind of education, would you not, without competition and all the other crippling things.

Question: If one does not know what truth is while living, will one know it when one is dead?

KRISHNAMURTI: Sir, what is truth? Truth is not something you have been told about by the church, the priest, the neighbor or through a book; it is not an idea or a belief. It is something vital, new; you have to discover it; it is there for you to find out. And to find out, you must die to the things that you already know. To see something very clearly, to see the rose, the flower, to see another person without interpretation, you must die to the word, to the memories of that person. Then you will know what truth is. Truth is not something far away, some mysterious thing which can only be discovered when you are physically dead, in heaven or in hell. If you were really hungry, you would not be satisfied with explanations about food. You would want food, not the word *food.* In the same way if you want to find out about truth, then the word, the symbol, the explanations are just ashes; they have no meaning.

Question: I see that one must be free of fear to have this energy, and yet it seems to me that in some ways fear is necessary. So how is one to get out of this vicious circle?

KRISHNAMURTI: Surely, a certain amount of physical fear is necessary; otherwise, you would find yourself under a bus. To a certain degree, self-enlightened self-protection is necessary. But beyond that there must be no fear of any kind. I am using the word *must* not as a command but because it is inevitable. I do not think we see the importance, the necessity of total freedom from fear, inwardly. A mind that is afraid cannot proceed to discover in any direction. And the reason we do not see this is because we have built up so many walls of security around ourselves, and we are afraid of what will happen if those guarantees, those resistances are destroyed. All we know is resistance and defense. We say, "What will happen to me if I have no resistance against my wife, my husband, my neighbor, my boss?" Nothing may happen, or everything may happen. To find the truth about it, there must be freedom from resistance, from fear.

Question: While we are listening to you, perhaps we do live in that state, but why don't we live in it all the time?

KRISHNAMURTI: You are listening to me, are you not, because I am rather insistent, because I am energetic, and I love what I am talking about. Not that I love just talking to an audience—that does not mean a thing to me. To find out what it means to live with death is to love death, to understand it, to go into it completely, totally, every minute of the day. So you are listening to me because I am forcing you into a corner to look at yourselves. But afterwards you will forget all about this. You will be back in the old rut, and then you will say, "How am I going to get out of this rut?" So it is really much better not to listen at all than to create another problem of how to continue in another state. You have enough problems—wars, your neighbors, your husbands, wives, children, your ambitions. Do not add another. Either die completely, knowing the necessity, the importance, the urgency of it, or carry on. Do not create another contradiction, another problem.

Question: What about physical death?

KRISHNAMURTI: Does not all machinery wear out? Machinery, however precisely put together, beautifully oiled, must wear out eventually. By eating rightly, taking exercise, finding the right drug, you may live for a hundred and fifty years, but the machinery will collapse in the end, and then you will have this problem of death. You have the problem at the beginning, and you have the problem at the end. Therefore it is much wiser, saner, more rational to solve the problem now and be finished with it.

Question: How are we to answer the child who asks about death?

KRISHNAMURTI: You can only answer the child if you know what death is yourself. You can tell the child that fire burns because you have burned yourself. But you cannot tell the child what love is, can you, or what death is. Neither can you tell the child what God is. If you are a Catholic, a Christian with beliefs and dogmas, you will answer the child accordingly, but that is merely your conditioning. If you yourself have inwardly entered the house of death, then you will really know what to say to the child. But if you have never tasted what it means to die, actually, inwardly, then whatever answer you give the child will have no validity at all; it will merely be a lot of words.

September 19, 1961

Eighth Talk in Paris

In this talk we need to cover a great deal of ground, and it may be rather difficult, or perhaps the right word is *strange*. I am going to use certain words which may mean one thing to you and a very different thing to me. To really commune with each other at all levels, we must have a mutual understanding of the words we use and their significance. Meditation, which I propose to go into with you, has for me a tremendous significance, whereas perhaps for you it is a word which one uses rather casually. Perhaps for you it may mean a method to achieve a result, to get somewhere; and it may involve the repetition of words and phrases to calm the mind, and the attitude of prayer. But, for me, the word *meditation* has quite an extraordinary meaning; and to go into it fully, which I propose to do, one has first to understand, I think, the power which creates illusion.

Most of us live in a make-believe world. All our beliefs are illusions; they have no validity at all. And to strip the mind of every form of illusion and of the power to create illusion needs really clear, sharp perception, the capability of good reasoning without any escape, any deviation. A brain that has no fear, that is not hiding behind secret desires, a brain that is very quiet, without any conflict—such a mind is capable of seeing what is true, of seeing if there is God. I do not mean the word *God* but what that word represents, something which is not measurable in terms of words or time—if there is such a thing. To discover, surely every form of illusion and the power to create illusion must come to an end. And to strip the mind of all illusion is, for me, the way of meditation. I feel that through meditation there is a vast field of immense discovery—not invention, not visions, but something entirely different which is actually beyond time, beyond the things which have been put together by the mind of man through centuries of search. If one really wants to find that out for oneself, one must lay the right foundation, and the laying of the right foundation is meditation. The copying of a pattern, the pursuit of a system, the following of a method of meditation—all that is too infantile, too immature; it is merely imitation and leads nowhere, even if it produces visions.

The right foundation for the discovery of whether there is a reality beyond the beliefs which propaganda has imposed upon each one's mind comes about only through self-knowing. The very knowing about oneself is meditation. The knowing about oneself is not the knowing of what one should be; that has no validity, no reality; it is just an idea, an ideal. But to understand *what is,* the actual fact of what one is from moment to moment—that requires the freeing of the mind from conditioning. I mean by that word *conditioning* all the impositions which society has laid upon us, which religion has laid upon us through propaganda, through insistence, through belief, through fear of heaven and hell. It includes the conditioning of nationality, of climate, of custom, of tradition, of culture as French, Hindu, or Russian, and the innumerable beliefs, superstitions, experiences which form the whole background in which consciousness lives, and which is established through one's own desire to remain secure. It is the investigation into that background and the undoing of that background which constitutes laying the right foundation for meditation.

Without freedom one cannot go very far; one merely wanders off into illusion, which has no meaning at all. If one wants to find out if there is reality or not, if one wants really to go to the very end of that discovery—not merely to play about with ideas, however pleasant, intellectual, reasonable, or apparently sane—there must first be freedom, freedom from conflict. And that is extremely difficult. It is fairly easy to escape from conflict; one can follow some method, take a pill, a tranquilizer, a drink, and one is no longer conscious of conflict. But to go into the whole question of conflict deeply requires attention.

Attention and concentration are two different things. Concentration is exclusion, narrowing down the mind or the brain so as to focus on the thing it desires to study, to look at. That is fairly simple to understand. And the concentration of exclusion creates distractions, does it not? When I wish to concentrate and the mind wanders off on to something else, the something else is a distraction, and therefore there is a conflict. All concentration implies distraction, conflict, and effort. Please do not merely follow my words, my explanations, but actually follow your own conflicts, your distractions, your efforts. Effort implies conflict, does it not? And there is effort only when you want to gain, to achieve, to avoid, to pursue, or deny.

This, if I may say so, is a very important point to understand—that concentration is exclusion, a resistance, a narrowing down of the power of thought. Attention is not the same process at all. Attention is inclusive. One can attend only when there are no barriers to the mind. That is to say, I can see the many faces in front of me now, listen to the voices outside, hear the working or not working of the electric fan, see the smiles, the nodding of heads in approval—attention includes all that and more. Whereas if you merely concentrate, you cannot include all that; it becomes distraction. In attention there is no distraction. In attention there can be concentration, but that concentration has no exclusion. Whereas concentration excludes attention. Perhaps this may be something new to you, but if you will experiment with it for yourself, you will find that there is a quality of attention which can listen, see, observe without any sense of identification; there is a complete seeing, observing, and therefore no exclusion.

I am talking a little bit about all this because I think it is very important to understand that a mind in conflict about anything—about itself, its problems, its neighbor, its security—such a mind, such a brain, can never be free. So you must find out for yourself whether it is possible, living in this world—having to earn a livelihood, living a family life with all the daily boredom of routine, the anxieties, the sense of guilt—to penetrate very deeply, to go beyond consciousness and to live without inward conflict.

Conflict exists, surely, when you want to become something. Conflict exists when there is ambition, greed, envy. And is it possible to live in this world without ambition, without greed? Or is the ultimate course for man to be everlastingly greedy, ambitious, seeking fulfillment and feeling frustrated, anxious, guilty, and all the rest of it? And is it possible to wipe all that out?—because without wiping it out you cannot go very far; it binds thought. And the wiping away from consciousness of this whole process of ambition, envy, greed, is meditation. An ambitious mind cannot possibly know what love is; a mind that is crippled with worldly desires can never be free. Not that one must be without shelter, food, clothing, a certain measure of physical comfort; but a mind that is occupied with envy, hate, greed—whether it is greedy for knowledge, for God or for more clothes—such a mind, being in conflict, can never be free. It is only the free mind that can go very far.

So self-knowing is the beginning of meditation. Without knowing yourself, repeating a lot of words from the Bible, from the Gita, or from any so-called sacred book has no meaning at all. It may pacify your mind, but you can do that with a pill. By repeating a phrase over and over again, your brain naturally becomes quiet, sleepy, and dull; and from that state of insensitivity, dullness, you might have some sort of experience, get certain results. But you are still ambitious, envious, greedy, and create enmity. So learning about oneself, what one actually is, is the beginning of meditation. I am using the word *learn* because when you are learning in the sense of which I am talking, there is no accumulation. What you call learning is the process of adding more and more to what you already know. But, for me, the moment you have acquired, gathered, that accumulation becomes knowledge, and knowledge is not learning. Learning is never accumulative, whereas acquiring knowledge is a process of conditioning.

If I want to learn about myself, find out actually what I am, I have to watch all the time, every minute of the day to see how it expresses itself. Watching is not condemning or approving but seeing what I am from moment to moment. Because what I am is changing all the time, is it not; it is never static. Knowledge is static, whereas the process of learning about the movement of ambition is never static; it is living, moving along. I hope I am explaining myself. So learning and acquiring knowledge are two different things. Learning is infinite; it is a movement in freedom; knowledge has a center which is accumulating, and the only movement it knows is a further accumulation, a further bondage.

To follow this thing which I call the 'me', with all its nuances, its expressions, its deviations, its subtleties, its cunningness, the mind must be very clear, alert, because what I am is constantly changing, being modified, is it not? I am not the same as yesterday or even a minute ago because every thought and feeling is modifying, shaping the mind. And if you are merely concerned with condemning or judging from your accumulated knowledge, your conditioning, then you are not following, moving along with the thing, observing. So learning about yourself has a far greater significance than acquiring knowledge about yourself. You cannot have static knowledge about a living thing. You can have knowledge about something which is past because all knowledge is in the past; it is static, already dead. But a living thing is ever changing, undergoing modification; it is different every minute, and you have to follow it, to learn about it. You cannot understand your child if you are all the time condemning, justifying, or identifying yourself with the child; you have to watch it without judgment when it is asleep, when it is crying, when it is playing, all the time.

So learning about yourself is the beginning of meditation, and as you learn about yourself, there is the elimination of all illusion. And that is absolutely essential because to find out what is true—if there is truth, something beyond measure—there must be no deception. And there is deception when there is the desire for pleasure, for comfort, for gratification. That process, of course, is very simple. In your desire for gratification you create the illusion, and there you are stuck for the rest of your life. There you are satisfied, and most people are satisfied when they believe in God. They are frightened of life, of the insecurity, the turmoil, the agony, the guilt, the anxiety, the misery and sorrow of life, so they establish something at last, which they call God, and go to that. And having committed themselves to belief, they have visions and become saints, and all the rest of it. That is not trying to find out if there is a reality or not. There may be, or there may not be; you have to find out. And to find out, there must be freedom at the beginning and not at the end—freedom from all these things like ambition, greed, envy, fame, wanting to be important, and all that infantile business.

So when you are learning about yourself, you proceed into yourself, not only at the conscious level, but at the deep, unconscious level, bringing out all the secret desires, the secret pursuits, urges, compulsions. Then the power to create illusion is destroyed because you have laid the right foundation. As the mind, the brain examines itself, watches itself in the movement of living, never allowing a single thought or feeling to escape without looking at it, understanding it, then the totality of all that is awareness. It is to be aware of yourself entirely, without condemnation, without justification, without choice—as you look at your face in the mirror. You cannot say, "I wish I had a different face"; it is there.

And through this self-understanding, the brain—which is mechanical, everlastingly chattering, responding to every influence, every challenge—becomes very quiet, though sensitive and alive. It is not a dead brain; it is an active, dynamic, alert brain but very quiet, silent, because it has no conflict. It is silent because it has put away, understood, all the problems it had created for itself. After all, a problem comes into existence only when you have not understood the issue. When the brain has completely understood, examined ambition, then there is no further problem about ambition; it is finished. And so the brain is quiet.

Now, from this point we can proceed, go together, either verbally or actually take the journey together and experience, which means to put away ambition completely. You know you cannot put away ambition or greed little by little; there is no question of "later on" or "in the meantime." Either you must put it away totally or it is not put away at all. But if you have gone that far so that there is no greed, no envy, no ambition, then the brain is exceedingly quiet, sensitive, and therefore free—which is all meditation—and then, but not before, you can go further. Going further, if you have not gone thus far, is mere speculation and has no meaning. To go further this foundation must be established, which is really virtue. It is not the virtue of respectability, the social morality of a society, but an extraordinary thing, a clean, true thing which comes into being without effort, and which is in itself humility. Humility is essential, but you cannot cultivate it, grow it, practice it. To say to oneself, "I will be humble," is too silly; it is vanity covered with the word *humility*. But there is a humility which comes into being naturally, unexpectedly, unsought, and then there is no conflict in it because that humility is never climbing, wanting.

Now, when one has gone that far, when there is complete silence, when the brain is completely still and therefore free, then there is a different movement altogether.

Now, please realize that for you this state is speculative. I am saying something of which you do not know, and therefore for you it has very little significance. But I am saying it because it has significance in relation to the whole, the total existence of life. Because if there is no discovery of what is true and what is false, if there is truth or not, life becomes extraordinarily shallow. Whether you call yourself a Christian, a Buddhist, a Hindu, or what you will, most of our lives are very shallow, empty, dull, mechanical. And with that dull mind we try to find something which cannot be put into words. A petty mind seeking that which is immeasurable is still petty. Therefore the dull mind has to transform itself. So I am talking about something which you may or may not have seen, but it is important to learn about it because that reality includes the totality of all consciousness; it includes the whole action of our life. To find that out the mind must be completely quiet, not through mesmerizing itself, through discipline, through suppression, conformity; all that is merely substituting one desire for another.

I do not know if it has ever happened to you—to have a very still mind. Not the sort of stillness you get in a church or the superficial feeling you have when you are walking down the street, or in a wood, or occupied with the radio, with cooking. These exterior things can absorb you and they do, and there is a temporary form of stillness. That is like a boy playing with a toy; the toy is so interesting that it absorbs all his energy, his thought, but that is not stillness. I mean the stillness which comes into being when the totality of consciousness has been understood, and there is no longer any seeking, searching, wanting, groping; and therefore it is completely quiet. In that quietness there is a totally different movement, and that movement is without time. Do not attempt to capture these phrases, for as such they have no meaning. Our brains, our thoughts are the result of time, so thinking about the timeless has no meaning. Only when the brain has quietened down, when it is no longer seeking, searching, avoiding, resisting, but is completely still because it has understood this whole mechanism, only then, in that stillness there comes a different kind of life, a movement which is beyond time.

Question: Is there not a right kind of effort?

KRISHNAMURTI: For me there is no right effort and wrong effort. All effort implies conflict, does it not? When you love something, in that there is no effort, no conflict, is there? I see that there must be a tremendous change in this world. With all the political leaders, the communists, the capitalists, the authoritarians everywhere, a fundamental change is essential in the world, inwardly. There must be mutation, and I want to find out exactly what the change means. Can it be brought about by effort? When you use the word *effort* it implies, does it not, a center from which you are making an effort to change something else. I want to change my ambition, to destroy it. Now, who is the entity that wants to destroy ambition? Is the ambition something separate from the entity? The entity who is observing the ambition and wanting to change it, to transform it into something else, is therefore still ambitious, so it is no change at all. What brings about a mutation is just watching, seeing—not judging, evaluating, but merely observing. But that seeing, that observation, is prevented because we are so conditioned—as to condemn, to justify, to compare. It is the unconditioning of the brain that brings about mutation.

One has to see the whole absurdity of being conditioned, influenced—by the parents, education, society, the church, the propaganda of ten thousand years or two thousand years. There is a center, inwardly, which has been formed around all that; the center is that. And when that center finds something to be unprofitable, it then wants to be something else which it thinks is more profitable. But we are prevented from seeing this because of our conditioning as being Christian, French, English, German, because of the influences of other people, of our own choice, of the example, the heroes, and so on. All this prevents mutation. But to realize that you are conditioned, to see the fact, without cunning, without the desire for profit—just to see, not verbally, intellectually, but actually to come into contact emotionally with that conditioning—is to listen to what is being said. If you listen now, as the thing is being said, you are emotionally in contact with the fact, and then there is no choice; it is a fact, like an electric shock. But you do not get that emotional shock because you guard yourself, you verbally protect yourself, you say, "What is going to happen to me if I lose everything, psychologically?" But a man who really wants to find out, who is hungry after this, has to free the mind from all influences and propaganda.

You know it is very strange how important propaganda has become in our lives. It has been there for centuries, but now it is becoming more and more rampant—the double talk, the selling; you are begged to buy; the churches repeat their words over and over and over again. And to be free of all that is to observe every thought, every emotion as it arises from moment to moment, to learn all about it. Then you will see, as you observe completely, that there is no process of deliberately lengthening the period of unconditioning; it is there immediately, and therefore no effort is needed.

Question: How can people, including myself, have this love for reality?

KRISHNAMURTI: You cannot have it, sir; you cannot buy it. For those who do not know love, no sacrifice, no exchange will bring it. How do you get love? By practice, by effort, by being told to love day after day, year after year? Mere kindliness is not love, but love includes kindliness, gentleness, concern about another. You see, love is not an end-result, and in love there is no attachment. Love comes only when there is no fear. One can be married, one can live with a family and love without attachment. But that is incredibly arduous; that requires watching all the time.

Question: Is the energy needed to find out about death different from the energy required for meditation?

KRISHNAMURTI: I was explaining the other day that to live with death or to live with anything—with your wife, your husband, your children, your neighbor—you need energy. You need energy to live with a lovely thing or with an ugly thing. If you have no energy to live with beauty, you become accustomed to beauty. And if you have no energy to live with something ugly, that ugliness corrupts, corrodes you. And in the same way to live with death, which is to die to everything, every day, every minute, requires energy. And then there is no fear of death—which we went through the other day. And that same energy is required in the understanding of oneself. How can you understand yourself if you have not got the energy for it? And this energy comes into being when there is no fear, no attachment to your property, your husband, your wife, children, country, gods, and beliefs. This energy is not something which can be measured out little by little; you must have it completely to go into this thing. There is no difference between energies—there is only energy.

Question: What is the difference between concentration and attention?

KRISHNAMURTI: The gentleman wants to know what is the difference between concentration and attention. I will go into it very succinctly. Where there is concentration, there is a thinker, and the thinker separates himself from the thought, and therefore he has to concentrate on thought to bring about a change in thought. But the thinker himself is the result of thought. The thinker is not different from the thought. If there is no thinking, there is no thinker.

Now, in attention there is no thinker, there is no observer; the attention is not from a center. Experiment with this; listen to everything about you; hear the various noises, the movement of people while one is talking, taking out a handkerchief, looking at a book—all that is going on now. In that attention there is no thinker and therefore no conflict, no contradiction, no effort. To observe outwardly is fairly easy, but to be attentive inwardly to every thought, every gesture, every word and feeling requires energy. And when you are so attentive, you are through with all the mechanism of thinking, and then only is it possible to go beyond consciousness.

September 21, 1961

Ninth Talk in Paris

This is the last talk. I would like to talk this morning about sorrow and the religious mind. There is sorrow everywhere, outwardly and inwardly. We see it in high places and in low. For thousands of years it has existed; many theories have been spun around it, and all the religions have talked a great deal about it, but it continues. Is it possible to end sorrow, to be really, inwardly, completely free from sorrow? There is not only the sorrow of old age and death but the sorrow of failure, of anxiety, of guilt, of fear, the sorrow of continued brutality, the ruthlessness of man against man. Is it ever possible to root out the cause of this sorrow—not in another, but in oneself? Surely, if any transformation is to take place, it must begin with oneself. After all, there is no separation between oneself and society. We are society, we are the collective. As a Frenchman, a Russian, an Englishman, a Hindu, we are the result of collective reactions and responses, challenges and influences. And in transforming this center, the individual, perhaps we may alter the collective consciousness.

I think this is not so much a crisis in the outward world but a crisis in consciousness, in thought, in one's whole being. And I think it is only the religious mind that can resolve this sorrow, that can dissipate entirely, wholly, the whole process of thought and the result which thought brings about as sorrow, fear, anxiety, and guilt.

We have tried so many ways to get rid of sorrow: going to church, escaping into beliefs, dogmas, committing oneself to various social and political activities, and innumerable other ways of running away from this everlasting gnawing of fear and sorrow. I think it is only the truly religious mind that can solve the problem. And by a religious mind I mean something entirely different from the mind, the brain, that believes in religion. There is no religion where there is belief. There is no religion where there is dogma, where there is the everlasting repetition of words, words, words, whether in Latin, Sanskrit, or any other language. Going to Mass is just another form of entertainment; it is not religion. Religion is not propaganda. Whether your brain is washed by the church people or by the communists, it is the same thing. Religion is something entirely different from belief and nonbelief, and I want to go into the whole question of what is the religious mind. So let us be very clear that religion is not the faith you believe in; that is too immature. And where there is immaturity, there is bound to be sorrow. It requires great maturity to discover what is a truly religious mind. Obviously it is not the believing mind, not the mind that follows authority of any kind, whether it be the greatest teacher or the head of a certain sect. So obviously a religious mind is free from all following and therefore from all authority.

May I here digress a little and talk a bit about something else? Some of you have been listening to these nine talks during the last three weeks fairly regularly. And if you go away with a lot of conclusions, with a new set of ideas and phrases, you will be going away empty-handed, or your hands will be full of ashes. Conclusions and ideas of any kind do not resolve sorrow. So I deeply hope you will not cling to words but rather journey together with me so that we may go beyond words and discover for ourselves, through self-knowing, what is factual, and from there take the further journey. The discovery of what is in oneself, actually and factually, brings about quite a different response and action. So I hope you will not carry away with you the ashes of words, of memory.

As I was saying, a religious mind is free of all authority. And it is extremely difficult to be free from authority—not only the authority imposed by another, but also the authority of the experience which one has gathered, which is of the past, which is tradition. And the religious mind has no beliefs; it has no dogmas; it moves from fact to fact, and therefore the religious mind is the scientific mind. But the scientific mind is not the religious mind. The religious mind includes the scientific mind, but the mind that is trained in the knowledge of science is not a religious mind.

A religious mind is concerned with the totality—not with a particular function, but with the total functioning of human existence. The brain is concerned with a particular function; it specializes. It functions in specialization as a scientist, a doctor, an engineer, a musician, an artist, a writer. It is these specialized, narrowed-down techniques that create division, not only inwardly, but outwardly. The scientist is probably regarded as the most important man required by society just now, as is the doctor. So function becomes all-important, and with it goes status, status being prestige. So where there is specialization, there must be contradiction and a narrowing down, and that is the function of the brain.

Surely, each one of us functions in a narrow groove of self-protective responses. It is there that the 'me', the 'I', is brought into being, in the brain with its defenses, its aggressions, its ambitions, frustrations, and sorrows.

So there is a difference between the brain and the mind. The brain is separative, functional; it cannot see the whole; it functions within a pattern. And the mind is the totality which can see the whole. The brain is contained within the mind, but the brain does not contain the mind. And however much thought may purify, refine, control itself, it cannot possibly conceive, formulate, or understand what is the total. It is the capacity of the mind that sees the whole, and not the brain.

But we have developed the brain to such an amazing extent. All our education is the cultivation of the brain because there is profit in the cultivation of a technique, the acquisition of knowledge. The capacity of seeing the whole, the totality of existence—such perception has no profit motive; therefore, we disregard it. For us, function is far more important than understanding. And there is understanding only when there is the perception of the total. However much the brain may work out the reason, the effect, the cause of things, sorrow cannot be solved by thought. It is only when the mind perceives the cause, the effect, the whole, total process and goes beyond that there is the ending of sorrow.

For most of us, function has become very important because with it goes status, position, class. And when status comes into being through function, there is contradiction and conflict. How we respect the scientist and look down on the cook! How we look up to the prime minister, the general, and disregard the soldier! So there is contradiction when status is allied to function; there is class differentiation, class struggle. A society may try to eradicate class, but so long as there is status accompanying function, there must be class. And that is what we all want. We all want status, which is power.

You know, power is a most extraordinary thing. Everybody pursues it: the hermit, the general, the scientist, the housewife, the husband. We all want power: the power that money gives, the power to dominate, the power of knowledge, the power of capacity. It gives us a position, a prestige, and that is what we want. And power is evil, whether it is the power of the dictator, the power of the wife over the husband or the husband over the wife. It is evil because it forces others to conform, to adjust, and in that process there is no freedom. And we want it, very subtly or very crudely, and that is why we pursue knowledge. Knowledge is so important to most of us, and we look up to the scholars with their intellectual tricks because with knowledge goes power.

Please listen not merely to me but to your own minds, brains, and hearts. Watch it there, and you will see how eagerly most of us want this power. And where there is the search for power, there is no learning. Only an innocent mind can learn; only a young, fresh mind delights in learning, not a mind, not a brain burdened with knowledge, with experience. So a religious mind is always learning, and there is no end to learning. Learning is not the accumulation of knowledge. In holding to knowledge and adding to knowledge, you are ceasing to learn. Do please follow this to the very end.

When you observe all these things, you are aware of an extraordinary sense of isolation, of loneliness, of being cut off. Most of us have experienced at one time or another this sense of being completely alone, enclosed, without a relationship with anything or anyone. And being aware of that, there is fear; and when there is fear, there is at once the urge, the demand to escape from it. Please follow all this inwardly because this is not a lecture; we are actually taking the journey together. And if you can take the journey, you will leave here with quite a different mind, with quite a different quality of brain.

This sense of loneliness must be gone through, and you cannot go through it if you are afraid. This loneliness is actually created by the mind through its self-protective responses and self-centered activities. If you observe your own brain and your own life, you will see how you are isolating yourself in everything you do and think. All the business of "my name, my family, my position, my qualities, my capacities, my property, my work"—it is all isolating you. So there is loneliness, and you cannot avoid it. You have to go through it, as factually as you have to go through a door. And to go through it, you must live with it. And to live with loneliness, to go through it, is to come upon a much greater thing, a much deeper state, which is aloneness—to be completely alone, without knowledge. By that I do not mean being without the superficial mechanical knowledge which is necessary for daily existence; the brain does not need to be washed out, but I mean that the knowledge which one has acquired and stored up should not be used for one's psychological expansion and security. I mean by aloneness a state which no influence of any kind can touch. It is no longer a state of isolation because it has understood isolation, it has understood the whole mechanical process of thinking, of experience, of challenge and response.

I do not know if you have ever thought of this problem of challenge and response. The brain is always responding to every form of challenge, conscious or unconscious. Every influence impresses itself upon the brain, and the brain responds. You can fairly easily understand the outward challenges; they are very petty, and if you go fairly deeply, you can see through the inward challenges and responses. Please follow this because when you go still deeper, there is neither a challenge nor a response—which does not mean that the mind is asleep. On the contrary, it is completely awake, so awake that it does not need any challenge, nor is there any necessity for a response. That state, when the mind is without challenge or response because it has understood the whole process—that state is aloneness. So the religious mind understands all this, goes through it, not in the course of time, but in perceiving immediately.

Does time bring understanding? Will you have understanding tomorrow? Or is there understanding only in the active present, now? Understanding is to see something totally, immediately. But that understanding is prevented by any form of evaluation. All verbalizing, condemnation, justification, and so on prevents perception. You say, "It takes time to understand. I need many days for it." And while you are taking many days, the problem takes deeper root in the mind, and it is much more difficult to get rid of it, whatever the problem is. So understanding is in the immediate present, and not in terms of time. When I see something very clearly, immediately, there is understanding. It is the immediacy which is important, not the postponement. If I clearly see the fact that I am angry, jealous, ambitious, and so on, without any opinion, evaluation, or judgment, then the very fact begins to operate immediately.

So you will see that the quality of aloneness is the state of a completely awakened mind. It is not thinking in terms of time. And it is really quite extraordinary if you go into it. Therefore the religious mind is not an evolutionary mind because reality is beyond time. This is really important to understand, if you have gone so far in discovery.

You see, chronological time and psychological time are two different things. We are talking about psychological time, the inward demand for more days, more time in order to achieve—which means the ideal, the hero, the gap between what you are and what you should be. You say that to cover that gap, to bridge it over, you need time, but that attitude is a form of laziness because you can see this thing immediately if you give your whole attention to it.

So the religious mind is not concerned with progress, with time; it is in a state of constant activity, but not in terms of 'becoming' or 'being'. You can go into it now, though you will probably never go into it. Because you will see, as you go into it, that the religious mind is the destructive mind, for without destruction there is no creation. Destruction is not a matter of time. Destruction takes place when the totality of the mind has given its attention to *what is*. The seeing of the false as false, completely, is the destruction of the false. It is not the destructiveness of the communist, the capitalist, and all that immature stuff. The religious mind is the destructive mind, and being destructive, the religious mind is creative. What is creation is destruction.

And there is no creation without love. You know, for us, love is a strange thing. We have divided love into passion, lust, profane and sacred, carnal and divine, into family love, love of the country, and so on and on, dividing it and dividing it. And in division there is contradiction, conflict, and sorrow.

Love, for most of us, is passion, lust; and in the very process of identification with another, there is contradiction, conflict, and the beginning of sorrow. And for us, love goes. The smoke of it—the jealousy, hate, envy, greed of it—destroys the flame. But where there is love, there is beauty and passion. You must have passion, but do not immediately translate that word into sexual passion. By *passion* I mean the passion of intensity, that energy which immediately sees things clearly, burningly. Without passion there is no austerity. Austerity is not mere denial, having only a few things, controlling yourself—which is all too small, too petty. Austerity comes through self-abandonment, and with self-abandonment there is passion, and therefore there is beauty. Not the beauty put together by man, not the beauty which the artist creates—though I am not saying there is no beauty there. But I am talking of a beauty which is beyond thought and feeling. And that can only come about when there is high sensitivity of the brain as well as of the body and mind. And there can be no sensitivity of that nature and quality when there is not complete abandonment, when the brain is not completely giving itself over to the totality which the mind sees. Then there is passion.

So the religious mind is the destructive mind. And it is the religious mind that is the creative mind because it is concerned with the totality of existence. It is not the creativity of the artist because he is only concerned with a certain segment of life, and he tries to express what he feels in that, as the man of the world tries to express himself in business—though the artist thinks he is superior to anybody else. So creation comes into being only when there is total understanding of the whole of life, not of one part of life.

Now, if the brain has gone as far as that and has understood the whole process of existence, and has put away all the gods that man has manufactured—his saviors, his symbols, his hell and his heaven—then, when there is complete aloneness, there is quite a different journey to be undertaken. But one must come to that before one can deny or assert if there is God or no God. From then on there is true discovery because the brain, the mind, has totally destroyed everything it has known. Then only is it possible to enter the unknown; then there is the unknowable. It is not the god of the churches, the temples, the mosques, not the god of your fears and beliefs. There is a reality which is to be found only in the total understanding of the whole process of existence, not one part of it.

Then the mind, you will find, becomes extraordinarily quiet and still, and the brain also. I wonder if you have ever noticed your own brain in operation, whether the brain has ever been aware of itself in action! If you have been so aware, choicelessly, negatively, you will see that it is everlastingly chattering, talking to itself, or talking about something, accumulating knowledge and storing it away. It is all the time acting, consciously at the upper levels and also deeply in dreams, hints, intimations of ideas, and so on. It is constantly moving, changing, acting; but it is never still. And it is necessary for the mind, the brain, to be completely, utterly quiet and still, with no contradiction, no conflict. Otherwise there is bound to be the projection of illusion. But when the mind and brain are completely quiet, without any movement—every form of vision, influence, and illusion having been absolutely wiped away—then, in that stillness, the totality will go further in the journey to receive that which is not measurable by time, that which has no name, the eternal, the everlasting.

Question: Is not the whole problem a matter of eliminating something which is not, in order to receive that which is?

KRISHNAMURTI: Surely, to seek confirmation is rather absurd, if I may say so. What we have been talking about does not need any confirmation. Either it is so, which is all right, or it is not so, which is also all right. But you cannot seek confirmation from another; you have to find out.

Question: Is the state of mind in which there is no challenge and response the same as meditation?

KRISHNAMURTI: I said very carefully that there is no meditation if there is no self-knowing. The laying of the right foundation, which is meditation, is actually to be free of ambition, envy, greed, and the worship of success. And if, after laying the right foundation, one goes further, deeper, there is no challenge and no response. But that is a long journey, not in time, not in days and years, but in ruthless self-knowing.

Question: Is there not a fear which is not the result of thought?

KRISHNAMURTI: We have said that there is instinctive, physical fear. When you meet a snake or a bus goes roaring by, you withdraw—which is natural, healthy, sane self-protection. But every form of psychological self-protection leads to mental illness.

Question: In dying, is there not a new being?

KRISHNAMURTI: In dying, as we have been going into it, there is no becoming, and there is no being. It is another state altogether.

Question: Why are we not always in that marvelous state?

KRISHNAMURTI: The actual fact is that you are not. All that you are is the result of your conditioning. To go through with the total understanding of what you are is to lay the right foundation for further discovery.

You see, I am afraid what has happened is that you have not listened at all to what we have been talking about. This is the last talk, and it would be a pity if you select the parts that suit you and try to take those ashes home with you. What has been said, from the first talk to the last, is all one. There can be no choice or preference in it. Either you must take the totality or nothing at all. But if you have laid the right foundation, you can go very far—not, as I have said, in terms of time, but far in the sense of the realization of an immensity which can never be put into words, into paint, or into marble. Without that discovery our life is empty, shallow, without meaning.

September 24, 1961

Madras, India, 1961

First Talk in Madras

To establish the right contact between the speaker and yourself and to establish communion on a proper basis, we must understand the significance of words. We interpret words to mean something that will be convenient or suitable to us, or interpret them according to a certain tradition. Words help us to reason, and most of us act according to words. Words have become extraordinarily significant. The words *nationalism, communism, God, brotherhood,* and so on have a certain significance; and if we would understand them fully, we must go beyond the words. We must not only see the significance of words in common usage but also see that the mind is not a slave to them. It is quite a difficult thing to do. The word *Hindu* or any other word has immense significance. Words like *reincarnation, karma, nationalism* have an extraordinary sway over the mind. The Christians, the Buddhists, and all the various people who belong to innumerable classes have their own jargons, their own approach, their own way of looking at things through words. So one becomes a prisoner to words. I think you have to realize that we are enslaved by words, and that you cannot possibly establish the right relationship between yourself and the speaker if you are merely listening to words and not going beyond the significance of words.

For me, words have a limited meaning, a very limited meaning—whether used by Buddha, Christ, or anybody else. Words that are used in the Upanishads or the Gita or the Bible have a very, very limited meaning, and the mind acting on those words in those traditions cannot possibly go very far. And it seems to me that it is very important now, in the present circumstances when there is a tremendous crisis going on in the world, that we should break through the barriers of words, whether used by me or somebody else, and examine very clearly, precisely, and definitely the world situation, and also how we react to challenges, because there are always challenges in life. Every moment there is the challenge, the demand, the question; and we respond to that challenge, to that demand, to that question according to our background, according to the words which we are used to. And I am afraid the present crisis cannot be translated or understood in terms of the Upanishads or the Bible or the Gita or any other book. One has to respond to it totally anew, as the present circumstances are entirely new. Life is not just the life of everyday incidents and accidents and happenings which are also there, but it is also much more vast and much deeper. To understand all these and to respond to them truly and rightly without conflict, it seems to me that it is very necessary to have a new mind, a totally new mind—not the mind that interprets the present in terms of the old, not the mind that responds to this everchanging challenge according to Shankara or Buddha or the various religious denominations or sects that one belongs to. All this has to be thrown aside completely in order not only to understand the present, but also to understand these enormous things that are going on in the world—this sorrow, this anxiety, this restlessness, and the never-ceasing guilt.

Let us understand each other: the speaker is only concerned with bringing about a new mind, a totally new mind, and not at all concerned with how to interpret the Gita or any of the books that one reads. The mind that acts in tradition, that acts in knowledge, however wide, however significant—such a mind is incapable of apprehending or understanding the quality of a new mind. As I was saying, to bring about this new mind, there must be a total revolution. And I mean by that word *revolution*—what it means in the dictionary—a total revolution, not mere acceptance, not conformity, not imitation. We need a new mind, and a new mind cannot be created by merely saying we are inquiring after the new mind—then it becomes a new jargon. But one can find out the new mind, what the quality of the new mind is, if one begins to examine very closely, pertinently, definitely, and precisely the mind that we have at present, the mind that we accept with such ease, the mind with which we function.

So, I would like to be perfectly clear from the beginning that we are concerned with revolution, with a new approach, and not with that which just suits the modern society—not reformation, not the patching up of the old, because those have utterly failed in misery, in conflict, and in confusion. The books, however sacred they are, have not solved them. On the contrary, there is more division, there is more orthodoxy, more provincialism, more authority and tyranny, more gurus, and more disciplines and less freedom. So you see all this—that progress denies freedom; the more prosperous one is, the more and more you want things to remain as they are. This is happening in America; they do not want any disturbance; all the sense of adventure, the sense of the new has gone. They go to the moon, but the sense of discovery of something totally new—which cannot be if there is security—is going. In this country too, though there is enormous poverty, degradation, and great tyranny of the past, the mind is in decay. They are becoming very clever experts in techniques; there are new jobs, clever engineers, electronic experts, and clever lawyers. But these are not going to solve any of our human problems, and they never did. The ancient Shankaras and the modern Shankaras cannot solve your problems. You may shave the head or put on a different cloth, but your mind and your heart are unchanged. And to meet the present crisis requires an enormous understanding. You require a real revolt, not reaction, not returning to the past, not the revival of religion, but a complete destruction of everything that one has held as sacred. One must question everything and find out. And I do not think we question, I do not think we know what it means to question. I wonder if you have asked anything really wanting to find out what is true, so that your questioning is not merely trying to find out an answer.

There are two ways to question. One is to question so as to find out a suitable, convenient, satisfactory answer—which is no questioning at all. And the other is to question so as to tear everything out to find out, to question so as to disturb the mind which is so completely secure, which has gone to sleep, to tear down all the barriers to find out what is true. There are these two ways of questioning: one merely to find a satisfactory, convenient, happy answer, and the other to bring down the walls, to tear down the walls of our own prison. The former has no meaning at all; both the educated and the uneducated are doing that. But to destroy—and I mean it, to really destroy—not the outer things, not merely the superficial customs, not merely the convenient and inconvenient traditions, but to tear down the walls that one has built inside oneself, within which one lives in security, to tear down all the gods, all the Masters, all the teachers, and to inquire and to find out the false and what is truth—that is true questioning, and that requires abnormal energy. You have to pursue your own thoughts and your own fears so as to discover what is false, and that is what we propose to do during these coming discussions or talks here, so that at the end of these talks or before, when you are made uncomfortable by questioning, asking, demanding in your mind, perhaps you will then see life entirely differently.

We lead a very mediocre life. Our life is made up of many fears. And we live within this enclosure all our life with infinite beliefs, conflicting theories, never discovering anything for ourselves, always depending, always copying, always following. At the present time the world is facing total destruction, total physical destruction; the world is asking not how to go to the moon—that is fairly simple; any mechanic with a little brain can do that, and they are doing that—but what it is all about and where we are going, not what is the object of life, not what is the purpose of life, not any formulation of theories and conforming to them. So, it seems to me that it is very important that you must find out for yourself as a human being, not as a mechanic, what it means to live.

I do not think we, in this country which has had no war for a long time, understand what is taking place in the rest of the world. We may read this in newspapers, we may talk to tourists or visitors. But I do not think we are aware, as a group of people living in this unfortunate country, what man is capable of doing. I mean not the capacity to go up to the moon, or to invent a new machine or an electronic brain, but the capacity to go within.

The distance to the moon is fairly small compared to the distance to be traveled in order to discover what is true within oneself. I do not think we have taken a journey within. We are taught about it; the sacred books which are of little value have said it is necessary. We have accepted—or rather, you have accepted—their explanations. But you have never taken the journey. And you can only take a journey within when you are capable of discarding everything outside. In the case of most of us, the mind becomes insensitive in the daily process of living, and it is much more difficult for such people to perform the journey, to break down the pattern of existence. And the young people in this country are only concerned with having a good job, with making money, and so on. There are a few people who really want to take a journey within, a psychological journey, which makes for a very clear mind—a mind that is capable of attention, capable of seeing what is true. To see what is true—not the ultimate truth, there is no ultimate truth; truth is only from moment to moment—first you must discard what is false. To find out what is false, you must look, ask, demand, question ceaselessly and endlessly. You cannot look, you cannot see for yourself if there is fear.

We are afraid. One of our major concerns in life is fear—fear of many things, fear of wife, fear of husband, fear of losing a job, fear of public opinion, fear of insecurity, fear of not being successful, not fulfilling, not becoming somebody important in this rotten world, not making a name, not being somebody. All that is fear. Without really understanding that fear and thereby putting it away entirely, totally and completely, pure seeing, total transformation, mutation, is not possible.

Please pay attention to what is being said. Fear is a deadly thing and is creating more and more trouble in the world—not less. And this fear, though unconscious, is there and shows itself in obedience. Where there is fear, there is confusion and therefore the demand for tyranny. It has brought communism, socialism, capitalism, all through the tyranny of the politician. Where there is fear, there is demand for order—order brought about under any circumstances. And that is what is happening in the world. We must have order; we are afraid. That is why there is the authority of the guru, the authority of the politician, the authority of the book, the authority of tradition, and it is very difficult to put away authority. I wonder if you are aware of authority and put away authority—not the bigger authority but, say, the authority of the wife. I know you will laugh; it shows it has very little meaning to you because you take for granted the authority of the wife or the authority of the husband. But authority begins there. It means the authority of the parent over the child; gradually this is built up into the authority of the nation, the authority of the guru, the authority of the politician, the authority of the Masters, or the authority of the representatives of God.

I wonder if you can put away every kind of authority, put it away completely, get rid of it because you have understood it. If you do this consciously, deliberately, with sanity, then you will know the beginning of that freedom in which all sense of compulsion, all sense of imitation has completely stopped. Therefore, one begins to have a smell, a taste, an apprehension of what is true freedom.

But when you see authority, you say, "Revolt." With most of us, such revolt is merely a reaction. You know what I mean. If I do not like something, I revolt. If I like something, I hold on to it. A revolt against the pattern of society is not revolution, is not mutation. Communism which is a revolt against capitalism is incapable of revolution. They may talk about revolution, but communism, being intrinsically a reaction, is incapable of acting truly. You understand what I mean? As long as we are reacting, action is not possible. Such reaction leads inevitably to inaction—inaction is a repetition of the old pattern only modified, and this modification is inaction, because it produces more misery, more confusion. Whereas an action without reaction is an action which arises when you have understood all the processes of revolt. This action which is not a reaction destroys all that is false because it is an action which is pure, clean, without root. I wonder whether you understand what I am talking about. To be a Hindu and then to become a Buddhist is a reaction. You may do all kinds of things in that reaction, but you still act as the same person. Communism, which is a reaction to capitalism, is reverting to the old form. The communists have their own privileged classes, the rich and the poor, their class divisions; they have armies, navies, and all the rest of the business—it is the same thing as capitalism, repeated in a different way. We have been talking of something entirely different. It is easy to revolt against modern society because it is fairly silly. Modern society—going to the office every morning, earning a livelihood, getting bored with it, getting more and more money, getting more and more tired, without any thought, without any feeling, without any real life—to revolt against that is fairly simple. But the revolt against it only creates another pattern, and the action in the pattern is inaction because it still continues the sorrow, confusion, and misery.

If we understand this clearly, then mutation, revolution, has quite a different meaning, because then you see what is false, and the denial of the false is the beginning of true action. To see the false in authority is quite a difficult thing to do. To examine the anatomy of authority requires a great deal of intelligence, a great deal of watching, searching, inquiring. The authority of the policeman, the authority of the law, and the authority of the government perhaps are necessary in modern society. But you have to deny every other form of authority because you understand it and inquire; then only can you find out what is true in authority and therefore be capable of putting away authority. Then it is not a reaction nor a revolt which is a reaction. But in that inquiry into the whole structure of authority, there begins the mutation of the mind. And it is only the new mind that can respond to the present challenge of life—not withdrawing, not returning to the old, not the revival of the old.

You have to consider the present world situation. Machines, electronic brains, are taking over the functions of the human mind. They are clever, they can learn much more rapidly, they can give you the most complicated mathematical answers in a few seconds; they are doing things which man has been doing—that is one thing. And then the other thing is that throughout the world, the rulers, the powers that be, are trying to control the mind, make it adjust itself to the patterns of existence. This is actually happening, this is not my invention. There is prosperity not only in Europe, in America, but also it is coming here—rapid industrialization, and with it everybody is wanting to live a more secure life; therefore, there is more competition than ever before. I do not know if you have followed the things in Russia, where the competition to destroy one's comrade is as urgent as to destroy capitalism. And here, too, because of industrialization, there is competition to make more and to have position, power. Where there is confusion, there is increase of authority, tyranny. There is also the attempt to revive the old religions, hoping thereby to save the ship from being wrecked.

When you see all this actually taking place daily around you and within you, obviously, you see the need for a different quality of mind, a different way of looking at life, different values. But a different existence is not possible within the old pattern, and so the destruction of the old pattern is absolutely essential—which means not throwing bombs on governors, kings, and rulers but breaking the pattern that one has built up psychologically, inwardly, within oneself; it is there that the change has to take place.

That is why one has to understand fear. You cannot cover up fear. You cannot escape from it through worship in the temples, through gurus. Do what you will, you cannot run away from it; it will follow you. You have to look at the whole phenomenon of fear and understand it. But to inquire into fear deeply means self-knowledge, knowing yourself, knowing what you are, what you actually are at every moment of the day—not what you think you are, not what the books say you are, not invent what you are. You have to know what you are, and that is very arduous and demands great attention, a great quality of awareness to see what is actually taking place—the way you sit, the way you talk, the way you walk, the way you look at the sky, the way you talk to your wife and children, the way the children talk to you. To be aware of all those things is the beginning; that is the basis of understanding.

Without knowing yourself, you cannot go very far, and if you think you can go very far, you are deluding yourself. If you want to delude yourself, that is quite a different matter; go on with it—you will soon be disillusioned. But if you want to find out what is truth, if there is God, if there is truth, if there is a thing which is beyond time, if you want to understand what is creation, what is life and such things, you have to know yourself from day to day, from moment to moment. If you are not capable of doing it, you cannot go far, you cannot move at all, you are in a prison; you can play with words. But the man who does not know himself from moment to moment cannot learn.

You know learning and knowing are two different things. The mind that is accumulating knowledge can never learn. Learning in life means constant inquiry, and you cannot inquire if you are merely accumulating. If I accumulate knowledge, that is information; and if from that accumulated knowledge, information, I begin to inquire, that inquiry is merely a further addition; it is merely added to what has been accumulated. But learning implies a constant inquiry, which means freedom from acquisition. If I want to learn a language, what happens is that I will have to read, search, ask, inquire, repeat; and gradually I also learn. Knowing a language is not learning. It is only the young mind that learns. It is only the clear mind that learns and not the mind that accumulates, and not the mind that says, "I know." It is only the mind that says, "I don't know. I will look," it is only the mind that has humility that is capable of learning. But a mind that has acquired knowledge can never have humility; therefore, it has ceased to learn.

So to inquire into yourself to find out what you are from day to day, you cannot accept anything of what you have been told, and that is really dangerous because that way leaves you completely alone. When you deny the authority of your wife or your husband, you are isolated, and naturally you are afraid to stand alone. Therefore, we have to be aware of what we are doing constantly. Because, without self-knowing, whatever you think, whatever you do, whatever you are—it can only lead to frustration and misery. If you understand this, then meditation is something extraordinarily beautiful.

Meditation, then, is not a repetition of words or understanding of phrases or looking at a picture. Meditation, then, is the beginning of self-understanding, the understanding of oneself; that is wisdom. And this wisdom cannot be taught by anybody; it is not in any book; no teacher, no guru, nobody can hand to you this wisdom. This wisdom cannot be handed to you; it is found by knowing yourself from moment to moment. You should die to what you have known from moment to moment so that your mind is fresh and young. The act of pure seeing is a miracle in itself. It is that which is going to transform, which will bring in the new mind.

You must begin with yourself, but not as opposed to the collective. Perhaps you are the collective, and so you think what society thinks; what you feel, your neighbor and a thousand neighbors feel. You are being conditioned by society; you are of the collective. Psychologically you have to face and understand the collective and be aware of every movement of the mind. It is only then that you can discover if there is God or no God; you will find for yourself what it is to live. You will be fully alive—every part of your life, physically, emotionally, being immensely, totally, fully active. Then there is no death. Then you are dying every minute to everything that you have known. Then you are aware of what you actually are every minute of the day, and there is no analysis but mere observation, which is the act of pure seeing, and which releases energy. And it is this energy that will carry you deeply and far; therefore, you will discover for yourself what is true.

November 22, 1961

Second Talk in Madras

We were saying last time when we met here that there was a deep crisis not only in the conscious, outwardly in the world, but also in the unconscious, deep within oneself. There is a crisis, and most of us agree that there must be a deep radical change of some kind. Thoughtful persons who are aware of the situation that exists in the world today more or less come together in saying that there must be some kind of a revolution, some kind of an immediate change, a mutation that is not merely an intellectual, emotional outcome, but one that takes place totally in the whole consciousness. A mere change in any particular direction of consciousness generally implies a change according to a certain particular pattern—a pattern created by circumstances, by very clever, erudite people, by people who have investigated past changes and how those changes have been brought about, what influences, what circumstances, what pressures and strains have brought about a certain change in the human mind. These people have studied these facts extensively.

You see the change brought about by the communists, and their intention. And you see the change brought about by the desire of so-called religious people—which is either revival or going back to tradition. And there are those who through propaganda force the mind to conform to a certain, particular pattern of thought. There are various ways to bring about a change. Before we begin to inquire into what is true change, we must look at the condition that exists and not avoid it. It is very important to face a fact because it is the fact itself—if it could be understood—and not what we bring to the fact that brings about a crisis; and that crisis demands, brings about, a challenge which you have to meet completely. I would like to talk about that this evening.

One sees that more and more, throughout the world, freedom is going. Politicians may talk about it. You can see prosperity, industrialization, education, the family, religion—all these are wiping away slowly, perhaps deliberately, all demand for freedom. That is a fact. Whether you like it or not, it is an irrefutable fact that education, propaganda, industrialization, prosperity, and so-called religion, which is really propaganda, the continuous repetition of tradition—all these are conditioning the mind so heavily, so deeply, that freedom is practically gone. That is the fact which you and I must face, and in facing it, perhaps we shall see how to break through it.

We must break it; otherwise, we are not human beings, we are mere machines recording certain pressures and strains. So we must face the fact that through deliberate propaganda, through various pressures, man is being denied freedom. There is the whole mechanism of propaganda—religious propaganda, political propaganda, the propaganda that is being done by certain political parties, and so on and so on. The constant repetition of phrases or words means constant dinning into the mind of certain ideas which are destroying the mind, controlling the mind, shaping the mind according to the phrases of the propagandists. That is a fact. Because, when you call yourself a Hindu or a Buddhist or a Chinese or whatever you like, it is the result of your being told over and over again, for centuries, that you are a Hindu, that you have a vast tradition—which has been shaping the mind—which makes you react as a Hindu according to certain established practices, by tradition. Please see this. Don't accept or deny because I am not out to do any propaganda or to convince you of anything, but I really think, if we could come together and intellectually, rationally observe certain facts, then out of that observation of facts, a change will come about, which is not predetermined by a conditioned mind.

To see a fact purely is all-important and not to try to change the fact according to the pattern, or the condition in which one has been brought up, because such a change is predetermined, and creates another pattern to which the mind becomes a slave. So it is very important to see the fact as it is and not bring an opinion, an idea, a judgment, and an evaluation upon the fact, because the evaluation, the judgment, the opinion is conditioned—it is the result of the past, it is the result of your culture, of the society in which you have been brought up. So if you look at the fact through the background of your culture, of your society, of your beliefs, then you are not looking at the fact. You are merely projecting what you believe, what you have experienced, what your background is, upon the fact. Therefore, it is not a fact. Please bear that very clearly in mind. This pure act of observation, seeing a thing very clearly without distortion, brings about a challenge to which you have to respond totally, and a total response frees the mind from the conditioning.

It is important that you and I, the speaker and you, should understand what we are trying to get at together. First, this is not a lecture. You do not come here merely to listen, to hear certain ideas, which you may like or dislike and go away agreeing or disagreeing. You may have come here with the idea that you are going to hear and not participate in what is being said. But we are participating together; therefore, this is not a lecture. We are sharing together the journey which we are going to take, and therefore it is not the work of the speaker only. You and I are going to work together to find out what is true, and therefore you are participating or sharing and not merely listening.

Then it is also very important to understand what is positive thinking and negative thinking, because seeing the fact is negative thinking. But if you approach the fact with an opinion, a judgment, an evaluation, that is positive thinking which destroys the fact. If I want to understand something, I must look at it and not have an opinion about it. That is a very simple fact. If I want to understand what you are saying, I must listen to you attentively. I will agree or disagree at the end, but I must listen to it. I must gather everything that you have said from the beginning to the end and not mere bits here and there. You must listen to the totality of what is being said, and then you can decide, if there is a decision to be made; you will not then choose but will merely see the fact.

So we must be very clear from the very beginning that this is not a propaganda meeting, that I am not out to convince you of anything. I literally mean it; I do not care whether you accept or reject. It is a fact. To understand the fact, you must come to it inquisitively, not positively. The positive mind, the positive attitude is one of determined opinion—a conditioned outlook, with a traditional point of view which is established, to which you automatically respond. It is positive thinking which most of us indulge in. You see something of national freedom, or you refer to the Gita, the Upanishads, or some other book, and respond; you respond according to what somebody has thought out for you or said what you should think about the fact. The book, the professor, the guru, the teacher, and the ancient wise people or group—those have done all the work of thinking and have written it down, and you just repeat them when you meet a fact; and your meeting the fact with a traditional outlook, with a conditioned response, is called positive thinking—which is no thinking at all. Every electronic machine does this if it has already been told what to think; when it is given certain problems to solve, it will respond automatically. The electronic brain is based on the working of the human brain.

So, when an opinion is given about a fact, it is not thinking at all. It is merely responding, the response being conditioned by previous experience. Please see what I am saying. It is something entirely different from that to which you are accustomed. Because, you and I are looking now at a fact without an opinion. I will show you something. There is a way, a botanical way of looking at a flower. You know the botanical way—to look at the whole structure of the flower in a scientific way. There is a way of looking at the flower, without referring to knowledge—to look at the flower purely, directly, without the intervention, without the screen of what we know. I wonder if I am making myself clear on this point. If it is not clear, I must make it clear because we cannot proceed further without understanding this intrinsic issue. To understand you as a human being, I cannot say, "You are a Hindu; you are that; you are this"; I must study, I must look at you without an opinion, without an evaluation, as a scientist does.

So you must look, and the looking is all-important, not the opinion. Please do give your attention to this, because you are so used to the so-called positive thinking. The Gita or the Upanishads says this, your guru says this, your traditional family education has told you this; and with the machinery of your memory, with that accumulated knowledge, you look at something and respond to what you see—that is what you call thinking. I do not think that it is thinking at all. It is merely the repetition of memory and the response of memory. It is conditioned by the past, by the culture, by society, by religious experience, by education, by the book; and that machinery is set going when you meet a fact and that machinery responds, and so it is sheer nonsense. But if you can approach a fact negatively—which is to look at it and not bring your opinion or knowledge to condemn or to condition it—you keep on looking at the fact, purely. I hope this is clear. If this is clear, then when you are capable of looking purely at a fact of any kind—the fact of memory, the fact of jealousy, the fact of nationalism, the fact of hatred, the desire for power, position, prestige—then, the fact reveals an immense power. Then, the fact flowers, and in the flowering of the fact is not only the understanding of the fact but the action which is produced by the fact.

So, we are concerned with many facts. The fact of extraordinary confusion in the world, the fact of increasing human misery, the fact of not lessening but increasing sorrow, a greater sense of frustration, confusion, strife even among the communists and among the so-called democratic politicians and in ourselves. The fact that all religions have failed, that they have no longer any meaning, that people belonging to these organized religions repeat some sets of words and feel marvelously happy, just like people who take a drug—all these are the many facts which you have to look at. It is only out of the pure act of seeing the fact that there comes the action, the mutation in human consciousness. And that is what is needed, not reversely going back to the old—revivalism or the invention of a new set of theories because they will not answer the present crisis. We know the present crisis—the extraordinary possibility of a few so-called political leaders destroying the world completely, according to their theories and ideas. Those leaders are not concerned with humanity at all, with you and your neighbor; they are concerned with ideas and their power and position. The religious leaders are not concerned with the betterment of man; they are concerned with theology. There is the fact of immense, deep frustration in man. I am sure you all know it—the anxiety, the sense of guilt, the despair. And the more you observe, the deeper is the sorrow. The indissoluble life that one leads, the boredom of going to the office day after day for fifty years, destroying every faculty, every sensitivity, earning a livelihood to support an increasing family, the pressure of civilization—you know these as well as I do. I do not go to the office, but you do; you have a family. You have gone to the office every day of your life for about fifty years, and then you casually turn to God; then you become religious by doing some stupid ceremonies. Those who are younger are going to do exactly the same, tomorrow. Don't laugh. This is a serious meeting, not an entertainment. I am merely describing the fact.

Another great fact is that we are no longer free. You are outwardly free. We talk here, but probably this cannot be done in China or Russia—that is not freedom. Freedom is something entirely different. It is freedom from ambition, greed, envy, fear. The mind can go very deeply within itself beyond the limits of time and space. But you cannot go on an immense, long, indefinite journey if your mind is tied to the brutality of ambition, to the cruelty of greed, to the destruction through envy. There is no freedom inwardly; outwardly you may say you have freedom. You can say what you like or don't like about the government in this country or in Western Europe or in America, but you may not be able to do that in Russia or China—but that does not constitute freedom. You cannot as a Hindu seek beyond what you have been taught, nor the Christian who has his Savior. Now, knowing all these facts, how do we change? How does mutation take place?

Change and mutation are entirely different. Change implies change towards something, change to something which you already know or which you have preconceived, preformulated, thought about, laid down the pattern for. And therefore such a change has a motive, has a purpose; it is brought about through compulsion, through conformity, through fear, through invention. Such a change has a purpose behind it, and that purpose is always conditioned by the past. Therefore that change is the continuity of what has been already, modified. Is it not? Therefore, it is not a mutation at all. It is like a person who goes from one religion to another—he is changing. A person leaves one society and joins some other society, leaves one club and joins another, because it is convenient; thereby, he thinks he has changed. There may be innumerable reasons why there should be such a change, but such a change is an escape from the fact. A change is really no change if there is a motive behind that change, if there is a purpose. The purpose is conditioned by the pattern, by tradition, by hopes and despairs, by your anxieties, guilt, ambitions, envy, jealousies. That change is a continuity of what has been, modified, so that is not mutation. And therefore the response which comes through such a change does not alter the world at all; it merely alters the pattern. It does not bring about a radical mutation in consciousness.

What we are talking about is a complete mutation in consciousness. And that is the only thing that will bring about a new world, a new civilization, a new way of living, and a new relationship between man and man. This is not a theory because mutation is possible—and mutation has no purpose at all. You know we are using the word *love* very easily. If you love with a motive, it is no longer love; it is merchandise. If you love with a purpose, it is mean, degrading. Love has no purpose. In the same way, mutation comes about without purpose, without motive. Please see that, please see the difference between a change with a purpose—a change brought about through compulsion, through adjustment, through pressure, through necessity, through fear, through ambition, through industrialization, all of which have motives—and the mutation which has no purpose at all. The very act of seeing brings about that mutation. That is, when you see something, you understand it immediately; the truth of that brings about the total alteration in one's attitude towards life.

Hearing and listening are two different things. To hear something, to hear what is being said, is one thing, and to listen to what is being said is another thing. Most of us hear; and hearing, we accept or deny. If we like it, we accept; if we don't, we reject; and such hearing is very superficial—it has no profound effect. Whereas, listening is something entirely different. I wonder if you have listened to anything so that you understand, you feel, you love what you are listening to, whether it is pleasant or unpleasant. Please do listen very attentively, without effort; then, in the very act of listening, you will see what is true and what is false, without any interference, so that it is not mechanical. You have to listen with all your being to find out, to see what is true in itself—not according to your opinion or your experience or your knowledge.

Take a very simple thing. The believer in God and the nonbeliever in God are about the same. To find God, if there is one, you have to inquire, you have to search, you have to find out, you have to dig very deeply, throwing aside every belief, every idea, because it may be something astonishing, something that has never been thought about—and it must be. To find out something, every form of knowledge, belief, condition, must be put aside. That is a fact. Is it not? To find something, you must come with your mind completely fresh, not with a traditional mind, not with a mind crippled with grief, with sorrow, with anxiety, with desire. The mind must be young, fresh, and new, and then only you can find out. Similarly, to find out what mutation is and how mutation can take place is very important, because change does not lead anywhere. Change, like any economic or social revolution, is merely a reaction of what has been, just as communism is the reaction to capitalism—they are obviously of the same pattern but in a different way, with a different set of people in power. But we must be concerned with mutation because the challenge now is not of your choosing but something entirely different. Challenge is always new, but unfortunately we meet it with the old, with our memory, and therefore the response is never adequate; therefore, there is sorrow, there is misery.

So, our concern is: What is the act that brings about this mutation in consciousness? Now, I do not know if you are serious. I mean by seriousness the capacity to follow a thought, an idea, a feeling right to the end, irrespective of what happens, irrespective of what is going to happen to you or your family, your nation, or anything else, to go to the very end irrespective of the consequences, to find out what is truth. Such a person is a serious person; the rest are really playing with life, and therefore they do not lead a full life. So, I hope that you have come here with a serious intent—which is to go together to the very end to find out what this mutation implies; to go to the very end irrespective of your family, your job, your present society, everything else, putting everything aside. Because, to find out you have to withdraw, to find out you have to cast away everything.

We, the old people as well as the young people, have never questioned. There is always the authority of the specialist—the specialist in religion, the specialist in education, the specialist in politics—there is the authority of the Gita, the Upanishads, the guru; they are never questioned. You have constantly been told, "He knows and you do not know. Therefore do not question, but obey." The mind that obeys, that accepts, is a dull mind; it is a mind that has gone to sleep and therefore is not creative; it is a dead mind, destructive of everything true; it is mechanically opposed to what it cannot understand, what it cannot penetrate. It cannot question sweetly and innocently to find out. That is why you and I are here together, to question. I am not your guru. I do not believe in authority of any kind, except the authority of government which says that you must have a passport to travel, that you must pay taxes, that you must buy stamps in order to send a letter. But the authority of the guru, of the Upanishads, the authority of one's own experience, the authority of tradition—they must be totally destroyed to find out what is true. And that is where we are going together, to discover what is true by questioning. The moment you question for yourself, you may find that you are wrong. What is wrong with it? A young mind, an innocent mind, makes mistakes and keeps on making mistakes; in the very making of the mistake, there is a discovery, and that discovery is truth. Truth is not what the old generation, the old people have told you, but what you discover. Therefore you have to question night and day, ceaselessly, until you find out. Such a mind is called a serious mind. You have to question incessantly, look at the fact innocently, putting away every fear that may arise in your questioning, never following anybody. Then out of that innocence, out of that inquiry, you find out what is truth. In the same way, you and I will find out how, in what way, in what manner, this mutation can take place.

You know, the word *how* implies pattern. When you and I say how, that very word implies the search for a pattern or a method of practice—it implies that you will tell me, and I will follow it. I am not using the word in that sense at all; the "how" is merely a question mark. It is not for me to tell you but for you to put that question and not fall into the trap of the pattern imposed by society so that your mind, which has been made dull through centuries of authority and tradition, can awaken, can become alive to question with intensity. Is it possible to bring about that mutation in each one of us? Don't say it is or it is not. If you say it is possible, you do not know. If you say it is not possible, you do not know either; you have already prevented yourself from examining, from questioning. So keep your mind free, unadulterated, so that you can find out for yourself.

Is mutation possible? It is not possible when you have started thinking in terms of change. When you start thinking in terms of change, change implies duration, change implies time, change implies from here to there. Whereas mutation is a process which takes place instantly. You have to see the truth of these two, change and mutation—"see" in the sense not merely intellectually, because that is mere verbal communication. Verbal communication is not the fact; the word *tree* is not the tree. But most of us, especially the so-called intellectual people, are caught in words, they are merely dealing in words. Life is not words. Life is living, life is pain, life is torture, life is despair—not words and explanations. You have to see the fact that there must be mutation, not change—a total revolution, not a modified adjustment.

Change implies that it is a gradual process. You have heard people say that you must have ideals and that when you have the ideal of nonviolence, gradually you will change to that ideal. I say that is absurd and immature thinking. Because, the fact is you are violent, and your mind can deal with it, but not with the ideal which is merely a theoretical invention. The fact is you are envious, you are ambitious, cruel, brutal. Deal with the fact, and not with the supposed ideal which is merely an invention to postpone action. Now we are not dealing with ideals, we are not dealing with suppositions; we are dealing with facts. You see the fact that change implies time, a gradual process which is postponement. Please understand this. A man who postpones, destroys his mind; when the facing of the problem is postponed, the problem is eating his mind and heart out, and therefore his mind is not young, fresh, innocent. What you are dealing with is the fact that all change according to our own tradition, according to what the professors, the teachers, the gurus, and others have said, is no change at all, but it is deterioration, destruction. If you see that fact, then you will be aware of the act of mutation taking place. You are following all this?

You know, consciousness is time, and so it is also time which says, "I will change tomorrow or a year later." That is merely being a slave to time, and therefore it is no change at all. Mutation implies a complete reversal of what has been, a complete, radical uprooting of everything that has been—you know there was mutation in the genes after the atomic bombing of Hiroshima and Nagasaki, and a different human entity came into being. Now a mutation has to take place in us so that the mind which is being crushed, destroyed, made ugly, brutal, stupid, dull, becomes overnight a young mind, a fresh mind. And I say that it can be done only when you approach the problem negatively, not positively. The negative approach is to deny totally all change, all reformation, because you understand it. It is not a reaction because you see what is implied in change. When you deny change because you have understood it and not because somebody tells you, then you are really changed. When you let the "change" flower, you see the quality of it; then you can destroy it, put it away completely, never thinking in terms of change, ideals, and all that. The moment you deny change, your mind is in a different state. It is already getting a new quality. You understand? When you deny something, not as a reaction, the mind is already fresh. But we never deny because it is not convenient; it may bring fear, so we imitate, we adjust, we modify ourselves according to the demands of the society we live in. You deny because you have understood what you deny.

For instance, take nationalism for which people are prepared to die. I deny nationalism; therefore, I am not a national; nationalism does not mean anything to me. Therefore when I deny something, it is significant. When you deny, your mind has already become fresh, new, because you have gone into the question of nationalism, inquired into it, searched out the truth, and discovered. When you deny anything, when you deny the false, there is truth. But to deny the false, you have to go to it negatively—which means, you have to look at it without any prejudice, without any opinion, judgment, evaluation. You try this, not because I say so, but because your life demands it, because your life wants it.

See your society, the conflict, the misery, the power, the striving for something, the endless gathering of money, the constant repetition of phrases; see your own empty, sordid life, full of fear and anxiety and guilt—such a living is not living at all, and you cannot change such a mind; you can only destroy that mind and create a new mind.

And the destruction of the old is absolutely imperative—the old being fear, ambition, greed, envy, search for security; it is this that makes the mind dull, never questioning, always accepting, bound to authority, and therefore never having freedom. It is only in freedom you can discover if there is truth or not. It is only in freedom you can find out what love is.

November 26, 1961

Third Talk in Madras

We were talking the other day about mutation. If I may, I would like to talk more about it, go much deeper into the problem. All change, however thoughtful, however premeditated, however desired, must still be within the limitation of time and condition. So we need a real revolution—not a mere superficial coating of color which may be called a change. We do need a deep, radical revolution in our thinking, feeling, behavior, in the way of our life. I think the more one watches oneself and the world, the more obvious that is. Superficial reformation, however necessary, is not the problem, is not the solution to our difficulties because reformation is still a conditional reaction and is not total action. By total action, I mean an action out of time—not within the limits of time. So, there is only one possibility, and that is a complete revolution, a complete mutation.

Is it possible for an individual to bring about this mutation? Obviously, the mutation is not in the physical, not in the superficial, not in the exterior—that is impossible—but it is a mutation in consciousness. I wonder what consciousness means to each one of you. Sirs, if I may most respectfully suggest, do not just accept words and live on words. We have done that—or at least you have done that—for centuries, and look where you are! But could you examine each word that has a connotation, like *consciousness,* and find out yourself what it means, not translate it in terms of what some teacher has said? You have to feel it out, to examine and to discover for yourself the borders of consciousness, the borders of your thinking, the borders of your feeling, how far and how deeply tradition goes, and how far experience shapes your conduct. The whole of this framework of conduct, of thought, of feeling, of tradition, of memories, of racial inheritance, of the innumerable experiences that one has or a family has, the tradition of the family, the tradition of the race—all that is consciousness.

Is it possible to break this and bring about a mutation? That is the real question, which should be urgent and important to most of us, because the world is in an awful mess—not only the world, but also our own lives. If one is satisfied with mere reformation, then that is all right; but if one wants to go more deeply, one must inquire into the question of change and of mutation, and see that change by thought, by persuasion, by compulsion, by a process of gradual adjustment, or by the influence of propaganda, surely, is no change at all. Therefore, unless there is action without motive, mutation without motive, it is not a change at all. I think we should be very clear on this point. And perhaps, it might be worthwhile to discuss the question: whether any other change is possible than the change by persuasion, the change brought about through expansion of knowledge, the change through fear, the change through example. Unless one has understood the nature of change psychologically, inwardly, to agree or to disagree seems quite futile. But having examined it, a change by persuasion seems to be no change at all. And yet it has been taught in your books and by your gurus that the business of culture and civilization is to bring about a change through gradual influence, through gradual pressure, imitation, or example. If you accept it consciously, not traditionally without much thought, if you accept that actually, then you have to examine the fact of this acceptance, and why you accept it; and I would like, if I may, to go into that.

Why should not jealousy, ambition, etc., be immediately brushed aside? Why should there be this postponement, the gradual change, the acceptance of idealistic authority? I hope, sirs, you are thinking it out with me and not merely listening to me. We accept this gradual process of change because it is more easy, and postponement is more pleasurable. The immediate gives you a great deal of excitement, and to see its value is much more difficult and requires much greater attention and energy. I do not know if you have realized that in facing a fact there is a release of energy, and it is this facing the fact, from which energy is derived, which has the quality that brings about mutation. And we cannot face the fact if we are convinced that change through a gradual process, through influence, through fear, through compulsion, is the only way. In the very act of facing it, you will find there is release of energy, psychologically.

Most of our lives are wasted through conflict. We do not face facts but run away from them, seeking various forms of escape. This is dissipated energy, and the result of that dissipation is confusion. If one does not escape, if one does not translate the fact in terms of one's own pleasure and pain, but merely observes, then that act of pure seeing in which there is no resistance is the releasing of energy.

Please listen. If I may point out, this is quite important to understand. The man who is ambitious wants to succeed and climb the hill; he wants success and fame. In that there is dissipation of energy, there is frustration, there is conflict, there is misery. He may succeed in achieving, but it is always followed by a shadow of fear, which we all know. But one has to observe the total fact of ambition—what is involved in it, its cruelty, its ruthlessness—and also the fact that when one acts in the name of the country, in the name of the family, in the name of the nation, and goodness and all the rest of it, one is primarily concerned to achieve, to fulfill. In that are involved several psychological factors such as brutality, ruthlessness, and these psychological factors take away one's energy. In that there is always contradiction. Where there is a contradiction, there is energy, as in the case of a man who is mentally ill. The man who is mentally ill is not in conflict, and he has tremendous energy. I do not know if you know some people who are somewhat unbalanced, not healthy mentally. They identify themselves with certain ideas, and this total identification gives them an extraordinary sense of energy because there is no resistance at all. But the mind that is ill cannot see things as they are.

When one observes the fact without any resistance, neither accepting nor denying nor judging it, neither condemning nor identifying oneself with the thing that one observes, in that pure act of observation, pure act of seeing, there is no resistance, there is no contradiction at all. Therefore that seeing of the fact releases total energy, and quite unlike the mentally ill person who also has got an extraordinary sense of energy, the mind that is clear, not ill, sees things actually as they are. A mere change will not bring about this energy which is released by the act of pure seeing—because change implies postponement, implies resistance, implies dissipation, contradiction, control; and so there is an increasing contradiction between *what is* and 'what should be'. I do not know whether you are following this. As I said, we are concerned with immediate mutation and not with gradual change. It seems to me it is very important to understand what is involved in change before we can understand what is meant by mutation.

What is implied in change when you say, "I must change"? What is involved in this process of change? Exercising the will—which is, after all, resistance. The more you exercise the will, the greater the contradiction, the greater the control, and thereby the greater is the dissipation of energy through friction, through contradiction. If you see this fact very clearly, that all process of change involves dissipation of energy because any change means resistance, then you must obviously deny it; you no longer think in terms of change in time.

Then there is the question of sensitivity, being sensitive. Being sensitive means love. Without sensitivity—being sensitive to nature, to people, to ideas—there is no affection. Our mind is not sensitive at all; it may talk about love, it may talk of affection, but it does not know how to love. Is it possible to be instantly sensitive and not build up sensitivity? You see the difference? I am not at all sure that I am conveying what I mean by sensitivity. You know, to appreciate beauty—the beauty of a person or of nature or of a tree or of a lovely river—your senses must be alert and fully alive. But you have been taught for centuries that you must not be a slave to the senses, and so the monks, the sannyasis, deny beauty. When you deny beauty, where is love? Sensitivity is to be sensitively aware of your children, of the tree, of the family, of a lovely face, and of the beauty of sensitivity. To be sensitively aware of all that is to be affectionate. If you deny that, you have no affection, though you may talk about it, though you may indulge in good works.

Now, you have to see that fact. I mean by "seeing," not explaining, not saying, "I must have sensitivity," or "It is good to have sensitivity." The process of accumulation of sensitivity is absurd. Through accumulation, probably you will become superficially clever, but you will still remain dull. If one is capable of seeing what is implied in sensitivity, then the very act of seeing makes the mind astonishingly sensitive. In the same manner, one has to be aware, sensitively, of what is implied in change. It is like changing your dress, but you remain the same inside. If you see it as you see the speaker sitting on this chair, then that very act of seeing puts an end to the change, and you are directly facing the fact.

You are so used to ideals—I am not. I have no ideals. You are so used to worshiping the ideal, like nonviolence, but it does not mean anything either to me or to you, really. There is the actual fact, and the ideal of nonviolence is merely the postponement of the fact, the covering up of the fact, and the pursuit of the ideal is the dissipation of the energy which we need to tackle the fact. And a mind that is being brought up in ideals, in postponement, says, "Eventually, I will be nonviolent." In the meanwhile, it is violent. To such a mind, the idea of facing the fact immediately becomes impossible. To say, "I am angry" and remain with that fact without trying to change, without trying to explain it away, is very difficult. I do not know if you have noticed that to live with an ugly thing without its corrupting you is very difficult. To live with an ugly picture and not let it pervert your sensitivity is very difficult because to live with an ugly thing releases a tremendous amount of energy, just as living with a beautiful thing does. You see a lovely tree in your garden, and you are proud of it, or you are used to it. Or, you see a filthy road, and you get used to it. To live with it and not let that dirty road corrupt you, or to live with something very beautiful without getting used to it, you need a great deal of energy, you need a great deal of sensitive awareness, don't you? Otherwise you get used to both; you become dull to beauty and to ugliness. So a mind that has become accustomed to ideals has become dull; it accepts postponing, and postponement is a facile habit. If you deny ideas, if you deny ideals, then you are free to face the fact. We have to understand all this.

We have to understand also the question of time—time, that is tomorrow or many tomorrows. Will time bring about change? Will time bring about a radical change or merely an adjustment? You have been Hindus for ten thousand or five thousand years now; the pressure of Western civilization is changing your habits or your way of life. Is that a radical change, or merely an adjustment to circumstances and therefore being a slave to circumstances? You see, you may call yourself a communist because that is the latest thing today; it pays you more, and so you adjust yourself to a system that is tyrannical, and you call that "revolution." But is it a revolution? Is adjustment to pressure, to the system, to an idea—is this adjustment a real, radical mutation?

Do you see yourself as you are? Have you ever been self-critically aware of yourself? Have you known what you are—angry, jealous, envious, ambitious, hating, and all the rest of it? Now, what will make you change? Let us start with it. How do you change? What makes you change? Do you change because it helps you? Do you change because it is pleasurable? Do you change because fear is involved? Or because you think that by changing, you will be a better man? Or because if you conform, you will get more money, you will be more respectable, and so on? Is that the way you change, if you have changed at all? And have you changed in anything? Do ask these questions, please. Don't let me put these questions to you; you are asking the questions yourself. Have you changed in anything? And if you have, what made you change?

What is the reason, the motive, the force, the compulsion, the urge, that made you change? Is it the external urge or social morality, or an inward compulsion based on your own fears and all the rest of it that made you change? Have you noticed, have you observed, that you have changed? What has made you change? If you say that disgust has made you change, is the change brought about in yourself by disgust a change? It is a mere reaction. If you pursue a thought to the very end, not stopping halfway, then you will see that the pursuit of that thought leads to the ending of that thought. You must give that thought full freedom to flower.

We are now allowing freedom for the flowering of disgust. What is implied in it is: I am envious; I am disgusted with it, and I say, "I must not be envious." That "must" is the reaction, isn't it? You say you are disgusted because it is a very simple psychological phenomenon, isn't it? You are disgusted because society has told you that envy is wrong. Also, you have found out for yourself that it is painful, that it does not pay, it is not profitable; and so these reasons have made you say that you are disgusted with *what is*. If you don't mind, please don't use the word *disgust*. If you say that one change is similar to all changes, and all change is empty, then you are left with a mind that does not accept change.

You do not want to change when change means danger, lest you lose your job or your wife. You may ask, "What is the need for change?" If you do not change, you are dead, obviously. Life means moving, and not stagnation. If you deny life, you are dead. Life and change are synonymous. You are changing, your body is changing, you are getting older, your senses are changing. And inwardly you do not want to change because you have found a belief, an idea, some superstition, a conclusion, and an experience; from that you do not want to move because it is pleasurable, profitable. If it is painful, you want to change it, you put it away.

Question: Does change come from within or without?

KRISHNAMURTI: What do we mean by "without" or "within"? Is it so clearly defined? Is not "without" the same as "within" and "within" the same as "without"? It is like a tide going out and coming in. You do not say that is "out" and this is "in." It is a movement, but we separate it. It is one movement, and that is the beauty of it. By understanding the outward movement, you begin to understand the inward movement. Then you see that the two are not separate. But if you separate the outer as not the real and the inner as the real, there is terrible confusion. But if you see that there is no division between the outer and the inner, then in the understanding of the outer—society, the morality of society, the whole pressure of the outer—you begin to understand also how the inner is the same thing as the outer. What we are talking about is the need to bring about a mutation in this process.

Most of us psychologically resist every form of change. We have found some form of security, some form of permanence; that gives us tremendous satisfaction, and we build a wall around that satisfaction and remain. The pressure outside is merely a casual and necessary acceptance—going to the office and all the rest of it. When one sees that mutation can take place, not only inwardly, but also outwardly, and that mutation is not change, then one will have to inquire very, very deeply and question every step of what we call change.

Do please inquire. Can you put away all thoughts of change? You have to put away change, not verbally, but emotionally, which is much more important than the verbal. When you put away all thoughts of change, what is taking place in the mind? What is the state of the mind that has finished with change? Let me put it this way. What is the state of mind that denies? How do you deny? There is Catholicism or Hinduism, and you deny it. What is the state of the mind? Do you deny it because you are going to join something else? Or do you deny all propagandist, organized religions? The denial of one because you are joining the other is not denial at all. I understand the whole implication of organized religion, and I deny it. But I do not know what is beyond the organized religion. I deny it totally. I do not join anything. Therefore my mind is totally insecure, uncertain. When I see the futility of change, I deny it; then the fact remains, and I do not think in terms of changing it or changing myself in relation to it. When the mind is free of this conflict of change, it has become sensitive in its awareness, and it realizes that it is dull.

When I say my mind is dull, do I know that dullness because I have been told, or because I have compared myself with somebody who is cleverer? How do I recognize the dullness? This involves a process of recognition. This involves the question of knowing. There are two ways of knowing—one is knowing because you have learned it, because somebody has told you; the other is knowing because you yourself have discovered. How do you discover? Do you discover through comparison? When you have put all these questions and have seen the futility of change, then is there dullness? Then how do you look at the thing? Do you look at it verbally?

As I said before, the word is not the thing, and to separate the look from the word is extraordinarily difficult. You understand? We are looking at the fact without seeing the word, and the word *dullness* has conveyed its meaning. Now to look at something without the word is to look at it directly without the interpretation through the word, through the symbol. What happens to the fact—anger, jealousy, whatever it is—without the word? Do not answer me, sir. This requires immense penetration. It means that the mind itself must be free from the word, and to be free from the slavery of words, you must have gone into it. To look at the fact, you have to understand the futility of change, and also the mind must not be a slave to words. You see what is involved. You live on words. You are a Hindu, or you are a Christian, or you are a Buddhist, or you are a communist—all words. Indian nationality—a word. The Gita is a word, and the word has become tremendously important. So, it is extraordinarily difficult for the mind to be free from the word, the word being a symbol. Now if you are free of the word, what is the fact? Is the fact a word? Do not answer me. Look at it. But I have used the word to denote the fact. When you remove the word, when the word is no longer influencing your look, then that observation is a pure act, isn't it? Can you look at the Gita, your favorite book, without the word *Gita?* You can't. Because the whole world of tradition, the whole world of respectability, authority, the recognition by society that it is a sacred book—all this holds you, and you are a slave to words. But to look at the fact requires an enormous inquiry into "change" and not the word. Then, you have understood "change," and you are free from the word.

A man who resists change is a dead man—he may live, he may go to the office, he may have children; but he is a dead man, he is not alive. And most of us are dead because we resist change; we remain what we have been from the beginning and die as we are. Life—not Indian life nor American life, but living—demands that you shatter through every form of change. And when you begin to inquire into change, you are bound to find out the emptiness of it, the meaninglessness of it. And, therefore there is no meaning in having ideals. When you have got cancer, you cannot think about ideals—the disease is eating you out. So in inquiring into change, you put away all ideals, therefore all examples, therefore all patterns, therefore all authority.

Do you inquire with words? We have to use words to communicate, to do, to act. But also there must be a look without the word. You must look at the flower without the botanical knowledge—which is a very complex process of looking. When you look in that way, you require immense, great penetration and meditation. Just listen to me while I am talking; you have to go into it, penetrate into it, in order to know. Then, if you have emotionally gone into the fact—not with words nor symbols nor a conclusion—then you will find for yourself that the fact has undergone a change because you have allowed it full freedom to flower. The flowering of the fact is important, not the word. It must flower, and in the flowering there is immense significance. But that significance cannot be understood or gone into if the mind is not highly sensitive, and there is no sensitivity if there is resistance to change.

November 29, 1961

Fourth Talk in Madras

The last few times when we were here, we were talking about the necessity of a new mind. We mean by a new mind, not a mind that has been brought about through various forms of changes, but a new mind which is only possible in mutation, a complete, radical revolution. It is not mere fancy, it is not something to be desired, but it is to be worked for very arduously. One has to go into the whole problem and the machinery of thinking very deeply. It is not something that you meditate about, sitting under a tree. It is not brought about by following some philosophy or attending some of these talks. It cannot be brought about casually, facilely. It has to be brought about, worked out in daily life. I mean by "being worked out," not complying to a particular pattern laid down by any of us through imitating, conforming, disciplining, but rather by inquiring into every activity, into every thought, into every feeling that happens during the day. Because without self-understanding, without knowing the ways of thought and feeling, this is a mere conjecture, a mere speculation of what the new mind should be.

It is definitely possible to bring about a totally new mind. But there are certain indications, certain necessary characteristics which do bring about that quality of newness. They are affection, or love, and integrity. Most of us do not know what it means to be affectionate. To us, it is a word which we casually use without much significance. Love is of course something very carefully guarded, something with which we are not familiar, though we use the word so glibly, so facilely—love of the country, love of truth, love of life, and many, many loves that we talk about; and I do not think it has anything to do with this. The ingredient—if I may use that word—which is absolutely necessary is the quality of affection and integrity. I don't mean by integrity any form or pattern of belief, nor do I mean it as integrity according to the experience through which one has to live, but I mean that integrity that comes about when you begin to observe every movement of your own thought and when no thought is hidden. You do not wear a mask, you do not any longer pretend to be something other than what you actually are; and therefore there is no discipline, no fancy, no worship; and out of that comes the external sense of integrity. I mean that kind of integrity, not the man who has belief and lives according to that belief, not the man who is sincere, but with certain ideals, not the man who follows a certain discipline or tries to bring about an integration emotionally or intellectually. Such efforts do not bring about integrity. On the contrary, they increase conflict, misery. Whereas the integrity that we are talking about is the quality of seeing the fact every minute, not trying to translate the fact in terms of pleasure and pain, but letting the fact flower without choice, without opinion—out of which seeing comes integrity which is never altered. Now these two, affection and integrity, are necessary.

You see, affection or love is a rare thing. It does not exist in the family. It does not exist in any relationship. It comes out of emptiness in the mind—not seeking, not wanting, not desiring. But that cannot come if we do not understand the urgent need for the ending of sorrow. Because, for most of us, sorrow is our shadow; it is always there; the sorrow that we are aware of—sorrow of death; sorrow of quarrel; sorrow of a smile; sorrow that exists when you see a villager going day after day, carrying burdens and working night and day for hours; sorrow that comes when you see poverty, when you see a man so dull and stupid; sorrow that comes when there is no fulfillment, when there is only frustration and bitterness; sorrow that exists with anxiety, with guilt. There are so many kinds and varieties of sorrow, and each one of us is caught in it in some manner or other, by force of circumstances or through our own ignorance. Sorrow is always there like a shadow from which you cannot possibly escape. You know your own sorrow. It is necessary to go into the whole process of sorrow and literally end it, without continuing with it for a single day, because any problem that continues day after day perverts the mind and disintegrates the quality of the brain. Every problem has to be dealt with immediately and solved, and not be carried over to the next minute, so that the mind and the brain are eternally young, innocent, fresh, unspoiled by any problem or experience.

So the quality of a new mind cannot be brought about if there is sorrow. Sorrow must be understood quite differently, and one cannot escape from it. You may be free from the pain of sorrow, but you create greater problems of sorrow. Your gods, books, ceremonies, your wife, your husband have all become mere means of escape from the fact that the mind is empty, sorrowful. How can there be a new mind which demands freshness, youth, and innocency if this is not understood? What I mean by understanding is the facing of the fact that one is in sorrow—not merely to find the cause of sorrow which is real. You seek the cause, and the cause may be desires, ambition, or perpetual discontent. The cause may be that you are not loved, and you want to be loved, or that you want to have more money, more capacity, more power. We know the reasons, but we go with that sorrow like a burden, day after day, year after year, until we end in the grave. Knowledge will not wipe away sorrow, however wide, however extensive be the frontiers of knowledge. Nothing will wipe it away, and so there is no escape. No religion, no leader, no guru, nothing can wipe it away; you will have to do it yourself—which means facing it and cutting at the root of it. That is one of the problems.

Then the other is that you have the real thing, a fresh, innocent mind. For this, the mind must be stripped of authority, and it is a difficult thing to be free of authority. You may be free from external authority or compulsion, or perhaps consciously or unconsciously you may do away with the law. You may not want to pay taxes, but you are forced to pay taxes, though you want to cheat the government in some way or other. But you obey, and you have got to obey external demands, the external laws. Then there is the internal authority; in trying to seek the light of experience, the light of understanding, the very light of knowledge becomes the authority. So the experience, the knowledge, the memory, becomes a burden which prevents the innocency of the mind.

So you have to understand authority—which is basically the desire for success, to be somebody, not only in this external world, in this rotten society, but also inwardly. We set up authority—the authority of the guru outwardly, the authority of the book, either the Gita or the Marxist, outwardly, and also the authority inwardly which is experience, which is more demanding, much more restrictive, much more insistent. One has to understand this. The response to a challenge is experience. We cannot escape from challenge. Life is all the time giving us challenges every minute, and we have been responding every minute, consciously or unconsciously. And the response is according to our background, the culture in which we have been brought up socially, morally, the values of that particular society with its religious sanctions and respectability. So we are constantly piling up experience. If you observe and go into the question of experience very deeply, you see that experience does not bring freedom from conflict. I do not know if you have noticed it. Every fact, every feeling or thought, translates itself in terms of the past, consciously or unconsciously; the present response is conditioned according to the past and added to the past, which again responds to a new challenge and thereby conditions the further response.

If I may point out, this is not a mere talk. This is not a thing to which you are listening, agreeing, or disagreeing; but you are actually investigating your own mind, and actually examining your own heart so that you will be able to perceive the working of your own brain with all its reactions, memories, wounds, and incidents, so that when you leave here—if you have really, deeply understood—you will not merely repeat certain phrases that you have heard or compare with what you have heard already, what you have learned already, but you will have found out for yourself; otherwise, this seems to me to be a real waste of time. So you have to listen genuinely, honestly.

Listening is quite difficult. When you actually compare what you listen to with something else that you have read, you are actually not listening at all. Or when you do listen to a word, to a phrase, to an idea, you resist it because it is something new; it must be disturbing; therefore, that prevents you from listening. Or when you hear, you translate it immediately into action and see the impossibility of such an action, and therefore you resist what you hear. But if you could really listen—that is, listen without any resistance, neither accepting nor rejecting, neither translating nor comparing, but actually listening—then you would find such listening—not that you agree with it or disagree with it—sets a new movement going. That listening is not the acceptance of propaganda, it is not something to which you will take avidly, hoping to resolve your problems. So there is the act of listening, which in itself is an extraordinary thing if you do it, unconcerned with the immediate problem. You know, most of us are concerned with the immediate—"immediate" being in terms of the future, in terms of many tomorrows, but those many tomorrows are still in terms of the immediate. The short view is translated in terms of the long view, which every politician throughout the world does, as also, unfortunately, the so-called spiritual people do. What we are talking about is neither the short nor the long, but the understanding of everything that is taking place in us, psychologically, inwardly, facing every fact from moment to moment and moving with that fact.

So authority is an evil thing, like power—whether the authority is the domination of the wife over the husband or the domination of the husband over the wife, or the authority of the parents over the children, though they say that they are the new generation, the new hope. But we see that the children conform to the pattern that we have established. This is what we call education. And so there is no new generation, no new hope; it is always the past carrying on through the new generation.

So, authority is really the desire to be secure, and the desire to be secure is expressed as ambition and authority. We are never for a single moment without authority—the authority of morality, the authority of the state, the authority of law, the authority of what is right and what is wrong. Do follow all this please, do listen please. We must do something about it, for which we have to be tremendously revolutionary. But the old are not going to do anything about it because they are fairly secure, their minds are half-asleep and half-dead. And the young obviously want the pleasures of life; they want to enjoy themselves, they want to make a success of life, and so, they won't listen either. But, perhaps, between the two, there may be somebody who will listen and perhaps will like the freedom of revolution—not the economic, social revolution, but that revolution that comes into being when you actually and really deny all authority.

There is a most extraordinary sense of freedom that comes into being when you are no longer carrying the burden of authority of anybody. You have no guru, no book, no Krishnas, no Ramas and Sitas, and no gods that man has created out of his fear and imagination, so that you are awake every minute of the day, even in the darkness of the night.

To be free, you have to examine authority, the whole skeleton of authority, tearing to pieces the whole dirty thing. And that requires energy, actual physical energy, and also, it demands psychological energy. But the energy is destroyed, is wasted when one is in conflict. The moment you begin to understand the whole process of conflict, inwardly and outwardly, then you will not only see that facing the fact gives you abundant energy, but also begin to understand this conflict—between belief and yourself, between yourself and 'what should be', between your ideals and yourself, in the desire to be superior or to fulfill, and in all the things that man has invented. You also understand the accepting of conflict as inevitable, and so making conflict as something extraordinary. So when there is the understanding of the whole process of conflict, there is the ending of conflict, there is abundance of energy. Then you can proceed, tearing down the house that you have built throughout the centuries and that has no meaning at all.

You know, to destroy is to create. We must destroy, not the buildings, not the social or economic system—this comes about daily—but the psychological, the unconscious and the conscious defenses, securities that one has built up rationally, individually, deeply, and superficially. We must tear through all that to be utterly defenseless, because you must be defenseless to love and have affection. Then you see and understand ambition, authority; and you begin to see when authority is necessary and at what level—the authority of the policeman and no more. Then there is no authority of learning, no authority of knowledge, no authority of capacity, no authority that function assumes and which becomes status. To understand all authority—of the gurus, of the Masters, and others—requires a very sharp mind, a clear brain, not a muddy brain, not a dull brain. But you are so unfortunate. Those of you who are listening do not apply yourselves consistently and persistently to go into this. Perhaps you may do it for a couple of days or for an hour or two, or you are not listening at all, but inevitably you will revert to the pattern because in that pattern is safety; there is respectability, there is money and profit, there is something to be gained, and so you become slaves to authority; otherwise, no religion could possibly exist.

The authority of the priest is very strong throughout the world because each of us wants to be secure, safe in what he is doing, never to be disturbed—that is what we really want. We do not want truth. We do not want God, we do not want understanding; we want more and more safety, more and more security, and therefore we pile up authority—not only the authority of the book, of the guru, but also our own authority of theory and knowledge. But when you tear down the house of authority totally, destroy it completely, then there is the freedom which has its own extraordinary sense of security. The free mind has no fear, and therefore in that state there is security—not the security of a petty, little mind because such a mind is merely seeking security, safety. But the mind that is free, having no fear of any kind, not wanting to be anything, has no authority, and therefore is everlastingly capable of affection and integrity. The man who loves is completely, everlastingly fearless.

But you see, unfortunately, most of us here will do very little about it. When you go home, go into yourself, step by step, to discover where is your authority, and why you cling to it. Please go into it very deeply yourself; take time off and go into it. You see for yourself the authority of your wife, the domination of your family, your children, and also wherein you dominate—the whole process of authority. If you go into it very deeply, step by step, then you will find out how completely, how unknowingly the burden of authority falls off; you do not have to do anything about it. Just follow the fact where it will lead you. Let the flower of authority blossom, and watch it blossoming without preventing it because it is an extraordinary flower, and you will see the outward symptoms of it. Please follow the outward symptoms, the outward facts; go into it every minute, every second, as you talk to your wife or your husband, as you talk to your boss when you go to the office—watch it every minute. Out of that watching, listening, looking, you will find yourself out of it all.

Or instead of watching, looking, seeing, you are so sensitive a man, so sharp, clear, that you jump to it immediately, totally; in a flash you have understood the whole structure. That is, God, the temples of God, books, knowledge, experience—everything has gone, and you are left with a mind that is no longer burdened. Therefore, the mind is capable of understanding the significance and the importance of knowledge and not being burdened by it. So either way one has to work, and nobody wants to work this out because he wants something. Nobody wants to go and search it out because in that there is no success, no prospect. They do not come out of it with more money, with bigger houses, with more cars. But that is all that most of us want—profit, gain. There are so very few of us who are not money-minded, who are not profit-minded, who are not utilitarian. Very few go into themselves sharply, incessantly, clearly, so that every movement, every thought, every feeling is uncovered and understood. Try it sometime and see what an extraordinary thing it is. But you will block yourself if you condemn or if you justify. If you give value to what you see, then you stop it; then you stop the flowering of the fact of what you are actually. You love authority. Don't you? You love to be B.A.'s, engineers, scientists, and so on, and you fall on your knees before a person who is the president of something or other. You never find a man without degrees, without a title. We have valued words, words which bring profit. That is all we are concerned about—so that all our life becomes very shabby, empty, dull. Very few of us see immediately the truth of a fact because we have never kept the mind free, sharp, clear, sensitive. When you see something very clearly, that acts immediately. Even to follow deeply to the root of authority, you need to have a sensitive mind, but that sensitivity is not brought about by fancy, meditation. It comes into being when you watch a tree, birds, animals, ants, etc.

Please watch yourself—how you walk, talk, dress, eat. See, and try sometimes when you have leisure, how you are making yourself very important. Go and try. Then you will see for yourself what an extraordinary thing it is to love, to have affection. Any love, any affection which has a motive, which has a purpose, is no love at all, and we only love when we have no motive.

You are listening here obviously hoping to get something or other. But you are not going to get anything at all. You will go empty-handed. You are not really listening to what the speaker is saying. You are only hearing something which is going on. So you are not tearing down the house that you have built about yourself.

The ending of sorrow is the denial of authority. It is only the dull mind that is a sorrowful mind, not the sensitive mind. It is only the mind that has accumulated knowledge and is held by it that has sorrow—not the sensitive mind, not the inquiring mind, not the mind that is questioning, asking. Such a mind is not asking for a reply, is not questioning to find out, but it puts the question because it is a marvelous thing to put the question without seeking an answer, because the question then becomes unraveled; it begins to open the doors and windows of your own mind. And so, through this questioning, watching, listening, your mind becomes extraordinarily sensitive. Therefore, such a mind is capable of affection, and that affection has its own integrity. And such affection, such integrity, has the catholicity to bring about a new mind. Not ideas, not theories, not listening to innumerable talks and reading innumerable books and repeating endless phrases, but only these two—affection without motive, and integrity—bring about a new mind. Then you will know for yourself what is a new mind.

You know there is a difference between the brain and the mind. The brain is essentially sensuous. It has been built up through the centuries, educated, and conditioned. It is the storehouse of memory. And this brain controls all our thoughts, shapes our thinking; and every thought shapes the brain to function in a particular way. If you notice a scientist, an engineer, a specialist, or a technician, you find that when he has been trained, year after year, for a particular groove endlessly, he may become an excellent mechanic, a marvelous technician. But his mind, the totality of his mind, is very little because he has not investigated the whole question of the mind. To him, the little thing—the specialized life—is everything. Its response answers to every demand of the immediate. So our brain becomes all-important. It has its own importance, but to go beyond the brain, it is necessary to have a brain that is highly sensitive and quiet, not asleep, not drugged by all the mechanical things.

After all, the greater part of the brain is the residuary result of the animal—as the biologist will tell you—and the remaining part of the brain is still undefined. We live our life in the very small part, never investigating, never stirring, never jumping out of that little place with which we are familiar. So you will find as you go into yourself, as you observe every thought and follow every emotion flowering, that the brain can be extraordinarily sensitive and quiet, the brain can be completely still. Then out of that stillness, the flowering of the mind begins. But that is mutation, and we will discuss it another time.

I am only pointing it out because unless authority and sorrow have come to an end completely, totally, deep down in the hidden recesses of our heart and mind, unless the mind is completely free of authority and sorrow, you can never have the brain still. An angry, distorted brain that is being trodden down by society, by frozen respectability—that brain can never be quiet; and when it is quiet, it is a dead brain. It is only a quiet, sensitive, alert brain that can begin to function and is the foundation for the discovery of a different mind.

Therefore, one has to begin very near to go very far. To begin, what is near is yourself. You are the nearest thing to yourself—not your property, not your wife, not your children, and not your gods, but only yourself. If you begin to unravel authority, then you will find out how easily it slips away from you, though it looks fearful, though it may be shattering for the moment. If you begin in spite of the fears, of the hopes and despairs, then, after that, sweetly and innocently comes a mutation; and it is that mutation that can answer all the problems in society, in civilization, in any culture. Without that we just become machines—not even very clever machines. So, if you are to be completely, totally free, look into yourself, and you cannot look into yourself if you have authority and if there is sorrow.

December 3, 1961

Fifth Talk in Madras

The other day when we met here, we were talking about integrity, the capacity to live totally, wholly. And it seems to me that it is very important to understand that factor because most of us worship the intellect. For us knowledge has become extraordinarily important, and the theorizing factor, the building up of words, has assumed immense importance, and not the way or the know-how to act totally, as a whole being—not as a divided, contradictory entity. And it seems to me when we worship the intellect as we do, we are inviting not only deterioration but also an immense gap between the intellect—which is the capacity to think, to reason—

and life, which is total, complete, which is whole. The capacity to live wholly, totally, is the ending of deterioration. I mean by "deterioration" not only the physical but also the emotional, the intellectual sensitivity of the human being which gradually withers away. The deteriorating factor is much stronger than the capacity to live totally.

I would like this evening, if I may, to discuss or talk about this factor of deterioration, not only of the brain—the capacity to think, the capacity to feel—but also of the capacity to live as a whole human being, without contradiction, without tension, without fear. To understand the whole problem of fear which, it seems to me, is really the major factor of withering away, we have to understand the whole process of thinking; and without going into the process of thinking rather deeply, merely to discuss fear seems to be a waste of time. But before we go into the whole process of thinking, should we not also inquire why human beings have given such an extraordinary importance to thought, to the intellect, to knowledge?

Now, there are two ways of questioning—the questioning that comes out of a reaction, and the questioning which is not out of a reaction at all. I could question something because I am uncomfortable, I am anxious, fearful; and out of that fear, out of that anxiety, out of that guilt, I question existence, realities, society. I question because my questioning has come from a reaction, and such questioning finds an answer, but it will be limited, incomplete—for all reactions are incomplete. This is what most of us do—we question out of a background, out of a reaction.

Now, there is a different questioning which, it seems to me, is more significant, of greater depth, which is: to question not out of a reaction, but understanding the reaction and putting aside the reaction, and then inquiring. I could question the value of the present society however right it may be, I could question its morality, the whole setup. That questioning arises because I do not find a place in it, or I see no value in it, or I have certain ideals which I want to pursue, and therefore I react to the present society; and such reaction will find an answer according to my conditioned thinking. That is fairly clear, simple, I think. But the other questioning is much more difficult, much greater, much more significant—that is, to be aware of the environment, of the social structure, its morality, its religious, political, economic values; being aware of all this and not reacting to it, and therefore not choosing a particular course of action, but questioning without reaction.

If we can do that, it is quite an arduous task because we live on reactions, and those reactions we call positive actions—"I don't like this," so I do something; this doing is a positive action, and it creates other problems. But if I can look at the fact and question the fact without reaction, then the fact gives me energy which will help me to go further into the fact. What we are talking about is not an intellectual feat. To me the intellect is only a very small part of the total existence, the total life. So, living only with the intellect is like cultivating a corner of a vast field and living on the products of that corner. Whereas to live totally is to cultivate and live on the whole of the field—to have the intellect with all its reason, to have the emotional sensitivity, to be able to be externally sensitive to everything: to thought, to beauty, to what one says, to all the doubts and innocuous feelings, to all the height and the narrowness of thought, and to the limitations of all thought. To live totally is to be totally aware and, out of that awareness, not to react but to question. That questioning then becomes entirely different because the answer is not according to what we want, not according to our reaction, but according to the fact of *what is*—which is to allow the fact to flower.

So, we are not discussing fear or any of the other things that we talk about, intellectually, verbally. The word is never the thing. To question the fact, the thing, one has to realize how strongly, how deeply—consciously and unconsciously—one is enclosed in words. Words have become the thing. When we are talking about fear, and when we are going very deeply, if we do not understand the whole mechanism of the word, the symbol, the word becomes important; we take the words for the experience. To live in experience is extremely arduous; therefore, the words satisfy, and it is easier to confine our activity, our being, our feeling, our thinking in terms of words. If you have watched yourself, you must have found out that thinking is merely verbal. A great deal of our thinking is verbalization, playing with words; every thought expressed or felt out is in terms of words, in symbols.

If you remove the word, is there thinking? I do not know if you have thought it out, gone into that question. What happens to the brain which is not thinking in terms of words? If the brain becomes aware that it is a slave to words, and realizes its limitations and puts away the significance of the symbols, then what happens to thinking? Then thought will not create a problem because then you are living with the fact, from moment to moment, but not with the idea about the fact. So if we could really grapple with the word and see its limitations and therefore put it aside, it will have no significance except merely as a means of communication. The usage of words creates a lot of misunderstanding. I may use a certain word like *love*, and you will translate it in so many different ways—what should be, what should not be, what is sacred, what is divine, and all the rest of it, which are all divisions. To me, it is not at all a division; it is being, it is a quality of existence, of life. To you the word means one thing, and to me the word means an entirely different thing. So communication becomes almost impossible because you are always interpreting words according to what you know, what you have been told, or what you have experienced. So one has not only to use the word to communicate but also to see how extraordinarily difficult the word becomes in usage, how it leads to misunderstanding—which means one has to be extraordinarily aware to see the danger of the word and of getting used to the word.

Now let me define it a little bit, if I may, and go into this question of awareness because all this is in relation to what we are going to talk about, which is fear. Without understanding all this, we will not understand fear. I am not talking away from the thing that we want to discuss or talk about this evening, but the talk is directly related to it. So please do follow it.

To be aware of something is quite an extraordinarily complex process. I am aware of you and you are aware of me—you see me and I see you. You see me in certain terms, in certain words, with a certain knowledge; you do not know me; you know my reputation, you know what I think. I do not know you at all, actually. But if I want to know you, I cannot have any preconceived idea about you—which means no judgment, no evaluation, but merely the fact that you are there and I am looking at you. This is extraordinarily difficult because I may or may not have an opinion. To look at something without an opinion, without choice is, really, awareness. This is not complicated, nor something mysterious. Being so aware, you begin to understand the immensity, the extraordinary vision of the things of life, of every thought, every feeling. Now, to be aware of these trees—most of us never look at the trees, never know what they look like; we are not acquainted even botanically with them—is to be sensitive enough to see the beauty of the tree or the beauty of the sunset. Please follow all this. This is not something extraneous but is relevant to what we are going to say.

So awareness, to us, has merely become a habit—going to the office, getting into the bus, talking to the wife, quarreling, and so on. We fall into a habit, and the mechanism of habit is never to be disturbed. We never want to feel something other than what we are used to because to feel something deeply, vitally, is very disturbing. So, in order to avoid this disturbance, pain, suffering, we gradually build a wall of resistance, and within that wall we live, and so gradually grow dull, bored, insufficient. Now we have to be aware of this factor—that we are dull because we have got innumerable traditions, ideas, opinions, judgments, and it is all this that makes us petty, dull, stupid. We have to be aware of that and not say, "I will keep this, and I will not keep that." We have to be aware without any choice, totally, of influence, of habit, of tradition, of the conditioning of the mind as a Hindu, a Christian, etc. To be totally aware of all this is to be totally sensitive. So, awareness is not merely of the external facts—the filthy road, the stupid society, the rotten, corrupt religion which has no meaning at all, the repetition of the Gita, the authority of the books. You have to be aware of all these facts and also be aware that you never look at a tree, you never have any communion with nature which has extraordinary beauty. To be aware of all things outwardly and then of your reaction to those outer things—which is the inward movement of the outer and which is not something separate—to be aware of the facts outside and the inward reactions to them and the experiences of those reactions is to be aware totally. And to be totally aware requires a very alert mind, a brain that is very sensitive, not made stupid by fifty years of the office. Being a specialist in a particular profession for fifty years does something to your brain; do what you will, it destroys your capacity. The moment you stop working, you wither away, you die. If you are alive all the time, sensitive, observing, alert, aware of the dirty road, of the office boss and his ugly ways and his domination, of the whole of this civilization, every minute, then going to the office is not a destructive thing.

For most of us, the word has become extraordinarily significant. Take the word *God*. It is really quite extraordinary what immense impact that word has on you! If the same word is used in Russia, in the communist world, they laugh at it. Now, to find out if there is or if there is not such a thing as God, the word must go with all the experience that word has given to human beings. All the images, the symbols, the ideas of all the teachers—all must go, to find out if there is or if there is not God. That requires immense energy, vitality, drive; and you can only have that drive, that energy, if you deny the false which is the word. The word God has no meaning at all because you have been conditioned by that word.

So one begins to realize to what depth, not only consciously, but unconsciously, deep down in the very remote corners of our being, the word has become extraordinarily significant. We are slaves to words—such as the wife, the husband, the son, the family, the nation. Now, we have to be aware of these words without choosing, without saying, "I will keep this word, but I will not keep that word because it does not satisfy me." When you are aware of what the word implies, of all the implications of that word, then that word loses its significance; then you are no longer a slave to that word. You must come to that state to find out; and as most people live on words, you are thrown out; and that is what you do not like, to stand constantly alone. So you are relying on words and so again you play with society. You have to see the whole implication of the word; then, being aware of it, you are out of the word altogether, you are dealing with facts and not with words.

Knowledge has become very important to us, and the electronic brains are taking over our knowledge. You can give them orders verbally now. They have all the knowledge that human beings have or are going to have. So the machines are taking over and, presently, knowledge will have no meaning. So, being aware of the word, without being entrapped in the word, you have to tear down all that you have learned, all that you have heard, all tradition; tear down everything, destroy everything in order to find out—that is, to question without reaction. Then you may find out if there is or if there is not. And what you find out cannot be experienced by another.

So we see that we are slaves to words, that we are not sensitive but merely repetitive, imitative, because in imitation and repetition there is security, psychological as well as physiological. It gives a great deal of security to live in a prison of words, to belong to a nation, to a group, to your family. Behind the word *group,* behind the word *nation,* there is a great feeling of security, a sense of living safely. So, after saying all this, let us talk about what is fear.

Each one of us is afraid. We have different kinds of fear, or we have multiple fears, many, many fears—fear of death, fear of public opinion, fear of society, fear of losing the job, fear of not being loved, fear of not fulfilling, and a dozen other things. You know what you are afraid of—of your wife, of your husband, afraid of your neighbor, afraid of not arriving just in time before the door closes, and all the other kinds of fear.

Take your fear and go through it. I will verbally go into it, but you must go through it; otherwise, it has no meaning. You take your particular form of fear and then, by listening to the speaker, you will discover how to face that fear and totally dissolve fear—not one particular form of fear, but all fear. I say it is possible.

Don't accept my word because I am not an authority or a guru. But you can find out for yourself that there is a state of the mind or the brain, whatever you like to call it, where there is complete freedom from fear and therefore no illusion. But to understand fear, you must understand thought because thought creates fear. Thought is time. Without thought, there is no fear. Without time, there is no fear. Because we have time and because we have thought, there is fear. If we are faced with something factual, there is no fear. If you are going to die the next instant, then you accept it; there is no fear. But if I say that you are going to die the day after tomorrow, then you have forty-eight hours to worry about it, to get sick about it. So time is fear, thought is fear, and the ending of thought, the ending of time, is the ending of fear. I don't know if you are following all this.

So, unless one understands the machinery of thought, fear will go on. Do whatever you like, go to any temple, seek any escape, go to women, cinemas, read the Gita backwards and forwards—you cannot possibly end fear. To end fear, you have to understand the machinery of thinking and also the question of time.

What is thinking? Surely thinking is a response to a challenge, isn't it? And there is a challenge all the time, pushing in upon you. There is not a moment when a challenge is not there, and so there is always this reaction, which we call thinking, to that challenge. I say to you, "What is thinking?" The moment you are asked, you try to find out an answer. The trying to find an answer, the period, the time lag between the question and the answer is the machinery of thought, which is the momentum or movement of that reaction. So thinking is entirely mechanical, and it can be very reasonable or unreasonable, unbalanced, irrational, stupid, or very, very clever, instructive, and so on. So, as you observe your own thinking, you will see that all thought is the response of memory. Please, sirs, do pay attention to this. This has to be understood very deeply. All experience is the accumulation of knowledge and therefore memory. Therefore thinking becomes merely the reaction; it is limited, conditioned, and therefore mechanical. Every thought shapes the mind, every thought conditions the mind, the outlook, the response, the reaction; and so one has to understand thought—not the thought of somebody else, but the thought with which you are familiar, which is operating in you when you are going to the office, when you talk to your wife, when you are listening here, when a question is asked, when you see something ugly or beautiful. Everything, every response is the product of memory which is recognition, which is based on experience. Unless you understand this mechanism, there is no ending of thought and therefore no ending of fear. You can say, "I will defy fear, I will escape from fear," and do all kinds of tricks in order to avoid fear—which most of us do—but it is always there. But if you want to go into it very deeply and eradicate fear totally—I say it is possible—you have to understand this mechanism which is called thinking and see if it can come to an end.

You know there is fear out of self-protection in a sense: for instance, you see a snake and the body reacts immediately. That is the normal, sensitive reaction. I am not talking of such fear. That is a natural self-protective response. But to find out where the self-protective response is psychological and not physical, and to be aware that the psychological fears control our action, our ideas, our activity, our thought, requires very sharp, clear, objective thinking; nothing can be taken for granted. One sees very clearly, not only consciously, but deep down in the unconscious, that there are various forms of fear with which you are totally unfamiliar—racial fears, fears of tradition, fear that you may not go to heaven, about which you have been told from your childhood. If you are a Catholic or a Protestant, there is hell awaiting you; it is there; you may deny it, you may say, "I have gone out of the church," but deep down there is fear, and you have to bring it out into your consciousness. And you can only do it by inquiring into the whole process of thinking and therefore being aware of every thought, every minute of the day, and therefore never dreaming at night. As you are conscious, aware, alert all the day, every minute of the day—watching, looking, examining, questioning—the unconscious gives out all its hints to the conscious, and therefore there is no need to dream; when you sleep, it is quite a different sleep. We will not go into it for the moment. Please do not say, "I will wait for that."

So, it is very important to understand thought. Thought creates fear—fear of what people may say, fear of death, fear of disease. You fall ill, feel the pain; you think of the past, and you do not want pain any more. So fear has come into being through thought of the thing known. You know you have to die; you are bound to die, and so you think about it, and there is the awakening of fear about death. That creates time, psychological time—not the time by the watch, but the psychological time of yesterday, today, and tomorrow.

So, to be aware of all this—that thought creates fear—and the understanding of thought most profoundly leads to the ending of thought, and therefore there is looking at life only with facts and not through the screen of words, ideas, tradition. This means really that the mind has no problem. After all, the problem exists only because we have not understood the fact—whatever be the fact, human fact or scientific fact. Fear becomes a problem—I am afraid of losing my job, I am afraid of public opinion, and a dozen other things. Fear ceases when you face the fact. And you can only face the fact if you have no opinion about it, if you do not deny, if you do not translate according to your background. An intelligent person must do all this because fear destroys, fear corrupts, fear creates illusion; all the gods that have been created are out of fear. When you have actually done all this, the mind is no longer frightened and therefore no longer guilty, and therefore there is no longing, no hope, no despair; and therefore the mind is living with the fact only, and there is no problem. This can be done, but it requires extraordinary alertness to be aware of every movement of thought and feeling.

This must be the foundation for meditation. This is the basis for meditation, for further inquiry. But the mind, which is frightened, which has not gone into it very deeply, cannot do this. You have to tear down every wall, every security, every idea, every word; then only you won't be creating illusions—most of your gods are illusions; they are not realities. So this is the foundation. A mind, a brain that has understood the verbal dangers, that has been made sensitive through awareness, a brain that has no problem—that mind, that brain, becomes extraordinarily quiet, though very sensitive; and it is only then that a different mutation can take place, the mutation of a new mind that is young, fresh, innocent. It is only such a mind that can travel very far. It is only such a mind that can find out if there is or if there is not the immeasurable. But a mind that is narrow, petty, thinking about gods, fearful, has no meaning at all. That is why we need to have a tremendous, deep revolution, a psychological revolution, a mutation that comes about when you face the fact—not the change that comes about through thought. And so there is the ending of thought, and therefore there is the ending of time, and thereby there is a timeless state.

December 6, 1961

Sixth Talk in Madras

I would like to talk over with you a rather complicated problem. I mean by a problem something which we do not understand. Every problem seems to dog us, and everything that we touch with our mind or with our heart becomes a problem. A problem is surely something which you have not resolved, a fact which you have not completely understood, an experience that pursues us with its unfinished, unresolved questions and answers.

And this evening, if we can, we will pursue something which demands all our attention. I mean by attention, not concentration at all. Concentration, for me, is rather a narrowing destructive process, though it has its utility at a certain level. But awareness is something entirely different, and I would like to discuss that at the beginning of this talk. Because, I feel we should understand what the difference is between awareness and concentration. We need desperately to change. The world situation and our own lives, which are so mediocre, so dull, without much meaning, demand it. We do need a radical, deep change, a mutation rather than a change.

And this change, this mutation, cannot be brought about by thought because, as we discussed the other day, thought is very limited. Thought is merely a reaction of memory, and memory is very limited. The concentration of memory in action is not the same as awareness in action. Memory becomes a technique in action, the know-how. Having learned something, I can carry it out—which most of us do as a habit, mechanical knowledge, or capacity. But such capacity, knowledge, or the know-how restricts, limits, our freedom. I am using the words deliberately, knowing what they mean.

If I may suggest, please listen in order to find out what the speaker has to say. But to find out, do not begin to interpret, do not say, "This is what he means, that is what he does not mean." Please listen to the very end of the talk. It is quite a difficult art to listen, to listen very attentively—not with knowledge, not with concentration—because you bring the whole memory of reactions. Whereas attention is entirely different—which I will go into presently. Concentration you can have, the more you have knowledge or capacity. The more capacity you have, the better can you force your concentration on something, to carry it out. You know action through concentration—that is what most of us have. The mechanic, the lawyer, the engineer, the specialist, the technological expert—they concentrate in action, which is the result of knowledge, of experience, the know-how; so that limits their awareness, their fullness of life. Now if you will experiment with what I am saying as I am talking, you will see that there is a difference between concentration and awareness.

Awareness is that state of mind which takes in everything—the crows flying across the sky, the flowers on the trees, the people sitting in front, the colors they are wearing—being extensively aware, which needs watching, observing, taking in the shape of the leaf, the shape of the trunk, the shape of the head of another, what he is doing. To be extensively aware and from there acting—that is to be aware of the totality of one's own being. To have a mere sectional capacity, a fragmentation of capacity or capacity fragmented, and to pursue that capacity and derive experience through that capacity which is limited—that makes the quality of the mind mediocre, limited, narrow. But an awareness of the totality of one's own being, understood through the awareness of every thought and every feeling, and never limiting it, letting every thought and every feeling flower, and therefore being aware—that is entirely different from action or concentration which is merely capacity and therefore limited.

To let a thought flower or a feeling flower requires attention—not concentration. I mean by the flowering of a thought giving freedom to it to see what happens, what is taking place in your thought, in your feeling. Anything that flowers must have freedom, must have light; it cannot be restricted. You cannot put any value on it, you cannot say, "That is right, that is wrong; this should be, and that should not be"—thereby, you limit the flowering of thought. And it can only flower in this awareness. Therefore, if you go into it very deeply, you will find that this flowering of thought is the ending of thought. And that is what I want to talk about this evening—which is really the beginning of meditation. I am using that word *meditation* very advisedly because for each one of us it has a different meaning. For some it has a meaning of repeating words, going into a corner, shutting one's eyes and repeating certain phrases, or concentrating on an idea or an image—which are all the actions of concentration—which is to limit thought and therefore to restrict life. To allow a thought to flower or a feeling to expand fully, and go to the very end of it, does not mean indulging in thought, indulging in feeling. As each feeling, each thought arises, to give it freedom to be what it is, to inquire into it, to search every corner, every breath, every angle to find out what it is—that is not possible if you merely limit it.

We need action. There must be action in life; otherwise, life cannot be. But if you examine your action very carefully, you will see that it is based on knowledge, on capacity, on memory, on motive. And such action invariably limits the totality of expression. The inquiry into the totality, into the whole process of thinking and feeling, to find out what is behind all this, is the process of meditation.

So that is what I want to talk about this evening. I may be using words with which you may not be familiar. They are not technical words or jargon with special meanings, but they are ordinary words with the ordinary dictionary meaning. There are several things that we have first to understand, such as experience, and we have to understand what is necessary as the foundation for meditation. I will begin by inquiring what is necessary for meditation—the foundation, not what you will get through meditation, not whether you will have peace of mind or not; it is too immature, too silly, too foolish to say, "I must have peace of mind." You cannot have peace of mind if you are ambitious, and the desire for peace of mind—unfortunately, it is called peace of mind, whatever that may mean—merely becomes stagnation. So I want to go into the question: First what is necessary—the necessary foundation for meditation? This means action, not just theory. And mutation is the very essence of the foundation.

Most of our minds are petty, shallow, and rather dull—which is mediocre. A mediocre mind can repeat endlessly the sacred books, East or West. It can follow a system and have certain stimulations and excitations, but it will remain always a petty mind, a shallow mind. That is a psychological fact. Whether you accept it or not, it is a fact that a petty mind thinking about God will remain still petty because its god is petty. So, the breaking of the petty mind is important. The mediocre outlook, the narrow family concern, the limited inquiry are all the indications of a petty mind, a narrow, limited, shallow, dull mind.

Now, how is that dull mind to be broken up, the petty mind to tear down the walls, to shatter all its images, its ideas, its hopes, its despairs? That is the first inquiry. Please don't say that your mind is something exceptional, that you are not mediocre but somebody else is. Let us make this inquiry personally, individually, so that as you are inquiring into it, your own pettiness is being broken up.

So our concern is, there must be mutation in the petty mind, something totally new must take place in the petty mind—which means a petty mind is no longer a mediocre mind—because the petty mind, the mediocre mind cannot inquire; it can only follow, it can repeat, it can have gurus, leaders, and all the rest of it. Now the whole world is more or less petty, limited, following leaders. It seems to be an obvious necessity to break up this petty mind. How is this to be done? Will thought do it? Certainly not. A petty mind thinking about its own pettiness and producing a thought which is still petty cannot break up this pettiness. So, thought is not the way out—which does not mean that we should not be reasonable, but one can see the limitation of thought. This is important to understand.

As I said, please listen to me, just listen neither agreeing nor disagreeing. Because, I am not trying to do any propaganda, I am not trying to persuade you to do anything. So, you can relax. You can go back to your patterns afterwards, or do what you like. But as you have taken the trouble to come here, please listen to find out. You cannot find out if you are merely translating what you are listening to in terms of what you have heard, what you have known, what some authority has asserted. But, please listen—which does not mean that you must put aside your critical capacity, it does not mean that you must not be questioning everything that is being said. You can only question if you are alert, if you are aware, and you can only listen if you are not concentrated on one part of the talk and letting the rest go. You need attention, not concentration, to listen.

So, a petty, narrow mind cannot answer the enormous problems of life. Going back to the past, to the tradition of a Hindu, or the revival of Christianity, or this or that is not going to solve these problems at all. You need a new mind, a totally new mind—not the petty mind that has developed certain capacities.

So, you need a new mind with a new series of responses and a new series of actions. That new mind can only come about when we understand how to break up the present condition of our existence, not sociologically nor economically, but inwardly, psychologically, spiritually. I am using the word *spiritually* in a very hesitant manner; I do not mean by that word, religiously—because for most of us, religion is such a shoddy affair with very little meaning. Going to the temple or doing some puja, reading the Gita ten times or whatever it is you do—that is not religion at all. Nor do I mean belonging to certain organizations or groups—all that is the action of a petty mind. Nationalism is essentially the state of a petty mind. And the world demands not only economically, socially, but also spiritually, inwardly, psychologically, a totally different variety of new actions. So, a mutation is necessary. And, this mutation can only take place in attention.

How to bring about this attention?—not as a method because method implies a practice, and a practice implies a repetition and therefore habit, and habit is the very essence of mediocrity. You have to see, first of all, the difficulty that, as we are, we are petty, mediocre. But, we have to find an answer, a way out of this mess. And it demands a totally different mind—not a reformed mind. Is it possible to bring it about and how? That is what I want to discuss this evening with you.

Now, we are going to inquire into different things, like experience, envy, thought producing visions, action, and so on. So, we will inquire into that—that is, question that, go into that very, very deeply. Please be good enough to follow this not merely verbally but actually, factually—which is to observe your own reaction, observe your own state of mind, your state of experience.

What do we mean by experience? Because, apparently, what guides most of us is the knowledge that we have derived from experience, either of our own or of another or of the community or of the race. Experience is what the race might have inherited, a certain knowledge, a certain tradition; that tradition, that knowledge is the derivation from experience, experience being response to stimuli, and that stimulated response leaves a residue which we call knowledge. This is very simple if you observe it. You have experience. That experience is the result of a challenge and a response. You are stimulated and you respond according to your memory, and this whole process is called an experience. Now, we live on sensation, on experience—which is on knowledge, on information, on memory. Every experience strengthens our memory according to its conditioning. So experience is not the factor of liberation. Experience will teach you mechanical things—what to do and what not to do, mechanically. If you are an engineer, you must have a great deal of knowledge to build a bridge or a skyscraper or an engine. For that, you must have knowledge; for that, you must have experience, the experience of many people—which is called science. But, experience, psychological inward experience, which is merely the response to a stimulus from the outside and which response is according to its conditioning, limits the mind, does not bring about a new quality of the mind. If I am a Hindu, and I have, psychologically, certain memories, certain traditions, according to those traditions I experience. Those experiences further strengthen the past, and from that past I respond, I act.

But the present world crisis, the present existence, demands a different mind, a different approach and not the response of the old. Therefore, a new action is necessary, and therefore it cannot rely on experience, pragmatic or actual. You cannot rely on experience because, if you do, you evoke the past—which will become mechanical. And life is not mechanical. So, you must approach it with a mind that has understood the whole nature of experience and has given the fullest scope to experience and gone away from the demand for further experience.

All of us want experience, don't we, more and more experience, more and more pleasure, more fun, more this and that, more visions and more peace—all that we want. Because we are fed up with the present experience of life, we want more. But when we ask for more experience, it means more sensation which will be translated in terms of the past and therefore will strengthen the past; therefore, it is not a breaking up of the past but merely the continuity, modified, of the past. If you see this very clearly, then you will see that there is a state of mind which does not seek experience at all.

I will put it round the other way. Most of us depend on challenge and response—outward challenge and a response to it. That is our existence; otherwise, we would go to sleep. There is the pressure of the world, of industry, of science, of war, and we have to respond to this. There is an external challenge and a response to it. And that response is from our background, from the know-how, knowledge, capacity. Now, if you do not rely on the external stimulus, the external challenge, but you have your own challenge every minute, then you are challenging everything—which is much more potent and has much more significance than the external challenge. If you reject both, which you do when you have gone into and done away with the whole problem of experience, then you will find that there is a new quality of the mind, which is not looking to experience as a means of knowing what to do—not in mechanical things, but in life.

I hope I am making this clear. A mind that has had experience is a very limited mind. It has capacity in a certain direction, but we are dealing not with fragmentation but with the totality of life. And to understand the action of the totality of life, the stimuli and the responses to it—either outward or inward—must come to an end, and a new quality of action must take place. That action can only take place if we understand the whole significance of experience, racial as well as personal, group, family.

Then, if we have understood the intricacies and the extraordinary immensity of experience and its pettiness, we will see that that experience will not produce a fresh, young, and innocent mind which is the very nature of mutation, the mind which has gone through mutation.

Then we will have to inquire into the whole question of envy and ambition. An ambitious mind is a corrupt mind. An ambitious mind cannot possibly understand what it is to meditate; it is thinking in terms of achievement, of success, of fulfilling. Is it possible to live in this world without ambition? You know what ambition means. It involves ruthlessness in which there is no love, no sympathy, no affection—each one out for himself in the name of the country, in the name of peace, in the name of God. And therefore such a mind is always in conflict with itself and with the neighbor. Ambition involves all that, and an ambitious man never loves what he is doing. He is using what he is doing to get somewhere else, and therefore his action is a means to something else; such a mind has no virtue.

The very essence of virtue is humility. And virtue is order. Order is not a continuity of what has been—that is a habit—but order from moment to moment, cleaning the room from moment to moment, every minute, so that there is no accumulation, there is no arrogance, no pride, and there is humility. An ambitious mind can never have the sense of humility, and therefore it is not a virtuous mind; the ambitious mind is the very essence of conflict. But you will say, "How can we live in this world without ambition? How can I go to the office and remain as a clerk for the rest of my life? I want to climb, I want to become big, I must be ambitious to survive." That is so. As the social structure is, that is the penalty. But if you begin to inquire into ambition—not saying, "We must live; it is necessary, as the social structure is, that we conform to it, and therefore we must be ambitious"—you will find that you can live in this world without being ambitious, and that, in the very process of inquiry into ambition, you will begin to love the thing itself—not what it will bring—and therefore you will do the thing much more capably, with greater intensity. Also, you will not always compare what you are doing with what somebody else does. Therefore, function and status are two different things. If you love what you are doing, there is no search for status—which is ambition, using the thing in order to have prestige, power, position.

So, a man who would have a new mind, a fresh mind, a young mind, has to be free totally from ambition. Because, ambition implies competition, which is what we are brought up on from our childhood—to compete in our school and to be somebody there and so on right through the world, right through our existence—to be somebody, which means violence, ruthlessness, no love or sympathy in this.

How can a mind which is ambitious in daily life know what meditation is? How can it possibly meditate? It can take tranquilizers to bring about peace of mind, it can repeat phrases, it can deceive itself, it can have visions of Buddha, Christ, X, Y, or Z, but it will still be ambitious in daily life. Therefore, such meditation, such inquiry, such a way of finding peace is mere trickery; it has no meaning—and that is what we are all doing; we have our hands in the other man's pocket and talk about God. Society respects the man who is ambitious, respects the man who is famous, notorious, with pictures that have appeared in the papers—because each one of us wants to see his face in the pictures. We are all ambitious. Therefore we are corrupt, though we talk of love, talk of family, of goodness, of virtue, of God, of religion. So, an action springing from ambition—whether that ambition be for the individual or for the collective or for the nation or for the world—is inaction because such an action produces misery, as you can see in the world factually. So, nationalism is becoming a poison.

When you understand this whole question of ambition and are aware of it—not verbally, not ideologically or as an idea, as an ideal eventually to be achieved, but actually be aware of it—in your daily existence, you will see that from that awareness, a new action is coming into being, which is an action without effort, without struggle, because you have understood. You are seeing the truth of it, and therefore the perception of what is true liberates. And therefore you are acting freely without any compulsion, without any fear. The same applies with regard to envy.

Our society which is corrupt is based on acquisition—not only the acquisition of things, but also the acquisition of knowledge, capacity. If you have great capacity, you are respected; if you have great knowledge, you are considered to be a very learned person. And acquisitiveness—acquiring, gathering, accumulating, not only inwardly, but outwardly—is the fashion, is the thing to do. And the very essence of envy is acquisitiveness. If you cease to acquire, you are no longer envious. Please follow all this; you may not do it; you probably won't do anything at all about what we are talking.

Please listen to what is being said. See how your life has become what it is—the misery, the sorrow, the everlasting struggle from the moment you are born to the moment you die, the pain, the ache, the anxiety, the fear, the guilt, the innumerable aches that one has, the boredom, the responsibilities, the duties in which there is no love, no affection; there is nothing left. That is your life, and you are not going to alter it because I am talking. But you will alter it without your knowing it if you listen to something which is factual, which is true, which is not propaganda, which is not trying to force you to do something or to think in one way or another. If you are aware of the very factual existence of your life—the pain, the misery, the shallowness of it all—from that awareness of the fact, there comes the mutation, without effort. All that is all we are concerned with, just to see the facts. And with what clarity you see the fact is important—not what you are going to do about the fact. You cannot do anything about the fact because your life is much too limited; you are conditioned. Your family and your society are too monstrous; they won't let you. Only a few can break through, unfortunately. But if you are merely listening, if you are merely seeing the fact—what it is actually, how miserable, how boring, how shallow all of it is—that very observation of the fact is enough. It will do something to you if you don't oppose it, if you don't say, "I can't do anything about it, and therefore I will run away from it." Look at it every day of your life, be aware of it first. And then, out of that awareness, there comes an action without effort, and therefore that action is never envious, never acquisitive.

So when you have understood experience, when you have understood ambition and envy which are the very nature of our petty, shallow, social existence and economic life, that is the foundation for further inquiry. Without that foundation—do what you will—you can go no further. Without that foundation—without understanding, both at the conscious level and also at the deep unconscious level, the whole process of experience, the corrupting influence of ambition, and the shallowness of envy—you cannot proceed further. That foundation becomes the foundation for meditation. That is the beauty of meditation. Meditation is something extraordinary. Now I am going to go into that, not theoretically, not for you to say that Buddha has said this or Shankara or Christ has said that—they are all repetitive, shallow, empty words.

That foundation for meditation is the foundation in righteousness—not the social righteousness or economic righteousness, but the righteousness of self-understanding. When the mind has laid that foundation, what happens to thinking? Then what is the place of thought? We have exercised thought in order to acquire; we have exercised thought in order to fulfill, in order to become; we have exercised thought in order to experience more and to choose and to avoid experience.

So when you have understood experience, ambition, and envy, what is the place of thinking? Is there thinking at all then? Or is there a different action taking place which is not the result of thought, which is a response of memory? So, the inquiry into the meaning of thought and what is the place of thought and of action—both the collective and the individual—is the inquiry which comes when you have laid the foundation. Without that foundation you cannot possibly inquire into the nature and the ending of thought, or what happens to thought. Mere control of thought is still a contradiction. Control implies suppression, control implies restriction, control implies discipline. A mind that is disciplined according to a pattern—social, religious, or other kind of pattern—can never be free. It will always be disciplined according to patterns; therefore, it is incapable of being free, and therefore incapable of laying the right foundation, and of inquiring into the significance of thought.

As I was saying, we see the significance of control, its limitation. In control there is discipline, limitation, suppression, and therefore perpetual conflict. When you have understood that, gone into it very, very deeply, then there comes out of it an awareness, and that awareness can concentrate without limitation. But a mind which has disciplined itself to control itself can never be aware, whereas awareness can concentrate without making itself limited. So you will see that when you have understood that awareness, when you have the understanding of experience, of the significance of ambition, and of the nature of envy, you have laid the foundation in yourself—not through effort, because you have understood by merely seeing the fact. The understanding of the fact gives you energy. Therefore, the fact never creates a problem. You create a problem of the fact, but the fact never creates a problem if you can look at the fact scientifically, objectively. Then you can proceed to find out, you can see what the place of thought is.

Is there thinking if you are no longer seeking experience? Your mind is driven by ambition, by success, and wants to reach God—that is also ambition. If you are no longer acquisitive, either in worldly things or inwardly—which means no longer acquiring, demanding more and more experience, more and more sensations, more and more feelings, more and more visions—then there is no place for thought. Then from that you will find the brain becomes extraordinarily quiet. The brain so far has been used for these purposes, and when these purposes are gone into, examined rationally, sanely, healthily, and understood, the brain is out of all that. Then that brain becomes extraordinarily quiet naturally—not because it wants to get somewhere, not because it has not understood the monstrous discontent, failure, and despair. It has understood all these, and therefore the brain becomes highly sensitive, very alert, but very quiet. Again, that is the basis for meditation.

Now, a quiet brain can watch without distortion. Because it has understood thought and feeling, it is no longer seeking experience. And therefore such a brain observes without distortion. Because it is not concerned with any experience, it is like watching the fact, the bacilli, through a microscope. You can only watch that way if you have laid the foundation, and if you have gone into yourself very, very deeply. No books, no guru, no teacher, no savior can lead you further—they can only tell you, "Do this, don't do that, don't be ambitious, or be ambitious." When you yourself have laid the foundation, you become aware of this brain which is absolutely quiet and yet highly sensitive. Then that brain can watch what is actually going on; then it is not concerned with experience, not concerned with how to translate what it sees into words and therefore communicate it to another; it is merely watching. When you have gone that far, you will see that there is a movement which is out of time.

A mind, a brain, that is completely quiet without any reaction—which is an extremely difficult thing to do—is only an instrument of observation and therefore is extraordinarily alive and sensitive. Now all that, from the beginning of what we have been talking about until now, is meditation. When you have gone so far in meditation, you will find for yourself that there is a movement, an action, out of time, a state which is immeasurable—and that you may call God; it has no meaning at all. That state is creation—not the writing of a poem, nor the painting of a picture, nor putting a vision in marble; they are not creation, they are all mere expressions.

There is creation which is beyond time. Until we know that—know in the sense not as knowledge—until there is a tremendous awareness of that state, our actions in daily life will have very little meaning. You may be very rich, you may be very prosperous, you may have a very good family, you may have all the things of the world, or you may be hankering after the things of the world. But if you have not understood that thing, life becomes empty, shallow.

And mutation is only possible when you have brought about through awareness, without any effort, the ending of all the things we have talked about—ambition, experience, conflict. Then, out of that comes something that cannot be conveyed in words. It is not to be experienced. It is not something that you are going to seek, because all search has ended. All that is meditation. That has extraordinary beauty. There is a great sense of marvelous reality which cannot possibly be understood by a petty mind, by a mediocre mind that is repeating the Gita and the Upanishads, that is going after the guru and the mantra, the everlasting word. All that must come to an end. The brain must be totally empty of the known. Then only can the unknowable perhaps come into being.

December 10, 1961

Seventh Talk in Madras

I would like this evening to talk about "death," if I may. But before we go into that, I think we should be able to approach it not in the usually accepted traditional way. Perhaps we can come to understand it by directly experiencing it. But before we enter into it, we ought to understand, I think, "fear"—fear of old age, fear of disease, and fear of loneliness, fear of the unknown. And before we explore those, we ought to understand also, I think, the question of effort.

All our life, we make effort of every kind—effort to arrive, effort to lose, effort to gain, effort to put aside, and effort to become and effort to deny. Everything we do is a process of effort, a struggle. And it seems to me that effort in any form perverts direct perception.

Is it possible to live in this acquisitive world—a world where everything is geared to struggle, where every form of competition, every form of achievement, success, is encouraged—without struggle at all, without effort? And why do we make effort? If we do not make effort, what would happen? From childhood, we are trained to make effort, to compete consciously as well as unconsciously, to acquire, to gain. Why do we make effort? If we do not make effort, shall we stagnate? Is there not a way of living without effort? I think we should be able to understand this because what we are going to discuss a little later this evening will not be fully understood if we do not go into the question of effort. Is it possible to see something directly, to see something true, and let that operate rather than we operate on that?

There is such a thing as "loneliness." We are all very lonely. We may have many companions, friends, a family, and we may go to the temple, to the church, occupy ourselves with innumerable things—our brains crowded with belief and dogma and the perpetual routine of the office. And yet, beyond all these, there is a sense of loneliness, and we try to escape from it in various ways, if we are at all aware of it. If we are not, then it is there waiting, and on occasion it catches you up; then you turn to the radio, go to the temple, or talk, or do something to run away from this extraordinary feeling of isolation. You all know it. When you become aware of your surroundings, when you are inwardly searching, you must invariably come upon it. That is a fact, and that makes us do all kinds of stupid and clever things to run away from it.

Please, if I may, let me stop here for a minute and not continue with that particular thing, and point out that this is not a talk which you casually hear of an evening and go away to discuss the ideas—whether they are right or wrong, whether they are workable or not, whether they are practical or theoretical. I believe you are here not merely to follow what the speaker is saying but also, as you are listening, to uncover in yourself what is being said, to find out for yourself, actually experiencing, as we go along, that which is being said. And to experience something directly, one must neither reject nor accept. You cannot accept a challenge or reject a challenge; it is there whether you like it or not. You can respond inadequately to it and thereby increase suffering, confusion, and misery, or you can respond to it totally and thereby wipe away the causes of misery. So, if you are merely listening to a lot of words—and there is no end to words—and if you are here merely to be entertained for an evening, then I say it will be an utter waste of your time. But if you could seriously, attentively, go into the matter of what is being said, to really inquire, question, demand, then perhaps you will find out for yourself not only what this loneliness is, but also perhaps you will be able to go even beyond.

Loneliness distorts, loneliness makes us attached, loneliness makes us compete, acquire, depend on others, which you call "relationship." And so it is important actually to go into this matter and see if we cannot wipe away this thing called loneliness, this isolation. You can only do that if you can go into it, step by step, factually, not theoretically. And when you do that, you will find that you are aware that not only is there loneliness but also there is a great deal of fear with it. Now fear is not concerned with what actually is there, but with what might be there. Fear is the process of time. Fear is the way of thought. We know that there is such a thing as loneliness. We are afraid. We have already made up our minds or come to a conclusion that we cannot understand it, that we do not know or have the capacity to understand; therefore, we are afraid. We are not afraid if we are not directly in contact with something that may be a temporary, instantaneous reaction, but there is immediate attention to that which causes fear. You don't run away. So, similarly, when you are lonely, you have to look at it, to go into it, and to understand it completely because if you don't understand it completely, you escape from it. And all the temples are filled with your gods and goddesses which have no meaning at all. All the Gitas, the rituals, the family, all relationship—these are of no avail if you don't understand this loneliness.

And, to understand loneliness, first you must understand the word *lonely*. The word is not the thing, the fact. So you must be aware of the word and not let the word frighten the approach—like the word *hate*, like the word *fear*, like the word *communist*, like the word *God;* they are just words. And to understand what is behind the word, one must be free of the word; the word must not engender, breed, fear. So, if one wishes to understand what this loneliness is, one must first put aside the word, and I hope you are doing it. It is quite a difficult thing to do, to put away the word *Gita*, the *Bible*, because the Gita and the Bible have such an immense authority, such significance, such tradition which weighs you down. And that is the final authority—you cannot question it; if you question, you are irreligious. But to find out, you must tear down the Gita, the Bible, the word, every authority. You can only do that if your intent is to find out what is true, what is false—not just merely talking about words which have no meaning. So, if you can put away the word and look at that thing called "loneliness," there is no fear because then you are faced with the fact, and not with the word which denotes the fact.

Please do this experiment with yourself as you are listening, and you will find how you are a slave to words. A mind that is a slave to words cannot go very far—like the word *atma* or *Vedanta* or any of those words which have no meaning and which you just repeat. You have absolutely to tear everything down to find out.

You are just beginning to find out how to tear down. So, when thought is free of the word, then you can look. You can see what loneliness is, which is caused by many isolating, self-centered activities. You may be married, have children, a family; and yet you are lonely. Therefore, your relationship with your family, with your neighbor, with your boss, and all the rest of it is self-centered. Because it is self-centered, there is always the fear of isolating, and the actual process of isolating yourself takes place, which ultimately results in this feeling of an extraordinary sense of loneliness. Now if you can stay with the fact, actually live with the fact that you are lonely, have cut off all avenues of escape—no more chatting, no more drink, no radio—and put away all the ugly gods that man has created—the saviors, the Masters, the gurus—then you are confronted with the fact; then you will be able to understand what it is and go through it. Then as you go through it, you come to quite a different thing—which is to be alone—because when you have put away all those, then only is the mind free from all influence, from all tradition, from the various masks imposed by the mind upon itself through life and put away now; then only is the mind alone. And it must be alone, completely naked, stripped of all ideas, of all ideals, beliefs, gods, commitments. Then you can take the journey into the unknown.

So, it is necessary to lay the foundation for inquiring into death. And also why do we make effort? Why can't we see things directly as things are? If I am stupid, dull-witted, heavy, as most of us are, insensitive, why can't I see, why can't I be aware of that fact? A dull mind does not become any brighter, sharper, cleaner, more useful by making an effort because a dull, petty mind making an effort will still be dull and petty. But when the dull mind is aware of the fact that it is dull, when you are aware of the fact that you are dull—not the word, not because somebody has told you you are dull, but you are aware of the fact that your mind is asleep, insensitive—then you will see that without effort, without struggle, without trying to become clever, sharp, sensitive, the very perception of the fact that the mind is dull, that very awareness begins to bring about sensitivity without your making any effort. Please listen to this. Because all your life is a dreadful struggle; from morning till night, you are fighting with somebody; all your relationships are resistance—battle, coming and going. When there is so little real life, so little joy, everything is a grief, a misery, a battle. And a mind that is in constant battle wears itself out; it is old before it begins to look around, it is already beginning to wither.

So do consider what is being said: that one can live in this world without effort, which is to look at the fact every minute of the day—at the fact, and not what you think about the fact, because what you think is merely tradition, your information, your knowledge which you are trying to impose on the fact. The fact is never conditioned, but your mind is conditioned. Your mind is conditioned as Christian, Hindu, Buddhist, communist—all those stupidities that we are caught in as a civilized people, not the villager; he is not caught in it, he is too poor a chap.

So, your mind is conditioned. With this conditioned mind that has imbibed tradition, that lives according to propaganda—either the propaganda of the Gita or the Bible or the newspaper or of the commissar—you try to understand the fact, and therefore create a problem out of the fact. But when you observe the fact, the fact does not create a problem; it is there. And so, a mind that is capable of observing the fact every minute, all the time, has no problem, and therefore it does not make any effort. There is no right effort and wrong effort; all effort prevents the understanding of the fact.

We are now going to inquire into "death," to question. As I pointed out the other day, you can question to try to find out an answer. Such questioning is based on reaction because you want some kind of favorable, happy answer, because you have already some fear, or your fear has already dictated how to seek an answer. So your questioning is reaction; it is born out of reaction, and therefore it is no questioning at all. There is a questioning without reaction—which is merely to question, not trying to find an answer. That very questioning opens the door through which you can find out, look, observe, and listen.

So we are going to inquire into death—not to find out what the life is after death. Who cares? Do you care to continue your life, as you are now, the misery, the squalor, the quarrels, the ambition, the frustration, and the enormous iniquity called morality? Do you want to continue that? So, we are going to inquire, to find out.

To inquire into a thing, you must never be satisfied, never seek a shelter. Obviously, the moment you find some satisfactory answer to your questioning, you are finished, you are no longer pursuing the inquiry, you have been sidetracked into a happy pool of contentment where you can decay happily. But to inquire means tearing down, tearing down your family, tearing down your ideas, tearing down everything to find out. And we are going to do that—I will do it, but you won't because you have your family, because you have your ideas so embedded that no bomb will break them up; even if there is a bomb, you take to a shelter and come back alive, to the same pattern of existence.

So we are going to inquire, not seeking an answer, because there is beauty in not seeking an answer, because then, every minute, you are living to find out what is actual, not what you think should be. So in inquiring, we must look into time. Death is time. Time is from here to there, the distance that needs time—the time to arrive, the time to gain, the time to cultivate the thing called virtue which you try to cultivate—every day, day after day, by repetition, by doing something over and over again, a habit which you call good. And that needs time.

And is habit virtue? The thing that you have cultivated day after day according to a pattern, projected by your own thought, by your race, by your family, or by your guru, by society—is that virtue? Or, is virtue something entirely different? Is it not totally unrelated to time, something which you see immediately and which does not require cultivation or gradation or a gradual process of coming to be good, getting to be noble like the vain man struggling to have humility? A vain man can never have humility, do what he will. All that he can do is to die to vanity.

So, time is the time by the watch, the chronological time of yesterday, today, and tomorrow, next year and so on. But there is another time; that is psychological time—"I will be; I am going to become a big man; I am going to have a big car, a big house; I am going eventually to be nonviolent." All that implies the psychological, inward time which is from here to there, inwardly the distance between *what is* and 'what should be'.

Please go with me. I am not your authority, your guru, but just listen.

Is that time a fact at all, or is it an invention of a clever mind or a stupid mind—the idea that I will eventually reach God? Therefore many lives, therefore many races, many experiences; I cultivate slowly various virtues until I am made perfect—which all indicates the employment of time as a means of postponing the understanding of *what is,* the fact. When you understand the fact that you are angry, the very understanding of the fact absolves you from time. Do inquire into this, and you will see how extraordinarily simple this is and therefore of immense significance. So, the idea of employing time as a means of gaining, as a means of fulfilling, is erroneous, is a folly.

You ought to have time to get home from here. You need to have time to learn a thing, to become an expert in some technique. There is mechanical time for acquiring knowledge, becoming proficient as a doctor, learning an electronic technique, and so on. These are mechanical processes which need time. And there is no other time. If you see the fact of that, actually there is no time in the psychological, inward sense of that word. Then your whole outlook has undergone a tremendous mutation. Then you are not thinking in terms of arriving, achieving, becoming; psychologically, you have wiped away the whole sense of 'becoming', which is to get caught in sorrow, in misery, in confusion—all the travail of every human being. And we create time psychologically by giving soil to the problem. Psychologically we have time because we do not know how to die to a problem—to die to a problem, not to continue it and carry it over to tomorrow. A problem is, as I said, existing only when you are not capable of looking at the fact. When you look at the fact, there is no problem because you are dealing with something directly, and therefore you eliminate time and the problem which is in time, which involves time.

So, in inquiring into, in questioning, what is death, we have to inquire surely, not what happens after, but what is death. You know very well you cannot argue with death. There is no argument. You cannot reason. It is an absolute finality. You may invent all kinds of things—that you will continue, that there is the atma or the higher self, that God will protect you—you invent a lot of theories which may or may not be facts. But it is absolutely final that you will die, whether you are young or old. Therefore, there is no question of arguing with it; you don't argue when death knocks at your door, you don't say, "Please wait a couple of days more, I have to see my family, I have to draw up my will, I have to settle my quarrel with my wife." There is no argument. But we argue with life, we cheat life, we play with life, we double-cross, we double-think, we do everything to cover up life. We can argue, we can choose, we can play around. We do not treat life as final as death. And if we do, then we have to deal with it every minute precisely, with decision—not postponement.

So, we have learned the trick of playing, choosing, arguing, covering up, running away from life, and so we approach death with that same attitude. You can play with life, but you cannot play with death; it is there and you are gone—not that there is a life hereafter; that becomes so unimportant. And besides, those of you who believe in life hereafter don't really mean it at all. If you meant it, you would instantly change everything of your life. Because you believe in karma, you say you will pay for it—just as you sow, so you will reap. You don't believe any of it because if you really felt it, if you were aware of the fact, you would not cover, even for one minute, the ugliness of your minds and hearts, the envies, the cruelties, the brutality; you would change, you would mutate immediately. So, your belief has no value at all.

So we have to deal with death. As I said, there is no argument. You can't argue with love, can you? Perhaps you do—which is to be jealous. Perhaps you don't love at all, you don't know what that means—because if you loved, do you know what would happen? You would have a different world; your children would be different—they would not pursue the pattern that you have set for them, the pattern of money, position, capacity, earning more and more and more, and becoming monstrously ugly, stupid. These are all what you are interested in when you talk about love—sex, children, and family. And in the family, you seek security for you in your old age; and, out of loneliness, you cling to your family, your sons, your daughters—you call that love, don't you? When you are concerned with yourself, you are frightened, and so you have no love, but you are lonely, and therefore there is fear of death.

Now to face death actually, not theoretically, you have to understand certain things. Obviously there is the death of the body. That you cannot help, unless some scientists or doctors invent a new drug which will make you last for fifty more years to continue in the same misery, the same shallow, narrow, stupid existence, going to the office perpetually, and breeding more children and educating them all in the same old pattern to carry on the filth of this civilization.

So the body will die—you have to accept that. And there is the fear of old age—getting old, forgetting, becoming blind, becoming deaf, having to have somebody to lean on; so you cling to the family, to the wife, to the husband—which you call love, which you call responsibility, duty, noble morality. Please follow this—not my words, but your own life. So the body will die. Now can't we also psychologically die to everything that we have known, because that means death, doesn't it? Don't you understand? To die to everything that you have known, to die to your family—this is very difficult for people to do because the family is such an extraordinary thing for most people; the family is their death.

So gradually we are afraid of death, the unknown, because you don't know anything about death, you have never met it—except that you have met the body that is being carried to the burning-ghat or to the grave, but you have never met death. You can meet death. And that is to die psychologically to your family, to your gods, to everything that you have gathered, to die every minute to every experience that comes and to leave it and die to it—which means to live at a tremendous height, not knowing what is going to happen the next minute because you have completely wiped away fear; you are dead to everything that you have gathered; you are no longer a Hindu, you are no longer a lawyer, you no longer have a bank account, you are no longer related to anything, least of all to your family. When you cling to your family, you want them to be conditioned as you are conditioned; you don't want them to change; you want them to have a good job, a good position, children, and carry on the same pattern. So, when you die psychologically, inwardly, to everything every minute of the day, then you will see that you can enter the house of death without fear. Then you know, while living, what death is, not during the last minute when you are almost unconscious, diseased, broken, unwilling.

But to live now and therefore die now in full vigor, in clarity, means really tearing down everything that one has built up in oneself, having no tradition, no experience, no capacity. And that is what you are going to have when you die—you have no capacity, you are left completely empty, though your thought may carry on. Thought is just words that have no meaning, a conclusion that may continue because you accept certain actions, certain vibrations, certain forces of being. Even to that you have to die; you have to die to your ideas, your experiences, your Masters, to everything.

You are afraid not of death but of the known, of leaving the known, leaving your family, your son, your experiences, your bank account, the country which you are used to, the things that you have gathered as knowledge. And leaving those behind—that is what frightens you, not the unknown. How can you be afraid of the unknown? Because you don't know anything of the unknown to be frightened. So one has to die to the known; that is quite an enormous task, and you can only do that when you are facing the fact of what you are and not introducing opinions, judgments, evaluations, traditions, what you would like and what you would not like—putting aside all that and tearing all that down, and facing the fact of what you are. That means destroying—nobody wants to destroy. The revolutionary—the economic revolutionary, the social revolutionary—he wants to destroy buildings or the social structure as a reaction; and that action of the revolutionary produces another set of reactions, modified but in the same old pattern. But we are talking of death—not revolution—a complete emptying of everything that one has known.

Then only, being free from the known, you can enter into the unknown—you don't have to enter then; it comes to you. Your mind then, being free of the known, will understand the unknowable. But you cannot come to it because you don't know what the unknowable is—you only know what your Gita tells you, what your Bible or your guru or your thousand years of propaganda have told you. But that does not mean you know the unknown. You have to die to all that. Don't say, "It is not for me. It is only the few that can do it." If you say that, that means you don't know what love is. You want love, you want sympathy, you want to understand this extraordinary thing called life and death. To understand it, to understand life which is death and death which is life, you have to tear down every psychological structure that you have built around yourself, around your family, around your security, around your hopes, desires, and purposes. When the mind is completely empty of the things put together by the mind, by the brain, when there is freedom from thought, then there is the unknowable which is life, which is death, which is creation. They are not separate things. Death is not separate from life. Life is death because there is life only when you are dying, not when you continue in the same old pattern of stupid existence.

There is creation only when you destroy totally, right from the beginning to the end, destroy your Masters, your society, your commitments, all the attachments to your family, to your ideas, completely wipe them away and stand alone. You have to—that is death. Therefore it is also life. And where life is, there is creation which is destruction, which is life.

December 13, 1961

Eighth Talk in Madras

This is the last talk. I would like, if I may this evening, to talk about the religious mind and the present-day scientific mind.

For most of us, symbols have an extraordinary meaning—for the Christian, the cross, the image, the church, the cathedral, and so on; for the Hindu, the various gods with innumerable arms, the temple, the ancient walls around the temple, the stone, the image graven either by the hand or by the mind—they have an extraordinary influence on us. They shape our thinking, they limit our endeavor, they enclose the wandering spirit, they minimize suffering, they give innumerable satisfactory explanations. And if we watch, observe our own thinking, we will see how easily a word, an explanation, a symbol satisfies us. A word, a phrase from the Gita or the Upanishads, from the Bible, from the Koran, or whatever book you hold sacred somehow seems to alleviate the ache and the pain and the despair and the boredom of existence. And a symbol, in any form, seems to cover many of our difficulties; and in the name of a symbol, we get very excited, we get very enthusiastic—as the Christians do, as the Hindus do, by words and by phrases and by a symbol.

As I have been saying during all these talks, please don't just listen to me, don't just hear words. One must go beyond words, beyond the name, beyond the symbol to really find out, to search very deeply, to inquire without restraint, without limitation. I would suggest most earnestly—if you care to do so, if you are serious enough—not merely to listen to an evening talk or a discussion of this kind, but also in the very act of listening to explore into yourself. In the very act of listening, if one does listen with awareness, without any effort, in that very act there is a strange miracle that does happen, which is like light penetrating into darkness. But that listening is not a mere acceptance of propaganda, nor being hypnotized by a series of words. Listening has importance only if, in the very act of that, you can go within yourself and uncover your own ways of thought, feeling, and discover how one is a slave to a symbol, to a word, and actually, emotionally, directly experience that thing which is being talked about. Then, it seems to me, what is being said will have significance. Otherwise what is said is mere trash, without much value, because we are concerned with our daily existence, with the daily torturing, boring, sorrowful events of our life.

How to bring about real mutation in our life, not to worship symbols, not to become a devotee of some god or some idea, not to worship flags which is the new religion all over the world, but actually, if it is possible, to bring about a radical change in our thinking, in our feeling, in the way of our daily existence—that is what is significant. We can only become aware of it and bring about a deep uprooting when we are capable of listening, not only to what is being said here, but also, every minute of the day, to listen to the birds, to watch the trees, to the talk of your neighbor, of your wife, of your children, so that every moment you are learning and therefore dispelling the dullness and the weariness of spirit.

So, in the same way, do listen so as to find out the workings of your own mind, the ways of your own heart, so that you know all about yourself—both the conscious and the unconscious, and all the influences, the enunciations, the ideas, the traditions that one has accumulated through the centuries. I don't see how one can go very far, either in thought or in deep affection, if one is caught in the daily turmoil, in the daily grind of misery, despair. And yet, we avoid that, we try to slur over it, cover it up and get lost in some idea, in some belief, in some symbol. So, if you are listening at all, it seems to me that it is very important to listen rightly. If you do listen rightly, then you are no longer influenced, no longer driven by circumstances, by your society; then you put all that aside, and then perhaps you will be able to understand what is really a religious mind.

The religious mind is the only mind that can solve our problems, not the scientific mind at all. To understand what a religious mind is, actually, not theoretically, one must not only investigate the symbol, question every symbol, but also go into the question of influence. How easily we are persuaded, how easily we become slaves to an idea which is, really, propaganda. How easily our emotions get entangled with a new, or a possibly new, escape. How slavish we are not only to symbols but also to all the influences of society, of tradition, of the family, of the name, of the occupation, the influence of papers, books, the influence of prominent people who are supposed to be very clever, who are supposed to be leaders. How easily and how disastrously we are influenced to think this way or that way, to act in a particular way and to pursue a system or habit. To be able to discern every influence, to be aware of that and yet not to be entangled in that, to be aware of the influence of a book as you are reading, to be aware of the pressures and the strains of the family, to be aware of the culture in which you are brought up—that is intelligence.

There are innumerable influences all the time penetrating into the very delicate mechanism of the mind; every word that is being said now is influencing the mind. You have to be aware of all these and yet not to be caught in them. The clothes you put on, the food you eat, the climate you live in, the books you read, and the tortuous years—fifty or thirty or forty years of business life or office life—how they distort, corrupt, make the mind petty. You have to be aware of all that, of all these subtle, conscious and unconscious influences, especially the unconscious influences—the old people have inherited so much influence and so many traditions, so many ways and habits of thinking, so deeply embedded in the unconscious. You have to be aware of them, to pull them out and examine them, question them, tear them to pieces so that not a single influence is left which you have not completely, totally understood.

That which is real has no influence. That which is true only liberates you from the false. It does not influence; you can leave it or take it. But to understand it, to go with it, to wander with it on the face of the earth, to penetrate into it deeply, you must be aware of the limiting, destructive influences that exist in the conscious mind as well as in the unconscious mind. Because, most of our consciousness is made up of influence; it is influence, if you examine it—the influence of the Buddhas, the Krishnas, the Shankaras, the political leaders—which is, really, propaganda—and it is there deeply embedded. And most of us are not aware of that; we are not even concerned—all that we are concerned about is mostly to earn a livelihood, to beget a few children, and to amuse ourselves around them, to carry on with a monotonous or rather a silly, stupid life. It is only when there is trouble, we awaken for a few minutes, try to solve it, know that we cannot solve it, and go back to sleep again. That is our life. To be aware of the many influences is necessary to liberate the mind because without a free mind there is no discovery. You cannot discover anything new when you are tied, tethered to some form of an idea, of a belief, of a dogma, of a family, of the innumerable attachments that one cultivates, gathers as one lives. Also, there is not only the symbol, the influence, but also the peculiar thing called *knowledge.*

It is strange how we worship knowledge. Knowledge always implies, doesn't it, the past. Knowing is always in the present, and knowledge is always of the past—like experiencing is in the present and experience is always in the past. For us, the past has an extraordinary significance—the past which is knowledge. Knowledge is necessary at the technical level, the mechanical level; and the more you have knowledge, the better—how to go to the moon, how to build a house, how to beautify the garden, how to enrich the earth. But knowledge also becomes an impediment to deep discovery because most of our lives are lived in the past. All that we know is the past. Do watch your own thinking, your own life; you will see this is a very simple thing—how knowledge corrupts. The knowledge of where you live is important; otherwise, you will have amnesia. But that very knowledge limits, creates fear, so that you don't want to go away from that which you have known. The mind which is held in knowledge is always anxious, guilty, fearful to inquire, to go into the unknown.

And so you are always living in the past, and therefore the present is only a passage to the future from the past, and so we live in a vicious circle, always in the field of the known, and therefore never discovering something new, fresh, young, innocent. You may know how to go to the moon, how to drive a car; you may know the extraordinary effort of building a bridge. But that is not creation, that is merely the functioning of mechanical knowledge. And that knowledge can be extensively added to year after year, century after century, but that is not creation. That does not open the door to something immense. So, symbol, influence, and knowledge, which are so important in our daily life, do corrupt, destroy, the right inquiry, right questioning.

If that is clear to each one of us, then we can begin to inquire what is a religious mind and what is a scientific, modern, twentieth century mind. The really scientific mind and the really religious mind are the only two minds that can exist in the twentieth century, not the superstitious, believing, temple-going, church-worshiping mind. The scientific mind is the mind that pursues fact. And to pursue materialistic fact—which is to discover under the microscope—needs immense accumulated knowledge. And such a scientific mind is the product of the twentieth century. So one begins to see that a scientific mind, the so-called educated mind, the mind that has learned a certain technique and thinks rationally and with knowledge, always moves from the known to the known, from fact to fact. Such a mind is absolutely necessary because it can reason logically, sanely, rationally, precisely. But such a mind cannot obviously free itself to inquire into what is beyond the accumulated knowledge—which is the function of religion.

So, what is the religious mind? You know there is a way of thinking which is negative, which is the highest form of thinking. That is to see what is false, not what is true. We are trained to think positively—which is to think imitatively, to think according to tradition, according to what has been known, following a particular method, a system, always projected from the past. This is what is called positive thinking. Whereas, there is negative thinking—which is to see the false which is the positive, and from there proceed. And that is what we are going to do, to find out what is the religious mind—seeing what is false and denying it totally, not accepting one breath of it. You cannot deny totally if you already know that you will gain something in denying the false. If you know the future, you would not be denying. If I deny all religious organizations as being false, as being without any foundation, and I know that I deny because I find hope in some other organization, then that is not a denial. I can only deny without knowing the next step, and that is the real demand, that is the real renunciation—not knowingly, but knowing that which is false. That is negative thinking.

So we are going to inquire into what is a religious mind, negatively. First, the religious mind is obviously not the believing mind because belief is based on the desire to be secure, to be safe, and so belief in any form prevents right inquiry, right questioning. If I believe in nationalism, then I cannot possibly investigate how to be truly brotherly with another. I must deny nationalism; then I shall find out what it is to live with another amicably, in a brotherly spirit. But most of our religions are beliefs. You believe that there is a God because you have been told for ten thousand years through propaganda that there is a God, that there is an atma—all kinds of verbal statements, spinning theories and words. You believe all that because you have been so brought up, educated. When you go to the other end of the world—to Russia and other parts—you find that they don't believe, they have been brought up not to believe. There is not much difference between one who believes in God and one who does not believe in God because they are both slaves to words, to propaganda—one for a thousand years and the other for forty years. I know you will laugh, I know you think it is funny, but you will still believe. A man who really inquires if there is God or if there is not, obviously must wipe away totally all his conditioning, all his belief in God.

So, the religious mind is not a mind that believes, not the mind which goes to the temple. You are going to the temple every day, repeating certain phrases, doing mantras and all the rest of it—that does not indicate you are a religious man at all. That may indicate that you are a superstitious man, that you are caught in habit which society has passed on to you. You may substitute religious rituals for parades, attending football, cricket, sitting by the hour by the radio—it is all the same thing. So, the ritualistic mind, the mind that goes to the temple or to the church and worships the symbol is not the religious mind at all. Why does one do it? Why do you do it? For various obvious reasons—first, you have been so trained; this has been instilled in you, to believe, to seek shelter in an idea. If you have no God, you have the state to worship, with its priests—one leader or another. We all want security because we are frightened of life. When we are troubled—someone dies, we lose our job, something happens to us—we do not go into it factually, with a scientific mind, and break through it. And so we turn easily, quietly, and darkly to something that, we hope, will give us security, some peace; and it does give peace, it does give security. A belief does give security. But that security is just a word, it is empty—it has no psychological security except to keep you completely asleep.

So the temple, the church, the symbol which is used to excite and organize man to worship God has no value at all for a religious mind. To deny that, to deny the whole religious structure in which you have been brought up, with the authority involved in it—the Shankaras, the Buddhas, the gurus, the Gita, the Bible—to deny all that totally is the beginning of the religious mind. That does not mean the mind becomes skeptical or accepts another authority. It denies the authority of any religion or any teacher and therefore of all the books, of all the temples and churches. To deny is very difficult because you may lose your job; there is your mother who cries, and you yourself are so frightened. Can you deny such gods who have been worshiped for so many centuries? And who are you to deny them?

You know the invention, the tricks we play upon ourselves. To deny and to remain in that denial—that is the beginning of the really religious mind. Because, when you deny what is false, your mind becomes very sensitive; when you deny the false, you have energy. You know, you need a great deal of energy to inquire and to discover, to live in that religious mind; you need energy, and an abundance of it. But, you cannot have that energy if you are in conflict—conflict between the fact of what you are and the idea of what you should be. Therefore a religious man has no ideal; he is only facing the fact from moment to moment. And virtue is in facing the fact. Out of facing the fact, you have an uncontrolled discipline—not the deadly practice of what you call discipline, which is habit, a resistance, a suppression.

So a mind which is inquiring into the quality and into the nature of the religious mind is a mind that is free from the ordained, rigorous, religious, traditional discipline. But it has its own extraordinary, unsuppressed, and uncontrolled discipline which comes into being when you look at the fact. You know, to look at a fact requires a great deal of energy. You can only look at a fact when you are not in conflict with the fact—the fact being what you are at a given moment, the fact that you may be jealous, ambitious, greedy, envious, ruthless, heartless. To face the fact, to look at it requires energy. You cannot live with the fact if you are in conflict with the fact. And when you look at the fact without conflict, that very fact releases energy which brings about its own discipline. And such discipline does not distort the mind because there is no suppression. All our disciplines are a means of suppressing what the fact is, because we worship and escape to the idea which is a nonfact. If you are listening—which I hope you are, not merely listening to the words which are very cheap and in abundance—if you are observing yourself through what is being said, you are bound to see the fact. If you are not in conflict with what is actual—which is yourself, not your atma and all the rest of it which has no meaning at all—then you will see that, as you are watching the fact, out of that watching comes a strange discipline. To watch something very clearly, you don't condemn, you have no judgment—like a scientific mind watching something dispassionately.

So, a religious mind has no authority, and therefore a religious mind is not an imitative mind. You will see also that the religious mind is not caught in time. It does not think in terms of evolution, growth, gradualism—that is the animalistic mind because the brain, some part of the brain is evolved from, grown out of, the animalistic instinct. The rest of the brain is still to be developed, and if it develops according to the animalistic instincts and experiences, it will still remain in time. Therefore, a religious mind never thinks in terms of growth, evolution. It is always jumping out of time. I think you will understand this, which may be rather new and strange to you, because that is what I mean by mutation.

A changing mind, a changing brain, is always moving from the known to the known. But a religious mind is always freeing itself from the known so that it is experiencing the unknown. The unknown is out of time, the known is in time. And so if you have gone very deeply into it, you will see that the religious mind is not a slave to time. If it is aware that it is ambitious or jealous or fearful, it does not think in terms of ideals, of postponement. It ends it immediately, at that instant; and the very ending of it is the beginning of that extraordinary, subtle, sensitive discipline which is uncontrolled, which is free.

So, the religious mind is the real revolutionary mind, not the revolution which is a reaction to what has been—like communism, which is only a reaction to capitalism; therefore, such a revolution is not a revolution at all. No reaction is a revolution, and therefore reaction cannot bring about a mutation. It is only a religious mind, a mind that is inquiring into itself, that is aware of its own movements, its own activity, which is the beginning of self-knowledge—it is only such a mind that is a revolutionary mind. And a revolutionary mind is a mutating mind—which is the religious mind.

So you will see our problem: The challenge of the present time and the challenge of every instant, if you are at all awake, is to respond totally to something that is new. I mean by responding totally—totally, with all your mind, with all your brain, with all your heart, with all your body, everything, with the totality of your whole being—responding not just intellectually or emotionally or sentimentally. I wonder if you do ever respond to anything so completely. You see when you do respond so completely, there is the absence of self-centered activity. When you respond to something totally, you will find at that moment, at that second, the self with all its activity, its fear, its ambitions, its cruelties, its envies, is gone. Therefore you can respond totally, and you do respond totally when there is sensitivity, which is life.

So, you find a religious mind is aware of what love is, not the love we all know, that we say is love—love of the family, carnal love, and so on, that is so divided, that is so shared, mutilated, spoiled, corrupted. When you love, you love one and the many. It is not: "Do you love all or the one?" You love. So the religious mind has no nationality, no religion, like belief and organized dogma. And a religious mind is a mind which has humility—in the sense, "to be humble." Humility is not to be acquired, is not to be cultivated; only the vain cultivate humility. But you have humility when you are listening to what is the fact. And virtue is that humility, for after all, virtue is order—order and nothing more than that—as you keep your room in order, tidy, clean. The function of virtue is that which arises from humility, but that order is to be maintained from moment to moment. You cannot say, "I have order." You have to watch it, clean it; and that cleansing, that virtue can only come when there is humility.

So, you begin to see that the religious mind is always freeing itself from the known—which is knowledge, which is experience, which is a thing that has been accumulated, which is the past. Don't say, "It is only reserved for the few." It is not. But if you have inquired, questioned deeply into yourself—that is when you are watching yourself, your thoughts, your emotions, your own way of eating, talking to your servant, your attachment to your family, to your son, to your daughter, despising some and respecting others, bending your knee to the symbol and kicking somebody else—when you watch all this, when you are aware of all this choicelessly, then you will find that your mind, your brain, becomes very quiet, still, alive, sensitive. Though it knows that it must function in knowledge, it is free of knowledge—and that is absolutely essential if it is to find out whether there is a reality or not. The mind must be totally free, completely free from the known—which is all the knowledge, all the experiences, all the tradition, the authority, the scratches of misery, the frustrations, the sorrow that one has accumulated which creates the illusion—all that must go; then only are you beginning to understand what a religious mind is.

Then you will find, if you have gone so far, that meditation is not the repetition of words, sitting in some dark corner, looking at your own projections and images and ideas. But meditation then is the unraveling of the known and freeing oneself from the known. Then you have the energy, that extraordinary energy which is needed—not the energy created by being a bachelor, eating one meal, putting on one loincloth, going away by yourself into a mountain and hiding yourself behind monastery walls and assuming a false name or number. That does not give you energy, that denies energy. But you must know all the dangers of it, be aware of all that, and therefore deny it. You must cut, as a surgeon cuts with a knife, all the cancerous, false things of life. Out of that you will find, if you have gone that far, that your brain is very still and yet very sensitive—it is only a very still thing that is sensitive.

Then you are beginning to understand what beauty is. You must have beauty, which is not good taste—good taste is a personal reaction. Good taste must go too—the personal good taste. Then you will know what beauty is. Beauty is not something that is put together by man, either on a canvas or on a page or on a stone. Beauty is not a mere response to a feeling which the artist has. Beauty is something far beyond all that. When you have gone so far, then you will see that there is creation.

Creation can never be put into words. Creation is not invention. The universe is not made of invention. So a religious mind is a creative mind because it has understood what living is, and therefore has freed itself of all the pettiness of daily existence. The daily existence is not living; it is a torture, and when that torture stops, only then do you begin to live. It is only a religious mind that can live that way. Therefore being free of all pettiness, and living—that is not an invention; it is the door through which the immeasurable, the unknowable comes into being.

December 17, 1961

Questions

New Delhi, 1961

1. Sir, what do you mean by *learn?* 1
2. Aren't you using *learning* in a very special sense? As we understand learning, it has a relation to knowledge—that is, getting more and more knowledge. There is no other meaning which can be put into that word learning. Are you not using it in a very special sense? 2
3. Sir, I am interested in understanding the mechanism of thinking. At times thought seems to come from the bottom of conclusions, and at times from the top surface, like a drop from above. I am confused. I do not know thought apart from the background. I am unable to evaluate what the word *thought* really means. 2
4. What is thinking? 3
5. Sir, can we temporarily suspend opinions from conclusions? 4
6. Sir, is it not like that one can go into the dark without even a torch? 5
7. If the mind is not interested, how is the mind to get it? 5
8. When I see a thing, my seeing is automatic; then interpretation comes in and also condemnation. 5
9. The difficulty is, sir, that we cannot just see ourselves without judging our action. Also when we judge, immediately we stop action. 5
10. But is action separate from that word? 6
11. How is observing different from thinking, sir? 6
12. It is not possible to observe without the thought process, which is memory coming into being. 6
13. My response to you now is one thing, and my response when I go outside is another. For maintaining my family and myself, certain basically essential things are necessary. In getting them, I also feel the need to ensure the continuity of these material things—food, clothing, and shelter—in the future also. My needs also tend to grow. Thus, greed steps in, and it develops. How is my mind to stop greed at any level? 6
14. A mathematician has an unresolved problem. How is his mind to be free of it? 9
15. Is that the result of prior knowledge? Sir, I love my children, I love my brother. I take their burden. I have a problem, and therefore I want to be free of that. 9

16. Sir, the use of the word *knowledge* is rather vague. You are covering so many things. Now take the instance of a car—that is technical knowledge. But that knowledge is quite different from a knowledge of the problem of life, or something where it is difficult to find a solution because of so many changing social conditions. And therefore knowledge does not always lead to a solution—it is not implied; sometimes in certain cases it may be implied, in certain cases it may not be. 9
17. Sir, what about intuition? 10
18. We want to come up to the standard we have set ourselves. 10
19. Only an insane mind has no problem. 11
20. Sir, what do you mean by "live"? 12
21. When you use the word *insufficiency,* does it not imply comparison? 13
22. Sir, is insufficiency different from the mind? Can the mind look at it? 13
23. But being conscious of all this, I get a feeling of being unhappy. 17
24. Can we run away from traditions, families, living on a desired pattern? 17
25. There is the will to live. If my mind were to know that it is dull, it wouldn't be able to live. 18
26. This is play. If I have no ambition, if I don't want to work for my children, why should I improve? 19
27. But we have no choice because of circumstances. 19
28. We usually see the minister and rarely the man. 20
29. Is there not such a thing as purposeless action, action without a purpose? 23
30. It seems to me that when I look at a flower, I have no purpose, and this is an action. When I hear a bird singing, that bird-song somehow affects me, and I have real joy in hearing that; this is an action, but without purpose. 23
31. I see a boy drowning and I rescue him. Is that action a purposive action? 24
32. I want to lead a life without contradiction. Does that become a purpose? 25
33. Why should not a mind which is violent try not to be violent? 25
34. Sir, do you advocate spontaneous love? 25
35. Do you think a detached action will lead to this? 29
36. Attachment is normal. It is instinct. And detachment is something you have to arrive at, a positive act. 30
37. One should not be attached as soon as the children can stand on their own legs. 30
38. Sir, if conformity leads to contradiction, absolute nonconformity may lead to absolute confusion. 32
39. Sir, conformity is essential to some extent. 32
40. May I know the technique for comprehension? 32
41. Status comes automatically if one functions effectively. Status, in that case, is not evil because it is got without pursuing it. 36
42. Would not that be a reaction, sir? 36
43. Sir, we have to function in some sphere or another in society, and that requires more and more knowledge relating to that sphere. Then, how can it be said that more and more knowledge takes us away from knowing? 36
44. Suppose I don't care for that status? 37

45. Sir, in the process of doing, there is recognition, and recognition becomes knowledge. 37
46. Sir, it is fear of the unknown. 38
47. It is some sort of total annihilation. 40
48. That totalization of the mind is an abstraction, withdrawing from the world. 45
49. If I find a cobra, I try to go back or do something, and that tells me afterwards that I was afraid of that cobra. 45
50. Is not fear an instinct born with the child? 47
51. This means that the instinctive response is not fear at all. 47
52. There are certain neurological responses which are awakened by thought which we call fear. How is it possible to observe the neurological responses of fear without the word *fear,* without the name? 47

Bombay, 1961

1. We are full of fear, we cannot get over this fear. 52
2. May I know what you mean by inquiry, or trying? 52
3. When you are talking, most of us are thinking of our own problems. That is the difficulty. 53
4. That is in appearance and it is something like a dream. 53
5. Is feeling an aspect of mind, sir? 53
6. It is somewhat difficult. 54
7. At a few moments one is aware. 55
8. How to be free from all these things? 56
9. You deny stages in this sort of revolution, or discovering in parts? 56
10. Try to probe into the cause of fear. 59
11. To observe fear alone—will it lead us to something? 60
12. It is so terrifying that we have not got the capacity to understand or look at it; instead of that, we try to imagine some divine power which will protect us. 60
13. The moment you understand it, it falls away by itself. 60
14. You say that all thought is mechanical, and yet you ask us to inquire and find out. Is not this reflection an aspect of thought? 64
15. Sir, is that energy God's? 65
16. To release tension, one writes—doesn't one? 65
17. In some moments we do feel that there are no contradictions and no confusion, and there is also no reference to time. Is that creativeness? 67
18. There is a response from the individual to the outer challenge. That response is from memory. How can the mind be devoid of memory so as to meet the challenge in the manner about which you are speaking? 71
19. The question is to find a solution. 71
20. Is it that one knows the answer, or is it the assembly of information? 72
21. What is the use of a mind when there is no response and challenge? Such a mind does not lead us anywhere. What will come out of such a mind? 72
22. You have described the final stage and the initial stage; the middle is not clear. 73
23. Does it mean one does not select between a response and a challenge? 73

24. It seems most of the people who come to listen to you come because they are desperate, because they are skeptics, cynics. Is it not difficult to wait, as far as the job is concerned? 74
25. I think, sir, you are doing an injustice to the scientist. For instance, there is the adventure of performing an experiment to challenge the statements of ages ago, which is something new. 77
26. Thinking is associated with word formation. When you use the words *negative thinking,* does it mean that word formation continues? 79
27. Could not that be real perception, instead of negative thinking? 79
28. The sense of recognition has always been there ever since our childhood; we have been brought up in that manner by means of our education, our background, and all that; therefore, whatever we see, whatever we observe, there is bound to be reaction. 84
29. The word disappears but comes again. 85
30. Is there not the undefined barrier of inchoate propensity beyond the word? 85
31. From a nonverbal state in childhood we have come to the verbal state. Now you tell us to eliminate all the past that we have gathered. Is it possible to go now, instantaneously, to that state of being nonverbal? 86
32. From the scientific, evolutionary point of view, we have developed from a nonword state to a word state. Can we reject the word now? 86
33. How would you then distinguish the preword state—that is, the primitive or the nondeveloped state—from the wordless state of which you are speaking? 87
34. When something happens unanticipated, it has a terrific impact on us, and at that moment there is a state which can be called timeless; in that state there is no word at all, and one is stunned. Would you call that experience a timeless experience? 87
35. Read a book. 88
36. The thought of fear is there. 92
37. We are in sorrow because when he was living, the person we loved was filling some space in us and helping us to live. 93
38. We instinctively avoid pain and sorrow. 93
39. Because we are not full, because our mind is not full. There is the utter emptiness of life. 93
40. Accept the fact that there is suffering. Attachment is the cause of sorrow. 93
41. What are the implications of suffering? 94
42. Sir, how did the first mind come into being? 96
43. Mind, time, and experience seem to be one thing, but memory cannot be time because memory is of the past. It is part of the conception of time. 98
44. When I listen to you, I am being influenced by your thought; then I say: I will investigate what you are talking about. Don't you think the question, "I will investigate," also involves time? 99
45. How do you ask us to be aware of facts without being influenced? 99
46. Has time any relationship with God? 99
47. The mind that has observed its own conditioning—can it transcend thought and duality? 102
48. There is the object towards which love is directed. Is there duality in love? 102

London, 1961

1. The mind seems to go round and round, but never seems to go beyond its own limitations. 119
2. One has to look with comprehension, not with the mind. 119
3. This instantaneous wiping away—surely, there can be no thought of any kind in it. 121
4. That seems to be something we are trying to grasp but cannot. 121
5. We can only say we do not know. 121
6. It seems to me that we can only see through words. 122
7. One might see for an instant, and then the mind comes in again. 122
8. Would that not be acting without thought? 123
9. I should say that thinking is a nervous reaction to that which has been experienced. We cannot react to something we do not know. 123
10. Is it not possible to have creative thinking—for example, to make new discoveries in science or mathematics? Is thinking entirely the result of conditioning? 124
11. Do you say that this process is not thinking? 124
12. If it comes from the unconscious, it is actually old stuff. It is not really new, is it? 125
13. I am sure that the conscious mind can be free, but it seems to me that a tremendous difficulty is the unconscious mind. 126
14. Not so clearly, because I belong to a group that is working for the United Nations, and I think that is a good thing. 126
15. We feel we are bound to our conditioning by our duties to society, to the family. 127
16. There is so much conditioning that is unconscious. 128
17. I think it happens to us occasionally; it comes and goes in spite of ourselves, like the wind in the trees, or the blowing along of dead leaves. 131
18. The conflict starts from wanting. 131
19. What about our want of God? 131
20. It is the resistance to the wanting that creates the contradiction. 131
21. I do not think I understand desire. 132
22. The memory of the experience. 132
23. The problem is that to prevent memory leaving its imprint on the mind, we must be possessed of a tremendous interest in every one of our experiences. 132
24. I suppose I should have said: How can this interest be brought about? 132
25. Is it rather: Why am I not interested? 133
26. It appears to me that I am frightened of being forced into circumstances, like living in some great city or working in a factory, where there is nothing I can love or feel is worthwhile. 136
27. Surely, you cannot do anything about it. 136
28. If one has work which one enjoys very much, is there fear in that also? 137
29. That seems to be the end of myself as I know myself, completely. 137
30. Habit forms quite a large part of what you are talking about, surely? 137
31. It may be a way of escape. 137
32. It is fear, is it not? It is greed also, I think. 138
33. Because the mind is occupation. 138
34. Those things are the mind on one level, but not all the mind. 138

35. The mind is all the time reacting to various stimuli. That is the process of being occupied. 138
36. It is impossible to try it because if the mind is empty, one cannot. 138
37. Does one perceive one's conditioning through the provocations, the challenges of life? 145
38. I suggest that the type of awareness or heightened perception which you are talking about is sometimes experienced when one is witnessing an accident. 145
39. How does one know if one is seeing the whole volume or only a page? 146
40. May I suggest that to find the correct answer, you must ask no questions and expect no answers. 146
41. We all have moments when there is an awareness of everything, and then one wants to trap it and keep it continuously. 146
42. Is not that anger a state of self-centeredness? 147
43. I should say that we never see anything. 147
44. We can only feel totally. 147
45. I think one needs to get drunk to know what drunkenness is. 151
46. It is the contradictions in desire that make it so impossible to deal with it. 151
47. We are afraid of what might happen if we give ourselves over entirely to one desire. 151
48. Is it possible ever actually to give oneself over to something insofar as there is always a schism between? 152
49. Is it possible to give oneself over to someone? 152
50. A desire is right and good when it does not damage anything else. 152
51. Is it possible to get rid of the object and stay with the essence of desire? 152
52. I have always thought that where there is space, there must be time, and you seem to make it rather different. Is not the space between two words, time? 162
53. Is not chronological time the same as psychological time? 162
54. After the stopping of the heart, is there thought as the person? 162
55. If you were told you were going to die tomorrow, would that have an effect on you personally? 162
56. Does the same mind create disorder and order? 173
57. I think you will agree that the state of human society leaves a lot to be desired. Is it possible for a religious person to act upon that society in an effective way against all the other people who are acting differently? 173
58. Would you tell us a little more of what love is? 179
59. In other words, in that moment one is love. 179
60. Christ taught us how to love in his words, "Love thy neighbor as thyself." 180
61. Is the process of cleansing the mind a process of thought? 180
62. At the moment of perception of *what is,* will you tell us what happens? 180
63. Can there be thinking without memory? 181

Saanen, 1961

1. Why do we find it difficult to put a right question? 186
2. What is it that is preventing us from going into a problem deeply? 187

3. It is very painful to go into a problem. 187
4. So to deal with this trouble in the world, we need order. 187
5. What is the price we have to pay for it? 187
6. Fear is no doubt one of our biggest stumbling blocks and prevents progress. But we cannot tear down everything right from the start. Should we not be satisfied for the moment with halfway measures? 188
7. But to reach that possibility of seeing immediately....... 188
8. I think more creative activity in the classroom would help to uncondition the mind. 192
9. How can one see the totality of fear? 193
10. What is the nature of creation? 196
11. One feels one must take a stand against the outer world, and in the very act of opposing the world, there is conflict. 196
12. I think there is no conflict if we live from moment to moment. 197
13. How do we know if we are facing the real fact or the idea about the fact? 197
14. If you go to the end of conflict for yourself, must you then just accept the conflict which is in the world? 197
15. Is understanding a capacity? 200
16. One seems to see the stupidity of desire and be free of it, but then it comes in again. 201
17. Is it possible to distinguish between being identified with what we see and to live with what we see? 201
18. If one does not identify oneself with things, then I suppose one can live outside it all? 201
19. In discovering, there is joy and pleasure; and is not discovering learning? 201
20. It seems to me that one of the first things is to know what the mind is made up of. 202
21. To know oneself requires a certain effort. 202
22. How does one get the energy for all this? 202
23. I don't quite understand that freedom must be at the beginning and not at the end because at the beginning there is all the past, and not freedom. 206
24. How can we see so clearly and forget every experience? 207
25. When there is sorrow, surely it is inevitable to want to do something about it? 210
26. In the case of physical pain should we not go to a doctor? 211
27. Is it possible for me to be free from sorrow when I see so much sorrow around me? 211
28. Of what use is a free person to another if he cannot help him? 211
29. To live with sorrow implies the prolongation of sorrow, and we shrink from the prolongation of sorrow. 212
30. Our preconceptions are in the way and we have to tackle them, and that may take time. 212
31. If we don't have the intensity, what can we do about it? 212
32. The state of total attention and desire without motive—are they the same? 217
33. Through the exploration of fear, will there not be a danger of mental disorder? 222
34. Can the religious mind be acquired through meditation? 227
35. Is it true that we cannot use reason to discover what is true? 227
36. One sees the absurdity of condemning things, outwardly and inwardly, but one keeps on condemning. So what is one to do? 228

Paris, 1961

1. How is one to come into contact with a fact emotionally? 233
2. Must one not be attentive to the dual process that is going on within us all the time, and is that not self-knowledge? 233
3. Is there a means to quieten the mind? 233
4. Does the mind carry within itself the elements of its own understanding? 237
5. Why is a free man not disturbed? 237
6. Is belief in God always based on fear? 238
7. How is it possible, without destroying or suppressing desire, to give it freedom; and does looking at desire without condemnation make it disappear? 242
8. What did you mean when you said the other day that we must be disturbed? 243
9. How can one find out what is one's main problem? 246
10. Can one liberate oneself by following any particular religion? 246
11. You have said that by believing in God one does not find God, but can one find God through revelation? 247
12. Why does fear come upon us when we become conscious of our own emptiness? 247
13. You have said that our essential needs are food, clothing, and shelter, whereas sex belongs to the world of psychological desires. Can you explain that further? 247
14. Can liberation be realized by everyone? 248
15. I have read a book by you on education. Could we not found a school of that kind while you are here in Paris? 252
16. Why do children have fear? 252
17. Is it possible to be always in the state of full attention which excludes fear? 252
18. Is all memory connected with knowledge, or is that silence a memory of a different kind? 252
19. If one visually sees the false as the false and drops it, is that denial, or is there something more to it? 257
20. When one comes to this sense of emptiness, how can one live in this world practically? 257
21. Can you tell us again why analysis is wrong? I didn't quite get it. 257
22. You spoke of freedom from all influence, but are not these meetings influencing us? 258
23. How are future generations to exist if one dies each minute? 261
24. If one does not know what truth is while living, will one know it when one is dead? 261
25. I see that one must be free of fear to have this energy, and yet it seems to me that in some ways fear is necessary. So how is one to get out of this vicious circle? 262
26. While we are listening to you, perhaps we do live in that state, but why don't we live in it all the time? 262
27. What about physical death? 262
28. How are we to answer the child who asks about death? 263
29. Is there not a right kind of effort? 267
30. How can people, including myself, have this love for reality? 268
31. Is the energy needed to find out about death different from the energy required for meditation? 268
32. What is the difference between concentration and attention? 269

33. Is not the whole problem a matter of eliminating something which is not, in order to receive that which is? 274
34. Is the state of mind in which there is no challenge and response the same as meditation? 274
35. Is there not a fear which is not the result of thought? 274
36. In dying, is there not a new being? 274
37. Why are we not always in that marvelous state? 274

Madras, 1961

1. Does change come from within or without? 291

Index

Abandonment: and *what is,* 165
Accumulation: versus learning, 157–58
Achievement: and frustration, 52
Acquisition: and society, 310–11
Acquisitiveness: as effort, 127; as social desire, 148; and thought, 312. *See also* Ambition; Envy; Power
Acquisitive society: and competition, 123
Action, 20–29, 31, 33–36, 40; and the absence of consciousness, 125; born of fullness, 75; and comprehension of the whole, 57; and condemnation, 5–6; without conditioning, 123; without conflict, 129; and conflict through contradiction, 130; and the confusion of challenge and response, 70; as destructive, 14; and discontent, 13–14; and idea, 102; and knowing what to do, 123, 128; as life essential, 307; and meditation, 42; and reaction, 79, 82–84; without reaction, 123, 128, 278; and sleep, 46; source of, 65–66; understanding, 278; and words, 6
Action and reaction: and the role of conflict, 131
Action without effort: and awareness, 311
Active mind: and dying, 160–61; limitations of, 163
Adjustment: and change, 254, 290–91; versus destruction, 225
Affection: and the empty mind, 294; and observation, 60; as quality of the new mind, 294, 297–98. *See also* Love
Alone: inability to be, 190; state of, 179. *See also* Aloneness; Loneliness
Aloneness: and the absence of fear, 157; and challenge and response, 272; defining, 87; and the desire to belong, 66; versus despair, 261; and dying every minute, 225; and energy, 260; fear of, 256; and reality, 231; and the religious mind, 89; and security, 135–36; state of, 271–72; as a state of revelation, 40; and the unknown, 315. *See also* Isolation; Loneliness; New; New mind
Ambition: and the absence of love, 130; awareness of, 56–57; and comparison, 14, 15; as conflict, 194, 264–66; and contradiction, 25; as corrupt, 309–10, 312; and the creative, 192–93; and the cruel mind, 67; and energy, 67; facing the fact of, 289; and fear, 45; freedom from, 17, 227; versus the good mind, 54; irrational and rational, 18–19; living without, 150; and love, 135; versus the mature mind, 205; and meditation, 266–67, 310; and psychological need, 244; and security, 296; and self-contradiction, 16; and time, 101
America: advertising in, 15; and the loss of adventure, 276; and prosperity versus freedom, 130; and subliminal advertising, 139. *See also* Authority; Conditioning; Identification; Nationalism; Words
Analysis: approaches to, 155; as hindrance to change, 254, 256, 257; and the unconscious, 126
Analyst: and conditioning, 257. *See also* Authority; Specialists
Analytic process: implications of, 141
Anger: and the center, 147; and self-image, 246. *See also* Feelings
Anonymity: as desirable, 89–90. *See also* Aloneness; Ambition
Answers: and problems, 8–10. *See also* Questioning
Artists: and the creative, 130–131; and creativity, 192–93, 273. *See also* Scientific mind
Aspiration: and time, 98. *See also* Ambition
Attachment: understanding, 30. *See also* Dependence
Attention: achieving, 308; and awareness, 102; without comparison, 12; versus concentration, 306; describing, 215; and effort, 41; and the exclusion of fear, 252; and fact, 181; and fear, 249, 251; and goodness, 134–35; and listening, 143–44, 248; and meditation, 44; and not-knowing, 251; process of, 264, 269; as a state of mind, 215; and stillness, 252; understanding, 167
Attentive: defining, 203
Austerity: defining, 165–66; and self-abandonment, 273. *See also* Simplicity
Authority, 234–38, 295–99; and conformity, 28; creation of, 203–4; as the death of truth, 167–68; and denial, 224–25, 250; and the desire for order, 189; and the desire for success, 295, 298; as evil, 296; and the false, 279; and fear, 278; freedom from, 204; and freedom from tradition, 171; government, 286; as hindrance, 180; as hindrance to the new mind, 114; inward and outward, 144; and positive thinking, 283; and questioning, 285–87; and reaction, 21; rejection of, 145; and the religious mind, 270, 323–24; and the ritualistic mind, 84; and social morality, 142–43; and thought, 205; tyranny of, 144, 145; and the word, 314–15; and world crisis, 283

Awareness, 305–6, 311–13; achieving, 266; of action, 68, 73; and ambition, 310, 312; and the center, 155; of challenge and response, 75–76; of contradiction, 24; and desire, 245; and discovery of the true, 280; without division, 101–2; and the dull mind, 17–18; of fact, 164–65; and fear, 43; and influences, 258, 321; of loneliness, 314–15; meaning of, 54–55; and meditation, 42; and the mind, 147; of the mind's limitations, 72; and mutation, 311; and the new mind, 114; of power, 56; process of, 43–44, 301–2; of the process of truth, 34; of self, 109, 114

Beatniks: as reaction, 144, 172
Beauty: and abandonment, 273; and the absence of fear, 156; and creation, 326; desire for, 131; and energy, 290; and living, 17; living with, 12, 136; and passion, 245; and the religious mind, 226; and the sensitive mind, 105, 165–66; and the state of negation, 255; without the word, 181
Becoming: and action, 128; and conflict, 264–65; as destructive, 127; as envy, 110. *See also* Ambition
Belief: and conditioning, 48, 238; as detriment to discovery, 126; and fear of death, 161; as hindrance to learning, 106; as hindrance to religion, 269–70; as illusion, 263; and Masters, 56; and propaganda, 251; and religion, 323; religious, 62; and the unconscious, 125; as valueless, 318–19
Believers: and the insensitive mind, 165; and nonbelievers, 323
Belonging: and commitment, 66; as hindrance to understanding, 200–201; need for, 33–34; and the positive state, 80–81; and the search for God, 127. *See also* Ambition; Competition; Identification
Beyond the mind: possibility of going, 125
Beyond time: need to go, 58
Bible. *See* Authority; Conditioning; Knowledge; Propaganda; Religion; Words
Bliss: state of, 102
Body: death of, 318
Books. *See* Authority; Conditioning; Knowledge; Propaganda; Words
Brain: and the absence of reaction, 213; as active and quiet, 213–14; and the conditioning of fragmentation, 191–92; development of, 226; function of, 191–92, 225–26, 229, 270–71, 273, 298; and memory, 224; and outward response, 225; and positive thinking, 213; and the process of existence, 273; as specialized, 270–71. *See also* Mind
Brain and the mind: differences between, 270
Brainwashing, 125
Buddhism. *See* Authority; Conditioning; Identification; Religious mind; Words

Capacity: and awareness and concentration, 306; and death, 319; and security, 137; and time, 200
Capitalism: and communism, 278. *See also* Authority; Conditioning; Identification; Nationalism; Tyranny; Words
Casual mind: and the serious mind, 58. *See also* Dull mind
Catholicism. *See* Authority; Conditioning; Conformity; Religious organizations; Saints; Tyranny; Words
Cause and effect: and time, 98, 100, 102
Center: absence of, 102; and accumulation, 199; and awareness, 147; as cause of conflict, 177–78; and conditioning, 267–68; and contradiction, 241; defining, 155, 166; as destructive, 87; dying to, 162; and experiencing, 120; and memory, 198; observation from, 83–84; and suffering, 95; and thought, 222
Ceremonies: and contradiction, 32
Certainty. *See* Fear; Security
Challenge: from the outside, 70
Challenge and response: and experience, 295, 308–9; as life process, 157; as limited, 68–81; response to, 285; and thinking, 250; understanding, 272; and words, 275
Change, 253–57, 288–93; and the center, 199; as escape from the fact, 284; and living things, 265–66; and the new mind, 121; process of, 200; as reaction, 285; types of, 120–21, 281; understanding, 284–87. *See also* Mutation; Revolution
Change and mutation: difference between, 284–86
Children: and educational conformity, 296; explaining death to, 263; and fear, 252
Choice: and challenge and response, 73–74; and time, 158
Choiceless awareness: and facing conflict, 241; and the free mind, 204; and the quiet brain, 325
Christ: and the hindrance of authority, 180. *See also* Christianity
Christianity: and suffering, 211. *See also* Authority; Conditioning; Identification; Religious mind; Words
Chronological time, 221, 272; as outward, 159. *See also* Psychological time
Class: and status, 271
Clear mind: and understanding authority, 297. *See also* Fresh mind; New mind
Collective: and awareness of the mind, 280; and death, 163. *See also* Individual
Collective action: and the individual, 253
Collective consciousness: altering, 269
Collective mind: and the unconscious, 253
Collective thinking, 162–63
Comfort: seeking, 209–10
Commitment: desire for, 33–34; and the desire to belong, 66; as hindrance to observation, 83; and the need to belong, 38; and security, 133–35; and self-forgetfulness, 110. *See also* Belonging; Conformity; Identification
Communication: and time, 158; and words, 86, 208, 229, 258, 301. *See also* Listening; Propaganda
Communism and capitalism, 278. *See also* Authority; Commitment; Conditioning; Conformity; Tyranny; Words
Comparison: comprehension of, 91; and creation, 217; and the creation of problems, 11–13; and discontent, 14; ending, 16; and the urge for power, 148, 149; and *what is,* 209; and the word, 181. *See also* Ambition

Compassion: and the new mind, 115; and the religious mind, 90; and the scientific mind, 90. *See also* New
Competition: versus efficiency, 20; and leadership, 19; and problems, 239, 241; and reaction, 36; and society, 15, 19; as time, 98; viewed as necessary, 239. *See also* Ambition; Power
Comprehension: inner and outer, 95; and the new mind, 57. *See also* Listening
Computers: and the human mind, 230; as mechanical, 106; and the process of thought, 123–24. *See also* Machines; Mechanical knowledge; Mind
Concentration, 305–6, 312; versus attention, 44; describing, 215; and duality, 102; limitless, 312; process of, 264, 269; and the process of exclusion, 143; understanding, 167. *See also* Listening; Meditation
Conclusions: and fear, 39; as hindrance, 45, 270; as hindrance to observation, 113. *See also* Conformity; Ideas
Condemnation: and action, 5–6; cessation of, 228; as escape from fact, 46; as hindrance to seeing, 61; as hindrance to understanding, 65, 242. *See also* Ambition; Comparison; Conflict
Conditioned mind: and fact, 316. *See also* Mind; Dull mind
Conditioned thinking, 282–83
Conditioning: versus anonymity, 90; and belief in God, 84; of the brain, 191–92; and the center, 267–68; and challenge and response, 75; and the conscious and unconscious, 124–25; defining, 263–64; and discussion, 2; and enslavement, 6; and experience, 224; and freedom from the past, 144; and illusion, 205; and influences, 139, 236–37; and loss of freedom, 281; and meditation, 42; and the mind, 145; and organized religion, 78; perceiving, 145–47; and response, 72–73; as the root of fear, 144; and time, 100–102, 159–60, 206–7; and visions, 167; and words, 4, 302
Conflict, 129–33, 153–57, 175–79, 193–98, 238–43; and the ambitious mind, 309–10, 312; and attention, 264; and attention and concentration, 215; and comparison, 13; and concentration, 264; and contradiction, 135; and desire, 148, 152, 245; desire to be free of, 123; and the destructive mind, 19; destructiveness of, 14; and dissipated energy, 289; and division, 134; and the dull mind, 176–77; between duty and fact, 127; and effort, 214; and energy, 63, 65, 110, 289; eradication of, 129–33; and fact, 323–24; between fact and desire, 104, 106; in life, 43; and the mind, 15, 110; between the observer and the observed, 177–78; between past and present, 208; and the religious mind, 175; and sorrow, 209; and time, 159; understanding, 129–33; understanding the process of, 296–97; and will, 158
Conflict of opposites: and learning, 199. *See also* Duality
Conformity: and the center, 177; and contradiction, 32; versus freedom, 235; versus the free mind, 142–43; and influence, 28; necessary, 32; and purpose, 23; types of, 28–29. *See also* Authority; Commitment
Confusion: and challenge and response, 68–74; as motive, 68–69; and the search for authority, 189. *See also* Conflict
Conscious: function of, 41, 111–13, 219–20. *See also* Mind; Unconscious
Conscious and the unconscious: absence of, 113; and divisions, 195; and influence, 321; and positive motive, 126; and the process of thought, 304. *See also* Mind
Consciousness: and change, 254; and conflict, 240–41; and the conflict of contradiction, 194; describing, 240; and effort and fear, 41, 304; function of, 256; meaning of, 288; and meditation, 265; and negation, 256; and the search for answers, 8; as thought, 220–21; and time, 240, 251, 287. *See also* Conscious; Mind
Contemplation: and action, 20; defining, 20–21
Contentment: and stagnation, 14
Continuity: versus the creative, 261; and death, 39; and fear, 161, 259; as habit, 146–47; as time and space, 160
Continuity of thought: and death, 221–22
Contradiction: as action in living, 24; and ambition, 15, 25; and broken action, 34; and challenge, 6; and challenge and response, 73; and conflict, 129, 194, 240–41; and confusion, 32; and the conscious and unconscious, 41–42, 125; and the creation of conflict, 177; and desire, 151; and energy, 63, 55, 66, 289; and experiencing, 44; and fact, 24; and fulfillment, 135; individual and social, 33; and the observer and the observed, 46; through reaction, 21–22; and the search for answers, 10; and seeing totally, 195; and tension, 26–27, 31; understanding, 22. *See also* Divisions
Control: limitations of, 312. *See also* Conformity; Discipline
Corruption: awareness of, 18; in leadership, 49–50
Courtesy: and the sense of beauty, 105
Creation: conditions for, 216–17; and creation, 199; defining the state of, 172; as destruction, 225–26, 272–73, 297; and dying, 261; and emptiness, 181; versus expression, 313; and invention, 64; versus mechanical knowledge, 322; as new, 216–17; and the religious mind, 82, 226, 326; and the unknowable, 319. *See also* God
Creation, love, and death: as one, 261
Creative: as destruction, 185; and energy, 64; versus the scientific, 77, 80. *See also* New; New mind
Creative mind: and the absence of conflict, 130; achieving, 48; as patternless, 185; as the religious mind, 273. *See also* Dull mind; Free mind; New mind
Creative state: achieving, 145; desire for, 67; need for, 123
Creative thinking: and discovery, 124
Creativity: and the artist, 192–93
Crisis: and challenge, 281

Daily life: and the insensitive mind, 277; and verbalization, 4

Death, 157–58, 160–63, 217–19, 221–22, 258–63, 315–19; and escape into beliefs, 209; and fear, 135; fear of, 304; learning about, 106–7; and permanency, 105; and sorrow, 92–93; understanding, 39. *See also* Continuity; Dying; Time
Death, fear, and time: relationship between, 217–23
Debate: versus discussion, 2
Deception: and gratification, 266
Denial: and change, 255–56; and the false, 322, 323; through knowledge or reaction, 224; and motive, 257; and the negation of the false, 255–56; and negative thinking, 287; and the religious mind, 323; state of mind of, 292
Dependence: and action, 33; and conflict, 242; and knowledge, 36; and psychological needs, 243–44. *See also* Attachment; Freedom
Desire, 148–53, 243–47; comprehension of, 217; and conflict, 131–32, 201, 242; understanding, 242; and will, 158. *See also* Acquisitiveness; Ambition; Despair; Power
Despair: and desire, 150; escape from, 175–76; and fear, 142; and hope, 170. *See also* Conflict; Feelings
Destruction: as creation, 225–26, 297, 319; and humility, 199–200; and the new, 223; and the religious mind, 272–73; as true questioning, 277
Detachment: understanding, 29–30. *See also* Dependence
Deterioration: and conflict, 13; and living without contradiction, 300
Differentiation: and fear, 48
Directional commitment: and envy, 110
Direct perception: versus the imitative experience, 146. *See also* Perception
Discipline: as escape, 130; and fear, 140; as hindrance, 149; types of, 324. *See also* Conformity; Effort; Resistance
Discontent: and action, 13–14; and change, 255–56; defining, 13–14; and desire, 150. *See also* Conflict; Dissatisfaction
Discovery: and the free mind, 204; and questioning, 286; and sorrow, 201–2; of true and false, 267; and the uncertain mind, 235
Discussion: meaning of, 1–2; and questions, 186–87
Disorder: defining, 172; and order, 189–90
Dissatisfaction: and comparison, 11–12; and seeking, 203. *See also* Conflict; Discontent
Distraction: and attention and concentration, 215, 264
Disturbance: avoidance of, 237; creating, 196–97; and the occupied mind, 243. *See also* Conflict
Divine power: and fear, 60
Divisions: in action, 68; and conflict, 194–95, 242; and consciousness, 240–41; as contradiction, 177–78; and desire, 152; and energy, 63; and fear, 45; of inner and outer, 70, 134, 197–98, 292; living without, 22, 25; between the observer and the observed, 255; and organized belief, 118; and specialization, 270; and tension, 63; between the thinker and the thought, 44, 177–78; and total action, 33; world, 191. *See also* Fragmentation; Totality; Whole
Dogma. *See* Belief; Tradition
Dreams: and the activity of the mind, 165; and analysis, 257; and conflict, 194; and the unconscious, 111
Drive. *See* Motive
Duality: absence of, 113; and time, 100–103; between *what is* and 'what should be', 155. *See also* Divisions
Dual process: meaning of, 233
Dull mind: and conflict, 129, 214; describing, 165; freedom from, 17; and living, 18; perception of, 315; recognition of, 292; transformation of, 267. *See also* Mind; New mind
Dullness: and observation, 45–46; recognition of, 31
Duty: versus freedom, 127. *See also* Conformity; Motive; Respectability
Dying: to action, 40; to the known, 318–19; while living, 160–61; to the mechanical, 107; to memory, 39, 259–60; and the mind alone, 225; and the new, 147; to a problem, 317; state of, 274; to thought, 221–22, 259; to time, 221–22. *See also* Death

Education: and competition, 209; and conformity in children, 296; and society, 37
Efficiency: achieving, 19; and ambition, 119; versus competition, 20
Effort and conflict, 264, 267; and fear, 41; futility of, 164; as hindrance to direct perception, 313; as hindrance to fact, 316; as hindrance to the new, 127; and living, 214; living without, 315; and negative thinking, 213–14; versus perception of the mind, 164; reasons for, 315; and self-knowing, 202. *See also* Conformity; Discipline
Ego. *See* Center
Electronic brains: and knowledge, 303. *See also* Computers
Electronic machines: and world change, 117. *See also* Computers; Electronic brains; Science
Emotional contact: and fact, 232–33. *See also* Feelings
Emptiness: of change, 293; and creation, 181; and daily living, 257; and discovery of the false, 256; and the new, 256. *See also* Isolation; Loneliness
Empty mind: and the absence of pressure, 25; and creation, 168; and dying to yesterdays, 161; and the immeasurable, 46–47; and the new, 154. *See also* Dull mind; Emptiness; Free mind; New mind
Ending: of thought, 138. *See also* Meditation
Energy: 63–67, 268; and the absence of conflict, 202; without beginning or end, 103; and cause and effect, 100; and condemnation, 242; and conflict, 196, 296–97; and the creative state, 145; dissipation of, 202–3; and envy, 110–11; and fear, 59; and freedom from authority, 46, 296; and the free mind, 171; and living with death, 260; and meditation, 325; and the mind, 111; and mutation, 289; of the new mind, 136–37; and pleasure, 45; and problems, 12; and the religious mind, 323–24; from seeing, 57, 62; types of, 57, 63–64, 110–11; wasting of, 12–13; and the whole, 56; and the word, 62, 302
Energy of purification: and the need to observe, 111. *See also* Energy
England. *See* Authority; Conditioning; Identification; Nationalism; Words

Enslavement: to time, 75, 85, 122; to words, 302–3, 315. *See also* Freedom; Free mind
Environment: and influence, 96–97, 100. *See also* Conditioning; Propaganda; Society
Envy: and acquisitiveness, 310–11; as basis of religious sanctions, 165; as the basis of society, 110–11; versus the mature mind, 205; and power, 28. *See also* Ambition
Escape: and the absence of understanding, 314; cessation of, 94; from conflict, 43, 129–30, 154, 156, 194, 241; from discontent, 14; and the dull mind, 175–76; from fear, 45, 59; forms of, 240; futility of, 9; from loneliness, 88; from problems, 8–9; from the shallow mind, 163; and sorrow, 208, 210, 269; from suffering, 91, 93–94; types of, 156
Evil: of authority, 180; of authority and power, 189; and power, 27–28, 34, 36
Evolutionary mind: versus the religious mind, 272. *See also* Dull mind; Time
Exclusion: and concentration, 264
Existence: and effort, 41. *See also* Life; Living
Experience: as the accumulation of knowledge, 236, 304; attempt to escape from, 132; and the center, 166; and challenge and response, 295; and conditioning, 224; as inner authority, 144; as the known, 120; meaning of, 236, 308–9; and memory, 132, 198; as a search for certainty, 134; and time, 98–99
Experiencer: and conflict, 198. *See also* Experiencer and the Experience
Experiencer and the experience: as source of conflict, 177–78. *See also* Divisions; Thinker and the thought
Experiencing: and attention, 102, 248; and challenge and response, 314; and contradiction, 44; while listening, 41; meaning of, 155; and the mind, 132; understanding, 16
Exploitation: by religions, 203. *See also* Authority
Exploration: and discussion, 2; versus exploring, 57; and mechanical thinking, 5
External authority: obedience to, 295. *See also* Outward authority; Society

Fact: and the absence of conditioning, 316; and the absence of fear, 247; and action, 5, 210; without adjustment, 205; as always moving, 169; approach to, 251; and the cessation of fear, 305; and chronological and psychological time, 159; and condemnation, 46; and conditioning, 311; and conflict, 240, 241; and contradiction, 24; and crisis, 281, 283; without effort, 165; and energy, 312, 324; versus fear, 303; and the hindrance of interpretation, 50; versus illusion, 61; versus judgment, 164, 282–83; and the mind as challenger, 76; as movement, 105; of need for security, 231–32; and the need to be casual, 58; as never still, 178; and observation, 89; and the observation of sorrow, 94; and opinion, 183–84; and perception, 67, 79–80; process of seeing, 232; recognition of, 30; and the release of energy, 289; and the religious mind, 89; and religious organizations, 80; and the scientific mind, 322; seeing, 228;and sorrow, 208–9, 295; and theory, 104; two stages of, 16; understanding, 281–87; versus 'what should be', 159; and the word, 180–81, 241, 303; without the word, 292–93; and world problems, 283. *See also What is*
Faith: destruction of, 69
False: and authority, 279; and the creation of the new, 141; and denial, 322; and questioning, 277; and the state of negation, 255–56; and time, 160. *See also* True
Family: and the conflict of freedom, 127–28; and death, 318
Fascism. *See* Authority; Conditioning; Identification; Propaganda; Words
Fear, 40–41, 43, 45–48, 58–62, 134–39, 139–42, 217–23, 248–52, 303–5; cessation of, 157; commonality of, 60; and conditioning, 144; and conflict, 157; and conformity, 28; and continuity, 259; creation of, 88; of death, 160–61, 258–59, 261, 318; and dependence, 33; and desire, 148; effects of, 248, 277–78; and energy, 65; and enslavement to words, 18; and escape, 247; freedom from, 262; and the free mind, 200; as hindrance to creative energy, 63; as hindrance to inquiry, 52; as hindrance to transformation, 277–78; and illusion, 148; of isolation, 244; and knowledge, 322; of the known, 319; of loneliness, 271, 314–15; and the mediocre life, 277; and meditation, 43; nature of, 38–39; and the need for security, 38–39; need to be aware of, 279; and the occupied mind, 234; and progress, 188; reluctance to probe into, 187; and security, 231–32; self-protective, 140; and suffering, 91–93, 95; and thinking, 300; and time, 58; types of, 249, 303–4; and the unhealthy mind, 59
Fear, time, and death: relationship between, 217–23
Feelings: as an aspect of mind, 53–54; and the center, 147; and conflict, 194; and desire, 148, 149; without division, 178; living with, 164; without naming, 44; and observation, 88; and the urge for power, 55; without words, 197, 241
Feeling and thinking: as one, 151
Fertile mind: as empty, 108. *See also* Free mind; Innocent mind
Followers: and the death of truth, 167–68; and the desire for saints, 82; desire to be, 27; free from the demand for order, 191. *See also* Authority; Leaders
Following: and discontent, 203; reasons for, 143–44, 235. *See also* Followers
Food, clothing, shelter: as essential, 17
Fragmentary action: and authority, 204. *See also* Action; Divisions; Totality; Whole
Fragmentation: of governments and organizations, 184–85. *See also* Fragmentary action
Freedom, 234–38; from authority, 234–38, 296; and the brain and mind, 230; and conditioning, 6; from conditioning, 282; from conflict, 154, 239; from conformity, 28–29; from fear, 46, 61, 218–19, 259, 262, 303–4; futility of search for, 200; from influence, 97; inward and outward, 231; from the known, 319; and looking at need, 246; loss of, 281, 284; meaning of, 284, 287; of the mind, 144; from power, 28; from problems, 12; and progress, 169;

from suffering, 94–95, 176; from time, 221; from the word, 88–89, 293
Free mind: and aloneness, 157; and conflict, 242; and discovery of the true, 232; and fear, 142; as fearless, 277; and meditation, 204–5, 263–65; and the religious mind, 325; and seeing, 191. *See also* Mutation
Freudians: and new approaches, 155
Fulfillment: and conflict, 239, 241; and desire, 150, 151, 153; and fear, 135; and sorrow, 98. *See also* Ambition; Belonging
Function: and education, 17; of knowledge, 35–37; and specialization, 270–71; and status, 34–36, 310
Fundamental transformation: and listening, 144. *See also* Change; Mutation; Revolution
Future: and fear of pain, 92. *See also* Time
Fresh mind: and mutation, 287. *See also* Free mind; New mind

Gita. *See* Authority; Conditioning; Knowledge; Propaganda; Words
God: belief in, 84; and conditioning, 323; and conflict, 14; as the creative state, 145; and the desire for permanency, 105; and discovery, 280; and energy, 65; and fear, 238; and freedom from conflict, 130; and gratification, 266; and the hindrance of belonging, 127; and the hindrance of illusion, 263; and the innocent mind, 40, 103; and the new mind, 119; and permanency, 162; and propaganda, 256; and revelation, 247; as security, 235; seeking, 142; and time, 99; as unknowable, 179; and the word, 85. *See also* Immeasurable
Good mind: versus ambition, 54. *See also* New mind
Goodness: versus conformity, 143, 144. *See also* Virtue
Gratification: process of, 266
Greed: and material needs, 6. *See also* Ambition; Power
Group: as reactionary, 22–23. *See also* Collective
Guilt: of the East and West, 141–42; and fear, 59
Gurus: as escape, 88. *See also* Authority; Power

Habits: and awareness, 302; and the difficulty of change, 253–54; as hindrance to understanding, 109; versus learning, 106; versus meditation, 167; and the occupied mind, 137; and time, 316. *See also* Conditioning; Conformity; Discipline
Happiness: search for, 203. *See also* Feelings; Sorrow
Hearing: and listening, 285
Hereafter: belief in, 317–18. *See also* Death; Religion
Hinduism. *See* Authority; Condition; Conformity; Divisions; Identification; Religion; Words
Hope: and the creation of frustration, 52; and despair, 170
Humility: and aloneness, 40; cultivation of, 36; defining, 198–99; versus knowledge, 36; and learning, 158, 198, 200; and power, 143; and the religious mind, 325; and self-understanding, 206; and virtue, 266, 310; and *what is,* 199–200

'I': and the center, 102; and the observer and the observed, 100–102. *See also* Center
Ideals: and fact, 16; versus the fact, 290; and *what is,* versus 'what should be', 159. *See also* Ideas
Ideas: and action, 24, 102, 130; and attachment, 30; and conditioning, 117; and conflict, 194; enslavement to, 231; versus fact, 225; and feeling, 193. *See also* Illusions; Words
Identification: and conflict, 177; and energy, 63; and meditation, 205; as partial, 151–52; reasons for, 133–34; and security, 135; versus *what is,* 201; and words, 197. *See also* Authority; Belonging; Commitment; Verbalization
Identity: and attachment, 30
"I don't know": and the new, 3–4; and the state of learning, 106; as a state of love and innocence, 107; states of, 121–22; and states of mind, 214
Illusions: and authority, 205; and conflict, 157; eliminating, 265–66; and fear, 305; and God, 247; as hindrance to meditation, 263–65; and meditation, 42; as the power of desire, 225; and world problems, 53. *See also* Ideals; Ideas
Image. *See* Words
Imitative experience: versus direct experience, 146. *See also* Experience; Experiencing
Imitative process: and seeking power, 143. *See also* Ambition; Power
Immature mind: as mediocre, 29. *See also* Dull mind; Mind
Immeasurable: and the creative mind, 48; discovering, 186; and fear, 45, 48; and meditation, 313; and the religious mind, 227. *See also* God
Immediate change: versus gradual change, 288. *See also* Change; Mutation; Revolution; Time
Immediate perception: and escape, 212; possible, 126; and progress, 188. *See also* Immediate change; Perception
"I must not": and "I must," 83
Incentive: and efficiency, 19. *See also* Motive
Inclusion: and attention, 264
India: and the lack of questioning, 276; and the patterns of belief, 118. *See also* Authority; Conditioning; Identification; Naming; Nationalism; Words
Individual: and change, 253; and the collective, 253; and machines, 117–18, 185
Individual change: and collective change, 253; and society, 269
Individual thinking, 162–63
Industrialism: and scientific spirit, 169
Industrialization: and control of the mind, 279. *See also* Progress; Science; World problems
Influences: and action, 22; and aloneness, 315; and challenge, 75–76; and conditioning, 139, 141, 144–45, 236–37; and the creation of authority, 258; freedom from, 125; inner and outer, 71; and power, 28; and propaganda, 15; and the religious mind, 321; and self-contradiction, 24; and symbols, 319–20, 321; understanding, 96–97, 100
Inner: as the unconscious, 70, 111. *See also* Inner and outer
Inner and outer: and conflict, 129; as one, 134–35; as unitary process, 90. *See also* Inward and outward
Inner comprehension: and the religious mind, 95

Inner problems: defining, 218. *See also* Inner and outer; Problems
"Inner voice": as source of action, 66
Innocent mind: and the absence of conflict, 129; and authority, 295; and clarity, 207; and freedom from knowledge, 35; and God, 103. *See also* New mind
Inquiry: and attention, 215–16; and change, 293; into death, 315–17; and energy, 111; as foundation for meditation, 311–12; and the good mind, 165; as hindrance to fear, 249; meaning of, 316; and the mind, 5, 52, 54, 110–11; negative and positive, 215; and the petty mind, 307–8; and power, 55–56; and the problem, 186; and the process of thought, 304; and the religious spirit, 170; and the scientific spirit, 169; two ways of, 140–41; into the unconscious, 219–20; understanding, 52–54. *See also* Questioning
Insane mind: and problems, 11. *See also* Dull mind; Mind
Insensitivity: and habit, 46. *See also* Sensitivity
Instinct: and fear, 47
Insufficiency: as a problem, 11, 13
Integrity: as a quality of the new mind, 294, 297, 298; understanding, 294. *See also* Intuition
Intellect: worship of, 299–300
Intellectuals: and conflict, 239; and words, 286. *See also* Authority; Specialists
Intelligence, 7–10; defining, 144–45, 321. *See also* New mind
Intelligent awareness: and the absence of apprehension, 6–7
Intelligent mind: achieving, 145; and dividing life, 22. *See also* Mind; New mind
Intensity: and desire, 149; and destruction, 212–13; as passion, 226
Internal authority: and the hindrance of knowledge, 295. *See also* Authority; Inner
Interpretation: as distortion, 218; as hindrance to fact, 50; as hindrance to listening, 67; and naming, 43; and seeing, 5. *See also* Authority
Intuition: defining, 10. *See also* Instinct
Invention: and creation, 64. *See also* Machines; Progress; Science
Investigation: need for, 100. *See also* Inquiry
Inward and outward: as one, 231; order, 189–90; as a single state, 57. *See also* Inner and outer
Inward authority, 144; defining, 234. *See also* Authority; Inner
Inward movement: and change, 291–92; defining, 171–72. *See also* Inward and outward
Inward revolution: and the scientific spirit, 169
Inward security, 235
Isolation: and the discovery of beauty, 156; fear of, 60–61, 280; living with, 271–72; and loneliness, 315; process of, 87–89. *See also* Alone; Aloneness
"It may be possible" and the new mind, 52–54. *See also* "I do not know"

Jargon: and the use of words, 275
Jealousy: and the feeling without the word, 241; perception of, 181
Jesus: as escape, 201. *See also* Authority; Conditioning; Identification; Religion; Religious mind; Words
Jungians: and new approaches, 155. *See also* Psychiatry
Justification. *See* Acquisitiveness; Conflict; Envy

Karma: and the fear of death, 160
Know-how: and challenge and response, 309; and mechanical knowledge, 306. *See also* Invention; Machines; Progress; Science
Knowing: versus knowledge, 34, 36–37; meaning of, 155; as the present, 37; process of, 7, 280; two ways of, 292
"Knowing" and "not-knowing": states of, 121–22
Knowledge: as an accumulative process, 198; and authority, 236; and the creation of problems, 7–10, 72; and electronic brains, 303; as hindrance to freedom, 35; as hindrance to knowing, 34, 37; as invention, 77, 80; inward and outward, 9–10; and learning, 1–2, 158; as mechanical, 63; and mechanical time, 317; and the new mind, 114; and the past, 7, 10, 321–22; and permanency, 105; and power, 271; and recognition, 37; and the religious mind, 325; and the scientist, 112; and the sensitive mind, 108; and thought, 304; versus the unburdened mind, 298; understanding, 265. *See also* Memory
Known: and the past, present, and future, 322; and the religious mind, 324–25; and unknown, 160–61, 163; as yesterday, 161. *See also* Time
Koran. *See* Authority; Conditioning; Knowledge; Power; Propaganda; Religion; Words

Label, *See* Identification; Words
Laziness: and passivity, 206
Lazy mind: and time, 159. *See also* Dull mind; Mind; New Mind
Leaders: and the creation of patterns, 16; and fear, 59; and power, 27–28; and world problems, 49–50. *See also* Authority
Leadership: and competition, 19. *See also* Authority; Power; Society
Learning, 198–200; conditions for, 157–58; and the empty mind, 32–33; and humility, 198–200; versus knowledge, 280; meaning of, 1–2; and the new mind, 114; and not-knowing, 250; versus power, 271; process of, 105–7, 280; understanding, 265. *See also* Attention; Listening
Liberation: and perception, 310; and self-knowing, 248. *See also* Freedom
Life: arguing with, 317–18; as challenge and response, 68–69; lack of awareness of, 321; as mechanical, 185; as movement, 291; as one movement, 9–10; as pain, 259–60; as problem, 8; and sorrow, 92–93. *See also* Living
Life and death: as one, 319
Limitations: of challenge and response, 68–81
Limited mind: and fragmentation, 309. *See also* Dull mind; Whole
Listening: and attention, 248, 306; and choicelessness, 268; without comparison, 188–89, 295–96; without contradiction, 67; without effort, 204; and fear, 252; versus following, 143; and hearing, 285; importance

of, 320; and perception, 1–2; process of, 58; and the quiet brain, 229; and the religious mind, 320; significance of, 90. *See also* Listening
Living: and the absence of purpose, 25; as action, 23–24; as annihilation, 40; with clarity, 195–96; without contradiction, 25; with death, 259–60; difficulty of, 54; and the dull mind, 18; and dying, 40, 160–61; without effort, 313; without fear, 260; as influence, 96; and meditation, 42; and the past, 137; with sorrow, 212; as timeless movement, 16–17; types of, 16–17. *See also* Death; Life
Living and dying: as one, 161, 222, 261
Living totally: defining, 300–301; and deterioration, 300. *See also* Whole
Logic: limitations of, 107–8. *See also* Science; Scientific mind
Loneliness, 87–89; and desire, 246; escape from, 156, 313–14; and sorrow, 208. *See also* Alone; Aloneness; Isolation
Looking: without the word, 293. *See also* Observation; Seeing
Love: and the absence of effort, 267; and the absence of fear, 268; and accumulation, 158; and aloneness, 40; and ambition, 309–10; versus ambition and envy, 205; and attention, 144; and desire, 149; and dying to yesterday, 161; and freedom from conflict, 20; and freedom from the word, 85; and future generations, 261; and the hindrance of ambition, 135; and the hindrance of the brain, 217; and knowing dying, 260–61; lack of, 318–19; meaning of, 179, 273; and meditation, 168; particular and universal, 10; and the quality of the new mind, 294, 297–98; and the religious mind, 325; and self-centeredness, 14; and sorrow, 210; as total versus fragmentary, 220; understanding, 171, 172; word, 122; of work, 309–10
Love and beauty: as one, 226
Love, creation, and death: as one, 261
Love, passion, and desire: as related, 243, 246

Machines: capability of, 246; proliferation of, 279
Marxism: as reaction, 22. *See also* Authority; Conditioning; Power; Tyranny; Words, World problems
Masters. *See* Authority
Mature mind: describing, 29. *See also* Dull mind; Free mind; New mind
Maya. *See* Illusion
'Me': and the clear mind, 265. *See also* Center
Mechanical: dying to, 107; energy, 63–64; time, 221; time and knowledge, 317
Mechanical invention: versus creation, 230
Mechanical knowledge: and experience, 308; as necessary, 321–22; nondenial of, 256–57. *See also* Invention; Science; Scientific approach; Scientific mind
Mechanical learning: and the center, 199
Mechanical living: and consciousness, 256
Mechanical mind: and thought, 232. *See also* Dull mind; New mind
Mechanical process: versus learning, 106–7
Mechanical response: and thoughts, 3
Mechanical thinking: and conditioning, 214; and reason, 64
Mediocre mind: defining, 307. *See also* Dull mind; Mind; New mind
Meditation, 203–6, 263–69; and awareness, 306–13; basis for, 305; and change, 200; conditions for, 274; and conformity, 29; defining, 42–43, 139; and fear, 43; foundation for, 307–13; and freedom from the known, 325; meaning of, 280; and the mind, 163, 168; and the process of time, 99; and the quiet mind, 166; and the religious mind, 227; understanding, 41–46, 48; and understanding conflict and effort, 213. *See also* Attention
Meditative mind: as essential, 168. *See also* Meditation
Memory: as the center, 155–56; and conditioning, 2, 6; and conflict, 178; and conformity, 29; and the creation of problems, 132; defining, 100; and experience, 166, 198, 224; and influence, 97; and knowledge, 252–53; versus love, 260–61; as mechanical, 180; and permanency, 105; and response, 71–72, 124; and thinking, 79; and thought, 304; and thought process, 3; and time, 58–62, 97–98. *See also* Past
Memory and the center: as cause and effect, 166
Memory in action: versus awareness in action, 305–6
Mental illness: causes of, 222–23; and conflict, 194; and energy, 289; and fear, 58–62; and fear of uncertainty, 235
Method. *See* Patterns; Tradition
Mind, 107–15, 163–68; and the absence of conflict, 14–15; and the absence of the need to escape, 94; and action, 22; alone, 80–81, 135–36, 225; and aloneness, 256; and ambition, 14, 15; approach to freeing, 61–62; and awareness, 55, 101–2; and the barrier of the word, 86; beyond challenge and response, 70, 72, 73–75; and the brain, 299; challenged, 76–77; as challenger, 76; conditioned, 100–102; and conflict, 13–15, 155, 176–77; and conformity, 28–29; and death, 39–40; defining, 202; and desire, 150–53; and the destructiveness of conflict, 104–5; deterioration of, 185; and discontent, 14; and energy, 46; enslaved by time, 99–100; and enslavement to words, 4–6, 44, 48; and experiencing death, 222; and feelings, 54–55; and freedom from authorities and followers, 180; and freedom from conflict, 20, 197; and freedom from conformity, 29; and freedom from fear, 140, 142, 305; and freedom from influences, 89, 139; and freedom from memory, 71–72; and freedom from sorrow, 208–9; free from authority, 204–5; free from challenge and response, 157; free from conditioning, 144; free from the word, 197, 216, 228; freeing, 67; freeing through self-knowledge, 16; function of, 120; and the hindrance of problems, 7–8, 10, 11; and the hindrance of time, 58–62; and illusion, 61; influences on, 321; inner and outer, 90; as insensitive, 16–17; and insufficiency, 13; as limitless, 85; as loneliness, 156–57; and love, 179; and meditation, 43; and the need to inquire, 5; and not knowing, 3–4; and the problem of comparison,

11–12; process of, 45, 119; and purpose, 24; and science, 51; and the search for security, 134–35, 137; as self-enslaver and liberator, 237; serious, 183; and sleep, 41–42; and society, 97; and the state of learning, 107; and suffering, 175–76; three states of, 52–54; and time, 66, 100–103, 159; and the timeless, 84; totality of, 95; as totally alive, 73–75; and understanding, 237; and understanding isolation, 89; and world problems, 230; worship of, 122. *See also* Brain
Mind and the brain: differences between, 270
Mind control: and loss of freedom, 281
Mistakes: and discovery, 286
Modern society: revolt against, 278. *See also* Industrialism; Society; World problems
Mohammed. *See* Authority; Conditioning; Identification; Religious mind; Words
Moment to moment: and self-knowing, 265–66
'More'. *See* Ambition; Fulfillment
Motive: and action, 66, 73; and affection and love, 298; and change, 255–56, 291; and confusion, 68–69; and the desire to be socially helpful, 66; as hindrance, 284–85
Motiveless action: and change, 288. *See also* Motive
Movement: and change, 291–92; and the religious mind, 171–72; and the truth, 252. *See also* Inner and outer
Muslim. *See* Authority; Conditioning; Identification; Religion; Religious mind; Words
Mutating mind: as the religious mind, 325
Mutation, 253–54, 256–57, 288–93; and the absence of authority, 299; achieving, 267; and attention, 308; and awareness, 311, 313; and consciousness, 256; how to achieve, 320; and meditation, 307; need for, 305; and the new mind, 305; and the petty mind, 307–9; understanding, 284–87. *See also* Change; Revolution; Transformation
Mutation and change: difference between, 284–86

Naming: as fact, 232; and understanding, 43–44; and the word. *See also* Identification
Nationalism: and belief, 126–27; and cruel energy, 64–65; and denial, 287; and viewing from the center, 95; and world problems, 75–76, 118. *See also* Power; Society
Needs: dependence on, 243–44; understanding, 244
Negation: and attention, 113; and the inquiring mind, 103; and inquiry into the religious mind, 224; and love, 179; and understanding action, 26–27. *See also* Negative approach
Negative approach: and the absence of reaction, 154; and denial, 287; and truth, 83–84; to the unconscious, 220; understanding, 170. *See also* Negation; Negative thinking; Thinking
Negative thinking: defining, 213–14, 322; as the highest form, 220; process of, 78–81, 255–56; and the religious mind, 322–23; and the religious spirit, 170. *See also* Negation
Neurological fear: types of, 47–48. *See also* Fear
New: versus belief, 321; challenge and response to, 325; and creation, 216–17; and emptiness, 256; and the innocent mind, 207; and living with death, 260; and revolution, 185; and science, 77; and the state of quietness, 227. *See also* Mutation; New mind
New mind, 293–95, 298; and the absence of ambition, 310; and the absence of conflict, 154; achieving, 115, 254, 308–9; and awareness, 56; and the challenge of life, 279; and the conscious and unconscious, 112; defining, 113–14, describing, 50–51, 55, 236; and dying to the past, 161; and energy, 114–15; as essential, 118; and family and societal obligations, 127; and inquiry, 293; need for, 50–54, 174, 275–76; as the religious mind, 107–8, 113–14; and seeing the total, 57–58; and sorrow, 294–95, 298; and time, 58; versus "what to do," 128. *See also* Change; Mutation; New mind; Revolution
New world: and mutation, 284
Nonviolence: as nonreality, 61; and time, 101
Nothingness: state of, 161
Not-knowing: and attention, 250–51; and fear, 250–51; state of, 215–16. *See also* Knowing; Knowledge

Obedience: and the dull mind, 286–87; and fear, 278
Observation: and the absence of resistance, 289; and change, 267; without comparison, 11–12; and conditioning, 100–101; and dullness, 45–46; and enslavement to words, 122; and the fact, 311; and feeling, 88; without the observer and observed, 113; process of, 43–46, 48; and the quiet brain, 312–13; and reaction, 83–84; and total response, 282; and true denial, 224; and understanding, 60, 109, 112; and understanding sorrow, 94; and the unity of inside and outside, 231; without the word, 89. *See also* Seeing
Observer: absence of, 102. *See also* Observer and the observed
Observer and the observed: and change, 253–54; and contradiction, 46; and duality, 100–102; and the whole mind, 44, 48. *See also* Thinker and the thought
Observing: versus thinking, 6
Occupied mind: and fear, 234; understanding, 137–38. *See also* Dull mind; Empty mind; Mind
Old age: fear of, 318
Old mind: describing, 236
Opinion: versus fact, 283
Opposites: overcoming, 100, 102. *See also* Divisions; Duality
Order, 189–92; desire for, 187–88, 189–90; and virtue, 310
Organized religion: as conditioned, 78; as escape from suffering, 175; as poisonous, 127. *See also* Authority; Power; Religion
Outer: and challenge, 75–76; defining the function of, 70–71. *See also* Inner
Outer and Inner: as unitary process, 90. *See also* Inner and outer; Inward and outward
Outer problems: defining, 218. *See also* Society; World problems
Outside. *See* Outer
Outward and inward movements: and the desire to belong, 184–85. *See also* Inner and outer

Outward authority, 144; defining, 234. *See also* Authority; Outer
Outward change: rapidity of, 200. *See also* Industrialism; Progress; Society
Outward movement: affecting, 185; and change, 291–92; defining, 171–72
Outward security, 235

Pain: and fear, 96. *See also* Sorrow; Suffering
Part: and whole, 176. *See also* Total action
Particular: and the universal, 10
Passion: and austerity, 166; and conflict, 194; defining, 149, 273; as foundation for the free mind, 205; meaning of, 245; and the religious mind, 226; versus sex, 245. *See also* Desire; Feelings; Love
Passionate mind: and the absence of conflict, 154. *See also* Mind; New mind; Quiet mind
Passion, love, and desire: as related, 243, 246
Passive awareness. *See* Choiceless awareness
Passivity: and laziness, 206
Past: as the conscious and unconscious, 127; dying to, 221–22, 260–61; and dying to yesterday, 37; enslavement to, 6; and experience, 224, 309; freedom from, 137; and influence, 97; and knowledge, 321–22. *See also* Knowledge; Memory; Time
Past, present, and future: and conflict, 177
Patterns: and conformity, 235; destruction of, 254, 279; versus meditation, 263. *See also* Tradition; Words
Peace: and conflict, 242, 298; desire for, 8, 238; meaning of, 190. *See also* God; Immeasurable; Reality; World problems
Perception: achieving, 24; and death, 258; and effort, 41; and freedom, 234; and liberation, 310; and listening, 67; and the negative approach to, 27; and the state of being alone, 225; and time, 160. *See also* Awareness; Seeing
Permanency: and the desire for security, 104–5; and the thinker and the thought, 177–78; and thought, 241; and time, 98; and time, death, and love, 162. *See also* Continuity
Persuasion: and change, 288
Petty mind: defining, 307–8. *See also* Dull mind; Empty mind; Mind
Philosophy of action. *See* Action
Physical continuity: desire for, 160. *See also* Permanency
Physical death: solving the problem of, 262. *See also* Continuity; Death
Physical fear: necessity of, 262; and psychological fear, 304. *See also* Fear
Physical needs: as necessity, 243
Physical needs and psychological needs: discerning between, 247
Physical pain: versus psychological suffering, 211
Physical security: need for, 135. *See also* Security
Physical sorrow, 208, 210. *See also* Sorrow
Physics: and applying the light of silence, 90. *See also* Science: Scientific mind
Pleasure: dying to, 161; and sorrow, 210. *See also* Feelings
Political mind: as destructive, 90. *See also* Authority; Power
Political problems: and challenges, 76. *See also* Authority; Power; Society
Political tyranny: increase of, 49–50. *See also* Authority; World problems
Politicians: as destructive, 50; and fear, 59; and world problems, 230. *See also* Authority; Power
Politics: and power, 37–38. *See also* Politicians
Positive: action and reaction, 300
Positive and negative: approaches to, 26–28
Positive process: and inquiry, 140–41
Positive thinking: and conflict, 154; and conformity, 78; defining, 213–14, 322; explaining, 282–83; and formulas, 255; as limited, 220; process of, 78–81; as reaction, 153. *See also* Negative thinking
Postponement and change, 289–90
Poverty: and action, 23; approach to, 187; and guilt, 140–41; and prosperity, 184. *See also* Society; World problems
Power: and authority, 236; and the desire to commit, 66; dying to, 40; evil of, 171, 189; and inquiry, 55–56; and knowledge, 35–36; meanings of, 171; seeking, 143; and society, 36; and status, 34–37, 271; understanding, 27–28. *See also* Ambition
Present: and fear, 249, 251. *See also* Time
Primitive: versus the cultivated state, 87
Problems: approach to, 117, 133, 246; and cessation of escape, 241; and conditioning, 53; and conflict, 15, 239; and fact, 317; and hopelessness, 174; and inquiry, 186–87; inward and outward as one, 218; need for an immediate end to, 294; and questions and answers, 71–72; and the religious and scientific approaches, 169; reluctance to probe, 187; and sorrow, 295; understanding, 7–12, 132; and understanding effort, conflict, and contradiction, 123
Profession: and capacity, 302. *See also* Specialists; Work
Profit-minded: and the desire for success, 298. *See also* Ambition
Progress: and comparison, 14; as denial to freedom, 276; and fear, 188; and freedom, 169; and time, 51. *See also* Change; Inventions; Revolution; Society
Propaganda: and belief, 251; and commitment, 231; and the denial of freedom, 281; enslavement to, 139; freedom from, 268; and influence, 96, 321; and the mechanical mind, 230; and tradition, 15. *See also* Conditioning; Conformity
Prosperity: and the loss of freedom, 130; and poverty, 184
Protective reaction: and fear, 140. *See also* Reaction
Psychiatry: and the unconscious, 111
Psychological death: and the known, 318. *See also* Death
Psychological fear: and physical fear, 304. *See also* Fear
Psychological needs, 243–44
Psychological security: as nonexistent, 190. *See also* Security
Psychological sorrow, 208, 210. *See also* Sorrow
Psychological time, 272; as inward, 159; and *what is* and 'what should be', 317. *See also* Time
Psychologists: and the hindrance of interpreters, 254. *See also* Authority; Specialists

Public opinion: and fear, 61
Purpose: and action, 23–25
Purpose of life: futility of search for, 163–64; and world problems, 277

Questioning: as dangerous, 235; and fact, 301; as irreligious, 315; need for, 285–87; without reaction, 316; two types of, 276–77; two ways of, 300. *See also* Inquiry
Questions: right and wrong, 186–87; and solutions, 71–72
Questions and responses: and the interval between, 124; and the process of thought, 250
Quiet brain: and the absence of conflict, 263, 266–67; and the absence of thought, 312; and listening, 229; and sensitivity, 326. *See also* Free mind; Innocent mind; Mind; Mutation; Quiet mind
Quiet mind: and the agitated mind, 233–34; defining, 216; and fact, 178–79; and meditation, 166; and mutation, 305; and the quiet brain, 273–74. *See also* Free mind; Innocent mind; Mind; New mind

Radical change: as the breaking of patterns, 253–54; and the need for change, 121. *See also* Change; Mutation; Revolution
Reaction, 21–22, 24–29, 31; and action, 83–84; and the brain, 192; and conflict, 156; and the creation of misery, 25; defining, 173; as hindrance to truth, 128; level of, 76–77; and living, 24; meaning of, 141; and negative and positive thinking, 213; and order, 190; and the positive and negative approaches, 153–54; and the process of thinking, 214, 250; and questioning, 300, 303, 316; and revolution, 159, 172, 278–79; understanding, 278. *See also* Challenge and response
Real: and the absence of influence, 321
Reality: and being alone, 225; and creation, 231; discovering, 264; and the free and silent mind, 216; and freedom from belief, 238; and total understanding, 273. *See also* Fact; Immeasurable; Truth; Unknown
Reason: as limited, 227; need for, 64
Reasoning: and the scientific mind, 322
Recognition: defining, 82; and fear, 48; and God, 85; and knowledge, 37. *See also* Identification
Reform: and determination, 23; versus revolution, 276. *See also* Change; Progress; Society
Reformers: and conflict, 130. *See also* Reform
Reincarnation: and continuity, 259; and escape, 91; and fear of death, 160. *See also* Religion; Security
Relationship: and aloneness, 136; and change, 105; and continuity, 222; and the desire for permanency, 134; and fear, 244; and the individual and the collective, 253; and loneliness, 156
Religion: and age, 171–72; and division, 134; and the existence of authority, 297; and the exploitation of seekers, 203; and the hindrance of belief, 269–70; and power, 27–28; and revolution as synonymous, 223; and self-liberation, 246–47. *See also* Religious mind
Religious: defining, 173
Religious approach: and problems, 169
Religious mind, 168–74, 223–27, 269–73, 319–20, 322–26; defining, 81–82, 87, 89; as directionless, 107, 113–14; function of, 174–75; and negative thinking, 78–81, 84–85, 89–90
Religious mind and the scientific mind: as the only real states of mind, 169, 172. *See also* Dull mind; Mind; New mind
Religious organization: and the enslavement of the mind, 83; failure of, 49–50; futility of, 114; as hindrance to truth, 79–80
Religious spirit: describing, 170–71; and the scientific spirit, 77, 80; versus tradition, 78. *See also* Religious mind; Scientific mind
Religious structure: and religious belief, 323
Religious tyranny: increase of, 49–50
Resistance: living without, 136, 138–39, 210. *See also* Effort
Respectability: attachment to, 212; and security, 135; and virtue, 142
Response: as the product of memory, 304. *See also* Challenge
Response and challenge: as limited, 68–81. *See also* Reaction
Resurrection: and the fear of death, 160
Revolt: as reaction, 278–79. *See also* Revolution
Revolution: absence of stages in, 56; and the analytic process, 141; defining, 223–24; and emptiness, 256–57; and freedom from authority, 235; and God, 173; as instantaneous, 159; need for, 49; need for an inward, 118, 119; and the new, 185; and the new mind, 276; and religion as synonymous, 223; and the religious spirit, 170; versus revolt, 278–79. *See also* Change; Mutation; Reform
Revolutionary mind: as the religious mind, 82, 324–25
Right action: and the challenged mind, 76–77; and living, 23. *See also* Action
Right problems: and right questions, 232–33. *See also* Problems
Ritual: versus the religious mind, 323
Ritualistic mind: versus the religious mind, 84
Russia. *See* Authority; Conditioning; Identification; Nationalism; Words

Saints: and fear, 59; recognition of, 82; and the timeless, 100. *See also* Authority; Religion
Saints and sinners: and conflict, 128
Sanity: and inquiry into fear, 223; and the insane world, 62
Sannyasi: and the mischievous mind, 90
Science and knowledge, 308; and the mind, 51. *See also* Knowledge; Scientific mind
Scientific approach: benefits of, 169; and problems, 169
Scientific mind, 168–74, 319, 322; and comparison, 95; defining, 81, 83; as directive, 107; and the religious mind, 80, 81, 85, 89–90, 270
Scientific mind and the religious mind: as the only real states of mind, 169, 172
Scientific spirit: describing, 169–70; and the religious spirit, 77, 80. *See also* Religious mind; Scientific mind

Scientist: approach of, 89, 112; and dualism, 81; and the spirit of inquiry, 90; and the spirit of knowledge, 77, 80. *See also* Specialists
Security, 133–37; and attitudes to war, 169; and authority, 296; and belief, 323; and consciousness, 195; desire for, 38; as destructive, 38; and disturbance, 237; and the dull mind, 18; and fear, 251; and following, 235; and hope, 162; and order, 190; and religion, 297; versus the religious spirit, 170; and resistance to change, 292; search for, 223; and the tradition of belief, 96; and the unconscious, 166–67; and words, 303; world search for, 230–31. *See also* Authority
Seeing: and the absence of fear, 251; and divisions, 195; and the free mind, 184; and interpretation, 5; and learning, 199; meaning of, 191, 235–36; and mutation, 285; and the new mind, 57–58, 280; process of, 119–20; and sensitivity, 290; significance of, 57, 62; without thought, 61–62; and time, 159; versus the word, 228. *See also* Observation; Perception
Seeing the fact: and action, 283. *See also* Fact; Seeing
Seeing totally: importance of, 193
Seeking: exploitation, 203; and fear, 252; and God, 256; and the need for commitment, 33–34; and the superficial mind, 164
Self: awareness of, 109, 112, 114. *See also* Center
Self-centered: and loneliness, 315
Self-centered activity: and love, 14; and total response, 325
Self-contradiction: and activity, 31; and conflict, 16; and the creation of conflict, 123; as a way of life, 68. *See also* Contradiction
Self-denial: and energy, 65, *See also* Denial
Self-forgetfulness: and commitment, 110
Self-fulfillment: and the conflict of opposites, 195. *See also* Divisions; Duality; Fulfillment
Self-importance: and observing *what is,* 246
Self-knowing, 9; and the beginning of meditation, 206; and the beginning or end, 217; and the conscious and unconscious, 320; and the creative state, 145; defining, 84; and freedom from fear, 260; and meditation, 263, 265–66; from moment to moment, 279–80; as one process, 231; process of, 166–67; and the process of thought, 250; and reality, 247; and the religious mind, 107–8, 175; and the silent mind, 216–17. *See also* Knowing; Self-knowledge
Self-knowledge: and the free mind, 16; meaning of, 233; and meditation, 48; and observation, 109–114; and the present, 7–9; and the religious mind, 324; and total action, 40. *See also* Center; Self-knowing
Self-protection: and fear, 304. *See also* Security
Self-understanding: and meditation, 311; and the new mind, 293–95. *See also* Center; Self-knowing
Sensitive mind: achieving, 17; and adjustment to fact, 105; defining, 108; and desire, 153; and learning, 106; and sorrow, 298. *See also* New; New mind
Sensitivity: and the absence of conflict, 176; and conflict, 194; and desire, 151; and the dull mind, 315; and the fertile mind, 108; meaning of, 290; need for, 37–38; and passion, 194; and the quiet brain, 326; and the unburdened mind, 298. *See also* New; New mind
Serious mind: defining, 202; and the discovery of the true and false, 223. *See also* Empty mind
Seriousness: defining, 193, 285; understanding, 183–85
Sex: importance of, 244; as psychological and physical fact, 247. *See also* Passion
Shallow mind: and increased activity, 163–64; nature of, 164. *See also* Dull mind; New mind
Silence: and the approach to problems, 90; and experiencing, 20; and the free mind, 266–67; and inquiry, 216. *See also* Meditation; Quiet mind
Simple: meaning of, 207–8
Simple mind: and freedom from words, 207. *See also* Dull mind; Free mind; New mind
Simplicity: and beauty, 165; and sorrow, 208
Sin: and love, 20
Slaves. *See* Enslavement
Sleep: and meditation, 46; understanding, 41–42, 46. *See also* Dreams
Social divisions: and problems, 10. *See also* Divisions; Society
Socialism. *See* Authority; Conditioning; Identification; Propaganda; Words
Social structure: and ambition, 310
Society: and acquisition, 310–11; as acquisitive, 36; and action, 22–24; and aloneness, 40; and commitment, 66; and competition, 15, 19; and the conflict of freedom, 127–28; and the confusion of challenge and response, 70, 72–74; and contradiction, 25; and the demand for order, 172; and the desire for power, 27–28; and education, 37; and envy, 110; and the mind, 97; and the religious mind, 173, 175; and the religious person, 173–74; and respectability, 212–13; and tension, 26. *See also* Authority
Society and the individual: as one, 269. *See also* Collective; Individual
Soldiers: as machines, 40
Solutions: and questions, 71–72; and the search for answers, 8–10. *See also* Problems
Sorrow, 91–95, 207–12, 269–71, 273; and authority, 298; and discovery, 200–202; escape from, 91, 93; and fear, 92–93, 95; and modern man, 283–84; physical and psychological, 92–93, 95; understanding, 294–95, 298–99. *See also* Pain; Suffering
Soul: and energy, 65–66
Space: existence in, 160
Space travel: versus the inner journey, 277
Specialists: and creation, 35; and education, 37; and knowledge, 306; and limited challenge, 75; and problems, 9; and questioning, 285–86
Specialization: and divisions, 270
Status: and class, 271; and function, 34–37, 310
Still mind: and the nameless, 200. *See also* Free mind; New mind
Stillness: and the absence of continuity, 252–53. *See also* Quiet mind
Strength: defining, 226–27
Stupid mind. *See* Dull mind

Subjugation: as the price for order, 187–88. *See also* Tyranny
Subliminal advertising: and influence, 15
Success: and authority, 234; and social recognition, 212–13. *See also* Ambition; Envy
Suffering, 175–77; acceptance and nonacceptance, 93; dying to, 161; and fear, 92, 95; and the mind, 175–76; as a reaction from the center, 87; types of, 91; understanding, 90–95. *See also* Conflict; Pain; Sorrow
Superficial change, 253–54. *See also* Change
Superficial life: and loneliness, 246
Superficial mind: and the process of thought, 124. *See also* Conscious; Mind
Suppression: futility of, 148–49. *See also* Discipline
Swamis. *See* Authority
Symbols: as influence, 319–20, 322. *See also* Words
System. *See* Patterns; Tradition

Tension, 26–27, 31, 36; and contradiction, 31, 65, 66; and energy, 63
Theory: and fact, 104; as reaction, 27
Theosophy. *See* Conditioning; Conformity; Identification; Religious organizations; Words
Thinker: and attention, 269; and authority, 205; and concentration, 269. *See also* Mind
Thinker and the thought: and conflict, 194–95, 240–41; and division, 177–78; and the duality of time, 101–2; and naming, 44, 48. *See also* Experiencer and the experienced; Observer and the observed
Thinking, 1–6; and the absence of the word, 126; collective and individual, 162–63; and conformity, 29; as limited, 124; as mechanical, 214; as a mechanical process, 126; nature of, 31; process of, 2–3, 121–22, 123–24, 250, 303–5; as a reaction between challenge and response, 250; and response, 283; as a response to a challenge, 303; without the thinker, 241; and time, 99; and verbalization, 85–86, 301; and the word, 79, 301. *See also* Mind; Thought
Thinking and feeling: as one, 151
Thought: and action, 21; as breeder of fear, 220–21; as cause of fear, 259; and the creation of the center, 241; as the creator of time, 221; ending of, 138; and energy, 64; and fear, 47–48, 60, 62, 303–4; and the field of the known, 260; inquiry into, 311–12; limitations of, 305, 311–12; as limited, 227; and limited energy, 66–67; as mechanical, 63; as a mechanism of thinking, 2–3; need to understand, 64; as never free, 180; process of, 303–5; as a process of memory, 58; as time, 47, 249–50; versus the unknown, 260; and the word, 62, 181. *See also* Mind; Thinking
Time, 95–103, 157–62, 217, 220–22, 314, 316–17; and the absence of creative disorder, 173; and aloneness, 272; and ambition and envy, 205; and authority, 237; and the beginning and the end, 206; and the brain, 226; as cause of fear, 259; and change, 199, 287, 290–91; and creation, 226, 313; and the creation of fear, 47; and death, 316; and energy, 66; enslavement to, 75; and fear, 135, 140–41, 249–50, 314; and freedom from fear, 62; as hindrance to seeing, 57–58; and influence, 96–97; need to understand, 62; and progress, 51; and the religious mind, 226, 272, 324; and revolution, 56; and sorrow, 209; as thought, 58, 62, 303–4; types of, 98–99; and understanding, 272; and verbalization, 86; and violence, 201. *See also* Past; Yesterday
Time and space: as life boundaries, 232
Time, death, and fear: relationship between, 217–23
Time intervals: and the process of thought, 3, 250
Timeless: and the ending of thought, 305; mind, 84; and the past, 137; and silence, 267. *See also* God; Immeasurable; Time
Timelessness, 95–103; and the absence of beginning and end, 97; defining, 58; and revolution, 159; and space and time, 162. *See also* Timeless
Today. *See* Time
Tomorrow. *See* Time
Total action: as action without reaction, 128; and complete mutation, 288; as meditation, 204; understanding, 33, 40; and the whole of life, 204. *See also* Action; Whole
Total awareness: and the absence of fear, 259; state of, 302. *See also* Awareness
Total commitment: and the unbalanced mind, 177. *See also* Commitment
Total death: versus organic death, 221. *See also* Death
Totality: as approach to seeing conflict, 195; of the mind, 120; and the religious mind, 270
Totality of being: and awareness, 306
Totality of consciousness: and fear, 251; understanding, 221
Totality of life: versus the limited mind, 309; understanding, 109
Totality of mind: and fear, 60–62; and meditation, 203, 205
Total response: and sensitivity, 325
Total revolution: and the religious mind, 175
Total seeing: and the brain, 192
Total transformation: achieving, 256. *See also* Change; Revolution
Total understanding: state of, 273
Total world: versus the fragmented world, 191
Tradition: versus fact, 104; freedom from, 170–71; and the Gita, 293; as hindrance to the new mind, 276; as limitation, 28; and the mind, 17; need to break with, 230; and the past, 96; as propaganda, 15, 281; versus the religious man, 78. *See also* Conditioning; Conformity
Transformation: need for immediate, 51. *See also* Change; Mutation; New; Revolution
True: versus the conflicted mind, 196; and freedom from motive, 141; and observation, 231; and the quiet brain, 263, 267; and the state of negation, 255–56. *See also* God; Immeasurable
True and false: and listening, 143–44
Truth: and conflict, 14; discovery of, 261–62, from moment to moment, 277; as timeless, 86. *See also* True
Tyranny: and action, 22; spread of, 22. *See also* World problems

Ugliness: and energy, 290; and living, 16–17; living with, 12, 136; and the sensitive mind, 105, 165. *See also* Beauty
Uncertain mind: as young, 237. *See also* Innocent mind
Uncertainty: and freedom from conflict, 292; and mental illness, 239
Unconscious: and change, 254; describing, 166–67; function of, 41, 70, 96; inquiry into, 218–20; as a positive process, 126; and the process of thinking, 124–25; understanding, 111–13. *See also* Conscious; Mind
Understanding: action, 20–29, 31, 33–36, 40; authority, 234–38, 295–99; challenge and response, 68–81; change, 253–57, 284–87; conflict, 129–33, 153–57, 175–79, 193–98, 238–43; death, 157–58, 160–63, 217–19, 221–22, 258–63, 315–19; defining, 41; desire, 148–53, 243–47; and the end of knowledge, 114; energy, 63–67; fact, 284–87; fear, 40–41, 43, 45–48, 58–62, 134–39, 139–42, 217–23, 248–52, 303–5; freedom from authority, 234–38; and freedom from conflict, 239; and the hindrance of conflict, 123; influences, 236–37; intelligence, 7–10; meditation, 41–46, 48; mind, 107–15, 203–6, 263–69; mutation, 284–87; observation, 43–46, 48; order, 189–92; problem, 7–12; reaction, 21–22, 24–29, 31, 36; religious mind, 223–27, 319–20, 322–26; response and challenge, 68–81; security, 133–37; self, 109–10, 114; seriousness, 183–85; sorrow, 91–95, 207–12; state of, 218; suffering, 90–95, 175–77; time, 95–103, 157–62, 217, 220–22; versus time, 272; timelessness, 95–103; words, 301–3
Unhappiness: knowing, 17. *See also* Sorrow; Suffering
Universal: and the particular, 10
Unknowable: achieving, 313
Unknown: achieving, 273; and death, 107, 260; fear of, 318–19; as indescribable, 107; and known, 160–61, 163; and space and time, 160–61; and the timeless, 324. *See also* God; Immeasurable
Upanishads. *See* Authority; Conditioning; Knowledge; Propaganda; Words
Usefulness: and the free person, 211–12

Verbal: and conformity, 28–29
Verbalization: as hindrance, 44; and thinking, 3–4. *See also* Communication; Words
Violence: and change, 199; and the conflict of opposites, 199; freedom from, 25; and peace, 190; as reality, 61; and time, 201
Virtue: as attention, 144; and denial of social morality, 206; and the desire for security, 134; and humility, 266, 310, 325; meaning of, 142, 44; and the state of negation, 255; as timeless, 316
Virtuous man: and conditioning, 147
Visions: and conditioning, 167; versus creation, 216

Waiting: fear of, 68–70, 74
Welfare society: as security, 38. *See also* Society; Welfare state; World problems
Welfare state: and the lack of incentive, 19
West: and the desire for security, 118; and knowledge, 114
What is: and the absence of fear, 259; and the center, 155; disgust with, 291; versus divisions, 195; and an end to seeking, 164, 165; and energy, 12, 202; versus escape, 209–10; and freedom from conditioning, 263–64; and the mechanical process, 199; need to understand, 25; and the negative approach, 27; and psychological needs, 243–44; and time, 317; and 'what shall be', 98. *See also* Fact
What is and 'what should be': and conflict, 155; and contradiction, 289; and duality, 102–3; gap between, 159; and time, 140. *See also What is*
'What should be': and the shallow mind, 164; and what actually is, 29. *See also What is*
"What to do": as hindrance to action, 123, 128
Whole: and the approach to the unconscious, 220; and the brain and the mind, 270–71; comprehending, 176; and ending, 212; experiencing, 120; seeing, 146–47; understanding, 172; and understanding influence, 97. *See also* Total action; Totality
Whole mind: achieving, 44, 48
Wholeness: awareness of, 54–57
Will: and choice, 158; and contradiction, 289; and fear, 140. *See also* Effort; Resistance
Words, 301–3; and communication, 229; and creating divisions, 180–81; as different from the thing, 108–9; and energy, 62; enslavement to, 18, 20, 44, 187, 207; and fear, 45; and feeling, 241; freedom from, 292–93; and freedom from comparison, 20; importance of, 4–5; and influence, 139–40, 320; and loneliness, 314–15; and meditation, 166; and the mind, 86; mind as slave to, 120, 122; and negative thinking, 79; as not the thing, 228, 301–2; and observing the feeling, 88; and the process of thought, 126; and purpose, 24; satisfaction of, 109; and seeing totally, 191; significance of, 263, 275; as symbols, 258; and the thought, 62; thought without, 210; as time, 85–86
Work: and fear, 136, 137
Work routine: versus inward response, 74
World: as chaotic, 15–16; and externalized events, 121; and industrialization, 279; need for clarity in, 223; viewed as a totality, 183
World change: and electronic brains, 117. *See also* Machines; World problems
World problems: and the desire for order, 189–90; as immediate, 230; increase of, 49–50; and the need for a new mind, 174; and outward and inward movements, 184–85; and the religious and scientific spirits, 81; and the scientific spirit, 169; and sorrow, 211
Worship: and the decaying mind, 217

Yesterday: dying to, 161; as hindrance to today, 38. *See also* Memory; Past; Time
Yesterday and tomorrow: and fear, 249. *See also* Yesterday
Yogis. *See* Authority; Conditioning; Identification; Religious mind; Words
Young mind: and dying to thought, 222; and learning, 271; as revolutionary, 38. *See also* Innocent mind

CPSIA information can be obtained
at www.ICGtesting.com
Printed in the USA
JSHW040015180223
37768JS00002B/9

9 781934 989456